PRICES, QUANTITIES AND
EXPECTATIONS

PRICES, QUANTITIES AND EXPECTATIONS

Keynes and Macroeconomics in the Fifty Years since
the Publication of the *General Theory*

EDITED BY

P. J. N. SINCLAIR

CLARENDON PRESS · OXFORD

1987

Oxford University Press, Walton Street, Oxford OX2 6DP

Oxford New York Toronto
Delhi Bombay Calcutta Madras Karachi
Petaling Jaya Singapore Hong Kong Tokyo
Nairobi Dar es Salaam Cape Town
Melbourne Auckland

and associated companies in
Beirut Berlin Ibadan Nicosia

Oxford is a trade mark of Oxford University Press

Published in the United States
by Oxford University Press, New York

British Library Cataloguing in Publication Data

Prices, quantities and expectations: Papers on macroeconomics fifty years
after the publication of the general theory of employment interest and
money by John Maynard Keynes
—— *(Oxford economic papers: special issue).*
1. Macroeconomics
I. Sinclair, P. J. N.   1558640
339   HB172.5
ISBN 0-19-828589-2

Library of Congress Cataloging-in-Publication Data

Prices, quantities, and expectations.
1. Keynesian economics.   2. Macroeconomics.
3. Keynes, John Maynard, 1883–1946.   I. Sinclair, P. J. N.
HB99.7.P74   1987   330.15′6   87-7770
ISBN 0-19-828589-2 (pbk.)

Printed in Northern Ireland at
The Universities Press (Belfast) Ltd.

CONTENTS

PREFACE

PRICES, QUANTITIES AND EXPECTATIONS: KEYNES AND MACROECONOMICS IN THE FIFTY YEARS SINCE THE PUBLICATION OF THE *GENERAL THEORY*

By P. J. N. SINCLAIR

Fifty years have now elapsed since the publication of Keynes' *General Theory of Employment, Interest and Money*. No book written since can have exerted greater pull upon events. In a longer span of history, it ranks with the *Wealth of Nations* and *Das Capital*. The present volume marks the General Theory's golden jubilee by presenting a number of important papers devoted to different aspects of macroeconomics. It honours Keynes' memory not so much by reexamining his writings (although some contributors do this) as by gathering contemporary analyses of the issues upon which Keynes initiated discussion. The major themes that run through this volume are the laws governing the evolution of economic aggregates, the causes and effects of incomplete flexibility in wages and prices, and the implications of different assumptions about expectations and the quality of information. They can be summed up in the words of the volume's title, Prices, Quantities and Expectations.

This introduction attempts a brief appraisal of Keynes' major achievements. It then traces some of the ways in which macroeconomic thought has evolved in the fifty years since the *General Theory's* publication, by looking at the curious changes in how certain propositions have been viewed, and by highlighting the major developments of each of the five decades that followed. It concludes with a short summary of the contributions to the volume.

Keynes hacked a path through the tangled undergrowth of conventional and unconventional wisdom. This has since turned into a crowded highway. The excitement and challenge of journeying upon it have faded. But the familiarity of the path must never blind us to the magnificent intellectual audacity of its first traveller. First traveller he was. Parts of the route may have been glimpsed before. His Swedish contemporaries, Myrdal (1931) and Ohlin (1937) were developing ex-ante/ex-post models of income and spending that bear striking resemblances to Keynes' General Theory at the time that he was writing it. Kahn had *rediscovered* the Multiplier in 1930. Hegeland (1954) traces it back to L. Johannsen and J. Wulff, both of whom were writing in the late nineteenth century. Irving Fisher (1930) had a "propensity to consume", although he put it to different uses. The distinction between money hoarded and money circulating as a means of

payment was stressed by Marx,[1] and the essentials of Keynesian liquidity preference were at least implicit in David Hume. Keynes himself enlisted Petty (1689), Malthus (1836) and Mummery and Hobson (1889) as posthumous allies in his battle to show that aggregate demand might insuffice. But the crucial point, as Klein (1948) emphasizes, is that it was Keynes who first brought all these ideas together, and propelled them forward. It is emphatically Keynes' road on which we tread today.

Keynes had inspired intuitions about economic behaviour, both in the small and in the large. Subsequent econometric studies, conducted on far richer data than Keynes could have used, have widened the set of influences operating on the key macro variables, and told us much about timing. But they have never overturned his major claims. Money demand does indeed depend on income and interest rates. Labour is not traded in a spot auction market, and money wages do not react instantaneously to changes in economic conditions. Investment plans can collapse and jump in the face of sudden changes in expected profits. Consumption depends on income and its own lagged value (". . . (a man) is apt to save the difference which discovers itself between his actual income and the expense of his habitual standard . . ." (*General Theory*, p. 97)), and the influence of interest rates is relatively weak. The changes in unemployment that follow in the wake of macro disturbances are not immediately self-correcting, and may take several years to fade.

Keynes' *General Theory* ensured that macroeconomics would always be a largely empirical science. His work led directly and quickly to the collection and publication of detailed statistics on economic aggregates. Good theorists tend to be fastidious, and laudably anxious to avoid asserting what they cannot prove. The assumptions from which inferences are drawn are a guide to thought, an admission required by intellectual honesty, a spur to generalization and extension. Perhaps from truthfulness and modesty, perhaps from lack of boldness—but above all because of the Herculean nature of creative modelling in economics—theorists find it easier to remain incarcerated in an Erewhon of the mind that obeys convenient premises (such as perfect information and full market clearing), and to address problems that such a framework renders tractable. Not so with Keynes. Keynes is all *a posteriori*. Analysis and synthesis are directed at the facts. By enhancing the status and supply of evidence, Keynes encouraged theorists to develop models that could account for phenomena, and exerted an undying effect upon the agenda on which research proceeds. In this sense, the scholars who have constructed New Classical Economics are as much Keynes' heirs as those who have stayed closer to the tenets of the *General Theory*.

No encomium convinces or concludes without a few words on less positive effects of its subject's achievements. It is sad that Keynes' writings could be

---

[1] *Capital,* ch. 3 part 3.

reduced to extreme and oversimplified slogans. One such is a kind of anti-Say's Law, "Demand creates its own supply". Another is a macroeconomic travesty of the Samuelson (1951)—Georgescu Roegen (1951) Non Substitution Theorem:[2] "Costs determine price, demand determines quantity". Propositions of this sort neglect important interdependencies and qualifications. In each repetition of Keynes' arguments, a little more is lost. Corners are cut, complications ignored. Keynes is unfortunately often reduced to a set of one-sided crudities that is bound to induce rebellion. All this is palpably unjust to Keynes. Similarly, valuable technical expositions (among which Hicks (1937), Klein (1948) and Champernowne (1936) stand out) are unreasonably criticized for misconstruing Keynes, or leaving out too much, when they are in fact far subtler (and exegetically more faithful) than often portrayed. These expositions tied up some of the General Theory's loose ends, and sharpened up its central message. What enhanced their utility to an increasingly numerate profession was Keynes' understandable wish to appeal to a very broad audience, and eschew technicalities. Algebra was still less the weapon of persuasion in 1936 than today.

Keynes' intellectual victories imposed some costs. The brilliant informalism with which he wrote tempted some followers to substitute dogma and description for rigorous analysis. The *General Theory* did not delay the development of general equilibrium modelling, for example. But it lowered the esteem with which such endeavours were regarded, and did not help to release them from the realm of the optional and the esoteric. His deemphasis on incentives facing economic agents, and issues of resource allocation, shifted attention from factors governing supply to financial management and aggregate demand, at just the time when aggregate demand was arguably ceasing to act as a binding restraint on national incomes. Supporters became trapped in a time-warp. Subsequent decades reveal an obsessive concern about the risk of mass unemployment, which had all but disappeared.

Perhaps it is inevitable that the economy works exactly opposite to the way in which it is fashionable to think it works. The thirty or forty years after 1936 are, by and large, the least Keynesian of periods in recorded recent economic history. Unemployment was lower and steadier than in the past. The predictions of the Quantity Theory of Money come closer to verification than in perhaps any previous period of comparable length for which data are available. Many would contend that the happy experiences of these decades owed most to private agents' beliefs that government would step in to stop violent macroeconomic swings. Ironically, the very stability and success of the long Keynesian boom that was to break in the 1970s, furnished growing econometric evidence that could be taken to imply

---

[2] The Non Substitution Theorem shows that, in an economy displaying no joint production, using a single scarce primary input, and constant returns technology in every sector, relative prices will not depend upon the pattern of final demand. For a simple summary, see Sinclair (1983), pp 121 et ff.

that Keynesian doctrines were wrong. Monetarism and New Classical Macroeconomics started to win academic converts, and influence policy, at just the time when, for example, the income velocities of monetary aggregates seem to become more volatile, and unemployment climbs. When Keynesian doctrines prevail, Keynesian phenomena vanish. As soon as macroeconomic policy is subordinated to the goal of stability in finance and prices, back they come!

What are Keynesian doctrines? The Keynesian would agree with Aristotle that "... production must be worth buying; but expenditure should match the product, if not outstrip it".[3] The Scylla of slumps is worse than the Charybdis of inflation, although both should be avoided if possible.[4] The vocabulary keeps changing, as each generation has the fun of bringing new guns to bear on old targets. Keynesian economics is a catastrophe, a singularity, a stochastic supergame, a pathological set of discontinuities, an application of Jensen's inequality, an anomalous graph, a semiotic dysfunction. Each new metaphor is as clever and teasing as it is arcane. More important, one can identify some curious shifts of substance in what counts as a Keynesian claim. Consider the following propositions:

A: Money does not affect output.
B: Money demand is interest-elastic.
C: Aggregate employment varies negatively with the real wage.

Proposition A was taken as a limiting case of Keynesian orthodoxy in the 1940s and 1950s. Suppose real balance effects on consumption can be ignored. Suppose that the same is true of the ratio of two interest elasticities (of that of expenditure to that of money demand): this will happen in the case of a liquidity trap, when the money supply cannot affect interest rates, or if expenditure is completely insensitive to them. In that case, aggregate demand is independent of the stock of money, and (presumably) output will be too.

By the late 1960s, everything had changed. In his presidential address to the American Economic Association, Friedman (1968) argued that monetary policy could have no enduring impact upon output or employment. Adaptive expectations made real wage rates and employment, and consequently aggregate supply, independent of the money supply in the long run. The New Classicals took the argument further. Predictions of the money supply, *inter alia,* would govern expectations of future prices, upon which

---

[3] ὥστε τὸ μὲν ἔργον τῆς δαπάνης ἄξιον δεῖ εἶναι, τὴν δὲ δαπάνην τοῦ ἔργου, ἢ καὶ ὑπερβάλλειν.
Nic. Eth., IV. ii.6. Aristotle was in fact prescribing purchasing rules for the discerning rich, rather than propounding Keynesian macroeconomic sentiments.
[4] "Thus inflation is unjust and deflation is inexpedient. Of the two, perhaps deflation is ... the worse ... But it is not necessary that we should weigh one evil against the other. It is easier to agree that both are evils to be shunned" (Keynes, 1923).

money wage bargains were struck. Only surprises in the money supply, or other relevant macro relationships, could cause actual and expected prices to diverge, given rational expectations. Output would be completely invariant to money supply changes that had been forecast. This point was stressed by Barro (1976), and Sargent and Wallace (1975, 1976). Their Keynesian opponents found themselves arguing that money supply changes *did* matter for output—an almost complete *bouleversement* from the earlier, stylized claim!

Proposition B at first occupied a central place in Keynesian orthodoxy. It helped to imply, for instance, that fiscal policy instruments could achieve a bigger "bang per buck" on national income than, say, open market operations. Friedman pooh-poohed this, and claimed that the interest-elasticity of money demand in the U.S. differed insignificantly from zero (1959), although Laidler (1966) later showed that this inference from the data was illicit. But by 1970, positions began to reverse. Friedman (1969) showed that the welfare costs of sustained inflation increased with the interest-elasticity of money demand, because that way inflation increases destroyed more surplus under the money-demand curve. The Keynesian tradition had it that inflation mattered less than unemployment. So its adherents could find themselves arguing that if money-demand were relatively interest-*inelastic,* inflation might prove a relatively efficient tax source in a second best world.

Proposition C was insisted upon repeatedly by Keynes in the *General Theory.* Perfect competition and producer equilibrium kept the marginal product of labour equal to the real wage, and labour was subjected to diminishing returns. Two decades later, Keynes' heirs in Cambridge, England, argued forcefully that the use of a well-behaved aggregate production function, and a negative link between the level of employment for a factor on the one side and its reward and marginal productivity on the other, were wholly unwarranted.[5] Just as Logical Positivism seemed to make a nonsense of the notion of marginal utility, references to factors' marginal products, especially in an aggregate sense, were derided like a form of academic nail-biting: a dirty habit, afflicting the nervous young and the untutored, never to be indulged in public, and which maturity should ultimately break. It was these New Keynesians' opponents, labelled "neoclassical", who sought to establish conditions under which aggregate production functions might be put to legitimate use. Perfect competition and diminishing returns to factors are hallmarks of New Classical writing today; many Keynesian writers, such as Weitzman (1982), experiment with increasing returns instead.

Yet a further instance of tergiversation is provided by the treatment of expectations. Keynes spoke loudly and eloquently of expectations, and their

---

[5] Kaldor (1956) and Robinson (1953, 1956) were the most celebrated advocates of this position.

central role in governing investment and money demand (if not consumption). In the conventional wisdom he was attacking, expectations receive scarcely a mention. Four decades later, Keynesiansism faced its most dangerous challenge on precisely the same battleground. But it was now the New Classicals that invoked expectations to their side, while some Keynesians were reduced to claiming that they were sluggish or relatively unimportant. Today it is the anti-Keynesians, then, who claim most strongly that money matters little for output, that money demand is significantly interest-elastic, that employment varies negatively with real wage rates, and that expectations are central to macroeconomic equilibrium. These were once Keynesian claims! What counts as Keynesian, then, never stands still. It displays all the tumult and tempo of a dance. It is the major twists and turns in post-Keynesian macroeconomics to which our attention must now be directed.

Five decades have now passed since the *General Theory* appeared. The first ten years, 1936–46, may be termed the **Decade of Distilling**. The central task in macroeconomics was to expound, and develop, the theories advanced in that work: to distil the essence of Keynes. By far the most influential account is due to Hicks (1937). He rounded off some missing links in Keynes' own summary (Chapter 18), and reduced the whole book's complex, many-sided arguments to a system of less than a dozen equations, and a single diagram, the "SI-LL" curves. The wider publicity provided by Hansen (1953) led to its relabelling as "IS-LM". Hicks' system is far richer than subsequent textbooks allowed. The money supply is permitted to vary with the rate of interest, for example, and there is a fully-developed set of producer optimization conditions that give rise to product supply and labour demand functions for firms in both consumer and capital goods industries. Another review of the *General Theory*, by Champernowne (1936) deserves to be better known than it is. He anticipates and explores the modern distinction between the natural rate ("basic unemployment", due to real factors) and deviations from it attributable to mispredictions or misperceptions of the aggregate price level ("monetary unemployment"). Other landmarks in the Decade of Distilling include Samuelson's powerful demonstration (1939) that trade cycles could develop from the interaction of lagged accelerator and multiplier; Harrod's seminal early work on dynamics (1936, 1939), which sketched a theory of the momentum of capital and output, and can be seen as a twin contribution to the theories of cycles and growth; and the notable contributions to cycle analysis provided by Kaldor (1940) and Kalecki (1937). These four authors were keen to repeal Keynes' short-run, Marshallian assumption of a given stock of capital, and explore the interdependent paths of investment and output. Kaldor and Kalecki opened a new seam that was to dominate the Cambridge, England post-Keynesian research programme, by trying to endogenize and extend the theory of distribution.

The monetary facet of the General Theory was taken up by Brown

(1938), who furnished the first econometric investigation of money demand (in this case, on the part of banks). Empirical inquiries into the impact of interest rates on investment were initiated by Andrews and Meade (1938). Brown confirmed that money demand was significantly interest-elastic, while the Andrews–Meade survey evidence concluded that investment was not. A lively debate conducted by Dunlop (1938) and Tarshis (1939) appeared to undermine the General Theory view that firms operated more or less continuously on relatively steady, downward sloping labour demand curves, by showing that real wage rates moved pro-cyclically.

The Decade of Distilling (1936–46) gave way to the **Decade of Data and Dispute**. Kuznets revealed that the average propensity to consume in the United States varied countercyclically but displayed no long-term time trend, despite growing real income per head. Competing explanations for this were offered by Duesenberry (1949), Modigliani with Brumberg (1954) and Friedman (1957). In the monetary arena, Baumol (1952) and Tobin (1956) established influential inventory-theoretic models that extended Keynes' interest elasticity to transactions money demand, while Friedman's restatement of the quantity theory (1956) added equities and durables to Keynes' portfolio and dressed it in maximizing garb. Rival theories, liquidity preference and loanable funds, contended for primacy in the determination of interest rates. Hicks condemned this as a "sham dispute": both were simply particular cases of his (1937) simultaneous system. Kaldor (1956) offered a theory of distribution that had its roots in Keynes' *Treatise*, while Robinson developed pugnacious and highly individual models of capital (1956). Notable empirical studies of the cycle were complemented by Hicks' theoretical work (1950). Keynesian exegesis continued with Klein (1948). The decade closed with the first edition of Patinkin (1956), which sought to sharpen the links and differences between neoclassical general equilibrium theory and Keynesian doctrines, among other objectives.

The next ten years, 1956–66, are the **Decade of Dynamics**. Solow (1956) replaced Harrod's rigidities in factor prices or technology with a model of growth where capital and labour were substitutes, and perfect competition reigned in its fullest sense (perfect foresight and price flexibility, and marginal productivity factor pricing). Solow's positive, one-sector model was extended to two sectors (Meade (1961) and Uzawa (1962)), to welfare issues (Phelps (1961)) and to money (Tobin (1965)). Growth theory was widened to encompass endogenous technical progress (Kaldor and Mirrlees (1962) and Weizsaecker (1966)), and supplemented by more technical analysis that returned to earlier, neglected models by Neumann (1938) and Ramsey (1928). Sraffa (1960) urged a return to still older concepts, and offered a reformulation of Ricardian principles of relative price formation and growth. In a sense, the climax of dynamic analysis was marked by Hicks (1965); the various ideas that led up to this work form the subject matter of Malinvaud's contribution to the present volume. The dynamics of expectations under the assumption that available information is used optimally were first studied by Muth (1961). Rational expectations also provided illuminating insights into the markets for goods where a time dimension is important; these are studied in this volume by Bray. Rational expectations were to dominate much of the research in macroeconomics in our fourth decade.

These ten years, 1966–76, are the **Decade of Disillusion**. The disillusion took many forms. First, it was claimed that workers and their employers would sooner or later escape from illusions about the price level: this led to the hypothesis of the expectations-augmented Phillips curve, due first to Phelps (1967), but echoing the earlier ideas of Champernowne (1936). It helped to explain why the rising inflation of the late 1960s was not accompanied by falling unemployment. The argument was extended by Barro (1976), Lucas (1975) and Sargent and Wallace (1975, 1976). They became known as the New Classical Macroeconomic or Rational Expectations School. They argued that previous macroeconomic analysis had been built on two inconsistent pictures. One picture was painted of how the economy worked, while a second, typically much cruder portrayal was provided of how the private agents within the economy *believed* it worked. The hypothesis of rational expectations removed this inconsistency. At least the systematic features of the actual economy must be fully reflected in agents' beliefs, and hence in their forecasts: 'You were not made to be brutes, but excel and prosecute knowledge'.[6] As Greenwald and Stiglitz emphasize in this volume, the policy conclusions that these authors drew—chiefly that the mean levels of output and employment could not be affected by systematic (and hence anticipated) monetary policy rules—were no less premised upon an assumption of continuous market clearing, which really drove their results. Andersen, in this volume, reminds us that inferences about policy impotence are highly sensitive to the other assumptions of the model into which rational expectations are inserted.

Disillusion also characterized other aspects of macroeconomic thinking in this decade. Leijonhufvud (1968) argued that Keynes had been misunderstood by his "Keynesian" expositors. At the root of Keynes' thinking, Leijonhufvud claimed, lay a fundamental failure of information and coordination. Keynes could not be reduced to a clean set of simultaneous equations, he maintained. A not dissimilar view, not so much about Keynes in particular as on the nature of discourse about any economic issue involving choice under uncertainty, had been propounded by Shackle (1938, 1949, 1961). Majority opinion in the profession chose to set aside the Shackle-Leijonhufvud genre of criticisms, chiefly on the ground that theoretical and econometric inquiry and policy evaluation cannot proceed constructively unless upon an explicit and relatively simple formal basis that attempts to split, however unconvincingly, the deterministic from the random. Disillusion centred, furthermore, on the apparent lack of microfoundations in Keynesian macroeconomics. One answer to this was offered

[6] Fatti non foste a viver come bruti
   Ma seguir virtute e canoscenza (Dante (1265)).

by the Rational Expectations School (which usually insisted on perfect price flexibility); another by the Quantity Rationing or Fix Price School (which asserted the exact opposite). The latter group is perhaps best exemplified by Barro and Grossman (1971) and Malinvaud (1977), and was anticipated in some respects by Solow and Stiglitz (1968) and Clower (1965). Another source of disillusion in the years from 1966 to 1976 was the sudden jump in oil prices in 1974. The advanced nations were rudely reminded that output does not depend on capital and labour alone. Energy also limits supply. A final manifestation of disillusion in this decade was provided by Barro's resurrection of Ricardo's claim that a society could not enrich itself by the sale of government bonds to its citizens (1974).

1976–86 can be called the **Decade of Debt, Doubt and Deflation**. Barro's argument that a bond-financed deficit could be equivalent to current taxation led to a lively debate on the consequences of debts and deficits, in which Buiter (1983, 1985), Feldstein (1980), Sargent and Wallace (1981) and Tobin (1980) stand out. This theme continues in the present volume in the contributions by Buiter, Rankin and Sheen. Mounting State indebtedness has created acute problems of financial management in the United States and elsewhere in the OECD area, and above all in the third world (examined most recently by Heffernan (1986) and the *European Economic Review* Symposium (1986)).

Doubts entered macroeconomics in this decade in the form of asymmetries in information, and their effects. Akerlof (1970) argued that markets could fail to clear if a seller knows something about the quality of the item to be traded that the buyer does not. Prices would then have two roles. They would allocate resources; but they would also carry information, or quality signals, too. This idea has been pursued by many writers, but particularly Stiglitz, from the mid 1970s on. It has been applied to the markets for credit, insurance and labour; to education, sharecropping and unemployment; and to the theory of agency and delegation. In credit markets, for example, Stiglitz and Weiss (1981, 1983) do not share the optimism of the psalmist:

A good man sheweth favour, and lendeth (Psalm 112, v. 5).

Much of this research programme may be though of as a quest for the macrofoundations of microeconomics. Several of its implications are discussed in this volume by Greenwald and Stiglitz. Asymmetric information may also infect the relation between the policymaker and the public: different aspects of this are studied here by Andersen and by Vickers. In the monetary sphere, doubts surround the role of banks and the need for Central Bank intervention, examined in this volume by Goodhart.

Doubts underlie 1976–86 macroeconomics in a wider sense, too. The student and the policymaker are painfully aware that the subject is once again as unsettled as in Keynes' day. Proponents of two sharply differing families of theories, the Keynesian and the New Classical, claim to account for aggregate time series phenomena. They can look almost exactly alike in a statistical sense, and yet their implications for policy could hardly diverge more. The macro modeller and theorist are faced with an awkward set of choices about assumptions. Who knows what about whom? Are agents' expectations to be endogenous, and if so how? Are prices flexible or frozen? Is competition in labour and product markets perfect or imperfect? Is the economy closed or open to international influences and what differences does it make which? Should macroeconomic analysis be widened to incorporate events like energy price shocks, and if so how?

What gives such questions added bite is the besetting worry of this decade, the ugly return of mass unemployment in so many parts of the world. "Deflation" is registered in output below trend, weak primary product prices, falling inflation, and, above all, increased unemployment. Empirical analyses of labour markets are provided in this volume by Andrews and Nickell, and by Hersoug, Kjaer and Rodseth, while the likely consequences of profit-sharing, and faster adjustment of money wage rates, are explored by Blanchflower and Oswald, and by Flemming, respectively. Some macroeconomic consequences of imperfect competition are investigated by Dixon. International aspects of policy coordination are examined in the papers by Darby, by Hughes Hallett, and by Levine and Currie, and other open economy issues by Fender and by Turnovsky; and the implications of energy price changes and energy policy are studied by Buffie and by Flemming in his review of Bruno and Sachs (1985), and by Anand and Nalebuff.

So much for the chronicle of the five decades that separate us from the *General Theory*. One can identify ten major post-Keynesian research programmes that span the half-century. The contributions to this volume have something to say, between them, on all of them. They are:

   (i) dynamization;
   (ii) internationalization;
  (iii) microfoundations;
  (iv) imperfect competition;
   (v) endogenizing expectations;
  (vi) endogenizing government;
 (vii) reexamining debts and deficits;
(viii) reexamining the role of money;
  (ix) asymmetric information;
   (x) endogenizing distribution.

Dynamization began with the endogenization of capital, and the early cycle and growth studies by Harrod (1936, 1939) and Samuelson (1939); a further stimulus was provided by the hypothesis of intertemporal optimization, and the work of Lucas and Rapping (1969). Internationalization had been anticipated by Harrod (1933), and more recent work is well represented by Dornbusch (1976), Neary (1980) and Buiter and Marston (1985), reviewed here by Darby. The quest for microfoundations began with Hicks

(1939), and continued with Patinkin (1956), Phelps (1970) and Barro and Grossman (1971), while the macroeconomic implications of imperfect competition have been explored by Negishi (1979), Hart (1982) and Weitzman (1982). Endogenizing expectations was pioneered by Muth (1961)—the hypothesis of rational expectations is probed here by Bray— and applied to macroeconomics most influentially by the Rational Expectations School. Recent work on the endogenization of government behaviour, such as Vickers' contribution to this volume, has proceeded rapidly on lines laid down by Barro and Gordon (1983a, 1983b), and it was also Barro (1974) who initiated (vii). Programme (viii) owed much to Friedman and Tobin, and the agenda has widened recently to topics embraced in the July 1983 symposium of the *Journal of Monetary Economics* on Alternative Monetary Standards. Programme (ix) began with Akerlof and develops apace. The endogenization of distribution is, as we saw, a central feature of Kaldor and Kalecki's writings; it also forms the subject matter of much of a recent book, Marglin (1984), reviewed here by Hahn.

My final task is to describe the volume and offer brief sketches of the contributions to it. The first twelve papers are due to appear in the March 1987 issue of *Oxford Economic Papers*. Of the other fourteen, three have been published in 1985 or 1986, while the rest will come out in the November 1986 issue. The contributors are affiliated, between them, to over 20 universities, research institutes or central banks, in seven countries (Australia, Belgium, Britain, Denmark, France, Norway and the United States). I should like to record my gratitude to the large team of anonymous reviewers to whom these papers have been sent. All contributions have been subjected to intensive refereeing. Referees are the all too often unsung heroes of any publication; I thank them all in the very warmest terms.

The volume begins with a paper on Employment. Weitzman has recently argued (1984, 1985) that the tendency to unemployment in contemporary western economies could be removed if workers' remuneration were based upon a share of their employers' profits, and not on wage rates alone. This proposal is subjected to critical scrutiny by Blanchflower and Oswald. They find that neither available empirical evidence nor theoretical reasoning lends strong support to Weitzman's policy recommendations.

The next five papers are devoted to different facets of Interest and Money, to continue the echo of the title of Keynes' work which this volume commemorates. Turnovsky examines the optimal monetary response to supply disturbances which are anticipated in advance or inferred indirectly from other variables. No matter whether current shocks are fully observed as they occur, or inferred from other signals, Turnovsky shows that all that is needed to be known to operate an optimum monetary rule is last period's forecast or the current forecast for the next. The other four papers in this group examine international policy coordination, banks, fiscal policy and inflation.

Levine and Currie ask whether international economic policy cooperation is sustainable. If it does not pay (as in the models of Miller and Salmon (1985) and Rogoff (1985)), it will not last. Levine and Currie's private agents expect governments either to act as they would wish ex post ("time-consistently"), or to optimize with a reputation for consistency ("reputa-tionally"). They suggest that reputational behaviour is necessary for cooperation to pay (and cooperation for reputational behaviour to pay, too). But it is not sufficient: disturbances must keep happening, or be symmetrical.

Goodhart examines what distinguishes banks from other financial inter-mediaries. What marks them out, he maintains, is their specialist role in taking up liabilities that problems of asymmetric information render unmarketable. He concludes that central banks have a vital role in supervising this. Sheen is concerned with the fiscal policy choices of, and constraints upon, policymakers with different political objectives, and the relation between fiscal policy and inflation. Conservative governments will go to greater lengths than liberal ones to avoid instability in the market for public debt, and will secure lower inflation in the long run but perhaps from a higher short run level. Buiter explores a neglected aspect of Sargent and Wallace's celebrated paper (1981) on the interaction of monetary and fiscal policy instruments. He applies a "Laffer curve" to the authorities' seig-norage revenue from inflation, and demonstrates that fiscal indiscipline may generate not hyperinflation but hyperdeflation—if agents are allowed to spend time on an ultimately unstable path.

The next four papers are addressed to central Keynesian themes. Greenwald and Stiglitz provide an essay on the macroeconomic implications of asymmetric information, and the imperfections in capital and labour markets to which this gives rise. They propound the intriguing view that Keynes was not nearly Keynesian enough. Dixon looks at the macro-economic consequences of imperfect competition in the product market, and paints a modified Walrasian picture where fiscal policy, and the quality of competition, will "matter", but money does not. Flemming explores Keynes' contention (General Theory, chapter 19) that faster downward adjustment of money wage rates in slumps may aggravate unemployment. He finds that Keynes was quite right: greater flexibility of money wages can indeed make matters worse. Rutherford reminds us of the importance of Keynes' earlier volume on Macroeconomics, the Treatise on Money, and scrutinizes the links between Malthus and Keynes.

The next group of papers is devoted to different aspects of the economics of energy. The sharp movement in oil prices witnessed since 1973, and the complex repercussions that ensued, have caused macroeconomists to recast their habits of thought. Flemming reviews a recent book, The Economics of Worldwide Stagflation by Michael Bruno and Jeffrey Sachs (1985), which seeks to explain the faltering levels of growth and employment that most OECD countries have experienced since the early 1970s—conditions not unlike those that must have framed the thinking of Keynes fifty years ago.

Anand and Nalebuff furnish a framework for evaluating the costs and benefits energy projects in developing countries that import oil. Expected net benefits need to be adjusted to reflect their impact upon the riskness and distribution of income, and other variables, they show. Buffie works with the Keynesian theme of sticky prices to explore some of the effects of oil price changes in a small, oil-importing country. One curious conclusion is that the output-squeezing effects of dearer oil can be accompanied by downward pressure on goods prices, and by an increase in the demand for labour (in Keynesian Unemployment, firms face an incentive to switch to more labour-intensive, less energy-intensive methods of production for a given level of demand).

The group of papers that follow falls under the general heading of Expectations and Dynamics. Bray provides an introduction to rational expectations, and illustrates their implications, under a variety of assumptions, in the context of a market for a good for which the decision to produce precedes delivery and sales. Andersen is concerned with the policy implications of rational expectations, in a world there is disparate information held by firms and government. He shows that systematic monetary policy is not neutral; a suitably constructed set of rules will achieve an outcome superior to the best alternative that the private sector can attain on its own through a system of wage indexation. Rankin examines the effects of government bonds in a dynamic, overlapping generations model where prices may or may not be flexible. When prices are sticky, Rankin finds, bond issues will generally raise both output and welfare. Rankin extends the analysis by allowing the labour supply to be endogenous. In such conditions, more bonds may imply lower welfare, under both fixed and flexible prices, although output may rise in the latter case.

Fender examines the determination of employment and unemployment in a small open economy, where prices are sticky, and agents have perfect foresight about the next period. He explores a variety of assumptions about the exchange rate regime. One surprising finding is that expectations of monetary expansion in the future may cause the exchange rate to appreciate now, because the resulting increase in future real income strengthens the demand for money in the present. Darby reviews an important recent collection of papers, edited by Willem Buiter and Richard Marston (1985), entitled *International Economic Policy Coordination*. This is also the subject of Hughes Hallett's paper, which follows next. He investigates the period of the late 1970s, following the 1974 oil price shock, and finds that the independent, "competitive" macroeconomic policies of the member states of the European Communities, and the United States, that were actually employed in these years, imposed considerable costs, particularly upon Europe.

Three papers now follow on different aspects of Growth and Distribution. Hahn reviews Stephen Marglin's recent book (1984) on this topic. Ginsburgh, Henin and Michel provide an interesting application of quantity rationing analysis to growth theory, and describe the various different non-clearing regimes that can emerge, and the intertemporal paths associated with them. The volume then continues with the text of the third Hicks Lecture, delivered in Oxford in May 1986 by Professor Malinvaud. Malinvaud gives the reader a Grand Tour of the theories of capital and growth, following much of the route mapped out in the writings of Sir John Hicks (and above all Hicks (1965)). Among the issues that receive particular attention in Malinvaud's paper are the concept of the traverse (the phase of transition towards long-run equilibrium growth), and the merits of assuming less than perfectly flexible prices in long-term dynamic analysis.

The last four contributions to this volume return to the subject with which it begins: issues bearing upon employment. Andrews and Nickell examine the determination of aggregate employment in a world consisting of numerous distinct labour markets, and price flexibility is incomplete. In some markets, employment will be limited by the demand for labour; in others, by supply. Both demand and supply are affected by sector-specific as well as macroeconomic disturbances. The authors strike new ground by proposing and employing an ingenious method of estimating aggregate employment in such circumstances. Testing their disequilibrium model on British post-war data, they find that it comfortably outperforms two rival hypotheses (that labour markets cleared continuously, or experienced only aggregate excess demand or supply). Yet they advise caution in interpreting the results, since the data may be still better explained within an imperfectly competitive setting, where prices are set by firms, and wage rates by unions, interdependently. The next paper, by Hersoug, Kjaer and Rodseth, examines Norwegian macroeconomic data in a simplified version of just this framework. Their findings are mixed; but their hypothesis that wages are set by utility-maximizing unions certainly describes the data at least as well as strong versions of alternative theories. Van der Willigen applies the temporary equilibrium, fixprice or quantity rationing method to a developing country, Tanzania. Tanzania has suffered a sharp fall in cash crop production in recent years, which led in turn to growing trade deficits. This country offers a clear instance where official price-setting policies make a market-clearing, flexible-price approach especially inappropriate. Van der Willigen has a curious result: improving the rural sector's terms of trade could tend to weaken agricultural production, not increase it. The final contribution to the volume is by Vickers. He is concerned with the authorities' choices governing output (and hence, indirectly, employment) on the one side, and inflation on the other. He contributes to the growing literature on the positive theory of inflation and inflation expectations, viewed as a game between the government and the public. A government, or policymaker, may be "dry" or "wet". A dry cares most about achieving low inflation: a wet is more concerned with keeping output and employment high. The policy-maker's true preferences are not known, and not necessarily directly observable. Wets may have an incentive to pretend to be dry, since this could bring down the costs of expected inflation; predicted inflation is assumed to be damaging, while surprise inflation is beneficial since it increases output. In a two-period setting, Vickers shows how recent games-theoretic results can be applied to rule out cases where wets and dries behave alike, and ensure that dries do indeed reveal their preferences by their actions.

The state of macroeconomics today is as unsettled and exciting as it was when Keynes wrote fifty years ago. The contributions to this volume will, it is hoped, honour Keynes' memory and serve the reader by providing a detailed perspective on the central macroeconomic debates and issues of current concern.

REFERENCES

AKERLOF, G. A. (1970) 'The Market for Lemons: Qualitative Uncertainty and the Market Mechanism', *Quarterly Journal of Economics,* 84, 488–500.

ANDREWS, P. W. S. and MEADE, J. E. (1938), 'Summary of Replies to Questions on the Effects of Interest Rates', *Oxford Economic Papers,* 1, 14–31.

ARISTOTLE, *The Nicomachean Ethics.*

BARRO, R. J. (1974), 'Are Government Bonds Net Wealth?', *Journal of Political Economy,* 82, 1095–1107.

BARRO, R. J. (1976), 'Rational Expectations and the Role of Monetary Policy', *Journal of Monetary Economics,* 1, 1–32.

BARRO, R. J. and GORDON, R. (1983a) 'Rules, Discretion and Reputation in a Model of Monetary Policy', *Journal of Monetary Economics,* 12, 101–21.

BARRO, R. J. and GORDON, R. (1983b) 'A Positive Theory of Monetary Policy in a Natural Rate Model', *Journal of Political Economy,* 91, 589–610.

BARRO, R. J. and GROSSMAN, H. I. (1971) 'A General Disequilibrium Model of Income and Employment', *American Economic Review,* 61, 82–93.

BAUMOL, W. J. (1952) 'The Transactions Demand for Cash: an Inventory Theoretic Approach', *Quarterly Journal of Economics,* 66, 545–56.

BROWN, A. J. (1938) 'The Liquidity Preference Schedules of London Clearing Banks', *Oxford Economic Papers,* 1, 49–82.

BRUNO, M. and SACHS, J. (1985) *The Economics of Worldwide Stagflation,* Blackwell, Oxford.

BUITER, W. H. (1983) 'Measurement of the Public Sector Deficit and its Implications for Policy Evaluation and Design', *International Monetary Fund Staff Papers,* 30, 306–49.

BUITER, W. H. (1985) 'A Guide to Public Sector Debt and Deficits', *Economic Policy,* 1, 13–60.

BUITER, W. H. and MARSTON, R. C. eds., (1985) *International Economic Policy Coordination,* Cambridge University Press.

CHAMPERNOWNE, D. G. (1936) 'Unemployment, Basic and Monetary: The Classical Analysis and the Keynesian', *Review of Economic Studies,* 3, 201–16.

CLOWER, R. W. (1965) 'The Keynesian Counter-Revolution: a Theoretical Appraisal', in R. W. Clower, ed. *Monetary Theory,* Penguin, Harmondsworth.

DANTE ALIGHIERI (1265) *La Divina Commedia,* ed. C. Tagliavini, IBM Italia, 1965.

DORNBUSCH, R. (1976) 'Expectations and Exchange Rate Dynamics', *Journal of Political Economy,* 84, 1161–76.

DUESENBERRY, J. S. (1949) *Income, Saving and the Theory of Consumer Behavior,* Harvard University Press, Cambridge, Mass.

DUNLOP, J. T. (1938) 'The Movement of Real and Money Wage Rates', *Economic Journal,* 48, 413–34.

European Economic Review (1986), Vol. 30, No. 3, International Seminar on Macroeconomics, ed. G. de Menil and R. J. Gordon.

FELDSTEIN, M. (1980) 'Fiscal Policies, Inflation and Capital Formation', *American Economic Review,* 70, 636–50.

FISHER, I. (1930) *The Theory of Interest,* New York.

FRIEDMAN, M. (1956) 'The Quantity Theory of Money: a Restatement' in Studies in The Quantity Theory of Money, Chicago.

FRIEDMAN, M. (1957) *A Theory of the Consumption Function,* Princeton University Press.

FRIEDMAN, M. (1959) 'The Demand for Money: Some Theoretical and Empirical Results' *Journal of Political Economy,* 67, 327–51.

FRIEDMAN, M. (1968) 'The Role of Monetary Policy', *American Economic Review,* 58, 1–17.

FRIEDMAN, M. (1969) 'The Optimum Quantity of Money' in *The Optimum Quantity of Money and Other Essays,* Macmillan, London.

GEORGESCU–ROEGEN, N. (1951) 'Some Properties of a Generalized Leontief Model' in T. C. Koopmans, ed., *Activity Analysis for Production and Allocation,* Cowles Commission, New Haven.

HANSEN, A. H. (1953) *A Guide to Keynes,* McGraw Hill, New York.

HARROD, R. F. (1933) *International Economics,* Nisbet and Cambridge University Press.

HARROD, R. F. (1936) *The Trade Cycle,* Oxford University Press.

HARROD, R. F. (1939) 'An Essay in Dynamic Theory', *Economic Journal,* 49, 14–33.

HART, O. D. (1982) 'A Model of Imperfect Competition with Keynesian Features', *Quarterly Journal of Economics,* 96, 109–38.

HEFFERNAN, S. A. (1986) *Sovereign Risk Analysis,* George Allen and Unwin, London.

HEDGELAND, H. (1954) *The Multiplier Theory,* Lund, Sweden.

HICKS, J. R. (1937) 'Mr Keynes and the Classics', *Econometrica,* 5.

HICKS, J. R. (1939) *Value and Capital,* Oxford University Press (first edition; second edition, 1946).

HICKS, J. R. (1950) *A Contribution to the Theory of the Trade Cycle,* Oxford University Press.

HICKS, J. R. (1965) *Capital and Growth,* Oxford University Press.

HOBSON, J. A. and MUMMERY, A. F. (1889) *The Physiology of Industry,* London.

Journal of Monetary Economics (1983) Vol. 12, No. 1, Symposium on Alternative Monetary Standards.

KALDOR, N. (1940) 'A Model of the Trade Cycle', *Economic Journal,* 50, 78–92.

KALDOR, N. (1956) 'Alternative Theories of Distribution', *Review of Economic Studies,* 23, 83–100.

KALDOR, N. and MIRRLEES, J. A. (1962) 'A New Model of Economic Growth', *Review of Economic Studies,* 29, 174–92.

KALECKI, M. (1937) 'A Theory of the Business Cycle', *Review of Economic Studies,* 4, 77–97.

KEYNES, J. M. (1923) *A Trace on Monetary Reform,* London.

KEYNES, J. M. (1930) *A Treatise on Money,* Macmillan, London.

KEYNES, J. M. (1936) *The General Theory of Employment, Interest and Money,* Macmillan, London.

KLEIN, L. R. (1948) *The Keynesian Revolution,* Macmillan, London.

LAIDLER, D. (1966) 'The Rate of Interest and the Demand for Money: Some Empirical Evidence', *Journal of Political Economy,* 74, 545–55.

LEIJONHUFVUD, A. (1968) *On Keynesian Economics and the Economics of Keynes,* Oxford University Press, New York.

LUCAS, R. E. (1975) 'An Equilibrium Model of the Business Cycle', *Journal of Political Economy,* 83, 1113–44.

LUCAS, R. E. and RAPPING, L. (1969) 'Real Wages, Employment and Inflation', *Journal of Political Economy,* 77, 721–54.

MALINVAUD, E. (1977) *The Theory of Unemployment Reconsidered,* Blackwell, Oxford.

MALTHUS, T. R. (1836) *Principles of Political Economy,* second edition; Augustus Kelley, New York, 1968.

MARGLIN, S. A. (1984) *Growth, Distribution and Prices,* Harvard University Press, Cambridge, Mass.

MARX, K. (1976) *Capital,* Vol. I, ed. E. Mandel, Penguin, Harmondsworth.

MEADE, J. E. (1961) *A Neoclassical Theory of Economic Growth,* George Allen and Unwin, London.

MILLER, M. H. and SALMON, M. (1985) 'Dynamic Games and the Time Inconsistency of Optimal Policy in Open Economies', *Economic Journal Supplement,* 95, 124–37.

MODIGLIANI, F. and BRUMBERG, R. (1954) 'Utility Analysis and the Consumption Function: an Interpretation of Cross-Section Data', in K. Kurihara, ed., *Post-Keynesian Economics,* Rutgers University Press, New Brunswick, N.J.

MUTH, J. F. (1961) 'Rational Expectations and the Theory of Price Movements', *Econometrica,* 29, 315–35.

MYRDAL, G. (1931) 'On Penningteoretisk Jämvikt', *Ekonomisk Tidskrift.*

NEARY, J. P. (1980) 'Non-Traded Goods and the Balance of Trade in a neo-Keynesian Temporary Equilibrium', *Quarterly Journal of Economics,* 95, 403–29.

NEGISHI, T. (1979) *Microeconomic Foundations of Keynesian Macroeconomics,* North Holland, Amsterdam.

NEUMANN, J. VON (1938) 'Ueber ein Oekonomisches Gleichungssystem und eine Verallgemeinerung des Brouwerschen Fixpunktsatzes' in K. Menger, ed., *Ergebnisse eines Mathematischen Seminars,* Vienna, Translated as 'A Model of General Economic Equilibrium', *Review of Economic Studies,* 13, 1–9.

OHLIN, B. 'Some Notes on the Stockholm Theory of Savings and Investment I and II' *Economic Journal,* 47, 53–69 and 221–40.

PATINKIN, D. (1956) *Money, Interest and Prices,* Harper Row, New York (second edition, 1965).

PETTY, SIR WILLIAM (1689) *Political Arithmetick.*

PHELPS, E. S. (1961) 'The Golden Rule of Accumulation', *American Economic Review,* 51, 638–43.

PHELPS, E. S. (1967) 'Phillips Curves, Expectations of Inflation and Optimal Unemployment over Time', *Economica,* 34, 254–81.

PHELPS, E. S. et al. (1970) *Microfoundations of Employment and Inflation Theory,* W. W. Norton, New York.

RAMSEY, F. P. (1928) 'A Mathematical Theory of Saving', *Economic Journal,* 38, 47–61.

ROBINSON, J. (1953) 'The Production Function and the Theory of Capital', *Review of Economic Studies,* 21, 81–106.

—— (1956) *The Accumulation of Capital,* Macmillan, London.

ROGOFF, K. 'Can International Monetary Policy Cooperation be Counterproductive? *Journal of International Economics,* 18, 199–217.

SAMUELSON, P. A. (1939) 'Interactions between the Multiplier Analysis and the Principle of Acceleration', *Review of Economics and Statistics,* 21, 75–8.

SAMUELSON, P. A. (1951) 'Abstract of a Theorem Concerning Substitutability in Open Economy Leontief Models', in T. C. Koopmans, ed., *Activity Analysis of Production and Allocation,* Cowles Commission, New Haven.

SARGENT, T. J. and WALLACE, N. (1975) 'Rational Expectations, the Optimal Monetary Instrument, and the Optimal Money Supply Rule', *Journal of Political Economy,* 83, 241–77.

SARGENT, T. J. and WALLACE, N. (1976) 'Rational Expectations and the Theory of Economic Policy', *Journal of Monetary Economics,* 2, 169–83.

SARGENT, T. J. and WALLACE, N. (1981) 'Some Unpleasant Monetarist Arithmetic', *Federal Reserve Board of Minneapolis Quarterly Review,* 5, 1–17.

SHACKLE, G. L. S. (1938) *Expectations, Investment and Income,* Oxford University Press and Humphrey Milford.

SHACKLE, G. L. S. (1949) *Expectations in Economics,* Cambridge University Press.

SHACKLE, G. L. S. (1961) *Decision Order and Time,* Cambridge University Press.

SINCLAIR, P. J. N. (1983) *The Foundations of Macroeconomic and Monetary Theory*, Oxford University Press.

SOLOW, R. M. (1956) 'A Contribution to the Theory of Economic Growth', *Quarterly Journal of Economics*, 70, 65–94.

SOLOW, R. M. and STIGLITZ, J. E. (1968) 'Output, Employment and Wages in the Short Run', *Quarterly Journal of Economics*, 82, 537–60.

SRAFFA, P. (1960) *Production of Commodities by Means of Commodities: Prelude to a Critique of Economic Theory*, Cambridge University Press.

STIGLITZ, J. E. and WEISS, A. (1981) 'Credit Rationing in Markets with Imperfect Information', *American Economic Review*, 71, 393–410.

STIGLITZ, J. E. and WEISS, A. (1983) 'Incentive Effects of Terminations: Applications to Credit and Labor Markets', *American Economic Review*, 73, 912–27.

TARSHIS, L. (1939) 'Changes in Real and Money Wage Rates', *Economic Journal*, 49, 150–54.

TOBIN, J. (1956) 'The Interest Elasticity of Transactions Demand for Cash', *Review of Economics and Statistics*, 38, 241–7.

TOBIN, J. (1965) 'Money and Economic Growth', *Econometrica*, 33, 671–84.

TOBIN, J. (1980) *Asset Accumulation and Economic Activity*, Blackwell, Oxford.

UZAWA, A. (1962) 'On a Two-Sector Model of Economic Growth', *Review of Economic Studies*, 30, 105–18.

WEITZMAN, M. L. (1982) 'Increasing Returns and the Foundations of Unemployment Theory', *Economic Journal*, 92, 787–804.

WEITZMAN, M. L. (1984) *The Share Economy: Conquering Stagflation*, Harvard University Press, Cambridge, Mass.

WEITZMAN, M. L. (1985) 'The Simple Macroeconomics of Profit Sharing', *American Economic Review*, 75, 937–53.

WEIZSAECKER, C. C. VON (1966) 'Tentative Notes on a Two-Sector Model with Induced Technical Progress', *Review of Economic studies*, 34, 245–51.

Oxford Economic Papers 39 (1987), 1–19

PROFIT SHARING—CAN IT WORK?

By DAVID G. BLANCHFLOWER and ANDREW J. OSWALD

1. Introduction

IN July 1986 the British government published a Green Paper proposing important changes to the way workers are paid. This government initiative has been stimulated in part by the belief that something has gone wrong with the 'wage system', under which employees are paid a roughly fixed wage and unemployment fluctuates severely. The Green Paper argues that Britain's economic prospects would be improved by a move to a method of remuneration which would make pay more flexible.

There are at least two ways to have workers' remuneration change more readily with firms' commercial performance. One is to link wages to profits by using cash-based profit sharing (where workers are made cash payments which vary with their employer's profitability). A second is to have workers paid partly in their firm's own shares. At present Britain provides certain tax advantages to the latter.

In this paper we attempt to assess the case for a radical reform of the remuneration system. We begin with an examination of the theoretical arguments, and then turn to the empirical evidence.

2. The macroeconomic role for profit sharing

2.1. *The background*

There seems little doubt that it is Britain's disappointing macroeconomic performance which has stimulated government interest in the possible macroeconomic role for, and microeconomic effects of, profit sharing. Unemployment now stands at approximately 3.3 million (it would be higher still, but for recent changes in definition) compared to 0.3 million in 1960. Yet the real wage rate in Britain continues to rise faster than productivity, and there is a widely held belief that workers are being priced out of jobs. The latest and best empirical research supports this view and provides measures of the responsiveness of aggregate employment to the cost of labour. Numerous studies by economists now show that, put crudely, a 1 per cent rise in the real wage leads eventually to an approximate 1 per cent fall in employment. This result emerges from Layard and Nickell (1985a, 1985b, 1986), Newell and Symons (1985), Bean, Layard and Nickell (1986) and Carruth and Oswald (1986), *inter alia*. Similar findings can be seen throughout the articles in Greenhalgh, Layard and Oswald (1983) and the Unemployment symposium issue of *Economica*, 1986.

We have benefited enormously from discussions with, and comments from, Laurie Brennan, Peter Elias, Saul Estrin, Felix Fitzroy, Dan Mitchell, Peter Sinclair and Sushil Wadhwani.

It has been suspected for some time that the unconstrained behaviour of wage rates can produce undesirable results. Ten years ago the (Labour) government of the day attempted to use a statutory wages and incomes policy to influence pay. That is now believed by some to be politically unacceptable, so the search has started for new ways to intervene in the labour market. Advocates of profit sharing and employee share ownership programmes take the view that what is required is a change in the very method of remuneration.

It is natural to begin with an examination of what economic theory suggests about the possible consequences of 'sharing' arrangements. That is what Section, 2.2 does. The following Section, 2.3, summarises the empirical evidence. It describes tests done—by ourselves and others—of the various theories of profit sharing and employee share ownership.

2.2. *Theoretical underpinnings*

The macroeconomic case for sharing schemes has been dominated by the work of Martin Weitzman. In *The Share Economy,* published in 1984, and in numerous articles, especially 'The Simple Macroeconomics of Profit Sharing' in the 1985 *American Economic Review,* Weitzman outlines a theoretical argument in favour of remuneration systems based partly upon profit sharing. When workers are paid fixed wages, the author argues, an economy automatically behaves in an unsatisfactory way. Changes in demand or in world prices generate large fluctuations in employment; economic cycles occur and needlessly high unemployment is produced. The author believes that the way around this is to "vaccinate capitalism against stagflation". This would be achieved, Weitzman contends, by switching to a world in which workers' wages are tied explicitly and substantially to their employers' profit levels. Outside disturbances, according to Weitzman, then merely alter wages and prices, and unemployment is avoided.

Weitzman's 1984 book is deliberately polemical. It contains no formal theoretical framework and nothing an economist would regard as convincing empirical evidence. The rigorous version of the argument is the 1985 paper, although there is again no empirical proof. In it a formal model of the economy is constructed which is used to discuss the economics of profit sharing.

The Weitzman argument is probably widely misunderstood. Most of those who propound the merits of sharing schemes and cite Weitzman (1984) approvingly do so, in our view, for quite different reasons from the author. In fact there are three main ways to make a macroeconomic case for profit sharing and similar ideas. They may be described as:-
   (i) the morale and productivity argument
   (ii) the wage flexibility argument
   (iii) Weitzman's macroeconomic argument.
It is useful and topical to begin with the third.

Martin Weitzman's principal idea is that it might be possible to create a world in which there is constant excess demand for labour. Consider a typical East European nation in which there are always shortages of goods, prices do not move to clear markets and queuing is part of life. This is, in a nutshell, exactly what the author hopes might be possible in the *labour* markets of the industrialised West.[1] Firms in such a world could never get quite as many employees as they would like; they would continually queue up for the few available spare workers. Small macroeconomic shocks would then be quite harmless because the general shortage of workers would always exist. To quote Weitzman:

> "Although share and wage systems have identical resource-allocation patterns in stationary equilibrium, there is a marked difference in the degrees of tension of their respective labour markets. The wage system has supply *equal* to demand in the labour market. A wage firm wants to hire exactly as much labour as it is hiring under its current wage contract. But the share system has demand for labour *greater* than supply of labour. A share firm always wants to hire more labour than it is actually able to hire . . ." (1984, p. 91)

Although obviously extreme, this is a very original idea. That it occurred to Martin Weitzman may perhaps be because his professional work until recently was focused primarily on the study of the economies of the Eastern Bloc.

How could we create an economy in which there were perpetual shortages of labour? One way would be to make labour extremely cheap, which would induce firms to hire more labour than otherwise. One difficulty here is that workers must be paid enough to persuade them to work, another is that there would be undesirable effects on income distribution. The ideal, therefore, is a remuneration system in which the employer has to pay only a small amount for each extra worker, and where that extra individual's total pay is made up to the required amount by some other method. The Weitzman solution is to make an employee's remuneration the sum of two such components. First, there is a base wage as paid under the normal remuneration system. Second, there is a profit-related amount, the share, which is some proportion of the per capita profit earned by the company. The firm will wish to employ any worker who would contribute in extra sales revenue more than the base wage—because any profit produced above that base wage will be distributed in part to the company. Hence the trick for the 'sharing economy' to be successful is to ensure that base pay is sufficiently low that firms will be unable to find as many employees as they would like. In this kind of world, unemployment disappears. It is not clear, however, that those politicians and others who believe in the promotion of sharing schemes have anything like this in mind. The other and more popular ways to provide a rationale for profit sharing programmes are to

---

[1] We owe this point to Saul Estrin.

show that they either induce genuine wage flexibility or raise productivity by changing workers' attitudes.

The wage flexibility argument is the most straightforward and is somewhat like the Weitzman approach. If a sharing remuneration system worked efficiently, firms would have much less incentive to sack workers in a slump. An extreme example would be that of a company which employs a single salesman who works on a contract which says that he or she will receive one half of any profits. A reduction in sales, caused by a slump, will not automatically mean redundancy for this individual. Although disappointed by the fall in its own profits, the firm will still find it attractive to keep on the salesman. Both sides gain or lose as economic conditions alter.

In many ways it is the final possibility, the productivity argument for sharing schemes, which is the most tantalising. A rigorous account of it has yet to appear in this part of the literature, but the idea is a simple one. In a small firm where one individual's own efforts affect the whole enterprise's profit, the introduction of a profit sharing policy might encourage each individual to work harder. That this incentive argument might, in this case, be effective is hard to dispute. For a large organisation, however, it seems unlikely that there would be significant gains. Workers would be well aware that their individual efforts could never materially affect company profits.

The only obvious way to object to such pessimism is to claim that, after the implementation of a profit sharing scheme, workers' attitudes would change. If individuals do not behave in a rational and selfish way, balancing private gains with the private costs of higher effort, sharing schemes have a much greater chance of raising productivity. Such a view of human nature would be taken by certain psychologists. On this view a sharing arrangement might so improve the climate of industrial relations that employees would, perhaps unconsciously, improve their performance.

James Meade has recently proposed that the conventional wage system needs to be modified. Meade (1986a,b) argues that much of Britain's economic problem stems from "the sense of alienation between 'us', the workers, and 'them', the capitalist bosses". This difficulty would be dramatically reduced, he believes, by moving to a 'sharing economy.' Meade's suggestion is that workers should receive special share certificates in their own company, and that if necessary new workers should be hired on lower wage scales than existing employees.

There is now much other theoretical work on the economics of profit sharing and related ideas. This literature includes Bradley and Smith (1985), Estrin (1985), Grout (1985), Hart (1983), Jackman (1985), Kovenock and Sparks (1985), Nuti (1985), and Samuelson (1977). Although these differ in detail, all fall within the three-argument classification suggested earlier. Related work includes Hart (1983) and Oswald (1982, 1986).

Theoretical ideas ultimately need to be tested empirically, but it is possible before that to consider theoretical objections to those ideas. In the case of profit sharing schemes, there are a number of standard points, which for brevity are simply listed below.

1. Sharing programmes expose workers to a significant amount of income risk. This is ignored by Weitzman and nearly all the other writers in this literature, yet it is clearly a central part of union objections to income sharing arrangements.[2]
2. Under profit sharing, current workers will wish to prevent the firm from hiring extra individuals (which is not a difficulty under a conventional wage system), because any expansion in employment drives down the existing employees' remuneration.
3. If profit sharing is such a good thing, why is it necessary to subsidise it? Firms ought to see that it is in their own best interests. The reason why governments should become involved is not explained successfully in the literature although it is sometimes claimed, perhaps sensibly, that trade unions and firms need to be encouraged to take into account the interests of the unemployed.
4. Weitzman's claims for the attractiveness of the share economy rest upon the notion of an equilibrium in which there is continual excess demand for labour. This is not easy to take seriously. Competition amongst firms to hire the limited quantities of labour would naturally and gradually force up the wage level. The familiar wage system, in other words, might be expected to reappear.

There are also practical objections.

5. If the wage system is efficient, purely cosmetic sharing schemes may grow up. Significant economic resources may be needed simply to police any government subsidies of tax concessions.
6. Unions which agree to profit sharing are likely to want some control of the workplace, because under profit sharing programmes they are more like partners in the enterprise.
7. It seems undesirable to encourage workers to invest financial capital in their own firm's shares, because their human capital is already tied up in the enterprise. It is a standard point that risk averse agents prefer a diversified portfolio.

Similar objections are discussed in detail by Meade (1986b) and Wadhwani (1986). Mitchell (1986) is much less pessimistic.

2.3. Empirical evidence

In this section we examine the empirical evidence that exists on the role and influence of two broad forms of 'sharing' remuneration schemes. One is

---

[2] The implicit contract literature (Rosen (1985), for example) makes an interesting contrast. The principal *raison d'etre* of that literature has been that workers' aversion to risk makes fixed wage contracts optimal. It is curious that Weitzman and other proponents of profit sharing have disregarded all this influential work.

profit sharing, under which an employee receives a payment which depends on the size of the employer's profits. The second is employee share ownership, under which workers receive, or have an option to purchase cheaply, the shares in the employing company. In some cases firms make profit sharing payments in the form of shares which cannot immediately be sold. Initially we examine the rather limited amount of evidence that exists for the United Kingdom. We then draw comparisons with the evidence from other countries such as West Germany, Japan and the United States where profit sharing tends to be more prevalent.

(1) *United Kingdom*

Various governments in the United Kingdom have tried to encourage profit sharing and share ownership. The Finance Act of 1972 provided tax advantages for certain executive share options and for share based profit sharing schemes, whilst the 1973 Finance Act extended to all employees tax advantages which were related to Save As You Earn (SAYE) contracts. The statutory wages and incomes policy referred to earlier suspended these schemes via the Finance Act of 1974. But there then came a succession of Finance Acts which all made significant changes and provided extra tax relief, notably the Finance Acts of 1978, 1980, 1982, 1984 and 1985. (For further information see Outram (1985), Bradley and Gelb (1986) and Creigh, Donaldson and Hawthorn (1981).) Currently there are three kinds of approved employee share schemes which attract tax relief.

(a) Share schemes introduced in the 1978 Finance Act covering all employees. As can be seen from Table 1, by December 1985 the Inland Revenue had approved 510 schemes out of the 708 submissions it had received. The early growth in these schemes was partly the result of companies such as ICI, which already practised profit sharing, taking up a the tax concessions after 1978 for approved schemes (Incomes Data Services, 1986 p. 8).

TABLE 1
Submissions to the Inland Revenue (cumulative totals).

	Finance Act 1978			Finance Act 1980		
	Submitted	*Dropped*	*Approved*	*Submitted*	*Dropped*	*Approved*
Up to March 1979	96	—	3	—	—	—
1980	228	—	117	—	—	—
1981	327	—	210	82	—	22
1982	400	—	278	195	—	137
1983	476	89	344	267	12	215
1984	552	107	392	362	20	288
1985	635	116	462	516	27	403
Up to Dec. 1985	708	133	510	597	45	499

Source: Incomes Data Services (1986, p. 8).

TABLE 2

Distribution of participating employees by age of share ownership scheme in the private sector.

Age of scheme	% of all participating workers
Less than 1 year	16.0
1 year/less than 2 years	22.3
2 years/less than 10 years	29.1
More than 10 years	32.3
Not stated	0.3

Source: Blanchflower and Oswald (1986).

(b) Savings related share option schemes for all employees, introduced in the Finance Act of 1980. Table 1 illustrates that by December 1985 the Inland Revenue had approved 403 out of the 516 proposals submitted to it under this legislation.

(c) Discretionary share option schemes introduced in the 1984 Finance Act. By December 1985, 1,831 executive schemes had been submitted to the Inland Revenue and 1,210 had been approved.

There are no reliable estimates of the large number of companies who operate their own non-tax concessionary schemes. These usually take the form of cash based profit sharing schemes covering all employees.

The most comprehensive set of estimates of the number of *individuals* covered by share ownership schemes is available from the 1980 Workplace Industrial Relations Survey (WIRS). This was a nationally representative survey of approximately 2,000 establishments of at least 25 employees (full and part-time) in both the private and public sectors.[3] Managers were asked to report whether or not a share ownership scheme operated in their establishment. If a scheme was operated, managers were asked when it was introduced, the number of individuals who were eligible and the number who actually participated in the scheme. Table 2, based on the survey, confirms the fact that share ownership schemes have become more common since 1978. Despite the recent growth, however, in 1980 one third of all participating workers were in schemes more than ten years old. Table 3 reports the distribution by industrial sector of British workers in share ownership schemes. They were particularily important in chemicals; retail food; mining, quarrying and construction; printing and banking. They were especially unusual in shipbuilding; post and telecommunications; and paper. Roughly ten per cent of workers in the private sector were eligible to participate in such schemes by 1980 and half of those actually did so. Data were not available on the average value, or the variation in the value. of holdings across individuals.

[3] For further details of these data see Daniel and Millward (1983), Blanchflower (1984) and Blanchflower and Corry (1986).

TABLE 3
Coverage of share ownership schemes across employees.

	% employees eligible to participate	% of eligible employees who participate	Number of employees who participate (000's)
Food	13.3	19.9	13.5
Drink & tobacco	15.0	60.4	24.6
Chemicals	21.4	80.3	69.9
Metal manufacture	7.2	7.1	2.2
Mechanical engineering	3.8	13.4	4.5
Instrument engineering	3.4	—	—
Electrical engineering	10.1	0.7	0.1
Other electrical	7.9	36.9	17.1
Shipbuilding	—	—	—
Motor vehicles & tractors	11.1	41.6	14.8
Other vehicles	4.9	27.6	3.3
Metal goods n.e.s.	12.9	26.8	15.7
Man-made fibres, spinning & weaving	—	—	—
Other textiles and leather	7.8	2.7	0.7
Clothing & footwear	3.2	100.0	7.9
Bricks, pottery & glass	11.8	23.8	5.2
Timber & furniture	16.4	14.0	6.2
Paper	—	—	—
Printing	5.1	46.2	35.5
Other manufacturing n.e.s.	0.1	40.2	0.8
Mining, quarrying & construction	5.5	76.2	32.9
Gas, electricity & water	2.0	100.0	6.4
Road transport	1.2	14.3	0.4
Rail, sea & air transport	2.8	78.0	8.2
Posts & telecommunications	—	—	—
Wholesale distribution	12.7	59.6	25.0
Retail food	10.9	30.5	10.0
Other retail distribution	28.0	69.1	95.2
Dealing in materials	6.0	11.4	1.5
Insurance	13.8	63.2	12.4
Banking	55.0	65.8	65.2
Other business services	11.5	77.6	22.7
Education	—	—	—
Medical services	—	—	—
Other professional services	0.5	100.0	1.6
Hotels & pubs	1.3	96.1	5.5
Other miscellaneous services	—	—	—
Other services	—	—	—
Private manufacturing	9.0	40.6	222.0
Private non-manufacturing	10.5	64.5	287.0
Private sector	9.6	51.3	509.0

Source: Blanchflower and Oswald (1986) and 1980 Workplace Industrial Relations Survey—own calculations.

What do we know about the effects of these and similar schemes? This is now an active area of research in economics and a number of papers have already appeared.

Blanchflower and Oswald (1986a,b) have examined a sample of 637 manufacturing establishments, drawn from the 1980 WIRS data, in an attempt to determine whether or not the existence of share ownership schemes had beneficial effects on employment and investment. They could find no rigorous statistical evidence that the existence of such schemes affected firms' decisions about the number of jobs. This was true whatever the age of the scheme or the proportion of individuals who actually participated. Similarly, the presence of share ownership schemes was found to have had no significant influence upon an establishment's investment behaviour over the preceding two to three years.

In a recent paper Estrin and Wilson (1986) studied 52 firms in the UK engineering and metal working sectors over the period 1978–1982. The main concentration of firms was in the West Midlands and West Yorkshire. Five firms had introduced a profit sharing scheme under the 1978 Act and sixteen had their own non-tax concessionary value added scheme; one firm had both. Typically, bonuses paid were around 3 per cent of pay, although they reached 10 per cent in some firms. As would be expected, these bonuses varied significantly with the firm's economic situation over the trade cycle. In contrast to the results on share ownership reported by Blanchflower and Oswald, Estrin and Wilson found that the introduction of profit sharing increased employment in their sample of firms by around 13 per cent. In addition, total remuneration in firms with profit sharing was found on average to be 4 per cent lower than in firms without profit sharing. These estimates are surprisingly large. Because they are based upon a small sample of firms drawn from a narrowly defined sector, it is difficult to conclude anything about the overall representativeness of the authors' results. It should be said, however, that the authors themselves warn that their results should be treated as preliminary.

"These findings are fairly strong evidence that the macroeconomic benefits for employment predicted by Weitzman may also hold at the enterprise level. The shift in employment may in part be associated with improved motivation and labour productivity, but the combined results of increased employment and reduced remuneration is consistent with Weitzman-type effects or a weakening of union power. However, these findings are preliminary and shed no light on the important proposition about the adjustment of profit sharing firms through the trade cycle. Further research is required before any final evaluation of the profit sharing proposal can be made." (1986, p. 31)

Richardson and Nejad (1986) analysed the impact of financial participation schemes on share price movements over the period 1978–1984 using a sample of 41 firms chosen from the UK multiple stores sector. This sector was chosen because it is reasonably competitive, relatively free from foreign competition and unlikely to have its profit levels affected by the vagaries of the exchange rate. By the end of 1984, out of their sample of 41 firms, 23 were operating at least one employee share ownership scheme. Their main finding is that companies which introduced the schemes had a 5 per cent higher share appreciation than those that did not. This difference was statistically significant at the 10 per cent confidence level. However, it is questionable that one can infer from these results that share ownership schemes raise share prices. Indeed, as Richardson and Nejad point out:-

"It may well be that the innovating firms introduced, or extended, financial participation as part of a much wider review of their management strategy. In this case, the use of financial participation might be an excellent index of improved management but not the sole cause of, or even an important contributor to, improved performance. Employee share ownership may, therefore, have been merely one element among many". (1986, p. 24)

It is apparent, therefore, that the limited amount of quantitative work that exists for the UK has produced conflicting evidence on the importance of sharing schemes in altering company performance. The evidence from a number of studies which have provided qualitative data on the effects of profit sharing is rather less equivocal. Wallace and Hanson (1984), for example, found that "profit sharing does significantly improve employee attitudes and employee views of the company". Their principal results, which were derived from interviews with 2,703 employees in 12 companies, are presented in Table 4 opposite. As can be seen from the sixth row of the Table, 51 per cent of respondents reported that they agreed, or strongly agreed, that profit sharing makes people try to work more effectively so as to help the firm be more successful. Interestingly enough, 96 per cent said that they agreed, or strongly agreed, that profit sharing should not be seen as a substitute for an adequate wage.

Broadly similar results were obtained by the Wider Share Ownership Council in their survey of *company* attitudes towards employee share ownership schemes. 138 companies were asked what effect they believed profit sharing or share savings schemes had on employee attitudes. As can be seen from Table 5, three quarters of firms reported that share schemes had resulted in some improvement in employee loyalty or attitudes. Moreover, approximately one third of all firms reported that such schemes had a significant effect. This compares with 40 per cent and 20 per cent, respectively, in the case of savings related schemes. Evidence regarding the effects of these two types of schemes upon productivity, staff turnover, recruitment etc. was much less clear cut.

To sum up the evidence for the United Kingdom, there is only a little *quantitative* evidence of a significant impact of profit sharing schemes upon company performance or employment. The two studies that have found significant effects (Estrin and Wilson, 1986 and Richardson and Nejad, 1986) were based upon relatively small samples of firms drawn from two

TABLE 4

The Industrial Participation Association Survey, 1980. (%)

	Agree strongly	Agree	Don't Know	Disagree	Disagree strongly
1. Profit sharing creates a better atmosphere in the firm	10	55	16	18	1
2. It is popular because people like to have the bonus	24	69	4	3	—
3. It makes people take a greater interest in profits and financial results	11	65	7	16	1
4. It is good for the company and the employees	14	72	11	3	—
5. It strengthens people's loyalty to the firm	6	41	17	34	2
6. It makes people try to work more effectively so as to help the firm be successful	6	45	15	31	3
7. It is welcomed by the participants but should not be seen as a substitute for an adequate wage or salary	44	52	3	1	—
8. Most people are apathetic about profit sharing	2	22	25	47	4
9. It can cause disappointment or bitterness, because profits can go down as well as up.	3	39	10	45	3

Source: "Profit sharing and employee shareholding attitude survey" published by the Industrial Participation Association.

narrowly defined sectors—metal working and multiple stores. A plausible explanation for their results is that it is the well managed, well run firms that introduce profit sharing. The danger then is of attributing to profit sharing what should more correctly be attributed to the overall efficiency of the organisation.

TABLE 5
Comments on effectiveness of profit sharing schemes, 1981.

	% of respondents with profit sharing schemes answering		% of respondents with savings related schemes answering	
	Small effect	Significant effect	Small effect	Significant effect
Increased productivity	41	4	23	4
Improved loyalty or attitudes	45	32	40	20
Helped negotiations	36	4	18	2
Facilitated recruitment	35	9	30	5
Reduced staff turnover	36	3	23	5

Source: "Employee share schemes" by Copeman Paterson; from the Wider Share Ownership Council

Such *qualitative* evidence that exists does suggest that profit sharing has small, but significant, effects upon employees' attitudes to work. If this evidence is to be believed, however, we would expect to observe some productivity enhancement in firms with profit sharing which, in principle, should be measurable.

2) *International evidence*

In the United States in 1985, according to a recent survey (United States General Accounting Office, 1986), more than seven million individuals participated in approximately 4,174 Employee Stock Ownership Plans (ESOPs). Collectively, by 1985 they held assets of nearly $19 billion. To create an ESOP, a company establishes an Employee Stock Ownership Trust (ESOT) which borrows capital and buys company stock. The trust is guaranteed by the company, which is allowed to place up to 25 per cent of its payroll into the ESOT to pay off the loan. As the loan is paid off, stock is allocated to each employee's ESOP account. When employees leave or retire they sell their stock back to the ESOP.[4] ESOPs are of four basic types.

(a) Tax credit. An ESOP originating in the Tax Reduction Act of 1975, which allows employers to claim a tax credit for contributions to an ESOP. From 1975–1982 the credit was based upon an employer's eligible investment; a 1 per cent credit could be claimed for contributions up to that amount and an additional 0.5 per cent could be claimed for contributions that matched employees' contributions up to that amount. Since 1983, a credit of 0.5 per cent of employee payroll has been allowed.

(b) Leveraged ESOP. An ESOP in which money is borrowed by the ESOT for the purpose of buying stock of the employer. The stock is

---

[4] For further details see Bradley and Gelb (1986) who provide an interesting discussion of potential abuses of ESOPs.

normally held as security by the lender and released for allocation to participant accounts as the loan is paid off.

(c) Leverageable ESOP. An ESOP that is permitted to lever under the terms of the plan documents but has not done so by a given date.

(d) Nonleveraged ESOP. An ESOP other than a tax credit ESOP that is not permitted to lever under the terms of the plan document. Although these plans do not take advantage of the special tax credit or levering provisions of the tax code, employers may establish them to take advantage of higher tax limits on deductions for contributions that are available. Also some employers may be unaware that they may establish and maintain a stock bonus plan that is not an ESOP.

The distributions of participants and assets in these various schemes in 1985 are presented in Table 6. Overall, 90.1 per cent of all ESOP participants were in tax credit ESOPs. The median tax credit ESOP had 430 participants, and held much larger amounts of assets than other types, although leveraged ESOPs had the highest asset value per participant. On average in 1985 participants had holdings of $5,226.

Since 1974, ESOPs have been granted increasingly favourable tax advantages; the legislation has had three main goals:

(1) the broader ownership of corporate stock
(2) the provision of more funds for capital formation
(3) improved performance of the sponsoring corporation.

Attention in the literature has focused particularly on the last of these goals; as in the case of Great Britain the evidence is conflicting. Marsh and McAllister (1981) found that the productivity growth rate of a sample of 125 ESOPs was greater in 1975–1979 than the national rate for their industries. However, Hamilton (1983) found that 10 matched firms had productivity at

TABLE 6
Estimates of the participants in and assets of ESOPs.[a]

	Participants			Assets[b]			
Type	Number	%	median per plan	Total (millions)	%	median per plan	median per person
Tax credit	6,391,029	90.1	430	14,800	79.3	864,446	2,952
Leveraged	158,238	2.2	54	1,450	7.8	444,708	8,660
Leverageable	293,274	4.1	37	1,445	7.7	272,663	7,149
Nonleveraged	238,406	3.4	40	961	5.2	209,397	5,098
Other	1,842	*	10	1	*	0	0
	7,082,789	99.8[c]	54	18,660	100.0	334,606	5,226
Total							

Notes: [a] based on plans active in 1983. [b] in constant 1983 dollars. [c] total does not equal 100.0 due to rounding. * less than 0.05%.

Source: "Employee stock ownership plans. Interim report and related trends" United States General Accounting Office, February 1986 Table 7.

least as high or higher than 10 ESOP firms in the same industry in
1978–1981.

One of the better known US studies is Conte and Tannenbaum (1978).
They analysed whether firms which were partly or wholly owned by their
employees behaved in a different way from conventional firms. Approximately 100 companies were studied. One third of those were directly owned
by workers; the rest had large employee stock ownership plans. The authors
obtained profit data from 30 of these companies, and showed that they had
an average pre-tax profits to sales ratio equal to 1.7 of the overall average in
the relevant industries. In other words, worker-owned firms appeared to be
more profitable. However, there are two criticisms of this conclusion. First,
the authors admit that the results are not formally statistically significant.
Second, it is not hard to believe that the 30 firms willing to release their
profit figures were those proud of their profitability levels. One of the few
statistically significant effects discovered by Conte and Tannenbaum was
that firms were more profitable the greater the amount of equity held by
workers. The authors also interviewed managers and concluded that
employee ownership "contributed substantially to the motivation of workers
and . . . productivity and profitability". Subsequent work with a matched
comparison of firms (Tannenbaum, Cook and Lohman, 1984), however,
found no difference in the profitability of the two groups of firms.

Rosen and Klein (1983) found that 10 ESOP firms were not significantly
more profitable than 10 matched firms on three measures of profitability
(the ratios of net profits to net sales, to net worth and to net working
capital) but outperformed the non-ESOP firms on a fourth measure (the
ratio of net sales to net worth). However, Brooks, Henry and Livingstone
(1982) found that employee share ownership had no significant effect on
company profitability, whilst both Bhagat, Brickley and Lease (1984) and
Livingston and Henry (1980) found that firms with such schemes were *less*
profitable than comparable firms without them.

A number of US studies have examined the impact of participation
schemes on attitudes and morale. Marsh and McAllister (1981) found an
increase in employee morale after the introduction of an ESOP. Kruse
(1984) surveryed attitudes at two U.S. firms with employee stock ownership
plans and concluded that the existence of the plans had no effect. Long
(1982) conducted a case study at an electronics firm that made changes in its
participation structure. He contrasted the attitudes of individuals who had
acquired small numbers of shares with those acquiring large numbers of
shares and reported that:-

"given the differences between the two groups in terms of personal characteristics,
as well as stock ownership, the pattern of results is remarkably similar, and seems
to suggest that the quantity of stock acquired had little impact on the extent to
which changes in attitudes or perceptions took place." (1982, p. 208)

Using a sample of 65 medium-sized firms in the West German metal working industry in 1977–79, Fitzroy and Kraft (1985a,b) examined the effects of profit sharing on productivity (1985a) and profitability (1985b). (These data are directly comparable to those used in Great Britain by Estrin and Wilson, 1986). In Fitzroy and Kraft (1985a) a strong positive relationship was found between profit sharing and total factor productivity; there was no correlation between hourly earnings and profit sharing after controlling for other relevant factors.[5] In Fitzroy and Kraft (1985b) it was found that profit sharing and employee ownership both have

> "strong and robust effects on profitability with none of the 'feedback' from profits to profit sharing which is sometimes posited" (1985b, p. 1)

The authors do accept the possibility, however, that it could be the best and most successful firms who provide profit shares to avoid worker discontent.

An interesting paper by Freeman and Weitzman (1986) has recently appeared. It uses time series macroeconomic data from Japan, for the years 1958–1982, to examine the behaviour of employment, wages and bonuses. Because Japanese workers are paid large profit-related bonuses (they constitute 25 per cent of workers' pay and 10 per cent of net domestic product), the country might be thought of as a good example of a 'share economy'. Freeman and Weitzman show that bonuses behave much more cyclically than basic wages, and that higher bonuses are positively correlated with higher employment. Employment is negatively correlated with the basic wage. Although these are intriguing conclusions, it is not clear that they help us to decide whether profit sharing has desirable consequences. On the face of it a reduction in bonuses would in fact act to *reduce* the size of employment fluctuations. Nevertheless, the authors point out that wages are lower than they would be without any profit sharing. They argue that this is likely to have raised Japan's level of employment.

Wadhwani (1985) also looks at the macroeconomic implications of profit sharing in the Japanese economy. His conclusions are generally negative. The author shows, counter to conventional wisdom, that between 1950 and 1981 Japan did not have lower cyclical variability of output or lower inflation than other industrial countries. In addition, his empirical tests demonstrate that changes in aggregate demand do not produce smaller effects upon Japan's output than is true elsewhere. However, Japan's unemployment rate over the period was lower than the rate in almost all other OECD countries, which the author argues is impressive but is unwilling to attribute to profit sharing.

---

[5] Work on producer cooperatives in a number of countries has also reported a positive effect of profit sharing on productivity. Examples are Jones and Backus (1977) and Jones (1977) for Great Britain, Jones and Svejnar (1985) for Italy, Cable and Fitzroy (1980 a,b) for West Germany, Defourney, Estrin and Jones (1985) for France and Conte and Svejnar (1981) for the United States.

3. Conclusion

The purpose of this paper has been to summarise and assess the debate about the merits of profit sharing and employee share ownership. We have identified three ways to make the case for more income sharing in the British economy. They are, in our terminology, (i) the morale and productivity argument, (ii) the wage flexibility argument and (iii) Martin Weitzman's macroeconomic argument. We believe that the third is widely misunderstood (Weitzman's idea is that profit sharing could create an economy with perpetual labour shortages) and that it has attracted much enthusiastic attention because it produces what many see, if for different reasons, as the correct prescription. Our examination of the evidence makes us believe that there is little to be said for the view that, for employment reasons, the Government should do more to encourage employee share ownership schemes. The major studies in the UK and abroad have produced no evidence that such schemes influence employment. Blanchflower and Oswald's (1986) analysis of more than 600 British plants, for example, finds no effect. Those investigators abroad, like Conte and Tannenbaum (1978), who favour such schemes commonly draw conclusions which even they agree are not proved by their statistical work.

The argument for cash based profit sharing is less weak and more interesting. There is a little empirical evidence in its favour (Estrin and Wilson (1986), for example), although series research has only recently started. However, it is hard to believe that wider profit sharing will make any significant difference to unemployment. We are not convinced that there is a case for tax concessions to encourage profit sharing.

Those who propound profit sharing would be best served by stressing three points. First, Britain appears to have severe economic problems and it may therefore be worth experimenting even with untested, radical solutions. Second, profit sharing may change certain kinds of employee attitudes. Third, the success of the Japanese economy, and of UK firms like John Lewis, is intriguing and may—although this is merely a conjecture—be something to do with their adoption of cash-based profit sharing.

Can profit sharing work? There is little empirical evidence that it can, and there are probably better ways of stimulating employment, such as by cutting National Insurance contributions. However, if the British government is determined to alter the whole system of remuneration,[6] tax relief for cash based profit sharing is less objectionable than further expansion of employee share ownership.

University of Surrey
London School of Economics

---

[6] At the time of writing the Chancellor of the Exchequer seems firmly committed to this idea.

REFERENCES

BEAN, C., LAYARD, R. and NICKELL, S. (1986), 'The Rise in Unemployment: A Multi-Country Study', *Economica*, Vol. 53, No. 210(s), pp. s1–s22.

BHAGAT, S., BRICKLEY, J. A. and LEASE, R. C. (1984), 'Incentive Effects of Stock Purchase Plans', *Journal of Financial Economics*, (forthcoming).

BLANCHFLOWER, D. (1984), 'Union Relative Wage Effects: A Cross-Section Analysis Using Establishment Data', *British Journal of Industrial Relations*, Vol. 22, pp. 311–332.

—— and CORRY, B. (1986), 'Part-Time Employment in Great Britain, 1980', Department of Employment Research Paper, (forthcoming).

—— and OSWALD, A. J. (1986a), 'Improving the Workings of Western Labour', *The Guardian*, March 19.

—— (1986b), 'Shares for Employees: a Test of Their Effects' London School of Economics, Mimeo.

BRADLEY, K. and GELB, A. (1986), *Share ownership for Employees, London*: Blackrose Press.

BRADLEY, M. D. and SMITH, C. S. (1985), 'Some Microeconomic Analysis of Income-Sharing Firms', George Washington University, Mimeo.

BROOKS, L., HENRY, J. and LIVINGSTONE, D. (1982). 'How Profitable are Employee Stock Ownership Plans?', *Financial Executive* May.

CABLE, J. and FITZROY, F. (1980a), 'Cooperation and Productivity: Some Evidence from West German Experience', *Economic Analysis and Workers' Management*, Vol. XIV, pp. 163–190.

—— (1980b), 'Production Efficiency, Incentives and Employee Participation: Some Preliminary Results for West Germany', *Kyklos*, Vol. 33, pp. 100–121.

CARRUTH, A. A. and OSWALD, A. J. (1986), 'Testing for Multiple Natural Rates of Unemployment in the British Economy', London School of Economics, Mimeo.

CONTE, M. and SVEJNAR (1981), 'Productivity Effects of Participatory and Worker Ownership Schemes, Profit-Sharing and Trade Unions in U.S. Manufacturing', Paper presented at the 1981 North American Meetings of the Econometric Society, Washing D.C., December.

—— and TANNENBAUM, A. (1978), 'Employee-Owned Companies: Is the Difference Measurable?', *Monthly Labor Review*, pp. 23–28.

CREIGH, S., DONALDSON, A. and HAWTHORN, E. 'A Stake in the Firm. Employee Financial Involvement in the Firm.' *Employment Gazette* May 1981, pp. 229–236.

DANIEL, W. and MILLWARD, N. (1982), *Workplace Industrial Relations in Britain*, London: Heinemann.

DEFOURNEY, J., ESTRIN, S. and JONES, D. C. (1985), 'The Effects of Worker Participation in French Cooperatives', *International Journal of Industrial Organisation*, Vol. 3, pp. 197–218.

ESTRIN, S. (1985), 'The Microeconomic Effects of Profit-Sharing', London School of Economics, Mimeo.

—— and WILSON, N. (1986), 'The Microeconomic Effects of Profit-Sharing: The British Experience', Center for Labour Economics Discussion Paper, London School of Economics.

FITZROY, F. and KRAFT, K. (1985a), 'Cooperation, Productivity and Profit Sharing'. *Quarterly Journal of Economics* (forthcoming).

—— (1985b) 'Profitability and Profit Sharing' *Journal of Industrial Economics* (forthcoming).

FREEMAN, R. and WEITZMAN, M. (1986), 'Bonuses and Employment in Japan'. National Bureau of Economic Research, Working Paper No 1878.

GREENHALGH, G. A. LAYARD, R. and OSWALD, A. J. (1983), *The Causes of Unemployment*, Oxford, Oxford University Press.

GROUT, P. A. (1985), 'Employee Share Ownership Schemes', University of Birmingham, Mimeo.

HAROLD HAMILTON, (1983), *The Effects of Employee Stock Ownership Plans on the Financial*

Performance of the Electrical and Electronic Machinery, Equipment, and Supplies Industry. (Ann Arbor, Mich.)

HART, O. D. (1983), 'Optimal Labour Contracts Under Asymmetric Information: an Introduction' *Review of Economic Studies* Vol. 50 pp. 3–35.

HOERR, J. A. (1982), 'Why Labour and Management are both Buying Profit Sharing' *Business Week* January.

Incomes Data Services (1986), 'Profit Sharing and Share Options' Incomes Data Services Study No. 357. London.

JACKMAN, R. (1985), 'Professor Weitzman and the Unions, or Why Profit-Sharing is Just Another Wage Tax: a Note' Centre for Labour Economics Working Paper No. 776. London School of Economics.

JONES, D. C. (1982), 'British Producer Cooperatives, 1948–1968. Productivity and Organisational Structure' in Jones, D. C., and Svejnar, J. (eds.), *Participatory and Self-managed Firms: Evaluating Economic Performance* Lexington Books. Lexington MA.

JONES, D. C. and BACKUS, D. (1977), 'British Producer Cooperatives in the Footwear Industry: and Empirical Investigation of the Theory of Financing' *Economic Journal* Vol. 87 pp. 488–510.

—— and SVEJNAR, J. (1985), 'Participation, Profit Sharing, Worker Ownership and Efficiency in Italian Producer Cooperatives' *Economica* Vol. 52 pp. 449–465.

KOVENOCK, D. and SPARKS, R. (1985), 'An Implicit Contract Approach to Employee Stock Ownership Plans' University of Essex, Department of Economics, Working Paper.

KRUSE, D. (1984), *Employee Ownership and Employee Attitudes: Two Case Studies* Pennsylvania: Norwood Editions.

LAYARD, R., and NICKELL, S. J. (1985a), 'The Causes of British Unemployment' *National Institute Economic Review* Vol. 111, pp. 62–85.

—— (1985b), 'Unemployment, Real Wages and Aggregate Demand in Europe, Japan and the U.S.' *Journal of Monetary Economics,* Carnegie–Rochester Conference Series, No. 23 Supplement.

—— (1986), 'Unemployment in Britain' *Economica* Vol. 53, No. 210(s), pp. s121–s170.

LIVINGSTON, D. and HENRY, J. B. (1980), 'The Effect of Employee Stock Ownership Plans on Corporate Profits' *Journal of Risk & Insurance* pp. 491–505.

LONG, R. (1982), 'Worker Ownership and Job Attitudes: A Field Study', *Industrial Relations,* 21. pp. 196–215.

MARSH, T. and MCALLISTER, D. (1981), 'ESOP's Fables: A Survey of Companies with Employee Stock Ownership Plans', *Journal of Corporation Law,* 6.

MEADE, J. (1986a). 'Different Forms of Employee Remuneration and Participation', paper for the Bank of England's Panel of Academic Consultants, February.

—— (1986b), *Different Forms of Share Economy,* Public Policy Centre, London.

MITCHELL, D. J. B. (1986), 'The Share Economy and Industrial Relations: Implications of the Weitzman Proposal' *Industrial Relations* (forthcoming).

NEWELL, A. and SYMONS, J. S. (1985), 'Wages and Employment in the OECD Economies', London School of Economics, Mimeo.

NUTI, D. M. (1985), 'The Share Economy: Plausibility and Viability of Weitzman's Model', European University Institute Working Paper No. 85/194.

OSWALD, A. J. (1982), 'The Microeconomic Theory of the Trade Union', *Economic Journal,* Vol. 92, pp. 576–596.

OSWALD, A. J. (1986), 'Unemployment Insurance and Labour Contracts under Asymmetric Information: Theory and Facts', *American Economic Review,* (forthcoming).

OUTRAM, Q. (1985), 'Weitzman in Historical Perspective', Leeds University, Mimeo.

RICHARDSON, R. and NEJAD, A. (1985), 'The Impact of Financial Participation Schemes on Share Price Movements', London School of Economics, Mimeo.

ROSEN, S. (1985) 'Implicit Contracts: a Survey' NBER Working Paper No 1635, June.

ROSEN, C. and KLEIN, K. (1983), 'Job Creating Performance of Employee-Owned Firms, *Monthly Labor Review,* 106, August, pp. 15–19.

SAMUELSON, P. A. (1977), 'Thoughts on Profit-Sharing', *Zeitschrift fur die Gesamte Staatswissenschaft,*' Special Issue on Profit-Sharing.

TANNENBAUM, A., COOK, A. and LOHMANN, J. (1984), *The Relationship of Employee Ownership to the Technological Adaptiveness and Performance of Companies*' (Ann Arbor, Mich.; Institute for Social Research).

WADHWANI, S. (1985) 'The Macro-Economic Implications of Profit-Sharing: Some Empirical Evidence', LSE, Centre from Labour Economics Discussion Paper no. 220.

—— (1986), 'Profit Sharing as a Cure for Unemployment: Some Doubts' Mimeo, London School of Economics.

WALLACE, B. D. and HANSON, C. (1984), 'Profit-Sharing and Employee Shareholding Attitude Survey', Industrial Participation Association, November.

WEITZMAN, M. L. (1982), 'Increasing Returns and the Foundations of Unemployment Theory', *Economic Journal,* Vol. 92, pp. 787–804.

—— (1983), 'Some Macroeconomic Implications of Alternative Compensation Systems', *Economic Journal,* Vol. VM 93, pp. 763–83.

—— (1984), *The Share Economy,* Harvard University Press, Cambridge.

—— (1985), 'The Simple Macroeconomics of Profit-Sharing', *American Economic Review,* Vol. 75, pp. 937–953.

Oxford Economic Papers 39 (1987), 20–37

SUPPLY SHOCKS AND OPTIMAL MONETARY POLICY

By STEPHEN J. TURNOVSKY*

1. Introduction

THE sharp increases in the price of oil during 1973–74 focused attention on the question of the appropriate monetary response in the face of supply disturbances. Should monetary policy be accommodative and finance the higher level of prices or should it be contractionary to offset the inflationary effects of such disturbances? These issues have occupied the attention of macroeonomists for over a decade now; see, e.g., Gordon (1975, 1984), Phelps (1978), Blinder (1981), Aizenman and Frenkel (1986), Fischer (1985). With the current fall in oil prices, the topic promises to be relevant for some time, although the direction of the shocks has been reversed.

At this point, there does not seem to be any consensus as to what the appropriate monetary response should be. In his early study, Gordon argued for monetary accommodation in response to an adverse supply shock (higher oil price). On the other hand, Blinder (1981) argues that certain types of disturbances may require a monetary contraction. By contrast, Fischer (1985) argues that as long as there is no real wage resistance by workers, supply shocks by themselves should require no monetary response. However, his results depend upon very specific assumptions regarding the form of the money demand function. Marston and Turnovsky (1985a) show how the macroeconomic effects of supply disturbances depend crucially upon wages policy, while Aizenman and Frenkel (1985) stress how this in turn is important in determining the role of monetary policy.

This paper analyzes the optimal monetary response to supply disturbances, taking up several issues which have thus far not been addressed in the literature. First, while several authors note the distinctions between: (i) permanent and transitory shocks on the one hand, and (ii) unanticipated and anticipated shocks on the other, and recognize that the required response to each type of disturbance will be different, a systematic general treatment of these different disturbances is thus far lacking. Secondly, the policy rules typically considered specify the adjustment of the money stock to *current* disturbances in supply.[1] Yet it is also possible and reasonable for the monetary authorities to respond to *anticipations* of both current and future supply shocks. Indeed, an important result of our analysis is that more general policy rules of this kind turn out to require less information about the nature of the supply disturbances than do 'simpler' rules based only on information about current shocks. They are therefore likely to lead

---

* The comments of an anonymous referee are gratefully acknowledged.
[1] An exception is Blinder (1981) who considers a rule in which the money stock is adjusted in response to anticipated and unanticipated supply shocks.

to improved stabilization performance. Thirdly, the existing literature assumes that the monetary authorities observe and respond to the current supply disturbance instantaneously.[2] This may not always be a plausible assumption. We therefore also investigate the case where the stochastic disturbances impinging on the economy are not observed instantaneously, but must be inferred from the movements of other variables, such as the price level and the interest rate, which are likely to be observed with greater frequency. It turns out that the optimal monetary response to a supply shock is virtually identical to that under complete information. The only difference is that the actual disturbance is replaced by the perceived disturbance determined by solving the appropriate signal extraction problem.

The remainder of the paper is structured as follows. Sections 2 and 3 outline the framework and provide the general solution to the model. The next two sections then determine the optimal monetary response under the assumptions of full and imperfect information respectively. The main results are reviewed in the final section.

2. The framework

Our analysis assumes a closed economy described by the following equations. These are expressed in deviation form about a stationary equilibrium so that all constants are suppressed.

$$Y_t = -d[r_t - (P^*_{t+1,t} - P_t)] + u_t \qquad d > 0 \tag{1a}$$

$$M_t = P_t = \alpha_1 Y_t - \alpha_2 r_t + w_t \qquad \alpha_1 > 0, \qquad \alpha_2 > 0 \tag{1b}$$

$$Y_t = \left(\frac{1-\theta}{\theta}\right)(1-\tau)(P_t - P^*_{t,t-1}) + \left(\frac{1-\theta}{\theta}\right)\left[E_t(v_t) - \frac{v^*_{t,t-1}}{1+n\theta}\right] + v_t$$

$$0 < \theta < 1, 0 \leqq \tau < 1, \qquad n > 0 \tag{1c}$$

where

Y_t = real output, expressed in logarithms
r_t = nominal interest rate,
P_t = price level, expressed in logarithms
$P^*_{t+1,t}$ = forecast of P_{t+1}, formed at time t,
M_t = nominal money supply, expressed in logarithms,
u_t = stochastic disturbance in the demand for output,
w_t = stochastic disturbance in the demand for money,
v_t = stochastic disturbance in supply of output,
$v^*_{t,t-1}$ = forecast of v_t, formed at time $t-1$,
$E_t(x_t)$ = perception of disturbance x_t, formed at time t, $x = u, v, w$.

---

[2] Aizenman and Frenkel (1985) allow for supply shocks which are not observed instantaneously. But the focus of their analysis is quite different, being on the tradeoff between wage indexation and monetary policy, rather than on stabilizing for supply shocks themselves. Marston and Turnovsky (1985b) allow for firm-specific productivity disturbances which may, or may not, be observed generally. Their analysis too is directed at different issues from those being pursued here.

The model contains three stochastic disturbances u_t, v_t, and w_t, which in general need not be observed contemporaneously. While our main interest is in the supply shock v_t, the introduction of the two demand disturbances u_t, w_t, is required in order to generate a potential situation of imperfect information. If the only disturbance is v_t, its value can always be inferred precisely from movements in other variables such as the interest rate, which may more reasonably be observed instantaneously.

Equation (1a) is the economy's IS curve, expressed as a negative relationship between output and the real interest rate, while (1b) is the LM curve. Equation (1c) describes the aggregate supply function; being less familiar, it is derived in the Appendix. Basically, it incorporates a one-period Fischer–Gray wage contract model, in which the contract wage adjusts to expected price movements and expected supply shocks.[3] The current wage is then determined by indexation to unanticipated movements in the price level, with the rate of indexation being τ. As is clear from (A.2) in the Appendix, the aggregate supply shock v_t can be interpreted as a shock in productivity, while $(1 - \theta)$ is the exponent on labour in the underlying production function. The remaining parameter n is the elasticity of labour supply with respect to the real wage. Equation (1c) is written on the assumption that the current supply disturbance is not observed instantaneously. In the event that v_t is observed, $E_t(v_t) = v_t$ and (1c) becomes

$$Y_t = \left(\frac{1-\theta}{\theta}\right)(1-\tau)(P_t - P^*_{t,t-1}) + \frac{1}{\theta}\left[v_t - \frac{1-\theta}{1+n\theta}v^*_{t,t-1}\right] \qquad (1c')$$

Finally, expectations are rational so that

$$P^*_{t+s,t} = E_t(P_{t+s}) \quad \text{for all } s$$

Monetary policy is assumed to be specified by a rule of the form

$$M_t = \mu_0 E_t(v_t) + \mu_1 v^*_{t+1,t} + \mu_2 v^*_{t,t-1} + \lambda_1 E_t(u_t) + \lambda_2 E_t(w_t) \qquad (1d)$$

That is, on the one hand, the money stock is adjusted to perceptions of the current stochastic disturbances, $E_t(v_t)$, $E_t(u_t)$, $E_t(w_t)$. At the same time, it is adjusted in anticipation of the next period's supply shock, as well as in response to the anticipated supply disturbance for the present period. It can be shown that for the objective function to be introduced below, this rule suffices to achieve minimum welfare costs. If, for example, the rule was augmented to allow the money stock to respond to $v^*_{t+j,t}$, the anticipated supply shock for time $t+j$, it can be shown that the corresponding coefficient μ_j say, in the optimal rule, would be zero; see, e.g., footnote 5 below. As already noted, our main concern is with the coefficients μ_0, μ_1, μ_2, which pertain to supply disturbances.[4] Further, in the case where the

---

[3] See Fischer (1977), Gray (1976).

[4] It is also possible to augment the rule to respond to anticipated demand shocks, analogous to those for supply. Including $v_1 u^*_{t+1,t} + v_2 u^*_{t-1,t}$, for example, it can be shown that v_1, v_2, satisfy

$$v_1 + v_2\left(\frac{\alpha_2}{1+\alpha_2}\right) = 0$$

and since our interest does not lie in demand shocks, we have chosen the simplest solution $v_1 = v_2 = 0$.

stochastic disturbances are observed instantaneously, the rule (1d) is modified to

$$M_t = \mu_0 v_t + \mu_1 v_{t+1,t}^* + \mu_2 v_{t,t-1}^* + \lambda_1 u_t + \lambda_2 w_t \qquad (1d')$$

To conclude the model requires the specification of a stabilization objective. As a benchmark, we consider a frictionless economy in which wages and prices are perfectly flexible so that labour markets clear. It is well known that the supply of output in such an economy is given by

$$Y_t^f = \frac{n(1-\theta)}{1+n\theta} E_t(v_t) + v_t \qquad (1e)$$

In the case that firms observe v_t instantaneously, (1e) reduces to

$$Y_t^f = \left(\frac{1+n}{1+n\theta}\right)v_t \qquad (1e')$$

The stabilization objective is then taken to be to minimize the variance of output Y_t above the frictionless level Y_t^f. This criterion can be shown to be equivalent to minimizing the welfare losses arising from labour market distortions due to the existence of wage contracts and the rigidities they impose; see Aizenman and Frenkel (1985).

3. The solution

The system outlined above is a standard rational expectations macro model. The solution procedures are familiar, enabling our description to be brief.

For notational convenience let

$$Z_t \equiv \left(\frac{1+n}{1+n\theta}\right)\left(\frac{\alpha_2}{d} + \alpha_1\right)v_t + w_t - \frac{\alpha_2}{d}u_t \qquad (2)$$

so that

$$Z_{t+j,t}^* = \left(\frac{1+n}{1+n\theta}\right)\left(\frac{\alpha_2}{d} + \alpha_1\right)v_{t+j,t}^* + w_{t+j,t}^* - \frac{\alpha_2}{d}u_{t+j,t}^* \qquad (2')$$

and

$$E_t(Z_t) \equiv Z_{t,t}^* = \left(\frac{1+n}{1+n\theta}\right)\left(\frac{\alpha_2}{d} + \alpha_1\right)E_t(v_t) + E_t(w_t) - \frac{\alpha_2}{d}E_t(u_t) \qquad (2'')$$

Taking conditional expectations of equations (1a)–(1c) at time t, for time $t+j$, and eliminating the conditional expectations variables $Y_{t+j,t}^*$, $r_{t+j,t}^*$ leads to the following difference equation in price expectations

$$\alpha_2 P_{t+j+1,t}^* - (1 + \alpha_2)P_{t+j,t}^* = Z_{t+j,t}^* - M_{t+j,t}^* \qquad j = 1, 2, \ldots \qquad (3)$$

where

$$M_{t+j,t}^* = (\mu_0 + \mu_2)v_{t+j,t}^* + \mu_1 v_{t+j+1,t}^* + \lambda_1 u_{t+j,t}^* + \lambda_2 w_{t+j,t}^* \qquad (4)$$

The solution to (3) is

$$P^*_{t+j,t} = \frac{1}{1+\alpha_2} \sum_{k=0}^{\infty} [M^*_{t+j+k,t} - Z^*_{t+j+k,t}] \left(\frac{\alpha_2}{1+\alpha_2}\right)^k \tag{5}$$

and setting $j = 1$,

$$P^*_{t+1,t} = \frac{1}{1+\alpha_2} \sum_{k=0}^{\infty} [M^*_{t+1+k,t} - Z^*_{t+1+k,t}] \left(\frac{\alpha_2}{1+\alpha_2}\right)^k \tag{5'}$$

Price expectations therefore reflect the net discounted effects of the expected future money stocks and the various stochastic disturbances impinging on the economy.

Setting $j = 1$ and $t = t - 1$ in (3), equations (1a)–(1c), (1e) can be solved for the deviation in output from its frictionless level, $Y_t - Y_t^f$ in the following form

$$Y_t - Y_t^f = \frac{d}{D} \left(\frac{1-\theta}{\theta}\right) \Big\{ (1-\tau)[(M_t - M^*_{t,t-1}) - (E_t(Z_t) - Z^*_{t,t-1})]$$

$$+ \alpha_2(1-\tau)[P^*_{t+1,t} - P^*_{t+1,t-1}] + \frac{1+\alpha_2}{1+n\theta}[E_t(v_t) - v^*_{t,t-1}]$$

$$+ (1-\tau)\left[\frac{\alpha_2}{d}[u_t - E_t(u_t)] - \left(\frac{\alpha_2}{d} + \alpha_1\right)[v_t - E_t(v_t)] - [w_t - E_t(w_t)]\right] \Big\} \tag{6}$$

where $D \equiv (1-\tau)[(1-\theta)/\theta](\alpha_2 + \alpha_1 d) + d(1+\alpha_2) > 0$ and price expectations are given by (5) and (5'). Written in this way, we see that the deviation in output from its frictionless level depends most critically upon revisions to information between time $t - 1$ and time t. Most importantly, it depends upon updates to the forecast of the price level for time $t + 1$, made between time $t - 1$ and time t. It is through these revisions that expected future supply shocks, and the expected future monetary response, impact on the current behavior of the economy. But $(Y_t - Y_t^f)$ also depends upon the differences between the actual and perceived disturbances at time t.

Substituting for $M^*_{t+k+1,t}$, $Z^*_{t+k+1,t}$ into $P^*_{t+1,t}$, $P^*_{t+1,t-1}$, and thence into (6), the solution can be expressed explicitly in terms of the policy parameters and current and expected future shocks as follows

$$Y_t - Y_t^f$$

$$= \frac{d}{D} \left(\frac{1-\theta}{\theta}\right) \Big\{ (1-\tau)(\mu_0 - \phi)[E_t(v_t) - v^*_{t,t-1}] + (1-\tau)\mu_1(v^*_{t+1,t} - v^*_{t+1,t-1})$$

$$+ (1-\tau)\left(\lambda_1 + \frac{\alpha_2}{d}\right)[E_t(u_t) - u^*_{t,t-1}]$$

$$+ (1-\tau)(\lambda_2 - 1)[E_t(w_t) - w^*_{t,t-1}] + \left(\frac{1+\alpha_2}{1+n\theta}\right)[E_t(v_t) - v^*_{t,t-1}]$$

$$+ (1 - \tau)\left(\sum_{j=1}^{\infty}\left[(\mu_0 + \mu_2 - \phi)(v_{t+j,t}^* - v_{t+j,t-1}^*) + \mu_1(v_{t+j+1,t}^* - v_{t+j+1,t-1}^*)\right.\right.$$

$$\left.\left. + \left(\lambda_1 + \frac{\alpha_2}{d}\right)(u_{t+j,t}^* - u_{t+j,t-1}^*) + (\lambda_2 - 1)(w_{t+j,t}^* - w_{t+j,t-1}^*)\right]\left(\frac{\alpha_2}{1 + \alpha_2}\right)^j\right)$$

$$\left. + (1 - \tau)\left[\frac{\alpha_2}{d}[u_t - E_t(u_t)] - \left(\frac{\alpha_2}{d} + \alpha_1\right)[v_t - E_t(v_t)] - [w_t - E_t(w_t)]\right]\right\} \quad (7)$$

where

$$\phi \equiv \left(\frac{1 + n}{1 + n\theta}\right)\left(\frac{\alpha_2}{d} + \alpha_1\right)$$

Before determining the optimal monetary policy rules, we briefly consider the case of full wage indexation, $\tau = 1$, when (7) reduces to

$$Y_t - Y_t^f = \frac{d}{D}\left(\frac{1 - \theta}{\theta}\right)\left(\frac{1 + \alpha_2}{1 + n\theta}\right)(E_t(v_t) - v_{t,t-1}^*)$$

The deviation in output about its frictionless level is independent of all monetary policy parameters, so that monetary policy becomes totally ineffective. Or, expressed differently, monetary policy can be effective only if wage indexation is partial, which is the reason for imposing the constraint on τ in (1c). As is well known, with full indexation, demand and monetary shocks have no effect on the output of the economy. More interestingly, the effect on output due to a supply shock depends solely on the revision of the estimate of the shock between $t - 1$ and t. Perfectly anticipated supply shocks, therefore, also have no effect on output. Further analysis of the case of full indexation would require investigation of the effects of shocks on the demand for, and supply of, labour. With failure to replicate the frictionless level of output, and therefore with disequilibrium in the labour market, supply of labour constraints may become binding.

4. Full information

We begin with the case where agents have perfect information on current disturbances, so that

$$E_t(v_t) = v_t; \qquad E_t(u_t) = u_t; \qquad E_t(w_t) = w_t$$

In this case, (7) simplifies to

$$Y_t - Y_t^f$$

$$= \frac{d}{D}\left(\frac{1 - \theta}{\theta}\right)\left\{(1 - \tau)(\mu_0 - \phi)(v_t - v_{t,t-1}^*) + (1 - \tau)\mu_1(v_{t+1,t}^* - v_{t+1,t-1}^*)\right.$$

$$\left. + (1 - \tau)\left(\lambda_1 + \frac{\alpha_2}{d}\right)(u_t - u_{t,t-1}^*)\right.$$

$$+ (1 - \tau)(\lambda_2 - 1)(w_t - w_{t,t-1}^*) + \left(\frac{1 + \alpha_2}{1 + n\theta}\right)(v_t - v_{t,t-1}^*)$$

$$+ (1 - \tau)\Bigg(\sum_{j=1}^{\infty} \Big[(\mu_0 + \mu_2 - \phi)(v_{t+j,t}^* - v_{t+j,t-1}^*) + \mu_1(v_{t+j+1,t}^* - v_{t+j+1,t-1}^*)$$

$$+ \left(\lambda_1 + \frac{\alpha_2}{d}\right)(u_{t+j,t}^* - u_{t+j,t-1}^*) + (\lambda_2 - 1)(w_{t+j,t}^* - w_{t+j,t-1}^*)\Big]\left(\frac{\alpha_2}{1 + \alpha_2}\right)^j\Bigg)\Bigg\}$$

$$(7')$$

The stabilization problem is to choose the policy parameters μ_0, μ_1, μ_2, λ_1, λ_2, to minimize $\mathrm{Var}\,(Y_t - Y_t^f)$. In fact, with full information, Y_t can be stabilized exactly at Y_t^f, thereby replicating the output of the frictionless economy and eliminating the welfare losses due to unemployment. This optimum is achieved by setting[5]

$$\lambda_1 = -\frac{\alpha_2}{d} \tag{8a}$$

$$\lambda_2 = 1 \tag{8b}$$

$$(1 - \tau)(\mu_0 - \phi) + \left(\frac{1 + \alpha_2}{1 + n\theta}\right) = 0 \tag{8c}$$

$$\mu_1 + (\mu_0 + \mu_2 - \phi)\frac{\alpha_2}{1 + \alpha_2} = 0 \tag{8d}$$

First, setting λ_1, λ_2, as in (8a), (8b) ensures that all current and expected future demand disturbances are eliminated entirely. Since these are not of direct concern, we shall not comment on them further. Substituting for μ_0, μ_1, μ_2, we see that the nominal money stock should be adjusted to supply disturbances in accordance with the rule

$$M_t = \left[\left(\frac{1 + n}{1 + n\theta}\right)\left(\frac{\alpha_2}{d} + \alpha_1\right) - \frac{1 + \alpha_2}{(1 + n\theta)(1 - \tau)}\right]v_t$$

$$+ \left[\frac{\alpha_2}{(1 + n\theta)(1 - \tau)} - \frac{\alpha_2\mu_2}{1 + \alpha_2}\right]v_{t+1,t}^* + \mu_2 v_{t,t-1}^* \tag{9}$$

where μ_2 is arbitrary. The rule specified in (9) describes the general form of accommodation and a number of cases require discussion.

---

[5] If the money supply here were augmented to include in addition a response to the expected supply shock two periods hence, $\mu_3 v_{t+2,t}^*$ say, we can show that in addition to (8a)–(8d), the optimally conditions will include

$$\mu_3 + \mu_1\left(\frac{\alpha_2}{1 + \alpha_2}\right) + (\mu_0 + \mu_2 - \phi)\left(\frac{\alpha_2}{1 + \alpha_2}\right)^2 = 0$$

This together with (8d) implies $\mu_3 = 0$. The same is true for all expectations beyond two periods ahead.

A. *White noise disturbances*

In the case of white noise disturbances, $v_{t+1,t}^* = v_{t,t-1}^* = 0$ and the optimal rule reduces to

$$M_t = \left[\left(\frac{1+n}{1+n\theta} \right) \left(\frac{\alpha_2}{d} + \alpha_1 \right) - \frac{1+\alpha_2}{(1+n\theta)(1-\tau)} \right] v_t \qquad (10)$$

This calls for monetary contraction or expansion in response to a positive supply (quantity) shock according to whether[6]

$$(1+n) \left(\frac{\alpha_2}{d} + \alpha_1 \right) \lesseqgtr \left(\frac{1+\alpha_2}{1-\tau} \right) \qquad (11)$$

On the one hand, the direct effect of a positive supply shock is to raise output in an economy with wages fixed by contracts above that in a frictionless economy, where the rise in real wages resulting from the shock inhibit the rise in output. On the other hand, the positive supply shock tends to lower the price level and this tends to reduce Y_t below Y_t^f. If the former effect dominates, monetary contraction is required to reduce Y_t back to Y_t^f; if the latter effect dominates, monetary expansion is required.

The optimal rule incorporates the tradeoff between monetary policy and wage indexation emphasized by Aizenman and Frenkel (1985) and Turnovsky (1983). For low degrees of indexation ($\tau \cong 0$), either the positive direct effect or the negative price effect of the supply shock may dominate and the optimal policy may call for either monetary contraction or expansion, depending upon which is larger. However, for a sufficiently high degree of indexation, the positive direct effect dominates, causing Y_t to increase above Y_t^f, and requiring a monetary contraction to generate a fall in price necessary to reduce Y_t back to the frictionless level.

Fischer's (1985) analysis, calling for a passive monetary policy, was based on a classical money demand function ($\alpha_1 = 1$, $\alpha_2 = 0$), with no wage indexation ($\tau = 0$) and with a fixed supply of labour ($n = 0$). For these parameter values, (10) implies the optimality of the passive policy $M = 0$ as well. With a classical money demand function, but with a positively elastic supply of labour, $n > 0$, a passive policy will be optimal if and only if money wages are partially indexed to unexpected price movements to the extent

$$\tau = \frac{n}{1+n} \qquad (12)$$

The reason for this is that with $n > 0$, the direct effect of a positive supply shock is to raise Y_t above Y_t^f, as already noted. The amount of indexation specified in (12) will induce a sufficient rise in the real wage to cut back the rise in output to exactly that in the frictionless economy.

------

[6] Note that whereas some authors refer to a positive supply shock in terms of an increase in input price, we are focusing on positive quantity shocks.

B. *General disturbances*

Returning to the optimal rule (9), it is seen that the optimal adjustment of the money stock to supply disturbances can be expressed in an infinite number of ways, depending upon the arbitrary choice of μ_2.

Substituting for the optimal policy parameters into (4), the expected money supply for time $t + j$ is given by

$$M^*_{t+j,t} = Z^*_{t+j,t} + \left[\mu_2 - \frac{1 + \alpha_2}{(1 + n\theta)(1 - \tau)} \right] \left[v^*_{t+j,t} - \left(\frac{\alpha_2}{1 + \alpha_2} \right) v^*_{t+j+1,t} \right] \quad (13)$$

so that (5), (5′) imply

$$
\begin{aligned}
P^*_{t+1,t} &= \frac{1}{1 + \alpha_2} \left[\mu_2 - \frac{1 + \alpha_2}{(1 + n\theta)(1 - \tau)} \right] v^*_{t+1,t}; \\[2mm]
P^*_{t+1,t-1} &= \frac{1}{1 + \alpha_2} \left[\mu_2 - \frac{1 + \alpha_2}{(1 + n\theta)(1 - \tau)} \right] v^*_{t+1,t-1}
\end{aligned}
\quad (14)
$$

The expected price for time $t + 1$ depends only upon the expected supply shock for that period. The optimal monetary rule neutralizes the effects of anticipated supply shocks for all subsequent periods. However, the response of the expected price level does depend upon the chosen value of μ_2 and two values are natural to consider.

(i) $\mu_2 = 0$: In this case the optimal monetary response to supply disturbances is given by

$$M_t = \left[\left(\frac{1 + n}{1 + n\theta} \right) \left(\frac{\alpha_2}{d} + \alpha_1 \right) - \frac{1 + \alpha_2}{(1 + n\theta)(1 - \tau)} \right] v_t + \frac{\alpha_2}{(1 + n\theta)(1 - \tau)} v^*_{t+1,t} \quad (15)$$

The optimal response to the current disturbance is the same as for white noise, discussed previously. But, in addition, the rule requires accommodation for the expected shock for next period, $v^*_{t+1,t}$. Moreover, this accommodation for the expected shock for next period, $v^*_{t+1,t}$. Moreover, this accommodation should be the same, whether the future shock is expected to last just one period, or indefinitely. The reason is simply that expectations of future supply shocks beyond one period are fully compensated for by the expected money supply and leave price expectations $P^*_{t+1,t}$ or $P^*_{t+1,t-1}$ unaffected.

While the adjustment to the current disturbance can be either expansionary or contractionary, as we have seen, the expected positive future shock calls for monetary expansion. The reason is that an expected positive future supply shock causes $P^*_{t+1,t}$ to fall. This in turn means that the real interest rate will rise and that current output will decline. In order to restore output to the level of the frictionless economy, an expansion in the money supply is required in order to offset this contractionary effect.

The optimal rule (15) implies further that a positive *current* supply disturbance which is expected to last for at least one period into the future (i.e., $v_{t+1,t}^* = v_t$) can be stabilized perfectly by setting

$$M_t = \left[\left(\frac{1+n}{1+n\theta}\right)\left(\frac{\alpha_2}{d} + \alpha_1\right) - \frac{1}{(1+n\theta)(1-\tau)}\right]v_t \tag{16}$$

Denoting the coefficient of v_t in (10) and (16) by μ_0, μ_0^* respectively, we see that $\mu_0^* > \mu_0$; i.e., the monetary policy should be more accommodating or less contractionary to such a disturbance than to a white noise shock.[7] The reason again is the negative price effect which needs to be offset in order to avoid the contraction in output which would otherwise occur.[8]

(ii) $\mu_2 = (1 + \alpha_2)/(1 + n\theta)(1 - \tau)$: For this choice of μ_2, the expected future supply disturbance drops out of the optimal rule, which now may be written as

$$M_t = \left(\frac{1+n}{1+n\theta}\right)\left(\frac{\alpha_2}{d} + \alpha_1\right)v_{t,t-1}^*$$
$$+ \left[\left(\frac{1+n}{1+n\theta}\right)\left(\frac{\alpha_2}{d} + \alpha_1\right) - \frac{1+\alpha_2}{(1+n\theta(1-\tau))}\right](v_t - v_{t,t-1}^*) \tag{17}$$

expressing the response in terms of the anticipated current shock, $v_{t,t-1}^*$ and its unanticipated component $(v_t - v_{t,t-1}^*)$. The response to the latter is the same as if it were white noise and can be either expansionary or contractionary. By contrast, a positive anticipated current supply shock requires monetary expansion. This is because an expected positive supply shock leads to a higher contract wage. This tends to reduce the demand for labor and output, unless offset by a monetary expansion which raises the price level and stimulates output.

It is interesting to observe that when μ_2 is chosen in this way, the monetary authorities need not forecast the future at all. They can simply base their policies on the anticipated and unanticipated components of the *current* supply disturbance. The reason is that when $\mu_2 = (1 + \alpha_2)/(1 + n\theta)(1 - \tau)$, $P_{t+1,t}^* = P_{t+1,t-1}^* = 0$. That is, the expected future price level is fixed and is independent of future supply disturbances.

Our analysis treats the degree of wage indexation as a given parameter. It is interesting to note that when τ is considered as a policy instrument, further degrees of freedom with respect to the determination of optimal

---

[7] It is also possible for monetary policy to be contractionary in response to a white noise disturbance, but expansionary to a permanent shift. This occurs if

$$(1 + \alpha_2) > (1 + n)(1 - \tau)\left(\frac{\alpha_2}{d} + \alpha_1\right) > 1$$

[8] With a classical supply function, $\alpha_2 = 0$ and price expectations disappear from the solution (6) for output deviations. In this case (10) and (16) are identical, so that both temporary and permanent supply shocks call for the same monetary response.

policy arise. For example, setting

$$1 - \tau = \frac{1 + \alpha_2}{(1+n)\left(\dfrac{\alpha_2}{d} + \alpha_1\right)} \tag{18a}$$

$$\mu_2 = \left(\frac{1+n}{1+n\theta}\right)\left(\frac{\alpha_2}{d} + \alpha_1\right). \tag{18b}$$

the coefficients of both v_t and $v_{t+1,t}^*$ in the optimal money supply rule (9) are zero. Optimal policy will consist of *partial* wage indexation, together with a monetary expansion based solely on the forecast of the supply shock at time t, formed at time $t-1$, namely

$$M_t = \left(\frac{1+n}{1+n\theta}\right)\left(\frac{\alpha_2}{d} + \alpha_1\right)v_{t,t-1}^* \tag{19}$$

In effect, the indexation eliminates the need to adjust the money to the unanticipated component of the supply shock in (17). A rule based entirely on past forecasts is obviously very convenient in an economy where there are lags in information.

C. *Effects on other variables*

So far, we have focused on the monetary rules which will ensure $Y_t = Y_t^f$, so that the contract economy replicates exactly the output of the frictionless economy. Combining (1c'), (1d') with (5'), it is seen that the adoption of the optimal monetary rule causes the current price level to respond in accordance with

$$P_t = P_{t,t-1}^* - \frac{(v_t - v_{t,t-1}^*)}{(1+n\theta)(1-\tau)} = \frac{\mu_2}{1-\alpha_2}v_{t,t-1}^* - \frac{1}{(1+n\theta)(1-\tau)}v_t \tag{20}$$

A current positive supply shock causes the current price level to fall, while to the extent that the monetary authorities accommodate to an anticipated positive current supply shock, the current price level will rise.

The demand for labour generated by the supply shock and resulting policy responses increases by an amount

$$N_t^d = \frac{Y_t - v_t}{1 - \theta} = \frac{n}{1+n\theta}v_t > 0$$

while the supply of labour

$$N^s = n(W - P) = n(\tau - 1)(P_t - P_{t,t-1}^*) + \frac{nv_{t,t-1}^*}{1+n\theta} = \frac{n}{1+n\theta}v_t > 0$$

rises by the same amount. The optimal monetary policy therefore ensures that the supply shock has no effect on unemployment. Upon reflection, this is hardly surprising, since the optimal rule ensures that the economy replicates the frictionless economy, in which the labour market always clears and the unemployment rate is therefore zero.

D. *A monetary rule based on only current supply shocks*

The striking feature of the optimal monetary rules (15) and (17) is their simplicity. Completely *general* supply shocks can be stabilized perfectly by using remarkably simple rules based on very limited information about the transitory or permanent nature of the shocks. The monetary authorities need consider only the current period and just one period ahead; they need *not* be concerned with what might occur in any subsequent periods beyond.

This form of rule is now compared to the usual kind of policy rule where the monetary intervention is in response to only current disturbances in supply. Analytically, this involves setting $\mu_1 = \mu_2 = 0$ in (1d'). Eliminating the demand disturbances by setting $\lambda_1 = -\alpha_2/d$, $\lambda_2 = 1$ in (7'), the deviation in output about its frictionless level, $Y_t - Y_t^f$, is given by

$$Y_t - Y_t^f = \frac{d}{D}\left(\frac{1-\theta}{\theta}\right)\left\{\left[(1-\tau)(\mu_0-\phi)+\frac{1+\alpha_2}{1+n\theta}\right](v_t - v_{t,t-1}^*)\right.$$

$$\left. + (1-\tau)(\mu_0-\phi)\left[\sum_{j=1}^{\infty}(v_{t+j,t}^* - v_{t+j,t-1}^*)\left(\frac{\alpha_2}{1+\alpha_2}\right)^j\right]\right\} \quad (7'')$$

The optimal rule for stabilizing white noise disturbances is obviously still given by (10), as before. But for any other forms of disturbances, to determine the optimal monetary response involves forming forecasts of the supply shocks, $v_{t+j,t}^*$, for *all* future periods $t+j$. The informational requirements are clearly severe.

In fact, perfect stabilization for Y_t about Y_t^f is possible for any arbitrary autoregressive moving average (ARMA) process generating supply disturbances v_t. Suppose, for example, v_t is generated by

$$v_t = \rho v_{t-1} + \varepsilon_t + \lambda\varepsilon_{t-1} \quad (21)$$

Then,

$$v_t - v_{t,t-1}^* = \varepsilon_t$$

$$v_{t+j,t}^* - v_{t+j,t-1}^* = \rho^{j-1}(\rho+\lambda)\varepsilon_t \quad j = 1, 2, \ldots$$

and substituting into (7''), yields

$$Y_t - Y_t^f = \frac{d}{D}\left(\frac{1-\theta}{\theta}\right)\left[\frac{(1-\tau)(\mu_0-\phi)(1+\alpha_2+\lambda\alpha_2)}{1+\alpha_2-\rho\alpha_2}+\frac{1+\alpha_2}{1+n\theta}\right] \quad (22)$$

We see from (22) that perfect stability of output Y_t about the frictionless level Y_t^f is attained by choosing the parameter μ_0 in accordance with

$$\mu_0 = \left(\frac{1+n}{1+n\theta}\right)\left(\frac{\alpha_2}{d}+\alpha_1\right)-\left(\frac{1+\alpha_2}{1+n\theta}\right)\left(\frac{1+\alpha_2-\rho\alpha_2}{(1+\alpha_2+\lambda\alpha_2)(1-\tau)}\right) \quad (23)$$

This rule depends upon ρ, λ, the two parameters characterizing the stochastic process generating v_t. It reduces to (10) when $\rho = \lambda = 0$ and v_t is a white noise process; it reduces to (16) when $\rho = 1$, $\lambda = 0$, and v_t follows a random walk with current shifts expected to be permanent.

In general, all parameters characterizing an ARMA process will appear in the optimal policy rule, and perfect stabilization is possible as long as information on all relevant parameters is correct. If, on the other hand, information is incorrect, perfect stabilization will not be achieved and indeed if the information is sufficiently inaccurate, intervention may serve only to destabilize the economy!

5. Imperfect information

We now determine the optimal degree of monetary response in the situation where information on the current disturbances is unavailable, so that only $E_t(v_t)$, $E_t(u_t)$ and $E_t(w_t)$ are known to all agents (both private and public). In this case, returning to the fundamental expression (7), we can easily show that $\mathrm{Var}\,(Y_t - Y_t^f)$ is minimized by choosing μ_0, μ_1, μ_2, λ_1, λ_2, precisely as before, in accordance with (8). Thus the response to the supply disturbance is now given by

$$M_t = \left[\left(\frac{1+n}{1+n\theta}\right)\left(\frac{\alpha_2}{d}+\alpha_1\right) - \frac{1+\alpha_2}{(1+n\theta)(1-\tau)}\right]E_t(v_t)$$

$$+ \left[\frac{\alpha_2}{(1+n\theta)(1-\tau)} - \frac{\alpha_2\mu_2}{1+\alpha_2}\right]v^*_{t+1,t} + \mu_2 v^*_{t,t-1} \quad (24)$$

This is of the same form as (9), the only difference being that the current perception of the supply disturbance, $E_t(v_t)$, replaces the actual shock. Thus the comments made previously with respect to the optimal policy rules in response to the various forms of supply disturbances applies to (24) as well.

There are, however, two differences which need to be considered. First, the perceived supply disturbance depends upon the information set available to agents. Secondly, the optimal rule may, or may not, yield perfect stabilization about the frictionless level of output.[9] That too, depends upon the information set. In general, we find that the minimized value of $\mathrm{Var}\,(Y_t - Y_t^f)$ is

$$(1 - \tau)^2 \mathrm{Var}\left\{\frac{\alpha_2}{d}(u_t - E_t(u_t)) - \left(\frac{\alpha_2}{d}+\alpha_1\right)(v_t - E_t(v_t)) - (w_t - E_t(w_t))\right\}$$

We shall consider two examples.

First, suppose that agents observe both the price level P_t and the interest rate r_t. Substituting (1a) into (1b) yields the relationship

$$M_t - P_t = -\alpha_1 d[r_t - (P^*_{t+1,t} - P_t)] - \alpha_2 r_t + \alpha_1 u_t + w_t \quad (25)$$

---

[9] In the case where perfect stabilization is not achieved, so that disequilibrium in the labor market exists, labor supply constraints might be binding and need to be considered.

The observability of M_t, $P^*_{t+1,t}$, along with r_t and P_t implies the observability of the composite disturbance $(\alpha_1 u_t + w_t)$. Similarly, substituting the supply function (1c) into (1b), the observability of M_t, $P^*_{t,t-1}$, $v^*_{t,t-1}$, $E_t(v_t)$, along with r_t and P_t implies the observability of $(\alpha_1 v_t + w_t)$. Optimal predictions of u_t, v_t, and w_t can be obtained by regressing these variables on the two observed composite disturbances. Assuming the underlying stochastic shocks are uncorrelated, the resulting expressions are given by[10]

$$E_t(v_t) = \frac{\sigma_v^2[\sigma_w^2 + \alpha_1^2\sigma_u^2](w_t + \alpha_1 v_t) - \sigma_v^2\sigma_w^2(w_t + \alpha_1 u_t)}{\alpha_1(\sigma_u^2 + \sigma_v^2)\sigma_w^2 + \alpha_1^3\sigma_u^2\sigma_v^2} \qquad (26a)$$

$$E_t(u_t) = \frac{-\sigma_u^2\sigma_w^2(w_t + \alpha_1 v_t) + \sigma_u^2[\sigma_w^2 + \alpha_1^2\sigma_v^2](w_t + \alpha_1 u_t)}{\alpha_1(\sigma_u^2 + \sigma_v^2)\sigma_w^2 + \alpha_1^3\sigma_u^2\sigma_v^2} \qquad (26b)$$

$$E_t(w_t) = \frac{\sigma_u^2\sigma_w^2(w_t + \alpha_1 v_t) + \sigma_v^2\sigma_w^2(w_t + \alpha_1 u_t)}{(\sigma_u^2 + \sigma_v^2)\sigma_w^2 + \alpha_1^2\sigma_u^2\sigma_v^2} \qquad (26c)$$

where σ_u^2, σ_v^2, σ_w^2, are the variances of u_t, v_t, and w_t, respectively. Notice that the absence of any one of u_t, v_t, w_t implies the observability of the remaining two.[11] This is because the observations contain two independent pieces of information, enabling the remaining two random variables to be inferred. Further, equations (26a)–(26c) imply

$$\alpha_1 E_t(u_t) + E_t(w_t) = \alpha_1 u_t + w_t \qquad (27a)$$

$$\alpha_1 E_t(v_t) + E_t(w_t) = \alpha_1 v_t + w_t \qquad (27b)$$

which together yield

$$\frac{\alpha_2}{d}[u_t - E_t(u_t)] - \left(\frac{\alpha_2}{d} + \alpha_1\right)[v_t - E_t(v_t)] - [w_t - E_t(w_t)] = 0 \qquad (28)$$

so that minimized Var $(Y_t - Y_t^f) = 0$; i.e., output is stabilized perfectly about its frictionless level.[12]

Thus, if the monetary authorities observe P_t, r_t, the appropriate prediction of the contemporaneous supply disturbance is given by (26a). It is clear that because of the signal extraction problem

$$\frac{\partial E_t(v_t)}{\partial v_t} = \frac{\sigma_v^2[\sigma_w^2 + \alpha_1^2\sigma_u^2]}{(\sigma_u^2 + \sigma_v^2)\sigma_w^2 + \alpha_1^2\sigma_u^2\sigma_v^2} < 1$$

---

[10] It is also possible to form predictions $E_t(v_t)$ from observations on $(\alpha_1 v_t + w_t)$ alone. However, by ignoring information, this yields a less efficient estimate than that given in (23a).

[11] These relationships also imply the observability of $(u_t - v_t)$.

[12] Much of the monetary policy literature specifies monetary rules in terms of responses to the directly observed variables, which in this case are P and r. Given that our forecasts of current shocks are just linear combinations of these variables, our formulation is clearly identical in terms of its stabilization performance. However, since the focus of our analysis is on responding to supply disturbances, we find our specification is more appropriate for our purposes.

As a consequence of the inability of the monetary authorities to identify unambiguously movements in the observed variables $(E_t(v_t))$ with actual supply disturbances, such disturbances are discounted somewhat, leading to less response in the money supply than if they were observed exactly. It is also possible for movements in the supply to be accompanied by concurrent movements in demand, so that while $v_t > 0$, the perceived supply disturbance, as determined by (26a), is negative. In this case, the direction of the monetary response will be reversed.

As a second example, suppose that the monetary authorities observe only the nominal interest rate r_t. In this case eliminating Y_t, P_t from (1a)–(1c), we find that the observability of r_t, along with the expectations and other predetermined variables, is equivalent to the observability of the composite term

$$\left[1 + \alpha_1\left(\frac{1-\theta}{\theta}\right)(1-\tau)\right]u_t + (\alpha_1 d - 1)v_t + \left[d + \left(\frac{1-\theta}{\theta}\right)(1-\tau)\right]w_t$$

The optimal prediction of the current supply disturbance is now

$$E_t(v_t) \equiv \frac{\Psi_2\sigma_v^2}{\Psi_1^2\sigma_u^2 + \Psi_2^2\sigma_v^2 + \Psi_3^2\sigma_w^2}\left[\Psi_1 u_t + \Psi_2 v_t + \Psi_3 w_t\right]$$

where

$$\Psi_1 \equiv 1 + \alpha_1\left(\frac{1-\theta}{\theta}\right)(1-\tau); \qquad \Psi_2 \equiv \alpha_1 d - 1; \qquad \Psi_3 \equiv d + \left(\frac{1-\theta}{\theta}\right)(1-\tau)$$

In this case we can now show that

$$\frac{\alpha_2}{d}[u_t - E_t(u_t)] - \left(\frac{\alpha_2}{d} + \alpha_1\right)[v_t - E_t(v_t)] - [w_t - E_t(w_t)] \neq 0$$

so that perfect stabilization of Y_t about Y_t^f is *not* achieved. We can also show that because of the deterioration in information from the first example, the response of $E_t(v_t)$ to v_t is damped even further.

6. Conclusions

Supply shocks continue to impinge on Western economies. This paper has analyzed the optimal monetary responses to such disturbances, emphasizing the distinction between disturbances that are transitory or permanent, on the one hand, and anticipated or unanticipated, on the other. Two main conclusions can be drawn from the analysis, although these are obviously subject to the specific assumptions of the model.

First, we have shown that if current shocks are observed instantaneously, output can be stabilized perfectly for completely general supply disturbances, by using remarkably simple monetary rules, requiring relatively little information about the nature of the disturbances. Specifically, the monetary authorities need consider only: (i) the current shock, (ii) the forecast of the current shock formed in the previous period, (iii) the forecast for just one period ahead. They need not be concerned with what might occur in subsequent periods beyond, and therefore do not need to determine whether an anticipated shock for the next period is temporary or permanent. The optimal rule will completely eliminate these subsequent effects from the current expected inflation rate, thereby neutralizing their effects on current output. In fact, the optimal rule can be expressed in an infinite number of different ways and only (ii) *or* (iii) need be considered, in conjunction with the current shock itself.

Perhaps the most convenient form specifies the monetary adjustment in terms of an expansion in response to the anticipated component of a (positive) current supply shock, together with an adjustment to the unanticipated component, which may be either expansionary or contractionary, depending upon the parameters. Expressed in this way, perfect output stabilization can be achieved for any form of supply disturbance without the need to forecast the future at all. If the degree of wage indexation is chosen optimally, the optimal monetary rule can be simplified further by eliminating the unanticipated component of the current supply shock from the optimal monetary rule. By contrast, monetary rules based on responses to current disturbances alone require substantially more information for optimal stabilization. Forecasts of supply shocks for all future periods are necessary.

Secondly, we have shown that if current shocks are not observed instantaneously, but are inferred from other signals such as the interest rate and price level, the optimal rules are of the same form, with the current perceived disturbance replacing the actual. The current perception of the shock depends upon the information sct and perfect stabilization of output may, or may not, be possible, again depending upon the information available.

University of Illinois at Urbana-Champaign, and
National Bureau of Economic Research

APPENDIX

Derivation of supply function

The supply function is based on the one-period wage contract model. We assume that the contract wage for time t is determined at time $t-1$ such that, given expectations of firms and workers, the labour market is expected to clear. The expected supply of labour at the contract wage is

$$N^s_{t,t-1} = n(W^c_{t,t-1} - P^*_{t,t-1}) \qquad n > 0 \tag{A.1}$$

where $N^s_{t,t-1}$ = expected supply of labour formed at time $t-1$, for time t, expressed in logarithms,
$W^c_{t,t-1}$ = contract wage, determined at time $t-1$ for time t, expressed in logarithms,
$P^*_{t,t-1}$ = forecast of P_t formed at time $t-1$.
Output is produced by means of a Cobb–Douglas production function

$$Y_t = (1-\theta)N_t + v_t \qquad 0 < \theta < 1 \tag{A.2}$$

where N_t = employment of labour, expressed in logarithms,
  v_t = stochastic disturbance in productivity.
  The expected demand for labour, $N_{t,t-1}^d$, (based on expected profit maximation), is determined by the marginal productivity condition

$$\ln (1 - \theta) - \theta N_{t,t-1}^d + v_{t,t-1}^* = W_{t,t-1}^c - P_{t,t-1}^* \tag{A.3}$$

The contract wage is determined by equating the expected demand and supply of labour in (A.1) and (A.3), yielding

$$W_{t,t-1}^c = P_{t,t-1}^* + \frac{\ln (1 - \theta)}{1 + n\theta} + \frac{v_{t,t-1}^*}{1 + n\theta} \tag{A.4}$$

The contract wage therefore depends upon the expected productivity disturbance as well as the expected price level.
  Actual employment is assumed to be determined by the short-run marginal productivity condition, after the actual wage and price are known. This is expected by

$$\ln (1 - \theta) - \theta N_t + E_t(v_t) = W_t - P_t \tag{A.5}$$

Introducing the current perceived productivity disturbance, $E_t(v_t)$, into the optimality condition (A.5), allows for the possibility that firms do not observe this disturbance instantaneously. If it is observed, then $E_t(v_t) = v_t$; otherwise they must infer it from available information on current observable variables, using the forecasting technique discussed in the text. Combining (A.2) and (A.5), current output is given by,

$$Y_t = \left(\frac{1 - \theta}{\theta}\right) \ln (1 - \theta) + \left(\frac{1 - \theta}{\theta}\right)(P_t - W_t) + \left(\frac{1 - \theta}{\theta}\right)E_t(v_t) + v_t \tag{A.6}$$

which depends upon both the firm's estimate of v_t and v_t itself. In the event that v_t is observed, (A.6) simplifies to

$$Y_t = \left(\frac{1 - \theta}{\theta}\right) \ln (1 - \theta) + \left(\frac{1 - \theta}{\theta}\right)(P_t - W_t) + \frac{v_t}{\theta} \tag{A.6'}$$

Finally, current wages are assumed to be determined in accordance with the indexation scheme

$$W_t = W_{t,t-1}^c + \tau(P_t - P_{t,t-1}^*) \qquad 0 < \tau < 1 \tag{A.7}$$

Combining (A.7) and (A.4) with (A.6) or (A.6'), yields the following alternative forms of supply functions, which correspond to the observability or otherwise of the productivity disturbance,

$$Y_t = \frac{(1 - \theta)n \ln (1 - \theta)}{1 + n\theta} + (1 - \tau)\left(\frac{1 - \theta}{\theta}\right)(P_t - P_{t,t-1}^*) + \left(\frac{1 - \theta}{\theta}\right)\left[E_t(v_t) - \frac{v_{t,t-1}^*}{1 + n\theta}\right] + v_t \tag{A.8}$$

$$Y_t = \frac{(1 - \theta)n \ln (1 - \theta)}{1 + n\theta} + (1 - \tau)\left(\frac{1 - \theta}{\theta}\right)(P_t - P_{t,t-1}^*) + \frac{v_t}{\theta} - \left(\frac{1 - \theta}{\theta}\right)\frac{v_{t,t-1}^*}{1 + n\theta} \tag{A.8'}$$

Suppressing the constant and measuring everything in deviation form, (A.8), (A.8') are equivalent to (1c), (1c') of the text.

REFERENCES

AIZENMAN, J. and J. A. FRENKEL, "Optimal Wage Indexation, Foreign Exchange Intervention, and Monetary Policy," *American Economic Review*, 75, 1985, 402–423.
AIZENMAN, J. and J. A. FRENKEL, "Supply Shocks, Wage Indexation and Monetary Accommodation," *Journal of Money, Credit and Banking*, 18, 1986, 305–322.

BLINDER, A. S., "Monetary Accommodation of Supply Shocks under Rational Expectations," *Journal of Money, Credit, and Banking,* 13, 1981, 425–438.

FISCHER, S., "Wage Indexation and Macroeconomic Stability," in K. Brunner and A. Meltzer (eds.), *Stabilization of the Domestic and International Economy,* Carnegie-Rochester Conference Series on Public Policy, Vol. 5, North-Holland, Amsterdam, 1977, 107–147.

FISCHER, S., "Supply Shocks, Wage Stickiness and Accommodation," *Journal of Money, Credit, and Banking,* 17, 1985, 1–15.

GORDON, R. J., "Alternative Responses of Policy to External Supply Shocks," *Brookings Papers on Economic Activity,* 1, 1975, 183–206.

GORDON, R. J., "Supply Shocks and Monetary Policy Revisited," *American Economic Review, Papers and Proceedings,* 74, 1984, 38–43.

GRAY, J. A., "Wage Indexation: A Macroeconomic Approach," *Journal of Monetary Economics,* 2, 1976, 221–235.

MARSTON, R. C., and S. J. TURNOVSKY, "Imported Material Prices, Wage Policy, and Macroeconomic Stabilization, *Canadian Journal of Economics,* **18,** 1985a, 273–284.

MARSTON, R. C., and S. J. TURNOVSKY, "Macroeconomic Stabilization through Taxation and Indexation: The Use of Firm-Specific Information," *Journal of Monetary Economics,* 16, 1985b, 375–395.

PHELPS, E. S., "Commodity-Supply Shock and Full-Employment Monetary Policy," *Journal of Money, Credit, and Banking,* 10, 1978, 206–221.

TURNOVSKY, S. J., "Wage Indexation and Exchange Market Intervention in a Small Open Economy," *Canadian Journal of Economics,* 16, 1983, 574–592.

Oxford Economic Papers 39 (1987), 38–74

DOES INTERNATIONAL MACROECONOMIC POLICY COORDINATION PAY AND IS IT SUSTAINABLE?: A TWO COUNTRY ANALYSIS

By PAUL LEVINE and DAVID CURRIE*

1. Introduction

THE purpose of this paper is to investigate the benefits and the sustainability of cooperation in the conduct of macroeconomic policy in the international economy. Recent work has highlighted the significant externalities between countries in the effects of policy particularly those arising through policy-induced exchange rate changes in a regime of floating rates. Thus Taylor (1985) finds that non-cooperative policy design results in an over-active use of monetary policy, relative to the cooperative case, as countries use tight monetary policy to induce exchange rate appreciation as part of an anti-inflationary package. This is true even if the real exchange rate must subsequently depreciate again, adding to inflationary pressures later on, for the pattern of real exchange rate appreciation and subsequent depreciation acts to redistribute inflation optimally through time, smoothing peaks and troughs. Currie and Levine (1985a, 1985b) obtain similar findings for monetary policy, and report also the incentive for individual governments to offset the output consequences of the resulting loss of competitiveness by means of expansionary fiscal policy. The consequent combination of tight money and expansionary fiscal policy is severely suboptimal for the system taken as a whole, and therefore for all individual countries if such policies are adopted generally, and, if adhered to, are found in some circumstances to be wholly destabilising.

These findings that international cooperation in macroeconomic policy is beneficial are at odds with other findings, notably by Oudiz and Sachs (1985), Miller and Salmon (1985) and Rogoff (1985), that the benefits of cooperation may be limited or even absent. It is clearly important to establish the source of these differences, and this is one aim of this paper. The principal source that we identify is whether governments are assumed to have sufficient credibility to commit themselves to the full optimal reputational policy. If governments lack credibility vis-a-vis their private sectors, international cooperation may be counter-productive. With credibility, the pursuit of reputational policies means that international cooperation will be beneficial and its absence may be damaging.

For those policies for which cooperation pays, there is still the question of whether cooperative behaviour will be sustained or whether it will be undermined by the incentive to free-ride. In this paper we therefore examine means by which cooperation may be sustained for reputational policies. In particular, we ask whether the threat by each country to revert

* The support of the National Institute of Economic and Social Research and of the Bank of England's Houblon Norman Research Fellowship is gratefully acknowledged.

to a Nash strategy in the event of a break-down of cooperation, precipitated by the other country, will create a sufficient incentive for all countries to sustain cooperative policies. As we discuss in the next section, this problem can be viewed formally as a supergame. If the Nash alternative is sufficiently unattractive, relative to the cooperative outcome, in all plausible circumstances, then this threat strategy will sustain cooperation provided that the threat is credible, that is, it is reasonable to suppose that it will be carried out. In the two country world which we consider here, the Nash threat is plausible (though our results point to some important caveats depending on the precise Nash concept used, a matter which we discuss later). In a multi-country setting, the appropriate choice of threat is less clear. Countries are unlikely to wish to punish reneging by a single country by abandoning cooperation altogether, even between countries that have not broken commitments. A more realistic threat is for the non-reneging countries to play a joint Nash strategy against reneging countries, while sustaining cooperation amongst themselves.

In this paper we examine whether the Nash threat will sustain cooperative rules of the full optimal reputational type derived from Pontryagin's maximum principle. Such rules are widely considered to be time-inconsistent, in that the mere passage of time leads to an incentive to reoptimise (Kydland and Prescott (1977)). Since the private sector can discern this, such policies will not be credible unless sustained by reputation or precommitment, and if not credible they will not be optimal even if adhered to. This potentially undesirable feature of the full optimal rule has tended to narrow interest to that class of policies for which no such incentive exists, namely time-consistent non-reputational policies. Cohen and Michel (1984) demonstrate how to derive the optimal rule within this subclass of rules, using dynamic programming.[1] Typically the time consistent non-reputational optimal rule gives a performance that is markedly inferior to that of the full optimal reputational rule (see, for example, Levine and Currie (1985)).

Elsewhere we have argued that the full optimal rule derived by means of Pontryagin's maximum principle is not without interest, particularly in a stochastic world (Currie and Levine (1985c)). Take the standard case considered in the literature of a government optimising a given objective function over an infinite time horizon with discounting. Assume that the private sector will believe credible policy announcements that are adhered to, but that reneging on the part of government will lead the private sector subsequently to place no faith in government announcements.[2] (Note that

---

[1] Levine and Currie (QMC PRISM Discussion Paper No. 5, April 1983, subsequently published as Levine and Currie (1985)) earlier derived this optimal time consistent rule as the limit of a Cournot-adjustment process in policy rules.

[2] This assumes an infinite punishment period. It would be of interest to examine the consequences of a finite punishment period (as in Barro and Gordon (1985) for a very simple model), but this is much more difficult to handle for the class of general models analysed in this paper.

this involves no strategic behaviour on the part of the private sector, and hence is consistent with an atomistic private sector.) If, after reneging, the private sector determines its expectations of future policy on the basis of what it is optimal for government to do given that its announcements now carry no weight, this leads to the time consistent non-reputational optimal policy.

With this set-up, it can be shown that the full optimal rule may be credible and sustainable in a stochastic world, provided that the rate of discount is not too high. In the deterministic case, the incentive to renege arises because at some point in the future it pays government to switch policies so as to deal more advantageously with the state of the system inherited from the previous policy.[3] But for the stochastic case, government must also consider the inferior performance that will be obtained subsequently in respect of future, currently unknown, disturbances as a consequence of reneging. If the discount rate is not too high, the inferior performance with respect to future disturbances will outweigh the gains in respect of past disturbances, and it will pay government not to renege. In effect, it pays government to sustain its reputation. And since the private sector can appreciate this, the full optimal rule is credible and therefore sustainable. In a stochastic world the class of sustainable policies is larger than in the deterministic world and may well include the full optimal rule.[4] The results reported by Currie and Levine for a simple open-economy model suggest that the full optimal rule is sustainable if the rate of discount is not unduly high: this reflects the superior performance of the full optimal rule relative to the time consistent non-reputational optimal rule.[5] In the following, we refer to the full optimal rule as the reputational optimal policy, and the Cohen/Michel rule as the non-reputational optimal policy.

Turning to a two-country world, the sustainability of the optimal cooperative policy requires one to examine the credibility of the policy with respect to both the relationships between governments and those between governments and the private sector. As the results will show, whether the environment is stochastic or not has an important bearing on the success of a cooperative agreement. This is for reasons similar to the issue of sustainability vis-a-vis the private sector. When reneging on cooperative agreements with other governments, a government must weigh the future

[3] Note, however, that if the only alternative policy is the optimal non-reputational time consistent policy such an incentive need not necessarily emerge. In the example examined by Currie and Levine (1985), it depends on the nature of the initial displacement of the system.

[4] This result is most obvious for the case of no-discounting, where future shocks necessarily assume an infinite weight relative to the current state of the system. Taylor (1985) suggests that the assumption of the case of no discounting is most appropriate for macroeconomic policy design. These findings are analogous to those obtained in the literature dealing explicitly with reputations (see, for example, Barro and Gordon (1983), Backus and Driffill (1984)). Note, however, that this analysis may be applied in a quite general class of models.

[5] The critical rate of discount is found to be so high that the argument could well survive the introduction of finite lived governments because of elections. Formally this may be modelled by assuming a given probability density of the government falling from power in any time interval.

consequences of a breakdown of cooperation, and these will be more deleterious if future shocks to the system are expected to occur.

The plan of the paper is as follows. In the next section, we discuss the details of the supergame, considering in particular the appropriate choice of Nash policy to be used in the threat strategy. Section 3 characterises the dynamics of the system under the Nash policy where governments have credibility and hence can pursue reputational optimal policies. Section 4 considers possible alternative equilibria. Section 5 characterises the system with cooperation under the full reputational optimal rule. Section 6 describes the two country model which we use to implement the analysis. Section 7 presents our results on the benefits and sustainability of cooperation, while Section 8 draws some conclusions.

2. Policy coordination as a supergame

We shall characterise the problem of policy coordination in a two-country world of market economies as a three-person game whose players consist of the two governments in the two countries and a homogeneous forward-looking private sector. In the model presented later in the paper, the forward-looking private sector consists of agents participating in the capital market. We further assume that the private sector is atomised so that only governments can act strategically, i.e. only governments can consider the effect of their own actions on the macro-environment and hence on their own objectives.

It is useful to consider separately relationships between governments and the private sector and between the governments themselves.

(i) Government/private sector relationships

The setting is dynamic in which governments and forward-looking agents plan for the future. For the government the choice of policy is first, between the reputational optimal policy and the non-reputational time consistent optimal policy. Second, policy announcements can be in feedback or open-loop form. Regarding the latter, whether *atomised* private agents perceive of policy as feedback (or closed-loop[6]) rules or as open-loop trajectories makes no difference to the game. Feedback rules define feedback between instruments and macroeconomic variables which an atomised private sector takes as given and not influenced by its decisions. If agents are large or collusive the manner in which rules are announced do affect government/private sector relationships, but we do not pursue this in this paper.

---

[6] Feedback control and closed-loop control are synonymous in our linear-quadratic framework in which "certainty-equivalence" applies. (See Bar-Shalom and Tse (1976)).

(ii) *Government/government relationships*

Governments can choose to cooperate and jointly select policies, in feedback or open-loop form, to minimise a global welfare loss function. In the absence of cooperation governments will act independently resulting in some non-cooperative equilibrium. We consider the various alternative non-cooperative equilibria in Section 2(iii).

We want to investigate whether the best form of cooperative behaviour (i.e., the reputational optimal policy) is sustainable in our two-country world. A useful framework for considering this problem is to use the concept of a *supergame*. A supergame (see, for example, Friedman (1977)) is a continuous repetition of a 'constituent game' which in the game described above consists of either the non-cooperative equilibrium or the cooperative agreement. A supergame strategy then gives the action for a constituent game as a function of all previous strategy choices by all players.

By analogy with Friedman's oligopoly game, the following supergame strategy may sustain a cooperative solution.

(a) Each government at time t honours the cooperative agreement if the other government has previously done so.

(b) If either government at time less than t deviates from the agreed policy, then the other government selects a non-cooperative policy.

There are two possible equilibria for this supergame: either both governments honour the cooperative agreement or both governments end up at some non-cooperative equilibrium. Irrespective of the initial policies, one of these equilibria will be reached. The supergame strategy is therefore sub-game perfect. The relationships between the various players of this supergame are summarised in Fig. 1 below.

The cooperative agreement is sustained in this supergame provided that two conditions are satisfied. First, the 'threat' (b) must be an effective deterrent, by which we mean that if each government knows that the other will carry out the threat (revert to non-cooperation) it will be deterred from reneging. Since reversion to some non-cooperative equilibrium by one country implies that the same equilibrium is the best policy for the other to follow, the threat is an effective deterrent if the non-cooperative equilibrium

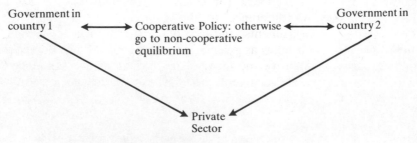

FIG. 1, The macroeconomic policy game.

yields a higher welfare loss *for both* countries as compared with the cooperative outcome. This condition is by no means guaranteed for two reasons. First, the optimal cooperative policy will be time inconsistent so that after the initial optimisation at $t = 0$, for $t > 0$ it ceases to be optimal. This means that the non-cooperative equilibrium calculated at $t > 0$ could in principle yield a lower global welfare loss. Second, even if the global welfare loss is always greater for the non-cooperative equilibrium, asymmetries between the countries either in the structure of the models or in the shocks hitting the two economies could mean that one country may still benefit by reneging.

The second condition for the supergame to sustain a cooperative equilibrium is that the threat should be credible; that is to say both governments believe it will be carried out. Threats in the form of 'optimal incentive strategies' such as those studied by Ehtamo and Hämäläinen (1985) (and see also references cited in that paper) do not address the question of credibility. If threats when jointly carried out constitute a non-cooperative equilibrium (i.e., the supergame is sub-game perfect) then they are credible in the (weak) sense that they constitute a feasible, non-enforcing outcome of a breakdown in cooperation. This rules out a Stackelberg leadership form of threat since it is not a non-cooperative equilibrium. However, the credibility of the threat to revert to some non-cooperative policy is not entirely straightforward because for a *given* deviation from the agreed cooperative policy by one country, it does not constitute the optimal policy for the other. Indeed it is conceivable that a form of reneging by one country can be found such that it is better for the second country to acquiesce and continue its side of the agreement than to switch to a non-cooperative equilibrium. However a more likely outcome of a breakdown of the cooperative policy is that each government in turn will optimise given the observed policy of the other. This will give rise to a Cournot-like adjustment process which will either diverge, resulting in enormous welfare loss for both countries, or converge to the non-cooperative equilibrium. Since both countries know this, the optimal policy in response to an act of reneging is in fact to carry out the non-cooperative equilibrium threat.

(iii) *The choice of non-cooperative equilibrium*

We consider together government/private sector and government/ government relationships to arrive at the possible forms of non-cooperative equilibria. Since we rule out the possibility of Stackelberg leadership this leaves the government/government relationship as either a *Nash* or a *Consistent Conjectural Variations* equilibrium (CCVE).

The CCVE has aroused considerable interest since the pioneering paper on the subject by Bresnahan (1981). Generally speaking, in a game with a CCVE each player has perceptions of how the other player's actions depend on its own. In equilibrium this perception of interdependence corresponds to the outcome in some sense. (Note this differs from Stackelberg games where one or both players have false perceptions of the interdependence). However there arc at least two problems associated with this solution concept.

First suppose that the two countries conduct policy in the form of feedback rules. In a CCVE, for each country, the coefficients in these rules will depend on expectations of the other country's rule and on its dependence on its own rule i.e., on each country's perception of the other country's reaction function. In most formulation of a CCVE consistency is imposed on both the levels and first derivatives of these reaction functions.

However, as Basar (1985) has pointed out consistency can be imposed on second derivatives as well and so on to give us any order CCVE, an n-order CCVE corresponding to consistency up to nth order derivatives (thus the Nash equilibrium is in fact a zero-order CCVE).

The multiplicity of solutions for a CCVE is not the only problem associated with this non-cooperative equilibrium. We shall show in Section 4(i) that even the zero-order CCVE (i.e. the Nash equilibrium) is exceedingly complex when countries pursue reputational policies in feedback form.[7] This leaves the possibility of a non-reputational time consistent CCVE. Hughes–Hallet (1985) describes an iterative procedure[8] for computing a 1st order CCVE which is time consistent by virtue of the fact that the model does not have rational expectations. Basar, Turnovsky and d'Orey (1985) tackle a time consistent 1st order CCVE but only for a rather simple rational expectations model. In the model of this paper there are 2 instruments and a state vector with 4 predetermined variables. This means the time-consistent feedback rule has 8 coefficients (see section 4(ii)). For a 1st order CCVE there are then 8 consistency conditions for the coefficients and $4^2 \times 2^2 = 64$ consistency conditions for their derivatives, making 72 conditions in all.

For these reasons we conclude that the CCVE is problematic even if we confine ourselves to a 1st order CCVE which is time consistent. We therefore restrict ourselves to Nash equilibria on this paper. In Section 3 we develop a solution procedure for an open-loop Nash equilibrium between countries when governments pursue time inconsistent policies. In Section 4 the closed-loop Nash equilibrium is examined for both the time inconsistent and time consistent cases.

---

[7] This is true only of reputational closed loop Nash strategies, which involves an element of strategic behaviour of each government vis-a-vis the other. It is not the case for non-reputational closed loop Nash, where this strategic element is absent.

[8] Hughes Hallet reports a general iterative procedure that may fail to converge and typically yields multiple solutions. A modified directed search was then implemented in which at least one country is better off and neither is worse off at each step. Since a 1st order CCVE is essentially a Nash-type game with perceptions of both levels and derivatives the justification for this is not altogether clear.

We finally consider the appropriate choice of a non-cooperative equilibrium for the 'threat point' of the supergame. In Sections 3 and 4 we shall narrow the choice down to an open-loop Nash equilibrium where each government has credibility and hence pursues an optimal reputational policy given the policy of the foreign country; and a closed-loop Nash equilibrium where only non-reputational policies are possible. Suppose the international agreement breaks down. If the private sector does not regard a switch to some non-cooperative policy as an act of reneging on itself and understands from the outset that the reputational cooperative policy is conditional upon a continuation of the international agreement, then it is conceivable that it will accept the governments' precommitment to a new non-cooperative reputational policy. Then the non-cooperative reputational Nash equilibrium of Section 3 is plausible. If, on the other hand, a breakdown in cooperation destroys the reputation of governments for honouring precommitments, then only non-reputational policies are available and the non-cooperative, non-reputational Nash equilibrium of Section 4(ii) is appropriate.[9] In what follows we shall keep both these options open so that we are looking for sustainability vis-a-vis both types of non-cooperative equilibria as threat points.

3. A non-cooperative equilibrium with reputation

In this section we set out a non-cooperative dynamic equilibrium for the case where the government has the credibility that it still pursues an announced policy. We refer to the resulting optimal policy as the optimal reputational policy. In the absence of reputation, this policy would be unsustainable because of the problem of time-inconsistency. However, credibility may be assured because of the presence of continuing stochastic shocks (see Currie and Levine (1985c)). Between countries the game is assumed to be of an *open-loop Nash* character, i.e. the policy instruments are perceived of by the two countries to be in open-loop (or trajectory) form and are taken as given.

The two-country model can be written in the following general form

$$\begin{bmatrix} dz \\ dx^e \end{bmatrix} = A \begin{bmatrix} z \\ x \end{bmatrix} dt + B \begin{bmatrix} w \\ w^* \end{bmatrix} dt + dv \qquad (3.1)$$

where z is an $(n-m) \times 1$ vector of predetermined variables, x is an $m \times 1$ vector of non-predetermined or free variables, dx^e is the rational expectation of dx formed at time t on the basis of the information set $I(t) = \{z(s), x(s) : s \leq t\}$ and knowledge of the model (2.1), w and w^* are $r \times 1$ vectors of control instruments,[*] indicating the instruments of the 'foreign'

---

[9] Another interesting possibility, which is not considered in this paper, is that the responsibility for the breakdown in the cooperative agreement can be directed at one of the countries only. Then this country is constrained to pursue time consistent policies but the other country can still pursue optimal time inconsistent policies.

country, dv is an $n \times 1$ vector of unobserved white noise disturbances independently distributed with $E(dv) = 0$ and $dv \sim N(0, V\,dt)$, A, B and V have time-invariant coefficients, and V is symmetric and non-negative definite. All variables are measured as deviations from some long-run trend equilibrium.

Let $s = \begin{bmatrix} z \\ x \end{bmatrix}$ and $B = [B_1, B_2]$ partitioned conformably with $\begin{bmatrix} w \\ w^* \end{bmatrix}$. Then in deterministic form, (3.1) may be written as

$$\dot{s} = As + B_1 w + B_2 w^* \tag{3.2}$$

where we have put $\dot{x}^e = \dot{x}$ by the rational expectations assumption. Consider a welfare loss function for country 1

$$W = \frac{1}{2} \int_0^\infty e^{-\rho t}[s^T Q s + w^T R w]\,dt \tag{3.3}$$

where $\rho \geqslant 0$ is a discount factor, Q and R have time invariant coefficients and, in addition R is symmetric and positive definite and Q is symmetric and non-negative definite.

The control problem for the country 1 is then to minimise (3.3) with respect to w, subject to (3.2). In the open-loop Nash game w^*, the instruments of the other country, are taken as given for this minimisation problem. Proceeding by Pontryagin's principle, we introduce a costate row vector λ and define a Hamiltonian

$$H = \tfrac{1}{2}e^{-\rho t}(s^T Q s + w^T R w) + \lambda(As + B_1 w + B_2^*) \tag{3.4}$$

Then the first order conditions are $\partial H/\partial \lambda = \dot{s}$, $\partial H/\partial w = 0$ and $\dot{\lambda} = -\partial H/\partial s$ from which (3.2) is obtained together with

$$Rw + B_1^T p = 0 \tag{3.5}$$

and

$$\dot{p} = (\rho I - A^T)p - Qs \tag{3.6}$$

where $p = e^{\rho t}\lambda^T$. The $2n$ boundary conditions for country 1's minimisation exercise are given by $z(0) = z_0$, $p_2(0) = 0$ and the transversality condition $\lim_{t \to \infty} e^{-\rho t}p(t) = 0$.

Repeating the argument for country 2 and denoting analogous variables and matrices with a^*, we arrive at

$$R^* w^* + B_2^T p^* = 0 \tag{3.7}$$

---

[10] Since the expected rate of inflation moves in a continuous way in this set-up, use of the nominal short term interest rate as the instrument is equivalent to use of the short term expected real rate of interest, r. We therefore treat r as the instrument, and associate instrument costs with movements in real, not nominal, interest rates.

and

$$\dot{p}^* = (\rho^* I - A^T) p^* - Q^* s \tag{3.8}$$

Combining (3.5)–(3.8) we obtain the following open-loop Nash equilibrium for the two countries under single-country optimal control

$$
\begin{bmatrix} \dot{s} \\ \dot{p} \\ \dot{p}^* \end{bmatrix} = \begin{bmatrix} A & F & F^* \\ -Q & G & 0 \\ -Q^* & 0 & G^* \end{bmatrix} \begin{bmatrix} s \\ p \\ p^* \end{bmatrix} \tag{3.9}
$$

where $F = -BR^{-1}B^T$, $F^* = -B^*R^{*-1}B^{*T}$, $G = \rho I - A^T$ and $G^* = \rho^* I - A^T$.

The stochastic case may be handled by an appeal to certainty equivalence which may be shown to hold in rational expectations models of the form (3.9) (Levine and Currie (1987)). For country 1, $w = -R^{-1}B_1 p$ is still the optimal rule in feedback form given $E(W^*)$. Similarly for country 2, $w^* = -R^{*-1}B_2 p^*$ applies so that the system under optimal control (3.9) becomes

$$
\begin{bmatrix} ds^e \\ dp \\ dp^* \end{bmatrix} = \begin{bmatrix} A & F & F^* \\ -Q & G & 0 \\ -Q^* & 0 & G^* \end{bmatrix} \begin{bmatrix} s \\ p \\ p^* \end{bmatrix} dt + \begin{bmatrix} dv \\ 0 \\ 0 \end{bmatrix} \tag{3.10}
$$

writing $ds^e = \begin{bmatrix} dz \\ dx^e \end{bmatrix}$.

In the stochastic problem the nature of the equilibrium is different. Each country plans its optimal rule on the basis of a prediction of the other country's trajectory of instruments. In the deterministic equilibrium the prediction turns out to be exactly right. In a stochastic environment the prediction will always be subject to forecast error due to current disturbances. But if each country can find an accurate ARMA representation of the other country's instruments, incorporate this ARMA, process into the dynamics of (3.1) and design its policy with feedforward on these exogenous variables, then the stochastic equilibrium (3.10) will be reached.

In the system under control (3.10) or, in the special case (3.14), there are $n + m$ predetermined variables $[z^T p_2^T p_2^{*T}]^T$ and $2n - m$ non-predetermined variables $[p_1^T p_1^{*T} x^T]^T$ where $p = [p_1^T p_2^T]^T$ and $p^* = [p_1^{*T} p_2^{*T}]^T$ are partitioned conformably with $[z^T x^T]^T$. It follows that a Nash open-loop equilibrium exists if and only if the transition matrix has the "saddlepoint property", namely $n + m$ eigenvalues with negative real part and $2n - m$ eigenvalues with positive real part. This condition is by no means guaranteed as we shall see in the results.

If the saddlepoint property is satisfied we can solve the system under control and find the welfare loss for the two countries. First rearrange the $3n$ equations in (3.10) so that the first $n + m$ define the dynamics of the predetermined variables, i.e. we rewrite (3.10) as

$$
\begin{bmatrix} dz \\ dp_2 \\ dp_2^* \\ dp_1 \\ dp_1^* \\ dx^e \end{bmatrix} = H \begin{bmatrix} z \\ p_2 \\ p_2^* \\ p_1 \\ p_1^* \\ x \end{bmatrix} dt + \begin{bmatrix} dv_1 \\ 0 \\ 0 \\ 0 \\ 0 \\ dv_2 \end{bmatrix} \tag{3.11}
$$

where H is formed from the transition matrix in (3.10) by appropriate rearrangement of rows and columns. Equation (3.11) is in the form of a standard rational expectations model with $n + m$ predetermined variables and $2n - m$ 'free' or 'jump' variables. The standard rational expectations assumption that the system is stable imposes the saddlepath relationship

$$
\begin{bmatrix} p_1 \\ p_1^* \\ x \end{bmatrix} = -N \begin{bmatrix} z \\ p_2 \\ p_2^* \end{bmatrix} \tag{3.12}
$$

where $N = M_{22}^{-1} M_{21}$ and M is the matrix of left-eigenvectors of H arranged so that the last $2n - m$ rows are associated with unstable eigenvectors and partitioned so that M_{11} is of order $(n + m) \times (n + m)$. Partitioning H as for M the dynamics of the predetermined variables are now given from (3.11) and (3.12) by

$$
\begin{bmatrix} dz \\ dp_2 \\ dp_2^* \end{bmatrix} = [H_{11} - H_{12}N] \begin{bmatrix} z \\ p_2 \\ p_2^* \end{bmatrix} dt + \begin{bmatrix} dv_1 \\ 0 \\ 0 \end{bmatrix} \tag{3.13}
$$

which has a solution

$$
\begin{bmatrix} z \\ p_2 \\ p_2^* \end{bmatrix} = e^{Jt} \begin{bmatrix} z(0) \\ 0 \\ 0 \end{bmatrix} + \int_0^t e^{J(t-s)} \begin{bmatrix} dv_1(s) \\ 0 \\ 0 \end{bmatrix} \tag{3.14}
$$

where $J = H_{11} - H_{12}N$ and we recall that $p_2(0) = p_2^*(0) = 0$. The feedback rules $w = -R^{-1}B_1p$ and $w^* = -R^{*-1}B_2p^*$ in Nash equilibrium now become, from (3.12),

$$
W = R^{-1}[K_1N_{11}, \; K_1N_{12} - K_2, \; -K_1N_{13}] \begin{bmatrix} z \\ p_2 \\ p_2^* \end{bmatrix} \tag{3.15}
$$

and

$$
w^* = R^{*-1}[K_1^*N_{21}, \; K_1^*N_{22} - K_2^*, \; -K_1^*N_{23}] \begin{bmatrix} z \\ p_2 \\ p_2^* \end{bmatrix} \tag{3.16}
$$

where $B_1^T = K = [K_1, K_2]$, $B_2^T = K^* = [K_1^*, K_2^*]$ and

$$N = \begin{bmatrix} N_{11} & N_{12} & N_{13} \\ N_{21} & N_{22} & N_{23} \\ N_{31} & N_{32} & N_{33} \end{bmatrix} \tag{3.17}$$

has been partitioned conformably with $[z^T p_2^T p_2^*]^T$.

The policy regimes for the two countries could be announced and implemented in the form of feedback rules (3.15) and (3.16) as far as the private sector is concerned. But since the countries are playing an open-loop Nash vis-a-vis each other this would be inconsistent. Instead, combining (3.14) and (3.15) we must envisage policy for country 1 being announced and implemented in the form

$$w = D \left[e^{Jt} \begin{bmatrix} z(0) \\ 0 \\ 0 \end{bmatrix} + \int_0^t e^{J(t-s)} \begin{bmatrix} dv_1(s) \\ 0 \\ 0 \end{bmatrix} \right] \tag{3.18}$$

where $D = R^{-1}[K_1 N_{11}, K_1 N_{12} - K_2, -K_1 N_{13}]$, with a similar equation for country 2. The policy (3.12) is now in open-loop form consisting of a *deterministic component* plus a *disturbance-contingent component*.

Turning to the calculation of the welfare loss W in equilibrium, for country 1 for the deterministic case, it will depend on both the initial state $z(0)$ and the policy of country 2, i.e. $W = W(z(0), w^*)$. From Pontryagin's principle we have

$$\left[\frac{\partial W}{\partial z(0)} \right]_{w^* \text{ fixed}} = p_1^T(0) = -N_{11} z(0) \tag{3.19}$$

from (3.12). Hence integrating

$$W(z(0), w^*) = \tfrac{1}{2} z^T(0) N_{11} z(0) + W(0, w^*) \tag{3.20}$$

From (3.20) we can see that W cannot be obtained directly from the costate vector due to the presence of the second term $W(0, w^*) > 0$. This term arises from spillover effects from the policy of country 2 into country 1. Rather than attempting to calculate $W(0, w^*)$ it is more straightforward to compute the covariance matrix for (3.11) directly and obtain the full welfare loss $W(z(0), w^*)$ from this.

Proceeding in this way writing $D = [D_1, D_2, D_3]$ in (3.18) we may express the welfare loss function for country 1 for the full stochastic problem as

$$E(W) = \tfrac{1}{2} \int_0^\infty e^{-\rho t} \text{tr} \, (\bar{Q} E(dd^T)) dt \tag{3.21}$$

where

$$\tilde{Q} = \begin{bmatrix} Q_{11} + D_1^T R D_1^T & D_1^T R D_2^T & D_1^T R D_3^T & 0 & 0 & Q_{12} \\ D_2^T R D_1^T & D_2^T R D_2^T & D_2^T R D_3^T & 0 & 0 & 0 \\ D_3^T R D_1^T & D_3^T R D_2^T & D_3^T R D_3^T & 0 & 0 & 0 \\ 0 & 0 & 0 & 0 & 0 & 0 \\ 0 & 0 & 0 & 0 & 0 & 0 \\ Q_{21} & 0 & 0 & 0 & 0 & Q_{22} \end{bmatrix} \tag{3.22}$$

and $d = [z^T p_2^T p_2^{*T} p_1^T p_1^{*T} x^T]^T$ is the state vector in (3.11). Then

$$E(W) = \tfrac{1}{2} \text{tr} \, (\tilde{Q}\tilde{D}) \tag{3.23}$$

where $\tilde{D} = \int_0^\infty e^{-\rho t} E(dd^T) dt$ can be shown to be obtained from

$$\tilde{D} = \begin{bmatrix} \tilde{Z} & -\tilde{Z}N^T \\ -N\tilde{Z}^T & -N\tilde{Z}N^T \end{bmatrix} \tag{3.24}$$

where $\tilde{Z}$ is an $(n + m) \times (n + m)$ matrix satisfying

$$(J - \tfrac{1}{2}\rho I)\tilde{Z} + \tilde{Z}(J^T - \tfrac{1}{2}\rho I) + Z(0) + \rho^{-1}\tilde{\Sigma} = 0 \tag{3.25}$$

with $\tilde{Z}(0) = \begin{bmatrix} z(0)z^T(0) & 0 \\ 0 & 0 \end{bmatrix}$ and $\tilde{\Sigma} = \begin{bmatrix} \Sigma_{11} & 0 \\ 0 & 0 \end{bmatrix}$ (see Levine and Currie (1987) for details). The welfare loss for country 2 follows similarly.

4. Other non-cooperative equilibria

(i) *Closed-loop Nash equilibrium with reputation*

Suppose that the Nash policies of the previous section were announced in the form (3.15) and (3.16). If both countries perceived the other country's policy in this form then the game would be of a closed-loop character. We consider now a Cournot-type adjustment process which we present not as so much as a feasible form of adjustment behaviour, but rather as a means of obtaining the closed-loop Nash equilibria. Country 1 announces its open-loop Nash policy in feedback form,

$$w^{(0)} = [D_1^{(0)} D_2^{(0)} D_3^{(0)}] \begin{bmatrix} z \\ p_2^{(0)} \\ p_2^{*(0)} \end{bmatrix} = D^{(0)} \begin{bmatrix} z \\ p_2^{(0)} \\ p_2^{*(0)} \end{bmatrix} \tag{4.1}$$

where $\begin{bmatrix} p_2^{(0)} \\ p_2^{*(0)} \end{bmatrix}$ is given by bottom $2m$ rows of (3.13)

The constraint facing country 2 then consists of

$$\frac{dz}{dx^e} = A\begin{bmatrix} z \\ x \end{bmatrix} dt + B_1 D^{(0)} \begin{bmatrix} z \\ p_2^{(0)} \\ p_2^{*(0)} \end{bmatrix} dt + B_2 w^* dt + dv \tag{4.2}$$

The dynamic system (4.2) has a state vector $[z^T p_2^{(0)} p_2^{*(0)} x]$ which is of order $n + 2m$. The optimal policy for country 2 will then take the form

$$w^{*(1)} = [D_1^{(1)} D_2^{(1)} D_3^{(1)} D_4^{(1)}] \begin{bmatrix} z \\ p_2^{(0)} \\ p_2^{*(0)} \\ p_2^{*(1)} \end{bmatrix} \tag{4.3}$$

where $p_2^{*(1)}$ is formed as for $p_2^{(0)}$ and $p_2^{*(0)}$.

After iterating n times (for n even) we arrive at

$$w^{*(n-1)} = [D_1^{(n-1)} D_2^{(n-1)} D_3^{(n-1)} \ldots D_{3+(n-1)}^{(n-1)}] \begin{bmatrix} z \\ p_2^{(0)} \\ p_2^{*(0)} \\ \vdots \\ p_2^{*(n-1)} \end{bmatrix} \tag{4.4}$$

and

$$w^{(n)} = [D_1^{(n)} D_2^{(n)} D_3^{(n)} \ldots D_{3+n}^{(n)}] \begin{bmatrix} z \\ p_2^{(0)} \\ p_2^{*(0)} \\ \vdots \\ p_2^{*(n-1)} \\ p_2^{(n)} \end{bmatrix} \tag{4.5}$$

for the two countries. Whatever the order of dynamics of the rule for one country, the response of the other is a higher order rule.

The existence of a closed-loop Nash equilibrium with reputation then rests on the convergence of the process described, i.e. on the conditions

$$\lim_{n \to \infty} D_{3+n-1}^{(n-1)} p_2^{*(n-1)} = 0 \tag{4.6}$$

$$\lim_{n \to \infty} D_{3+n}^{(n)} p_2^{(n)}(t) = 0 \tag{4.7}$$

or all t. Conditions (4.6) and (4.7) are necessary for $w^{(n)}(t)$ and $w^{*(n)}(t)$ to tend to finite values as $n \to \infty$.

The closed-loop Nash equilibrium with reputation, if it exists, is an extremely complicated rule and must be approximated by rules of the form

(4.4) and (4.5) for some (possibly large) n. In practical terms the possibility of countries actually engaging in games involving policy rules of such complexity seems remote. We therefore do not pursue this form of non-cooperative behaviour further in this paper.

If the closed-loop Nash equilibrium with reputation is to be ruled out on the grounds that either it does not exist or it is too complex, the same must apply with greater force for a CCVE. As we have seen in the discussion in section 2(iii), it is even more complex than the closed-loop Nash equilibrium and there is again no guarantee it even exists. Again, as for the closed-loop Nash equilibrium, we do not consider the CCVE (with reputation) to be a plausible form of non-cooperative solution.

(ii) *The non-reputational closed-loop Nash equilibrium*

If the government lacks the credibility to precommit itself to preannounced policies, optimal policies must be found which are time-consistent without reputation. The following is an iterative solution for a time consistent non-reputational closed-loop Nash equilibrium between two countries (see also Miller and Salmon (1985) and the discrete-time analogue of Oudiz and Sachs (1985)).

It is now well-established in the literature that time consistent non-reputational rules must take the form of proportional feedback on the predetermined variables, i.e. the rules must be of the form $w = Dz$, $w^* = D^*z$ (This is because feedback on additional costate variables of the optimisation decision introduces potential of time inconsistency: see, in addition to work cited above, Cohen and Michel (1984) and Currie and Levine (1985c)). Suppose the two countries begin with $w = D_0z$ and $w^* = D_0^*z$. Substituting into (3.1) the system under control will then be

$$\begin{bmatrix} dz \\ dx^e \end{bmatrix} = [A + B_1D_0 + B_2D_0^*]\begin{bmatrix} z \\ x \end{bmatrix}dt + dv \tag{4.8}$$

The rational expectations solution to (4.8) has a saddlepath given by

$$x = -N_0z \tag{4.9}$$

where $N_0 = N_0(D_0, D_0) = M_{22}^{-1}M_{21}$, with $M = \begin{bmatrix} M_{11} & M_{12} \\ M_{21} & M_{22} \end{bmatrix}$ being the matrix of left-eigenvectors of the transition matrix in (4.8) arranged so that the last m rows are associated with the unstable eigenvalues and partitioned conformably with $\begin{bmatrix} z \\ x \end{bmatrix}$.

Country 1 now takes N_0 as given (the time consistency constraint) and D_0^* as given (the closed-loop Nash assumption between countries). Substituting for x from (4.9) it then minimises $E(W)$ where

$$W = \tfrac{1}{2} \int_0^\infty e^{-\rho t}(z^T \tilde{Q} z + w^T R w)dt \qquad (4.10)$$

where $\tilde{Q} = Q_{11} - N_0^T Q_{12} - Q_{21} N_0 + N_0^T Q_{22} N_0$ and $Q = \begin{bmatrix} Q_{11} & Q_{12} \\ Q_{21} & Q_{22} \end{bmatrix}$ parti-

tioned conformably with $\begin{bmatrix} z \\ x \end{bmatrix}$. The dynamic constraint is

$$dz = [\tilde{A}_{11} - \tilde{A}_{12} N_0]z\, dt + B_1 w dt + dv^1 \qquad (4.11)$$

where $\tilde{A} = A + B_2[D_0^*, 0]$ and $\tilde{A}$, $[D_0^*, 0]$ and $dv = \begin{bmatrix} dv^1 \\ dv^2 \end{bmatrix}$ are all partitioned

conformably with $\begin{bmatrix} z \\ x \end{bmatrix}$.

The minimization of $E(W)$ with W given by (4.10) and subject to (4.11) is a standard control problem with solution $w = D_1 z$ where $D_1 = -R^{-1} B_1^T S_1$ and S_1 satisfies the Riccati equation

$$S_1(\tilde{A}_{11} - \tilde{A}_{12} N_0 - \tfrac{1}{2}\rho I) + (\tilde{A}_{11} - \tilde{A}_{12} N_0 - \tfrac{1}{2}\rho I)^T S_1 + \tilde{Q} - S_1 B_1 R^{-1} B_1^T S_1 = 0 \qquad (4.12)$$

There are a number of ways in which the iteration may now proceed. The following we found to be numerically successful for the model given in Section 6. Keeping $x = -N_0 z$ with $N_0 = N_0(D_0, D_0)$ we iterate between countries to obtain a convergent sequence $D_1, D_2, D_3, \ldots$ for country 1 and $D_1^*, D_2^*, D_3^*, \ldots$ for country 2, with stationary values D and D^* respectively. Then N_0 is up-dated based on the latest D and D^* and the process is repeated. This leads to a time consistent closed-loop Nash equilibrium.

Let the stationary values for the two coupled Riccati equations associated with countries 1 and 2 be S and S^* respectively. Then corresponding to (3.23) we have that the expected welfare loss is given by

$$E(W) = \tfrac{1}{2}\mathrm{tr}\,(S(Z(0) + \rho^{-1}\Sigma_{11})) \qquad (4.13)$$

where $Z(0) = z(0)z^T(0)$, for country 1 with a similar expression (with S replaced by S^* and ρ by ρ^*) for country 2.

5. The cooperative equilibrium

For the cooperative equilibrium the two countries combine to choose $\begin{bmatrix} w \\ w^* \end{bmatrix}$ to minimise a joint welfare loss function which is a linear combination of the individual countries' loss functions, i.e. $E(W)$ where

$$W = \frac{1}{2} \int_0^\infty e^{-\rho t}[s^T(\alpha Q + (1 - \alpha)Q^*)s + \alpha w^T R w + (1 - \alpha)w^{*T} R^* w^*]dt \qquad (5.1)$$

and $0 \leq \alpha \leq 1$. The choice of α is discussed in part (iii) of this section. The discount factor ρ is assumed to be the same for each country acting independently (i.e. $\rho = \rho^*$).

(i) *The optimal policy with precommitment*

The control problem for the two countries acting together is then to minimise $E(W)$ with W given by (5.1) subject to (3.1). Proceeding as before by Pontryagin's principle, we define a Hamiltonian

$$H = \tfrac{1}{2}e^{-\rho t}\left(s^T Q^C s + [ww^*]^T R^C \begin{bmatrix} w \\ w^* \end{bmatrix}\right) + \lambda\left(As + B\begin{bmatrix} w \\ w^* \end{bmatrix}\right) \tag{5.2}$$

where λ is a costate row vector, $Q^C = \alpha Q + (1 - \alpha)Q^*$ and $R^C = \begin{bmatrix} \alpha R & 0 \\ 0 & (1 - \alpha)R^* \end{bmatrix}$. Then the first order conditions give, for the deterministic problem

$$R^C \begin{bmatrix} w \\ w^* \end{bmatrix} - B^T p = 0 \tag{5.3}$$

$$\dot{p} = (\rho I - A^T) - Q^C s \tag{5.4}$$

where $p = e^{\rho t}\lambda^T$ and the $2n$ boundary conditions are given by $z(0)$, $p_2(0) = 0$ and $\lim_{t \to \infty} e^{-\rho t}p(t) = 0$.

By certainty equivalence the stochastic system under optimal control is then

$$\begin{bmatrix} dz^e \\ dp \end{bmatrix} = \begin{bmatrix} A & F^C \\ -Q^C & G \end{bmatrix}\begin{bmatrix} s \\ p \end{bmatrix}dt + \begin{bmatrix} dv \\ 0 \end{bmatrix} \tag{5.5}$$

where $ds^e = \begin{bmatrix} dz \\ dx^e \end{bmatrix}$, $F^C = -BRB^T$ and $G = \rho I - A^T$.

The saddlepath relationship is now

$$\begin{bmatrix} p_1 \\ x \end{bmatrix} = -N^c \begin{bmatrix} z \\ p_2 \end{bmatrix} \tag{5.6}$$

where N^c is defined analogously in (3.12) and the solution is as before with the feedback rule becoming

$$w = R^{c-1}[K_1^c N_{11}^c, K_1^c N_{12}^c - K_2]\begin{bmatrix} z \\ p_2 \end{bmatrix} \tag{5.7}$$

where $B^T = K^c = [K_1^c, K_2^c]$ and $N^c = \begin{bmatrix} N_{11}^c & N_{12}^c \\ N_{21}^c & N_{22}^c \end{bmatrix}$ has been partitioned conformably with $[z^T p_2^T]^T$.

The welfare loss calculation is now far more straightforward. For the deterministic case, $W = W(z(0))$ so that corresponding to (3.19) we have

$$\frac{dW}{dz(0)} = p_1^T(0) = -N_{11}^c z(0) \tag{5.8}$$

Hence integrating

$$W(z(0)) = -\tfrac{1}{2} z^T(0) N_{11}^c z(0)$$
$$= -\tfrac{1}{2} \text{tr} \, (N_{11}^c Z(0)) \tag{5.9}$$

where $Z(0) = z(0)z^T(0)$ and we have used $W(0) = 0$. For the full stochastic problem (5.9) is replaced with $E(W) = -\tfrac{1}{2} \text{tr} \, (N_{11}^c(Z(0) + \rho^{-1}\Sigma_{11}))$ where $\Sigma_{11} = \text{cov} \, (dv^1)$ (Levine and Currie (1987)).

$E(W)$ is the joint or global welfare loss. To obtain the individual welfare losses for the counties separately the method used for the non-cooperative open loop Nash equilibrium (equations (3.21)–(3.25)) must be employed.

(ii) *Non-reputational optimal*

The optimal non-reputational cooperative policy can be calculated as for the closed-loop Nash time consistent non-cooperative policy of Section 4(ii). Of course, for the cooperative case the iterations only precede between the collusive governments and the private sector.

(iii) *The choice of α*

The parameter α should be chosen in accordance with the 'bargaining power' or relative gains from cooperation for the two countries. In standard bargaining theory the outcome is usually taken to be the Nash arbitration point which maximises the product of the cooperative gains. Let $E(W^{CP})$ and $E(W^{NCP})$ represent the expected welfare loss for our chosen cooperative and non-cooperative solutions respectively for country 1 and let $E(W^{*CP})$, $E(W^{*NCP})$ be the corresponding values for country 2. Then the Nash point is given by the value of α that maximises the product

$$(E(W^{CP}) - E(W^{NCP}))(E(W^{*CP}) - E(W^{*NCP})) \tag{5.10}$$

(see Hughes–Hallet (1985) for a discussion of the Nash point and alternatives).

6. The model

We apply the methods developed in the previous sections of the paper to a two country model. The model consists of the following equations:

$$dy = \psi_1(\alpha_1 c + \alpha_2 y^* - \alpha_3 r - \alpha_4 s - y)dt + dv_1 \tag{6.1}$$

$$dp = (\beta_1 y + \beta_2 c)dt + dv_2 \tag{6.2}$$

$$dc^e = (r - r^*)dt \tag{6.3}$$

$$c^* = -c \tag{6.4}$$

with two further relationships analogous to (6.1)–(6.2) with starred variables and parameters replacing unstarred variables and *vice versa*, and where the following notation is used:

y = real output

p = price level

r = short-term expected real rate of interest

s = autonomous component of real taxes

c = real exchange rate

$\quad = e + p^* - p$ where e is the nominal exchange rate

dv_1 = white noise demand disturbance

dv_2 = white noise supply disturbance

All variables are measured as logarithms with the exception of the real rate of interest which is a proportion and all variables are measured as a deviation about a long run trend. All parameters are specified to be non-negative.

Equation (6.1) represents the IS curve, with output adjusting sluggishly to competitiveness, the real rate of interest, real taxes and overseas real output. Equation (6.2) represents a Phillips curve relationship with inflation depending on output deviations and on real competitiveness, this latter effect arising from the effects of shifts in the terms of trade on the real consumption wage and hence on potential supply. The model is then completed by an uncovered real interest arbitrage condition (equation (6.3)) which assumes that domestic and foreign bonds are perfect substitutes, so that the real rates of return, adjusted for expected real exchange rate changes, are equalised. We treat autonomous taxes and short term interest rates as the policy instruments.

Certain features of the model deserve further comment. The money market is not specified explicitly, but its inclusion would add nothing to our analysis. This is because, with interest rates acting as the instrument of policy, the money supply adjusts passively to clear the money market at prevailing interest rates. Our model also neglects the effects of changes in wealth resulting from current account imbalances or fiscal deficits. It also neglects expectations in the inflation equation, and aspects of forward looking behaviour that might arise in the determination of expenditures. There would be interest in working with a more developed model, preferably empirically based, that rectifies these omissions, and this will be the aim of future work by the authors. Nonetheless, our simple model incorporates key macroeconomic relationships of interest, and provides a useful testbed for an initial exploration of questions of international cooperation.

Our two country model may be set up in the form

$$
\begin{bmatrix} dy \\ dy^* \\ dp \\ dp^* \\ dc^e \end{bmatrix} = \begin{bmatrix} -\psi_1 & \psi_1\alpha_2 & 0 & 0 & \psi_1\alpha_1 \\ \psi_1^*\alpha_2^* & -\psi_1^* & 0 & 0 & -\psi_1^*\alpha^* \\ \beta_1 & 0 & 0 & 0 & \beta_2 \\ 0 & \beta_1^* & 0 & 0 & -\beta_2^* \\ 0 & 0 & 0 & 0 & 0 \end{bmatrix} \begin{bmatrix} y \\ y^* \\ p \\ p^* \\ c \end{bmatrix} dt
$$

$$+ \begin{bmatrix} -\psi_1\alpha_3 & -\psi_1\alpha_4 \\ 0 & 0 \\ 0 & 0 \\ 0 & 0 \\ 1 & 0 \end{bmatrix} \begin{bmatrix} r \\ s \end{bmatrix} dt + \begin{bmatrix} 0 & 0 \\ -\psi_1^*\alpha_3^* & -\psi_1^*\alpha_4^* \\ 0 & 0 \\ 0 & 0 \\ -1 & 0 \end{bmatrix} \begin{bmatrix} r^* \\ s^* \end{bmatrix} dt + \begin{bmatrix} dv_1 \\ dv_1^* \\ dv_2 \\ dv_2^* \\ 0 \end{bmatrix} \quad (6.5)$$

which is comparable to (3.1) with $z = [yy^*pp^*]^T$, $x = c$, $w = [rs]^T$ and $w^* = [r^*s^*]^T$.

The welfare loss function adopted for country 1 is $E(W)$ where

$$W = \frac{1}{2}\int_0^\infty e^{-\rho t}(ay^2 + bp^2 + r^2 + s^2)dt \quad (6.6)$$

so that in (3.3)

$$Q = \begin{bmatrix} a & & & 0 \\ & 0 & & \\ & & b & \\ 0 & & & 0 \end{bmatrix}; \quad (6.7)$$

and $R = I$. $E(W^*)$ is given similarly for country 2 with starred variables and parameters and

$$Q^* = \begin{bmatrix} 0 & & & 0 \\ & a & & \\ & & 0 & \\ 0 & & & b \end{bmatrix}; R^* = I \quad (6.8)$$

The analysis and associated software is quite general and can be used for asymmetrical economies. However in this paper we confine ourselves to identical countries. The starred and unstarred parameters are then equal. In the results that follow the following 'central' values are chosen: $\psi_1 = \psi_1^* = \alpha_2 = \alpha_2^* = 0.5$, $\alpha_1 = \alpha_1^* = 0.3$, $\alpha_3 = \alpha_3^* = 0.1$, $\alpha_4 = \alpha_4^* = 0.4$, $\beta_1 = \beta_1^* = 0.15$, $\beta_2 = \beta_2^* = 0.25$, $a = a^* = b = b^* = 2.0$, $\rho = \rho^* = 0.05$, $\alpha = 0.5$. Where alternative parameter values are used, this is indicated.

7. Results

In Sections 3 to 5 we have described four possible non-cooperative equilibria and two cooperative equilibria. Of the four non-cooperative solutions we have ruled out the closed-loop Nash with reputation (i.e. when governments can implement the full optimal policy) and all types of CCVE on the grounds of their complexity. This leaves two forms of non-cooperative behaviour. The equilibria concepts are summarised in Table 1 below with the abbreviations used subsequently.

TABLE 1

Taxonomy of Equilibria.

| | *Government/government relationships* | |
| *Government/private* | | *Non-cooperative* |
sector relationships	*Cooperative*	*Nash*
Optimal policy with		
reputation	CR	NCR (open-loop)
Optimal non-reputational policy	CNR	NCNR (closed-loop)

(i) *The trajectories of CR, CNR, NCR, and NCNR.*

Tables 4–11 show the deterministic trajectories and the corresponding welfare losses for the four equilibria for an initial negative displacement of real output, $y(0) = -1$, and a positive initial price level displacement, $p(0) = 1$, in country 1. For the two time reputational policies, CR and NCR, the importance of potential time inconsistency can be assessed by comparing the welfare loss before and after re-optimisation (or 'reneging') along the trajectories. These values are shown in the last two columns. (The first number in the brackets refers to country 1, the second to country 2 and the number above is the total.)

For the initial output displacement $y(0) = -1$ in country 1 all four policies involve a relaxation of fiscal and monetary policies. Both the real interest rates (r, r^*) and real taxes (s, s^*) fall immediately (and more in country 1), and then move gradually back to their steady-state values. The real exchange rate, c, rises immediately (representing a depreciation) and then falls gradually to its long-run equilibrium. Output rises, but with it still below its natural rate prices fall, returning eventually to their equilibria.

For the initial price displacement $p(0) = 1$ the picture is broadly reversed. Fiscal and monetary policies are tightened (and more so in country 1). The real exchange rate undershoots and then rises back to its long-run value. The price level falls but with output losses experienced by both countries.

For cooperative policy the time inconsistent and time consistent policies, CR and CNR respectively, differ principally in the use of the exchange rate. When governments can precommit themselves they can exercise a leadership role with respect to the forward-looking private sector. Thus with credible announcements, policy CR enables the governments jointly to utilise the exchange rate mechanism more and we see this in the greater degree of overshooting for the case of an output displacement and a greater degree of undershooting for a price displacement, especially the latter.

The consequence of this greater use of the exchange rate is that for CR there is a far more equal distribution of the welfare loss between the country experiencing the displacement and the second country. For instance in the case of $p(0) = 1$, for CR output falls to -0.21 in country 1, -0.18 in country 2 and the price level falls to 0.38 in country 1 and *rises* to 0.42 in country 2 by year 5. (Since the variables are in log form these represent % changes in the original variables.) For CNR by contrast output falls to -0.23 in country 1, -0.16 in country 2 and the price level falls to 0.68 in country 1 but only rises to 0.12 in country 2 by year 5.

Turning to the non-cooperative policies, again the reputational policy NCR involves a much greater use of the exchange rate than the non-reputational policy NCNR. This is particularly true for an initial price displacement. In this case country 1 "exports" its price level disturbance and its output loss to country 2. But whereas with CR the real interest rate in country 2 is kept below that in country 2 (and is even negative for a period), with NCR the Nash response of country 2 to an immediate tightening of monetary and fiscal policy in country 1 is to tighten its policy even more. The Nash equilibrium is a rather unusual response to a price displacement consisting of a relaxation of fiscal and monetary policy by both countries with eventually, after year 6, the interest rate in country 1 being above that in country 2. (The persistence of the price displacement means a 10 year time horizon is necessary to examine NCR fully.)

Non-cooperative Nash equilibria can of course give outcomes which no player wants (recall the Prisoner's Dilemma) and NCR is a case in point. Indeed we have found for high values of the discount rate in the region $\rho > 0.12$ (with the remaining parameters at their central values) NCR is actually *unstable* (i.e. has too many unstable roots for the saddlepath condition). For ρ at its central value 0.05 the model is stable at NCR but the performance is very bad for an initial price displacement. (For the initial output displacement there is not a great deal of difference in the performance across all four equilibria.) An interesting feature of NCR is that it is exhibits potentially extreme time inconsistencies in the sense that very large gains can be obtained if both countries re-optimise especially in later years. However, if re-optimisation takes place after year 1, country 1 actually loses out, all the benefits from reneging going to country 2. Again gives the Nash assumption that countries optimise given the actions of the other this is a quite possible unintended effect of 'reneging'.

(ii) *The gains from cooperation*

Consider first the *deterministic* case with displacements $y(0) = -1$, $y(0) = y^*(0) = -1$, $p(0) = 1$, and $p(0) = p^*(0) = 1$. Table 2 shows the initial welfare loss for the two countries separately (in brackets) and the total (above) for these four displacements for the equilibria CR, CNR, NCR and NCNR.

It should be emphasized that the welfare loss for the two cooperative solutions CR and CNR are for the case of equal weights ($\alpha = 0.5$) attached to the two countries, collective welfare loss function in (5.1). In this case, comparing CR with either NCR or NCNR, it can be seen that the country not faced with an output or price displacement loses out by cooperating. However for symmetrical displacements ($y(0) = y^*(0) = 1$ and $p(0) = p^*(0) = 1$), for which $\alpha = 0.5$ is appropriate, CR is superior to both non-cooperative solutions for both countries although the gains for this model and parameter values are not large unless NCR is chosen as the threat point.

TABLE 2
The Gains from Cooperation ($\alpha = 0.5$). Deterministic Case.

Equilibrium solution	$y(0) = -1$	$y(0) = y^*(0) = -1$	$p(0) = 1$	$p(0) = p^*(0) = 1$
CR	1.48	4.78	4.77	17.20
	(1.12, 0.35)	(2.39, 2.39)	(2.94, 1.83)	(8.60, 8.60)
CNR	1.51	4.78	6.10	17.20
	(1.24, 0.16)	(2.39, 2.39)	(5.51, 0.60)	(8.60, 8.60)
NCR	1.53	5.04	6.52	24.34
	(1.14, 0.39)	(2.52, 2.52)	(3.90, 2.62)	(12.17, 12.17)
NCNR	1.57	5.04	5.91	18.04
	(1.27, 0.30)	(2.52, 2.52)	(5.17, 0.74)	(9.02, 9.02)

A further interesting point is revealed by Table 2. It regards the gains from cooperation when the governments cannot precommit themselves and are thus constrained to pursue time consistent policies. Then cooperation can actually *increase* the total welfare loss of the two countries and thus be counterproductive. Comparing CNR with NCNR we can see this is true for a price level ($p(0) = 1$) but not the output displacement ($y(0) = -1$). This result confirms similar findings by Rogoff (1985) and Miller and Salmon (1985). It should be noted that for symmetrical displacements $y(0) = y^*(0) = -1$ and $p(0) = p^*(0) = 1$ the optimal policy is always time consistent since symmetry implies no exchange rate movement is possible. Policies CR and CNR then coincide since the exchange rate is the only forward looking variable that can give rise to time inconsistency, and these cooperative policies must always be superior to any non-cooperative equilibrium.

The conclusion that must be drawn from Table 2 is that in a deterministic setting the cooperative solution CR is possible on the basis of equal weights $\alpha = 0.5$ only for symmetrical displacements. For asymmetrical displacements α must be changed in favour of the country not facing any initial displacement. The results are displayed in Figs 2 and 3. The shaded regions

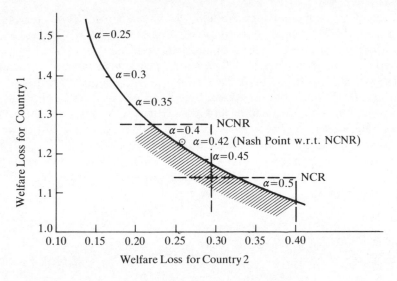

FIG. 2. Welfare losses under CR for $0.25 \leq \alpha \leq 0.5$. Initial displacement $y(0) = -1$.

are those pairs of welfare losses for the two countries which are Pareto-superior to the two non-cooperative equilibria NCNR and NCR. Thus for an initial displacement $y(0) = -1$ (Fig. 2) choices of α between about 0.38 to 0.45 give a CR equilibrium Pareto-superior to NCNR. The ringed point, $\alpha = 0.42$, is the Nash bargaining point with respect to a threat point NCNR.

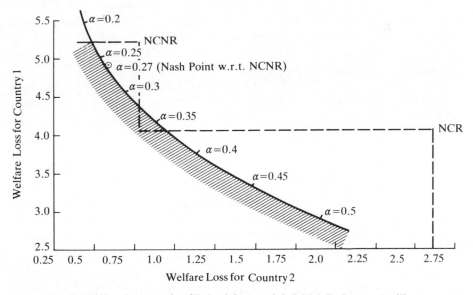

FIG. 3. Welfare losses under CR for $0.2 \leq \alpha \leq 0.5$. Initial displacement $p(0) = 1$.

However α must lie between about 0.47 to 0.58 for CR to be Pareto-superior to the alternative non-cooperative outcome NCR. The important point to note of course is that these intervals do not intersect, i.e. *there is no choice of α that will sustain CR against both non-cooperative equilibria NCNR and NCR*. From Fig. 3 we see that is also true for an initial price displacement $p(0) = 1$. We conclude that if NCNR and NCR are regarded as possible non-cooperative alternatives or threats following a breakdown in the cooperative agreement, CR, there is no choice of α that will make CR sustainable in a deterministic context.

This leaves the possibility that CR is sustainable in a *stochastic* setting. We start by assuming a particular covariance matrix Σ_{11} where $\text{cov}(dv^1) = \Sigma_{11} \, dt$ and $dv^T = (dv_1 dv_1^* dv_2 dv_2^*)$. We put

$$
\Sigma_{11} = \begin{bmatrix} 1 & & & 0 \\ & 1 & & \\ & & 1 & \\ 0 & & & 1 \end{bmatrix} \tag{7.1}
$$

so that shocks are uncorrelated and have the same unit variances.[11] In a stochastic world these disturbances are in addition to the initial displacement of the system considered for the deterministic case. Rather than choose an arbitrary relationship between initial displacements and the disturbance covariance matrix we scale the former with respect to the latter as follows.

Imagine the system in stochastic equilibrium under policy CR. Given Σ_{11} we can then derive the asymptotic variance matrix, $\tilde{Z}$, of the predetermined variables $z = (y, y^*, p$ and $p^*)$. (This is found by solving a Lyapunov equation analogous to (3.25).) Then for each z_i (i.e. each predetermined variable) in turn, we can calculate a 99% confidence region. We then choose two initial displacements by putting y and p in turn on the extreme boundary of this 99% confidence interval. Thus for Σ_{11} given by (7.1) this gives (Table 3) $z(0) = 3.01$ and $p(0) = 4.86$ for displacements 1 and 2 respectively. The other components of the initial displacements are calculated from the standard regression formula

$$
E(z_j(0)/z_i(0)) = \tilde{Z}_{ij}\tilde{Z}_{ii}^{-1}z_i(0) \tag{7.2}
$$

The consequence of this procedure is that initial displacements are chosen to be at the extreme 1% tail of the distribution of y, y^*, p, and p^* that would be observed in stochastic equilibrium under CR. In this sense the initial displacement is chosen to be large in relation to stochastic disturbances. This is done because large initial displacements relative to stochastic

---

[11] Symmetry is then maintained between countries in that they both experience uncorrelated disturbance of equal variances. But this is a minimal amount of symmetry which still leaves the possibility of considerable asymmetry in the displacements at any time.

TABLE 3

The Gains from Cooperation ($\alpha = 0.5$). *Stochastic Case.*

	Displacement 1	Displacement 2
	$y(0)$ 3.01	$y(0)$ −1.62
	$y^*(0) =$ 1.59	$y^*(0) =$ −1.41
	$p(0)$ −2.65	$p(0)$ 4.86
	$p^*(0)$ −2.89	$p^*(0)$ 3.98
Equilibria		
CR	322	528
	(165, 157)	(269, 259)
CNR	376	584
	(193, 183)	(309, 275)
NCNR	372	588
	(191, 181)	(310, 278)
NCR	420	719
	(214, 206)	(365, 354)

noise reduce the sustainability of CR with respect to both the two governments and the governments and the private sector. Thus if anything we are biasing our results *against* the possibility of sustaining CR.

The results for the initial welfare losses are shown for these two extreme initial displacements in Table 3. In contrast to the deterministic case for $\alpha = 0.5$ we now see that CR is easily Pareto-superior to both non-cooperative outcomes NCNR and NCR for both displacements. However all the results of this sub-section are for initial welfare losses at the time at which policies are calculated and announced. To establish the sustainability of CR we need to show that CR is Pareto-superior to NCNR and NCR at any point in time. The credibility of CR also requires that CR is Pareto-superior to CNR at all times. These matters are examined in the final sub-section.

(iii) *The supergame strategy*

We now turn to the supergame strategy discussed in Section 2. We wish to establish whether the cooperative, initially optimal solution CR can be sustained at all time $t \geqslant 0$. The first consideration is whether there exists an incentive for the two countries to renege jointly on the private sector. Because time inconsistency, CR is only initially optimal (at $t = 0$) and for $t > 0$ it is sub-optimal, the optimal policy then being (5.7) with $p_2(t)$ reset to zero. Re-optimising in this way, however, is not possible as time inconsistent policy announcements would then lack credibility with the private sector. But a switch to the *time consistent* policy is always a possible policy option because this is precisely the policy the private sector expects when the government loses its reputation for precommitment. (See Currie and Levine (1985) for a full discussion of this point.)

TABLE 4

Expected Trajectories and Welfare Loss for CR. Initial Displacement: $y(0) = -1$.

Time t (years)	$y(t)$	$y^*(t)$	$p(t)$	$p^*(t)$	$c(t)$	$r(t)$	$s(t)$	$r^*(t)$	$s^*(t)$	Welfare loss	
										Before reneging	After reneging
0	-1.00	0.00	0.00	0.00	0.277	-0.148	-0.591	-0.091	-0.366	1.48 (1.12, 0.35)	1.48 (1.12, 0.35)
1	-0.513	-0.113	-0.052	-0.068	0.174	-0.152	-0.404	-0.029	-0.319	0.77 (0.47, 0.30)	0.77 (0.48, 0.29)
2	-0.263	-0.109	-0.079	-0.115	0.066	-0.113	-0.294	-0.026	-0.262	0.52 (0.27, 0.25)	0.52 (0.28, 0.24)
3	-0.130	-0.068	-0.099	-0.136	0.005	-0.073	-0.224	-0.035	-0.210	0.41 (0.20, 0.21)	0.41 (0.20, 0.21)
4	-0.056	-0.027	-0.115	-0.141	-0.016	-0.047	-0.176	-0.039	-0.169	0.35 (0.17, 0.18)	0.35 (0.17, 0.18)
5	-0.012	0.005	-0.124	-0.138	-0.016	-0.032	-0.142	-0.037	-0.137	0.30 (0.15, 0.15)	0.30 (0.15, 0.15)

TABLE 5

Expected Trajectories and Welfare Loss for CR. Initial Displacement $p(0) = 1$

Time t (years)	$y(t)$	$y^*(t)$	$p(t)$	$p^*(t)$	$c(t)$	$r(t)$	$s(t)$	$r^*(t)$	$s^*(t)$	Welfare loss	
										Before reneging	After reneging
0	0.00	0.00	1.00	0.00	-1.095	0.091	0.366	0.148	0.591	4.77 (2.94, 1.83)	4.77 (2.94, 1.83)
1	-0.191	0.014	0.734	0.251	-0.830	0.317	0.379	-0.104	0.473	3.94 (2.18, 1.76)	3.90 (2.25, 1.65)
2	-0.254	-0.031	0.546	0.405	-0.410	0.276	0.317	-0.098	0.396	3.34 (1.71, 1.63)	3.31 (1.77, 1.54)
3	-0.250	-0.095	0.445	0.458	-0.119	0.179	0.279	-0.028	0.325	2.86 (1.41, 1.44)	2.85 (1.45, 1.40)
4	-0.228	-0.148	0.399	0.449	0.015	0.101	0.250	0.029	0.270	2.44 (1.20, 1.24)	2.44 (1.21, 1.23)
5	-0.207	-0.178	0.376	0.415	0.048	0.058	0.223	0.055	0.228	2.08 (1.03, 1.05)	2.08 (1.03, 1.05)

TABLE 6
Expected Trajectories and Welfare Loss for CNR. Initial Displacement: $y(0) = 1$.

Time t (years)	$y(t)$	$y^*(t)$	$p(t)$	$p^*(t)$	$c(t)$	$r(t)$	$s(t)$	$r^*(t)$	$s^*(t)$	Welfare loss
0	−1.00	0.00	0.00	0.00	0.101	−0.151	−0.605	−0.088	−0.351	1.51 (1.25, 0.26)
1	−0.528	−0.099	−0.092	−0.028	0.174	−0.152	−0.404	−0.029	−0.319	0.80 (0.59, 0.21)
2	−0.276	−0.095	−0.139	−0.055	0.036	−0.077	−0.036	−0.062	−0.250	0.54 (0.37, 0.17)
3	−0.136	−0.063	−0.161	−0.075	0.026	−0.058	−0.232	−0.051	−0.202	0.42 (0.28, 0.14)
4	−0.054	−0.028	−0.169	−0.087	0.020	−0.045	−0.181	−0.041	−0.164	0.36 (0.24, 0.12)
5	−0.007	−0.000	−0.169	−0.094	0.017	−0.036	−0.145	−0.033	−0.133	0.31 (0.20, 0.11)

The incentive for the countries jointly to renege on the private sector can then be assessed by comparing the cooperative optimal policy CR with the cooperative time consistent policy CNR. This is done in Tables 12 and 13 for the deterministic and stochastic cases respectively. For the deterministic case with $\alpha = 0.5$ we can see that for an initial price displacement $p(0) = 1$ the welfare loss under CNR, although considerably greater than under CR at $t = 0$, becomes less at times $t = 2$ and 3 years. It is then optimal for jointly optimising countries to renege to CNR at any time between 2 and 3 years. Whether the countries would agree to do this is another matter because in each case the benefits from reneging in this way accrue entirely to the second country and the first country loses out. The most likely outcome of

TABLE 7
Expected Trajectories and Welfare Loss for CNR. Initial Displacement: $p(0) = 1$.

Time t (years)	$y(t)$	$y^*(t)$	$p(t)$	$p^*(t)$	$c(t)$	$r(t)$	$s(t)$	$r^*(t)$	$s^*(t)$	Welfare loss
0	−0.00	0.00	1.00	0.00	−0.213	0.145	0.582	0.113	0.454	6.10 (5.51, 0.60)
1	−0.117	−0.059	0.941	0.045	−0.185	0.119	0.476	0.094	0.376	5.20 (4.66, 0.53)
2	−0.181	−0.104	0.874	0.076	−0.163	0.099	0.398	0.079	0.315	4.41 (3.93, 0.48)
3	−0.213	−0.133	−0.806	−0.096	−0.144	0.084	0.337	0.067	0.267	3.73 (3.29, 0.44)
4	−0.226	−0.150	0.740	0.109	−0.127	0.073	0.290	0.057	0.229	3.14 (2.74, 0.40)
5	−0.227	−0.158	0.676	0.115	−0.113	0.063	0.253	0.050	0.198	2.63 (2.27, 0.36)

TABLE 8

Expected Trajectories and Welfare Loss for NCR. Initial Displacement: $y(0) = 1$.

Time t (years)	$y(t)$	$y^*(t)$	$p(t)$	$p^*(t)$	$c(t)$	$r(t)$	$s(t)$	$r^*(t)$	$s^*(t)$	Welfare loss Before reneging	After reneging
0	-1.00	0.00	0.00	0.00	0.242	-0.098	-0.392	-0.030	-0.120	1.53 (1.14, 0.39)	1.53 (1.14, 0.39)
1	-0.544	-0.141	-0.062	-0.064	0.157	-0.052	-0.208	-0.026	-0.106	0.96 (0.56, 0.40)	1.03 (0.61, 0.42)
2	-0.295	-0.140	-0.094	-0.115	0.076	-0.023	-0.092	-0.014	-0.055	0.77 (0.39, 0.38)	0.82 (0.43, 0.39)
3	-0.147	-0.088	-0.115	-0.144	0.022	-0.003	-0.011	0.001	0.003	0.72 (0.35, 0.37)	0.68 (0.34, 0.34)
4	-0.050	-0.025	-0.127	-0.154	-0.005	0.013	0.050	0.014	0.057	0.70 (0.34, 0.36)	0.70 (0.28, 0.29)
5	0.020	0.032	-0.132	-0.151	-0.013	0.024	0.097	0.025	0.101	0.69 (0.34, 0.35)	0.44 (0.22, 0.22)

TABLE 9

Expected Trajectories and Welfare Loss for NCR. Initial Displacement: $p(0) = 1$.

Time t (years)	$y(t)$	$y^*(t)$	$p(t)$	$p^*(t)$	$c(t)$	$r(t)$	$s(t)$	$r^*(t)$	$s^*(t)$	Welfare loss Before reneging	After reneging
0	0.00	0.00	1.00	0.00	-0.911	0.011	0.044	0.029	0.116	6.52 (3.90, 2.62)	6.52 (3.90, 2.62)
1	-0.119	0.050	0.776	0.219	-0.754	0.019	-0.077	0.010	0.042	6.02 (3.28, 2.74)	5.96 (2.80, 2.46)
2	-0.192	-0.006	0.600	0.376	-0.460	-0.042	-0.169	-0.016	-0.065	5.70 (2.93, 2.77)	5.26 (2.80, 2.46)
4	-0.281	-0.186	0.417	0.462	-0.050	-0.077	-0.309	-0.068	-0.274	5.13 (2.53, 2.60)	5.26 (1.78, 1.79)
6	-0.281	-0.344	0.328	0.374	0.0424	-0.102	-0.407	-0.102	-0.406	4.35 (2.15, 2.20)	1.93 (0.95, 0.98)
8	-0.410	-0.417	0.229	0.240	0.023	-0.112	-0.447	-0.113	-0.447	3.38 (1.68, 1.70)	0.87 (0.43, 0.44)
10	-0.412	-0.416	0.110	0.108	0.003	-0.105	-0.422	-0.106	-0.420	2.42 (1.21, 1.21)	0.54 (0.27, 0.27)

TABLE 10

Expected Trajectories and Welfare Loss for NCNR. Initial Displacement: $y(0) = -1$.

Time t (years)	$y(t)$	$y^*(t)$	$p(t)$	$p^*(t)$	$c(t)$	$r(t)$	$s(t)$	$r^*(t)$	$s^*(t)$	Welfare loss
0	−1.00	0.00	0.00	0.00	0.123	−0.127	−0.507	−0.048	−0.190	1.56 (1.27, 0.29)
1	−0.544	−0.123	−0.089	−0.034	0.067	−0.063	−0.252	−0.045	−0.181	0.92 (0.43, 0.25)
2	−0.276	−0.095	−0.139	−0.055	0.036	−0.077	−0.306	−0.062	−0.250	0.54 (0.37, 017)
3	−0.165	−0.099	−0.163	−0.093	0.028	−0.048	−0.193	−0.039	−0.156	0.58 (0.35, 0.21)
4	−0.085	−0.063	−0.175	−0.112	0.021	−0.039	−0.155	−0.033	−0.133	0.51 (0.30, 0.21)
5	−0.035	−0.031	−0.179	−0.123	0.017	−0.032	−0.128	−0.028	−0.113	0.49 (0.28, 0.20)

this incentive to switch to a time consistent policy would be the non-cooperative time consistent equilibrium NCNR.

The second condition for the sustainability of CR is that there is no incentive for either country to switch to a non-cooperative policy. As we have seen in the previous section with equal weights attached to the joint welfare junction ($\alpha = 0.5$) CR is not Pareto-superior to either NCNR or NCR unless the shocks are symmetrical. Furthermore CR and NCR are so far apart that there is no value of α that makes CR Pareto-superior to both NCNR and NCR. Cooperation cannot even get off the ground in a deterministic world.

In a stochastic world we have seen that there are considerable initial gains from cooperation for both countries. In Table 13 we consider the passage of

TABLE 11

Expected Trajectories and Welfare Loss of NCNR. Initial Displacement: $p(0) = 1$.

Time t (years)	$y(t)$	$y^*(t)$	$p(t)$	$p^*(t)$	$c(t)$	$r(t)$	$s(t)$	$r^*(t)$	$s^*(t)$	Welfare loss
0	−0.00	0.00	1.00	0.00	−0.296	0.111	0.444	0.050	0.199	5.91 (5.17, 0.74)
1	−0.100	−0.013	0.925	0.066	−0.243	0.093	0.371	0.047	0.188	5.14 (4.39, 0.75)
2	−0.149	−0.038	0.850	0.118	−0.203	0.080	0.318	0.044	0.174	4.49 (3.73, 0.76)
3	−0.172	−0.062	−0.779	0.170	−0.170	0.070	0.278	0.040	0.161	3.93 (3.17, 0.76)
4	−0.181	−0.081	0.714	0.185	−0.144	0.062	0.247	0.037	0.149	3.45 (2.70, 0.75)
5	−0.182	−0.094	0.654	0.205	−0.121	0.055	0.055	0.221	0.139	3.03 (2.30, 0.73)

TABLE 12

Welfare Loss Along Trajectory of CR: Deterministic Case: $\alpha = 0.5$.

Time (years)	CR Before reneging	CR After reneging	Displacement $y(0) = -1$ After switch to CNR	After switch to NCNR	After switch to NCR	CR Before reneging	CR After reneging	Displacement $p(0) = 1$ After switch to CNR
0	1.48	1.48	1.51	1.57	1.53	4.77	4.77	6.10
	(1.12, 0.35)	(1.12, 0.35)	(1.25, 0.26)	(1.27, 0.30)	(1.14, 0.39)	(2.94, 1.83)	(2.94, 1.83)	(5.51, 0.60)
1	0.77	0.77	0.78	0.82	0.83	3.93	3.89	4.16
	(0.47, 0.30)	(0.48, 0.29)	(0.26, 0.51)	(0.53, 0.29)	(0.53, 0.35)	(2.18, 1.76)	(2.25, 1.64)	(3.17, 0.99)
2	0.52	0.52	0.52	0.56	0.65	3.34	3.31	3.32
	(0.27, 0.25)	(0.27, 0.24)	(0.25, 0.27)	(0.20, 0.23)	(0.27, 0.28)	(1.71, 1.63)	(1.77, 1.54)	(1.95, 1.37)
3	0.41	0.41	0.41	0.42	0.55	0.41	0.41	0.41
	(0.20, 0.21)	(0.20, 0.21)	(0.22, 0.19)	(0.22, 0.23)	(0.27, 0.28)	(1.41, 1.41)	(1.45, 1.40)	(1.39, 1.46)
4	0.35	0.35	0.35	0.37	0.48	2.44	2.44	2.45
	(0.17, 0.18)	(0.17, 0.18)	(0.19, 0.16)	(0.17, 0.20)	(0.24, 0.24)	(1.20, 1.24)	(1.21, 1.23)	(1.13, 1.32)
5	0.30	0.30	0.30	0.32	0.43	2.08	2.08	2.08
	(0.15, 0.15)	(0.15, 0.15)	(0.16, 0.14)	(0.15, 0.17)	(0.21, 0.22)	(1.03, 1.24)	(1.03, 1.05)	(0.97, 1.11)

After switch to NCNR	Switch to NCR	Displacement $y(0) = y^*(0) = -1$ CR = CNR	After switch to NCNR	After switch to NCR	Displacement $p(0) = p^*(0) = 1$ CR = CNR	After switch to NCNR	After switch to NCR
5.91	6.52	4.78	5.04	5.04	17.20	18.04	24.34
(5.17, 0.74)	(3.90, 2.62)	(2.39, 2.39)	(2.52, 2.52)	(2.52, 2.52)	(8.60, 8.60)	(9.02, 9.02)	(12.17, 12.17)
4.25	5.49	2.91	3.08	3.36	15.06	15.72	21.42
(3.11, 1.14)	(3.09, 2.40)	(1.45, 1.45)	(1.54, 1.54)	(1.68, 1.68)	(7.53, 7.53)	(7.86, 7.86)	(10.71, 10.71)
3.45	4.70	2.05	2.18	2.60	13.13	13.66	18.70
(1.46, 1.99)	(2.48, 2.22)	(1.03, 1.03)	(1.09, 1.09)	(1.30, 1.30)	(6.57, 6.57)	(6.83, 6.83)	(9.35, 9.35)
0.42	0.55	1.63	1.72	2.20	11.36	11.78	16.16
(1.45, 1.50)	(2.05, 2.00)	(0.81, 0.81)	(0.86, 0.86)	(1.10, 1.10)	(5.68, 5.68)	(5.89, 5.89)	(8.08, 8.08)
2.53	3.46	1.38	1.46	1.92	9.75	10.10	13.86
(1.35, 1.18)	(1.72, 1.74)	(0.69, 0.69)	(0.73, 0.73)	(0.96, 0.96)	(4.88, 4.88)	(5.05, 5.05)	(6.93, 6.93)
2.16	2.95	1.20	1.26	1.70	8.32	8.60	11.80
(1.02, 1.14)	(1.46, 1.49)	(0.60, 0.60)	(0.63, 0.63)	(0.85, 0.85)	(4.16, 4.16)	(4.30, 4.30)	(5.90, 5.90)

time along the average (expected) trajectory of CR. Now we see that CR is Pareto-superior by a large margin to both CNR and the two non-cooperative outcomes NCNR and NCR at all times. Thus the existence of stochastic disturbances renders the best form of cooperative behaviour CR sustainable. This proves to be true, for our model and parameter values, for both a possible joint reneging of the governments on the private sector and a reneging of one country on the other.

TABLE 13

Welfare Loss Along Trajectory of CR. Stochastic Case: $\alpha = 0.5$.

Time (Years)	Displacement 1 (see Table 3)					Displacement 2 (see Table 3)				
	CR		After switch to CNR	After switch to NCNR	After switch to NCR	CR		After switch to CNR	After switch to NCNR	After switch to NCR
	Before reneging	After reneging				Before reneging	After reneging			
0	322 (165, 157)	322 (165, 157)	376 (193, 183)	372 (191, 181)	420 (214, 206)	528 (269, 259)	528 (269, 259)	584 (309, 275)	588 (310, 278)	719 (365, 354)
1	305 (154, 151)	305 (154, 151)	359 (182, 178)	354 (179, 175)	398 (201, 197)	490 (247, 243)	490 (247, 242)	545 (280, 264)	548 (281, 267)	663 (334, 329)
2	293 (147, 146)	293 (147, 146)	348 (175, 173)	342 (172, 170)	382 (192, 190)	455	455	510 (257, 253)	512 (258, 254)	614 (308, 306)
3	284 (142, 142)	284 (142, 142)	339 (170, 169)	333 (167, 166)	370 (185, 185)	424 (212, 212)	424 (212, 212)	479 (239, 240)	478 (239, 239)	570 (285, 285)
4	277 (136, 136)	277 (136, 136)	332 (163, 163)	327 (164, 163)	360 (180, 180)	397 (199, 199)	397 (199, 199)	452 (225, 227)	451 (225, 226)	532 (266, 266)
5	272 (136, 136)	272 (136, 136)	327 (163, 163)	322 (161, 161)	354 (177, 177)	374 (187, 187)	374 (187, 187)	429 (214, 215)	427 (213, 214)	498 (249, 249)

8. Conclusions

In this paper, we have been concerned to examine whether international cooperation between governments in macroeconomic policy making is sustainable in a two country world. We use for this purpose a fairly standard illustrative model, which incorporates the key international spillover effects, though neglecting asset accumulation. Future work will be directed towards extending this analysis to empirically based models.

The difficulty with sustaining cooperative policies is that there may emerge, with the passage of time, a position at which it pays one or other of the governments to renege on the cooperative agreement. (In calculating whether this is so, account must be taken of the consequences of breaking associated commitments with the private sector.) If this is so, cooperative agreements will lack credibility, and will therefore not be entered into by rational governments.

In the analysis, questions of sustainability of cooperative policy intersect with questions of the credibility and reputation of government vis-a-vis the private sector. Without government reputation vis-a-vis the private sector, it turns out the cooperation between governments may not pay, and when it does the benefits are minimal (see Table 3). These results confirm in the context of our model the results of Rogoff (1985). They arise because non-reputational policies may be thought of as non-cooperation between the government and private sector, and with non-cooperation between certain players in the policy game cooperation between governments may not be advantageous.

Our results also suggest a converse: that without cooperation between governments, government reputations may not be advantageous. Thus non-cooperative reputational policy delivers a much worse policy pay-off than do the non-reputational policies, whether cooperative or not, and is actually unstable if the discount rate of policy makers is too high. (All are necessarily inferior to the cooperative reputational policy).

These results suggest that, without government reputation vis-a-vis the private sector, cooperation will not be advantageous and therefore, *a fortiori*, not sustainable. It remains therefore to ask whether, with reputations, cooperation is sustainable. Our results suggest that cooperation with reputation is difficult to sustain in a deterministic world, where the policy problem is one of setting policy so as to deal with an undesirable initial position of the system (e.g. reducing high inflation, recovering from recession). Only if the initial displacement is nearly symmetrical between the two countries will cooperation be sustainable. By contrast, cooperation with reputation is more easily sustained in a stochastic world, where repeated disturbances (e.g. inflationary shocks, demand fluctuations) continually move the system away from its desired position. In this case, when considering reneging on cooperative agreements, governments will need to weigh the advantages of reneging with respect to past shocks against the costs, in terms of poorer policy performance, of dealing with future shocks in a noncooperative manner. Provided that discount rate of policy makers is not too high, cooperation with reputation will prove advantageous and therefore sustainable. These benefits are measured relative to the non-reputational alternatives. Measured relative to the alternative of non-cooperation with reputation, the gains are still larger.

These results suggest an important message. Rogoff's finding is that a move towards international cooperation is not necessarily advantageous in a world where governments lack credibility with their private sectors. Our results suggest that government credibility with their private sectors may be most disadvantageous if unaccompanied by cooperation between governments. Further work will establish whether this result carries over to empirically based models of the international economy.

London Business School.
Queen Mary College, University of London
and CEPR

REFERENCES

BACKUS, DAVID and DRIFFILL, JOHN (1985). "Rational Expectations and Policy Credibility Following a Change in Regime"; *Review of Economic Studies,* Vol. 52, pp. 211–221.

BARRO, ROBERT J. and GORDON, DAVID B. (1983). "Rules, Discretion and Reputation in a Model of Monetary Policy"; *Journal of Monetary Economics,* pp. 101–121.

BASAR, TAMER (1985). "A Tutorial on Dynamic Games"; presented to the SEDC Conference, London, July.

BAR-SHALOM, Y. and EDISON, T. (1976). "Caution, Probing and the Value of Information in the Control of Uncertain Systems," *Annals of Economic and Social Measurement,* Vol. 5, No. 3, pp. 323–337.

BASAR, TAMER, TURNOVSKY, STEPHEN J. and J'OREY, VASCO (1985). "Optimal Strategic Monetary Policies in Dynamic Interdependent Economies"; presented to the SEDC Conference, London, July.

BRESNAHAN, T. F. (1981). "Duopoly Models with Consistent Conjectures"; *American Economic Review,* 71, pp. 934–945.

BUITER, WILLEM H. (1983). "Optimal and Time-Consistent Policies in Continuous Time Rational Expectations Models"; NBER Technical Working Paper No. 29.

CALVO, GUILLERMO A. (1978). "On the Time Consistency of Optimal Policy in a Monetary Economy"; *Econometrica,* Vol. 46, pp. 1411–1428.

COHEN, DANIEL and MICHEL, PHILLIPPE (1984). "Toward a Theory of Optimal Pre-Commitment: an Analysis of the Time-Consistent Equilibria"; paper presented to the CEPR Manchester Conference on the European Monetary System: Policy Coordination and Exchange Rate Systems, September.

CURRIE, DAVID A. and LEVINE, PAUL (1985a). "Macroeconomic Policy Design in an Interdependent World"; in Willem H. Buiter and Richard C. Marston (eds.), *International Economic Policy Coordination,* CUP, Cambridge.

CURRIE, DAVID A. and LEVINE, PAUL (1985b). "Simple Macropolicy Rules for the Open Economy"; *Economic Journal,* Vol. 95 (Supp.), pp. 60–70.

CURRIE, DAVID A. and LEVINE, PAUL (1985c). "Credibility and Time Inconsistency in a Stochastic World"; QMC PRISM Discussion Paper No. 36.

EHTAMO, HARRI and HÄMÄLÄINEN, RAIMO P. (1985). "On Affine Incentives for Dynamic Decision Problems", Helsinki University of Technology Systems Analysis Laboratory, Research report no. A14, presented to the SEDC Conference, London, July.

FRIEDMAN, JAMES W. (1977). *Oligopoly and the Theory of Games,* Amsterdam, North-Holland.

HUGHES-HALLET, ANDREW J. (1985). "How Much Could the International Coordination of Economic Policies Achieve? An Example from US-EEC Policy Making"; CEPR Discussion paper No. 77.

KYDLAND, FINN E. and PRESCOTT, EDWARD C. (1977). "Rules rather than Discretion: the Inconsistency of Optimal Plans"; *Journal of Political Economy,* Vol. 85, pp. 473–491. 473–491.

LEVINE, PAUL and CURRIE, DAVID A. (1985). "Optimal Feedback Rules in an Open Economy Macromodel with Rational Expectations"; *European Economic Review,* Vol. 27, pp. 141–163.

LEVINE, PAUL and CURRIE, DAVID A. (1987). "The Design of Feedback Rules in Linear Stochastic Rational Expectations Models"; *Journal of Economic Dynamics and Control,* (forthcoming).

MILLER. MARCUS H. and SALMON, MARK H. (1985). "Dynamic Games and the Time Inconsistency of Optimal Policy in Open Economies"; *Economic Journal,* Vol. 85 (Supp.) pp. 124–137.

OUDIZ, GILLES and SACHS, JEFFREY (1985). "International Policy Coordination in Dynamic Macroeconomic Models"; in Willem H. Buiter and Richard C. Marston (eds.) *The International Coordination of Economic Policy,* Cambridge University Press.

ROGOFF, K. (1985). "Can International Monetary Policy Cooperation be Counterproductive?"; *Journal of International Economics,* 18, pp. 199–217.

TAYLOR, JOHN (1980). "Aggregate Dynamics and Staggered Contracts"; *Journal of Political Economy,* Vol. 88, February, pp. 1–23.

TAYLOR, JOHN (1985). "International Co-ordination in the Design of Macroeconomic Policy Rules"; *European Economic Review,* Vol. 28, pp. 53–81.

Oxford Economic Papers 39 (1987), 75–89

WHY DO BANKS NEED A CENTRAL BANK?*

By C. A. E. GOODHART

1. Introduction

IN my earlier monograph, *The Evolution of Central Banks,* (1985), especially Chapter 3, pages 28–35, I sought to examine the key features that distinguished banks from other financial intermediaries, and, in particular, necessitated the support of a Central Bank. This paper continues and extends that work.

Fama, in his paper on 'Banking in the Theory of Finance', *Journal of Monetary Economics,* (1980), describes banks as having two functions, the first being to provide transactions and accounting services, the second being portfolio management. Yet transactions services are carried out by other institutions, e.g. giro, Post Office, non-bank credit card companies, etc., without much need for special supervision, etc, by a Central Bank.[1] More important, I shall argue that it would be perfectly possible, generally safer, and a likely development, for transactions services to be provided by an altogether different set of financial intermediaries, i.e. intermediaries providing mutual collective investment in (primarily) marketable securities. If this was to occur, would it make such mutual investment intermediaries, e.g. unit trusts, open-end investment trusts, into banks? Would such intermediaries then become subject to the same risks as banks, and need to be subject to the same kind of supervision/regulation?

I shall argue, in Section 2, that there is no necessary reason why banks alone among financial intermediaries should provide transactions services, and in their role as portfolio managers, banks have much in common with other intermediaries acting in this capacity (though, as I shall argue later, in Section 3, certain crucial distinctions remain between the characteristic form of portfolios held by banks as compared with those held by non-bank financial intermediaries). Nevertheless, it is this *joint* role that is held to give a special character to banking, and to require special treatment for banks through the establishment of a Central Bank, e.g. to provide Lender of Last Resort (LOLR) and other support services for banks in difficulties, support which goes beyond the assistance envisaged for other financial intermediaries that get into trouble.

* This paper was originally prepared for the Manhattan Institute Conference in New York, March 1986, and was also presented at seminars at Nottingham University and Brasenose College, Oxford. I have benefitted greatly from comments made on those occasions, notably by Max Hall, Mervyn Lewis, Bennett McCallum and Lawrence White, and subsequently by Gavin Bingham and my referees, but they should not be blamed for my remaining idiosyncracies.

[1] Except insofar as the Central Bank has a direct concern for the smooth and trouble-free operation of the payments' system itself, e.g. the working of the clearing house(s) and the settlement system(s), as contrasted with the institutions providing the transactions services.

Thus Tobin (1985), states on page 20, that

"The basic dilemma is this: Our monetary and banking institutions have evolved
in a way that entangles competition among financial intermediary firms with the
provision of transactions media".

But what actually are the problems caused by this entanglement? The
problem is often seen, and so appears to Tobin, as arising from the
propensity of banks, acting as competing financial intermediaries, to run
risks of default, which then, through a process aggravated by contagion,
puts the monetary system, whose successful functioning is an essential
public good, at risk.

I begin Section 2 by recording that Tobin's suggestion, in accord also with
Friedman's views, is that institutions (banks) seeking to offer deposits
involving payments' services should be required to segregate these in special
funds held against risk-free earmarked safe assets. As historical experience
shows, however, such a restriction would reduce the profitability, and not
just the riskiness, of banking. An alternative method of providing protection against runs, and systemic crises, could, however, be obtained by
basing the payments' on the liabilities of mutual collective investment funds,
the value of whose liabilities varies in line with the value of their marketable
assets. Since the banking system developed first, the banks established a
branch system, clearing houses, etc., which provided them with economies
of scale and familiarity in running the payments' system, but technological
change is eroding, and could even be reversing, banks' advantages in this
respect.

Indeed, non-bank mutual investment funds are already beginning to
provide payments' services and there is no (technical) reason why this
development should not proceed much further. It is often claimed,
however, that people would be unwilling to make payments against asset
balances which fluctuate in value over time. In practice, however, payments
already often incorporate a probabilistic element, in the sense that the payer
may have some uncertainty whether the balance, or overdraft facility,
available will be sufficient for the bank drawn on to honour the cheque. The
additional uncertainty involved could possibly be reduced sufficiently to
make people prepared to use payments' services offered by non-bank
investment funds.

Since these latter financial intermediaries would be protected from
illiquidity by their holding of marketable assets, and from insolvency by the
fact that the value of their liabilities varies in line with their asset values, a
Central Bank should welcome their entry into the provision of payments'
services and need impose no further supervisory/regulatory constraints on
them. This development would, however, raise further questions about the
meaning of money, since the estimated nominal value of balances capable of
being used in payments would vary automatically with the prices of the
assets held by these intermediaries. Indeed, the central intuition of Section

2 is that the monetization of assets is *not* necessarily limited to a restricted set of financial intermediaries, i.e. banks.

So, I demonstrate in Section 2 that the provision of payments' services jointly with portfolio management does *not, per se,* require the involvement of a Central Bank—if, for example, the joint function is undertaken by mutual collective investment funds. Clearly it is not so much the joint function, but rather the particular characteristics of banks' liabilities and asset portfolios that makes them especially vulnerable. Indeed I try to highlight this by enquiring, in Section 3, whether the banking system would still require Central Bank support even if banks were to withdraw altogether from providing payments' services, i.e. funding their asset books only through time deposits and C.D.s.

The reason why the answer to this question is 'Yes' lies in the fundamental raison d'être of banking. Why do borrowers seek loans from banks and depositors place savings with banks rather than transact directly through the market place? In part the answer lies in the costs of obtaining and assessing information on the credit worthiness of (most) borrowers. Banks have a specialized advantage in this function, but, even so, the costs and limitations of such information induce banks to extend (non-marketable) loans on a *fixed nominal value basis*. With their assets largely on such a fixed nominal value basis, it is less risky for banks also to have their deposit liabilities on the same, fixed nominal value, terms: and the same concerns with only having access to limited information about their bank's 'true' position also makes the depositor prefer fixed nominal value bank deposits.

The resulting combination of uncertain 'true' bank asset valuation, and fixed nominal value deposits, leads to the possibility of bank runs: lengthening the maturity of bank deposits slows down the potential *speed* of such runs, but does not prevent them. What is, however, particularly interesting in recent analysis of banking is that it has been realized that much of the economic damage caused by bank crises and failures rebounds on bank *borrowers*. The loss of wealth to depositors, and the dislocation of the payments' system, have already been fully appreciated in the literature. What is new now is the view that the added pressures placed on bank borrowers by such crises, e.g. the removal of access to new loans, the need to obtain facilities elsewhere at an awkward time, and, in some cases, the demand by receivers for the repayment of their outstanding borrowing, can represent an additional deleterious effect.

2. The provision of payments' services by banks and by other financial intermediaries

Tobin, *op. cit.,* (1985, *page* 23) *states*:

"Even if bank managers act with normal perspicuity in the interests of the stockholders, even if all temptations of personal gain are resisted, sheer chance will bring some failures—insolvency because of borrowers' defaults or other capital losses on assets, or inability to meet withdrawals of deposits even though the bank would be solvent if assets' present values could be immediately realized. The probability is multiplied by the essential instability of depositor confidence. News of withdrawals triggers more withdrawals, sauve qui peut, at the same bank, or by contagion at others. For these reasons the banking business has not been left to free market competition but has been significantly regulated".

On page 24 Tobin notes:

"Government deposit insurance in the U.S. protects not only means-of-payment deposits but all other deposits in eligible institutions, including non-checkable savings accounts and time deposits. Similar obligations of mutual funds and other debtors not covered by deposit insurance are not guaranteed. It is not clear why all kinds of liabilities of covered institutions should be insured, except that the assets are so commingled that withdrawals of non-insured deposit liabilities would imperil the insured deposits. That indeed is why the insurance guarantee was *de facto* extended beyond the statutory limit".

Tobin's suggestion is:

"This problem could be avoided by segregating and earmarking assets corresponding to particular classes of liabilities permitting a depositor in effect to purchase a fund which could not be impaired by difficulties elsewhere in the institution's balance sheet. In this way, a bank would become more like a company offering a variety of mutual funds, just as these companies—which are not insured—are becoming more like banks,"

In particular, Tobin, following an earlier suggestion made by Friedman, advocated 100% reserve-backed funds for checkable deposits, as has also Henry Wallich, in his paper, 'A Broad View of Deregulation', and several other US economists. Thus Tobin continues,

"The 100%—reserve deposit proposed, . . . , would be one such [mutual] fund, but there could be others. For example, many households of modest means and little financial sophistication want savings accounts that are safe stores of value in the unit of account. *They can be provided in various maturities without risk by a fund invested in Treasury securities. They can be provided as demand obligations either by letting their redemption value fluctuate with net asset value or by crediting a floating interest rate to a fixed value*", [emphasis added here, not in original].

With such illustrious, and wide, support from economists why has this idea not had more practical success? The concept of a 100% segregated reserve against checkable deposits would, however, reverse the evolution of banking. Initially goldsmiths received deposits of gold coin from customers and acted purely as safety vaults. It was the realization that it would be profitable, and under most circumstances relatively safe, to loan out some proportion of these reserves to prospective borrowers, in addition to the loans made on the basis of their own capital, that transformed such entrepreneurs into bankers. Naturally when such early bankers did run into difficulties, by over-trading, proposals were made to force such commercial bankers back to stricter segregation. Thus the fore-runner of the Swedish Riksbank, founded by John Palmstruch in 1656, was organized on the basis of two supposedly separate departments, the loan department financing loans on the basis of longer-term deposits and capital, and the issue department supplying credit notes on the receipt of gold and specie. But even when Palmstruch's Private bank had been taken over by Parliament,

"A secret instruction, however, authorized the advance by the exchange department to the lending department of the funds at its disposal, though on reasonably moderate terms".[2]

The reason why such segregation and hypothecation of certain safe assets to checkable deposits will not work in the case of commercial banks is that it largely removes the profitability of banking along with its risks. The regulatory constraint on the banks' preferred portfolio allocation, under such circumstances, would be seen—as historical experience indicates—as burdensome: attempts would be made to avoid, or to evade, such constraints, e.g. by the provision of substitute transactions' media at unconstrained intermediaries, which, being free of such constraints, could offer higher returns on such media. Only in the case of non-profit-maximising banks, such as the Bank of England, divided into two Departments on much the same theoretical basis by the 1844 Bank Charter Act, would such segregation be acceptable and not subject to avoidance and evasion. Of course, if the public sector were prepared to subsidize the provision of payments' services either by operating them directly itself, or

"by paying some interest on the 100%—reserves"

held by private sector intermediaries, then it could be done; but, in the light of Congress' recent response to suggestions for paying interest on required reserves in the USA, it seems difficult to envisage the public being prepared to vote tax funds for this purpose.

Anyhow, there is a simpler, and less expensive, alternative which Tobin almost reaches when he comments that the public's savings accounts could be

"provided as demand obligations, . . . , by letting their redemption value fluctuate with net asset value"

We are so used to having payments' services provided against checkable fixed nominal value liabilities, with 100% convertibility of demand deposits, that we have not—mostly—realized that payments' services could be just as easily provided by a mutual collective investment financial intermediary, where the liabilities are units representing a proportional claim on a set of marketable assets. The value of the units fluctuates, of course, with the underlying value of the assets in the portfolio. Because the (close-of-day)

[2] See A. W. Flux (1911), page 17, and also Goodhart (1985), pages 109–116 and 159–162.

market value of the portfolio is known, the value of the unit can be published each morning, and each depositor then knows how much his or her units are worth. Because there will be a period of float, during which underlying asset values will change, and because the attempt by the mutual funds to meet net outflows by net sales of assets could itself influence prices, one would expect a mutual fund to limit payments services and convertibility by requiring some minimum balance in units to be held normally, with a progressive penalty in terms of yield foregone for dropping below this balance, plus some emergency arrangements for occasional overdrafts, say from an associated bank. This concept of required minimum balance has been adopted often enough, by commercial banks, and the public is familiar with it. The cheques would, of course, have to be drawn in terms of the numeraire—otherwise they would not be useful in clearing debts. The value of the drawers' units would change between the date of writing the cheque and of its being presented,[3] and—in a period of falling asset prices—there would be a danger of the drawer being overdrawn at the latter date, while having had funds to spare at the earlier date; but this problem would seem also to be generally soluble by only providing guaranteed payments' services up to a minimum credit balance in units, (plus an emergency overdraft arrangement, perhaps with an associated bank).

I see no insuperable technical problem why payments' services could not be provided by mutual collective investment intermediaries in this manner. They would need to hold some liquid reserves, vault cash to pay depositors' demanding currency, and liquid assets to meet net outflows at times when the fund manager judged that it would be inopportune to realize investments, (n.b. this latter need is *neither* for liquidity *nor* for solvency purposes. Liquidity is always available from the ability to sell marketable assets, and solvency is assured because the value of liabilities falls with the value of assets. Instead, the desire for liquid assets would arise from desire to maximise the net asset value of units under varying market conditions,[4] and thus improve reputation, service fees, and managerial earnings). Nevertheless the need to hold vault cash, at least, might lower the expected return on the intermediaries' assets, but the effect of this on the demand for units should be (more than) counterbalanced by the improved liquidity to the unit holder of his investments, and the associated advantages of being able to use them for transactions purposes.

Be that as it may, the current trend already is for (limited) transactions' services to be provided by investment-managing non-bank financial intermediaries on the basis of depositors' funds, the value of which varies with the market value of the underlying assets. Merrill Lynch cash management service is one example. Certain other unit trusts and mutual funds, such as

---

[3] It would, of course, be just as simple to keep the value of each unit constant, but alter the number of units owned by each depositor as asset values changes. I cannot see why that shift in presentation should affect people's behaviour in any way.

[4] The analysis, of course, stems from Tobin (1958).

money market mutual funds, are also providing (limited) payments' services. Similarly certain building societies and certain mortgage businesses in other countries are considering allowing borrowers to draw additional top-up mortgages up to a stated proportion of the market value of their house.[5]

A common response to this idea is that, whereas it would be perfectly possible, as a technical matter, to provide payments' services against liabilities with a varying market value, the public would not happily accept it, and it would not succeed in practice. It is argued, for example, that there is a large psychological gulf between being absolutely certain that one has the funds to meet a payment, and being 99% certain of that. But is such 100% certainty a general feature of our existing payments' system? Unless one monitors one's bank account, outstanding float, etc., continuously, and knows exactly what overdraft limits, if any, the bank manager may have set, the willingness of the bank to honour certain cheque payments will have a probabilistic element.

Lawrence White, (1984, page 707) put this general case, *against* basing payments' services on liabilities with a varying market value, most persuasively:

> "Demand deposits, being ready debt claims, are potentially superior to mutual fund shares, which are equity claims, in at least one respect. The value of a deposit may be contractually guaranteed to increase over time at a preannounced rate of interest. Its unit-of-account value at a future date is certain so long as the bank continues to honor its obligation to redeem its deposits on demand. No such contractual guarantee may be made with respect to an equity claim. A mutual fund is obligated to pay out after the fact its actual earnings, so that the yield on fund shares cannot be predetermined. In the absence of deposit rate ceiling regulation, the range of anticipated possible returns from holding fund shares need not lie entirely above the deposit interest rate. Risk-diversifying portfolio owners might therefore not divest themselves entirely of demand deposits even given a higher mean yield on mutual funds. It is true that the characteristic pledge of money market mutual funds to maintain a fixed share price, or rather the policy of investing exclusively in short-term highly reputable securities so that the pledge can be kept makes fund shares akin to demand deposits in having near-zero risk of negative nominal yield over any period. The difference between predetermined and postdetermined yields—between debt and equity—nonetheless remains. The historical fact is that deposit banking did not naturally grow up on an equity basis."

Because the provision of payments' services by mutual funds, whose liabilities have a market-varying value, would not only be a somewhat novel concept, but would also worry those unused to any probabilistic element in

---

[5] Building societies, of course, will be entering more actively into the provision of payments' services, once the Building Societies Bill (December 1985), has been passed into law. But payments will normally be on the basis of their nominally fixed-value convertible liabilities. The example above, however, envisages building societies, in certain circumstances, also being prepared to monetize assets with a varying market value.

payments, I would expect its introduction to be gradual, and probably to start with richer customers better able to cope with such probabilistic concerns. Moreover, such a limited introduction could prevent the mutual funds making use of economies of scale in the provision of payments' services. There are, therefore, some observers who believe that this possible development will fail the practical test of success in the free, open market.

On the other hand there seems no technical reason why the trend towards the provision of payments' services against the value of units in a collective investment fund (up to a minimum balance) should not proceed much further, especially now that technological innovations in the provision of such services, e.g. shared automated teller machines (ATMs), electronic fund transfer (EFT) and home-banking, are transforming the production function of payments' services, especially in reducing the economies of scale to a network of manned branch buildings. White's arguments (*ibid*, page 707/8) that the provision of payments' services by non-bank (mutual fund) intermediaries has been more expensive could be reduced in force, or even reversed, by the new technologies in this field.

Moreover, there would seem considerable cause to welcome such a development, not only for the extra competition that this would inject in this area, but also because the characteristics of mutual, collective invest-ment funds should serve to make them naturally *more suitable* purveyors of payments' services than banks. In particular, both the likelihood of a run on an individual bank, and of systemic dangers to the monetary system arising from a contagion of fear, would be greatly reduced if payments' services were provided by mutual collective-investment intermediaries, rather than by banks. For example, the announcement of bad news reducing the market value of such an intermediary's assets, assuming an efficient market, would immediately reduce the value of depositors' units. There would be no risk of insolvency for the intermediary, and no advantage, again assuming an efficient market, for any depositor to withdraw his funds from that intermediary.[6] Again, since the asset portfolios of such intermediaries are publicly reported and their value at any time exactly ascertainable, there would seem little scope for rumour or fear to take hold. Certainly if a particular fund manager did significantly worse (better) than average, depositors would find it difficult to distinguish bad (good) luck from bad (good) management, and would probably switch funds in sizeable amounts to the ex post more successful, but such switching of funds between funds would hardly damage the payments' system, rather the reverse.

[6] Mutual funds seeking to attract depositors, in part on the grounds of an offer to provide payments' services, face a trade-off in this respect. Because of depositors' familiarity with fixed-nominal-value convertible deposits as a basis for the payments' system, some mutual funds, to attract such depositors, have given some commitments to hold the value of their liabilities (normally) at such a fixed nominal value. But this opens them up to runs as soon as the publicly observable value of their assets falls towards, or below, the (temporarily) fixed value of their liabilities. This happened with the UK Provident Institute in April 1986. White (1984, page 707) and Lewis, in personal discussion, have reported such behaviour among mutual funds in the US and Australia respectively.

There would still be a possibility of a sharp general fall in market values leading depositors to shift en masse out of market valued unit holdings into the fixed nominal value numeraire, thereby forcing the collective investment funds to have to sell further assets, and thereby deepening the asset price depression. Unlike the case of a run on the banks, which raises the subjective probability of failure elsewhere, and thus reduces the expected return on holding deposits, at least the fall in market values on the assets in the portfolio of the mutual fund should tend to increase the expected running yield on such units, and thus act as an offset to the inducement to hold cash. Moreover, it would still be possible for the authorities, perhaps the Central Bank, to undertake open market operations to offset the shift of unit holders into cash, possibly by buying the assets, say equities, that the funds were selling. There are precedents for such actions: at one time the Japanese intervened to support Stock Exchange values.

Thus a monetary system in which transactions' services were provided to unit holders of collective investment mutual funds would seem inherently safer and more stable than the present system, in which such services are provided to (a sub-set of) bank depositors. Indeed, the nature of bank portfolios, largely filled with nonmarketable assets of uncertain true value held on the basis of nominally fixed value liabilities, would seem remarkably unsuited to form the basis of our payments' systems. Why did it develop in this way? The answer is, I think, to be found in the accidents of historical evolution. Broad, well-functioning, efficient asset markets are a reasonably recent phenomenon. Because of people's need both to borrow and to find a secure home for savings, banks developed well before mutual collective investment funds. The historical form of bank development led them inevitably into the payments' business. Thereafter, the economies of scale involved in the existing structure of the payments' system, the clearing houses, branch networks and the intangibles of public familiarity and legal and institutional framework, left the banks largely—indeed in some Anglo Saxon countries absolutely—unrivalled in the provision of payments' services.

Owing to the various innovations noted earlier, such bank monopoly of the payments' system may now be coming to an end. The authorities should welcome the opportunity to encourage the development of a safer payments' system. They should certainly not put obstacles in the way of properly-run collective investment funds offering payments' services. Indeed there is a question exactly what concern the authorities (and/or the Central Bank) needs to feel about the amount of monetary units thereby created, and with the state of the intermediaries creating them.[7] So long as such intermediaries abided by their deeds of establishment and restricted their investments to marketable securities, of a certain class, with the value of the units adjusted continuously in line, solvency should never be in

---

[7] There would still have to be protection against fraud, but that is a common requirement, not particularly related to the provision of transactions' services.

doubt, and would not be affected by the additional offer of payments' services. Similarly liquidity would be assured by marketability. So it is not clear why a Central Bank should need to impose *any* additional regulation/ supervision over mutual funds offering payments' services.

Moreover, in a world where payments' services were predominantly pro- vided by monetary units of collective investment funds rather than by banks,[8] why should the authorities pay any particular attention to the quantity of money itself, particularly since its nominal value would shift automatically with asset market prices? In such circumstances how would the quantity of money be measured? Indeed, the intuition of this Section is that the monetization of assets is *not* necessarily limited to a restricted set of financial intermediaries, i.e. banks. A much wider range of financial intermediaries could, in principle, monetize a much wider set of assets than is currently done. Under these circumstances the definition of money would either have to contract, to become synonymous with the dominant, 'outside', base money, assuming that such still continues to exist,[9] or become an amorphous concept almost devoid of meaning.

3. Bank portfolios and central bank support

It would appear, therefore, that the provision of payments' (monetary) services on units offered by collective investment intermediaries would *not, ipso facto,* require the involvement of the authorities (the Central Bank) to monitor and regulate the provision of such services. The next question is whether the withdrawal of commercial banks from the provision of payments' services, (so that demand deposits, NOW accounts, and the like were no longer offered), would absolve the Central Bank from its central concern with the well-being of the banking system. If banks offered only

[8] Something of a half-way house between a monetary unit and a bank demand deposit would be an *indexed* demand deposit provided either by a bank or another intermediary. It might actually be slightly *more* difficult technically to organize payments services on the basis of these, than on mutual funds invested in marketable assets, since the latter are continuously revalued while the former have (partly unanticipated) jumps on discrete occasions with the publication of the (RPI/CPI) price index to which the deposit was related. Again payment might only be guaranteed up to some minimum real, or nominal, balance. Some way would also have to be found to allow continuous revaluing of the deposits through the month in line with the anticipated change in the forthcoming RPI. Still, these technical problems should be surmountable. Given that there are fiscal advantages to (most tax-brackets of) depositors in holding indexed rather than nominal deposits, (i.e. no Capital Gains Tax on the inflation element in the indexed deposit; whereas income tax on the whole nominal interest on ordinary deposits is charged less the allowance given against bank charges), and that, in the UK, riskless short-term assets for such an intermediary to hold exist in the form of Government indexed bonds, it is surprising that no intermediary has yet started to offer indexed banking, with both liabilities and assets in indexed form. Perhaps the most likely reason, besides inertia and set-up costs, is that intermediaries basically require a combination of riskier and higher yielding assets, together with safe assets, to hold against liabilities, all denominated in the same form. The disincentive for intermediaries in the UK from setting up as indexed bankers is an apparent absence of borrowers prepared to take loans in indexed form: why that should be so is beyond the scope of this paper.

[9] For surveys of this latter issue, see White (1984) and McCallum (1985).

time deposits, C.D.s, etc., leaving payments' and transactions' services to others, would there be any need for special support for the banking system?

The answer to this, I believe, is that cessation of payments' services would make little difference to banks' riskiness or to the real basis of Central Bank concern with the banking system. There is little, or no, evidence that demand deposits provide a less stable source of funds than short-dated time deposits, C.D.s or borrowing in the inter-bank market; rather the reverse appears to be the case.[10] Recent occasions of runs on banks have *not* involved an attempt by the public to move out of bank deposits into cash, but merely a flight of depositors from banks seen as now excessively dangerous to some alternative placement (not cash). The Fringe Bank crisis in 1973/74 in the UK, and Continental-Illinois, are instances of this, and earlier U.S. historical experience examined by Aharony and Swary (1983) points in the same direction. Earlier, it was suggested that flows of funds from one collective investment fund to another would *not* have damaging repercussions for the payments' system, were such funds offering monetized units and providing the (bulk of) such services. Yet I shall argue that, even were banking to be entirely divorced from the provision of payments' services, such flows between banks would be extremely damaging for the economy, and would require a continuing support role for a Central Bank to prevent and, if necessary, to recycle such flows.

The reasons why this is so are to be found in the fundamental *raison d'etre* of banking itself. In particular, consider why there is a need for banks to act as intermediaries in the first place? Why cannot people simply purchase the same diversified collection of assets that the bank does? There are, of course, advantages arising from economies of scale, and the provision of safe-keeping services, but these could be obtained by investing in a collective investment fund. The key difference between a collective investment fund and a bank is that the former invests entirely, or primarily, in marketable assets, while the latter invests quite largely in non-marketable (or, at least, non-marketed) assets.

Why do borrowers prefer to obtain loans from banks rather than issue marketable securities? The set-up costs required to allow a proper market to exist have represented, in practice, formidable obstacles to the establishment of markets in the debt and equity obligations of persons and small businesses. Underlying these are the costs of providing sufficient public information to enable an equilibrium fundamental value to be established (e.g. the costs of issuing a *credible* prospectus), and the size of the expected regular volume

---

[10] Of course the risk of a run still depends, in part, on a maturity transformation by the bank, with the duration of liabilities being generally shorter than that of assets. But even if there was *no* maturity transformation, a fall of asset values relative to the nominally fixed value of liabilities would make depositors unwilling to roll-over, or extend, further funds to the bank, except on terms which made such depositors preferred, earlier creditors (than depositors with later maturities), a course which would be subject to legal constraint. So, the absence of maturity transformation would delay, and slow, the development of a run, but would not stop depositors from running when, and as, they could.

of transactions necessary to induce a market maker to establish a market in such an asset. In this sense, as Leland and Pyle (1977), Baron (1982) and Diamond (1984) have argued, the particular role of banks is to specialize[11] in choosing borrowers and monitoring their behaviour. Public information on the economic condition and prospects of such borrowers is so limited and expensive, that the alternative of issuing marketable securities is either non-existent or unattractive.

Even though banks have such an advantage (*vis à vis* ordinary savers) in choosing and monitoring propective borrowers, they too will be at a comparative disadvantage, compared with the borrower, in assessing the latter's condition, intentions and prospects.[12] Even though there would be advantages in risk sharing resulting from extending loans whose return was conditional on the contingent outcome of the project for which the loan was raised, it would reduce the incentive on the borrower to succeed, and the bank would have difficulties in monitoring the ex post outcome. Businessmen, at least in some countries, are sometmes said to have three sets of books, one for the tax inspector, one for their shareholders, and one for themselves. Which of these would the banks see, or would there be yet another set of books.[13]

In order, therefore, to reduce information and monitoring costs, banks have been led to extend loans on a fixed nominal value basis, irrespective of contingent outcome (with the loan further supported in many cases by collateral and with a duration often less than the intended life of the project to enable periodic re-assessment). Even so, both the initial, and subsequent, valuation of the loan by a bank does depend on information that is generally private between the bank and its borrowers, or, perhaps, known only to the borrower.[14] Thus the true asset value of the bank's (non-marketed) loans is

[11] An interesting question, suggested to me by Professor Mervyn Lewis, is to what extent banks obtain useful information about borrowers' conditions from their (complementary) function in operating the (present) payments system. In so far as banks do obtain information that is useful for credit assessment from the handling of payment flows, this would provide a stronger economic rationale for the present combination of banking functions. Research into, and analysis of, the customarily private and confidential question of (informational) relationships between banks and their borrowers needs to be developed further, and we cannot say with any confidence now how far banks benefit in seeking to assess credit worthiness from their provision of payments services.

[12] At least this will be so until, and unless, a large borrower runs into prospective problems in meeting contractual repayment obligations. To a casual observer, banks seem to try to limit the informational costs of making the initial loans, e.g. by resorting to standardized grading procedures; but once a (sizeable) borrower runs into difficulties, the bank responds by greatly increasing its monitoring activities, becoming often very closely involved with that borrower's future actions.

[13] This is not, as it happens, a purely hypothetical question. The Muslim prohibition on interest payments is causing certain Islamic countries to require their banks to issue Mushariqi loans, which do represent a form of equity share in the project being financed. Students of banking theory and practice might find it informative to give closer study to Islamic banking. See, for example, the article, 'Islam's Bad Debtors' in the *Financial Times,* April 8, 1986.

[14] Much recent literature on banking and credit has assumed that the borrower's selection and management of projects may not be observed by any outside party, even the banker himself: see, for example, Stiglitz and Weiss (1981, 1983).

always subject to uncertainty, though their nominal value is fixed, subject to accounting rules about provisions, write-offs, etc. Under these conditions it will benefit both bank and depositor to denominate deposit liabilities also in fixed nominal terms. The banks will benefit because the common de-nomination will reduce the risk that would arise from reduced covariance between the value of its assets and of its liabilities (as would occur, for example, if its liabilities were indexed, say to the RPI, and its assets were fixed in nominal value, or, alternatively if its assets fluctuated in line with borrowers' profits while its liabilities were fixed in nominal value). The depositor would seek fixed nominal deposits from the bank for the same reason that the bank sought fixed nominal value terms from borrowers: depositors cannot easily monitor the actual condition, intentions and prospects of their bank, so that information and monitoring costs are lessened, and the incentives on the bank to perform satisfactorily are increased, by denominating deposits in fixed nominal terms.

The combination, however, of the nominal convertibility guarantee, together with the uncertainty about the true value of bank assets, leads to the possibility of runs on individual banks and systemic crises. Moreover, once the nominal convertibility guarantee is established, the effect of better public information on banks' true asset values is uncertain. For example, 'hidden reserves' were once justified by practical bankers as likely to reduce the likelihood of runs and to maintain confidence. Again, Central Bankers have been, at most, lukewarm about allowing a market to develop in large syndicated loans to sovereign countries, whose ability to service and repay on schedule was subject to doubt, because the concrete exhibition of the fall in the value of such loans could impair the banks' recorded capital value, and potentially cause failures. An economist might ask who was being fooled? Yet on a number of occasions financial institutions have been effectively insolvent, but, so long as everyone steadfastly averted their gaze, a way through and back to solvency was achieved.

Be that as it may, under these conditions of private and expensive information, and fixed nominal value loans, any major flow of funds between banks is liable to have deleterious effects on *borrowers,* as well as on those depositors who lose both wealth and liquidity by having been left too late in the queue to withdraw when the bank(s) suspended payment. Even if the prospects of the borrower of the failed bank are at least as good as on the occasion when the borrower first arranged to loan, the borrower will have to undergo expensive search costs to obtain replacement funds. Assuming the borrower searched beforehand, and found the 'best' deal, the likelihood is now that the borrower will obtain less beneficial arrange-ments.

Bank runs, however, tend to happen when conditions for many borrowers have turned adverse. The suspicion, or indeed the knowledge, of that is what prompted the run in the first place. Accordingly the expected value of the loans of many borrowers will have fallen. If they are forced to repay the

failing bank, by the receiver to meet the creditors' demands,[15] they would
not be able to replace the funds required on the same terms, if at all, from
other banks. Thus bank failures will place the economic well-being, indeed
survival, of many borrowers at risk, as well as impairing depositors'
wealth.[16] Consequently flows of funds from suspect banks to supposedly
stronger banks can have a severely adverse effect on the economy, even
when there is no flight into cash at all. A Central Bank will aim to prevent,
and, if that fails, to recycle such flows—subject to such safeguards as it can
achieve to limit moral hazard and to penalize inadequate or improper
managerial behaviour.[17]

4. Conclusion

To summarize and conclude, it is often claimed that banking is special
and particular, requiring additional regulation and supervision by a Central
Bank, *because* it is unique among financial intermediaries in combining
payments' services and portfolio management. I hope to have demonstrated
that this is false. Monetary payments' services not only could be provided,
(and are increasingly being provided), by other collective-investment funds,
but could also be provided more safely than by banks. Moreover, the
characteristics of such funds are such that their entry into this field (the
provision of monetary services) need not cause the authorities (the Central
Bank) any extra concern; they could be left to operate under their current
regulations. Similarly, if banks were to abandon the provision of payments'
services, and restrict their deposit liabilities to non-checkable form, it would
not much reduce bank riskiness. They would still require the assistance of a
Central Bank.

All this follows because the really important distinction between banks
and other financial intermediaries resides in the characteristics of their asset
portfolio, which, in turn, largely determines what kind of liability they can
offer: fixed value in the case of banks, market-value-related for collective
investment funds. It is these latter differences, rather than the special

---

[15] Insofar as constraints, either external or self-imposed, exist which stop the receiver from
calling in loans outstanding at failed banks, this source of potential loss to society would be
lessened. Even so, at a minimum, the borrower would lose the ability to obtain *additional* loans
from the failing bank, and that ability could be crucial to survival in a cyclical depression.

[16] This feature of banking, whereby calling of loans by failed banks causes economic
disruption, has been recently noted and modelled by Diamond and Dybvig (1983), and by
Bernanke (1983).

[17] Even in the absence of a Central Bank there will be some incentives for commercial banks
to act, either independently or collusively, in the same way, i.e. to recycle deposit flows to
banks facing liquidity problems and to support, or to take over, potentially insolvent banks.
But the public good aspect of such actions will be less compelling to competing commercial
banks, (e.g. why help a competitor that got into trouble through its own fault?), and the risk to
their own profit positions of such action more worrying to them than to a Central Bank.
Moreover the usual circumstances of a rescue, at very short notice under conditions of severely
limited information, makes it more difficult for commercial banks to act collusively, than for an
independent Central Bank to act swiftly and decisively.

monetary nature of certain bank deposits, that will maintain in future years the distinction between bank and non-bank financial intermediaries.

London School of Economics

BIBLIOGRAPHY

AHARONY, J. and SWARY, I. (1983), 'Contagion Effects of Bank Failures: Evidence from Capital Markets', *Journal of Business*, Vol. 56, No. 3, 305–22.

BARON, D. (1982), 'A Model of the Demand for Investment Banking and Advising and Distribution Services for New Issues', *Journal of Finance*, Vol. 37, No. 4, 955–76.

BERNANKE, B. S. (1983), 'Non-monetary Effects of the Financial Crisis in the Propagation of the Great Depression', *American Economic Review*, Vol. 73, No. 3, 257–76.

DIAMOND, D. W. (1984), 'Financial Intermediation and Delegated Monitoring', *Review of Economic Studies*, Vol. 51, No. 3, 393–414.

DIAMOND, D. W. and DYBVIG, P. H. (1983), 'Bank Runs, Deposit Insurance, and Liquidity', *Journal of Political Economy*, Vol. 91, No. 3, 401–19.

FAMA, E. (1980), 'Banking in the Theory of Finance', *Journal of Monetary Economics*, 6, No. 1, 39–57.

FLUX, A. W. (1911), 'The Swedish Banking System', from *Banking in Sweden and Switzerland*, National Monetary Commission, Vol. XVII, (Government Printing Office: Washington).

GOODHART, C. A. E. (1985), *The Evolution of Central Banks*, (LSE, STICERD monograph).

HOUSE OF COMMONS (1985), *Building Societies Bill*, (HMSO: London).

LELAND, H. E. and PYLE, D. H. (1977), 'Information Asymmetries, Financial Structure and Financial Intermediaries', *Journal of Finance*, Vol. 32, No. 2, 371–87.

McCALLUM, B. T. (1985), 'Bank Deregulation, Accounting Systems of Exchange, and the Unit of Account: A Critical Review', *Carnegie-Rochester Conference Series on Public Policy*, Vol. 23.

STIGLITZ, J. E. and WEISS, A. M. (1981), 'Credit Rationing in Markets with Imperfect Information', *American Economic Review*, Vol. 71, No. 3, 393–410.

STIGLITZ, J. E. and WEISS A. M. (1983), 'Incentive Effects of Terminations: Applications to the Credit and Labor Markets', *American Economic Review*, Vol. 73, No. 5, 912–27.

TOBIN, J. (1958), 'Liquidity Preference as Behavior Towards Risk', *Review of Economic Studies*, Vol. 25, No. 67, 65–86.

TOBIN, J. (1985), 'Financial Innovation and Deregulation in Perspective', *Bank of Japan Monetary and Economic Studies*, Vol. 3, No. 2.,

WALLICH, H. (1984), 'A Broad View of Deregulation', Paper presented at the FRB San Francisco Conference on Pacific Basin Financial Reform, mimeo, December.

WHITE, L. H. (1984), 'Competitive Payments Systems and the Unit of Account', *American Economic Review*, Vol. 74, No. 4, 699–712.

Oxford Economic Papers 39 (1987), 90–110

INFLATION DEBT AND FISCAL POLICY ATTITUDES

By JEFFREY SHEEN

Introduction

CONCERN about fiscal deficits arise for a number of reasons. To the extent that they are monetised, they are supposed to lead to inflation and, to the extent that they imply debt accumulation, they are supposed to impose a crowding out burden on the private sector. Most analysis of these issues is carried out by comparing the results of pure money financing to pure debt financing (for example, see Turnovsky (1977)). This involves the strong assumption that monetary authorities can and do precommit themselves to fixed growth targets of either money or debt. Such polar precommitment requires extremely strong conviction on the part of government and, given that both options involve political costs, it seems unrealistic to suppose that either will occur. In a recent paper, Liviatan (1982) studies the issue of debt neutrality in the context of the Sidrauski (1967)–Brock (1974) intertemporally optimal growth model, where the financing shares are precommitted away from zero and he shows that the existence of endogenous inflation taxes induces non-neutrality. Dornbusch (1977) also considered the mixed-financing assumption using a non-optimal growth model and established non-neutrality and the increased possibility of instability when the share of debt finance is raised.

Thus another policy concern about fiscal deficits involves the problem of servicing outstanding debt. In a survey of literature on the stability of models of debt finance, Christ (1979) showed that it may be appropriate, even necessary to introduce an endogenous component into the fiscal deficit. Indeed, the contribution of this paper relies on Christ's suggestion of endogenising fiscal policy to avoid instability. The degree to which fiscal deficits have to be and are endogenised, albeit in a model with flexible prices, is parameterised in this paper. The extent to which governments decide to cover themselves against possible instability can be shown to have important short and long run implications for inflation (and by implication, for output). In this context the concept of an excessively cautious or conservative government as opposed to an optimistic or liberal government is introduced, giving the paper a political economy flavour.

The paper shows that, at low rates of inflation, a shift in the money-debt finance share will fulfil "monetarist" predictions in the short and long run if the government is conservative but will not if it is liberal. The "monetarist" label is used here in the sense that a shift away from debt finance will

The author is grateful for helpful discussions with William Scarth and Mono Chatterji. The views expressed herein are solely those of the author.

raise the rate of inflation. This contribution is of interest because a consensus has emerged in the literature on debt finance accepting the somewhat paradoxial result that open market sales of debt raise output or prices (for example, see Blinder and Solow (1973), and Brunner and Meltzer (1976) for instantaneous open market operations and Dornbusch (1977) and Liviatan[1] (1982) for continuous ones). The logic underlying the paradox is that higher outstanding debt (and lower money) creates a budget deficit and thus further debt issue. Taxes in some form must be boosted by an overall increase in output or prices. Obviously, if the fiscal authorities consciously vary their instruments to encourage stability, the automatic stabilising role that needs to be played by output or prices is reduced. This paper sets out the conditions for the reversal of the paradox, relating these conditions to the attitude of the authorities to the possibility of instability.

The model employs a monetary transactions cost technology. The existence of money in utility functions can be defended (see, for example, Brock (1974)) on the grounds that money is a substitute for leisure in fulfilling transactions. Although not getting to the root of the use of money, a somewhat more acceptable alternative is to assume that transactions costs use up real output or real income, and that the use of money reduces these costs. This approach is studied by Dornbusch and Frenkel (1973) and by Gray (1984). In the former paper, the objective was to show that the steady state capital-labour ratio was not neutral with respect to inflation using a simple money and growth model. Gray (1984) focussed on the saddlepath characteristics of the transactions cost model with the objective of showing that it had broadly similar properties to the Sidrauski–Brock perfect foresight monetary models. By introducing the government budget constraint to a transactions cost model, the current paper displays a wider range of equilibria than those explicitly envisaged by Gray. The transactions cost model permits an indirect channel for the crowding out of private consumption which does not emerge in the Sidrauski–Brock model.

The paper is organised as follows. In Section 1, the constraint on and instruments of the government are discussed, followed by a discussion of the intertemporal optimal plan of the representative consumer. Section 2 describes the key differential equations of the perfect foresight model, the steady state and the associated stability characteristics. In Section 3, the effects of various ways of enforcing restrictive policy are discussed. Comparisons are made for a shift towards debt finance, for tax increases, for the reduction of utility-yielding or output-yielding government expenditure and for a balanced budget contraction. Section 4 provides concluding comments.

---

[1] Liviatan (1982), (1984) does show that alternative definitions of the authorities' desired autonomous deficit can give rise to different answers. However, he explicitly declines to rank or justify the choice of definition.

Section 1

1.1. *The government sector*

The government raises finance to support its spending and its interest payments by imposing taxes, issuing money or borrowing real short term debt. The government budget constraint, in real per capita terms is given by

$$g + rb = t + \mu m + \beta b \tag{1}$$

where μ and β are the (endogenous) nominal rates of growth of money and debt, m and b are values of real money and debt, g is real government spending, t is a lump sum real tax and r defines the real rate of interest on debt. Real, or indexed, debt is employed in this model merely to simplify the analysis. The major conclusions of the paper are not significantly affected.

The existence of debt introduces an element of possible instability because the perpetual issue of debt to finance its service has to be explicitly avoided. Although output is endogenous, only lump sum taxes are used. This means that the stabilising role of taxes has to be deliberately selected. It is straightforward to introduce automatic stabilisers and one may even like to think of equations (2) as a general formulation that nests automatic and non-automatic stabilisers. The fiscal instruments, g and t, will be assumed to be adjusted in response to the level of debt with

$$g = g_0 - \theta_g b \tag{2a}$$

$$t = t_0 + \theta_t b \tag{2b}$$

where θ_g and θ_t are the endogenous adjustment parameters of government expenditure and taxes relative to outstanding debt and their sum is defined as

$$\theta = \theta_g + \theta_t \tag{3}$$

The size of θ chosen will be seen to characterise the extent to which the government is concerned with the potential instability of the macroeconomic equilibrium. It will define the fiscal policy attitude to the possibility of instability. The exogenous elements of government expenditure and taxation are g_0 and t_0 and their difference is the autonomous deficit, D, such that

$$D = g_0 - t_0 \tag{4}$$

To understand the workings of this model, it is important to be aware of the distinction between the autonomous deficit and the total deficit, $D + (r - \theta)b$. With b endogenous, the two deficit measures can move in opposite directions.

The total deficit is financed by the debt and money issue. For generality, following Dornbusch (1977) and Liviatan (1982), the authorities are assumed to care at every instant about the composition of finance. The share of the total deficit financed by money issue is α where

$$\alpha = \frac{\mu m}{\mu m + \beta b} \tag{5}$$

Whilst μ and β are endogenous, they are restricted by equation (5). The policy parameter α can be thought to represent continuous or flow open market operations; the authorities may also undertake standard instantaneous or stock open market operations by trading money for real debt. The growth rate of money is thus endogenous (except when $\alpha = 0$) even if the authorities had set a target.[2] If $\alpha = 0$, deficits are debt financed and if $\alpha = 1$, they are money financed; these two polar cases will be seen to be associated with steady states in which the real value of the non-financing asset is zero (see (24) below). By specifiying α as a parameter of the system, one can sharply distinguish between autonomous and non-autonomous budgetary policy and yet permit interdependence of these decisions over time. The polar cases avoid interdependence and usually require further assumptions concerning non-cooperative behaviour between the fiscal and monetary authorities.

Defining n as the population growth rate, the equations governing money and debt can be written as

$$\mu m = \dot{m} - (\pi + n)m = \alpha(D + (r - \theta)b)$$
$$\beta b = \dot{b} - nb = (1 - \alpha)(D + (r - \theta)b) \tag{6}$$

1.2. Firms

The motivation for the production technology and the behaviour of firms will be kept to the barest minimum in this paper. The main focus is meant

---

[2] Sargent and Wallace (1981) initiated a literature where the fiscal authorities effectively Stackelberg-lead the monetary authorities. An alternative specification would be to introduce a target component into the growth of money so that

$$\alpha = \frac{\mu m}{D + (r - \theta)b - \bar{\mu}m}.$$

This allows for the possibility of having a constant growth rate when $\alpha = 0$ and would reproduce the Sargent and Wallace results; Liviatan (1984) provides a very clear analysis of the paradox of tight money generating higher inflation using the Sidrauski–Brock growth model.

to be on the equilibrium relationships between the government and consumers.

Per capita output, y, is produced by firms using effective physical capital and labour. Private physical capital accumulation is ruled out, y is assumed constant at its steady state level.

Constant returns to scale are assumed and so profits and wages exhaust output. In the steady state, this can be represented as

$$\hat{y} = \hat{w} + \hat{\rho}k \tag{7}$$

where $\hat{w}$ is the steady state real wage rate, k is the fixed capital/labour force ratio and $\hat{\rho}$ is the steady state level of the marginal productivity of capital. The capital stock is owned by households. Although the aggregate capital stock is fixed, the effective stock is assumed to grow at the rate n. Individual households are able to buy and sell instantaneous shares in the effective capital stock. Households do not make a fundamental distinction between wage and profit income.

1.3. *Households*

A representative household is infinitely-lived and chooses a path of expenditure, e_i, real money balances, m_i, debt, b_i, and shares, k_i, so as to maximise an integral of additively separable and subjectively discounted (δ) instantaneous utilities, u, which are functions of per capita private consumption, c_i, and a proportion, λ, of real government spending. Ignoring a subscript indexing the individual household, the problem to be solved is:

$$\max_{e,m,b,k} \int_0^\infty u(c(\tau) + \lambda g(\tau)) \exp(-\delta\tau) \, d\tau \tag{8}$$

subject to (i) its budget constraint

$$\dot{v} = y + (r-n)b - (\pi+n)m - t - e \tag{9}$$

where v is real non-human wealth defined as

$$v = m + b + k \tag{10}$$

and (ii) a transaction technology function which converts expenditure into consumption, with the help of money, such that

$$e = c + T(e, m) \tag{11}$$

Note that all household variables should be indexed (say by i). Since aggregation problems are assumed away, the index is not shown.

The utility function obeys diminishing marginal utility in total consumption. If domestic consumption and government expenditure were perfect substitutes, then the utility function involves only their sum, $c + g$. If they are less than perfectly substitutable or if a part of government expenditure is perceived to be irrelevant to private utility, the sum overstates utility. For simplicity, the sum $c + \lambda g$ is used to determine utility, where by definition λ is the proportion of total government spending generating private utility. It is assumed that the government incurs smaller (indeed zero) costs in getting goods to households than the households suffer in private trades.

To consume, households have to convert assets into final goods so as to reap the utility involved in their consumption. This conversion process is assumed costly since resources in the form of final goods have to be continuously devoted to such activities. What is observed is total household expenditure; utility-yielding consumption emerges after the incursion of transaction costs. The transactions cost function in (11) is assumed convex so that required expenditure increases faster than the consumption yield. The usage of money is assumed to reduce transactions costs at a diminishing rate. In this one good model, money plays the roles of a medium of exchange and a store of value, allowing the time path of consumption to be smoothed. However, money is not vital for the conduct of economic activity. There is a backstop transaction technology available, thus permitting an intertemporal barter economy to emerge. Debt and capital are also used for intertemporal smoothing, but the barter alternative is assumed to be generally socially dominated by the fiat money economy because of the relative virtues of money-verifiability, valuation, divisibility, availability and the implicit cost of supply. Of course, the usage of money will be seen to decline with inflation. Transaction costs can never exceed total income, thus assuring positive consumption in a barter economy.

The transactions cost function thus exhibits the following properties:

$$0 < T_e < 1; \qquad T_{ee} > 0; \qquad T_m < 0;$$
$$T_{mm} > 0; \qquad T_{me} \leqslant 0; \qquad T(e, 0) > y \tag{12}$$

From here on, T_{me} is fixed at zero. This simplifies the exposition at the cost of overstating the size of the interest elasticity of the demand for money.

A key assumption of monetary growth models is that financial transfers by the government are not regarded as interest on money by the private sector. A similar problem arises concerning endogenous taxes and government spending. To what extent does the private sector take account of this endogeneity? This raises issues of aggregation, information and co-ordination. Throughout this paper, it is assumed that the private sector is composed of independent atomistic agents who are unable to co-ordinate responses to government behaviour.[3]

---

[3] Fischer (1979) showed that money is transitionally super-non-neutral in the context of capital accumulation, if transfers are not regarded as interest on money. Otherwise money is always superneutral. Similarly, if households regarded endogenous fiscal policy as an implicit tax on government debt, that policy would be entirely neutral.

Defining the coefficient of absolute risk aversion as $A = -u_{cc}/u_c$, and following Brock (1974), the first order Euler conditions necessary for the solution to the calculus of variations problem[4] (8)–(10) become:

$$\frac{d}{dt}\left(\frac{\partial u}{\partial \dot{X}}\right) = \frac{\partial u}{\partial X} + \delta \frac{\partial u}{\partial \dot{X}} \text{ where } X = b, k, m$$

To compute the partial derivatives, insert (10) differentiated into (9), use e from (9) in (11) and substitute the resulting expression for c into the utility function.

The first order conditions are

$$A\dot{c} = r - \delta - n - \frac{T_{ee}}{(1 - T_e)}\dot{e} \tag{13a}$$

$$A\dot{c} = \hat{\rho} - \delta - n - \frac{T_{ee}}{(1 - T_e)}\dot{e} \tag{13b}$$

$$A\dot{c} = \frac{-T_m}{(1 - T_e)} - \delta - \pi - n - \frac{T_{ee}}{(1 - T_e)}\dot{e} \tag{13c}$$

Together these imply

$$\hat{\rho} = -\left(\frac{T_m}{(1 - T_e)} + \pi\right) = r \tag{14}$$

Individuals attempt to accumulate[5] shares, money and debt so that their net benefits are equated at the margin. On the left hand side of (14) is the marginal benefit from capital represented by the steady state rate of return. In the middle of (14), the marginal transaction cost reduction from money is countervailed by the inflation tax. On the right hand side is the net marginal benefit from debt which is just the real rate of interest because of the atomistic assumption about households.

Equations (11)–(13) would simplify dramatically if the utility function and the transaction cost function were linear so that $A = 0$ and $T_{ee} = 0$.[6] With

---

[4] The necessary second order Legendre condition for a maximum requires that the indirect utility function is concave in $\dot{X}$, i.e., that

$$\frac{\partial u_c \frac{\partial(c + g)}{\partial X}}{\partial \dot{X}} \leq 0$$

This condition depends on $-A(1 - T_e)^2 - T_{ee}$ which is negative.

[5] There are two transversality conditions which will be intimately related to the stability analysis of the macroeconomic equilibrium. Households will hold money and debt if $\lim_{t\to\infty} b_t u(c_t) \to 0$ and $\lim_{t\to\infty} m_t u(c_t) \to 0$. These conditions place upper bounds on these variables. Bearing these in mind, restrictions on government behaviour are necessary to ensure stability of the equilibrium.

[6] Gray (1984) shows that $A = 0$ and $T_e = 0$ in a transactions model implies similar dynamic properties to the Brock model where utility is separable in consumption and money.

linear utility, the accumulation of assets is not constrained by increasing marginal utility as consumption falls or by decreasing marginal transaction costs as expenditure falls. In certain circumstances, the perfect foresight equilibrium will be characterised by constant household expenditure ($\dot{e} = 0$). The simplest case arises in a closed economy model with no investment and exogenous government expenditure so that output is totally accounted for by households.

With the separability assumption on T, T_m is a function of m alone, and T_e is a function of e alone. Hence the right equality in (14) gives the level of real money balances demanded as a function of the nominal rate of interest, i, where $i = r + \pi$ and the level of expenditure, e; that is $m^d = L(i, e)$.

Section 2

2.1. *Equilibrium conditions and reduced form dynamic equations*

There are four markets which are assumed to always clear: goods, money debt, and shares in the capital stock. Goods prices are completely flexible and inflation is assumed to be perfectly foreseen. The paper assumes no problems of aggregation and so per capita definitions can be used in the macroeconomic equilibrium analysis that follows. I shall show that the system is recursive and can be reduced to two differential equations in debt and real money balances (or, inflation).

Goods market equilibrium is given by

$$y = e + g \tag{15}$$

With identical individuals, money and debt will be held in accordance with (13). Hence the rate of inflation and the real rate of interest will be given by

$$\pi = \frac{-T_m}{1 - T_e} - \hat{\rho} \tag{16}$$

$$r = \hat{\rho} \tag{17}$$

Money market equilibrium is described in (16). With predetermined nominal money balances, the price level adjusts to ensure equilibrium. Capital market equilibrium is given by (17). The constancy of the real rate of interest comes about because I have not allowed the possibility of capital gains on shares. This rather extreme assumption is the key to the recursive property of the model and endows analytic feasibility.

Differentiating (11) gives

$$\dot{c} = (1 - T_e)\dot{e} - T_m \dot{m}$$

Substituting this into (13b) gives $\dot{e}$ (and thus $\dot{c}$ through (13b)) as a linear function of $\dot{m}$ alone

$$\dot{e} = \frac{AT_m}{A(1 - T_e) + \dfrac{T_{ee}}{1 - T_e}} \dot{m} + \frac{\hat{\rho} - n - \delta}{A(1 - T_e) + \dfrac{T_{ee}}{1 - T_e}}$$

Using this in (16) differentiated gives $\dot{\pi}$ as a negative linear function of $\dot{m}$ alone

$$\dot{\pi} = \frac{-1}{1 - T_e}\left(T_{mm} + \frac{AT_m^2 T_{ee}}{A(1 - T_e)^2 + T_{ee}}\right)\dot{m} - \frac{T_m T_{ee}(\hat{\rho} - n - \delta)}{(1 - T_e)(A(1 - T_e)^2 + T_{ee})} \quad (18)$$

In fact, the last term in (18) will always be zero because I shall have to assume that $\hat{\rho} = \delta + n$ (see (27) below). We can thus discuss the dynamics of π, once we know the dynamics of m. In Section 3, I choose to focus upon π.

The actual evolution of per capita real money balances and debt can be obtained from (1) to (5) and the definitions of real money and bond growth

$$\left(\frac{\dot{m}}{m} = \mu - \pi - n, \frac{\dot{b}}{b} = \beta - n\right)$$

to give

$$\dot{m} = \alpha(D + (r - \theta_g - \theta_r)b) - (\pi + n)m \quad (19)$$

$$\dot{b} = (1 - \alpha)(D + (r - \theta_g - \theta_r)b) - nb \quad (20)$$

2.2. Steady states

A steady state occurs when per capital real assets are stationary. The steady state rate of growth of nominal money and debt are endogenous.

$$\hat{\mu} = \hat{\pi} + n \quad (22)$$

$$\hat{\beta} = n \quad (23)$$

By setting the left hand side of (19) and (20) to zero, the steady state relationship between money and debt becomes

$$\hat{b} = \frac{(1 - \alpha)}{\alpha n}(\hat{\pi} + n)\hat{m} \quad (24)$$

From this equation, it becomes clear that a meaningful long run with $0 < \alpha < 1$ necessitates $n \neq 0$. This is simply because *real* (or indexed) debt has been employed in the model. A steady state autonomous deficit is not sustainable by the part-issuance of real debt unless the growth rate of the economy is non-zero. With nominal debt, existence in the long run would not require positive growth.

From (15), (2) and (11), steady state private sector expenditure and consumption are given by

$$\hat{e} = \hat{y} - g_0 + \theta_g \hat{b}$$
$$\hat{c} = \hat{e} - T(\hat{e}, \hat{m})$$

(25)

With consumption constant in the steady state, the demand for per capita real balances $(\hat{m})$ is determined by

$$\frac{T_m}{1 - T_e} = -(\delta + \hat{\pi} + n) = -\hat{i}$$

(26)

At the classical optimal rate of inflation (see Friedman (1969)), T_m and, hence, the nominal rate of interest, $\hat{i}$, is zero; this is where no further marginal benefits are obtained from extra money. This concept will be used as a benchmark for later analysis and will only occur with an autonomous surplus $(D < 0)$.

The real rate of interest on debt is

$$\hat{r} = \hat{\rho} = \delta + n$$

(27)

As is well known, if a steady state is to exist, the net yield on real debt and capital must equal the rate of time preference plus growth. In this model, it needs to be assumed, although the condition can be endogenously generated by introducing either capital accumulation (for example, see Fischer (1977)), a second-hand market for existing capital (see Obstfeld and Rogoff (1983)) or endogenous time preference (see Uzawa (1968)). I do not pursue any of these options because they severely complicate the algebra.

Using (20) when $\dot{b} = 0$, (24) and (27), one verifies that

$$(\hat{\pi} + n)\hat{m} = \gamma \cdot D$$

(28)

if we define γ as the proportion of the autonomous deficit D that is financed by the growth and inflation tax on money in the steady state. So

$$\gamma = \frac{\alpha n}{n + (1 - \alpha)(\theta - \delta - n)}$$

(29)

Note that $\alpha = 0$ or 1 implies $\gamma = 0$ or 1. The right hand side of (28) must be positive if the inflation tax is positive. We shall consider equilibria such that $\gamma \geq 0$ and finite so that the steady state growth and inflation tax must be a positive share of the autonomous deficit. This restriction will be seen to be necessary and sufficient for ruling out instability at high rates of inflation.

Equations (26) (having used (24) and (25)) and (28) can be solved for steady state real balances and inflation. In Fig. 1, they are depicted as 'money demand' (MD) and a 'money supply' (MS) curves, showing two equilibria which will be seen to depend on the size of the interest elasticity of the demand for money. At A_0, this interest elasticity is less than unity, while at B_0, it is greater. Requiring $\gamma \geq 0$ and finite necessarily implies that

$$\theta > \delta - \frac{\alpha n}{1 - \alpha}$$

(30)

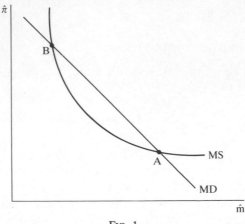

FIG. 1

If the government chooses to finance its autonomous deficit, D, with money alone $(\alpha = 1)$, the value of the debt stabilisation parameter, θ, becomes irrelevant. Alternatively, using debt finance alone $(\alpha = 0)$ requires the stabilisation parameter to exceed the rate of time preference, i.e. $\theta > \delta$. As α increases, the required θ decreases. When α approaches $\delta/\delta + n$, the minimum value of θ approaches zero; although for higher α, subsidies may be paid on debt, this is assumed away by fixing θ at zero. If θ were set at zero, a stable equilibrium will be guaranteed only if $\alpha > \delta/\delta + n$ which means that pure bond financing would be ruled out in an impatient economy $(\delta > 0)$. This is then a reason for introducing the parameter θ.

However, if condition (30) is only marginally satisfied, the relationship between γ and α is not necessarily monotonic. To achieve monotonicity and to ensure that $\gamma > 0$, it would be sufficient that $\theta > \delta + n$, where $\delta + n$ is the steady state real rate of interest. In this case $0 \leqslant \gamma \leqslant 1$, and it will be identified with excessively cautious, pessimistic or conservative governments. The implications of such unnecessary caution will become plain below.

Definition: (a) A *conservative* government will set the debt stabilisation parameter so that it exceeds the sum of the rate of time preference and growth

$$\theta > \delta + n \tag{31}$$

(b) A *liberal* government fulfils

$$\delta > \theta > \delta - \frac{\alpha n}{1 - \alpha} \tag{32}$$

Hence, under conservatism, growth *raises* the (sufficient) stabilisation parameter; under a liberal government growth *reduces* the (necessary and sufficient) stabilisation parameter by the factor $\alpha/1 - \alpha$. Note that there is a grey area $(\delta \leqslant \theta \leqslant \delta + n)$ when growth is non-zero.

2.3. *Stability Analysis*

The properties of the steady state are closely related to its local stability characteristics. Taking a linear approximation of (19)' and (20)' about the state where $\dot{m} = \dot{b} = 0$, the transition matrix, becomes

$$\Omega = \begin{bmatrix} \dot{m}_m & \dot{m}_b \\ \dot{b}_m & \dot{b}_b \end{bmatrix} = \begin{bmatrix} -\left(\pi + n - \dfrac{mT_{mm}}{1-T_e}\right) & \alpha(r-\theta) \\ 0 & (1-\alpha)(r-\theta) - n \end{bmatrix}$$

The stability properties of the model depend crucially on the determinant of the transition matrix. Using (29) and the following definition of the partial inflation or nominal interest rate elasticity of the demand for money

$$\varepsilon = \frac{(\pi + n)(1 - T_e)}{mT_{mm}} > 0$$

the determinant of Ω becomes

$$|\Omega| = \frac{\alpha n (\pi + n)\left(1 - \dfrac{1}{\varepsilon}\right)}{\gamma} \tag{33}$$

This determinant equals the product of the characteristic roots of the transition matrix. Since b is a predetermined variable whose current value is historically given, while m (through the flexible price level) is a non-predetermined variable free to assume any current value, the steady state is a saddle point if the characteristic roots are opposite in sign (see Buiter (1984)). Hence for a unique saddlepath, we require $|\Omega| > 0$. From the definition of γ in (29), for an autonomous deficit ($D > 0$), $(\pi + n)/\gamma$ must be positive; otherwise real money balances would be negative. Obviously, γ and $(\pi + n)$ must have the same sign if D is positive.

In the region of saddlepoint equilibria, speculative hyperinflations cannot be ruled out a priori unless money is deemed essential (c/f Brock (1974)), i.e. unless transactions costs become infinite as real balances approach zero. Since barter is not assumed impossible, the Brock solution is unavailable and some form of government intervention is required to rule out 'speculative bubbles'.[7] Henceforth, bubbles are ignored and only convergent solutions are discussed.

Although the rest of the paper will only deal with the saddlepath outcome ($\varepsilon < 1$), it is worth noting that the properties of the model will be quite different at sufficiently high rates of inflation. Ignoring the third derivative

---

[7] By introducing a market for existing capital, Obstfeld and Rogoff (1984) show how a government that owns a share of the capital stock can provide a credible guarantee to deter unwarranted speculation. Alternatively, the government could insist that its taxes be paid in fiat currency.

of the transactions cost function, the elasticity of money demand increases with inflation; hence, beyond some critical inflation rate, the saddlepoint property disappears.

If $\varepsilon = 1$ however, $|\Omega| = 0$ and the zero root problem[8] emerges whereby the steady state is unique for given parameter values, exogenous variables and initial conditions; the system exhibits hysteresis.

At even higher rates of inflation, $\varepsilon > 1$. In this case, the steady state may be locally stable, giving rise to multiple convergent paths.[9] Local stability requires $|\Omega| > 0$ and a negative trace $(\dot{m}_m + \dot{b}_b < 0)$ since the latter measures the sum of the characteristic roots. In this case, $\dot{m}_m < 0$ and

$$\dot{b}_b = \frac{-\alpha n}{\gamma} \qquad (34)$$

Since $(\pi + n) > 0$, for local stability it is necessary and sufficient to ensure that $\gamma > 0$. If the conservative condition holds $(\theta > \delta + n)$, stability is assured.

A further sense in which the government is pessimistic or excessively cautious is now apparent; it is because the conservative fiscal attitude is sufficient but not necessary to ensure $\gamma > 0$ and thus to rule out local instability in high inflation circumstances.

2.4. Transition paths

There can be a distinction between the short and the long run in this model because the process of debt issue takes time: b is a predetermined variable.

The transition paths of the linearised system can be easily displayed. For the sake of brevity, the analysis is pursued only for the saddlepath outcome. The implications of conservative or liberal governments are presented.

Since $\dot{\pi}$ is negatively related to $\dot{m}$ in (18), equation (19) can be reinterpreted as an equation for inflation change. The locus in $\{\pi, b\}$ space where $\dot{m} = \dot{\pi} = 0$ describes

$$(\pi + n)m = \alpha(D - (\theta - \delta - n)b$$

where m is a negative function of π. With $\varepsilon < 1$, an increase in π raises the tax on money $(\partial\dot{\pi}/\partial\pi > 0)$. If the government is conservative, an increase in b reduces the total deficit in the steady state $(\partial\dot{\pi}/\partial b = \alpha(\theta - \delta - n) > 0)$. In this case, the $\dot{\pi} = 0$ locus can be drawn as the negatively sloped PP curve as in Fig. 2. Everywhere above (below) this curve, the inflation rate will have to increase (decrease).

---

[8] For a discussion of this hysteresis issue in various models, see Giavazzi and Wyplosz (1985).

[9] See Taylor (1977), McCallum (1983) for solutions to the problem of multiple convergent rational expectations equilibrium paths. In this situation it seems reasonable to conjecture that the non-predetermined variables jump immediately to their steady state values.

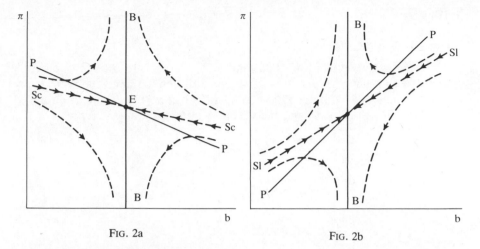

FIG. 2a

FIG. 2b

The BB curve depicting $\dot{b} = 0$ from (20) and (29) is given by

$$(1 - \alpha)D = \frac{\alpha m}{\gamma} b$$

An increase in b, for given π, will reduce the change in per capital debt $(\partial \dot{b}/\partial b < 0)$; the steady state fiscal return on debt must be positive. The BB locus must be vertical.

For a conservative government the saddlepath must be negatively sloped[10] and is drawn as the arrow-dashed line $S_c S_c$ in Fig. 2a.

If the government is liberal, $\partial \dot{\pi}/\partial b < 0$ and so the PP locus becomes positively sloped. The saddlepath will become positively sloped as in Fig. 2b. Observe that the slopes of the PP locus and the saddlepath depend critically on the particular definitions of the two types of government. But as mentioned above, there is a grey area between the two definitions i.e. $\delta \leq \theta \leq \delta + n$. Very different *short run* effects on inflation derive from this distinction as will be seen in the next section.

---

[10] For a conservative government, the transition matrix has the sign pattern

$$\begin{bmatrix} \dot{\pi}_\pi & \dot{\pi}_b \\ \dot{b}_\pi & \dot{b}_D \end{bmatrix} = \begin{bmatrix} + & + \\ - & - \end{bmatrix}$$

The solution to the linearised system must be of the form

$$\pi(t) - \hat{\pi} = a_{11} e^{st}$$
$$b(t) - \hat{b} = a_{21} e^{st}$$

where s is the negative eigenvalue, the term in the positive one having been deleted to meet the finite limit condition on $\pi(t)$ and $b(t)$. On differentiating one gets $\dot{\pi} = s(\pi - \hat{\pi})$ which, on comparison with the original equation, gives the saddlepath $(\pi - \hat{\pi}) = -(b - \hat{b})\dot{\pi}_b/(-s + \dot{\pi}_\pi)$ which is negatively sloped. For a liberal government, only $\dot{\pi}_b$ changes sign, and so its saddlepath is positively sloped.

Section 3

3.1. *Contractionary financial policy*

The qualitative effect on inflation of a change in the government's propensity to finance its deficit with money will depend upon its fiscal policy attitude. The steady state equations (24)–(29) can be solved for $\hat{\pi}$, $\hat{m}$, $\hat{b}$ and $(\hat{c} + \lambda \hat{g})$ as functions of γ (and then α) and differentiated to give

$$\frac{d\hat{\pi}}{-d\gamma} = \frac{-(\pi + n)}{\gamma(1 - \varepsilon)} < 0$$

$$\frac{d\hat{m}}{-d\gamma} = \frac{\varepsilon \hat{m}}{\gamma(1 - \varepsilon)} > 0$$

$$\frac{d\gamma}{d\alpha} = \frac{\gamma^2}{\alpha^2 n}(\theta - \delta) \gtreqless 0$$

$$\frac{d\hat{b}}{-d\alpha} = \frac{\gamma^2}{\alpha^2} D > 0$$

$$\frac{d(\hat{c} + \lambda \hat{g})}{-d\alpha} = (1 - T_e)\hat{i}\frac{d\hat{m}}{-d\alpha} + (1 - T_e - \lambda)\theta_g \frac{d\hat{b}}{-d\alpha} \gtreqless 0$$

From section 2.3, saddlepoint stability requires $\varepsilon < 1$; hence a decrease in γ is deflationary.[11] However the parameter, α, is the policy control variable. By definition, a conservative government sets $\theta - \delta > n$ implying that α and γ are positively related. Under these circumstances, a conservative government will lower the required long run inflation tax and hence the rate of inflation by a shift towards debt finance (a decrease in α).

For liberal governments, θ need only exceed $\delta - \alpha n/(1 - \alpha)$ with mixed financing, growth in the economy reduces the required size of θ. Therefore, since this government allows $\theta < \delta$, we get the perverse result that a shift towards debt financing in normal circumstances raises inflation. The reason for this is that outstanding debt is decidedly greater in the new steady state (while the effect of a change in debt on the total deficit is positive since, $\delta + n - \theta > 0$). Hence a higher inflation tax is required and a higher inflation rate ensues. It is worth noting that this result will not emerge in the grey area of policy attitudes. The inflation paradox is not merely the result of the endogenous policy response being less than the real rate of interest.

In terms of Fig. 1, the MS schedule shifts towards (away from) the origin for conservative (progressive) governments after a decrease in α. If θ_g were zero, the MD schedule would be stationary. The saddle-point stable equilibrium at A_0 moves down (up) MD. If θ_g is positive, MD would shift down but would not affect the conclusion, so long as $\varepsilon < 1$.

---

[11] At very high rates of inflation, such that $\varepsilon > 1$, local stability requires $\gamma > 0$ and this result is reversed.

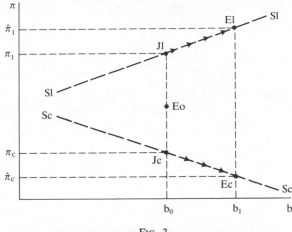

FIG. 3

Consider the transition to the steady state after an unexpected decrease in α when saddlepath stable. For conservative governments, the long run is at E_C south-west of E_0 in Fig. 3 (in which the BB and PP curves have been suppressed). At impact, b is predetermined but π collapses to π_C at J_C thus initially undershooting the required long run fall in inflation. At J_C, the movement down $S_C S_C$ implies $\dot{\pi} < 0$. Compare these outcomes with those of a fiscally liberal government. $\hat{\pi}$ rises shifting the steady state to E_l and the saddlepath to $S_l S_l$ in Fig. 3. Inflation therefore jumps to π_l and along $S_l S_l$, $\dot{\pi}$ is positive.

To summarise, the choice of θ implies critically different outcomes for the time path of inflation after a change in government financing. In low inflation circumstances, the monetarist presumption of pessimistic conservative governments will be correct. Conversely, optimistic liberal governments will find that its antimonetarist presumptions are fulfilled. The liberal result is analogous to the perverse effects of a once and for all open market operation in the Blinder–Solow (1973) model. It also emerges in Dornbusch (1977) and Liviatan (1982) for continuous open market operations. In all these papers, stability requires endogenous tax revenues in response to output. Our conservative result specifies precisely the degree of endogeneity which can eliminate the perversity; since debt and inflation are linearly related along the saddlepath, there is a unique linear relationship between our tax on debt, θ, and a non-neutral tax that operates through inflation.

Finally, observe that the effect on steady state private sector utility is ambiguous. For conservative governments, disinflation raises real money balances, reduces transactions costs and enhances consumption. However, the extra debt issued may involve an endogenous reduction in government expenditure. If government expenditure is a perfect substitute for private consumption ($\lambda = 1$), the fall in government expenditure must be utility reducing. If only taxes were used as a stabilising fiscal instrument ($\theta_g = 0$) and if the classical optimum rate of inflation was chosen ($i = 0$), disinflation would be neutral.

3.2. *Contractionary fiscal policy*

Fiscal policy in this model can be discussed in terms of tax and/or government expenditure changes that are neutral or not neutral with respect to the autonomous deficit, D. Only if θ is set at $\delta + n$ will the long run deficit and D be identical. We proceed with non-neutral tax increases and government expenditure cutbacks followed by a balanced budget contraction.

Higher taxes

The long run effects of an increase in exogenous taxes are similar to those of a decrease in γ.

In particular, from (24)–(29), one can calculate

$$\frac{d\hat{\pi}}{dt_0} = \frac{-(\hat{\pi} + n)}{D(1 - \varepsilon)} < 0$$

$$\frac{d\hat{m}}{dt_0} = \frac{\varepsilon \hat{m}}{D(1 - \varepsilon)} > 0$$

$$\frac{d\hat{b}}{dt_0} = \frac{-(1 - \alpha)\gamma}{\alpha n} < 0$$

$$\frac{d(\hat{c} + \lambda \hat{g})}{dt_0} = (1 - T_e)\hat{i} \frac{d\hat{m}}{dt_0} + (1 - T_e - \lambda)\theta_g \frac{d\hat{b}}{dt_0} \gtrless 0$$

If $\hat{\pi} + n > 0$, tax increases reduce inflation, raise real balances and reduce real debt. Similar partial derivatives were obtained for a shift towards debt finance with conservative governments but not with liberal ones. The transition paths are of some interest. In Fig. 4, the long run outcome of lower inflation and debt after fiscal contraction is shown as the shift to E_1. The conservative and liberal government saddlepaths at the new equilibria are drawn as $S_C S_C$ and $S_l S_l$. The relative fall in inflation on impact, to J_C for the conservative and J_l for the liberal government indicates that fiscal contraction leads to a more dramatic initial fall in inflation with conservative governments. The quite different effects on inflation for the two types of government occurs because of the different implications on the total government deficit of the anticipated retirements of debt on the way to the new steady state. With conservatives, easier deficits and thus rising inflation will be anticipated. Therefore an overshooting impact is required because the inflation rate must ultimately be lower. The converse occurs with liberal governments.

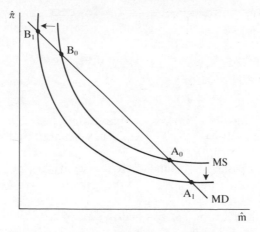

FIG. 4

Again the long run utility effects are ambiguous. With positive nominal interest rates, tax increases encourage steady state consumption and, hence, utility. This occurs because the fall in inflation can induce people to hold larger real money balances and thus to reduce their transactions costs. At the classical optimal rate of money growth, this mechanism is inoperative. In addition, the tax increases means lower debt and can raise endogenous government expenditure if $\theta_g \neq 0$. Costly private expenditure is crowded out, but a portion of government expenditure, λ, is utility inducing. If $\lambda = 1$, utility must increase.

Government expenditure cutbacks

An extra complication is introduced with autonomous government expenditure cutbacks because output can be temporarily lower and private

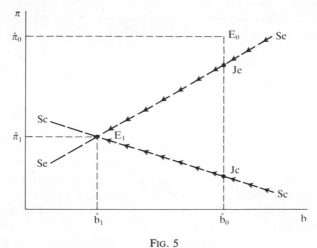

FIG. 5

sector expenditure crowded in (see (15)). However, the short and long run effects on inflation, real money balances and debt are qualitatively the same as those obtained with tax increases.

The long run effect on utility is measured by considering

$$\frac{d(\hat{c} + \lambda\hat{g})}{-dg_0} = \hat{i}\,\frac{d\hat{m}}{-dg_0} + (1 - T_e - \lambda)(1 + \theta_g)\,\frac{d\hat{b}}{-dg_0} \gtreqless 0$$

and the utility comparison between government expenditure falls and tax rises is indexed simply by $(1 - T_e - \lambda)$. If government and private spending are perfect substitutes, a tax rise is the preferred option when the autonomous deficit must be reduced. If the items of government expenditure to be cut were entirely useless to the private sector $(\lambda = 0)$, then such cuts must be preferable to tax rises.

Up to now, a proportion, λ, of government expenditure was assumed to contribute to the utility of households while $(1 - \lambda)$ was wasted. Instead, the former could be assumed to raise firm's output at the margin (for example, throught the benefits of capital spending on infrastructure or public goods). Let $y = f(\lambda g)$ such that $f' > 1$, $f'' < 0$. Once again, the only result is the utility difference between cuts in government spending and tax rises which is $(1 - T_e)(1 - \lambda f')$. If all expenditure were productive $(\lambda = 1, f' > 1)$ it would always be better to raise taxes when the deficit must be reduced.

A balanced budget contraction

If the autonomous components of government expenditure and taxes are reduced so that the deficit, D, remains constant, the total steady state tax on money and outstanding debt are unchanged in the steady state. Private expenditure is crowded in raising the demand for money. Steady state inflation decreases. Since this policy is neutral with respect to debt, the type of government is irrelevant and the impact and long run effects on inflation coincide. For utility-yielding government expenditure, the long run effect on utility is just $(1 - T_e - \lambda)$. For $\lambda = 1$, utility must fall since the crowded in private expenditure suffers from extra transactions costs.

An alternative balanced contraction involves an equal, opposite shift in the *endogenous* fiscal response parameters: $d\theta_t = -d\theta_g = d\theta^* < 0$. Qualitatively, similar results are obtained as in the autonomous case.

4. Conclusions

This paper has established a catalogue of possibilities for the relationship between fiscal policy and inflation. In particular, the outcomes will depend on the attitude of the government towards its outstanding debt. A fiscally conservative government, with its natural inbuilt high aversion to bad outcomes, will give an inordinate amount of attention to the margin needed to pre-empt unstable outcomes. On the other hand, a liberal government will display far less aversion to the possibility of instability.

These differences will generate the result that conservative governments give rise to inflation outcomes which accord with a monetarist's outlook, but with the reverse occurring with a liberal government. Positive short run deviations are obtained for conservatives even though long run inflation is lowered. Financial policy is always associated with undershooting inflation rates. However, alterations to planned budget deficits will present much more violent, short run effects on inflation with conservative governments because the inflation rate is made to overshoot.

The model has some major omissions which forbid categorical statements. First, there is no genuine market for ownership of existing capital and therefore no possibility of capital gains. This feature ensured a constant real rate of interest on debt, and permitted analytic tractability. The alternative raises the dimension of the differential equation system (see Brock and Turnovsky (1981) for a detailed model of the corporate sector.) Second, investment and capital accumulation have been ruled out. Third, a closed economy has been analysed. Fourth, all markets have been assumed to be in full equilibrium at all times. This paper has achieved the limited purpose of showing that necessarily endogenous fiscal policy matters.

University of Essex

REFERENCES

BLINDER, A. and SOLOW, R. "Does Fiscal Policy Matter?" *Journal of Public Economics*, 2, 1973 p. 319–337.

BROCK, W. A. "Money and Growth: the Case of Long Run Perfect Foresight", *International Economic Review*, October 1974, p. 750–777.

BROCK, W. A. and TURNOVSKY, S. "The Analysis of Macroeconomic Policies in Perfect Foresight Equilibrium", *International Economic Review* February 1981, p. 179–209.

BRUNNER, K. and MELTZER, A. H. "An Aggregative Theory for a Closed Economy" in J. L. Stein (ed.) *Monetarism*, North Holland, 1976, p. 69–103.

BUITER, W. H. "Saddlepoint Problems in Continuous Time Rational Expectations Models: a General Method and Some Macroeconomic Examples", *Econometrica*, May 1984, p. 665–680.

CHRIST, C. "On Fiscal and Monetary Policies and the Government Budget Restraint", *American Economic Review*, Sept. 1979, p. 526–538.

DORNBUSCH, R. and FRENKEL, J. A. "Inflation and Growth: Alternative Approaches", *Journal of Money, Credit and Banking*, Feb. 1973, p. 141–156.

FISCHER, S. "Capital Accumulation on the Transition Path in a Monetary Optimising Model", *Econometrica* 47, November 1979, p. 1433–1439.

FRIEDMAN, M. *The Optimum Quantity of Money*, Chicago: Aldine, 1969.

GIAVAZZI, F. and WYPLOSZ, C. "The Zero Root Problem: A Note on the Dynamic Determination of the Stationary Equilibrium in Linear Models", *Review of Economic Studies*, April, 1985, pp. 353–357.

GRAY, J. A., "Dynamic Instability in Rational Expectations Models: An Attempt to Clarify", *International Economic Review*, February, 1984, p. 93–122.

LIVIATAN, N. "Neutrality of Government Bonds Reconsidered", *Journal* of Public Economics, 19, 1982, p. 261–270.

LIVIATAN, N. "Tight Money and Inflation", *Journal of Monetary Economics*, 13, 1984, p. 5–15.

McCALLUM, B. "On Non-Uniqueness in Rational Expectation Models: an Attempt at Perspective", *Journal of Monetary Economics*, 112, 1983, p. 139–168.

OBSTFELD, M. and ROGOFF, K. "Speculative Hyperinflation in Maximising Models: Can we Rule Them Out?" *Journal of Political Economy*, August 1983, p. 675–705.

SARGENT, T. J. and WALLACE, N. "Some Unpleasant Monetarist Arithmetic", *Federal Reserve Bank of Minneapolis Quarterly Review* 5, 1981, p. 1–17.

SIDRAUSKI, M. "Rational Choice and Patterns of Growth in a Monetary Economy", *American Economic Review Supplement,* May 1967, p. 534–544.

TAYLOR, J. "Conditions for Unique Solutions in Stochastic Macroeconomic Models with Rational Expectations", *Econometrica,* 45, September 1977, p. 1377–1385.

TURNOVSKY, S. *Macroeconomic Analysis and Stabilisation Policy,* Cambridge University Press, 1977.

UZAWA, H. "Time Preference, the Consumption Function and Optimum Asset Holdings" in J. N. Wolfe (ed.) *Value Capital and Growth: Essays in Honor of Sir John Hicks,* Chicago: Aldine 1968.

Oxford Economic Papers 39 (1987), 111–118

A FISCAL THEORY OF HYPERDEFLATIONS?
SOME SURPRISING MONETARIST ARITHMETIC

By WILLEM H. BUITER

IN a paper that has already become a classic, Sargent and Wallace (1981, 1984) (reprinted in Sargent (1986)) explored some unfamiliar implications of the government budget constraint and proposed a "fiscal theory of inflation." Once the real per capita stock of non-monetary, interest-bearing government debt stabilises (say because it reaches some upper limit reflecting real resource constraints), and with the primary deficit (the public sector deficit net of interest payments) treated as exogenous, monetary growth is endogenously or residually determined by the requirement that the real value of seigniorage (the real value of nominal money stock increases) should satisfy the government budget constraint. Their paper then goes on to analyse the consequences for inflation, in the short run and in the long run, of short-run changes in monetary growth not accompanied by changes in the primary deficit. Elsewhere I have commented at length on that issue (Buiter (1983, 1984)). This short note focuses on a neglected aspect of the Sargent-Wallace model: its implications for the nascent theory of hyperdeflations. It is shown how, according to the equation of motion alone, a sufficiently large fiscal deficit will result in unstable, explosive behaviour of the money growth rate, the inflation rate, and the stock of real money balances. This explosive process, however, is not a hyperinflation but a hyperdeflation: the rates of money growth and inflation decline and the per capita real money stock increases without bound. Such behaviour obviously is not sustainable, and the model's side-conditions make this clear. In the Sargent-Wallace two-period, two-class overlapping generations model, the real stock of money balances equals the saving out of period one income (and the purchases of consumption goods in the second period of their lives) by the poor. Income and the supply of consumer goods are bounded; an unbounded real money stock therefore cannot characterize an equilibrium. That notwithstanding, I will suggest that the Sargent–Wallace model may temporarily generate a bit of hyperdeflation, before the unsustainability of their trajectory dawns on the inhabitants of the Sargent–Wallace universe and the model disappears off the page.

In any case, whatever the merit of hyperdeflations, in the Sargent–Wallace model deficits can never generate hyperinflations. In spite of this, the spirit, although not the letter (or the formal structure) of this model underlies Sargent's well known empirical study of four hyperinflations (Sargent (1982), reprinted in Sargent (1986)). Dornbusch and Fischer (1986) in their study of four hyperinflations note the possibility that if the deficit is too high no stationary equilibrium may exist in the Sargent–Wallace model.

They infer that "Hyperinflation would be a strong possibility (Dornbusch and Fischer 1986, p. 5)." This note shows that, with rational expectations, hyperinflation is impossible but hyperdeflation may get under way. The paucity of empirical data on hyperdeflations (indeed their absence) should not be a deterrent to a thorough theoretical analysis of the phenomenon. After all, a large fraction of the profession has worked and is now working on the theory of general competitive equilibrium.

I shall present the model in continuous time, rather than in the original discrete-time format, because of the presentational usefulness of continuous time phase-diagrams. The exact same points can, however, be made using the discrete time model. m denotes the real per capita stock of money balances; b the real per capita stock of interest-bearing public debt; δ the real per capita primary deficit; r the exogenous real interest rate; n the exogenous proportional growth rate of the population; and π the rate of inflation. The real per capita stock of debt is kept constant at a given value $b = \bar{b}$. Nominal bond issues, $\dot{B}$ are therefore just sufficient to offset the erosion in the real per capita stock of bonds due to population growth and inflation: $\dot{B} = (n + \pi)B$. The government budget constraint then implies that

$$\dot{m} = \delta + (r - n)\bar{b} - (\pi + n)m \tag{1}$$

It is assumed until further notice, that $\delta + (r - n)\bar{b} > 0$. The per capita demand for real money balances depends inversely on the expected rate of inflation. Rational inflation expectations prevail

$$m = \gamma_1 - \gamma_2\pi \qquad \gamma_1, \gamma_2 > 0 \tag{2a}$$

$$0 \leq m \leq \bar{m}. \tag{2b}$$

$\bar{m}$ is the upper bound on the real per capita money stock referred to earlier. Substituting (2a) into (1) we obtain

$$\dot{m} = \delta + (r - n)\bar{b} - (\gamma_2^{-1}\gamma_1 + n)m + \gamma_2^{-1}m^2 \tag{3}$$

This differential equation either has two, one or zero stationary equilibria. The three cases are illustrated in Figure 1a, b, c. In Fig. (1a) m_1^* is the locally unstable low inflation stationary equilibrium. m_2^* is the locally stable high inflation stationary equilibrium. It is easily checked that

$$m_{1,2}^* = \frac{\gamma_1 + n\gamma_2 \pm [(\gamma_1 + n\gamma_2)^2 - 4\gamma_2(\delta + (r - n)\bar{b})]^{\frac{1}{2}}}{2} \tag{4}$$

The case with two stationary equilibria corresponds to "small" deficts $\left(\delta + (r - n)\bar{b} < \dfrac{(\gamma_1 + n\gamma_2)^2}{4\gamma_2}\right)$. The case with no stationary equilibrium corresponds to "large" deficits $\left(\delta + (r - n)\bar{b} > \dfrac{(\gamma_1 + n\gamma_2)^2)}{4\gamma_2}\right)$.

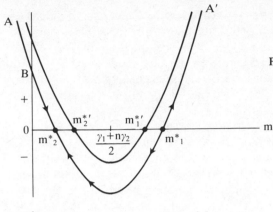

FIG. 1a. $0 < \delta + (r - n)\bar{b} < \dfrac{(\gamma_1 + n\gamma_2)^2}{4\gamma_2}$

FIG. 1b. $\delta + (r - n)\bar{b} = \dfrac{(\gamma_1 + n\gamma_2)^2}{4\gamma_2}$

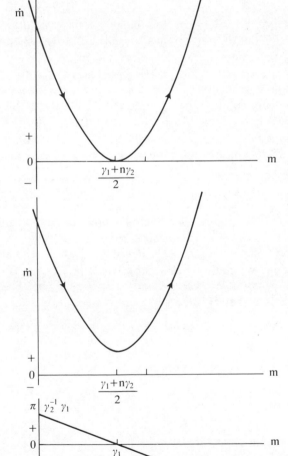

FIG. 1c. $\delta + (r - n)\bar{b} > \dfrac{(\gamma_1 + n\gamma_2)^2}{4\gamma_2}$

In their paper Sargent and Wallace considered only the small deficit case depicted in Fig. (1a). They also opted for the locally unstable low inflation steady state m_1^*. Presumably, this choice was prompted by analogy with the common practice, in linear rational espectations models, of associating non-predetermined state variables with unstable eigenvalues. The general price level in this classical, flexible price model is non-predetermined and so therefore is m.

The transversality or terminal boundary condition that the system should converge continuously (except possibly at moments when 'news' arrives) to a steady state, for constant values of the forcing variables, only suffices to determine a unique initial value for m if the steady state equilibrium in question is m_1^*. If the terminal boundary condition required convergence to m_2^*, any initial value of m on AA' to the left of m_1^* and to the right of B would be eligible. There would seem to be no economic rationale for choosing m_1^* rather than m_2^*. If m_1^* is a feasible stationary solution ($m_1^* \leqslant \bar{m}$) then so is m_2^*. No economic or physical constraints will impede solutions moving toward m_2^* from anywhere between B and m_1^*.

The issue as to whether there exist, for the small deficit case depicted in Fig. (1a), reasonable economic restrictions that allow one to choose a unique convergent solution from among the continuum of solutions that converge to m_2^* is not resolved here. Instead I propose to focus on the two diagrams in Fig. (1c), which depict the explosive, non-stationary behaviour that will be exhibited when this economy has large deficits $(\delta + (r - n)\bar{b} > \frac{(\gamma_1 + n\gamma_2)^2)}{4\gamma_2}$.

When the real per capita debt stock is constant, large deficits (strictly speaking larger inflation-and-real-growth-corrected government full employment current account deficits) require more seigniorage revenue, that is, a greater yield of the inflation tax. Let μ denote the proportional rate of growth of the nominal money stock and σ real per capita seigniorage: $\sigma \equiv \mu m$. In a steady state $\sigma = \gamma_2^{-1} m^2 - (\gamma_2^{-1} \gamma_1 + n)m$. The value of m, $\hat{m}$ say, that maximizes steady-state seigniorage is given by:

$$\hat{m} = \frac{\gamma_1 + n\gamma_2}{2} \tag{5a}$$

The maximum steady-state value of seigniorage is:

$$\hat{\sigma} = \frac{(\gamma_1 + n\gamma_2)^2}{4\gamma_2} \tag{5b}$$

The steady-state seigniorage maximizing rate of inflation is

$$\hat{\pi} = \tfrac{1}{2}(\gamma_1 \gamma_2^{-1} - n) \tag{5c}$$

Not surprisingly, the large deficit case depicted in Fig. (1c) is the one for which it is not possible to find a steady state in which the inflation tax is sufficient to close the budget gap $(\delta + (r - n)\bar{b} > \hat{\sigma})$. It is possible, however, (at least until $m > \bar{m}$) to generate the necessary seigniorage revenue in a non-steady state manner. While the high deficit economy depicted in Fig. (1c) cannot raise the necessary seigniorage at a constant rate of inflation and a constant value of m, it can generate the required inflation tax revenue with a steadily rising stock of real per capita money balances and steadily falling rates of inflation and nominal money stock growth.

A lower rate of nominal money growth will be associated with an increase in real per capita seigniorage if the elasticity of money demand with respect to the rate of monetary growth exceeds unity $\left(\eta_{m\mu} = \dfrac{-\mu \, dm}{m \, d\mu} > 1\right)$. From the money demand function (2a) we see that the effect on real seigniorage of a reduction in money growth is given by

$$\gamma_1 - \gamma_2 \pi - \mu \gamma_2 \frac{d\pi}{d\mu}$$

In steady states, $\pi = \mu - n$ and the steady-state effect on real seigniorage of a permanent reduction in the rate of growth of nominal money is positive if $\mu > \frac{1}{2}(\gamma_1 \gamma_2^{-1} + n)$, the steady-state real seigniorage maximizing rate of money growth. This will occur, for example, if in Fig. (1a) the initial stationary equilibrium is the locally stable m_2^*. A larger deficit will in that case be associated with a new long-run equilibrium such as $m_2^{*\prime}$ with a lower rate of money growth and a lower rate of inflation. Both m_2^* and $m_2^{*\prime}$ are on the wrong side of the long-run "seigniorage Laffer curve." If the relevant stationary equilibrium is the locally unstable m_1^*, a lower rate of money growth will, comparing steady states, be associated with a smaller real seigniorage revenue. Larger deficits are associated with increased inflation in the long run.

For a given real per capita deficit (i.e., along a given solution parabola in Figures 1a, b, or c above), constant real per capita seigniorage revenue equal to $\delta + (r - n)\bar{b}$ is generated at every instant, both when the *long-run* money demand schedule is elastic (for high π) and when it is inelastic (for low π).[1] Consider, for example, the explosive large deficit case depicted in Fig. (1c). With m rising, $\pi = -\gamma_2^{-1}m + \gamma_2^{-1}\gamma_1$ falling, and $\mu = \dfrac{\delta + (r - n)\bar{b}}{m}$ falling, the same amount of real seigniorage is raised with a steadily falling inflation tax rate and a steadily expanding inflation tax base.[2]

---

[1] Obviously along any given solution parabola, the instaneous elasticity of money demand with respect to the rate of money growth, $\eta_{m\mu}$ equals unity.

[2] Note that, if $m > 0$ and $\delta + (r - n)\bar{b} > 0$, μ always remains positive for finite values of m. π is a linear decreasing function of m and will be negative for $m > \gamma_1$. There will be an increasing divergence between the growth rate of the nominal money stock and the rate of inflation, since $\dfrac{d\pi}{d\mu} = \dfrac{m^2}{(\delta + (r - n)\bar{b})\gamma_2}$ increases with m.

Thus the price of fiscal irresponsibility appears to be hyperdeflation. Clearly, if such a process got underway if could not be sustained because of the real resource constraints that set an upper bound on m. There exists a view of rational expectations models which holds that a process that cannot be sustained would not get started. I consider such a view to be unnecessarily restrictive and would regard as admissable those solution trajectories that spend some time on an explosive, unsustainable course.

Even if one rejects the conclusion that the Sargent–Wallace model generates hyperdeflation as a result of large inflation-and-real-growth corrected public sector current account deficits, there is no way in which that model can ever generate hyperinflation. If the hyperdeflation case (Fig. (1c)) is ruled out, then there is simply *no* solution to the large deficit $[\delta + (r - n)\bar{b} > \hat{\sigma}]$ case. There isn't a hyperinflation solution. If we are in the small deficit case $(0 < \delta + (r - n)\bar{b} < \hat{\sigma})$ of Fig. (1a) an increase in the deficit can either raise the long-run rate of inflation (if we choose the locally unstable equilibrium) or lower the long-run rate of inflation (if we choose the locally stable equilibrium). Even when the long-run inflation rate increases, this increase is a finite one, not a run-away explosive hyperinflation.

Now consider the case where the inflation-and-real growth connected government current account deficit is negative: $\delta + (r + n)\bar{b} < 0$. This government surplus economy is depicted in Fig. (2). $\delta + (r - n)\bar{b}$ is measured by the intersection of the parabola with the vertical $\dot{m}$ axis at B.

Note that as long as $\gamma_1 + n\gamma_2 > 0$, there will still be one stationary

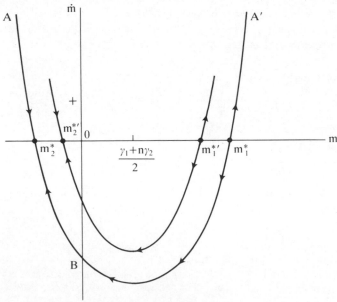

FIG. 2. $\delta + (r - n)\bar{b} < 0 < \dfrac{\gamma_1 + n\gamma_2}{2}$

equilibrium with a positive value of m, the unstable one at m_1^*. If we conside only non-negative values of m to be admissable and if we impose the "no-bubble" transversality condition that if there exists a convergent solution, the economy will pick it, solutions will be unique. The response of the system to a reduction in the surplus then is the same as the response to an increase in the deficit in Fig. (1a) when the locally unstable stationary equilibrium m_1^* is considered to be the relevant one. The long-run effect (and also the impact effect if the reduction in the surplus is unanticipated, immediate and permanent) is a finite increase in the rate of inflation. If we admit bubbles, the system could either move north-east along $m_1^* A'$ (the hyperdeflation case) or along $m_1^* B$ with a falling m and a rising rate of inflation. Even when m hits zero, at B, the rate of inflation is only $\gamma_2^{-1} \gamma_1$. This may seem paradoxical until it is realized that m becomes equal to zero not because the price level becomes infinite with a positive nominal money stock, but because the nominal money stock declines to zero with a finite (if rising) price level as the government uses its surpluses to contract the nominal money stock. The grounds for confining the analysis (in Fig. (1a, b, and c) as well as in Fig. (2)) to a non-negative real money stock then become rather shaky. It is indeed simple to modify the Sargent–Wallace model in such a way as to permit the poor private agents to borrow from the government by issuing monetary liabilities. Negative values of m then simply reflect negative values of the nominal money stock, i.e., a net creditor position of the government vis-à-vis its poor citizens. The case of Fig. 2 then becomes in all important respects the same as the small deficit case depicted in Fig. (1a). Whichever way one turns it, the model cannot generate a hyperinflation.

One might be tempted to try and save the model for the analysis of hyperinflations by restricting the analysis to the range of 'small' deficits for which there are two stationary equilibria and identifying as hyperinflation the transition from the low inflation stationary equilibrium to thc high inflation stationary equilibrium. This, however, would be a bit silly. Both stationary equilibria are just that: well-behaved long-run equilibria with constant, finite rates of inflation. There is nothing "runaway" or exploseve about the transition from the low to the high inflation steady state. In fact the move from the low inflation equilibrium to the high inflation equilibrium involves initially an accelerating rate of inflation ($\dot{\pi}$ rises) but ultimately a decelerating rate of inflation ($\dot{\pi}$ falls) with $\dot{\pi}$ smoothly approaching zero as the economy eases into the high inflation steady state. (See the transition from π_L to π_H in Fig. 3). To describe the traverse from π_L to π_H as a hyperinflation is akin to describing a mild summer breeze as a hurricane. Unlike the adaptive expectations (Cagan (1956)) version of this model, the Sargent and Wallace (1984) rational expectations version cannot generate hyperinflations.

While there is a certain scarcity of empirical observations on hyperdeflations, one can take encouragement from the thought that among the many

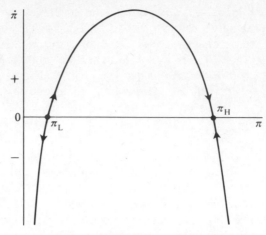

FIG. 3.

countries now facing intractable budgetary deficits, there may well be a few that will be compelled to monetize these deficits at ever decreasing rates of monetary growth. The United States might even be the place where this new chapter in monetary history is written.

REFERENCES

BUITER, W. H. (1983). "Deficits, Crowding Out and Inflation: The Simple Analytics," *NBER* Working Paper No. 1078, February 1983.

BUITER, W. H. (1984) "Comment on T. J. Sargent and N. Wallace: Some Unpleasant Monetarist Arithmetic," in B. Griffiths and G. E. Wood eds. *Monetarism in the U.K.,* MacMillan, London, pp. 42–60.

CAGAN, P. (1956) "The Monetary Dynamics of Hyperinflation," in M. Friedman, ed. *Studies in the Quantity Theory of Money,* Chicago, University of Chicago Press.

DORNBUSCH, R. and S. FISCHER (1986) "Stopping Hyperinflations Past and Present." *NBER* Working Paper No. 1810, January.

SARGENT, T. J. and N. WALLACE (1981) "Some Unpleasant Monetarist Arithmetic," *Federal Reserve Bank of Minneapolis Quarterly Review* 5, Fall, pp. 117.

SARGENT, T. J. (1982) "The Ends of Four Big Inflations," in R. E. Hall ed. *Inflation: Causes and Effects,* University of Chicago Press, pp. 41–97.

SARGENT, T. J. and N. WALLACE (1984) "Some Unpleasant Monetarist Arithmetic," in B. Griffiths and G. E. Wood eds. *Monetarism in the U.K.,* MacMillan, London, pp. 42–60.

SARGENT, T. J. (1986) *Rational Expectations and Inflation,* Harper & Row, New York.

Oxford Economic Papers 39 (1987), 119–132

KEYNESIAN, NEW KEYNESIAN AND NEW CLASSICAL ECONOMICS

By B. GREENWALD *and* J. E. STIGLITZ[1]

1. Introduction

FOR more than two centuries, there have been two opposing views of the capitalist economy. One stresses its virtues, and the efficiency with which prices carry information between consumers and producers, and allocate resources. The other spotlights the shortcomings of the market system, and particularly its episodes of massive unemployment of capital and labour. Adherents of the first group usually treat unemployment as a temporary aberration that market forces will cure if left to themselves. The New Classical Economists have gone further. They interpret changes in employment levels as rational agents' responses to perceived changes in relative prices: workers in 1932, for example, took more leisure because relative wages looked low. They liken unemployed capital to a spare tyre—spare capacity held for those few times when it is really needed. To the critics of capitalism, such views are dangerous, unscientific nonsense, misleading governments into acquiescing in the grave social and private costs of high unemployment. Keynes reconciled these conflicting views of capitalism. He confronted the unemployment problem, and argued that limited government intervention could solve it. Once unemployment was removed, the classical vision of the efficient market could be restored. Samuelson dubbed this the Neoclassical Synthesis.

The Neoclassical Synthesis was taken as an article of faith. Fundamental questions about the failures of the market system, such as the causes of periodic depressions and the unemployment that accompanied them, were avoided. Keynesian economics created schizophrenia in the way that economics was taught: microeconomic courses, in which students were introduced to Adam Smith's invisible hand and the fundamental theorems of welfare economics, were followed by macroeconomic courses, focusing on the failures of the market economy and the role of government in correcting them. Two sub-disciplines developed. Microeconomists criticized macroeconomists for their lack of rigour and theoretical foundations. Macroeconomists castigated microeconomists for the unrealism and inappropriateness of their theories. Dissatisfaction with Keynesian economics was also based on the want of explanation for some of its central assumptions, particularly concerning the sluggishness of prices and wages. Why did wages and prices not fall enough in recessions? Why didn't firms that wanted to sell more simply lower their prices? A quarter of a century of research failed to provide convincing answers to these questions. This state of affairs could not continue for long.

[1] Financial support from the National Science Foundation and the Hoover Institution is gratefully acknowledged. The authors wish to thank Peter Sinclair for comments on an earlier draft of this paper.

There were two ways in which the two sub-disciplines could be recon-
nected. Macrotheory could be adapted to microtheory; and the converse.
New Classical Economics took the first approach. Its advocates aimed to
derive the dynamic, aggregative behaviour of the economy from the basic
principles of rational, maximizing firms and individuals. The School
recognized the importance of dynamics for understanding macro-behaviour,
and the central role of expectations in shaping those dynamics. It focused
attention, then, on the consequences of rational expectation formation, and
it is this aspect of their work which has given the School its alternative
name, the Rational Expectations School.[2]

The other approach seeks to adapt microtheory to macrotheory. For the
want of a better term, one can refer to it as the New Keynesian Economics.
The phenomena of unemployment, credit rationing and business cycles are
inconsistent with standard microeconomic theory. New Keynesian Economics aims to develop a microtheory that can account for them. There are
numerous different strands to New Keynesian Economics, taken in its
broadest possible sense. One major element is the study of imperfect
information and incomplete markets.

This paper aims to present a broad outline of this aspect of the New
Keynesian Economics, and to show how it resembles and differs from
traditional Keynesian Economics. Keynes himself had a novel, and markedly non-neoclassical vision of how the economy worked. Keynes used
picturesque language to describe the behaviour of entrepreneurs: they were
moved by "animal spirits". But when Keynesian economics came to be
codified, and presented in the form of a simple model (as in chapter 18 of
the *General Theory,* and the expositions of others, such as Hicks (1937) and
Klein (1948)), earlier modes of thinking crept back. We contend that this
vision, captured so well in many of his brilliant passages, provides greater
understanding of unemployment and business cycles than do the formal
Keynesian models.[3]

2. Some important Keynesian insights

Four of Keynes' many insights we regard as essential to the explanation of
unemployment and business fluctuations. These are:

---

[2] The leading proponents of the New Classical Economics, Barro, Lucas, Sargent and
Wallace, have consistently based their models upon rational expectations. But their central
doctrines derive not from rational expectations *per se,* but from the *old classical* assumption
that markets always clear. It is this last assumption that leads directly to the conclusions that
(involuntary) unemployment cannot exist, and that macro stabilization policy may well be
ineffective. Neary and Stiglitz (1983) have shown that with rational expectations and price
rigidities, government policy is even more effective than under myopic expectations: multipliers
are even larger; and Buiter (1981) and Taylor (1985) provide numerous other examples where
rational expectations do *not* imply policy impotence.
[3] Leijonhufvud (1968) expresses a not dissimilar view, although in terms of his distinction
between Keynesian Economics and the Economics of Keynes, we would wish to classify
chapter 18 of the *General Theory* as an early example of the former.

1. A general theory must account for the *persistence* of unemployment
2. A general theory must account for the *fluctuations* in unemployment
3. Savings and investment must be carefully distinguished
4. Disturbances in demand, not supply, underlie the cyclical behaviour of macroeconomic aggregates.

2.1. *The persistence of unemployment*

Keynes attributed the persistence of unemployment to the failure of wages to adjust with sufficient speed to clear labour markets, while at the same time stressing, in chapter 19 of the *General Theory,* that greater flexibility in money wage rates need not exert stabilizing effects. An assumption that money wage rates are frozen is integral to the Fixed Price School, exemplified, among others, by Barro and Grossman (1971). But this premise fails to square with evidence (money wage rates fell by one third in the Great Slump in the United States), and cries out for theoretical justification. In fact, Keynesian conclusions do not require absolute rigidity in money wage rates. All that is needed is that wages fail to fall to market clearing levels. As we shall see below, efficiency wage models offer a compelling set of explanations for the critical Keynesian contention that wage rates fail to clear the markets for labour.

2.2. *The fluctuations in unemployment*

Turning to the second issue, the fluctuations in unemployment, we face two questions. What is the source of shocks which cause them? Why do changes in prices fail to dampen their effects? The shocks that generate macroeconomic fluctuations are rarely, if ever, wholly exogenous to the economic system. Evidence suggests that they often take the form of changes in the demand for investment, and in particular for inventories. Yet if production functions are concave, and recessions are characterized by relatively low real wage and/or interest rates, intertemporal production smoothing should occur. Inventories should serve to limit fluctuations, not exacerbate them. Keynes rightly stressed the role of investment in macro-economic fluctuations. But he attributed the changes in investment to animal spirits, to unexplained changes in expectations. His story is less than complete.

To account for fluctuations in unemployment, Keynes invoked changes in the demand for investment; but he also had to say why prices, and in particular interest rates, failed to change by enough to offset them. In the *General Theory,* he argued that nominal interest rates would fall little if money demand were highly interest-elastic. One difficulty here is that it is real, not nominal, interest rates that should matter for investment; real rates take account of the rate of price inflation. In fact, the slump of the 1930s saw prices fall, and real interest rates rose somewhat. There must also be doubts (vented by Keynes himself, if with greater emphasis in the *Treatise on Money* than in the *General Theory*) about how much extra investment a given fall in interest rates could secure (and when).

The New Keynesian Economics offers a somewhat different account of the determination of investment, and in particular for the likely failure of interest rates to clear credit markets. These will be examined below. It also provides firm foundations for the tendency for swings in macroeconomic activity to become self-amplifying. But it has yet to furnish a complete explanation for the business cycle. It shows how shocks can induce protracted, major changes in investment and employment, but it treats such shocks as exogenous, not endogenous, phenomena.

2.3. *Savings and investment*

Keynes' third important insight that merits stress at this point is his distinction between savings and investment:

> "Those who think ⟨that an act of individual saving leads to a parallel act of investment⟩ . . . are deceived . . . . They are fallaciously supposing that there is a nexus which unites decisions to abstain from present consumption with decisions to provide for future consumption; whereas the motives which determine the latter are not linked in any simple way with the motives which determine the former" (*General Theory*, p. 21)

One aspect of this distinction is the difference between funds within the firm, and funds at the disposal of households. If capital markets were perfect, this difference would carry no particular implications for the spending of households and firms. In his *Treatise on Money*, Keynes had written at length about what he called the Fringe of Unsatisfied Borrowers, and the wider economic significance of credit rationing (chapter 37, section (iii)(b), and elsewhere). These powerful ideas are almost eclipsed in the *General Theory*, although a definite echo can be found on p. 158. One can rationalize Keynes' claim that it is current income that exercises the dominant influence upon consumers' spending two ways: either current income may be taken as a good forecast of (unobservable) future income, or else capital market imperfections may be adduced to explain it. It is the latter view, pursued by Flemming (1973) among others, upon which the New Keynesian Economics lays most stress.

2.4. *Supply and demand*

Keynes needed, as we said, to find a source of fluctuations in economic activity. It was apparent that changes in technology, in supply, could not account for what was occurring in the Great Depression. He therefore naturally turned to changes in demand. Those brought up in the Marshallian tradition were schooled in analysing demand and supply disturbances separately.

Keynes' reliance on the Marshallian demand/supply framework posed problems which he, and his followers, never satisfactorily resolved. For the

Marshallian theory suggested that equilibrium ought to be at the intersection of demand and supply; if firms were on their supply curves, real product wages should rise as employment falls. This was one of the first empirical propositions of Keynesian economics to fall by the way-side. But just as Marxian economics was never abandoned by its proponents, simply because its predictions turned out to be wrong, so too Keynesian economics was not to be abandoned simply because one of its empirical predictions was unconfirmed. There are three ways of dealing with uncomfortable facts: (a) to deny them, e.g. by asserting that wages and prices are measured incorrectly (just as the New Classical economists approach the unemployment problem by denying the relevence of the unemployment statistics); (b) to provide a new interpretation, e.g. by asserting what is relevant is not the spot wage, because of the existence of long term (implicit) contracts, ignoring the fact that real product wages of newly hired workers or workers on spot contracts also did not rise significantly; (c) to assert that the empirical proposition was not central to the theory. Thus, a large literature developed, asserting that firms, while solving quite complicated intertemporal maximization problems, acted as if the price and quantities they faced were fixed. It was simply asserted that firms did not use price policy to affect sales, an implausible and counterfactual assumption.[4]

3. The New Keynesian Economics

The New Keynesian Economics begins with Keynes' basic insights. But it recognizes the need for a more radical departure from the neoclassical framework, and for a much deeper study of the consequences of imperfections in capital markets, imperfections which can be explained by the costs of information. The major ingredients of this new perspective are:

1. Efficiency wage theories
2. Capital market imperfections
3. Credit rationing
4. A revised view of the role of monetary policy

We examine each in turn.

3.1. *Efficiency wage models*

Efficiency wage models[5] are based on the hypothesis that there is imperfect information about the characteristics of workers; that the actions

---

[4] Models which postulate imperfectly competitive firms explain why real wages may not equal the value of the marginal product; but they have little to say about involuntary unemployment (indeed, in contrast to models with classical unemployment, with real wages in excess of the value of the marginal product, here real wages are less than the value of the marginal product; whether employment is higher or lower in equilibrium simply depends on the (uncompensated) labour supply elasticities) or about its fluctuations. Below, we provide an explanation for cyclical variability in mark-ups. See also Stiglitz (1984).

[5] For surveys of efficiency wage theories, see Stiglitz (1986a, 1986b).

of individual workers cannot be adequately monitored; and that it is not possible to write contracts that ensure that the worker bears all the consequences of his actions.

As a result, the quality of the labour force, its productivity (and hence the firm's profits) may increase with the wage paid. Similarly, labour turnover may decrease with an increase in the wage, and since the firm must bear some part of the turnover costs, again profits may increase with an increase in wages, up to some point. In the face of unemployment, wages may not fall, for firms will recognize that if they lower wages, productivity will decrease, turnover may increase, and profits will fall. In this perspective, firms are competitive; there are many firms in the market; but nonetheless firms are wage setters, at least within a range. If the Walrasian wage, where the demand for labour equals the supply, is too low, any firm has the option of raising its wage and thus increasing its profits. The *efficiency wage,* the wage that maximizes the firm's profits, may of course vary with economic circumstances; hence the wage is not absolutely rigid. But wages need not fall to market clearing levels.[6]

It can be objected that the presence of wage rigidities in some sector(s) of the economy is not sufficient to explain unemployment.[7] So long as there is some sector with flexible wages, any individual who chooses not to work there is voluntarily unemployed. We view this to be largely a semantic objection: the fact is that individuals who are observationally indistinguishable from the unemployed individual are being employed at higher wages; that the market equilibrium is inefficient; and that resources which could be productively employed remain idle.[8]

Efficiency wage theories explain why wages may fail to clear labour markets. Analogous models for capital markets can explain why interest rates may fail to achieve equality between the demand and supply of credit (Stiglitz and Weiss 1981, 1983, 1985). More generally, Akerlof and Yellen (1985) have pointed out that even when firms should change the wages they pay they may not do so; they show that the loss of profits from this

---

[6] Thus, the policy implications of these theories may be markedly different from those of the standard fixed wage-price models. The latter assume that economic policy has no effect on the wages paid. The efficiency wage models recognize that certain policies (e.g. unemployment compensation) may have strong effects on equilibrium wages, and the consequences of this need to be taken into account.

[7] This is, of course, not the only objection to efficiency wage theory. For a more extended discussion, see Stiglitz (1986b).

[8] Elsewhere (Greenwald and Stiglitz (1986b)) we have discussed a variety of reasons why it may be rational for an individual to reject a low wage now, if he believes that a better paying job will become available in the near future. These have to do with asymmetric information, with the information conveyed by the individual's willingness to accept a low wage job as well as with the fact that once someone is unemployed, he becomes "used labour" with adverse effects on future wages similar to those that arise in Akerlof's (1970) lemons model (see Greenwald (1986)). We have also discussed why a worker might wish to decline an employer's offer of a low wage now, coupled with a higher wage in future if the firm survives, because to accept it would, in effect, make the worker take an equity position in the firm (Greenwald and Stiglitz (1987)).

near-rational behaviour may be small, even though the loss to society may
be large. Indeed, if firms are risk averse (as we argue below they will be),
and if there is some uncertainty about the consequences of wage changes,
keeping wages unchanged in the face of certain disturbances is fully-
rational. Again, similar arguments hold for the capital market.

Moreover, the efficiency wage models further show why the wages of
firms are interdependent: the optimal wage for any one firm depends on the
wages paid by all other firms. This interdependence may lead to multiple
equilibria, in which no firm changes its wage even in the face of changes in
its demand.[9] Thus, by explaining wage, interest rate, and price rigidities,
these theories help to explain why certain disturbances are amplified as a
result of the repercussions they induce within the economic system, rather
than dampened.

There is a further set of reasons for the "multiplication" of disturbances.
In the presence of incomplete markets and imperfect information, the
actions of one firm or individual exerts externality-like effects on others; the
reduction of production by one firm, in response to increased uncertainty or
a reduction in its working capital, increases the uncertainty and reduces the
working capital of other firms. While price adjustments tend to dampen
disturbances, externality effects may (and in these instances do) exacerbate
them.

3.2. *Capital market imperfections*

Capital market imperfections derive from imperfect information. There
are asymmetries of information between managers of firms and potential
investors, asymmetries which can give rise to what one can call "equity
rationing." Equity rationing matters because it means that if firms wish to
obtain more capital, to invest or to increase production, they must borrow
the funds; and even if they are able to do so, they must expose themselves
to considerable risk, including the risk of bankruptcy (the risk of not being
able to pay back the promised amounts).

The consequences of this are exacerbated by the absence of futures
markets. Thus, firms cannot sell the goods which they plan to produce until
after they have produced them. Every production decision is a risk decision,
a risk which they (the managers and equity holders) must bear, and which
they cannot easily shift on to others. The absence of futures markets implies
that firms cannot sell their output at the time of production.

Thus, an analysis of firm behavior must focus on its willingness to
undertake these risks. Unexpected changes in its working capital base
(caused for instance by unexpected changes in the prices at which it can sell
its existing stock of goods) could, for instance, have a deleterious effect on
its willingness to produce.

---

[9] Again similar arguments hold for the capital market and the product market.

3.3 Credit rationing

While at times considerations of potential risk limit the amount that firms are willing to produce, at other times, firms' access to capital is limited; there is credit rationing. The reasons that suppliers of capital do not raise interest rates in the presence of an excess demand for capital are analogous to the reasons that firms do not lower wages in the presence of an excess supply of labour: increasing interest rates may lower the expected return to the supplier of capital, either because of selection effects (the mix of applicants changes adversely) or because of incentive effects (borrowers are induced to undertake riskier actions.)

3.4. A revised view of the role for monetary policy

Monetary policy exerts its influence—when it does—not so much through the willingness of individuals to hold cash balances, but through the availability of credit. Asymmetries of information imply that if banks decide to lend less, there are not other potential lenders who are perfect substitutes. Banks' decisions to lend are analogous to those determining firms' willingness to produce. The monetary authorities can take actions which affect banks' willingness to lend (or the terms under which they are willing to lend.) Though, depending on the economic circumstances, other lenders may take partially offsetting actions, their actions can never be fully offsetting.

3.5. A new general theory

The New Keynesian Economics provides a general theory of the economy, derived from micro-economic principles (and thus integrates the two sub-disciplines.) It succeeds both in filling the lacunae in traditional Keynesian theory (e.g. by explaining partial wage rigidities, rather than simply assuming rigid wages) and resolving the paradoxes and inconsistencies of more traditional Keynesian theory (both the internal inconsistencies, e.g. concerning how expectations are formed, and the inconsistencies between its predictions and observations.) It provides an explanation both for an equilibrium level of unemployment (through the efficiency wage theories) and for business fluctuations.[10] The theory of business fluctuations it provides is simple: in broad outline, certain shocks to the economy affect the stock of working capital of firms. Even if firms had perfect access to the credit markets (that is, they could borrow as much as they wished, at the actuarially fair interest rate), the amount they would be willing to borrow is limited by their willingness to bear risk; the fixed commitments associated

---

[10] This is not to say that there are not important gaps in the theory which remain. The theory developed so far does not provide an entirely endogenous business cyle; it only explains how the economy responds to certain shocks.

There remains a controversy over whether an entirely endogenous business cycle theory is required, or whether one should be content with a theory which translates certain kinds of shocks into disturbances in which the economy persists below "full employment" for a number of periods. We do not take a position on that issue here.

with loan contracts implies that, as the working capital which is available is reduced, the risk (bankruptcy probability) associated with any level of borrowing increases. Thus, if their working capital is reduced, their desired production level (given that they do not have fixed commitments to sell their products[11]) is lowered; and it takes time to restore working capital to normal levels. The theory explains not only why both aggregate shocks (like an unexpected decrease in the price level, resulting from a monetary shock) and sectoral shocks (like an unexpected shift in demand, or the unexpected formation of an oil cartel) would exert aggregative effects: willingness to produce will, in general, be a concave function of working capital, and hence a redistribution of working capital will have aggregative effects.[12]

In the discussion below, we shall show how this theory provides an explanation for several of the phenomena which seemed so hard for more traditional Keynesian theory to explain: (a) it explains why firms do not lower prices in recessions, i.e. it explains cyclical movements in mark-ups; (b) it provides an explanation of cyclical behaviour of investment and inventories; (c) it provides an explanation for why unemployed workers do not succeed in getting hired by offering to work for lower wages, and even in industries where efficiency wage considerations are not important, it provides a partial explanation for why workers do not offer to work for lower wages, in return for the promise of higher wages in the future; and (d) it provides an explanation for why an unanticipated wage-price reduction might actually serve to exacerbate the recession, rather than alleviate it (by further deteriorating the working capital base of firms).

4. Some shortcomings in Keynes, and the new Keynesian resolution

It is a matter for regret that Keynes' summary of his arguments in chapter 18 of the *General Theory*, and the formal modelling of Keynes' thinking by many later writers, relied so much upon the neoclassical and Marshallian tools which then, as now, were the style of the day.[13] A much richer picture emerges from the *General Theory* taken as a whole. Yet this picture is

---

[11] Even if they have commitments, potential purchasers may not honour those commitments, particularly in the event of their bankruptcy. In recessions, the risk associated with any "commitment" is increased.

[12] These redistribution effects seem to be at least as important as others sometimes postulated with government debt policy (the change in the maturity structure of the debt having either an intertemporal or an intratemporal redistribution effect) or with some forms of insurance.

The redistribution resulting from insurance associated with implicit labour contracts, a redistribution from the corporate to the household sector, operates essentially through the mechanism described above. In the presence of perfect capital markets, the only effects arising from that redistribution would be those associated with differing marginal propensities to consume between capitalists and workers.

[13] Quite possibly the reason for this was that, to win acceptance for the new ideas, Keynes and his expositors wished to demonstrate that only a few changes in the basic assumptions that underlay much conventional thinking about the economy, could lead to dramatically different results.

defective in certain respects, particularly in its treatment of the firm and the role of money, and, underlying these, its analysis of capital markets.

4.1. *Equities and bonds*

One weakness was Keynes' aggregation of long term bonds and equities (as may be seen, for example, in footnote 1 on p. 151 of the *General Theory*). Even in the absence of bankruptcies, these two sets of assets differ in their risk properties. Recessions raise bond values; equities fall. This makes them highly imperfect substitutes from the investor's standpoint. Still more important are the differences in the nature of the firm's commitment: with bonds and loans, the firm is committed to paying back a certain amount on a particular date; with equities, no such commitment exists. As a result, for firms as well as investors, there two securities are far from perfect substitutes. Particularly in recessionary periods, firms seldom resort to the equity market to raise needed capital: investors suspect that any firm wishing to do so is in bad straits, unable to obtain capital from banks or other sources. Elsewhere, we (Greenwald, Stiglitz, and Weiss (1984)) have provided a simple adverse selection model in which only the worst firms will in fact resort to the equity market to raise capital.

4.2. *Supply and demand again*

Keynes' attempt to explain economic fluctuations in terms of demand considerations alone not only posed the quandary we have referred to before—why don't firms use price policy to increase their sales—but posed another problem: how could a small open economy ever face Keynesian unemployment problems? Simply by changing its exchange rate, it could face unlimited demand for its products.

In our theory, there is not a clean distinction between demand and supply. Firms would be willing to produce more, if they could have an assured demand. In this sense, demand is limiting production. Firms are not willing to produce more, given the risks associated with production in the absence of an assured demand. In this sense, firms are on their supply curve. Our theory thus explains why the amount of goods firms are willing to supply, at any expected real product wage, may change over the business cycle.

Our theory can also explain why firms, in setting their prices, might attempt to have a higher mark-up over costs in recessionary periods. In markets with imperfect competition and imperfect information, firms must recruit customers. They do so partially by using price policies. They thus face a trade-off, lower prices today leading to higher future sales, higher future profits, but lower current profits. The price they choose depends on the *implicit* cost of capital (not the market rate of interest), and in the presence of equity rationing, this may be higher in recessionary periods.

4.3. Investment

Keynes argued that the primary determinant of the level of investment, for a given set of expectations, was the interest rate. Though there has always been some ambiguity about whether this is the real or nominal interest rate, the only sense that one can make of this is that it must have been the real interest rate. But real market interest rates have fluctuated relatively little (until the 1980s). A good theory should never take a constant (or an almost constant) as an explanatory variable.

In our theory, credit availability at certain times is the major determinant of the level of investment. It is precisely at those times that monetary policy can affect the level of economic activity. In recessionary periods, however, banks may be willing to lend to any "good" prospect at the going interest rate, but there is a shortage of willing borrowers. In such circumstances, monetary policy is likely to be ineffective.

The Keynesian-neoclassical theory simply cannot explain inventory fluctuations, the fact that inventories serve to exacerbate rather than to dampen fluctuations. Our theory can Again, the increase in the effective cost of capital—the result of equity rationing and the decrease in the supply of working capital—implies that firms will wish to decrease their inventories in recessionary periods.

4.4. The monetary mechanism

The mechanism by which the monetary authorities affected the level of economic activity in Keynesian analysis is implausible. There are three steps: (a) the government takes actions which affect the money supply; (b) given individuals' demand functions for money (a function presumably of interest rates and income), interest rates change; (c) as a result of interest rate changes, investment changes.[14]

There are problems with each of the steps: while the government may be able to affect the supply of outside money, there are close, near money substitutes, at least for transactions purposes. Moreover, money is not required for most transactions, only credit. (This is what makes those models which are based on the cash-in-advance constraint so implausible.) And to the extent that money is required for transactions purposes, one must explain why that is so. Moreover, the relationship between transactions and income is tenuous: many, perhaps most, transactions are exchanges of assets, and the kinds of economic changes associated with the

---

[14] This is obviously an oversimplification. In some variants of the theory, the demand for money depends only on income, and hence, given rigid prices, a decrease in the supply of money must be accompanied by a decrease in income. No plausible mechanisms by which this is effected have been put forward.

In other theories, the demand for investment is a function of expected future incomes, which in turn are a function of current income. The fluctuations in investment then become as much a consequence as a cause of income fluctuations. It is hard to reconcile such naive accelerator models with rational behaviour.

business cycle are often accompanied by changes in wealth, and hence in asset distribution.

To the extent that money demand is based on asset considerations, what is relevant, of course, is not income, but wealth. And since there are short term bonds which are, except for transactions purposes, perfect substitutes for money, the relevant opportunity cost of holding money is the short term money rate of interest; but if any interest rate is relevant for investment, it should be the real rate of interest.[15] Moreover, as the recent development of Cash Management Accounts makes clear, it is clearly feasible to provide interest bearing "money," in which case the only relevant question facing the individual is the maturity structure of the debt which he wishes to hold.

More recent Keynesians (e.g. Tobin (1969)) have proposed another mechanism by which monetary policy affects economic activity: In the general portfolio approach, different assets (short term, long term bonds) are seen as imperfect substitutes, and changes in the relative supply affect different interest rates, and, in particular, the price of equities. This can be criticized on several grounds. First, firms do not, for the most part, resort to the equities market to raise capital. Thus the price of equities is not directly relevant. How can we explain the observed correlations? In our theory, optimistic expectations, say about future sales, will be reflected in a high price of equities (high future profits), and in managers' willingness to produce. There is a correlation, but not causation.

To put it another way, what managers and controlling stockholders are concerned about is not the price of equities today, but the price of equities when they go to sell their shares. The current price may be a good forecast of future prices, but businessmen are more likely to base their judgments concerning particular investment projects not on the judgments of some relatively uninformed outsider, but on their more well informed insider views.

Secondly, in theory, changes in the maturity structure of the government's debt should have no effect on the market equilibrium, provided that there are not significant redistributive consequences of that change (and these seem implausible.) For those changes represent changes in the (stochastic) future tax liabilities of individuals. Individuals, in deciding on their optimal portfolios, should take into account other aspects of the risks which they face, including wage and tax risks; and if they do this correctly, there will be no effects on real interest rates. The Tobin approach would, in a perfect capital market, seem to rely on irrational behavior.

Actually, we are sympathetic with the Tobin portfolio approach, because

---

[15] It is not clear whether it should be the long term or short term real interest rate. When the question is, when should a project be undertaken, the short term real interest rate is presumably relevant; when the question is, should a project be undertaken, it is presumably the long term real interest rate. Since the information relevant to undertaking a project (the set of suppliers, the prices at which factors can be purchased, etc.) becomes obsolete so rapidly, in many cases at least the question posed by firms is more the latter than the former.

these results on the Irrelevance of Public Financial Policy depend critically on the existence of a perfect capital market, an assumption which we have previously called into question. But the mechanism by which investment is affected is not through the change in interest rates or the price of equities, but through the availability of credit.

5. Concluding remarks

5.1. *On methodology*

Capitalist economies are complicated. A model is supposed to capture its central features, not reproduce it exactly. Decisions of individuals and firms today are based on future expectations, and are affected by past decisions. Individuals do not have perfect foresight or rational expectations concerning the future. The events which they confront often appear to be unique, and there is no way that they can form a statistical model predicting the probability distribution of outcomes. And there is little evidence that they even attempt to do so. At the same time, individuals are not myopic. They do not simply assume that the future is like the present.

Markets are not perfect. But markets do exist. Prices do adjust. Wages fall in the presence of massive unemployment. These "facts" pose some important strategic decisions for the modeller: within the foreseeable future, it is not possible to construct a dynamic model adequately reflecting all of them. Polar cases are easier to study. Should one assume perfect wage or price flexibility or no wage or price flexibility? Rational expectations or myopia? Any set of choices is open to criticism, but equally, can be defended as part of a long term research strategy.

In our view, the choices must be dictated by the phenomenon to be studied. If this is unemployment, to begin the analysis by assuming market clearing is to assume away what is to be explained. Important as it is to understand the dynamic maximization problems individual and firms are engaged in, ignoring the important constraints they face (e.g. on the accesss to capital markets) results in models which are of little relevance. We suspect that in many instances, myopic models focusing on the constraints are far better than "rational" models ignoring them. Indeed, in some cases, one can show that the rational models with constraints look identical to the standard myopic models (e.g. with rule driven behaviour, all of profits and none of wages saved.)

5.2. *On policy*

There has been a long standing controversy over what governments should do in the face of unemployment: (a) nothing; (b) encourage wage reductions; (c) use monetary policy; or (d) increase government expenditures. The success of Keynesian theory has much to do with the fact that it provided a theoretical justification for those who wished to take the fourth course. The success of the New Classical theory has much to do with the fact that it has provided a theoretical justification for those who wished the government to do nothing.

In our view, Keynes' policy conclusions were basically correct. Government policy can affect the outcome; in recessionary periods, monetary policy is likely to be of limited efficacy; and wage cuts may not be effective.[16]

5.3. *On the efficiency of the market economy*

Though a half-century of experience may make us less sanguine about the government's ability to eliminate business fluctuations, a half-century of experience with alternative forms of economic organization have made us even less sanguine about the ability of these alternatives to provide the basis of a more efficient system of resource allocation. Like the emperor's new clothes, we may not be able to see the invisible hand because it is not there; or perhaps more accurately, because it is so invisible, we do not see how palsied it is. Unemployment is but the worst manifestation of pervasive market failures which arise in the presence of imperfect information and incomplete markets. But if the invisible hand of the market is palsied, the visible hand of the government *may* be far worse. Leibniz[17] and J. B. Cabell's optimism[18] was wrong: we do not live in the best of all possible worlds. We live in an imperfect world. And we must learn to live with those imperfections. Might not limited government intervention—correcting the worst manifestations of market failures, including massive unemployment—after all be the wisest policy to follow? In the end, Keynes, and Keynesian policies, are vindicated.

Bell Communications Research, Morristown, N.J.
Princeton University, and
The Hoover Institution, Stanford University

REFERENCES

AKERLOF, G. (1970), 'The Market for Lemons: Qualitative Uncertainty and the Market Mechanism', *Quarterly Journal of Economics*, 84, 288–300.

[16] In Keynes' *General Theory,* wage cuts may reduce aggregate demand (ch. 19). In more modern treatments, where consumption is based on permanent income, such wage cuts might have a negligible effect on demand. Our theory provides an explanation of why wage cuts could have a significant effect: imperfect capital markets results in some individuals having to reduce their consumption. On the other hand, there are circumstances in our theory where a wage cut would be effective: when each firm chooses not to reduce its wage, given the wages paid by other firms, a coordinated wage change can increase the demand for labour. Our theory suggests, however, that there are other circumstances where lowering real wages (below the efficiency wage) would actually result in a reduction in the demand for labour.

To the extent that lower wages lead to lower prices, wage reductions can have future deleterious effects, in reducing the working capital available to firms, and in making them more reluctant to produce, if they extrapolate current declines in prices to continue in the future.

[17] Leibniz (1710), First Part of the Essays on Divine Justice, Human Freedom and the Origin of Evil, § 8.

[18] Cabell (1926), book iv, ch. 26.

AKERLOF, G. and YELLEN, J. (1985), 'A Near Rational Model of The Business Cycle with Wage and Price Inertia', *Quarterly Journal of Economics*, 99, 832–8.

BARRO, R. J. and GROSSMAN, H. I., (1971), 'A General Disequilibrium Model of Income and Employment', *American Economic Review*, 61, 82–93.

BUITER, W. H. (1981), 'The Superiority of Contingent Rules over Fixed Rules in Models with Rational Expectations', *Economic Journal*, 91, 647–70.

CABELL, J. B. (1926), *The Silver Stallion*.

FLEMMING, J. S. (1973), 'The Consumption Function when Capital Markets are Imperfect: The Permanent Income Hypothesis Reconsidered', *Oxford Economic Papers*, 25, 160–72.

GREENWALD, B. and STIGLITZ, J. E. (1986a), 'Externalities in Economies with Imperfect Information and Incomplete Markets', *Quarterly Journal of Economics*, March.

—— (1986b), 'Information, Finance Constraints and Business Fluctuations', *Proceedings of the Taiwan Conference on Monetary Theory*, Taipei, Chung–Hua Institute.

—— 'Imperfect Information, Credit Markets, and Unemployment' (1987) *European Economic Review* (forthcoming).

—— and WEISS, A. M. (1984), 'Informational Imperfections and Macroeconomic Fluctuations', *American Economic Review* papers and proceedings, 74, 194–9.

HICKS, J. R. (1937), 'Mr Keynes and The Classics', *Econometrica*, 5.

KEYNES, J. M. (1930), *A Treatise on Money*, Macmillan, London.

—— (1936), *The General Theory of Employment, Interest and Money*, Macmillan, London.

KLEIN, L. R. (1948), *The Keynesian Revolution*, Macmillan, London.

LEIBNIZ, G. W. (1710), *Essais de Théodicée sur la bonté de Dieu, la liberté de l'homme et l'origine du mal*, Amsterdam.

LEIJONHUFVUD, A. (1968), *On Keynesian Economics and The Economics of Keynes*, Oxford University Press, New York.

NEARY, J. P. and STIGLITZ, J. E. (1983), 'Towards a Reconstruction of Keynesian Economics: Expectations and Constrained Equilibria', *Quarterly Journal of Economics* Supplement 97, 199–228.

STIGLITZ, J. E. (1984), 'Price Rigidities and Market Structure', *American Economic Review* papers and proceedings, 74, 350–6.

—— (1986a), 'Theories of Wage Rigidities', paper presented to Conference on Keynes' Economic Legacy, University of Delaware, 1983, in *Keynes' Economic Legacy*, Praeger, New York.

—— (1987), 'The Causes and Consequences of the Dependence of Quality on Price', *Journal of Economic Literature* (forthcoming).

STIGLITZ, J. E. and WEISS, A. M. (1981), 'Credit Rationing in Markets with Imperfect Information', *American Economic Review*, 71, 393–410.

—— (1983), 'Incentive Effects of Terminations: Applications to the Credit and Labor Markets', *American Economic Review*, 73, 912–27.

—— (1985), 'Credit Rationing and Collateral', paper presented at CEPR conference, Oxford, September 1985.

TAYLOR, J. (1985), 'Rational Expectations Models' in K. J. Arrow and S. Honkapohja (eds.) *Frontiers of Economics*, Blackwell, Oxford.

TOBIN, J. (1969), 'A General Equilibrium Approach to Monetary Theory', *Journal of Money Credit and Banking*, 1, 15–29.

Oxford Economic Papers 39 (1987), 134–160

A SIMPLE MODEL OF IMPERFECT COMPETITION WITH WALRASIAN FEATURES

By HUW DIXON

IMPERFECT competition is a pervasive part of modern industrial economies, where high levels of concentration in product markets often coexist with unionised labour markets. Most standard macroeconomic models, however, assume that markets are perfectly competitive. This paper provides a *simple* framework in which we are able to explore some of the implications of imperfect competition for the macroeconomy, and to evaluate the adequacy of competitive macroeconomic models as "convenient simplifications". The results of the paper suggest that whilst some general features of competitive macromodels do carry over to an imperfectly competitive framework, others do not. Imperfect competition in the labour and product market can have a significant impact on the level of employment and the effectiveness of macroeconomic policy. Imperfect competition provides an explicit account of price and wage determination, and thus gives us a far greater insight into the microeconomic structure of macroeconomic equilibrium than is possible in competitive models.

This paper presents a simple model of imperfect competition with Walrasian features. The model is "Walrasian" both in some of its assumptions,[0] and also in the properties of the model. What we have attempted to do is to take a standard neoclassical synthesis macromodel (e.g. Patinkin (1965), Branson (1979)) and introduce imperfect competition into the product and labour markets. We feel that this is a useful exercise for two reasons. Firstly, it provides a simple macro model of imperfect competition in which the causal mechanisms are very clear. In general, models of imperfect competition have tended to be rather complex, despite a recent trend towards simpler versions (e.g. Hart (1982), d'Aspremont *et al.* (1985)). Secondly, by adopting the standard neoclassical synthesis framework, it is easy to relate the model of imperfect competition to more familiar models.

Imperfect competition in the product is modelled using conjectural-variations Cournot equilibrium which captures a wide range of possible market solutions, encompassing perfect competition, Cournot, and joint profit maximisation as special cases. This approach contrasts with existing

I would like to thank Ben Lockwood and Dennis Snower for many useful conversations. The first section of the paper was used for the M.Sc. macroeconomics course at Birkbeck in March 1985. The current revision owes much to comments made at the time. Financial support from the ESRC is gratefully acknowledged. Faults, alas, remain my own.

[0] These Walrasian assumptions include that of Leontief technology in Section 1. It is often forgotten that Walras made wide use of "coefficients de fabrication" in his work.

models which adopt a Chamberlinian framework with differentiated products and price-setting firms (Blanchard and Kiyotaki (1985), Layard and Nickell (1985), Svensson (1986)), and generalises Hart's (1982) assumption of Cournot competition. We explore the model with a competitive labour market in Sections 1-2, and with a unionised labour market in Section 3.

With an imperfectly competitive product market and competitive labour market, we can use familiar Aggregate Demand and Aggregate Supply analysis to evaluate the influence of the degree of imperfect competition on the level of employment, the government expenditure multiplier, and the neutrality of money. There are three main results. Firstly, equilibrium employment is inversely related to the degree of monopoly in the product market. With perfect competition employment is at its Walrasian level. Since the labour market is competitive there is no involuntary unemployment and this deviation of employment from its Walrasian level can be interpreted as underemployment. Secondly, if money is neutral the underlying Walrasian equilibrium then it will also be neutral in the imperfectly competitive equilibrium. This follows since the behavioural equations are all homogeneous to degree zero (Hodo) in money and prices. Thirdly, the government expenditure multiplier is in a very precise sense "Walrasian" in this model. By this we mean that the mechansims underlying the Walrasian multiplier are the same with imperfect competition. There will be crowding out, and the multiplier has the Walrasian value as its lower bound, is strictly less than unity, and strictly increasing in the degree of monopoly. In Section 1 the model is presented assuming constant returns to scale, a convenient simplification which enables us to derive an explicit solution to the model. In Section 2, however, we make the more orthodox assumption of diminishing returns: the analytical properties of the model are not affected by this.

In Section 3 we consider the impact of unions in an imperfectly competitive macromodel. A union may wish to set the wage above the market clearing level, so that there may be "excess supply" in both the labour and product markets.[1] In this sense the economy has a "Keynesian" equilibrium. However, we consider two alternative models of wage determination (bargaining, monopoly union) for which the equilibrium is very unkeynesian in its implications for macroeconomic policy. Both fiscal and monetary policy are neutral,[2] so that macroeconomic policy has even less impact here than in a Walrasian economy, despite the presence of excess supplies. The basic reason is that the equilibrium level of employment and

---

[1] The use of the terms "excess supply" and "market clearing" are the suoject of disagreement. My own favoured uses are (a) market clearing means competitive—hence any non-competitive equilibrium is a non-clearing equilibrium, (b) excess supply means that at a given price suppliers would like to sell more than they do. Others who dislike this may translate into their own terminology.

[2] Throughout this paper we will use the term "fiscal neutrality" to mean that the fiscal multiplier is zero. We do not use the term in the technical sense of monetary theory, i.e. that no real variables are affected (although money is neutral in this sense too).

real wages are unaffected by government policy, so that changes in the money supply or government expenditure feed through entirely into nominal wage and price increases. The only role for macroeconomic policy in a unionised economy in the examples presented is in the presence of multiple equilibria: macroeconomic policy can be used to ensure that the equilibrium with the highest level of employment is attained rather than a low employment equilibrium. The results of this section relate most closely to Layard and Nickell's (1985) model of NAIRU. The main conceptual difference between the two models is that Layard and Nickell adopt an essentially partial equilibrium approach for the purpose of deriving a tractable econometric model. The model we present adopts an explicit—if simple—general equilibrium framework.

Whilst the models presented in this paper are very specific, and have no claim to generality, we believe that the results should not be dismissed as simply special examples. Most of the assumptions made are absolutely standard, and the originality of the paper consists not in the ingredients but the recipe. For this reason we believe the specific models presented have conceptual implications over and beyond their mathematical implications.

1. Imperfect competition with a competitive labour market

We shall first lay out the basic assumptions about households, firms, and the government.

(a) The household

There is one price-taking household which has initial endowments of money M^0 and leisure T and derives utility from consumption C, real money balances M/p and leisure l (money is being used as numeraire). The houlehold also receives all the profits from the two firms in the economy. The household has Cobb–Douglas utility:

$$U = \alpha \log C + \beta \log l + \gamma \log \frac{M}{p} \qquad (1.1)$$

The household is a price-taker, and so maximises (1.1) subject to the budget constraint:

$$pC + lw + M \leq wT + M^0 + \pi \qquad (1.2)$$

Where π are distributed profits, to be explained below. The solution to (1.1–2) yields the familiar Walrasian demand functions for money and consumption, and supply of labour $N = T - l$. Whilst (1.1) is assumed throughout the paper, we shall often write these demand functions in general form:

$$C = C\left(\frac{w}{p}, \frac{M^0 + \pi}{p}\right) = \alpha \frac{(wT + M^0 + \pi)}{p} \tag{1.3}$$

$$N = N\left(\frac{w}{p}, \frac{M^0 + \pi}{p}\right) = T(1 - \beta) - \frac{\beta p}{w}\left(\frac{M^0}{p} + \frac{\pi}{p}\right) \tag{1.4}$$

$$\frac{M}{p} = \frac{M}{p}\left(\frac{w}{p}, \frac{M^0 + \pi}{p}\right) = v\left(\frac{wT}{p} + \frac{M^0 + \pi}{p}\right) \tag{1.5}$$

As is clear from (1.3), the household's demand for consumption has a unit elasticity (as do (1.4) and (1.5)). Furthermore, all the demand functions are homogeneous of degree zero (Hodo) in prices, money balances and profits (p, w, M^0, π). This is because (a) the budget constraint (1.2) is unaffected by an equiproportionate change in (p, w, M^0, π) (b) utility is Hodo in (p, M). Of course, we might prefer to interpret the model as being a temporary equilibrium, in which case *nominal* rather than real money balances would enter the household's utility function. The condition for an indirect utility function to be Hodo in (p, M) are very restrictive (see Grandmont (1984)). However, it suits our purposes to have real money balances in the utility function because we aim to demonstrate that imperfect competition *per se* does not invalidate the "classical dichotomy": if the underlying competitive equilibrium is unaffected by the money supply M^0, then so will the imperfectly competitive economy. The treatment of profits in imperfectly competitive general equilibrium models is problematic (see Hart (1985)).

(b) *The firm*

There are two firms in the output market (this obviously generalises). They are price-takers in the labour market and there is a conjectural variations Cournot model in the output market. The assumption of price-taking in the labour market and price-making in the output market can be justified by the fact that the firm is "small" in the labour market (there are lots of firms from the many output markets), but "large" in its particular product market. Furthermore, the firms have no "general equilibrium" awareness: in taking their output decisions, they do not calculate the effects of this on the labour market (this contrasts with models such as Hart (1979) and Roberts (1980) where firms do calculate the full effect). However, the firms know the "true" household demand curve (taking w as given), which from (1.3) has unit elasticity. In this section it is assumed that firms have constant-return to scale production with one input—labour. This is a convenient simplification that enables us to derive explicit results; in Section 2 we show that the introduction of diminishing returns does not invalidate our analytical results. The output—labour ratio is normalised to unity:

$$y_i = N_i \tag{1.6}$$

where y_i and N_i are the i firm's output and employment respectively. Under (1.6) firms have constant marginal cost w. We further assume that firms have the same conjectural variations parameter ϕ. With two firms, unit elasticity demand, and constant marginal cost we have the equilibrium price-cost margin μ:[3]

$$\mu \equiv \frac{p - w}{p} = \frac{1 + \phi}{2} \tag{1.7}$$

and hence real wage and profits:

$$\frac{w}{p} = 1 - \mu \qquad \frac{\pi}{p} = \mu \cdot N \tag{1.8}$$

For the competitive case with Bertrand conjectures $(\phi = -1)w/p = 1$ and $\mu = 0$; there are no profits, and all income is wages. In the Cournot case $(\phi = 0)$, $w/p = \mu = \frac{1}{2}$: wages are half of income. For ϕ close to 1, the equilibrium price-cost margin μ becomes close to 1 and real-wages close to 0 (note that for $\phi \geqslant +1$ no conjectural variation equilibrium exists with unit elastic demand). Following Lerner (1934), we shall call μ the "degree of monopoly".

(c) Government

Government expenditure can be in two forms: levels of *real* expenditure g are predetermined, or *nominal* levels ("cash limits"). Whether government expenditure is planned in real or nominal terms will have a big influence on the effects of that expenditure on the macroeconomy (this is discussed in more detail in Dixon (1986)). The results of this paper will apply to *real* government expenditure plans, as is standard in the macroeconomic literature. The simplest way to model g is to conceive of the government purchasing output at a price p_g determined by bilateral bargaining between the industry and government, the corresponding markup being μ_g. The important point is that the price which the government pays is not (directly) influenced by, and will not influence the price paid the household. This

---

[3] Those unfamiliar with the conjectural variations model of Cournot oligopoly are referred to Waterson (1984, pp. 18–19). The equilibrium condition that marginal revenue equals marginal cost is:

$$p\left(1 + \frac{1 + \phi}{2}\right) = w$$

from which (1.7) comes directly. The markup μ is constant because with Cobb–Douglas preferences there is constant elasticity of demand. Alternatively, with Cournot competition, the markup can be seen as varying with the number of firms ($\mu = 1/n$).

assumptions seems reasonable: the government is a big buyer, and does not enter the market as a price-taker.

Since p_g is determined independently of p, the conjectural variations equilibrium μ (1.7) will not be influenced by g (since the revenue gained from government contracts is fixed at $p_g g$, it does not enter into *marginal* revenue). Again, purely for simplicity, we assume that although independently determined, $p_g = p$: the price paid by government and households happens to be equal. This can easily be relaxed.[4] For a wide range of industrial products, bilateral contracts between firms and government is more realistic than the usual treatment of simply adding g to industry demand.

Lastly, there is the question of the governments budget constraint: how does it finance its expenditure? This is not analysed in any detail here. However, the results of this paper are consistent with a proportional profits tax. Alternatively, the government can be viewed as financing the expenditure by printing money, which appears in the next period's money balances. Neither of these possibilities is made explicit, since our main interest does not lie in the government's finance policy. In what follows, a change in government spending is analysed in its own right, independently of any monetary repercussions that could ensue.

(d) *Equilibrium and macroeconomic policy*

We have now outlined the assumptions underlying the model. Since the household is unrationed in all markets, consumption, employment and the demand for money are all given by notional demands (1.3–5). The equilibrium in the economy can be represented by four equations:

$$y = N\left(\frac{w}{p}, \frac{M^0 + \pi}{p}\right) \tag{1.9}$$

$$y = c\left(\frac{w}{p}, \frac{M^0 + \pi}{p}\right) + g \tag{1.10}$$

$$\frac{w}{p} = \frac{1 - \phi}{2} = 1 - \mu \tag{1.11}$$

$$\frac{\pi}{p} = \mu y \tag{1.12}$$

(1.9) is the equilibrium condition for the competitive labour market (y is total output); (1.10) is the equilibrium condition for output (output is demand determined); (1.11) is the real-wage determined by the equilibrium price-cost margin; (1.12) is total real profits determined by the equilibrium

---

[4] For example, a common form for government contracts is cost-plus, in effect a markup μ_g. The model would then simply require a different markup for government and private consumption. For example, profits would become: $\pi = \mu_g \cdot g + \mu(N - g)$ (see (1.12)).

price-cost margin and output. We omit the money market equilibrium condition, since (1.3–5) satisfy Walras' Law. The endogenous variables determined the equilibrium are $\{w, p, y, \pi, N\}$, and the exogenous variables are $\{M^0, \phi, g\}$.

The equilibrium in this economy can be represented by the usual aggregate supply and demand equations in (p, N) space. From the price-cost equation (1.7), the mark-up of price over the wage is fixed due to CRTS, hence things look the same in (w, N) and (p, N) space. The **Aggregate Supply** curve (AS) is derived by combining (1.9) and (1.12):

$$\text{AS} \qquad N = N\!\left(1 - \mu, \mu N + \frac{M^0}{p}\right) \qquad (1.13)$$

By total differentiation:

$$\left.\frac{\mathrm{d}N}{\mathrm{d}p}\right|_{\text{AS}} = \frac{-N_2 M^0}{p^2(1 - N_2\mu)} > 0 \qquad (1.14)$$

where $N_2 = \mathrm{d}N/\mathrm{d}W < 0$ from (1.4). If the price rises *given the real wage*, then the real balance effect will elicit an increased supply of labour (since with Cobb–Douglas preferences (1.1), leisure is normal). Note that the AS curve is upward sloping not due to the presence of "money illusion", but rather due to the real balance effect which operates in the labour supply (with leisure a normal good). In many received textbooks accounts, the labour supply depends only on the real wage w/p, which implicitly suppresses the real balance effect. The resultant vertical AS function is at best a misleading heuristic device (the origin of this "simplification" is probably Patinkin (1965, pp. 202–5)). Similarly:

$$\left.\frac{\mathrm{d}N}{\mathrm{d}\mu}\right|_{\text{AS}} = \frac{-(N_1 - N_2 N)}{1 - N_2 N} < 0 \qquad (1.15)$$

At a given price, a rise in the markup μ will reduce the real wage and increase profits for any level of employment. Both of these effects lead to a reduction in the labour supply at a given price. Thus the AS function is upward sloping, and a rise in μ shifts it to the left, as in Fig. 1.1.

The analysis of aggregate demand is a little more complicated. The real balance effect will of course lead to a downward sloping **Aggregate Demand curve** (AD), which is defined by

$$\text{AD} \qquad N = C\!\left(1 - \mu, \frac{M^0}{p} + \mu N\right) + g \qquad (1.16)$$

Hence:

$$\left.\frac{\mathrm{d}N}{\mathrm{d}p}\right|_{\text{AD}} = \frac{-C_2 M^0}{p^2(1 - c_2\mu)} < 0 \qquad (1.17)$$

The effect of a change in μ on N given p is a little less obvious. A rise in μ

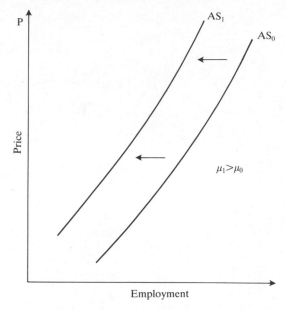

FIG. 1.1. Aggretate supply and the degree of monopoly

leads to a fall in the real wage, but a rise in profit income. If consumption is normal, these effects work in opposite directions. However, with Cobb–Douglas preferences the real-wage effect predominates:

$$\frac{dC}{d\mu} = -C_1 + C_2 N = \alpha(N - T) < 0 \tag{1.18}$$

Hence a rise in μ shifts the AD leftwards as in Fig. 1.2

$$\left.\frac{dN}{d\mu}\right|_{AD} = \frac{-(C_1 - C_2 N)}{1 - C_2 \mu} < 0 \tag{1.19}$$

(Note that $1 - C_2\mu > 0$, since from (1.3) C_2, the marginal propensity to consume from real balances is of course less than unity).

An equilibrium in this economy is represented by the intersection of the aggregate demand and aggregate supply functions. Inspection of (1.13) and (1.16) reveals that the classical dichotomy holds in this model since the equilibrium equations are homogeneous of degree zero (Hodo) in w, p, m. The classical dichotomy thus stems from homogeneity, and not a vertical AS curve nor the assumption of a competitive economy.

Proposition 1: Let $\lambda > 0$. If $\{w^*, p^*, \pi^*, N^*\}$ is an equilibrium given M^0, then $\{\lambda w^*, \lambda p^*, \lambda \pi^*, \cdot N^*\}$ is an equilibrium given λM^0.

Whilst the introduction of imperfect competition into this model does not upset the homogeneity of the economy, the level of equilibrium employment is decreasing in the degree of monopoly.

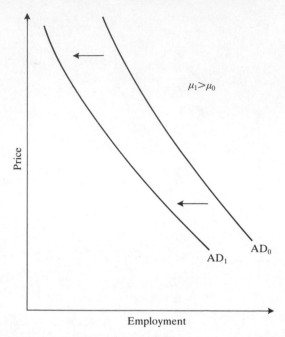

FIG. 1.2. Aggregate demand and the degree of monopoly

Proposition 2: Equilibrium employment is inversely related to the degree of monopoly μ.

Proof.
Total differentiation of (1.13) and (1.16) yields:

$$\frac{dN}{d\mu} = \frac{N_2 C_1 - N_1 C_2}{C_2 - N_2} < 0 \qquad\qquad \text{QED}$$

The maximium employment attained in this economy occurs at the Walrasian equilibrium, with $\mu = 0$. The labour market is of course competitive, so that there is no involuntary unemployment (in any possible sense of the word), merely underemployment. The presence of imperfect competition in the product market leads to a lower level of equilibrium employment in the competitive labour market.

What of the effectiveness of fiscal policy in this model? If we consider equations (1.13–16) which define the AS and AD curves, fiscal policy affects only the AS curve. The fiscal multiplier *taking μ and p as given* is a "Keynesian" multiplier:

$$\left.\frac{dN}{dg}\right|_{AD} = \frac{1}{1 - C_2\mu} > 1 \qquad\qquad (1.20)$$

where C_2 is the marginal propensity to consume out of (real) income.

Essentially, what happens is that government expenditure increases profits initially by μg, this increases consumption, and this leads to a feedback from output to profits to increased consumption. The increase in output due to an increase in g in (1.20) is represented in Fig. 1.3 by a shift from initial position A to B. However, the increase in output at initial price p_0 leads to excess demand for labour, and hence wages and prices will rise to p_1. The full fiscal multiplier can be derived if we totally differentiate the AS and AD functions with respect to g:

$$
\begin{bmatrix} 1 - N_2\mu & N_2\dfrac{M}{p^2} \\[2ex] 1 - C_2\mu & C_2\dfrac{M}{p^2} \end{bmatrix}
\begin{bmatrix} \mathrm{d}N/\mathrm{d}g \\[1ex] \mathrm{d}p/\mathrm{d}g \end{bmatrix}
= \begin{bmatrix} 0 \\ 1 \end{bmatrix}
$$

Using Cramer's rule this yields:

$$
\frac{\mathrm{d}N}{\mathrm{d}g} = \frac{-N_2}{C_2 - N_2} > 0 \tag{1.21}
$$

$$
\frac{\mathrm{d}p}{\mathrm{d}g} = \frac{p^2 C_2(1 - N_2\mu)}{M^0 C_2 - N_2} > 0 \tag{1.22}
$$

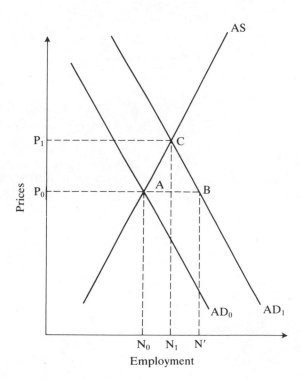

FIG. 1.3. Fiscal policy

Clearly, the fiscal multiplier is less than one and strictly positive. Using (1.3) and (1.4) the explicit solution is:

$$\frac{dN}{dg} = \frac{\beta}{\beta + (1-\mu)\alpha} \tag{1.23}$$

Using (1.7) we can relate firms' conjectures ϕ to the markup μ and hence the multiplier by (1.23). This is done in Table 1.

Recall that when $\phi = 1$ there is no equilibrium in the product market: we include $\phi = 1$ since from (1.23) as μ tends to 1 from below, the multiplier tends to unity. The cartel is then a limiting result. As is clear from (1.23) and Table 1, the greater the degree of monopoly μ, the more effective is fiscal policy. In general since $-1 \leqslant \phi < +1$,

$$1 > \frac{dN}{dg} \geqslant \frac{\beta}{\alpha + \beta} \tag{1.24}$$

Whilst the value of μ does influence the fiscal multiplier, there is always crowding out. Furthermore, the mechanisms underlying the multiplier are essentially the same—as indicated by the general formula (1.21). In this sense, the multiplier is basically "Walrasian" rather than Keynesian. We summarise the foregoing discussion in Proposition 3.

Proposition 3: for $0 \leqslant \mu < 1$ the fiscal multiplier is

$$\frac{dN}{dg} = \frac{-N_2}{C_2 - N_2} = \frac{\beta}{\beta + (1-\mu)\alpha}$$

Hence

$$\frac{\beta}{\beta + \alpha} \leqslant \frac{dN}{dg} \leqslant 1$$

and is *increasing* in μ.

We shall now show that a profits tax will leave these results unaffected. This is important, since it shows that we are justified in not treating the

TABLE 1

Imperfect competition (Duopoly) and the fiscal multiplier

Conjecture	Markup μ	Multiplier
-1 (Bertrand)	0	$\dfrac{\beta}{\beta + \alpha}$
0 (Cournot)	$\frac{1}{2}$	$\dfrac{2\beta}{2\beta + \alpha}$
1 (Cartel)	1	1

government budget constraint explicitly. Suppose we assume that only a proportion t of profits appears in households budget constraints (1.2) (where $0 \leq t \leq 1$). In this case, AD and AS become:

$$N - C\left(1 - \mu, \frac{M_0}{p} + t\mu N\right) - g = 0 \quad \mathrm{AD}(t)$$

$$N - N\left(1 - \mu, \frac{M^0}{p} + t\mu N\right) = 0 \quad \mathrm{AS}(t)$$

Total differentiation of $\mathrm{AD}(t)$ on $\mathrm{AS}(t)$ with respect to t shows that $dN/dt = 0$. The equilibrium is unaffected by the proportion of profits distributed to the shareholder. Furthermore, total differentiation with respect to g yields the *same* fiscal multiplier as in (1.21) and (1.23). The effectiveness of fiscal policy is not influenced by the proportion of profits distributed. This is a surprising result given that the aggregate demand multiplier derived from $\mathrm{AD}(t)$ holding price constant is sensitive to t (e.g. if $t = 1$, then $dN/dg|\mathrm{AD} = 1$). The crucial point here is that if t increases, real distributed profits at the equilibrium output fall by $\Delta t\mu N$. The price level will fall so that real balances increase by $\Delta p M^0/p^2$. The increase in real balances exactly offsets the fall in real distributed profits, so that total wealth remains unchanged. Since the real wage remains constant, equilibrium output and employment are unaltered. In one sense, therefore, an ad valorem profits tax can be said to have no real effects, only nominal effects. Similar exercises can be conducted for an employment tax (which reduces the real wage and share of profits in income), a (real) lump sum tax (which increases equilibrium output via the wealth effect), and an income tax (which alters the real wage and the proportion of profits which households receive). The imposition of these taxes to finance government expenditure would alter the specific results stated in this paper, as they would in a Walrasian economy. However, we hope to have convinced the reader that the Walrasian features would still shine through.

2. Imperfect competition with diminishing returns

In the previous section, we made the simplest possible assumptions that enabled us to derive explicit formulae for policy multipliers. One of these—the "Walrasian" assumption of constant returns—is not standard in textbook macroeconomics. Since Keynes, it has been usual to view the macroeconomic equilibrium as occurring in the "short-run"; capital is fixed. This leads to the standard assumption that there are diminishing returns to labour—output is a concave function of employment; $y = f(N); f' > 0 > f''$.

In this section we shall see that constant returns was merely a convenient simplification. Whilst we are unable to derive explicit formulae for the multiplier, the overall logic and conclusions of the previous section are not changed.

With diminishing returns, the only additional complexity is that the real wage becomes a function of employment as well as the degree of competition in the product market. The profit maximising duopolist chooses its output so that marginal revenue equals marginal cost. Rather than being constant, marginal cost increases with output, and is given by w/f';

$$\mu = \frac{p - w/f'}{p} = \frac{1 + \phi}{2} \tag{2.1a}$$

$$\frac{w}{p} = f' \frac{(1 - \phi)}{2} = f' \cdot (1 - \mu) \tag{2.1b}$$

In the case of a perfectly competitive product market ($\phi = -1$), this simply means that the real wage equals the marginal product of labour. With imperfect competition, however, labour receives less than its marginal product. In the case of Cournot Duopoly ($\phi = 0$) the real wage equals only one half of the marginal product. Equation (2.1a) is often referred to as the "demand curve" for labour. This is misleading, as we shall discuss below. Rather, it simply tells us the relationship between nominal wages, prices and employment that must hold with imperfectly competitive product markets.

If we now define the real wage $\omega \equiv w/p$, our macroeconomic system becomes:[5]

$$Y = c\left(\omega, \frac{M^0}{p}\right) + g \tag{2.2}$$

$$Y = f(N) \tag{2.3}$$

$$\omega \equiv w/p = f' \cdot (1 - \mu) \tag{2.4}$$

$$N = N\left(\omega, \frac{M^0}{p}\right) \tag{2.5}$$

Note that we are omitting profits from our analysis for simplicity.

Aggregate demand and supply analysis is still valid in this framework, so long as we include the real-wage equation (2.4). Turning first to aggregate demand (AD) in (N, p) space, we have the three equations (2.2)–(2.4). As the price increases, this reduces real balances as before, but also leads to an increase in the real wage. To see this, substitution reduces (2.2)–(2.4) to the AD relation

$$\text{AD} \quad f(N) = c\left(f'(N)1 - \mu, \frac{M^0}{p}\right) + g \tag{2.6}$$

[5] There is an aggregation problem here which is skirted around, as is usual. In (2.1) the marginal productivity condition holds for the firm's production function. In (2.3) and (2.4) we have the aggregate production function. So long as firms are identical and the equilibrium symmetric, as here, there is no problem. Let the firm's production function be defined as $g(N_i)$, and the economies as $f = 2g(N/2)$: then $f' = g'$.

Total differentiation of (2.6) yields

$$\frac{dN}{dp}\bigg|_{AD} = \frac{-c_2}{f' - f''(1-\mu)\cdot c_1} < 0 \tag{2.7}$$

Note that since $c_1 > 0$ (leisure is normal) then the "real wage" effects of increases in price via the price cost equation (2.4) reinforces the real balance effect. As in the Walrasian model, an increase in monopoly μ shifts the AD curve to the left in (N, p) space.

Aggregate supply (AS) is defined by the two equations (2.4) and (2.5). For comparison with text-books, we can consider the AS relationship in real-wage/employment space. Equation (2.4) gives the real-wage as a function of employment, as in Fig. 2.1. The supply of labour is upward sloping in the real-wage. However, because of real balance effects, there are a family of labour supply curves which correspond to different price levels. The higher the price level, the lower are real balances, and the higher the labour supply at any given real wage (in terms of Fig. 2.1, $p_0 < p_1$). Thus for price level p_0, the corresponding employment is N_0, and N_1 corresponds to p_1.

The AS function is upward sloping, as can be verified by total

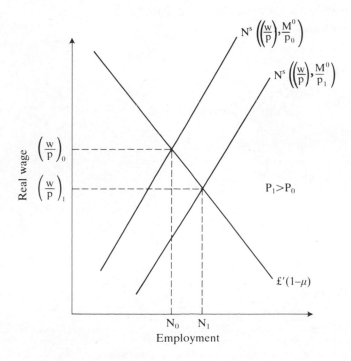

FIG. 2.1. Real wages, employment and the price level

differentiation of (2.4) and (2.5):

$$\left.\frac{dN}{dp}\right|_{AS} = \frac{-N_2\dfrac{M^0}{p^2}}{1 - N_1 f''(1 - \mu)} > 0 \tag{2.8}$$

Note that an increase in the degree of monopoly (a decrease in ϕ) will shift the relationship between real-wages and employment to the left. In Fig. 2.2 we depict the relationship for $\phi = 1$ (perfect competition, $\phi = -1$) and $\phi = 1/2$ (Cournot). There is an inverse relationship between the degree of monopoly and employment.

The analysis of monetary and fiscal policy can be carried out analogously to the previous section. Equations (2.2)–(2.5) are Hodo in (w, p, M^0), so that the classical dichotomy holds and money is neutral. An increase in government expenditure shifts the AS curve to the right, leading to an increase in employment and prices. The fiscal multiplier is:

$$\frac{dN}{dg} = \frac{-N_2}{c_2(1 - N_1 \cdot (1 - \mu) \cdot f'') - N_2(f' - c_1 \cdot f'' \cdot (1 - \mu))} > 0 \tag{2.9}$$

Again, there is crowding out: $0 < dN/dg < 1$.

Note that as the degree of monopoly increases the multiplier increases. The "Walrasian" multiplier corresponds to the case when $\mu = 0$: again, the basic mechanisms underlying the expansionary effect of g are the same as in the Walrasian case.

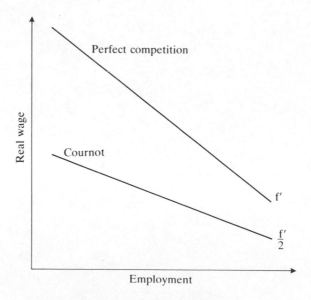

FIG. 2.2. Real wages and employment

3. Unions and the natural rate of unemployment

In this section, we relax the assumption that the labour market is competitive, and introduce a union which bargains with the firms over the nominal wage w. This introduces the possibility of an excess supply of labour: the union can push up the nominal wage, and hence the real wage, above the market clearing level. The resultant equilibrium will be "Keynesian" in the sense that there will be an excess supply in both the product and labour markets. However, as we shall demonstrate, the model is very un-Keynesian in that the classical dichotomy still holds (money is neutral) and fiscal policy can be less effective than in the Walrasian case. Indeed, we provide examples in which the fiscal policy multiplier is zero, and there is complete crowding out.

The model presented seems a good interpretation of Friedman's conception of the Natural Rate of Unemployment (NRH), (Friedman (1968), (1975)). Friedman's original article on the natural rate defined it as "the level ... ground out by the Walrasian system of general equilibrium equations, provided that there is embedded in them the actual structural characteristics of labour and product markets, including market imperfections, the cost of gathering information about job vacancies and so on" (1968, p8). Some economists have focussed on the word "Walrasian" in the above quote, and interpreted the NR as simply the Walrasian equilibrium (eg. Hahn (1980 p, 293)). Others focus on search models of unemployment (Mortensen (1970), Diamond (1985), Pissarides (1984), Lockwood (1985)). The model here focusses on imperfect competition in the labour and product market—the NR as a non-Walrasian equilibrium. At the end of this section we will show how the equilibrium can be interpreted as the Natural Rate.

How should unions be introduced into this model? A first point is that we can no longer think of there being one "representative" household. There will be two types of households in equilibrium: the employed and the unemployed. The union may act in the interests of its employed members, to maximise their welfare. Secondly, since there will be rationing in the labour market, the notional consumption function will have to be altered to become an *effective* demand function. We will first outline the model of the household and labour market, and then the union.

(a) *Households*

There is a continuum H of households with identical preference and money balances as represented by (1.1–5), except that for simplicity profits are not distributed. This corresponds to the idea that each household is very "small" and that to obtain market demand/supply you have to add up (in fact integrate) each household's demand/supply. If we look first at the labour supply, we integrate over the set H of households, so that market supply is given by:

$$N^s(\omega, M^0/p) = \int_H N^s(\omega, M^0/p, h) \, dh \qquad (3.1)$$

If there is insufficient demand for the labour supplied, we assume that the first households in the queue (or seniority system) are employed, and the rest are unemployed. Thus if labour demand is N, then the employment and unemployment rates are:

$$e = N/N(\omega, M^0/p) \qquad (3.2a)$$

$$u = 1 - e \qquad (3.2b)$$

Those households which are employed will receive income consisting of wages from employment plus money balances, the unemployed live off their money balances. Since households have Cobb–Douglas preferences, we can aggregate over employed and unemployed households. Consumer demand in the product market thus:

$$c^d\left(\omega, \frac{M^0}{p}, N\right) = e.C(w/p, M^0/p) + (1 - e)\frac{\alpha}{\alpha + \gamma}\frac{M^0}{p} \qquad (3.3)$$

The effective demand function still has unit elasticity of demand, so our analysis of the firm in Section 1 still holds good.

For a given level of (w, M^0) then, the macroeconomic equilibrium is determined by:

$$y = c^d\left(\omega, \frac{M^0}{p}, N\right) + g \qquad (3.4)$$

$$y = f(N) \qquad (3.5)$$

$$\omega \equiv w/p = f'(1 - \mu) \qquad (3.6)$$

plus (implicitly) the three equations (3.1–3) used to derive c^d. (3.4) tells us that output is determined by *effective* demand $c^d + g$, which takes account of the fact that some households may be rationed in the labour market. Using (3.4–6) we can determine output, employment and prices *given* the nominal wage, money balances and government expenditure. We will define the Aggregate Demand function as solving (3.4–6) for employment, $AD(w, M^0, g)$. If we hold (M^0, g) as fixed, this yields the true "demand for labour" relationship. Total differentiation of (3.4–6) yields:

$$\left.\frac{dN}{dw}\right|_{AD} = \frac{-c_2^d f'(1 - \mu)M^0}{w^2(f' - f''(1 - \mu))c_1^d + c_2^d f''(1 - \mu)\dfrac{M^0}{w} + c_3^d} < 0 \qquad (3.7)$$

Thus a higher nominal wage leads to a lower level of employment. This is because a higher nominal wage leads to higher prices, and a higher real wage. As in the previous section, a rise in the degree of monopoly μ leads to an inward shift in the AD curve. The AD curve is the union's real demand curve: it gives the level of employment that will result if a particular nominal wage is set. Equation (3.4–6) also tells the union the real wage that will result. As in the previous sections, the behavioural equations are all Hodo in (w, p, M^0), as is the AD function.

(b) *The union*

Given the relationships between nominal wages, real wages, and employment contained in the AD curve and equations (3.4–6), how is the equilibrium determined? We need a model of nominal wage determination. In this section, we shall consider two different models: the monopoly-union model where unions have the power to unilaterally set the nominal wage, and a model where firms and unions bargain over the nominal wage. Given the nominal wages set, firms choose outputs and thus prices. This seems very reasonable: in practice unions have a direct say only on the wages they get, not on the prices which firms set.

There are many alternative assumptions that can be made about the union's objectives in the wage determination process. In the bargaining model we adopt the simple yet plausible assumption that the union seeks to maximise the real wage. The rationale for this is that the union seeks to maximise the utility of those households which are employed—who presumably make up its membership. As Oswald (1984) argues, if there is a seniority system such as LIFO (Last In, First Out) which determines who get laid-off, then majority voting will lead to real-wage maximisation. In the context of the monopoly union model, however, the assumption of real wage maximisation is rather extreme (with diminishing returns, real wages are maximised with one employee), so we allow for a general utility function defined on employment as well as real wages (as is common—see Oswald (1985), Pencavel (1984)).

(c) *Bargaining over the nominal wage*

The firms and the union bargain over the nominal wage. The wage bargain is made at the industry level, so that the two firms act together. Given the nominal wage chosen, price is determined by the non-cooperative behaviour of firms in the product market. The firms' objectives are profits: the unions real wages. Out of the many possible bargaining solutions we will adopt the simple Nash-bargain. Thus the nominal wage is chosen to maximise the product of profits with real wages. Since (from the AD relation) there is a $1:1$ relationship between nominal wages and employment, it is most convenient to represent the bargain as a choice of *employment*. Real wages are $f'(1 - \mu)$: profits are $f - f'(1 - \mu)N$. Hence the

TABLE 2

Equilibrium employment and the degree of monopoly: example

| Equilibrium Employment | The degree of monopoly | | | |
	Competitive $\mu = 0$	$\mu = 1/4$	Cournot $\mu = 1/2$	Cartel $\mu = 1$
N	$\dfrac{1}{3\delta}$	$\dfrac{1}{\delta\sqrt{12}}$	$\dfrac{1}{4\delta}$	$\dfrac{2 - \sqrt{3}}{2\delta}$
% of $\mu = 0$ (3.s.f.)	100	86.8	75.1	40.2

Nash-product is:

$$\max_{N} (f - f'(1 - \mu)N)f'(1 - \mu) \qquad (3.8)$$

$$\text{s.t.} \quad N \leqslant N^s(f'(1 - \mu), M^0/p) \qquad (3.9)$$

Constraint (3.9) represents the notion that the union cannot force people to work, and p is given through (3.4–6). We will assume that (3.9) never binds, so that from the first order conditions for (3.8) we have for an inferior maximum:

$$N = \frac{f'^2\mu + ff''}{2f'f''(1 - \mu)} \qquad (3.10)$$

(the second-order condition will generally be satisfied—a sufficient condition is that $f''' \leqslant 0$). Given the equilibrium level of employment, the nominal wage is set so that AD yields N using (3.4)–(3.6). Of course an interior solution to (3.8–9) need not exist: however, that is not of interest here.[6] What is of interest is that the equilibrium level of employment defined by (3.10) is determined solely by the degree of monopoly μ, and the technology represented by the production function $f(N)$. If (3.9) is binding, then the labour market clears and we revert to the equilibrium examined in Section 2.

Suppose we consider a concrete example. Let $y = N - \delta N^2$, where we choose δ small enough so that $dy/dN = 1 - 2\delta N$ is positive for relevant N (e.g. $1/2\delta$ is greater than the Walrasian level of employment.) In this case we can solve (3.10) for the equilibrium employment level (assuming (3.9) is not binding). In Table 2 we have calculated the solution for different values of μ satisfied at these values, which give the global maxima over relevant ranges of N). In the second row we express the equilibrium employment levels as a percentage of the level when $\mu = 0$.

---

[6] No solution may exist at all, since the lower bound on N is given by the strict inequality $N > g$ (there is no upper bound on nominal wages). If a solution does exist, it may have (3.9) binding.

In this example, the degree of monopoly in the product market has a very strong influence on the equilibrium level of employment.

A generalisation of the classic Nash-solution is to allow for differential bargaining power, and have a *weighted* Nash-bargain. The objective function then becomes:

$$\max_{N} (f - f'N(1 - \mu))^{\lambda}(f'(1 - \mu))^{(1-\lambda)} \tag{3.11}$$

where a smaller λ represents greater union bargaining power, and $1 \geqslant \lambda \geqslant 0$. (3.11) yields the first order condition:

$$N = \frac{\lambda \mu f' + (1 - \lambda)ff''}{f'f''(1 - \mu)} \tag{3.11a}$$

Letting $\mu = 0$ a quadratic production function yields $N = \lambda/\delta(1 + \lambda)$. Thus the greater the bargaining power of unions (the smaller λ) the lower the equilibrium level of employment.[7]

In the particular model of bargaining we have considered, there is no role for macroeconomic policy to influence the equilibrium level of employment. Unions and firms are locked into a bargaining process, the outcome of which is not influenced by monetary or fiscal policy.[8]

(d) A monopoly union model

An alternative assumption to a wage-bargain is that the union sets nominal wages. Thus the union sets (nominal) wages and firms set prices given the wages set. A higher nominal wage causes lower employment (through aggregate demand) and a higher real wage. The real wage equation (3.6) gives the feasible combinations of real-wage and employment. We could assume a general union utility function defined on the real wage and employment (see Oswald (1985) for a survey). In this case, the union maximises its utility subject to the real wage equation.

$$\max_{N} u(\omega, N) \tag{3.12}$$

$$\text{s.t.} \quad \omega = f'(1 - \mu) \tag{3.13}$$

Should a solution to (3.12–13) exist, government monetary and fiscal policy will not effect the equilibrium level of employment. The impact of an increase in government expenditure is to crowd out the consumption of households, since the resultant price rise reduces the value of their real balances.[9]

---

[7] When $\lambda = 0$, $N = 0$ and the real wage is maximised: when $\lambda = 1$ then $N = 1/2\delta$ and profits are maximised. Clearly, we would expect the labour supply constraint to become effective for $\lambda < 1$, with the labour market clearing (as in Section 1).

[8] This is only true for an interior solution (3.10) and (3.11a), when (3.9) is not binding.

[9] Consumption by employed workers is $c(w/p, M^0/p)$; by the unemployed $(\alpha/(\alpha + \gamma))M^0/p$.

These strong results of fiscal neutrality stem from the assumptions made about the union's objective function. Although household utility depends upon consumption and leisure, it also depends upon real balances. In the two examples given above, the union's objective was expressed purely in *real* terms: the nominal price level played no direct role. This suppression of the real balance effect may seem a very reasonable step: after all, how many unions worry about the impact of wage settlements on their members real balances? However, the introduction of real balances to the union's objective function would undermine the fiscal neutrality result, although homogeneity and hence monetary neutrality still hold.

We have considered two models of nominal wage determination in a unionised economy. With a union influencing wage determination, and firms prices, the resultant equilibrium can have excess supply in both the output and labour markets. In this sense the equilibrium is very Keynesian. However, the policy implications for the economy are very unkeynesian: money is neutral, and the fiscal multiplier can be zero. The basis idea behind the classical dichotomy still holds in a unionised economy. The monopoly union case is depicted in Fig. 3.1. The equilibrium level of employment is determined in the labour market. Given the equilibrium level of employment, the nominal wage w^* is set to achieve this given AD. Since the AD function is Hodo in (w, M^0), an increase in M^0 to $M^{0'}$ will lead to an equiproportionate rise in the nominal wage set by the union, from w^* to w'.

To what extent do models of imperfect competition with unionised labour markets yield a model of the "natural rate"?. There are perhaps five crucial features of the NRH: (i) there exists a unique equilibrium in the economy, in which (ii) agents' expectations are confirmed and (iii) money is neutral, (iv) trade unions can influence the unique equilibrium[10] (v) the theoretical model is a general equilibrium model (this seems to be the import of Friedman's use of the phrase "Walrasian system"). Any equilibrium concept which has properties (i)–(v) will very much resemble Friedman's notion of the NRH.

Clearly, the model of imperfect competition in a unionised economy which we have presented satisfied (ii)–(v). Uniqueness is, however, rather less easy to guarantee. If we turn to the case of a Nash-bargain between firm and unions, over the nominal wage, uniqueness may or may not hold, depending on the nature of the production function. In the case of the monopoly union, uniqueness can only be guaranteed by fairly strong restrictions on both the production function and the union's utility function. For example, if the marginal product of labour is non-concave then there may be two or more "tangencies" with the union's indifference curve, as in Fig. 3.2. Recall that the concavity of the production function merely

---

[10] "Trade unions play an important role in determining the position of the natural level of unemployment" Friedman (1975, p. 30).

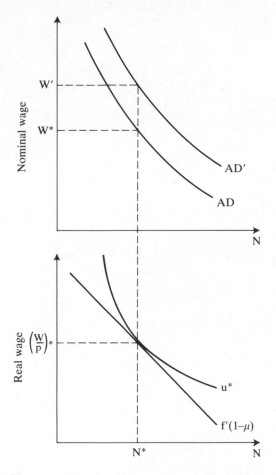

FIG. 3.1. The monopoly union: real wages, nominal wages and employment

requires the marginal product of labour to be decreasing, so for any shaped union indifference curve it is possible to construct multiple equilibria (a sufficient condition to ensure uniqueness given that the union utility is quasiconcave is $f''' \leq 0$).

Whilst non-uniqueness goes very much against the spirit of Friedman's NRH, it does not imply that the model is Keynesian, in the sense that there are multiplier effects. However, it is possible to conceive of macroeconomic policy causing the economy to switch from one equilibrium to another. Consider the following argument. In Fig. 3.2 there is a high-employment equilibrium at N_h, and a low-employment equilibrium at N_l. Suppose that the economy is at the low-employment equilibrium, and that wages are fixed in the short-run due to fixed-term contracts. Given initial government polict (M^0, g), the union has set wage w_1, as in Fig. 3.3. Given this wage, the

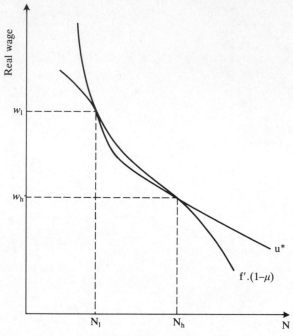

FIG. 3.2. Multiple Equilibria

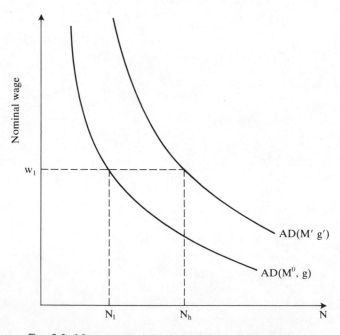

FIG. 3.3. Macroeconomic Policy with Multiple Equilibria

government can alter its macroeconomic policy to some (M', g'), such that:

$$N_h = \text{AD}(w_1, M', g')$$

With the new policy, the union finds itself at the high-employment equilibrium, and has no incentive to alter the nominal wage. This story is very plausible, and indicates that in the case of multiple equilibria, macroeconomic policy can be used to ensure that the highest level of equilibrium employment is attained, avoiding the low employment equilibria.

If we put aside problems of uniqueness, it is possible to generate the long-run Phillips curve model if we assume that wage-bargains are fixed in the short run and unions (and firms) have rational expectations. We can impose the following two-stage temporal structure on the model. In the first stage, unions and firms bargain over the nominal wage, or the union chooses w. In the second-stage, the nominal wage is fixed: the government announces its money supply and firms choose their output and employment (this structure of moves is used by Nickell and Layard (1985)). The agents in the economy have point expectations about the governments policy (M^e, g^e). Given the desired level of employment N^*, w is chosen to attain this given expectations, so w solves:

$$N^* = \text{AD}(w, M^e, g^e)$$

Given the wage set, actual employment is given by:

$$N = N^* + (M^0 - M^e)\partial\text{AD}/\partial M + (g - g^e)\partial\text{AD}/\partial g \qquad (3.17)$$

Where the derivatives of AD are obtained by total differentiation[11] of (3.3–6), and will include standard multiplier effects. Thus if monetary or fiscal policy are more expansionary than expected, employment will be higher than the equilibrium where they are fully anticipated (this model can be seen as a theoretical justification for the econometric model employed by Nickell and Layard (1985) in which only surprises in fiscal policy are effective). From the price-cost equation (3.6), $p = w/f'(1 - \mu)$. Hence an increase in employment will give rise to an increase in prices, due to diminishing marginal productivity:

$$\left.\frac{dp}{dN}\right|_w = -\frac{f'^2(1 - \mu)}{f''w} > 0 \qquad (3.18)$$

Hence it is possible to represent the deviation of actual from expected employment as a function of the deviation of the actual from expected prices:

$$N = N^* + \beta(p - p^e) \qquad (3.19)$$

---

[11] (3.15) can be seen as a linear approximation if derivatives are evaluated at (M^e, g^e), or an exact expression by the Mean Value Theorem if derivatives are evaluated at some intermediate value.

or

$$p = p^e + (1/\beta)(N - N^*) \tag{3.20}$$

where

$$\beta = \frac{dp}{dN} \left(\frac{\partial AD}{\partial M} (M - M^e) + \frac{\partial AD}{\partial g} (g - g^e) \right)$$

Of course, the causality does not run from surprises in prices to deviations in employment: rather it runs from surprises in aggregate demand to deviations in employment and prices. Note that this neutrality result is much stronger than in a Walrasian economy where money is neutral, but even fully anticipated fiscal policy is not.

Given the basic set-up of fixed-wage contracts, we are able to provide a rigorous story of deviations from the "natural rate", which is in effect the short-run Phillips-curve. If we combine this with an appropriate model of expectations formation, then we can tell the usual stories. With rational expectations, surprises in government policy will be a white-noise error term, and hence deviations from the natural rate will be purely transitory. With adaptive expectations, there can be short-run deviations, but employment will tend back to the long-run equilibrium.

Conclusion

This paper has explored some of the implications of imperfect competition for macroeconomic policy within the simplest possible macroeconomic model with proper microeconomic foundations. In the product market there is a conjectural variations Cournot oligopoly model which allows for a wide range of competitive behaviour from perfect competition to joint profit maximisation. In the labour market we considered the case of perfect competition and two models of wage determination in a unionised labour market. Whilst it is dangerous to draw general conclusions from specific models, we feel that the following broad lessons can be drawn.

Imperfect competition matters. Not only does imperfect competition infiuence the equilibrium levels of employment and prices, it also influences the effectiveness of fiscal policy. With a competitive labour market the fiscal multiplier is larger the less competitive is the product market (though there is still crowding out). With a unionised labour market we presented two examples where there was complete crowding out. All three examples presented point towards "classical" conclusions about fiscal policy—there is partial or complete crowding out. Of course, it may well be possible that alternative assumptions might yield more Keynesian results.

Perhaps the most crucial assumption in the models presented is that there is a single sector. In Dixon (1986) we present a two-sector model of a unionized economy, which shares most of the assumptions of this paper. The union in each sector sets its wage, given the wage set by the other union. With two sectors, the unionized equilibrium does not have a unique natural rate of employment, but rather a "natural range" of employment. Hence macroeconomic policy is not ineffective, as in this paper. There is a limited range of feasible levels of employment which can be achieved by an appropriate policy.

There is one aspect of a perfectly competitive economy that can carry over to an imperfectly competitive economy: the neutrality of money. The basic justification for neutrality is the homogeneity of the underlying behavioural equations. This homogeneity is unaffected by imperfect competition per se. However, even in a perfectly competitive economy homogeneity is an extremely strong assumption (see Grandmont (1984)). Whilst we have adopted a basic framework that includes homogeneity for simplicity, it is no more plausible here than in competitive macromodels.

Imperfect competition has an ambiguous relationship to keynesian economics. If firms set prices, and unions wages, it is possible to have a macroeconomic equilibrium which is Keynesian in the sense that if agents were price-takers, they would like to sell more at equilibrium prices. Imperfect competition leads to a non-Walrasian equilibrium. The implications for macroeconomic policy are very non-Keynesian. In the examples presented of a unionised economy, fiscal policy had no effect on equilibrium employment, because an increase in government expenditure causes wages and prices to rise, crowding out private consumption by the real balance effect.

Certainly, the models of a unionised economy presented seem to have more affinity with Friedman's Natural Rate. We argued that the imperfectly competitive equilibrium can be seen as a natural interpretation of the Natural Rate, and one of which Friedman is aware. If we combine the model of the unionised economy with short run wage rigidity, the usual Phillips curve stories arise. The only scope for macroeconomic policy in this context appears to be in the case of multiple equilibria. If wages are fixed in the short-run, the government can ensure that the equilibrium with the highest level of employment is attained.

Birkbeck College, London

BIBLIOGRAPHY

D'ASPREMONT, C., FERRIERA, R. and VARET, L. (1985) Monopolistic Competition and Involuntary unemployment. Mimeo, CORE.

BLANCHARD, O. and KIYATAKI, N. (1985) Monopolistic Competition and Aggregate Demand Externalities. NBER working Paper 1770.

BRANSON, W. (1979) *Macroeconomic Theory and Policy,* Harper Row.

DIAMOND, P. (1985) Wage determination and Efficiency in Search Equilibrium. *Review of Economic Studies,* (59).

DIXON, H. (1986) Unions, Oligopoly, and Macroeconomic Policy. Forthcoming Discussion Paper, Birkbeck College.

FRIEDMAN, M. (1968) The Role of Monetary Policy, *American Economic Review,* March.

FRIEDMAN, M. (1975) Unemployment Versus Inflation. Occasional Paper 44.

GRANDMONT, J. (1984) *Money and Value*. CUP.

HAHN, F. (1980) Unemployment: A Theoretical Viewpoint, *Economica*, (47) 285–298.

HART, O. (1979) Monopolistic Competition in a Large Economy with Differentiated Products. *Review of Economic Studies*, (46) 1–30.

HART, O. (1983) A Model of Imperfect Competition with Keynesian Features *Quarterly Journal of Economics*, (97) 109–138.

HART, O. (1985) Imperfect Competition in General Equilibrium: An Overview. In Arrow and Honkapohja (ed), *Frontiers of Economics*. Blackwell.

LAYARD, R. and NICKELL, S. (1985) The Causes of British Unemployment. *NIER* (Feb) 62–85.

LERNER, A. (1934) On the Concept of Monopoly and the Measurement of Monopoly Power, *Review of Economic Studies*, (1).

LOCKWOOD, B. (1985) Transferable skills, Job Matching, and the Inefficiency of the Natural Rate of Unemployment. Forthcoming, *Economic Journal*.

MORTENSON, D. (1970) Job Search, the Duration of Unemployment, and the Phillips Curve, *American Economic Review*, (60) 847–862.

OSWALD, A. (1984) Efficient Contracts are on the Labour Demand Curve. Mimeo, Oxford.

OSWALD, A. (1985) The Economic Theory of Trade Unions. *Scandinavian Journal of Economics*, (87) 160–193.

PATINKIN, D. (1965) *Money, Interest, and Prices* (2nd Ed) Harper Row.

PENCAVEL, J. (1984) The Trade-off between Wages and Employment in Union Objectives, *Quarterly Journal of Economics*, (99) 215–232.

PISSARIDES, C. (1984) Efficient Job Rejection, *Economic Journal* (94), conference supplement, 97–108.

ROBERTS, K. (1980) The Limit points of Monopolistic Competition, *Journal of Economic Theory*, (22) 112–27.

SNOWER, D. (1983) Imperfect Competition, Underemployment, and Crowding out. *Oxford Economic Papers*, (35) 245–270.

SVENSSON, L. (1986) Sticky Goods Prices, Flexible Asset Prices, Monopolistic Competition, and Monetary Policy. *Review of Economic Studies*, (53) 385–406

WATERSON, M. (1984) *Economic Theory of the Industry*. CUP.

Oxford Economic Papers 39 (1987), 161–174

WAGE FLEXIBILITY AND EMPLOYMENT STABILITY

By J. S. FLEMMING*

"To suppose that a flexible wage policy is a right and proper adjunct of a system which on the whole is one of *laissez faire,* is the opposite of the truth." JMK GT Ch. 19, p. 269.

I

THE issue of wage flexibility was central to Keynes' *General Theory* [1936] and in Chapter 19 he argued (as quoted above) that not only were wages in fact sticky but that their flexibility could be destabilising. It is easy to see that if price expectations are extrapolative such instability is possible. Demand falls, money wages and prices fall, real interest rates rise and the initial demand reduction is aggravated. This story depends on the dynamics of both wages and prices, so that the effects of nominal wage stickiness depend also on whether the money supply responds to shocks to the system. This paper analyses the effects of increased wage flexibility on the stability of employment under various monetary policy rules.

Although the preceding story can be told even if money wages are fixed, provided that real wages move inversely with output, Keynes is surely right to have believed that its plausibility was enhanced by money wage flexibility. What is, perhaps, surprising is that something similar can happen even if expectations are rational—provided that wage adjustment is not very rapid. It would not, for instance, occur if money wages were fixed each day for the next on the basis of rational, i.e., unbiassed, expectations of the next day's prices (the so-called 'auction' model). As long as money wages are fixed less frequently than employers adjust employment errors will be serially correlated. [Fischer 1977a][1]

The Keynesian instability with extrapolative expectations implied global instability. The model presented here with rational expectations is, by assumption, both globally and locally stable. However, it is specified as a stochastic model with a stochastic equilibrium, and it is the effect of wage flexibility on the *variance* of employment about its natural rate that may be perverse.

The analysis relates to the stochastic equilibrium of a model which deviates from pure neo-classicism only in that wages adjust less than

* Bank of England and Nuffield College, Oxford. This is a revised version of a paper prepared before I joined the Bank and first published (in Spanish) in the Keynes' centenary edition of "Información Comercial Espaniola" Num. 593 (1983).

I am very grateful to Olivier Blanchard, Stan Fischer, Bennett McCallum, Don Patinkin, Jeff Sachs, Peter Sinclair, Steve Turnovsky, Ken Wallis and a referee, for valuable comments on previous drafts. I remain responsible for any errors.

[1] In Fischer's model of explicit overlapping contracts, unlike our model of partial adjustment, convergence occurs in finite time. See also J. Taylor (1985).

instantaneously; rather they adjust partially towards an equilibrium, the level and trend of which are rationally inferred. If the labour market does not clear we must not only invoke an equation to describe wage/price dynamics but also specify the determination of actual employment. In this paper we assume that employment is demand determined: the analysis carries over almost exactly to the case in which employment is the *minimum* of labour supply and demand if supply is totally inelastic, since the distribution of employment outcomes is then as in this paper with truncation at full employment. Although this is an extreme case it may extend the generality of the results a little. Apart from the Keynesian assumption of money wage stickiness necessary to generate serially correlated unemployment, our assumptions are as neo-classical as possible. In this case the criterion offers little guidance; although demand determination sounds Keynesian it is exponents of the new Keynesianism [Barro-Grossman (1976), Malinvaud (1977)] who have used the 'min-rule' while monetarist studies of the wage equation, generating the expectations-augmentated Phillips curve, are consistent with demand determination.[2]

Following Keynes (1936), rather than Barro and Grossman (1976), prices are assumed to adjust instantaneously to clear the goods market given the money wage.[3] If wages are sticky but not rigid their adjustment process makes their movements, and hence that of prices, partly predictable, at least if the money supply follows systematic rules. These anticipated price movements affect aggregate demand as was recognised by Keynes (1936, p. 141/2). Note that the wage adjustment we assume is symmetrical and does not represent only downward stickiness.[4]

Although greater wage flexibility accelerates the return to 'full employment' this may not compensate for its effect on the initial impact of disturbances. It will be shown that, given the assumed effect of expected price changes on demand, greater wage flexibility implies a reduced responsiveness of prices to wages and thus greater sensitivity of both real wages and employment to disturbances. The question is whether this increased impact sensitivity is offset by more rapid equilibration.

The model is set out in Section II and the dependence of impact effects on wage flexibility is demonstrated in Section III. Section IV looks at the dependence of the equilibrium variance of employment on wage flexibility under two alternative money supply rules. Finally, Section V considers an optimal money supply rule and the relaxation of the assumption that the natural rate of employment is observable.

It is implied by the focus of our analysis that employment variation is a

[2] The partial adjustment of the money wage assumed here generates a particular expectations augmented Phillips curve, as shown on p. 16 below, which is closer to that of Sargent/Wallace (1975) then Lucas (1975).
[3] For some reasons for wage stickiness which do not apply to goods. See Flemming (1975).
[4] On the comparative static implications of symmetrical wage stickiness when prices are flexible and labour supply responds to the real wage, see Buiter and Lorie (1977).

'bad thing'. On the other hand, one interpretation of the model is that agents accept unbiased estimates of expected price changes as certainty equivalents—the variance of expected price changes plays no part. This might be regarded as requiring that they have linear (or rather log linear) utility functions so that variances (or rather log variances) of other arguments, such as employment, should also be irrelevant.

This position is particularly plasuible if it is assumed that everybody always has a job 'unemployment' taking the form of a failure to sell as many hours of work as desired at the going real wage. In this case, if available work is shared equally, the variance of individual aggregate employment is a multiple of the variance of hours of work. However, I prefer to think of wage inflexibility as involving variation in the number of jobs—the hours per job being fixed. In this case it is both more plausible and consistent that the variance of employment has welfare significance—especially if capital market imperfection makes consumption very responsive to job loss.[5] If I knew how they affect behaviour I would gladly include variances of expectations. I use the rational expectations certainty equivalent model for convenience and coherence with the related literature—not because I accept all the assumptions required for its rigorous justification in this context.

II

The model consists of the following eight equations in which d is the logarithm of aggregate demand (and output), n is the logarithm of employment, p the logarithm of the price level, w the logarithm of the wage and m the logarithm of the quantity of money. r is the nominal (short) interest rate and π the expected rate of inflation. The system is assumed to be linear in these variables, e.g., the production function is Cobb–Douglas.

Those equations (1–5) relating to *levels* of variables are written below without explicit time arguments (or indices) and with error terms $\bar{u}_i$; the 'dynamic' equations (6–8) have error terms $\bar{e}_i$ and time subscripts particularly on the expectations operator $E(\cdot)$.

$$d = \delta_1 y - \delta_2 r + \delta_3 \pi + \delta_4 m - \delta_5 p + \bar{u}_1 \tag{1}$$

$$y = \alpha n + \bar{u}_2 = d \tag{2}$$

$$m = p + \gamma_1 d - \gamma_2 4 - \gamma_3 \pi + \bar{u}_3 \tag{3}$$

$$m = m_0 + \lambda(\bar{n} - n) + \mu_4 t \tag{4}$$

$$p = w + \eta n - \bar{u}_2 - \ln \alpha; \qquad \eta \equiv 1 - \alpha > 0 \tag{5}$$

$$\pi_t = E_t(p_{t+1} - p_t) \tag{6}$$

$$w_t = w_{t-1} + E_{t-1}(\bar{w}_t - \bar{w}_{t-1}) + \phi E_{t-1}(\bar{w} - w)_t + \bar{e}_{7t} \tag{7}$$

$$\bar{n}_t = \bar{n}_{t-1} + \bar{e}_{8t} \tag{8}$$

[5] For a fuller discussion of these issues, see Flemming (1973), (1975), (1978).

The $\bar{e}_i$ are independently and identically distributed random disturbances such that $\bar{e}_{it} = N(\mu_i, v_i)$ while $\bar{u}_i(t)$ is the cumulation of past values of $\bar{e}_i$, i.e., $\bar{u}_{it} = \bar{u}_{it-1} + \bar{e}_{it}$; $E\bar{e}_{it} = \mu_i$; $E\bar{e}_{it}\bar{e}_{is} = 0$, $t \neq s = v_i$, $t = s$, $E\bar{e}_{it}\bar{e}_{jt} = 0$, $i \neq j$.

Equation (1) expresses aggregate demand (d) as depending on income (y), the nominal short rate, expected rate of inflation and real balances. Given the production function (2), y and the disturbance $\bar{u}_2$ contain information on the level of income, its distribution between wages and profits, the real wage, and the level of unemployment. (This implies that $\bar{u}_1$ may not be independent of $\bar{u}_2$.) Only the assumption that $\delta_3 > 0$ is at all contentious; on the one hand, given r, a higher π means a lower real interest rate and hence more expenditure; on the other hand, for positive money balances m, expected inflation reduces real income by generating capital losses on cash.[6] We assume that the authorities control the trend of the money supply so that there is no long term inflation. Thus the effect of π on permanent real income is small compared to the opportunities to make capital gains by taking advantage of short term price fluctuations. We therefore assume, and this is a Keynesian[7] assumption, that $\delta_3 > 0$. The real balance effect implies $\delta_4 = \delta_5 > 0$. If m were varied by open market operations private wealth would not vary £ for £ with m; however, we do assume $\delta_4 > 0$.

Equation (2) is a well behaved production function and also states that output equals aggregate demand. Capital does not appear in the production function for the usual reasons, although the assumption that everything that adjusts does so more rapidly than the capital stock would appear to exclude very sticky, but not rigid, wages. The labour input relates to the number of men employed (N); the length of the work-shift is either invariable or employment adjustment is much faster than that of wages. The disturbance $\bar{u}_2$ may in general drift with capital accumulation or technical progress.

Equation (3) is a conventional demand-for-money equation, including both nominal interest and expected inflation effects while (4) is a reaction function describing money supply policy. The description involves two parameters λ and μ_4. λ is the elasticity of money supply to the deviation $(\bar{n} - n)$ of (log) employment from its natural level $(\bar{n})$. Given that this feedback is posited to be contemporaneous, depending on contemporary values of $\bar{u}_1$, $\bar{u}_2$, $\bar{u}_3$, etc, any disturbance $\bar{u}_4$ in this equation could be offset; v_4 is therefore set equal to zero. μ_4, the trend growth of money supply, is set to meet our requirement that there be no long term trend in prices, i.e., μ_4 is equal to the trend growth rate of demand for money.

It may be objected that giving the authorities knowledge of contemporaneous disturbances eliminates the stabilisation problem, or that it

---

[6] For evidence suggesting that inflation reduces aggregate demand, see Deaton (1977) (whose theoretical argument, however, relates to *unexpected* inflation) and Davidson *et al.* (1978), also references in Davis (1982).

[7] See *General Theory*, Ch. 19, pp. 141/2.

represents an informational advantage over private agents. To these objections there are three replies. First it may make optimal stabilisation trivial, and completely successful, but it does not make uninteresting the analysis of non-optimal policies such as fixed monetary growth or interest rate stabilisation. Secondly, even contemporaneous information may be incomplete, e.g., if the natural rate is not directly observable (even after a lag) and enters into equations with a stochastic disturbance which therefore itself ceases to be observable contemporaneously—or subsequently. Thirdly, far from representing an informational advantage it may represent the adoption by the authorities of the same procedure of decentralisation that enables private agents *in the aggregate* to react to contemporary aggregates not individually observable. McCallum and Whittaker (1979) have presented analysis in which they distinguish between automatic (decentralised) fiscal stabilisers operating without lags (eg, taxes and social security) from feedback rules which necessarily operate with a lag (public expenditure increases in response to unemployment in their case). Surprisingly they assumed that any monetary feedback rule would necessarily be of this latter type; it would, however, be quite possible to instruct the officers arranging for payment of unemployment insurance benefits to undertake open market operations, on government account, as a part of the registration procedure of individual unemployed men. In this way a monetary supply response to unemployment need not await the compilation of aggregate statistics and could, in principle, be as prompt as the response of the flow of unemployment benefits.

As far as λ is concerned we consider three policies; first, a fixed money supply trend $(\lambda = 0)$; this is the open-loop type of control rule without feedback advocated by Friedman. Second a policy under which λ is chosen to remove serial correlation from the nominal interest rate, which is the nearest we can get to a fixed interest rate rule, and finally employment stabilising policy. It might be thought that it would be more appropriate to vary the rate of growth, rather than the level, of money supply with the employment rate. The difference would be sharpest in a continuous time model, however, as all the disturbances would then follow a Brownian motion, money supply variation would be virtually continuous (through not differentiable) even in the analog of the form used in (4).

Equation (5) relates the price level to the money wage and to the marginal product of labour, while equation (6) defines the rationally expected rate of inflation. The price expectations π_t depend on knowledge of all the parameters and the current values of all the disturbances. In the case of $\bar{u}_1$, $\bar{u}_2$ and $\bar{u}_3$ this is straightforward; however as noted, $\bar{n}$ is not, in general, observable. Thus in a general model both public and private agents will, at best, have to rely on inferences about the natural rate—this generalisation is considered in Section V below. Our consideration of alternative values of the wage adjustment parameter ϕ and the monetary policy parameter λ involves considering the system operating with different dynamic properties. The response of a rational agent to each of the arguments of the demand functions (6) and (7) depends on ϕ and λ.

The endogeneity of the parameters δ_i, and γ_i of the demand function for goods and money is suppressed in this paper; it can, however, be shown that in a plausible model of these parameters, the qualitative conclusions of the present analysis survive.

Equation (7) describes the movement of money wages; $\bar{w}$ is (the log of) the "equilibrium" money wage at which employment n equals the inelastic equilibrium supply $\bar{n}$ (an expression for $\bar{w}$ is derived explicitly below). Money wages set at time $(t-1)$ are equal to w_{t-1} plus the expected change of $\bar{w}$ plus a proportion ϕ of the deviation of money wages from their equilibrium value (as expected for time t at time $t-1$); ϕ is thus an index of money wage flexibility.

In a largely neo-classical model such as this, the stability of employment is closely related to the flexibility of the real wage. We shall see that equation (7) implies that money wages converge to equilibrium at the rate $\phi/(1+\phi)$. Given the unique saddle point equilibrium of the (log) linear model of equations (1)–(8) all the endogenous variables, including the real wage, converge at the same rate. Thus *ex ante* the real wage also converges at the rate $\phi/(1+\phi)$ and ϕ can be regarded as an indicator of *ex ante* real wage flexibility. If, however, real wages were specified to adjust partially the impact of shocks would be quite different. As it is with sticky money wages real wages may jump in response to a shock. This would not occur if wage contracts were indexed; the implications of such contracts for employment stability are considered by Fischer (1977b).

III

The first step is to make rigorous the definition of the equilibrium value of the wage rate $\bar{w}$ and that of the other endogenous variables p and r. We have already said that the trend rate of growth of the money supply (μ_4) is to be chosen so as to make the trend inflation rate $\bar{\pi} = 0$. With little loss of generality we can remove the drift from all the stochastic equations by setting μ_1, μ_2, μ_3, μ_7 and μ_8 all equal to zero in which case the required value of μ_4 is also zero. Equilibrium requires $n = \bar{n}$, $w = \bar{w}$, $p = \bar{p}$, $r = \bar{r}$ and $\pi = \bar{\pi} = 0$; if also we choose units so that $\bar{m} = 0$ we have, from (4) $m = \bar{m} = 0$.

Then equations (1) and (2) imply that

$$\alpha(1 - \delta_1)\bar{n} = (\bar{u}_1 - (1 - \delta_1)\bar{u}_2) - \delta_2\bar{r} - \delta_5\bar{p} \tag{9}$$

while (3) and (4) imply that

$$0 = \delta_5\bar{p} + \alpha_1\gamma_1\delta_5\bar{n} + \delta_5(\gamma_1\bar{u}_2 + \bar{u}_3) - \gamma_2\delta_5\bar{r}. \tag{10}$$

By addition

$$(\delta_2 + \gamma_2\delta_5)\bar{r} = [\bar{u}_1 - \bar{u}_2(1 - \delta_1 - \gamma_1\delta_5) + \delta_5\bar{u}_3] - \alpha(1 - \delta_1 - \gamma_1\delta_5)\bar{n} \tag{11}$$

similarly

$$(\delta_2 + \gamma_2\delta_5)\bar{p} = [\gamma_2\bar{u}_1 + (\delta_2\gamma_1 + (1 - \delta_1)\gamma_2)\bar{u}_2 - \delta_2\bar{u}_3] - \alpha[\gamma_1\delta_2 + (1 - \delta_1)\gamma_2]\bar{n} \tag{12}$$

or, setting

$$A = \delta_2 + \gamma_2\delta_5 > 0$$
$$C = (1 - \delta_1)\gamma_2 + \gamma_1\delta_2$$
$$Z = (1 - \delta_1) - \gamma_1\delta_5$$

$$A\bar{r} = \bar{u}_1 - \bar{u}_2 z + \delta_5\bar{u}_3 - \alpha Z\bar{n} \tag{11a}$$

$$A\bar{p} = \gamma_2\bar{u}_1 + \bar{u}_2 C - \delta_2\bar{u}_3 - \alpha C\bar{n} \tag{12a}$$

while from (5)

$$\bar{w} = \bar{p} - \eta\bar{n} + \bar{u}_2 + \ln\alpha. \tag{13}$$

The subsequent analysis is more conveniently carried out in terms of deviations from these equilibrium values; we therefore define

$$\omega \equiv w - \bar{w}, \qquad \psi \equiv p - \bar{p}, \qquad v \equiv n - \bar{n}, \qquad \rho \equiv r - \bar{r}.$$

Under rational expectations

$$E_{t-1}\bar{w}_t = \bar{w}_t + \bar{\varepsilon} \tag{14}$$

where $\bar{\varepsilon}$ is a normal random variate with variance σ_ε^2 which can be derived from (8), (12) and (13) to be

$$\alpha_\varepsilon^2 = (\gamma_2/A)^2 v_1 + (C/A)^2 v_2 + (\delta_2/A)^2 v_3 + (\eta + \alpha C/A)^2 v_8 \tag{15}$$

Similarly, if the disturbance $\bar{e}_{7t}$ intervenes after the wage has been set for time t at time $t - 1$, $E_{t-1}w_t = w_t - \bar{e}_{7t}$. Thus equation 7 can be written as

$$w_t = w_{t-1} + (\bar{w}_t - \bar{w}_{t-1}) + \phi(\bar{w}_t - w_t) + (1 + \phi)(\bar{\varepsilon} + \bar{e}_7)$$

or $\omega_t = \omega_{t-1}/(1 + \phi) + \bar{e}_t$ where $\bar{e} = \bar{\varepsilon} + \bar{e}_7$ and has variance

$$\tilde{\sigma}_e^2 = v = \sigma_\varepsilon^2 + v_7. \tag{16}$$

Given $\bar{\pi} = 0$ the expected rate of change of prices and the expected change of the deviation of prices from their equilibrium are the same thing, ie $\pi_t = E_t p_{t+1} - p_t = E_t \psi_{t+1} - \psi_t$.

In stable dynamic models of this sort all variables converge at the same expected rate, thus

$$E_t \psi_{t+1} = \frac{\psi_t}{1 + \phi}$$

and

$$\pi_t = \left(\frac{1}{1 + \phi} - 1\right)\psi_t = -\frac{\phi}{1 + \phi}\psi t \tag{17}$$

while from (5)

$$\psi = \omega + \eta v. \tag{18}$$

Using equations (17) and (18), and writing ξ for $\phi/(1 + \phi)$, equations (1) and (2) now imply

$$\alpha(1 - \delta_1)n = (\bar{u}_1 - \bar{u}_2) - \delta_2 r - \delta_5 p - \delta_4 \lambda v - \delta_3 \xi(\omega + \eta v) \tag{19}$$

Substituting equation (9) and rearranging gives

$$0 = [\delta_4 \lambda + \alpha(1 - \delta_1) + \eta(\delta_5 + \xi\delta_3)]v + \delta_2 \rho + (\delta_5 + \xi\delta_3)\omega. \tag{20}$$

Similarly (3) and (4) now imply

$$0 = [\lambda + \alpha\gamma_1 + \eta(1 + \xi\gamma_3)]v - \gamma_2 \rho + (1 + \xi\gamma_3)\omega. \tag{21}$$

Equations (20) and (21) enable v and ρ to be expressed as functions of ω whose dynamics are given by (16) (and (15)). Thus,

$$v = \frac{-[(\delta_2 + \gamma_2\delta_5) + (\gamma_2\delta_3 + \delta_2\gamma_3)\xi]\omega}{\alpha(\gamma_2 + \gamma_1\delta_2) - \delta_1\gamma_2 + \lambda(\delta_2 + \gamma_2\delta_4) + \eta[\delta_2 + \gamma_2\delta_5) + (\gamma_2\delta_3 + \delta_2\gamma_3)\xi]}$$

$$= \frac{-(A + B\xi)\omega}{C + D\lambda + (A + B\xi)\eta} \tag{22}$$

where

$$B \equiv \gamma_2\delta_3 + \delta_2\gamma_3 > 0$$
$$D \equiv \delta_2 + \gamma_2\delta_4 > 0.$$

We can now see that changing wage flexibility has two opposing effects on the stability of employment. First raising ϕ (and thus ξ) almost certainly increases the responsiveness of employment to wage deviations steepening the $v(\omega)$ line. Secondly, of course, it accelerates the return to equilibrium.

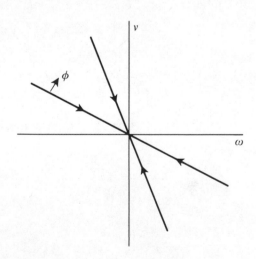

Consider the first effect: the absolute value of the slope of the line

$$s = \left| \frac{dv}{d\omega} \right| = -\frac{v}{\omega} = \frac{A + B\xi}{C + D\lambda + \eta(A + B\xi)} \tag{23}$$

$1 > \delta_1$ is sufficient for $C > 0$ to hold and is required if additional employment is to add more to output than to demand, ceteris paribus, ie, it corresponds to a marginal propensity to consume of less than unity. Whether the mpc of the GT should be regarded as 'large' or small depends on one's reference point. Patinkin (1976, p67) has written that the Keynes of the Treatise (1930) appears implicitly to have assumed mpc = 1(which roughly corresponds to $\delta_1 = 1$) whereas a more neo-classical position, eg, Friedman's permanent income hypothesis (1957), would make $1 \gg \delta_1 \approx 0$.

$ds/d\xi$ is obviously positive if $(C + D\lambda)$ is positive. C will be assumed positive from now on so that for $\lambda \geqslant 0$ increasing wage flexibility increases the impact effect on employment of any disturbance.

This is, perhaps, the key result in this paper; an inituitive account is as follows. Consider an adverse shock, nominal wages do not jump. The more flexible they are the more rapidly they will fall and the higher *ex ante* real interest rate for a given nominal rate (the nominal rate only falls if real balances rise, eg because prices jump down—but that, given the wage, can only happen at a lower level of output). The higher real interest associated with the expectation of more rapid wage adjustment depresses demand and employment; the more output and employment fall the lower the price. Thus the greater the flexibility of a wage that does not jump the greater the impact effect of shocks on the price level, the real wage, and output.

In the next section we examine the conditions under which this greater impact effect may, locally, outweigh the greater speed of equilibration in determining the asymptotic variance of employment. This variance is necessarily smaller if wages are immediately perfectly flexible than if they are rigid. Notice, however, that perfect flexibility in a discrete time model implies full adjustment next period—not an immediate jump response.

IV

The variance of employment deviations we write as V_v which is equal to $s^2 V_\omega$.

For a large enough value of t the variance, as of time zero, of ω_{t-1} and ω_t will be equal. This asymptotic variance can be derived by squaring and taking expectations of equation (16) to give

$$V_\omega \left[1 - \left(\frac{1}{1 + \phi} \right)^2 \right] = v$$

or

$$V_\omega = \frac{v(1 + \phi)^2}{\phi(2 + \phi)} = \frac{v}{\xi(2 - \xi)} \tag{24}$$

so that

$$\left(\frac{V_v}{v}\right) = \frac{s^2}{\xi(2 - \xi)} \tag{25}$$

Then

$$\frac{d(V_v/v)}{d\xi} = \frac{2s \dfrac{ds}{\delta\xi}}{\xi(2 - \xi)} - \frac{s^2 2(1 - \xi)}{\xi^2(2 - \xi)^2}$$

so that

$$\frac{d(V_v/v)}{d\xi} \gtrless 0 \quad \text{as} \quad \frac{\xi}{s}\frac{ds}{d\xi} \gtrless \frac{1 - \xi}{2 - \xi} \tag{26}$$

We consider first the case in which $\lambda = 0$, ie, monetary policy is non-accommodating—the money supply being fixed.

From (23), writing X for $(A + B\xi) > 0$

$$\frac{\xi}{s}\frac{ds}{\delta\xi}\bigg|_{\lambda=0} = \frac{[(C + \eta X)B - X\eta B]\xi}{(C + \eta X)X} = \frac{BC\xi}{X(C + \eta X)} \tag{27}$$

Thus, as ξ goes from zero to one the left hand side of (26) goes from zero to something strictly positive while the right hand side goes from a half to zero. Thus, in the region of $\xi = 1$ greater wage flexibility increases the asymptotic variance of employment if $C, \lambda \geqslant 0$. It is easy to see that the result holds for any positive value of λ independent of ϕ(or ξ)—it does not depend on a strictly non accommodating monetary policy, but the degree of accommodation must not depend on the degree of wage flexibility.

To explain the result, two points should be noted

(i) the opposing forces mentioned above; and

(ii) that while s rises monotonically with ξ (sign $\delta s/\delta\xi$ = sign $[C + D\lambda]$) for all finite ξ. V_ω goes asymptotically to its finite limit v as ξ goes to one.

The result is not entirely robust. As the time unit goes to zero—i.e., as a

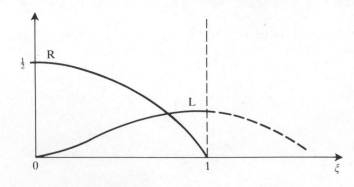

continuous time specification is approached—v, the lower limit of V_ω, goes to zero as the speed of adjustment (ϕ) becomes infinite. If this happens fast enough, the perverse region in which employment stability falls with increased wage flexibility, moves towards the middle of the range of values of the flexibility parameter and may well disappear, especially if the price level effect on expenditure (δ_5) is large and the interest rate effect on expenditure (δ_2) is large relative to its effect on the demand for money (γ_2).

Thus, Keynesian parameter values in a largely "laissez-faire" model, of the type envisaged in the cited passage, do indeed go some way to validate his claim. However this is conditional on a money supply policy other than that he assumed. Keynes seems more nearly, though not entirely consistently, to have assumed a fixed nominal interest rate policy (GT p. 245) than a fixed (or employment related) quantitative money supply rule such as is implied by a fixed value of λ in (4). In particular an exogenous nominal interest rate chosen by the authorities does much to rationalise the speculative element in the aggregated demand for money which features so prominently in the General Theory.

A fixed nominal interest rate is not compatible with our requirement that equilibrium be non inflationary; demand disturbances are liable to affect the equilibrium real interest rate and any failure of the nominal rate to follow must generate drifting prices. It is, however, feasible to choose a $\lambda = \lambda^*(\phi)$, or rather $\lambda = \lambda^*(\xi)$, such that r is always equal to $\bar{r}$ and follows a random walk.

Solving equations (20) and (21) for ρ in terms of ω and setting the coefficient of ω to zero gives

$$\lambda^*(\xi) = \frac{F + G\xi}{K + H\xi} \gtrless 0$$

where

$$\left. \begin{array}{l} F = \alpha\gamma_1 A - C \gtrless 0 \\ G = \alpha\gamma_1 B - C\gamma_3 \gtrless 0 \\ K = D - A \gtrless 0 \\ H = D\gamma_3 - B \gtrless 0. \end{array} \right\} \tag{28}$$

The general expression for the LHS of (26) when $\lambda = \lambda(\xi)$ is, writing λ' for $d\lambda/d\xi$,

$$\frac{\xi}{s} \frac{\delta s}{d\xi} = \frac{(BC - D\lambda'X)\xi}{(C + D\lambda + \eta X)X} \tag{29}$$

while from (28)

$$\lambda^{*\prime} = \frac{GK - FH}{(K + H\xi)^2}. \tag{30}$$

Unambiguous results are more clearly obtained for the special case in which the price level and money supply effects on aggregate demand are equal and opposite. In this real balance case $\delta_4 = \delta_5$ and $A = D$ (see (23)) so that $K = 0$ whence

$$\lambda^*(\xi) = \frac{(F + G\xi)}{H\xi} \gtrless 0 \qquad (28')$$

while

$$\lambda^{*\prime} = \frac{-F}{H\xi^2} \gtrless 0. \qquad (30')$$

Substituting from (28') and 30' into (29) and (26) gives the condition

$$\frac{d(V_v/v)}{d\xi} \gtrless 0 \quad \text{as} \quad \frac{BCH\xi^2 + DFX}{[CH\xi + D(F + G\xi) + \eta XH\xi]X} \gtrless \frac{1 - \xi}{2 - \xi}. \qquad (31)$$

As before the RHS of this condition falls from $\frac{1}{2}$ to zero as ξ rises from zero to 1. At $\xi = 0$, however, the LHS takes the value unity. In the absence of any restriction on the signs of F, G and H there is little point in speculating about the shape of the function. Thus the only conclusion we can draw is that in this more Keynesian case of maximum consistent interest stability, at least for values of ϕ (and ξ) close to zero, i.e., when wages are very sticky, an increase in wage flexibility would increase the variance of employment—further support for the Keynesian proposition with which we started.

V

So far we have considered the effects of varying wage flexibility on employment stability under two money supply rules; fixity, and interest stabilising. Clearly we should also consider a monetary policy designed not to stabilise interest but employment. From equation (22) it is clear that employment can be made independent of wage discrepancies if λ is made infinite. This is interventionist monetary policy 'à outrance' discussed in a Keynesian context by Leijonhufvud.[8]

More generally on the informational assumptions we have made, which imply that the authorities can observe all the variables and disturbances and adjust the money supply within the period, perfect stabilisation is quite feasible. Perhaps the least realistic of these assumptions, and thus a major contributor to the incompleteness of observed stabilisation, is the assumption that the natural rate of employment $\bar{n}$ is observable, although it does not enter directly into any behavioural equation other than that describing the monetary policy response to deviation of actual employment from it. Using equation (22) the $E_{t-1}(\bar{w} - w)_t$ term in the wage adjustment equation (7) could be replaced by one in terms of $E_{t-1}(n - \bar{n})_t$, and this in turn (as in (18)) by $v_{t-1}/(1 + \phi)$; giving $w_t = w_{t-1} + \mu_2 - \eta\mu_8 + \xi(n_{t-1} - \bar{n}_{t-1}) + \bar{e}_{7t}$. Even when knowledge of w_t is added to that of w_{t-1}, n_{t-1}, μ_8, η and ϕ the

[8] Axel Leijonhufvud (1968) pp. 20, 58 and elsewhere.

observable residual $z_t = \bar{e}_{7t} - \xi \bar{n}_{t-1}$ cannot be decomposed into its component parts.

Under these circumstances the authorities' money supply rule (4) has to be modified, $\bar{n}$ being replaced by n^*, the authorities' estimate of the natural rate. Under rational expectations this estimate will be formed optimally and the inference will itself be the subject of successful replication by private agents as an ingredient in their own forecasts.

It is fairly easy to see that these optimal forecasts will take an adaptive form such as:

$$n_t^* = n_{t-1}^* + \mu_8 + \beta \xi (\hat{n} - n^*)_{t-1} \frac{v_8}{v_7} \qquad (32)$$

where $\hat{n}_{t-1}$ is the value of $\bar{n}_{t-1}$ implicit in the emergence of w_t on the assumption that $\bar{e}_{7t} = 0$. That is, from $(\hat{7})$

$$\hat{n}_{t-1} = n_{t-1}[(w_t - w_{t-1}) - \mu_2 + \eta \mu_8]/\xi \qquad (33)$$

Equation (32) says that the weight given to the current implicit value $\hat{n}$ is directly proportional to the (known) variance (v_8) of the changes in $\bar{n}$, about which inferences are being made, and inversely proportional to the "noisiness" (v_7) of the process generating the wage adjustment on which the implicit estimate of $\hat{n}$ is based. The optimal policy under these informational conditions is not self evident. It is clear that monetary policy 'à outrance' can 'stabilise' employment an n_t^* but the discrepancies of n_t^* from $\bar{n}_t$ will be serially correlated under the adaptive rule (32). Thus attempts to "stabilise" n at n^* are liable to aggravate fluctuations in the level and rate of change of prices—the real world may present difficult choices between price and employment stabilisation which are not reflected in the analysis of Sections II.

Conclusion

In this paper we have set up a model of the type used by advocates of *laissez faire* with the minimum modification—a specification of sticky wages—necessary to analyse Keynesian propositions. It is a valid criticism both of Keynes, and of this paper, that no micro economic rationalisation of this wage stickiness is offered. One may however be possible in informational terms; see Yellen (1984) for a survey of such models.

Within the restricted framework we have gone some way to substantiating Keynes' claim. While the orthodox claim that more flexible wages make for a better outcome may not always be the opposite of the truth, one can certainly construct a number of counter examples as we have done above.

Since the discussion of "the theory of the second best" by welfare economists this should surprise us less. A policy designed to increase wage flexibility, which one might expect to be "a good thing", can only be relied upon to raise welfare if other policies—notably monetary policy—are also optimised. If wages are less than perfectly flexible, the optimisation of money supply policy is by no means trivial.

Bank of England and Nuffield College, Oxford.

REFERENCES

BARRO, R. J. and GROSSMAN, H. I. (1976) *Money, Employment and Inflation* Cambridge University Press, New York.

BUITER, W. E. H. and LORIE, H. R. (1977) 'Some Unfamiliar Properties of a Familiar Macroeconomic Model' *Economic Journal* 87, 743–754.

DAVIS, E. P. (1982) The Consumption Function in Macro-Economic Models' *Bank of England Discussion Paper* Technical Series No 1.

DAVIDSON, J. E. H., HENDRY, D. F., SRBA, F. and YEO, S. (1978) 'Econometric Modelling of the Time-Series Relationship between Consumers' Expenditure and Income in the UK' *Economic Journal* 88, 661–692.

DEATON, A. S. (1977) 'Involuntary Saving Through Unanticipated Inflation' *American Economic Review* 67, 899–910.

FISCHER, S. (1977a) 'Long Term Contracts, Rational Expectations and the Optimal Money Supply Rate' *Journal of Political Economy* 85, 191–206.

—— (1977b) 'Wage Indexation and Macroeconomic Stability' *JME* supp: Carnegie-Rochester Conference Series Vol 5, 107–147.

FLEMMING, J. S. (1973) 'The Consumption Function when Capital Markets are Imperfect' *Oxford Economic Papers* 25, 160–172.

—— (1975) 'Wage Rigidity and Employment Adjustment' in *Contemporary Issues in Economics,* Parkin M., and Nobay, A. R. (eds), Manchester University Press.

—— (1978) 'Aspects of Optimal Unemployment Insurance' *Journal of Public Economics* 10, 403–426.

FRIEDMAN, M. (1957) *A Theory of the Consumption Function* (NBER: Princeton).

KEYNES, J. M. (1930) *A Treatise on Monday* (Macmillan: London).

—— (1936) *General Theory of Employment, Interest and Money* (Macmillan: London).

LEIJONHUFVUD, A. (1968) *On Keynesian Economics and the Economics of Keynes* (Oxford University Press, New York.

LUCAS, R. E. (1975) 'An Equilibrium Model of The Business Cycle', *Journal of Political Economy,* 83, 473–91.

MALINVAUD, E. (1977) *The Theory of Unemployment Reconsidered* (Blackwell, Oxford).

McCALLUM, B. T. and WHITTAKER, J. K. (1979) 'The Effectiveness of Fiscal Feedback Rules and Automatic Stabilisers under Rational Expectations' *J. Mon. E.* 5, 1971–86.

PATINKIN, D. (1976) *Keynes' Monetary Thought* (Duke University Press, Durham NC).

TAYLOR, J. B. (1985) 'Rational Expectations in Macroeconomic Models' in Arrow, K. J. and Honkapohja, S. *Frontiers of Economics* (Oxford, Blackwell).

SARGENT, T. and WALLACE, N. (1975) 'Rational Expectations, The Optimal Monetary Instrument and The Optimal Money Supply Rule', *Journal of Political Economy,* 83, 241–54.

YELLEN, J. L. (1984) 'Efficiency Wage Models of Unemployment', *American Economic Review,* papers and proceedings, 74, 200–5.

Oxford Economic Papers 39 (1987), 175–189

MALTHUS AND KEYNES*

By R. P. RUTHERFORD

THE question of Malthus's stature as an early Keynesian has held a continuing fascination for historians of economic thought. While Keynes himself claimed Malthus as a forbear, most commentators have shared Schumpeter's judgement (1954) that Keynes was mistaken. This paper argues that Malthus did anticipate Keynes in important respects and that the literature has misjudged the relationship because of undue concentration on Keynes's General Theory.[1] After noting some problems in modern interpretations of the relationship, a justification is offered for turning instead to Keynes's Treatise on Money to establish the link. This is then explored with reference both to the theory of failure of effective demand and the policy solutions proposed.

Introduction

At least since Cannan (1917, p. 7) Malthus has been widely portrayed as a hopelessly muddled thinker. This view has been turned on its head in recent years and his reputation as a theoretician is deservedly higher than at any time this century. There has emerged a consensus over his basic theoretical framework of a cyclical model of economic growth based on the interaction of capital and labour cobwebs.[2] The Malthusian economy is pictured as having an inherent tendency to stall or become 'hitchbound' as Schumpeter puts it (1954, p. 566). However, views on Malthus's analysis of the post Napoleonic depression have differed widely and it is this work, including the proposed policy solutions, which is most pertinent to that of Keynes.

Perhaps the simplest position taken on Malthus's depression analysis is to regard it, with Sowell as the slump phase of a self correcting cycle in the growth process. The analysis of general glut is seen as 'a sketchy corollary on temporary unemployment' appended to 'an elaborate theory of economic development' (1963, p. 193). This interpretation conflicts with the many references which suggest a more serious breakdown in the economy. It also runs into difficulties because it strictly identifies Malthusian 'oversaving' with overinvestment, that is with capital accumulation overshooting in the cobweb. Many commentators have noted that, in analysing the depression resulting from the transition from war to peace, Malthus is not looking at a situation heralded by the collapse of an investment boom. There are two

---

* I would like to thank my colleagues, Alf Hagger and Ben Heijdra, for comments on an earlier version, and two anonymous referees for helping me to clarify the argument at some critical points. Any remaining errors are of course my own responsibility.

[1] All references to the works of Keynes are to the Collected Writings published by the Royal Economic Society and are given by volume number in Roman numerals and page number.

[2] Malthus's framework is derived chiefly from his *Principles of Political Economy*. Unless otherwise indicated all references are to the second edition of 1836.

problems here. Firstly, it has been too easily accepted that an overinvestment theory of depression would of necessity be non-Keynesian and this issue is taken up later in the paper. Secondly, if overinvestment is the basic cause of the slump phase of a cycle, how are we to integrate the discussion of the post Napoleonic depression with the discussion of the growth process? Hollander believes that our problems of interpretation arise because we persist in looking for a unified theory, while Malthus in fact had more than one theory of depression and therefore his account of post war events with regard to causes 'is not inconsistent with Keynesian analysis' (1969, p. 306). The attribution to Malthus of an analysis at variance with the basic model of capital accumulation results in serious problems of internal logical consistency with respect to the rationale lying behind Malthus's policy prescriptions. Hollander argues that the seemingly Keynesian solutions to unemployment are based on 'a markedly non-Keynesian set of arguments' because 'Malthus's logic frequently involves results derived from the basic model of capital accumulation' (1969, p. 307). Further these solutions themselves are 'not really consistent with his own basic model of accumulation' (1969, p. 334n). Hollander thus presents Malthus as a sophisticated theorist evolving new structures to grapple with the march of events but unable to successfully integrate these with his underlying model.

There lies a great challenge in presenting a coherent Malthusian model able to embrace both his views of the growth process and his post war depression analysis. This is exactly what Eltis attempts. After first developing, as he says uncontroversially (1980, p. 19), a Sowell like analysis of the interactions of the labour and capital cobwebs in a business cycle, he notes the failure of this analysis to explain the many references which suggest that something more serious can go wrong with the economy than merely a self correcting slump. The Eltis solution is a growth model in which it is possible for key variables to take on values such that effective demand fails to grow at the same rate as supply. The most daring and controversial element in this model is the introduction of functional dependence of the rate of technical progress on the rate of profit, a relationship which plays a crucial role in the failure of effective demand.[3] While Eltis is not specifically concerned with the relationship to Keynes, he in effect presents Malthus as the first 'Cambridge' growth theorist. That is to say, with separate investment and savings functions and classes with differing propensities to save, the dynamic equilibrium condition that planned saving equals planned investment will only be met if the distribution of income adjusts appropriately. It has long been acknowledged that such growth models contain Keynesian elements. Eltis clearly regards Malthus's model as being in some

---

[3] Eltis justifies this relationship with a series of quotations designed to show that Malthus believed motivation to be of central importance and that productivity growth is demand induced. The textual basis is a little thin but Malthus may well have echoed Smith on this point. The bold incorporation of endogenous technical progress is no doubt based on the methodological justification given for the assumption made. (1980, p. 19)

respects Keynesian though it is with Kalecki that he draws his fleeting comparison (1980, p. 39). In a recent paper, Costabile and Rowthorn (1985) also present Malthus as a 'Cambridge' growth theorist though their model differs in some important assumptions.

In evaluating Malthus as an early Keynesian reference will be made to a variety of Keynes's writings.[4] Since the original version of the Essay on Malthus dates from 1922, it is clear that Keynes thought highly of Malthus at a very early stage in the development of his own theories. Moreover, only a few years separate the General Theory from the Treatise on Money and an editorial note makes clear that the critical passages of the Essay, where Keynes makes his strongest claims for Malthus, were added at the beginning of 1933 thus falling squarely between the two works (Vol X. p. 71). In any case, we no longer see the General Theory as a revolutionary break with Keynes's previous work. The resurgence of interest in Keynes's economics following the work of Clower (1965) and Leijonhufvud (1968) has led us to an appreciation of the essential continuity in his thought. The evidence of the Treatise on Money is particularly valuable because the analysis of fluctuations in effective demand is there conducted using a model which assumes price flexibility. This takes us much closer to Malthus. It will be argued that the sequence of events analysed by Malthus in the post-Napoleonic depression bears close correspondence to the depression process outlined in the Treatise and that there is an essential similarity of conception over the crucial role of the rate of profit and the way in which changes in income distribution can result in a failure of effective demand.

Keynes made several specific claims for Malthus. He praised him for his conception of effective demand as determining prices and profits, (Vol X, p. 88) and for dealing with a specifically monetary economy (Vol X. p. 97). He credited him with a 'complete comprehension of the effects of excessive saving on output *via* its effects on profit' (Vol X. p. 99), and commended his policy prescriptions (Vol X. p. 101). The following is aimed at substantiating these claims which are currently dismissed or at best deemed overstated.

The depression process in Keynes's treatise

Since Keynes claimed that Malthus had seen the link between effective demand, prices and profits and how excessive saving could affect output through its effects on profit, we need to establish that these elements play a part in both Keynes's Treatise view of the depression process and Malthus's. Given that most economists are familiar not with the Treatise but with the later modelling of the problem in the General Theory, it seems appropriate to begin with a brief outline of the analytical apparatus of the Treatise, then show how a depression can arise and finally compare this to Malthus's analysis of depression.

[4] Most commentators have made their points against the implicit benchmark of the textbook Keynesian model with which they can safely assume the reader is acquainted and have directed their energies almost totally to careful textual analysis of Malthus.

It may come as a surprise to those whose Keynesianism begins with the General Theory to learn that Keynes explicitly worked with a concept of effective demand in the Treatise. He was quite clear that this amounted to saying aggregate output could vary. The analysis of effective demand takes place in a price-flex economy but the adjustment velocities of prices are not all the same. Effective demand is discussed without the multiplier and the modern reader faces the difficulty of a strong temptation to read it in. While Say's Law is not explicitly dealt with it is quite clearly dismissed, and moreover, in the sense of the modern proposition that we owe to Clower (1965), that the sum of excess demands for all goods including money is zero.[5] There is a clear distinction in the model between motives to save and invest, that is there are separate savings and investment functions. While not specified mathematically these functions are extensively discussed and the operation of the Fundamental Equations depends on them. The discussion of output and employment effects takes place as a process analysis with a definite sequence. The analysis is entirely of the short run and concerns disequilibrium as equilibrium is defined as occurring at full employment. While we may presume Keynes believed such an equilibrium to exist he clearly did not regard it as stable as the whole thrust of the book is to advocate an active monetary policy based on the rate of interest. It should be noted that he assumes that the market rate of interest is sticky and so are money wages. However, it is unclear whether the Keynes of the Treatise believed that these variables could move to restore equilibrium or that the economy was locked into 'disequilibrium'. This is not of great importance to us here since precisely the same thing can be said of the view of depression Malthus espouses. In this brief outline of how depression can arise in the 'Treatise' view I will assume that money wages and the interest rate are fixed.

Full employment equilibrium output exists in the situation where costs of production ex ante, including normal rewards to entrepreneurs, equal actual costs of production. However, expectations might not be validated in this way, in which case there will be a windfall gain or loss to entrepreneurs. There can also be windfall gains or losses to the suppliers of labour with fixed money wages if the price level of consumption goods changes but these gains and losses have no driving force in the model. Effectively we can assume that all wages are spent. The real action of the model lies in how the relative movement in the price level of consumer goods vis a vis the price level of investment goods imposes a windfall gain or loss on entrepreneurs and how this affects their decision to invest in the next period.

In Chapter 12 of the Treatise [Vol V, p. 154–165] Keynes was concerned

---

[5] This modern conceptual variant of Say's Law is employed as most pertinent to the mechanism by which excess demand failure occurs in both Malthus and Keynes. It in effect subsumes both "Say's Identity" and "Say's Equality" in Baumol's terminology (1977). Thweatt (1979) also reviews the early development of Say's Law, and discusses its connexion with both the nineteenth century orthodoxy rejecting general glut, and the twentieth century Treasury View attacked by Keynes.

to establish that a decision to save in terms of non-consumption was not a decision to invest in capital goods and that an exogenous shock, such as an increase in the savings ratio, could lead to depression precisely because it was not matched by an increase in investment. The mechanism he envisages is that an exogenous shock, be it a change in planned savings by consumers or planned investment by entrepreneurs, results in changes in the relative prices of consumption goods and these result in income distribution effects. A key analytic point is that aggregate output is sold at prices below the ex ante costs of production. Because in the model of the Treatise it is the decisions of entrepreneurs which drive the level of overall activity, the concentration is on the windfall gains and losses to entrepreneurs. It is important to note that either oversaving or 'overinvestment' can provide the exogenous shock leading to a depression. In order to use Keynes's own illustration of the 'banana plantation' and to facilitate comparison with the Malthus analysis of the post-Napoleonic depression, the oversaving shock will be discussed.

The sequence in the banana example [Vol V, p. 158–160] works this way. Consumers decide to save a higher proportion of their incomes. However, the entrepreneurs of the society do not increase their investment in new plantations. The same quantity of bananas comes to market and on the assumption that they are non-storable the price level of bananas falls. Consumers are better off since they have increased their savings but enjoyed the same consumption level as before at a lower price level with money wages unchanged. The bananas, aggregate output, have been sold below their ex ante costs of production and entrepreneurs have suffered a windfall loss which has been transferred to the workers via higher real wages. The losses are made good by the entrepreneurs borrowing the savings of the consumers. Keynes concludes that entrepreneurs will attempt to protect themselves by reducing wages and employment but that this will not help as long as planned savings exceed planned investment: 'there will be no position of equilibrium until either (a) all production ceases and the entire population starves to death; or (b) the thrift campaign is called off or peters out as a result of the growing poverty; or (c) investment is stimulated by some means or another so that its cost no longer lags behind the rate of saving.' [Vol V, p. 160]

It is not our concern here whether this represents good economics but only whether the analysis is similar to that used by Malthus.

The depression process in Malthus

The purpose of this section is to establish that the process by which depression can arise in Malthus's model is consistent with that outlined in Keynes's Treatise on Money. Furthermore, it will be argued that Malthus had only one theory of depression in the sense of the key elements of the process by which it occurred. However, he allowed either an exogenous shock of the overinvestment type when entrepreneurs were excessively optimistic about the profit rate or an exogenous shock of the underconsumption and underinvestment type when entrepreneurs were excessively pessimistic about the profit rate. Both processes are mirrored in Keynes and can be contrasted with crude underconsumptionist and overinvestment theories which lack an analysis of the process.

Many early commentators on Malthus as a Keynesian used as their litmus paper test the question of whether Malthus assigned a role to hoarding. The reason for this was their concern to establish whether Malthus like Keynes was allowing a role for the running up of idle money balances as a leakage from the circular flow of income. Since their view of Keynesian economics was confined to the General Theory we can construe this as positing an outward shift in the speculative demand for money function within an ISLM framework leading to an upward movement of the LM curve and a reduction in real output and employment.[6] This was perhaps understandable given the novelty value of the speculative demand for money in the General Theory. However, unfortunately for those who wished to show Malthus in this sort of Keynesian light, there were some formidable quotations which seemingly denied any significance to hoarding.

Sowell (1972, p. 97) draws attention to the following passages from the 'Principles' to argue that Malthus usually meant that saving was the same thing as investment:

'No political economist of the present day can by saving mean mere hoarding.' (1836, p. 38)
'If he did not choose to use it in the purchase of luxuries or the maintenance of personal services, it might as well be thrown into the sea. To save it, that is to use it in employing more labourers upon the land, . . .' (1836, p. 325)

There are serious objections to this view. The rational running up of idle balances might not have been thought of as hoarding by Malthus. Eltis (1980, p. 53) points out that the reference to hoarding is incidental to a discussion of the correct borderline between the productive and unproductive sectors of the economy. He goes on to argue that Malthus would have defined an act of saving as adding to the stock of wealth and an act of investment as adding to that component of stock used as capital to earn profits and provide investment and so clearly the two need not be the same. The essential point he attempts to establish is that planned savings are distinct from planned investment. Hollander (1969) also argues that savings and investment are distinct. Neither deals explicitly with the question of how a leakage occurs in the process leading to depression, whether the depression occurs in the wake of excessive capital accumulation or as a result of excessive saving which is not matched by investment.

[6] Since the Keynesian model against which Malthus is compared is never spelt out, it is possible that some actually saw this as accompanied by a shift in the investment function as opposed to a simple movement along it induced by the resultant higher interest rate.

The denials of hoarding should, as Eltis suggests, be viewed in context. We must remember that Malthus's Principles purported to be a 're-coinage' of Smith's Wealth of Nations. It is generally accepted by modern economists that Smith's distinction between unproductive and productive labour was the basis of a model for maximizing economic growth.[7] The denial of hoarding in the first quotation comes directly from the section where Malthus is concerned with the usefulness of Smith's distinction. It should come as no surprise to us that in the context of a growing economy all savings are invested for the precise reason that capital is earning its supply price. Malthus puts his views quite plainly:

'Parsimony, or the conversion of revenue into capital, may take place without any diminution of consumption, if the revenue increases first.' (1836, p. 326n)

Later after arguing the dangers of oversaving he writes:

"How then is this saving to take place without producing the diminution of value apprehended? It may take place, and practically almost always does take place, in consequence of a previous increase in the value of the national revenue, in which case a saving may be effected, not only without any diminution of demand and consumption, but under an actual increase of demand, consumption and value during every part of the process.' (1836, p. 365)

Thus in the context of discussing growth rather than stagnation it is entirely appropriate for Malthus to echo Smith on the relationship of capital accumulation to the growth process and, because expectations of the return to capital are being realised as output grows, to identify savings with investment. However, once we move away from the question of what best promotes the trend rate of growth of the economy to the question of short-run depression, when capitalists' expectations of the rate of profit are not realized, it seems equally clear that Malthus admits a role for the running up of idle balances.

There is a remarkable passage in the first edition of Malthus's Essay on Population which sheds considerable light on the hoarding issue. Malthus is arguing against Godwin's model of a perfect society on the grounds that it is divorced from economic reality:

'Dr Adam Smith has very justly observed that nations as well as individuals grow rich by parsimony and poor by profusion, and that, therefore, every frugal man was a friend and every spendthrift an enemy to his country. The reason he gives is that what is saved from revenue is always added to stock, and is therefore taken from the maintenance of labour that is generally unproductive and employed in the maintenance of labour that realizes itself in valuable commodities. No observation can be more evidently just. The subject of Mr Godwin's essay is a little similar in its first appearance, but in essence is as distinct as possible. He considers the mischief of profusion as an acknowledged truth, and therefore makes his comparison between the avaricious man, and the man who spends his

[7] See for instance Hicks (1965, p. 36–38).

income. But the avaricious man of Mr Godwin is totally a distinct character, at least with regard to his effect upon the prosperity of the state, from the frugal man of Dr Adam Smith. The frugal man in order to make more money saves from his income and adds to his capital, and this capital he either employs himself in the maintenance of productive labour, or he lends it to some other person who will probably employ it in this way. He benefits the state because he adds to its general capital, and because wealth employed as capital not only sets in motion more labour than when spent as income, but the labour is besides of a more valuable kind. But the avaricious man of Mr Godwin locks up his wealth in a chest and sets in motion no labour of any kind, either productive of unproductive.' (1798, p. 175–6)

This passage is interesting because this is the early Malthus using the Smithian argument, on the virtues of parsimony and its importance for growth, to dismiss Godwin's arguments as utopian outpourings. But very significantly he is open to the notion of hoarding as a phenomenon and once admitted he goes on to say that it can have serious economic repercussions:

'But Mr Godwin says that the miser really locks up nothing, that the point has not been rightly understood, and that the true development and definition of the nature of wealth have not been applied to illustrate it. Having defined therefore wealth, very justly, to be the commodities raised and fostered by human labour, he observes that the miser locks up neither corn, nor oxen, nor clothes, nor houses. Undoubtedly he does not really lock up these articles, but he locks up the power of producing them, which is virtually the same. These things are certainly used and consumed by his contemporaries, as truly, and to as great an extent, as if he were a beggar; but not to as great an extent as if he had employed his wealth in turning up more land, in breeding more oxen, in employing more tailors, and in building more houses. But supposing, for a moment, that the conduct of the miser did not tend to check any really useful produce, how are all those who are thrown out of employment to obtain patents which they may shew in order to be awarded a proper share of the food and raiment produced by the society? This is the unconquerable difficulty.' (1798, p. 180–1)

This point that 'hoarding' or saving without investing can lead to workers being dismissed and that this had repercussions in the product market because their current money incomes were constrained is of great importance as to why Keynes ascribed to Malthus an understanding of the operations of a money economy. It is evident that Malthus did not always assume that all savings were invested and that 'oversaving', depending on its context, may refer either to excessive planned investment or excessive non-consumption.

Hollander credits Malthus with a Keynesian analysis of the causes of the post-Napoleonic depression. However, he nowhere specifies what is meant by a Keynesian analysis of depression and argues that the basic model of excessive capital accumulation in the growth process leading to depression is distinctly non-Keynesian. With reference to the specific 'Treatise' Keynesian model discussed earlier, it will now be argued that both are essentially

Keynesian. In terms of textual exegesis of Malthus what follows is entirely uncontroversial and Hollander himself provides ample referencing to the excessive capital accumulation case (1969, pp. 308–312) and to the underconsumption case (1969, pp. 313–320). Here are only the bare bones of each sequence to facilitate comparison with Keynes.

The so-called basic model of capital accumulation starts with an exogenous shock of overinvestment. Capitalists, their 'animal spirits' raised perhaps, respond to a high profit rate by overinvestment. In order to do this they must reduce their own consumption. In Malthus this is much the same thing as spending less on unproductive labour. In effect they sack the 'minstrels' and hire them again to plant corn. The consumption of workers thus remains constant but the output of wage-goods rises. This produces a fall in the price level of wage goods. Money wages do not fall initially and hence the real wage rate rises and there is a transfer of real income from entrepreneurs to workers. A situation of general glut sets in as output as a whole is sold at prices which do not cover ex ante costs of production. The rate of profit is reduced below that expected ex ante. Capitalists respond to the income transfer by cutting investment or, what is the same thing in Malthus, by sacking workers or not advancing wage goods. The sacked workers are not re-hired as minstrels because of the income transfer. The rise in unemployment further depresses the price level of output because the unemployed while they have the 'will' to consume lack the 'power'. The economy thus goes into depression.

The post-Napoleonic depression commences with a different shock that of an excessive output of corn after a series of good harvests.[8] This leads to a fall in the price level of the food component of wage goods. With money wages constant, real wages rise. There is a transfer of income from farmers to workers. Malthus then has a downward multiplier process. The rise in agricultural unemployment reduces the effective demand for manufactured wage goods. It is quite clear that, while money wages are flexible, they lag behind the fall in the price level. He even considers the effect to spread to the export market with a fall in mercantile earnings.[9] It is also apparent that the sequence from an income transfer and fall in the rate of profit to reduced employment and reduced effective demand is no different to that outlined for the overinvestment case. Two points stand out for particular attention, the central role of the income transfer and the fact that it is not flexibility of money wages which is important but that money wages lag in the process:

'For the four or five years since the war, on account of the change in the

[8] Malthus (1836, p. 413–416) is quite clear that excessive capital accumulation is not involved and that capital is deficient but not in the sense of it not matching the growth in the labour force but in the sense of a deficient effective demand for it.

[9] Since Malthus is analysing real events and we are looking at his implicit model, I have not addressed his arguments as to how the depression is exacerbated by a contraction of the money supply, the increase in the labour force through natural growth and demobilisation, and reduced taxation bills leading to higher savings not investment.

distribution of the national produce, and the want of effectual consumption and demand occasioned by it, a check has been given to the rate of production. . . . . .Though labour is cheap, there is neither the power nor the will to employ it all; because not only has the capital of the country diminished, compared with the number of labourers, but, owing to the diminished revenues of the country, the commodities which those labourers would produce are not in such request as to ensure tolerable profits to the reduced capital.' (1836, p. 417)

The two depression processes are presented in order to show their similarity of process and that they differ only in the sense of the shock administered to the model. In outlining them I have neglected the analysis of the labour market 'cobweb' on the grounds that Malthus discusses this in both contexts and this merely exacerbates the effective demand problem which is in all essentials exactly the same as that outlined previously from Keynes's Treatise. Malthus himself would have regarded the overinvestment shock as a supply side shock and the collapse of prices in the wake of good harvest as a failure of effective demand. Furthermore, his definition of a situation of general glut is symmetric with respect to cause:

"A glut is said to be general, when, either from superabundance of supply or diminution of demand, a considerable mass of commodities falls below the elementary costs of production.' (1827, p. 247)

The common features of the two Malthusian depression stories and that of Keynes's Treatise can now be brought together. All descriptions start with a shock which leads to a fall in the price level of consumption goods. It is assumed that the product market always clears. All prices including money wages are flexible but there is a definite sequence of response so that money wages fall only after product prices fall. The central problem, in each case leading to a failure of effective demand, is due to the distributional consequences of the relative price movements. The rise in the real wage rate and fall in the profit rate leads to a reduction in employment. Current consumption is constrained by current money incomes, so that the initial fall in consumption prices is amplified and a downward spiral in output, expenditure and income sets in.

Interestingly, both Malthus and the Keynes of the Treatise are ambiguous on the question of automatic mechanisms by which full employment equilibrium could be restored. Malthus alternatively writes of 'a marked depression of wealth and population permanently'[10] (Ricardo II, p. 325) and that 'the question of a glut is exclusively whether it may be general, as well as particular, and not whether it may be permanent as well as temporary' (1827, p. 62). Keynes set up his formal equations with a fixed full employment level of output assuming there were forces to pull the economy

[10] The quotation given is from the 1st. edition of Malthus's *Principles*. Further evidence of Malthus's ambiguity here is that in the second edition the word 'permanently' is replaced by 'afterwards'. (1836, p. 326) Costabile and Rowthorn explicitly model Malthus as not having an automatic mechanism. (1985, p. 435)

back to this. However, the non-formal analysis frequently belies this. Both in any case argued for active policy intervention in the face of depression.

The Malthusian remedies

Keynes commended Malthus's policy proposals that 'public works and expenditure by landlords and persons of property was the appropriate remedy' (Vol X, p. 101). While both sound Keynesian, Hollander, as noted earlier, claims that the rationale Malthus presents is non-Keynesian because of Malthus's use of results from the excessive capital accumulation model.

It should be obvious from the foregoing analysis that, since we are dealing with the same model subjected to different shocks and that this model is Keynesian in the sense of the Keynes of the Treatise, this argument falls to the ground. Indeed, Hollander's own thorough and perceptive analysis, in particular of the public works policy proposal, fits in neatly with the link between effective demand and the profit rate discussed in our analysis of the Treatise model:

> 'Public works were not supported by Malthus because they represent a net injection of purchasing power into the economy which—together with multiplier effects—would lead to a higher level of activity. The argument is based upon the Malthusian position that any *transfer of funds from productive to unproductive expenditure will raise the level of effectual demand and accordingly the profit rate.*' (1969, p. 334).

The same, of course, can be said of any increase in unproductive consumption including hiring more minstrels.[11] The famous 'widow's cruse' argument of the Treatise (Vol V, p. 125) depends on exactly this mechanism.

In any case we must dispose of the view that Keynes's advocacy of a public works programme was something that sprang up with the General Theory. As Moggridge points out (1976, p. 82) Keynes held in the Treatise that monetary policy should be used to operate on the long term interest rate in order to restore aggregate demand. However, Keynes recognised a special case for a small open economy on a fixed exchange rate where this would not be possible and public works were then a reserve weapon. This is even illustrated in application to the depression of the 1890's in the applied volume of the Treatise (Vol VI, pp. 150–2). Moggridge also points to the advocacy of public works in the pamphlet, 'Can Lloyd George Do It? and gives this quotation from a talk given in the U.S. in June 1931:

> 'In Great Britain I have for a long time past agitated very strongly for a public works programme, and my argument has been that we are such a centre of an international system that we cannot operate on the rate of interest, because if we

---

[11] It should be noted that Malthus' arguments for public works are strictly qualified with respect to the source and use of funds. Corry (1958, 1962) has argued that Malthus was not an advocate of public works, but see Hollander's discussion of this position (1969, pp. 329–34).

tried to force the rate of interest down, there is too much lending and we lose our gold . . .' (1976, p. 84–5)

This view had been expressed before the amendments of the Essay on Malthus previously noted. It would therefore appear that those policy proposals which sound Keynesian are Keynesian in the true sense that the analysis behind them is akin to that Keynes used in the Treatise. One can even make a case for the policy proposals which were essentially long run and which therefore sound non-Keynesian. If planned saving is to equal planned investment in the dynamic setting of the growth process, this requires an appropriate distribution of income so that the rate of profit is maintained. As Eltis points out (1980, p. 42) the whole structure of the argument of sections VI to IX of 'The Progress of Wealth' in the Principles (1836, p. 361–413) is concerned with mechanisms by which demand side factors can maintain the rate of profit necessary for continued growth and this includes such things as the 'division of landed property' and the importance of unproductive consumption.

The general implications for the relationship of Malthus and Keynes

One of the criticisms this paper levels at past comparisons of Malthus and Keynes is that Keynes has been left implicit. By implication it has been the Keynes of the General Theory alone that has been the benchmark and, given some of the comments made, almost certainly in ISLM garb. In order to be specific in our comparison and with proper regard to the timing of Keynes's comments on Malthus, explicit attention has been given to the model of depression in the Treatise. However, this comparison can now be used to facilitate a wider perspective on the relationship and be linked to a more recent debate on the nature of Keynesian economics.

Many of the problems in seeing the link between Keynesian and Malthusian economics stem from the implicit use of a comparative statics model derived from the General Theory. Most observers would now agree with Leijonhufvud's contention (1968, p. 50–4), that the essentially dynamic analysis of the General Theory was obscured by the use of comparative statics.[12] This can be linked to the failure of commentators to understand the role of money in both Malthus and Keynes and the nature of the attack on Say's Law. Hence, they also fail to see the basis for Keynes's praise of Malthus. For instance Sowell, in the context of arguing that Malthus and others did not attach special significance to money, claims that classical economists 'put much more emphasis than do modern economists on causation in a sequential sense rather than in the sense of simultaneous determination of the values of related variables' (1972, p. 98).

He dismisses the fact that both Malthus (1836, pp. 315–6) and Keynes

[12] Moggridge makes the point that Keynes adopted comparative statics analysis because, while less suited to describing disequilibrium situations, it was extremely useful for getting his message across to non-specialists. (1976, p. 92)

(Vol. VII, pp. 18–22) claimed to be attacking Say's Law by warning that 'Say's Law has both lost and acquired meanings in the long process of theoretical refinement', and that 'it has led to grotesque distortions of history where the general glut controversy that reached its peak in the 1820's is treated as a debate over Say's Law in its modern sense . . .' (1972, p. 5).

An implication of the comparison made earlier is precisely that both Malthus and Keynes were making the same fundamental critique of the operation of a market economy and both correctly singled out the law of markets as the analytic lynchpin of the orthodoxy they opposed. We should remember that prior to Clower (1965) most economists would have accepted that Keynes attacked Say's Law as defined by Lange, that is the behavioural proposition that the sum of excess demands for all goods except money is zero. It is doubtful if any serious economist ever believed this to be true in the short run. Even Ricardo, who clearly believed in the long run neutrality of money, was aware that monetary movements had some short-run real effects.[13] The Keynesian model of the neoclassical synthesis appeared to be a special case of the general Walrasian model with institutional rigidities in money wages and the interest rate. These resulted in the failure of the labour market to clear. Aggregate output could be less than full employment output and the automatic mechanisms to restore full equilibrium were painfully slow.

Thanks to Clower we now have the distinction drawn between the planning budget constraint called Say's Principle (1965, p. 116) and the market principle of Walras' Law, the basic point being that the former requires that the sum of planned excess demands for all goods including money is zero whereas the latter is the much stronger proposition that the sum of effective excess demands for all goods including money is zero. Keynes's attack on the law of markets was an attack on the proposition with respect to effective excess demands. When people are thrown out of work there is an excess supply of labour but there is no offsetting effective excess demand for goods. Money plays a crucial role because it is only if we can trade our leisure for money that we can make our notional demand for goods effective in the absence of credit linked to the notional transformation possibilities of the economy. As Malthus would have put it there is no way the unemployed can obtain 'patents'. This problem has been characterised in a number of ways: the absence of forward markets; the reversal of the Marshallian adjustment velocities. Leijonhufvud even attempted to give it a choice theoretic basis with a generalisation of liquidity preference. The key elements though are simple. Money wages move more slowly than money prices. A shock to the economy produces income effects through so-called 'false trading', the most important of these being through the trades that *do*

---

[13] The relative importance to be ascribed to these, as qualifications to his main argument or as bearing the thrust of it, is a major issue of contention in Ricardian scholarship. See Hollander (1979, ch. 9) and O'Brien (1981)

not take place because the real wage is wrong. Workers become unemployed. Consumption is constrained by current money incomes so a downward multiplier process sets in. The ideas that prices lead money wages, that income distribution effects lead to quantity responses in the labour market and that consumption is money income constrained were all used in the depression processes previously outlined.[14]

While Malthus does not have a modern analytic apparatus to draw on he is emphatic on the need for goods to exchange for money so that demand can be effective and it is for this reason, no doubt, that Keynes credited him with an understanding that a modern market economy cannot be analysed in a model based on barter in the manner Ricardo proposed.

Conclusion

A lively debate has persisted for many years over whether Malthus deserved the accolades Keynes bestowed upon him. The early commentators who supported Keynes, for instance O'Leary (1942) and Lambert (1962), had their analysis dismissed by later commentators such as Sowell as being trivial in merely showing the employment of similar phraseology (1972, p. 6). The general consensus of the critical literature has been that Keynes foisted his own economics on to Malthus and misinterpreted him as a result. However, this paper has argued that the focus of the debate has been wrong. It has been consistently and usually implicitly assumed that the correct comparison is with the economics of Keynes's General Theory. This has led to undue concentration on whether by oversaving Malthus meant hoarding or overinvestment. Too little attention has been paid to the timing of the claims Keynes made for Malthus. The critical references to the principle of effective demand were added to the Essay on Malthus in 1933, suggesting that it is with the economics of the Treatise that we should make our comparison. When the depression process outlined in in the Treatise with its stress on relative price movements is juxtaposed with Malthus's analysis of the post-Napoleonic depression, a close correspondence can be discerned. It therefore becomes possible to grasp why Keynes, at this stage in the development of his thought, recognised the underlying similarities of their conceptions.

University of Tasmania

REFERENCES

BAUMOL, W. J. "Say's (at least) Eight Laws, or What Say and James Mill May Really Have Meant", *Economica*, Vol. 44, 1977.

---

[14] The argument presented does not depend on Clower's Keynes with an implicit Walrasian theory of household behaviour. Even those who take a more 'Cambridge' view argue that Keynes did attack Walras' Law and they emphasize the process analysis of the Treatise. See Chick (1978).

CANNAN, E., *Theories of Production,* 3rd ed., P. S. King Ltd., London, 1917.

CHICK, V., "The Nature of the Keynesian Revolution: A Reassessment", *Australian Economic Papers,* Vol. 17, 1978.

CLOWER, R. W., "The Keynesian Counter-Revolution: A Theoretical Appraisal", *The Theory of Interest Rates,* Hahn, F. H. and Brechling, F., (eds.), Macmillan, London, 1965.

CORRY, B. A. "The Theory of The Economic Effects of Government Expenditure in English Classical Political Economy", *Economica,* Vol. 25, 1958.

CORRY, B. A. *Money Savings and Investment in English Economics,* 1800–1850, Macmillan, London, 1962.

COSTABILE, L. and ROWTHORN, R. E., "Malthus's Theory of Wages and Growth", *Economic Journal,* Vol 95, 1985.

ELTIS, W. A., "Malthus's Theory of Effective Demand and Growth", *Oxford Economic Papers,* Vol. 32, 1980.

HICKS, J. R., *Capital and Growth,* Oxford University Press, London, 1965.

HOLLANDER, S., "Malthus and the Post-Napoleonic Depression", *History of Political Economy,* Vol. 1, 1969.

HOLLANDER, S., *The Economics of David Ricardo,* University of Toronto Press, Toronto, 1979.

KEYNES, J. M., A Treatise on Money. The Pure Theory of Money, *Collected Writings Vol. V,* Macmillan for the Royal Economic Society, London, 1971.

KEYNES, J. M., A Treatise on Money. The Applied Theory of Money, *Collected Writings Vol. VI,* Macmillan for the Royal Economic Society, London, 1971.

KEYNES, J. M., The General Theory of Employment, Interest and Money, *Collected Writings Vol. VII,* Macmillan for the Royal Economic Society, London, 1973.

KEYNES, J. M., Thomas Robert Malthus: the First of the Cambridge Economists, Essays in Biography, *Collected Writings Vol. X,* Macmillan for the Royal Economic Society, London, 1972.

LAMBERT, P., "Malthus and Keynes: Nouvel Examen de la Parenté Profonde des Deux Oeuvres", *Revue d'Économie Politique,* Vol. 72, 1962.

LEIJONHUFVUD, A., *On Keynesian Economics and the Economics of Keynes,* Oxford University Press, London, 1968.

MALTHUS, T. R., *Principles of Political Economy,* 2nd edition (1836), Augustus M. Kelley, New York, 1968.

MALTHUS, T. R., *An Essay on the Principle of Population,* 1st edition (1798), Ed., Flew, A., Penguin Books, Harmondsworth, 1970.

MALTHUS, T. R., *Definitions in Political Economy,* (1827), Augustus M. Kelley, New York, 1971.

MOGGRIDGE, D. E., *Keynes,* Fontana, Glasgow, 1976.

O'BRIEN, D. P., "Ricardian Economics and The Economics of David Ricardo", *Oxford Economic Papers,* Vol. 33, 1981.

O'LEARY, J., "Malthus and Keynes", *Journal of Political Economy,* Vol. 50, 1942.

RICARDO, D., Notes on Malthus, *Collected Works Vol. II,* ed., Sraffa, P., Cambridge University Press for the Royal Economic Society, 1951.

THWEATT, W. O. "Early Formulators of Say's Law", *Quarterly Review of Economics and Business,* Vol. 19, 1979.

SCHUMPETER, J. A., *History of Economic Analysis,* Oxford University Press, New York, 1954.

SOWELL, T., "The General Glut Controversy Reconsidered", *Oxford Economic Papers,* Vol. 15, 1963.

SOWELL, T., *Say's Law,* Princeton University Press, Princeton, 1972.

Oxford Economic Papers 39 (1987), 190–222

ISSUES IN THE APPLICATION OF COST-BENEFIT ANALYSIS TO ENERGY PROJECTS IN DEVELOPING COUNTRIES*

By SUDHIR ANAND *and* BARRY NALEBUFF

1. Introduction

THE THEORY behind cost-benefit analysis is relatively well developed [see Little and Mirrlees (1968), (1974); Dasgupta, Marglin and Sen (1972); Mason and Merton (1984)], but its application to real world problems is not always easy. This paper considers the application of cost-benefit analysis to energy problems in oil-importing developing countries (OIDCs).

The results are divided into four parts: Section 2 presents a methodology for handling uncertainty; Section 3 studies the implications of exhaustibility; Section 4 examines the externalities associated with exploration; Section 5 applies these tools in an analysis of the costs associated with importing oil.

In Section 2 we begin with a discussion of the theoretical issues involved in cost-benefit analysis in the presence of uncertainty. Problems arise when there are conflicting estimates of a project's chance of success. The analysis must consider how the range of possible outcomes affects both the total risk borne in the economy and the income distribution. Uncertain future returns have to be appropriately discounted to the present. Projects which deplete exhaustible resources are irreversible and therefore the cost-benefit analysis must take into account the value of current reserves.

In Section 3 Hotelling's rule is presented as the starting point for forming expectations about the price path of oil and other exhaustible energy resources. All project appraisals for programs ranging from new energy development to conservation or stockpiling are strongly influenced by the expected future price of energy, and oil in particular. Energy prices today and in the future depend on estimates of total world hydrocarbon reserves, their extraction costs, and the predicted availability of backstop technologies. Uncertainty about future reserves leads to variability in supplies and price, and causes an inefficiency in the intertemporal allocation of oil; depletion takes place more slowly in order to maintain flexibility in the event of worse-case scenarios. The gains from developing new energy supplies (and conservation) include lower prices, reduced vulnerability, and

* We are particularly grateful to Harinder Kohli for motivating this work and for providing continuous support and encouragement. We appreciate discussions with, or comments on earlier drafts from, Panos Cavoulacos, Angus Deaton, Kemal Dervis, William Hogan, Harinder Kohli, Deepak Lal, Alan Manning, Ricardo Martin, James Mirrlees, John Page, D. C. Rao, Paul Seabright, Edilberto Segura, Robert Stobaugh, Yannis Stournaras, Michael Webb, and two anonymous referees. Audrey Hiscock, Jean Ponchamni and Tony Tenorio typed the different versions of this paper, and we are extremely grateful to them. Financial support for the research was provided by the Industry Department of the World Bank. An expanded version of this paper appeared as World Bank Staff Working Paper Number 738 [Anand and Nalebuff (1985)].

greater competition in the world market. How countries respond to the expected price path of oil will depend on their discount rate. Oil-importing developing countries frequently have above average discount rates due to below average creditworthiness and constraints arising from imperfect capital markets or restrictions on foreign investment; from their perspective, the high price of oil today relative to the future should lead them to deplete their own resources at a faster rate.

Section 4 widens the scope of cost-benefit analysis to capture the externalities involved when research strategies for exploration are coordinated. The uncertainty concerning the total size of oil, gas and other energy reserves hurts all oil-importing countries. Because information is a public good, the gains to information gathering extend beyond a country's border. Projects that reduce the uncertainty associated with reserve levels should be evaluated from an international perspective. There may also be economies of scale in gathering information; a little knowledge may be useless but it is still costly to acquire. Related is the question of economies of scope: to develop renewable energy resources, how many competing directions of research should be financed? Since only the best solutions will be implemented, this reduces the advantages to diversification. With regard to diversification, there is an important distinction between risk-sharing and risk-pooling: sharing involves spreading risk among a larger number of individuals, while pooling involves accepting a larger number of less than perfectly correlated projects. Pooling together independent projects increases both the total expected return and the total variance. When the risks are already spread as thinly as possible, there is no safety in the law of large numbers.

Section 5 examines the options for an oil-importing developing country to reduce both its vulnerability and dependence on imported oil. Stockpiles can be an effective and inexpensive tool to lower a country's vulnerability to short-run supply disruptions. Other strategies which reduce dependence on foreign oil in the long-run include (i) increasing conservation, (ii) promoting renewable energy projects and, in the medium-run, (iii) depleting their stocks of exhaustible energy resources. Because of capital constraints and the difficulties associated with financing private contracts, there may be too little energy development taking place in oil-importing developing countries. The evidence presented by Blitzer et al. (1984) is quite striking. While 70% of worldwide exploratory wells in 1980 were drilled in the United States compared with about 3% for the entire group of oil-importing developing countries, the success rates were almost equal at 30%. During the 1970s the cost-effectiveness of developing countries was four times greater: 1.6 barrels of hydrocarbon reserves were generated per dollar of investment in developing countries compared with 0.4 barrels of reserves in the United States.

Section 6 brings together the theory and applications in a brief conclusion that summarizes the results.

2. Cost-benefit analysis under uncertainty

The first and most obvious problem in evaluating a project is the fact that nothing is certain. As a starting point the Expected Present Monetary Value (EPV) is used as a proxy for the expected welfare value of a project. If in period t the probability of an output worth Z is $p_t(Z)$, and r_t is the appropriate average discount rate between periods 1 and t, then

$$\text{EPV} = \sum_t \left[\int Z p_t(Z) \, dZ \right] \Big/ (1 + r_t)^t. \tag{1}$$

However, the expected present value index is only the first step in project appraisal. The following subsections discuss how this criterion must be adjusted to take account of: conflicting probability estimates $p(Z)$; the costs of uncertainty; income distribution effects; the appropriate discount rate for the project; the value of the status quo, and project timing.

2.1. Evaluating conflicting probability estimates

Probabilities are only estimates, and in practice they may be no better than rough guesses. Thus, there may be several conflicting estimates of the likelihood of any outcome. This uncertainty is contrasted in the next subsection with the different type of uncertainty caused by the possibility of multiple outcomes; for example, in a coin toss, the outcome, either heads or tails, is uncertain but the probability of heads is known to be 0.5 with certainty. Here we focus on how to evaluate EPV when the possible outcomes are known (e.g., heads or tails) but the probability of each event is uncertain.

Consider the following two situations. In Case A, there are two estimates: both show that the probability of a 1 million rupee return is 0.25. In situation B, there is uncertainty about the estimates. Estimate 1 shows the probability of a 1 million rupee return to be 0.10; estimate 2 shows the probability to be 0.40. In the second case there are conflicting estimates of the chance of success, one putting it at only 10% while the other more optimistically expecting a 40% chance of success. The probabilities are shown in the table below.

Case	A	B
Estimate 1	0.25	0.1
Estimate 2	0.25	0.4
Average	0.25	0.25

Since both estimates agree in Case A, it is straightforward that the expected present value should be calculated using a 0.25 probability of a 1 million rupee return. For Case B, assume that the two conflicting estimates

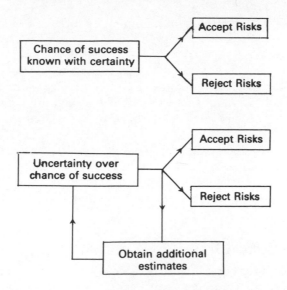

FIG. 2.1. Decision chart with uncertain probabilities of success.

are equally precise.[1] Both estimates are then given equal weight and the expected chance of a 1 million rupee return in Case B is

$$p(1,000,000) = (0.5 \times 0.1) + (0.5 \times 0.4) = 0.25,$$

which is the same as in Case A. The expected return, the variance, and all other moments are equal in the two situations.

The project in situation B should *not* be penalized because there are conflicting estimates about its actual chance of success. There is no risk aversion to uncertainty about the estimated probability of success. Indeed there can even be a benefit arising from uncertainty in the estimated probability of success.

The benefit from uncertainty becomes clearer in the context of sequential decision-making [Rothschild (1971)]. When the probability of success is known with certainty, there is no more information that can be found out. For example, the probability of heads when flipping an unbiased coin is known to be 1/2. With this information, the only remaining decision is whether or not to take the gamble. Alternatively, when the probability of success is unknown, there is the additional possibility of gaining further information (see decision chart in Fig. 2.1). This new information will lead to new probabilities and thus a potentially different decision. Of course, gathering this information may be expensive and thus it is not necessarily worthwhile.

---

[1] Technically, the probability estimate is the mean of some distribution of probabilities. The precision is inversely related to the variance of this probability estimate.

The value of the additional information depends on the extent to which the estimates diverge. When the probability is known (as in the case of the unbiased coin) there is no value to obtaining additional estimates. To the extent that the conflicting estimates are farther apart, there is more uncertainty to be resolved.[2] In our example, there is greater confidence that 0.25 is the actual chance of success in Case A since both estimates agree; in Case B at least one, and perhaps both, of the estimated probabilities must be wrong.

This point may be summarized by noting that once the decision is made to accept the risks, all that matters is the expected probability of each possible outcome. There is no reason to be risk averse due to divergent probability estimates. But, divergent estimates suggest that there may be a value to obtaining further information.

2.2. *The costs of uncertainty*

A cost from uncertainty can arise when a project has several possible outcomes. Individuals are averse to fluctuations in their income. The cost from bad outcomes is greater than the benefits from correspondingly good outcomes. Decision-makers prefer a sure thing to any pure gamble with the same expected outcome. And, except in the hypothetical case of complete contingent claims markets, it is not possible to purchase complete insurance and eliminate the effects of uncertainty [Arrow and Lind (1970)].

Risk aversion becomes important when the range of the possible income levels for *individuals* is more than trivially affected by the outcome of the project. For Bangladesh, with its population of about 100 million, even a large project having returns between $50 million and $150 million results in an income variation per person of at most a dollar. This may turn out to be a small risk relative to even a low per capita national income of $100.

There are two factors that complicate this straightforward example of a risk-sharing argument. Project outcomes are correlated with the state of the economy; because there are real costs to the risks associated with fluctuations in the economy, adding *incremental* risk will be important. Secondly, project risks may not be spread evenly across the population; appraisals must include consideration of the differential effects of a project on different groups of people. These points are taken up in Sections 2.3 and 2.5.

2.3. *Valuation of project output under uncertainty*

This subsection demonstrates the importance of taking into account the correlation between fluctuations in per capita income and project output when calculating the costs of uncertainty.

---

[2] While the value of additional information may be high, the existence of conflicting probability estimates does not in itself imply anything about the costs of additional information. As always, benefits must be compared with costs.

Let Y = national income per person; Z = net project output per person; $V(Y)$ = social valuation of representative person's income, where $V'(Y) > 0$ and $V''(Y) < 0$. A project Z should be done if it raises expected social welfare, i.e., $E[V(Y + Z)] > E[V(Y)]$, where $E[\ ]$ denotes the expectation operator.

Define the certainty equivalent z of a project as that income which the government would consider equally satisfactory as a project Z whose net output is random. In other words, z is defined through the equation:

$$E[V(Y + Z)] = E[V(Y + z)]. \tag{2}$$

Letting $\bar{Y} = E[Y]$ and $\bar{Z} = E[Z]$, we can expand the left-hand and right-hand sides of equation (2) around $(\bar{Y} + \bar{Z})$. The Taylor series expansions to second order of the left-hand and right-hand sides, respectively, are:

$$E[V(Y + Z)] = V(\bar{Y} + \bar{Z}) + V'(\bar{Y} + \bar{Z})E[Y - \bar{Y} + Z - \bar{Z}]$$
$$+ (1/2)V''(\bar{Y} + \bar{Z})E[(Y - \bar{Y}) + (Z - \bar{Z})]^2 \tag{3}$$

$$E[V(Y + z)] = V(\bar{Y} + \bar{Z}) + V'(\bar{Y} + \bar{Z})E[Y - \bar{Y} + z - \bar{Z}]$$
$$+ (1/2)V''(\bar{Y} + \bar{Z})E[(Y - \bar{Y}) + (z - \bar{Z})]^2 \tag{4}$$

Equating the right-hand sides of equations (3) and (4) yields

$$(1/2)V''(\bar{Y} + \bar{Z})[\text{Var}\,(Y) + \text{Var}\,(Z) + 2\,\text{Cov}\,(Y, Z)]$$
$$= (z - \bar{Z})V'(\bar{Y} + \bar{Z}) + (1/2)V''(\bar{Y} + \bar{Z})[\text{Var}\,(Y) + (z - \bar{Z})^2]. \tag{5}$$

Hence,

$$z = \bar{Z} + (1/2)\frac{V''(\bar{Y} + \bar{Z})}{V'(\bar{Y} + \bar{Z})}[\text{Var}\,(Z) + 2\,\text{Cov}\,(Y, Z) - (z - \bar{Z})^2]$$

$$= \bar{Z} - (1/2)\frac{R(\bar{Y} + \bar{Z})}{(\bar{Y} + \bar{Z})}[\text{Var}\,(Z) + 2\,\text{Cov}\,(Y, Z)] \tag{6}$$

where $R(y) = -yV''(y)/V'(y)$ is the relative risk aversion (or elasticity of marginal valuation of income) at income level y, and $(z - \bar{Z})^2/(\bar{Y} + \bar{Z})$ is assumed negligible compared with $(z - \bar{Z})$.

The costs of uncertainty can be broken up into two terms: the variance effect and the covariance effect. We look at these two terms sequentially in order to gauge their relative importance. As will be seen below, the cost due to the variance term will typically be significantly smaller than the benefit associated with the (negative) covariance term for energy projects in OIDCs.

Both terms are equally affected by the choice of the relative risk aversion parameter, denoted by R. The literature on alternative estimates of the elasticity of social marginal valuation of income has been reviewed by Stern (1977) [see also Anand (1973)], where values between 1.5 and 2.5 are suggested as being reasonable and broadly acceptable. We assume a constant value of $R = 2$ in the relevant range around $(\bar{Y} + \bar{Z})$, and hence the valuation function specified as $V(y) = a - by^{-1}$.

First we focus on the variance term. If national income per person is itself certain (i.e., Y is not a random variable), then $\text{Cov}(Y, Z) = 0$. In this case, equation (6) reduces to:

$$z = \bar{Z} - (1/2)R \frac{\text{Var}(Z)}{(\bar{Y} + \bar{Z})}. \tag{7}$$

Consider a large government project in which per capita income can vary by 1% over the range of possible outcomes. For the example of Bangladesh, this would perhaps be a project with an outcome that is uncertain over a $100 million range. Even for countries with smaller populations such as Mali, Burkina Faso, or Botswana where energy projects of $150 million would not be unrealistic, the *uncertainty* associated with the project outcome will almost always be less than 5% of per capita income.

Starting with a per capita income of $100, an example of a project with a 1% range is:

$$Z = \begin{cases} \$0.5 \text{ with probability } 1/2 \\ \$1.5 \text{ with probability } 1/2 \end{cases} \tag{8}$$

The project has an expected per capita return $\bar{Z} = 1$ and a variance $\text{Var}(Z) = 0.25$. The risk premium or proportion by which the expected monetary value of the project has to be deflated because of the uncertain return is:

$$\frac{(\bar{Z} - z)}{\bar{Z}} = (1/2)(R) \frac{\text{Var}(Z)}{\bar{Z}(\bar{Y} + \bar{Z})}$$

$$= (1/2)(2) \frac{0.25}{101} = 0.0025. \tag{9}$$

Thus, the risk premium is just under one-quarter of one percent—a miniscule amount which, for practical purposes, may be ignored.

When a per capita income of $100 is subject to a 5% risk, the risk premium is twenty-five times larger, and a downward adjustment of about 6% is required. Although this is now relevant, we see below that it may still be only one-eighth as large as a realistic correction for the corresponding *covariance*.

Economists are concerned with the value of the energy project conditional on the state of the economy and of the world. Knowing the correlation between the economy and the project is important both for determining the *value* to the economy of money from the project and for determining the *amount* of money the project is likely to generate. A small variation of the earlier examples shows how the *correlation* between national income and the project's return can have a much more significant effect on the certainty equivalent monetary value of the project.

The first example demonstrated that the risk adjustments associated with even large projects are relatively small (with the qualification that income distribution effects must also be considered). But to determine the monetary value of a project, it is essential to realize that the price of the output, especially in the case of energy, will in general be related to the state of the economy. The welfare value of the project will also depend on the state of the economy. We are not worried about causality, whether the project affects the economy or the state of the economy affects the project. Here, we are emphasizing that the swings in the economy may be *correlated* with the output of the project and this should be taken into account. For energy projects in oil-importing developing countries it is very likely that the marginal welfare value of the project's output, $ZV'(Y)$, and national income per person in the economy as a whole, Y, are *negatively* correlated since they are oppositely affected by variations in the world price of oil. An oil embargo will make the development of internal energy sources (including energy conservation) particularly attractive both because the economy will be depressed due to the embargo and because of the high price of the remaining available oil; the marginal welfare value of income will be high when the project output is high. That is, for an economy dependent on oil imports, oil will usually be expensive when the economy is depressed and vice versa. These effects would be further amplified by changes in the shadow price of foreign exchange, which are also likely to be negatively correlated with the economy.[3]

We can now make illustrative estimates of the extent to which the expected monetary value of output may have to be adjusted to take account of fluctuations in the marginal value of income. Consider the earlier example of a 1% variation again, but now suppose that when the output of the project is $0.5, national income per head is $110, and when the output of the project is $1.5, national income per head is $90. Again suppose that the two events occur with probability $1/2$. We continue to assume an elasticity of marginal valuation of income of 2 in this range, i.e., $V'(y) = by^{-2}$. In this case, there is a *negative covariance* between Y and Z, given by

$$\text{Cov}(Y, Z) = E[(Y - \bar{Y})(Z - \bar{Z})]$$
$$= -5. \tag{10}$$

The certainty equivalent monetary value for this project, z, is *greater* than its expected monetary value, $\bar{Z}$, and the proportional upward adjustment

---

[3] A project appraisal has to consider all the general equilibrium effects of changes in the economy. It is necessary to estimate changes both in the price of energy and in the prices of all other commodities (i.e. foreign exchange, interest rates, transportation, etc.). To calculate the EPV, the expectation of the shadow value of output has to be taken across all states of nature corresponding to oil price (or supply) shocks. Strictly speaking, this requires working out all the shadow prices in each state of nature contingent on assumptions about government policy. This is not an easy task!

can be obtained from equation (6) straightforwardly as

$$\frac{(z - \bar{Z})}{\bar{Z}} = -(1/2)(R)\frac{[2\,\mathrm{Cov}\,(Y,\,Z)]}{(\bar{Y} + \bar{Z})\bar{Z}}$$

$$= (1/2)\frac{(2)10}{101} = 0.099. \tag{11}$$

This ignores the (downward) adjustment for Var (Z) which was shown to be negligible (0.0025). The negative correlation between Y and Z therefore calls for an upward adjustment in $\bar{Z}$ of 9.9%. For $R = 4$ the increase is twice as large, almost 20% of the expected monetary value of the project. Such upward adjustments imply corresponding upward changes to the expected present value of the entire stream of returns from the project.

When the project outcome ranges over 5% of per capita income (e.g., $Z = -\$1.5$ when income is $110 and $Z = \$3.5$ when income is $90) then the covariance correction is five times larger at almost 50%. It is now important to include the 6% reduction due to the variance term, which still leaves a net upward correction of approximately 44%.

Our conclusion from this analysis is that it may be necessary to make significant adjustments to account for uncertainty. When calculating an example of the size of the effects associated with the uncertainty in the price and availability of oil imports, oil dependency can lead to a negative correlation between the output of an energy project and national income per head which is forty times more important than the variance in income from the project for the average individual. This ratio of 40 to 1 does not depend on the magnitude of the relative risk aversion, as changes in R affect both terms proportionally. However, the ratio does depend on the size of the project relative to national income; doubling the size of the project (or considering a country with half the per capita income) also doubles the *relative* importance of the variance effect. Even in the largest projects (5% case), though, the covariance term is still eight times larger and of the opposite sign.

A negative correlation between the return on asset i and the portfolio as a whole is beneficial because it reduces the variance of the total return.[4] Two important examples of energy projects negatively correlated with the economy—conservation for the long-term and stockpiling for the short-term—are considered in Sections 3.6 and 5.1, respectively.

The beneficial effects of this negative correlation are analogous to those associated with asset pricing in the literature on modern finance. Let r_i and r_m denote the random rates of return on stock i and on a portfolio of all

---

[4] If the negative correlation is sufficiently large, people would be willing to hold an asset which *loses* money on average. House insurance is such an asset; the expected return to the owner is negative (otherwise insurance companies would be unprofitable) but the payoff occurs precisely when the marginal utility of income is very high.

stocks in the market, respectively. Under the assumptions of the capital asset pricing model (CAPM), the *expected risk-adjusted* rate of return on stock i, $\bar{r}_i$, in an efficient market satisfies the equation

$$\bar{r}_i = r + \beta_{im}[\bar{r}_m - r] \tag{12}$$

where

$$\beta_{im} = \frac{\text{Cov}\,(r_i, r_m)}{\text{Var}\,(r_m)} \tag{13}$$

is a measure of risk, r is the risk-free interest rate, and $\bar{r}_m$ is the expected rate of return on the market portfolio [Sharpe (1964)]. In countries with well-developed capital markets, $\bar{r}_i$ is the appropriate risk-adjusted discount factor to use in evaluating a project's returns. This approach has the advantage that it is not necessary to estimate risk-aversion coefficients needed in equation (6); the cost of risk is determined by the required return on the market portfolio. In developing countries, it may be easier to estimate risk-aversion parameters and thus calculate certainty equivalents directly through equation (6) than to estimate the return on the market portfolio (even if it exists).

2.4. *Correcting for uncertainty through the discount rate*

Two caveats should be noted in applying CAPM to make risk adjustments in the required rate-of-return or discount rate in calculating EPV. First, the adjustments are made period-by-period. Second, discounting for risk continues only until the uncertainty is resolved.

A difficulty arises in attempting to aggregate the effects of multi-period risk into a single adjustment factor. Consider a typical investment project which becomes profitable after a set-up period in which there are losses. Initially, when the expected return in a period is negative, the marginal valuation of income increases, so the direction of the appropriate adjustment in the discount rate applied to the expected return is to *lower* the rate. Later, when the expected returns are positive, diminishing marginal valuation of income requires a *higher* discount rate. It follows that no single adjustment in the discount rate can be made to reflect risk correctly *at every point in time* if the expected return is positive in some periods and negative in others [Lind (1982)]. Even if there is some risk-adjusted rate $\bar{r}$ which equates the present value of expected returns ($\bar{Z}_t$) discounted at $\bar{r}$ to the present value of the certainty equivalent of these returns (z_t) discounted at the risk-free rate r, there will be no guarantee that $\bar{r} > r$.

Another, quite separate, point concerning the discount rate arises if it is known that the project risk will be resolved in the course of the project's life [Wilson (1982)]. Assume that the values of the uncertain return in each period are, in fact, correctly captured by discounting the expected returns by a risk-adjusted rate, $\bar{r}$. It is only correct to use the rate $\bar{r}$ to discount the expected returns *until* the uncertainty has been resolved. A return twenty years in the future that is uncertain today but will become known in five years should only be discounted for five years of risk. This can be seen by adapting our earlier example.

Suppose the project Z at the end of each period yields a return of $0.5 with probability 1/2 and $1.5 with probability 1/2. After the first period, the uncertainty becomes resolved one way or the other forever. Thus at the end of the first and all subsequent periods, the returns are either ($0.5, $0.5, $0.5,...) with probability 1/2 or ($1.5, $1.5, $1.5,...) with probability 1/2. For example, the project might be an oil-drilling project whose returns depend on the size of the reserves which become known only at the *end* of period 1.

For this project at the *beginning* of period 1, the expected present value of all future returns discounted at the rate $\tilde{r}$, EPV($\tilde{r}$), is given by:

$$\text{EPV}(\tilde{r}) = \sum_{t=1}^{\infty} \frac{1}{(1+\tilde{r})^t} = \frac{1}{\tilde{r}}. \tag{14}$$

On the other hand, the present value of the project at the *end* of period 1 will be either $(0.5)(1+r)/r$ with probability 1/2 or $(1.5)(1+r)/r$ with probability 1/2. Because this return is risky, it has to be discounted back to the beginning of the first period by the rate $\tilde{r}$. Hence, the correct measure of expected present value is:

$$\text{EPV}(\tilde{r}, r) = \frac{1+r}{r(1+\tilde{r})} = \frac{1+r}{r+r\tilde{r}}. \tag{15}$$

When $\tilde{r} > r$, this yields a higher present value because

$$\text{EPV}(\tilde{r}, r) = \frac{1+r}{r+r\tilde{r}} > \frac{1+r}{\tilde{r}+r\tilde{r}} = \frac{1}{\tilde{r}} = \text{EPV}(\tilde{r}).$$

Using a higher discount rate to value uncertain future returns underestimates their value if the uncertainty is resolved or diminished at some intermediate point in the life of the project.

2.5. *Income distribution considerations*

Project risks are not borne equally across the population. Although the earlier analysis in Section 2.3 with the representative individual assumes that the government *can* and *will* spread risks evenly over the entire population, in practice it may turn out that certain groups bear a disproportionate burden of the variations associated with the price of energy. Government policy could in principle correct the distributional consequences of price changes, but this cannot be taken for granted. On balance, and without strong evidence to the contrary, it is safer to assume that government policy will remain unchanged. Project choice must take into account sub-optimal policies of government, whatever the reason for their existence. However, identifying government policies is not always straightforward. For example, when energy import costs rise the government's financial position is affected. If its policy is to maintain a balanced budget then the government may be forced to raise taxes; if its policy is to maintain tax rates then the government may be forced towards a budget deficit. In advance, it is difficult to know whether government policy is to maintain tax rates or a balanced budget.

If government policy fails to spread risk evenly then the use of a representative individual can underestimate the costs associated with energy price fluctuations, and the appraisal of domestic energy projects should take such distributional implications into account.[5]

2.6. *Project appraisal in relation to the status quo*

Cost-benefit analyses often neglect the costs associated with depleting a finite reserve of an exhaustible resource. The price of oil in the ground is called its royalty value. This royalty value should be *subtracted* from the market (i.e. well-head) price of oil in a project appraisal. The reason is that oil extracted now cannot be extracted later: the total supply is fixed. This opportunity cost is a real cost. In particular, instead of extracting the oil it may be possible to sell it in its current form by auctioning the drilling and extraction rights. That is why it is important to emphasize that costs and benefits should be measured relative to the *status quo*. Currently the oil is in the ground. When developing exhaustible resources, the relevant measure of benefit is the *value added,* the difference between the price of oil and the royalty value of deposits.

The royalty value of an oil reserve is based on the market price of oil in the ground. A problem arises in countries whose reserves are not traded. Domestic conditions may prevent many LDCs from trading their coal, gas and oil reserves internationally. In the absence of complete markets, countries can at least begin to place bounds on the value of their reserves by comparing the relative profitability of their reserves with that of reserves traded in the market, such as off Alaska or in the North Sea.[6]

Project appraisals which include in the benefits the value of extracted oil but neglect estimated royalty costs can easily have *internal rates of return* of several hundred percent. Using this method of appraisal, however, can lead alternative projects to have still higher rates of return. For example, a country that sells its oil reserves in the ground to a foreign oil company receives a large positive payment and apparently incurs no costs. This leads to a practically infinite internal rate of return. This example helps illustrate

---

[5] The analyses in this paper consider the sum of a project's effects across a population and are thus cast in the framework of utilitarianism. Other ethical considerations may affect the results of cost-benefit analysis [Schulze and Kneese (1981)]. A Rawlsian criterion would focus on the utility of the worst-off individual. Interpersonal comparisons of utility can only be avoided if the project improves everyone's expected welfare (Pareto criterion).

[6] The value of the reserves depends on extraction costs, transportation costs to points of sale, and degree of uncertainty about reserve levels.

both the weakness of using the internal rate of return criterion and the mistakes that may be made if the royalty cost of depleting the resource is left out of the calculation.

It is also important to consider the timing of energy projects. Since oil reserves are exhaustible, complete extraction today precludes extraction tomorrow; that is, alternative programs for oil extraction are *mutually exclusive*. Even with renewable energy projects, timing decisions require comparisons of mutually exclusive options; the decision to proceed with a synthetic fuels program today precludes postponing the project for one year. Thus, even when the expected discounted value of one project option is positive, it may not be the optimal alternative. Project appraisal should choose the program with the *highest* (positive) *expected present value* among all of the mutually exclusive options.

3. Hotelling's rule and the price path of oil

Oil is an exhaustible resource; a barrel extracted today results in one barrel less for extraction tomorrow. When the timing of oil extraction and sales is chosen to maximize discounted profits, this leads to an expected price path due to Hotelling (1931). The technique for calculating an optimal extraction rule is first demonstrated in a general model, and then specialized to cases examining perfect competition, extraction costs, and imperfect competition.

Consider an entrepreneur who owns S barrels of oil reserves. If he sells at a rate of q_t barrels at time t, he expects to receive revenue at the rate of $R(q_t)$; in the case of perfect competition, $R(q_t)$ will be equal to expected price p_t times quantity q_t. His costs of extraction, $C(q_t, \dot{q}_t, t)$, depend on the time t at which the extraction occurs, and on both the extraction rate (q_t) and the change in the extraction rate $(\dot{q}_t)$; extracting a larger quantity is costlier as is the attempt to *speed up* the extraction rate.[7] The entrepreneur is constrained to sell no more than his total reserves, S.

Formally, the problem can be expressed as[8]:

$$\underset{q_t}{\text{Max}} \left[\int_0^\infty [R(q_t) - C(q_t, \dot{q}_t, t)] e^{-r_t t} \, dt \right], \tag{16}$$

subject to

$$\int_0^\infty q_t \, dt \leq S, \tag{17}$$

---

[7] The problem can be further complicated by permitting extraction costs to depend on the size of remaining reserves and by permitting storage (instead of sales) after extraction.

[8] We use r_t to represent the continuous time analogue of the average discount rate between 0 and t, i.e.,

$$r_t = \left[\int_0^t r(s) \, ds \right] \Big/ t$$

where $r(s)$ is the instantaneous discount rate at time s.

and

$$q_t \geqslant 0. \tag{18}$$

Letting subscripts denote partial derivatives with respect to the relevant argument, the Euler condition for an optimal path can be written as

$$[R_1(q_t) - C_1(q_t, \dot{q}_t, t)]e^{-r_t t} - \lambda \leqslant -d[C_2(q_t, \dot{q}_t, t)e^{-r_t t}]/dt \tag{19}$$

with strict equality whenever the extraction rate is positive, and where λ is chosen to ensure that the solution satisfies the exhaustion constraint (17).

3.1. *Perfect competition, costless extraction, and a constant discount rate*

The simplest and most idealized special case involves entrepreneurs acting under perfect competition with costless extraction and a constant discount rate, r. The optimality condition (19) reduces to

$$q_t > 0 \text{ and } p_t e^{-rt} = \lambda; \quad or \quad q_t = 0 \text{ and } p_t e^{-rt} \leqslant \lambda \tag{20}$$

where p_t is the market price. Thus oil is extracted and sold only in the period(s) in which its present discounted value is highest. The Lagrange multiplier is the maximum discounted price, $\lambda = \max_t [p_t e^{-rt}]$.

Unless the present discounted price for every period is the same, the market will not be in equilibrium. Thus if the price of oil is expected to rise more quickly than the nominal interest rate, then all suppliers will hold on to their oil anticipating higher profits. This raises the price of oil today relative to its price in the future and restores equilibrium. If the price of oil is expected to rise slower than the interest rate, suppliers will try to sell more oil today and invest their profits to receive the nominal interest rate. This flooding of the market leads to a lowering of the price today relative to the future and restores the equilibrium path.

Oil prices cannot continue to rise at the nominal interest rate if there is a backstop technology which can provide an unlimited supply of energy at a constant price. In this case, the oil price path must also be at the right level to ensure that the stock of depletable resources will be exhausted just at the time when the backstop technology is *expected* to become competitive. If entrepreneurs thought that an alternative supply would arrive before their stocks are exhausted, they would increase their oil supply now in order to prevent being stuck with excess oil in the future. This brings the market back into equilibrium as it results in a lower price and higher demand in each period.

Because of the boundary condition that leads to exhaustion, the price of oil today is sensitive to changes in long-run interest rates. A higher interest rate results in a price path of oil where prices rise faster over time. If today's price remains constant then all future consumption will be reduced. To ensure exhaustion, the equilibrium price today must fall to compensate for its swifter rise. Higher interest rates shift consumption from the future to the present. Similarly, because of the boundary condition, if new reserves are found or an increase in conservation takes place, the whole equilibrium price path must be lowered to stimulate the additional demand needed to ensure exhaustion; thus, today's price must fall.

Note that if different suppliers have differing discount rates then those with above average discount rates (typically OIDCs) will be the first to extract their reserves. The price will rise at the discount rate of the marginal supplier.

The recent dramatic rises and falls in the price of oil have caused many to doubt the validity of Hotelling's implied steady rise in the price of oil. But this conclusion depends on there being perfect competition, costless extraction and a constant discount rate. Even under these very stylized assumptions, Hotelling's rule only requires that the price of oil is *expected* to rise at the interest rate. The price path of oil will be changed by variations in the interest rate, by new discoveries that affect expected world oil reserves, by new technologies for the use of oil substitutes (coal, synthetic fuels, etc.) or for interfuel substitution, and by changes in consumption patterns (due for example to faster than anticipated conservation efforts). The volatility of nominal interest rates and fluctuations in the world's proven reserves are reflected in a high variance of oil prices around their expected (or average) growth path.

Several other factors can also interfere with the stylized Hotelling solution:

(1) Extraction is not costless. As illustrated in expression (16), costs depend both on the rate of extraction and on *changes* in the rate of extraction;

(2) Oil for the future is held by a monopolist who in the interest of profit maximization chooses not to sell today;

(3) Oil for the future is held by a cartel with conflicting objectives different from *joint* profit maximization;[9]

(4) Oil for the future is held by both a cartel and a competitive fringe, and either (i) the competitive fringe chooses to save rather than sell its oil for strategic reasons [Nichols and Zeckhauser (1977), Crawford and Sobel (1982)]; or (ii) the competitive fringe tries to sell oil as fast as it can but is constrained by a physical limit to the rate of extraction; or (iii) the relative market shares of the cartel and competitive fringe change.

The first two issues above are discussed in the subsections that follow. In the short run, the market may be out of equilibrium because most oil is located far away from where it is consumed; transportation is slow and expensive; there are lags in production; demand is volatile; and expectations

---

[9] For example, current revenue requirements or *individual* profit maximization may lead some members of the cartel to overproduce, thus disrupting production quota agreements and lowering price.

may turn out to be wrong. When prices are thought to be too high, competitive producers who try rapidly to increase their extraction rate often must pay much higher marginal costs and may even sacrifice some of their recoverable reserves (due to technological inefficiencies involved in excessively rapid extraction).

3.2. *Extraction costs*

Even in a perfectly competitive market with a constant discount rate, extraction costs can fundamentally alter the expected price path of oil. With constant unit extraction costs, $C(q_t, \dot{q}_t, t) = cq_t$, the Euler conditions lead to an equilibrium in which

$$(p_t - c)e^{-rt} = \lambda. \tag{21}$$

Price net of unit extraction costs rises at the discount rate; this implies that price rises *slower* than the discount rate. When unit extraction costs are constant with respect to output but fall over time with technical progress, the corresponding equilibrium is

$$(p_t - c_t)e^{-rt} = \lambda.$$

Here, falling marginal costs c_t further slows the rate of price appreciation. Only if marginal costs actually rise faster than the discount rate will price appreciation be faster than the discount rate. Significantly more complicated is the solution when extraction costs depend on changes in the rate of extraction.[10]

Extraction costs may also vary across different suppliers. For any price path, those with smaller unit extraction cost will choose to extract first. Marginal revenue net of marginal cost appreciates faster for suppliers with high marginal costs; high-cost suppliers have a relatively greater benefit from postponing their extraction costs into the future. The shift over time from low to high cost extractors (or from low to high cost techniques) will be partially offset through improvements from technological innovations.

3.3. *Imperfect competition*

Compared with the competitive solution, the price path of exhaustible resources may be different when the oil reserves are held by a cartel or monopolist. A monopolist will choose an intertemporal distribution of

---

[10] If speeding up extraction is expensive, it becomes necessary to evaluate the term

$$d[C_2(q_t, \dot{q}_t, t)]/dt \quad \text{from equation (19).}$$

The solution remains tractable in the special case where the cost function takes the linear form:

$$C(q_t, \dot{q}_t, t) = \gamma_0 + \gamma_1 q_t + \gamma_2 \dot{q}_t.$$

Then, along an equilibrium path,

$$p_t = \gamma_1 + r\gamma_2 + \lambda e^{rt}.$$

supply to maximize total discounted profit; this requires the present discounted value of marginal revenue minus marginal cost to be the same for any period. Unlike the competitive solution, the monopolist may choose *not* to exhaust the entire stock of resources by the time the backstop technology is expected to become competitive. Greater profits may result if the monopolist initially follows a higher price path and later when the competitive backstop technology constrains his ability to raise prices further he exhausts all remaining stock at the constant backstop price [Stiglitz and Dasgupta (1980)].

There are two potential differences to the solution of Hotelling's rule under a monopoly: (i) the price path may be different to the extent that marginal revenue is different from price; (ii) the whole price path may be higher if the monopolist finds it optimal not to exhaust supply by the stage at which the backstop technology becomes competitive. Under monopoly the rate of oil price rises can be either faster or slower than under competition. If extraction is costless and the price elasticity of demand is *constant*, then the price of oil rises at the monopolist's discount rate [Stiglitz (1976)]. Marginal revenue is given by $p(1 - 1/\varepsilon)$, where p is price and ε is the elasticity of demand. With costless extraction, marginal revenue and therefore price (which is a fixed multiple of marginal revenue) rises at the monopolist's discount rate. In this case, competition and monopoly imply the same rate of price increase if the discount rates in the two situations are the same.

The expected price path of oil may differ from Hotelling's rule to the extent that oil reserves are controlled by a monopoly and the price elasticity of demand changes over time. For example, an increase in the price elasticity brought about by gradually increased substitution possibilities will imply that prices rise slower than the monopolist's discount rate.

3.4. *The discount rate in developing countries*

The appropriate social discount rate for developing countries may be higher than the interest rates which prevail in the rest of the world. The suboptimality of domestic savings [Little and Mirrlees (1968), (1974)] and restrictions on foreign investment suggest that rates of return to domestic projects in developing countries may be higher than those obtainable elsewhere. Thus, these countries attempt to borrow funds from international development agencies and capital markets until they run up against lending constraints and large risk premia. In contrast, the discount rate for oil-exporting, capital-rich countries is likely to be lower than in the rest of the world.

There are several implications of an OIDC's discount rate being higher than that of oil-exporting countries. First, given any path for the world price of oil, it will pay an OIDC to deplete its own reserves at a faster rate than the oil-exporting countries if it has the same (or lower) extraction costs. To the extent that its marginal extraction costs rise with both the amount and the speed of extraction, this depletion policy will be moderated. Such a policy does have the side effect of increasing the OIDC's future dependence on oil imports.

A higher discount rate also raises the costs of stockpiling. Whatever the capital gain (or loss) from changes in the world price of oil over time, the annual opportunity cost of the capital tied up in the oil stockpile is higher. Other opportunity costs of storing oil will also be higher because the capital tied up (in extraction and storage facilities—see Section 5.1) has to be valued at the higher interest rate.

3.5. The cost arising from uncertain reserves

Unless future supplies of oil are known with certainty, it is impossible to allocate oil consumption efficiently over time [Gilbert (1976)]. If an unexpected bonus of oil is found, then too little consumption will have occurred; if a well runs dry unexpectedly soon, then too much consumption will have occurred. A cost to uncertainty arises because we assume the loss from a shortage is greater than the benefit from an equivalent surplus.[11] If it is increasingly difficult to find replacements for oil as shortages become more severe then prices must rise more steeply in the event of a shortage than they fall when there is a surplus. Resolving the uncertainty over oil reserves sooner will on average increase today's consumption and lower the price.[12]

Consider a two-period model in which the total quantity of oil is either 0.5 or 1.5 (each with chance 1/2). Extraction is costless. At the time when first-period consumption is decided, total supply is uncertain. Before the second period, the remaining supply becomes known. In a competitive market, second-period prices will lead to the resource just being exhausted. To capture the increasing difficulty of finding substitutes for oil, the demand function must be assumed convex in price. For example, let demand as a function of price be

$$q(p) = 1/p. \tag{22}$$

If consumption in the first period is q_1, then the first-period price is

$$p_1 = 1/q_1. \tag{23}$$

Second-period consumption q_2 will either be $(0.5 - q_1)$ or $(1.5 - q_1)$. Second-period prices $p_2(q_2)$ may be written as a function of the total stock Z

---

[11] Devarajan and Fisher (1982) highlight a benefit from uncertain reserves. When there are economies of scale, expected extraction costs of a random reserve are lower than for a certain reserve equal to the expected size of the random reserve.

[12] Resolving the uncertainty will not always result in oil stocks being equal to the expected reserves; oil stocks may be higher or lower than the average of all possibilities. The benefit of resolving the uncertainty is that we know the actual stocks sooner and can thus plan better.

and first-period consumption q_1 as follows:

$$p_2(q_2) = 1/q_2 = 1/(Z - q_1), \qquad \text{since } Z = q_1 + q_2. \qquad (24)$$

Hotelling's rule can be used to determine the equilibrium. The *expected* discounted second-period price must equal the first-period price. Thus, if r is the risk-free interest rate, this implies

$$p_1 = [(1/2)p_2(1.5 - q_1) + (1/2)p_2(0.5 - q_1)]/(1 + r). \qquad (25)$$

Hence first-period consumption q_1 is given as the solution to the equation:

$$2/q_1 = [1/(1.5 - q_1) + 1/(0.5 - q_1)]/(1 + r). \qquad (26)$$

In the two-period model, it is reasonable to think of the periods as each being ten years. Then if $r = 100\%$, this gives

$$q_1 = 0.39, \qquad p_1 = 2.5;$$
$$p_2(0.5 - q_1) = 9.1, \qquad p_2(1.5 - q_1) = 0.9; \qquad \text{hence } E[p_2] = 5.0.$$

If the stock Z were known with certainty at the *beginning* of the first period, the outcome would be either

$$\text{for } Z = 0.5: \quad p_1 = 3, \quad p_2 = 6; \quad q_1 = 0.33, \quad q_2 = 0.17$$

or

$$\text{for } Z = 1.5: \quad p_1 = 1, \quad p_2 = 2; \quad q_1 = 1.0, \quad q_2 = 0.5.$$

The average price and consumption levels are:

$$E[p_1] = 2, \ E[p_2] = 4;$$

and

$$E[q_1] = 0.67, \ E[q_2] = 0.33.$$

In this example, the cost of uncertainty in the first period results in a 25% higher price compared with the average of the paths when the reserves are known.

The inefficiency in intertemporal allocation arises because of the need to maintain flexibility in facing the uncertain second-period supply; this inefficiency is relative to the optimal depletion path in a world with no uncertainty. Caution in the first period reduces the costs of adjusting to a worse than expected outcome in the second period. When the elasticity of demand is lower, the cost of adjusting to a shortage is greater and more flexibility is needed; first-period consumption must be reduced even further which leads to greater inefficiency and higher prices.

This subsection illustrates an important externality associated with oil exploration projects. The evaluation of such projects should include the benefit of reducing the misallocation arising from uncertainty about the size of global reserves.

3.6. The effects of new energy supplies

In evaluating the benefits from the technologies of producing energy, it is important to make a distinction between the production of energy from exhaustible and from renewable resources. The development of known exhaustible resources in a world of certainty should not affect the world price because everyone knows that they will be extracted sooner or later.[13] Prices are lowered with the development of renewable energy resources (e.g., solar, hydro and nuclear) since this increases the world's total supply of energy.[14] This may also be accomplished through energy conservation. By using the available oil or coal more efficiently, the same outputs can be produced with less oil or coal [for estimates of this potential, see World Bank (1982)]. When conservation results in a 25% greater efficiency this is equivalent to an effective increase of 25% in the entire stock of reserves. This benefit must be weighed against the costs of conservation.

Reducing energy import needs either through developing renewable resources or conservation decreases dependency and hence vulnerability to oil-price shocks. Less dependency creates greater competition in world oil markets. This should benefit all oil-importing countries.[15]

A related issue is: when should importing countries extract their limited stocks of exhaustible resources [see Crawford and Sobel (1982) and Gilbert et al. (1978)]? The cartelization of the current market is moderated by the fact that many countries at present have sizeable reserves, i.e. there is a large *potential* competitive fringe. Without these reserves, there would be a much greater potential for cartelization in the future. But, this issue arises only if developing countries increase their production of *depletable* resources. Conserving energy and developing renewable energy resources have no such negative externality: the world's energy supply is increased.

4. Coordinating strategies

The advantage to coordinating strategies for information gathering and developing alternative energy sources has resulted in oil-importing countries forming the International Energy Agency (IEA).[16] This is only a first step in the right direction. Countries (or multinational oil companies) acting alone

[13] Other oil-exporting nations can cut back current production knowing that their supply will be more in demand later when other countries' exhaustible resources run out. This assumes that they can still meet their current revenue requirements by borrowing against their now larger future incomes; some of the effects of borrowing constraints are discussed below.

[14] Similarly, a new technology that improves the cost-effectiveness of alternative exhaustible resources (e.g., gas or coal) creates additional supplies of energy.

[15] The development of both renewable and non-renewable energy resources shifts revenues away from oil-exporters, but in the case of non-renewable resources these revenues are simply postponed until the future.

[16] Participants in the International Energy Plan hope to minimize the costs of a supply interruption by formalizing sharing rules in advance. However, Hogan (1981) argues that the sharing rules are poorly designed and may be expected to break down in the event of a major disruption.

collect too little information and wastefully duplicate or excessively diversify their research strategies. This section discusses externalities associated with exploration and research diversification.

4.1. *Information externalities in exploration*

The first step in developing energy resources is the gathering of information. There are important reasons why this should be done by a central authority rather than the free market (if it exists). Information is perhaps one of the only true public goods. It can be shared by an unlimited number of people and across countries. Thus everyone has an incentive to wait for others to gather the information rather than to pay the costs and duplicate efforts. There is an inefficiency when more than one group pays the costs to find out the same information. While there can be private advantages when information is withheld, the sum of the benefits is generally not reduced when the information is shared. Duplicating efforts to gather information frequently occurs in zero-sum games such as futures markets, where each trader tries to take advantage of another. Competitive information gathering affects the distribution of income but not the size of the pie.

At present, oil-importing developing countries all pay a risk premium because the world's total supply of oil (and its substitutes) is not known precisely. As demonstrated in Section 3.5, uncertainty leads to an inefficient intertemporal allocation of resources. No one country can eliminate this uncertainty by investing in exploratory drilling. Yet each country that investigates its level of reserves contributes to a reduction of the total uncertainty. Although developing countries might not be willing to do exploration on their own, the IEA could promote a quid-pro-quo policy where oil-importers agree to find out more about their own reserves provided others find out about theirs.

For oil-exporting countries, information gathering provides both advantages and disadvantages. More information about the level of a country's reserves decreases the risk of unanticipated future price variability for its own oil [Gilbert *et al.* (1978)]. However, each individual oil-exporting country will prefer greater uncertainty about others' reserves since its oil will then command a higher risk premium.

4.2. *Diversification and multi-project analysis*

The discussion has focused on oil but the issue is clearly one of energy generally. A country considering research and development strategies should examine the various approaches to producing both oil and its substitutes. For example, hydroelectric power and shale oil may prove equal to oil in their importance for many South American countries. How much should research be diversified, how should the eggs be spread among the baskets?

When there are several projects, all of which have goals that are substitutes for one another, it is important that they be evaluated simultaneously. Independent project evaluation can lead to excessive diversification; too many projects could be accepted.

Uncertainty usually motivates diversification. Even though research and exploration are inherently risky propositions, diversification may not be advantageous. There are two important special features of research projects that motivate specialization even in the presence of uncertainty. First, there may be economies of scale in producing information. Second, there may be diseconomies of scope; when there are several alternative solutions, only the best one is implemented.

A little information costs more than it is worth [Radner and Stiglitz (1975), Dasgupta (1982)]. Gathering information has a direct economic cost. The benefits can only be calculated indirectly. Actions are based on the information available. The information's value is then determined by the expected return from the ensuing action. When actions are chosen optimally (conditional on the information), a slight perturbation will not change the expected return. The value of incremental information arises from the distribution of actions becoming more appropriate given the outcomes. At zero information, only a single action is taken and hence there are no gains from redistributing actions more appropriately. Starting from ignorance, there is initially a cost to obtaining information but no benefit. Thus, research projects initially have increasing returns to scale.[17]

An example may help illustrate this point. Imagine that the information concerns the probability of finding oil in a given geological structure. In the extreme case of perfect information the probability of finding oil is either 0 or 1; drilling when undertaken will always be successful. At the other extreme of zero information, there is still a prior probability of finding oil. If this probability is above some critical value, then drilling for oil is expected to be profitable. Gathering only a very small amount of information can only make a small change from the prior probability of success. A small amount of information cannot be sufficiently favorable to induce drilling when, based on prior beliefs, drilling was inadvisable. Since the distribution of actions is the same, there is no expected gain from only a marginal amount of information. There is an analogy between fixed costs in production and the ineffectiveness of a small amount of information: the fixed cost associated with gathering information is the cost of obtaining the minimal amount of information needed to have a potential effect on the decision.

Diseconomies of scope may also provide an argument for specialization. If society is only interested in the single best technique for producing energy, and its research projects do not suffer from decreasing returns to scale, then as shown below it is indeed appropriate to put all the money into

---

[17] This argument relates to projects starting from scratch: small additions to ongoing projects may well be worthwhile.

one project [Nalebuff and Varian (1983)]. While this result is obvious if there is no uncertainty about the returns from the project,[18] its interest lies in the fact that it is also true when the fruits of research are uncertain. One goes with the expected winner. This result does not depend on the correlation between projects (positive, negative, or zero).

To formalize this proposition, consider a government allocating funds to various projects. Each project produces output $f_i(X_i, e_i)$ where X_i are the funds allocated to project i and e_i is a random variable determining the project's success. The government has a budget constraint that $\sum X_i = B$. The random variables may have any general joint probability density function $g(e_1, \ldots, e_n)$. Society only cares about the winner. The value of outputs $(f_1, \ldots, f_n)$ is $\text{Max}\,(f_1, \ldots, f_n)$. Conditional on any realization of $e = (e_1, \ldots, e_n)$, the value of each research project, $f_i(X_i, e_i)$, is assumed to be convex; as argued above, there are increasing returns to scale in gathering information. The expected return from following research strategy $X = (X_1, \ldots, X_n)$ is

$$E[\text{Max}\,[f_i(X_i, e_i)]] =$$

$$\int \ldots \int \text{Max}\,[f_1(X_1, e_1), \ldots, f_n(X_n, e_n)] g(e_1, \ldots, e_n)\, de_1 \ldots de_n.$$

For each realization of e, the valuation function $\text{Max}\,[f_i(X_i, e_i)]$ is the composite of two increasing and convex functions and is thus convex. The expectation of $\text{Max}\,[f_i(X_i, e_i)]$ is just a weighted average of the valuation function conditional on e_i; a weighted average of convex functions is still a (weakly) convex function. Because the maximum value of a convex function occurs at a boundary, it is optimal to fund only one project: for some i, $X_i^* = B$ and $X_j = 0$ for $j \neq i$.

A government does not care whether there is a *second* firm to discover a new technology; only the first discoverer counts. Specialization may hasten the time and improve the quality of the discovery. Diversification is only justified if the leading project encounters diminishing returns to scale or if there is diminishing marginal valuation with respect to increases in the value of the best outcome.

Initially it may seem counter-intuitive that specialization is optimal even in an uncertain world. On reflection it becomes clear: diversification is implied by the convexity of the constraints or the concavity of the objective function. If these conditions are not met, diversification is not necessarily optimal. The standard assumptions about concavity are likely to be violated when considering the returns from several simultaneous research projects.

4.3. *Risk pooling and multi-project analysis*

Outside of research and development, the total value of several projects is generally equal to the *sum* of the outputs. Then, one justification for accepting several simultaneous projects is the advantage from risk-pooling.

---

[18] With no uncertainty, the best project is known and only *it* should be funded.

As discussed earlier in the context of the capital asset pricing model (CAPM), when there are several projects which are negatively correlated there is a reduction in risk because the sum of the outputs becomes less risky. Often this intuition is mistakenly extended to include projects which have a less than perfect positive correlation, and the claim is made that accepting several *independent* projects also results in lower risk.

As the number of independent and identically distributed assets increases, the *average* return converges in probability to a constant. Thus, adding an additional asset *and* an additional shareholder (to an existing portfolio of n assets held by n people) results in lower risk to all; the additional asset increases the variance by a factor of $(n+1)/n$ while the additional shareholder lowers the portfolio's variance by a factor of $[n/(n+1)]^2$. But a government may not be able to increase its number of shareholders beyond its existing population. Investments will already be spread as thinly as possible. Given that the maximum risk-spreading has already taken place, a government cares about the *sum* of the returns rather than the *mean* return. Accepting additional independently distributed projects linearly increases both the total expected return *and* the total variance. This may or may not be beneficial.

The fallacy of large numbers [Samuelson (1963)] is designed to contrast with the law of large numbers; it shows that investing in a large number of independent and identically distributed assets may be undesirable. Consider an asset with a positive expected return but with sufficient variance so that an investor would choose not to hold this asset at *any* income level. The "fallacy" shows that holding any number of independent and identically distributed *replicas* of this asset is also undesirable. Thus, if the government of Monaco is sufficiently risk averse that it never wants to be the house for a single bet at Monte Carlo, then it will also refuse to play the house over a period of a day, year, or century. The proof follows by induction. Since by assumption accepting a single bet is never desirable, expected welfare is improved by eliminating the final replication. Continuing to remove each remaining final replication implies that expected welfare is maximized when none of the bets is left.

5. The costs of importing oil

There are two interrelated costs facing an economy which is heavily dependent on imported oil: the danger from disruptions in supply and a higher variance in the economy's performance due to fluctuations in the price of oil. Our discussion starts at supply disruptions.[19]

[19] Developing countries have at least two important reasons why they should be concerned about their supply of oil being cut off: embargos and wars. The history of 1973 proves the real possibility of an embargo. Wars have disrupted the flow of oil either by cutting off the producers (as in Iran–Iraq) or by blockades around the consumer (as in Malawi during the Tanzania–Uganda war and in Argentina during the Falklands crisis). The costs of a disruption include threats to national security (defence), massive inefficiencies from disturbances in production, and hardships suffered by individuals unable to obtain or to afford fuel for cooking and heating [Deese and Nye (1981), Plummer (1982)].

The responses to this danger include: (1) reducing domestic consumption through tariffs and quotas and through increased conservation; (2) buying on the spot market; (3) investing in backstop technologies; (4) strategic stockpiling of crude oil; and (5) carrying excess domestic production capacity. We consider each of these options.

The market price fails to reflect all the externalities associated with importing an additional barrel of oil. To reduce demand to the appropriate level, it may be optimal for a government to combine the use of tariffs and quotas. If demand is restrained solely by the use of quotas, then the oil-exporting country would raise its price until market demand is at the quota level. The importing country could capture this price increase by imposing a tariff on oil imports [Hogan (1982)]. Domestic consumers would be better off when part of the price of oil is paid to their own government rather than to sellers of oil abroad.

In the presence of uncertainty, there is an advantage to supplementing tariffs with quotas. A quota helps to limit a country's foreign exchange commitment in the importation of energy. In countries where oil imports form a very large proportion of export earnings, small fluctuations in the volume of energy imports can cause large changes in the balance-of-payments. With their capacities to borrow already stretched (and their foreign reserves exhausted), many OIDCs face the risk of sharp rises in the exchange rate. In such situations the costs to the non-traded sectors of the economy can be excessive.

Ideally, countries can reduce their risk by investing in assets that are negatively correlated with the supply, or positively correlated with the price, of oil (e.g., purchasing shares of oil companies). Subsidizing conservation has a high payoff in the event of a supply disruption. Similarly, the development of a contingent rationing scheme creates another negatively correlated asset; it is valuable only in the event of a supply disruption. Ration coupons which are tradable help protect the poor against oil-price shocks while maintaining the incentive for efficient allocation.

To a greater or lesser extent, all countries respond to threatened disruptions by buying on the spot market. There are two disadvantages to this approach: (i) the spot market has accounted for a relatively small proportion of the total oil traded, so that individual countries may face high prices if they all move to the spot market together to meet disruptions; (ii) oil purchased in spot markets may be at great distance from the home country and transport costs and time lags could entail considerable losses to the economy.

Reliance on renewable resources (such as alcohol from biomass) is not economic at present world oil prices but may become so in the future with a long-term increase in real prices. Because oil is an exhaustible resource whereas most synthetic fuels are not, we would expect the real price of oil to rise in the long-run but that of most synfuels to remain more or less constant. Thus, in due course, synfuels should become competitive in relation to oil supplies that are exhaustible. Some development of renewable resources at higher cost today may in any case be warranted as a way of reducing the uncertainty in supplies faced by oil-importing developing countries. The extent of such development would depend on the premium attached to security of supplies; this varies according to a country's circumstances and the technological possibilities open to it.

A further protection against interruptions of oil supply is for countries to keep a strategic stockpile of oil reserves.[20] The argument for public stockpiling must depend on an implicit belief that the private market does not have sufficient incentives to maintain an adequate stockpile [Wright and Williams (1982)]. There are several potentially large externalities that are not captured by the private incentives to stockpile. In the event of a shortage, private sellers expect (with good reason) that the government will impose a price ceiling. This cuts off part of the favorable tail of benefits. The expected value to society of the stockpile exceeds its market price when the government limits prices. A second factor mitigating competitive stockpiling arises when the size of the optimal stockpile is large enough to affect prices. Purchasing a large stockpile may force oil prices to rise if it restricts the supply available to consumers. The higher oil prices resulting from stockpiling creates a comparative advantage for the oil producers to hold the stockpiles. Having a stockpile may also provide strategic advantages not captured by the market. Hogan (1982) stresses the advantage of a stockpile in reducing the probability of a disruption; as the impact of an embargo is diminished, it is less likely to be deployed.

Countries that extract and refine some of their own oil have the option of keeping a safety reserve in the form of untapped wells that can be brought into immediate production (i.e. carrying excess capacity). The economic theory of exhaustible resources shows that this is essentially another form of stockpiling.

5.1. *The costs of stockpiling*

The true costs of stockpiling an *exhaustible* resource are likely to be lower than those associated with carrying inventories of ordinary (renewable) goods. The reason is that exhaustible resources such as oil are expected to reap capital gains from price rises along a Hotelling equilibrium path. Although there is a notional interest loss on the capital tied up in stored oil, this is offset by the extent to which the real price of oil rises over time. With perfect competition and zero extraction costs, the price of oil would be expected to rise at exactly the rate of interest. In this case there is no opportunity cost to the capital invested in the stockpile—it is simply another form of holding savings. Authors such as Samouilidis and Berahas [1982, p.

---

[20] There are several ways in which these reserves can in principle be held. They can be kept above ground in storage tanks, or underground—in leached salt caverns or abandoned salt, hematite, limestone, granite, chalk, or coal mines, or indeed in existing or disused oil-wells. Some new suggested systems for crude-oil storage include rubber bags and artificially created "lagoons", sometimes lined with impermeable synthetic plastics of polyethylene products. Idle tankers are also obvious potential storage facilities.

569] underestimate the returns to stockpiling because they attribute an interest cost to the stockpile but do *not* take into account the expected gains in its value.

The opportunity cost of capital tied up in stockpiling must be evaluated at the country's *own* internal discount rate. Yet the price path for oil is largely determined by the *lower* discount rates prevailing in capital-rich, oil-exporting countries (Section 3.4). Together with the effect of positive extraction costs in moderating the rate of price increase, this suggests that capital gains in the value of the stockpile are unlikely to offset the full opportunity cost of capital tied up in the stockpile.

There are additional costs of stockpiling. Building storage facilities for oil can be expensive[21] and there is generally some loss from evaporation (of the order of 1% to 2% per year). When extraction costs are incurred for oil extracted from own reserves, these could have been delayed until the oil was actually needed. The money spent on early extraction leads to an opportunity cost that should be evaluated at the country's discount rate. Extraction costs may also be falling over time with improvements in technology. The lost savings in extraction costs should be attributed to the costs of maintaining the stockpile. A developing country may not have adequate refining capabilities. Hence, it may need to stockpile refined instead of crude oil. The additional expense of purchasing refined oil could also have been postponed until the oil was just ready for use. Although refining costs do grow to keep up with inflation, real interest is lost on the capital spent on refining.

5.2. *Inventories and flexibility in production*

Even a country which produces some of its own energy has reasons to carry stockpiles. These inventories can be used to counter the disruptive effects of the second major problem associated with importing oil, viz. its price variability.

Inventories can be used to accommodate fluctuations in supply while reducing price variability. If inventories are not used (or run out), the price mechanism will act as a brake; during peak periods of demand, price will rise to choke off some of the excess demand. The optimal stabilization results in neither a constant price nor a band-width rule; it is the solution demonstrated by Gustafson (1958) to a dynamic optimization problem that turns out to be similar to Hotelling's rule [Newbery and Stiglitz (1982)]. The costs of oil supply shocks can be reduced but not eliminated through an optimal management of strategic oil reserves.

Note that price variation is in itself not always harmful. Random variation in input costs is *beneficial* because cost functions are concave in input prices.

---

[21] Costs presently range from $3 per barrel in existing salt mines to $16 per barrel in above-ground tanks.

Firms can take extra advantage of oil when it is a bargain and substitute away from it when it is expensive. The use of oil inventories accentuates this advantage if stockpiles can be built up when the purchase price is low.

Inventories illustrate one of the advantages of flexibility. This argument has been extended to claim that the choice of energy production techniques should be relatively more capital-intensive so as to have greater flexibility in meeting variations in demand. By paying a higher fixed cost, firms hope to exploit the opportunity of relatively efficient production over a range of output levels. *Yet, it may be preferable to use inventories rather than excess capacity to meet these types of unexpected fluctuations.* Making relatively large fixed cost investments takes away an even more important aspect of flexibility, the option of shutting down [see Mason and Merton (1984)]. If the price of imported oil becomes very low (for example, because of a technological break-through in offshore development) then one of the production options is to shut down and import oil.

The fact often overlooked is that for projects with a high marginal (i.e. variable) cost, there is a greater probability of the economy being able to take advantage of cheaper alternatives. The choice of a technology usually involves making trade-offs between high fixed costs and high marginal costs. It is optimal to choose projects with a relatively small fixed-cost component (and correspondingly higher marginal costs) when taking into account the often desirable option of temporarily shutting down and relying on imports if they become cheap.[22]

5.3. *Financing energy development in* OIDCs

A primary concern of many oil-importing developing countries is the financing of their imports. Countries that are constrained in their ability to borrow may also find it difficult to undertake the large investments needed to develop their own domestic energy sources.[23]

A loan to pay for current consumption of energy is an especially risky proposition. Moreover, the risk premium with loans may be expected to rise as the total outstanding debt grows. Countries such as Brazil are already beginning to find themselves in situations where borrowing money to buy oil has become prohibitively expensive. But at the same time that it is negotiating crippling loans, Brazil also has a large savings account in the

---

[22] For example, in the production of ethanol from corn, the marginal input costs (corn @ $2.50/bushel) form over 85% of the total production costs of a project with an output of 50 million gallons per year [Manassah (1981), Part A, Table I, p. 335]. Similarly, in the production of ethanol from sugarcane in South-east Brazil, biomass inputs made up almost 65% of the production costs while the levelized investment cost was less than 20% of the total expenditures [Gray (1981), p. 298]. These types of projects have the flexibility to be expanded or contracted depending on whether the world oil price is high or low.

[23] The cost of importing energy has formed a significant proportion of many developing countries' exports (in 1980 it was more than 50% for India, Brazil, etc.). The true cost of these imports is particularly high when account is taken of their overvalued exchange rates. Large expenditures on imported oil add pressure to the exchange rate and increase the risk premia on loans to such countries (e.g. Brazil, Turkey, and Jamaica).

form of shale oil deposits. Borrowing is one form of dissaving. Brazil has started "borrowing" from its future self by dissaving (i.e., depleting) its stocks of non-renewable resources. Although future generations are left with less savings in the ground, they will also have less external debt to carry. When servicing the debt costs more than the return on reserves, future generations are better off in net terms. A second advantage of this type of "borrowing" is that a risk premium is avoided; a corresponding disadvantage is that the country cannot default (on itself). Investors and banks realize that the risks associated with developing a country's supply of exhaustible resources are far smaller than financing a loan to pay for current energy consumption. Thus, developing countries often contract with multinational oil companies both for their access to capital and for their technical expertise. There are advantages and disadvantages to this approach [see Blitzer et al. (1982)].

Selling a contract for oil exploration and development can help a small country spread the risk associated with the uncertain size of its reserves and the uncertain cost of developing them. But, in addition to sharing risks, the contract should provide the outside developer with incentives to minimize costs and to explore efficiently. For example, efficiency is promoted if a developer could pay a *fixed sum* in return for the rights to all the costs and benefits; in this contract, the developer is also accepting all of the risks.

A difficulty arises if the contract can be broken. Most multinational oil companies have reason to fear that they will be nationalized or heavily taxed if oil reserves or oil prices prove much higher than expected. This uncertainty reduces their incentives to finance the exploration and development costs. This effect is especially severe if oil companies depend on their few large successes to cover their more frequent small losses.

A valuable area of ongoing research examines optimal contract design in a constrained environment: how should energy development contracts make tradeoffs between risk-sharing and incentives if the contract may be broken? Blitzer et al. (1984) compare four commonly used contract formulas: service contracts, toll or fee per barrel contracts, production-sharing contracts, and royalty contracts. They emphasize that the contracts should attempt to spread the different risks in proportion to each party's comparative ability to accept these risks. Consider the production-sharing contract; the developer is rewarded with a fixed fraction of the benefits for assuming a fixed fraction of the costs. If the fraction of benefits equals the fraction of costs then the developer has the correct incentives for efficient exploration and production. However, developers often do not expect to receive benefits above some maximum level (due to taxes, nationalization, currency restrictions). In this case, efficient incentives are provided only if the developer's fraction of benefits is larger than his fraction of costs to compensate for his loss of the upper tail of benefits. This uneven sharing of costs and benefits results in the host country bearing more risk—a result of its inability to commit itself credibly to contractual agreements.

6. Conclusions

The expected present value (EPV) of domestic energy production or conservation programs does not reflect their true social welfare benefits. The EPV must be adjusted upwards to account for the reduced variability in national income, and improvements in income distribution. A reduced dependency on foreign imports may also create externalities which help reduce the world price of oil.

The appraisal of domestic non-renewable energy projects must take account of the same insurance benefits, but there is also a large adjustment in the opposite direction. Calculations must include the opportunity cost of depleting the exhaustible resource. A royalty value per barrel should be subtracted from the market price of oil. With extraction, we are interested in the *value added* by the project as opposed to the *value* of the project. By the same token, when calculating the true costs of stockpiling, the opportunity cost of capital invested in the stockpile will be lower since it must be adjusted to include expected appreciation in the value of the stockpile.

No correction for depletion is necessary for renewable energy resources. Given a long-run increase in the expected price of exhaustible resources under Hotelling's rule, renewable energy projects will eventually become economic. When production technology has low fixed costs and high marginal costs, this allows greater flexibility in responding to the variability of world prices; there is the option of shutting down temporarily and relying on imports when these are cheap. A low fixed-cost technology becomes more attractive with a higher discount rate; owing to capital shortages, the discount rate is likely to be higher in OIDCs. Other things equal, this will also imply a faster depletion rate of its exhaustible energy resources.

The development of domestic exhaustible energy resources is a way of borrowing from future generations without paying a risk premium. In situations where many OIDCs are overexposed to foreign borrowing, a reduction in the risk premium on loans can represent a considerable gain.

Even after all the corrections have been made that translate expected present value into a measure of social welfare, this does not guarantee that the appropriate social welfare criteria will be used in the decision-making process. Cost-benefit analysis cannot be applied in isolation of the incentives of those who have the decision-making power. To implement decisions according to cost-benefit criteria, the decision-makers must either be benevolent or they must be rewarded according to the gain in social welfare. Designing incentive schemes that motivate implementation of cost-benefit rules is an important area for future research.

Cost-benefit analysis is an essential part of development economics. Energy is an essential ingredient. In order to implement the optimum development of OIDCs' exhaustible and renewable energy resources, it is first necessary to specify and then to use appropriate project evaluation criteria/guidelines. The special features associated with energy projects in oil-importing developing countries require significant adjustments from expected present discounted value.

St. Catherine's College, Oxford,
and Princeton University, USA.

REFERENCES

ANAND, SUDHIR (1973): "Distributional Weights in Project Analysis", mimeographed, Development Research Center, World Bank, Washington, D.C., July.

ANAND, SUDHIR and NALEBUFF, BARRY J. (1985): "Issues in the Appraisal of Energy Projects for Oil-Importing Developing Countries", World Bank Staff Working Paper Number 738, Washington, D.C., July.

ARROW, KENNETH J. and LIND, ROBERT C. (1970): "Uncertainty and the Evaluation of Public Investment Decisions", *American Economic Review*, Vol. 60 (June), pp. 364–378; reprinted in Richard Layard (ed.), *Cost-Benefit Analysis*, Penguin Modern Economics Readings, Penguin Books, England, 1972.

BLITZER, CHARLES R., LESSARD, DONALD R. and PADDOCK, JAMES L. (1982): "Risk Bearing and the Choice of Contract Forms for Oil Exploration and Development", Working Paper No. MIT-EL 82-053WP, International Energy Studies Program, Massachusetts Institute of Technology, Cambridge, September.

BLITZER, CHARLES R., CAVOULACOS, PANOS, LESSARD, DONALD R. and PADDOCK, JAMES L. (1984): "An Analysis of Financial Impediments to Oil and Gas Exploration in Developing Countries", Working Paper No. MIT-EL 84-005, Center for Energy Policy Research, Massachusetts Institute of Technology, Cambridge, January.

CRAWFORD, VINCE and SOBEL, JOEL (1982): "Strategic Considerations in the Stockpiling of Oil", mimeographed, University of California at San Diego.

DASGUPTA, PARTHA S. (1982): "Environmental Management Under Uncertainty", in Smith and Krutilla (eds.) (1982).

DASGUPTA, PARTHA S., MARGLIN, STEPHEN A. and SEN, AMARTYA K. (1972): *UNIDO Guidelines for Project Evaluation*, United Nations, New York.

DEESE, DAVID A. and NYE, JOSEPH S. (eds.) (1981): *Energy and Security*, Ballinger Publishing House, Cambridge, Massachusetts.

DEVARAJAN, SHANTAYANAN and FISHER, ANTHONY C. (1982): "Measures of Natural Resource Scarcity Under Uncertainty", in Smith and Krutilla (eds.) (1982).

GILBERT, RICHARD J. (1976): "Optimal Depletion of an Uncertain Stock", SEER Technical Report No. 10, University of California, Berkeley.

GILBERT, RICHARD J. and STIGLITZ, JOSEPH E. (1978): *Effects of Risk on Prices and Quantities of Energy Supplies*, Volumes I to IV, Report EA-700, EPRI, Palo Alto, California.

GILBERT, RICHARD J., NEWBERY, DAVID M. G., and STIGLITZ, JOSEPH E. (1978): *An Overview of the Economic Theory of Uncertainty and its Implications for Energy Supply*, EA-586-SR, EPRI, Palo Alto, California.

GRAY, DALE F. (1981): "Methods for the Economic Evaluation of Petroleum Exploration and Synthetic Fuels Production: An Application to Brazil", Ph.D. Thesis, Massachusetts Institute of Technology, Cambridge, Massachusetts.

GUSTAFSON, R. L. (1958): "Carryover Levels for Grains", U.S. Department of Agriculture, Technical Bulletin No. 1178, Washington, D.C.

HOGAN, WILLIAM W. (1981): "Energy and Security Policy", Energy and Environmental Policy Center, Discussion Paper E-81-09, John F. Kennedy School of Government, Harvard University, Cambridge, Massachusetts, September.

HOGAN, WILLIAM W. (1982): "Policies for Oil Importers", Energy and Environmental Policy

Center, Discussion Paper E-82-02, John F. Kennedy School of Government, Harvard University, Cambridge, Massachusetts, February.

HOTELLING, HAROLD (1931): "The Economics of Exhaustible Resources", *Journal of Political Economy*, Vol. 39, pp. 137–75.

LIND, ROBERT C. (1982): "A Primer on the Major Issues Relating to the Discount Rate for Evaluating National Energy Options", in Lind *et al*. (1982).

LIND, ROBERT C. *et al*. (1982): *Discounting for Time and Risk in Energy Policy*, published by Resources for the Future, Inc., Washington, D.C., The Johns Hopkins University Press, Baltimore, Maryland.

LITTLE, IAN M. D. and MIRRLEES, JAMES A. (1968): *Manual of Industrial Project Analysis in Developing Countries, Vol. 2, Social Cost-Benefit Analysis*, Development Center, Organization for Economic Cooperation and Development, Paris.

LITTLE, IAN M. D. and MIRRLEES, JAMES A. (1974): *Project Appraisal and Planning for Developing Countries*, Basic Books, New York.

MANASSAH, JAMAL T. (ed.) (1981): *Alternative Energy Sources, Parts A & B*, Academic Press, New York.

MASON, SCOTT P. and MERTON, ROBERT C. (1984): "The Role of Contingent Claims Analysis in Corporate Finance", mimeographed, Sloan School of Management, M.I.T., Cambridge, Massachusetts, January.

NALEBUFF, BARRY J. and VARIAN, HAL (1983): "Some Aspects of Risk Sharing in Non-Classical Environments", in (ed.) Dale W. Jorgenson, *Proceedings of the Arne Lynde Symposium on Social Insurance*, North Holland.

NEWBERY, DAVID M. G. and STIGLITZ, JOSEPH E. (1982): "Optimal Commodity Stock-Piling Rules", mimeographed, Princeton University, New Jersey, February.

NICHOLS, ALBERT L. and ZECKHAUSER, RICHARD J. (1977): "Stockpiling Strategies and Cartel Prices", *The Bell Journal of Economics*, Vol. 8, No. 1, Spring.

PLUMMER, JAMES L. (ed.) (1982): *Energy Vulnerability*, Ballinger Press, Cambridge, Massachusetts, U.S.A.

RADNER, ROY and STIGLITZ, JOSEPH E. (1975): "Fundamental Non-Convexities in the Value of Information", mimeographed, Stanford University, California.

ROTHSCHILD, MICHAEL (1971): "A Two-Armed Bandit Theory of Market Pricing", Working Paper No. 10, University of California, Berkeley.

SAMUELSON, PAUL A. (1963): "Risk and Uncertainty: A Fallacy of Large Numbers", *Scientia*, Vol. 6, April/May.

SAMOUILIDIS, J. E. and BERAHAS, S. A. (1982): "A Methodological Approach to Strategic Petroleum Reserves", *Omega*, Vol. 10, No. 5, pp. 565–574.

SCHULZE, WILLIAM D. and KNEESE, ALLEN V. (1981): "Risk in Benefit-Cost Analysis", *Risk Analysis*, Vol. 1, No. 1, March, pp. 81–88.

SHARPE, W. F. (1964): "Capital Asset Prices: A Theory of Market Equilibrium Under Conditions of Risk", *Journal of Finance*, Vol. 19, September, pp. 425–442.

SMITH, V. KERRY and KRUTILLA, JOHN V. (eds.) (1982): *Explorations in Natural Resource Economics*, published for Resources for the Future, Inc., The Johns Hopkins University Press, Baltimore, Maryland.

STERN, NICHOLAS H. (1977): "Welfare Weights and the Elasticity of the Marginal Valuation of Income", in M. Artis and A. R. Nobay, (eds.) *Current Economic Problems*, Basil Blackwell, Oxford.

STIGLITZ, JOSEPH E. (1976): "Monopoly and the Rate of Extraction of Exhaustible Resources", *American Economic Review*, Vol. 66, pp. 655–61.

STIGLITZ, JOSEPH E. and DASGUPTA, PARTHA S. (1980): "Market Structure and Resource Depletion: A Contribution to the Theory of Intertemporal Monopolistic Competition", Econometric Research Program Research Memorandum No. 261, Princeton University, Princeton, New Jersey, March.

WILSON, ROBERT (1982): "Risk Measurement of Public Projects", in Lind *et al*. (1982).

WORLD BANK (1982): *Potential for Industrial Energy Conservation in Developing Countries,* by Edilberto Segura and staff of the Industry Department, Washington, D.C., October.

WRIGHT, BRIAN D. and WILLIAMS, JEFFREY C. (1982): "The Roles of Public and Private Storage in Managing Oil Import Disruptions", mimeographed, Yale University and Brandeis University, March.

Oxford Economic Papers 39 (1987), 223–232

THE ECONOMICS OF WORLDWIDE
STAGFLATION: A REVIEW*

By J. S. FLEMMING

THIS is not an easy book. Roughly half of it is devoted to a very thorough exposition of the macroeconomic theory of an economy with an imported intermediate product (energy). This clearly introduces the possibility of an exogenous supply shock if the terms on which energy can be bought shift. This section ends with some simulation exercises on a complete general equilibrium dynamic model of 35 equations.

Thus when one turns to the empirical work in the second half of the book, which relates to the experience of oil importing countries over the last two decades, one has two expectations: that the estimated models will be complete simultaneous systems, and that the oil price will play a key role. Both expectations are disappointed. The main focus is not on the energy market but on the labour market, where the key contribution is in the use made of a notion of a real wage gap in the modelling of industrial country price and output dynamics. The real wage gap is the proportion by which real wage rates exceed their full employment equilibrium value. This modelling is not done in a consistent simultaneous structural framework, indeed it is not only rather scrappy in theoretical terms but also econometrically unsophisticated.

The link between these two sections might be found in the determination of real wage gaps by energy price changes. They do indeed have a role to play but other factors can also generate gaps; thus the authors see the spontaneous European wage explosion of the late 1960's as opening up a gap, and likewise the widespread increase in payroll taxes. Another possible contributor is a productivity slowdown not reflected in wage trends; this is recognised, but is treated as being in large part endogenous.

The authors' purpose is not to displace Keynesian demand considerations by a variant on new classical rational-expectations supply-side models, but to try to synthesise demand and supply factors in a model with alternative regimes the demarcation of which is blurred by aggregation. This is a very worthy task on which they have made considerable advances, although their particular mixture of rigorous theoretical and relatively casual empirical argument will not be to everyone's taste.

With Keynesian features to support policy effectiveness the question of international co-operation arises naturally in the context of an open economy model and a comparative study. The case for co-operation is strong, but is complicated by the recognition that economies differ in ways which significantly affect not only their responses to their own policies, but

* This is a review of the Economics of Worldwide, Stagflation, by M. Bruno and J. Sachs (Blackwell, Oxford, 1985).

also the repercussions of those policies on other countries. Successful co-operation thus requires agreement not on a single model of the representative economy but on a set of models one for each economy.

The copious empirical results reported emphasise differences between economies but the structural differences identified are not explained. To some extent they are political and might be changed; in other respects they may be endogenous and respond to economic developments. The first possibility leaves it open to a major government to refuse to accept the structure of another country as a constraint on any joint maximisation exercise.

The general story that emerges in the second half of the book is one that I find eminently plausible—indeed I have put forward similar, if fragmentary, interpretations from time to time myself. My only regret is that the story is not more coherently and consistently presented in the book. I shall try to make good that defect here.

Stagflation in industrial countries in the 1970s arose thus: raw material price rises, of which the oil price increase of 1974 was only the most dramatic and most apparently exogenous, reduced the terms of trade of manufacturing industry. Real wages were slow to adjust; their excess led to adjustment of employment; though relatively rapid this too took time. The low level of employment implied lower utilisation of capacity, and the excess real wage implied reduced profits. For both reasons investment was diminished, and with it the growth of productivity. This implied a fall in the warranted rate of growth of real wages. Since wage growth depends both on the expected warranted increase and the extent of any disequilibrium, failure to recognise the cut in warranted growth slowed the adjustment process. The falls in output would have been associated with higher equilibrium prices even if the money supply were exogenous. It may in fact have responded to raised unemployment, or to fiscal problems as Keynesian policies were tried, or because public expenditure plans posited on continued growth had a momentum of their own. These fiscal problems may also have led to increases in tax rates with cost inflationary consequences.

To capture these effects one needs a model; what follows is about as simple as possible and differs somewhat from the simulation model presented in Chapter 7. If an excess real wage "gap" is to be identified one needs a system to determine the warranted real wage and equilibrium employment level. These can be derived from the demand and supply for labour

$$L^D = D(K, Pm, Wc, M/P, G, \text{Comp}) \qquad (1)$$
$$ + \quad ? \quad - \quad + \quad + \quad +$$

$$L^S = S(V, Wc, T, B, \text{Pop}) \qquad (2)$$
$$ - \quad ? \quad ? \quad - \quad +$$

where K is the capital stock, Pm the relative price of imported raw materials, and Wc the wage in consumption units. The last three arguments of the demand function (real money balances, real government expenditure and international competitiveness) proxy the state of aggregate demand which may be relevant under imperfect competition. Labour supply depends on wealth (the capitalisation of non-labour income), wages, taxes, unemployment benefits and demography. From these two equations, and denoting equilibrium values by a tilde ($\sim$) we derive

$$\tilde{W}_c = \tilde{W}_c(K, Pm, V, T, B, \text{Pop}, M/P, G, \text{Comp})$$
$$\quad\quad\quad + \quad ? \quad + \; + \quad ? \quad - \quad + \quad + \quad + \tag{3}$$

and

$$\tilde{L} = \tilde{L}(K, Pm, V, T, B, \text{Pop}, M/P, G, \text{Comp})$$
$$\quad\; ? \quad ? \quad - \; ? \quad - \quad + \quad ? \quad ? \quad ? \tag{4}$$

Most of the signs indicated in (1) and (2) are self-evident and imply those shown in (3) and (4); the effect of material prices on labour demand is, in principle, ambiguous, depending as it does on the pattern of substitutability between the three factors in the production process, in practice it is assumed to have a negative effect. How real wages, and the taxes they bear, affect labour supply, is ambiguous, as it depends on the balance between income and substitution effects.

Next we need to model the adjustment processes for both the money wage and the level of employment. Using lower case letters for logs a particularly simple structure would be

$$\dot{w} = f(\dot{p}^e, \dot{\tilde{w}}_c^e, w_c - \tilde{w}_c, l - \tilde{l})$$
$$\quad\quad + \quad + \quad\;\; - \quad\quad + \tag{5}$$

$$\dot{l} = g(\dot{l}^e, w_c - \tilde{w}_c, l - \tilde{l})$$
$$\quad\quad + \quad\quad - \quad\;\; - \tag{6}$$

The first term in the wage adjustment equation is the now familiar inflation expectation effect; the second is a slightly less familiar equilibrium real wage expectation effect. This is necessary if the equilibrium level of employment is not to be very sensitive to the rate of e.g. Harrod neutral technical progress (the argument for a unit coefficient on this term may be found less compelling than that relating to price expectations).[1] The inclusion of both the disequilibrium labour price and quantity effects are required for generality. They would be proportional to one another in a log linear world with instantaneous adjustment of employment to the level of labour demand. This set of special assumptions is not made.

Bruno and Sachs' simulation model ignores the problem of employment adjustment in equation (6) and excludes the wage gap from the wage

---

[1] Note that a unit coefficient on both the price and real wage expectations makes persistent unemployment difficult under rational expectations if $\dot{p}^e$ and $\tilde{w}_c^e$ are replaced by $\dot{w}^e$.

adjustment equation (5) despite the dynamic specification of the empirical employment equations and the emphasis elsewhere on the role of wage gaps.

Both the expected trends in real wages and employment depend on the dynamics of the capital stock. If

$$\tilde{K} = \tilde{K}(R, Pm, V, B, T, \text{Pop}, M/P, G, \text{Comp}) \tag{7}$$

where R is the (real) cost of capital, net investment might be given by

$$\dot{k} = h(\dot{\tilde{k}}^e, w_c - \bar{w}_c, l - \bar{l}, k - \tilde{k}) \tag{8}$$
$$+ \quad - \quad + \quad -$$

This specification reflects in some measure both the capacity utilisation $(l - \bar{l})$ and profitability $(w_c - \bar{w}_c)$ effects on investment given the conditioning of $\bar{w}_c$ and l on the actual capital stock K rather than its equilibrium level $\tilde{K}$. $\dot{\bar{w}}_c^e$ and $\dot{\bar{l}}^e$ should thus depend, under rational expectations on $\dot{k}^e$ rather than on $\dot{\tilde{k}}^e$ so that productivity expectations $\dot{\bar{w}}_c^e$ reflect the effects of disequilibrium on capital formation. More generally, however, many of the relevant expectations, particularly of real variables, are more likely to be adaptive than rational.

If the public sector were to be endogenised it might consist of the accounting identity

$$\frac{M}{P} + \frac{D}{(R + \dot{p}^e)P} + T(Q - P_m I) \equiv G + BU + D \tag{9}$$

where D is the nominal annual service cost of a debt consisting of nominal consols, $R + \dot{p}^e$ the nominal interest rate, $Y = (Q - PmI)$ is aggregate value added (and the tax base), subject to tax at the rate. T. Then policy responses might be

$$\dot{g} = (\dot{y}^e, d, g, t, y), \quad \dot{m} = (\dot{y}^e, \dot{p}^e, \dot{p}), \quad \dot{i} = ((\dot{y}^e, \dot{p}^e, t, y, \dot{g}, \dot{d})$$
$$+ \; - \; - \; - \; + \qquad\qquad + \; + \; - \qquad\quad ? \; + \; - \; - \; + \; + \tag{10a-c}$$

How many of the features of this structure are discussed and estimated by Bruno and Sachs?

At different points they emphasise oil prices (Pm), monetary policy (M/P), taxation (T), public expenditure (G) and competitiveness (Comp). Changes in other exogenous variables of equations (3) and (4) (the capital stock, private wealth, unemployment benefits and demography) have typically varied rather slowly and are represented by time trends, quite often with shift or slope dummies for the period 1975–81. This reflects a relative lack of attention to tracking down productivity effects of capital formation and its determinants; no equation for investment such as (8) is estimated in the book though one is reported by Michael Bruno in a subsequent Discussion Paper (NBER 1696). Nor is any attempt made to model public sector responses as in equations (10a–c).

Thus the main estimation effort goes into the wage and employment equations (3) and (4) or their dynamic forms (5) and (6). Here, in addition to the economic variables mentioned, considerable space is devoted to discussing social, institutional, and legislative factors, relating to incomes policies and an index of "corporatism", which are difficult to pin down empirically.

The empirical approach is to use fairly basic econometric techniques to estimate different parameters for each of six to nine OECD countries for which macro time series are available for the last two or three decades. No attempt is made to impose parameter uniformity across the countries: indeed one of the main themes is the difference in real and nominal wage responsiveness between different countries, particularly between the United States and the rest; and the relation between these differences and social structure especially as represented by an index of "corporatism" derived from the work of Colin Crouch (1986). The index reflects the incidence of strikes, the coverage of unions, their centralisation, employer organisations and the political role of labour, as well as aspects of work-place participation.

The empirical section starts with a review of the growth, inflation, unemployment and labour productivity record, of all 24 OECD countries since 1960. The authors then consider the contribution of demand factors, where M1 growth is emphasised, and its reflection of a policy of not accommodating OPEC II is highlighted statistically, before looking at the more endogenous supply-side indicators (factor shares, profitability and investment) as well as the relative prices of raw materials and supply and demand for oil.

The second set of estimated equations is designed to establish the role of real wages in determining employment; labour input, as measured by the log of man-hours, is regressed on its own lagged value, the wage deflated by the price of value added, and split time trends, separately for nine countries. This is used to demonstrate that in all cases but one (the US) the real wage has a (statistically significant) negative effect on employment, as argued by neo-classical economists, rather than being as irrelevant as urged by some Keynesians. the difference from previous findings (which are not rigorously "encompassed" in the treatment here) is attributed to inappropriate data and concentration on the (untypical) US case. It is not clear that the equation is identified as a labour demand function (our (1)); regarded as a dynamic employment adjustment equation (our (6)) not only are all the expectational terms missing but so also is the employment disequilibrium term $(l - l)$ and the real wage term enters in level rather than divergence form. This last point is remedied later (on pps 184–5) where the change in the growth of man hours between the 1960s and 1970s in six countries is shown to be negatively (partially) related to the change in a measure of the wage gap $(w_c - \bar{w}_c)$.

If we add the rate of change of equilibrium employment to both sides of a linearisation of our equation (6) and recognise that $\dot{w}^e$ should enter with a unit coefficient, that (under rational expectation) expectational errors might be white noise, and that if the natural rate can be represented by suitable time trends $(l - \bar{l})$ is linearly related to unemployment, then (6) becomes, in continuous time,

$$\dot{U} = \alpha_0 + \alpha_1 U + \alpha_2 t + \alpha_3(w_c - \bar{w}_c)$$

or in discrete time

$$U_t = \beta_0 + \beta_1 U_{-1} + \beta_2 t + \beta_3(w_c - \bar{w}_c) \tag{11}$$

The results of estimating this equation for the same six major countries are given in Table 9.4 (p 185). In this form the real wage term is everywhere positive in its effect on unempolyment, though not significantly so in either the US or France. Tests of "Granger causality" are also reported which support the claim that causation runs from excess wages to unemployment— except in the US (and perhaps France).

Table 10.6 shows that the equation is improved in nearly all cases by the addition of a lagged real money balance term. Though not explicitly modelled as a monetary surprise, long run homogeneity of P in M would make this interpretation relatively plausible. In our model the effect of a rise in M/P on (un)employment should work through the wage gap and expectational terms, but given the omission of the latter and the proxies for $w - \bar{w}$ used by Bruno and Sachs it is not surprising that the real balance effect itself comes through quite strongly.

Bruno and Sachs use two methods of estimating series for the real wage gap. The first assumes that production is Cobb–Douglas so that marginal productivity is proportional to average productivity. Full employment marginal product of labour is therefore proportional to average product at cyclical peaks if they are assumed to correspond to full employment. A log-linear trend is used to interpolate between peaks and the average of these trends is used to extrapolate after 1981. The second approach adjusts average productivity for changes in the level and rate of change of unemployment according to a fitted equation. In each case the "gap" is between estimated full employment productivity and the observed real wage, so scaled as to average zero between 1965 and 69.

The two different measures produce very similar results. Very modest gaps in Canada and France (on US BLS data) slightly larger in France (on INSEE data) and the US. Quite large in Germany, very large (20%) in Japan in 1975 and 1979 and inexorably rising in the UK, to 20–25% by 1981. (It is not clear how the bonus element in Japanese wages, highlighted by Weitzman's analysis (1984), is treated in these figures.)

Bruno and Sachs refer (at several points) to the possibility that real wage growth "targets" might exceed the underlying trend rate of increase of productivity, with consequences for rising unemployment or inflation. This terminology has been familiar in the UK since the work of Sargan (1964) and the CEPG. It is not, however, one that I find congenial or helpful. The crucial question is the exogeneity of the real wage growth target.

We have already seen that there is a role for $\dot{w}^e$ in the wage equation (5) but this is defined as an endogenous equilibrium concept, even if modelled as adjusting slowly, and not as an exogenous source of disequilibrium. In earlier work (e.g. Henry, Sawyer & Smith (1977)) a, time trend which could just as well have been interpreted as, say, a rising trend in the natural rate of unemployment, was interpreted as a target wage trend. In any case such trend terms are likely to be attenuated in the presence of an adequate proxy for $\dot{w}^e$.

Even excluding the perverse response in the US the response of unemployment to the estimated wage gap differs widely with little response in Japan in either the short or long run, ten times as large a short run response in Canada and Denmark and 20 times as large a long run response in the UK where the impact effect is not much above the mean.

Turning now to the inflation equation, Bruno and Sachs work with prices rather than the wages of our (5). They start from a "basic" equation

$$\dot{p} = \alpha_0 + \alpha_1 U + \alpha_2 \dot{p}_{-1} \qquad (12) \ 10.1 \ \text{pp. } 200/203$$

fitted separately to each of eight countries, in which α_1 is negative for all except Denmark and France. Equation (5) implies that such an equation, if derived by a mark-up on wages, should include a wage gap term.

Applying a fixed markup on wages, or assuming that the markup changes with things which change wages, (5) implies

$$\dot{p} = (\dot{p}^e, \ \dot{w}^e_c, \ w_c - \bar{w}_c, \ l - \bar{l}) \qquad (12a)$$

Bruno and Sachs present similar equations in which the two expectational terms are represented by a lag on price changes, the wage gap by w^x and the employment gap by unemployment U. They derive it, however, from a wage equation which does *not* include the wage gap and a price equation which does.

The argument seems to be that $\dot{p} = \dot{p}^e + \lambda \ (q - \bar{q})$ where the last term captures output relative to desired supply. It is then argued that this output gap is imperfectly proxied by unemployment (suppose boatloads of eligible immigrants arrive with an impact effect on u but not w, why should p fall?) which needs to be supplemented by the wage gap as excess wages reduce desired supply. Classical unemployment does nothing to restrain prices. I don't find this derivation very satisfactory as it is not clear that it is the price change rather than the price level that responds to the output gap. The latter would bring the change in the output gap (or unemployment) into this inflation equation (of which more anon).

In explaining consumer prices, import prices and (full employment) trend productivity growth, are also included and jointly enormously improve the explanatory power of the equation. Unemployment is now appropriately signed, but not significant, for Denmark, and wrongly signed (though not significant) only for France. The wage gap has a positive effect in all eight countries but is significant in only half of them. The productivity trend is appropriately signed everywhere but Canada, while significant only in the US. Given the "markup" argument for including the wage gap in the price adjustment equation it is surprising that when the authors do briefly consider wage equations they revert to a "basic" Phillips curve

$$\left.\begin{aligned} \dot{w} &= \beta_0 + \beta_1 u + \beta_2 \dot{p} + (1 - \beta_2)\dot{p}_{-1} \quad \text{or} \\ \dot{w}_c &= \dot{w} - \dot{p} = \beta_0 + \beta_1 u - (1 - \beta_2)(\dot{p} - \dot{p}_{-1}) \end{aligned}\right\} \tag{13}$$

in which $\beta_2 \approx \frac{1}{2}$ in North America and 1 in Europe and Japan so that there is *de facto* wage indexation in the latter but a real wage that grows less rapidly as inflation rises in North America.

The model of equations (1)–(10) above says nothing directly about productivity. The key equation is that for investment which, as mentioned, is not seriously addressed by B/S. B/S do, however need to model productivity in order to generate their wage gap. It may seem odd, for reasons urged elsewhere by the authors (p 200), that they use unemployment rather than the wage gap to make a cyclical adjustment to productivity (why should a boatload of eligible immigrants impinge on current productivity?) even though what is sought at this stage is a cyclical adjustment to the wage gap itself. A rather more careful model of productivity growth is presented on pages 263–4. This proxies the investment effects of low capacity utilisation by using cumulative unemployment but continues to use u rather than the wage gap. The relative change in input prices (e.g. oil) adds little to this explanation.

A possible merit of the model set out above is that it suggests an approach which might avoid the measurement problems involved in constructing w^x. The wage gap can be eliminated from (5) and (6) to give

$$\dot{w} = F(\dot{p}^e, \dot{w}_c^e, \dot{l}^e, l - \bar{l}, \dot{l})$$

or

$$\dot{l} = G(\dot{p}^e, \dot{w}_c^e, \bar{l}, l - \bar{l}, \dot{w}) \tag{14}$$

An interesting point about equation (14) is its inclusion of both the employment gap (i.e. unemployment) and the change in employment (or unemployment). Many estimated Phillips curves have lagged unemployment rates and the relative weight on the change in unemployment is often interpreted in terms of the wage adjustment equation alone as reflecting the impact of the employment gap on wages. In this context a strong effect from the change in (un)employment relative to its level tends to be seen in an unfavourable light—only rising unemployment makes workers exercise any restraint.

An alternative story is that rising unemployment may reflect employment ajdustment to the wage gap which has been omitted from the wage adjustment equation. This could have the more favourable interpretation that wage bargains too are sensitive to the wage gap, possibly more so than to the employment gap. In principle, if wages were so sensitive to the wage discrepancy, the path back to equilibrium would require little, if any, quantity adjustments. That would be welcome. Along these lines the ideal would be that wages adjust slowly to the employment gap and rapidly to the wage gap while employment adjusts slowly to both—with the implication that the wage change should be extremely sensitive to the (very small) changes in unemployment. Clearly this ideal does not hold but we cannot reject it on the basis of the relative coefficients on u and $\dot{u}$ in an unidentified reduced form combining elements of both wage and employment adjustment equations.

Thus the empirical work in this book is seriously flawed in specification, estimation and interpretation. Nevertheless it is probably better than most of what is available in the field. The lack of theoretical coherence is highlighted by the contrast with the simulation model of the earlier sections, while the whole gains from the authors' open-minded combination of (neo)-classical and Keynesian features—though catholicism, eclecticism and casual empiricism may be hard to distinguish.

The main competition to the B/S account comes from some of the most recent work of the Centre of Labour Economics at LSE—notably the work of Richard Layard and Stephen Nickell. This differs from the model sketched above in that instead of wage and employment adjustment equations they have separate equations for price and wage determination, each given the other, and depending *inter alia* also on employment and price surprises. These two equations thus determine both the equilibrium real wage and the equilibrium level of employment (and thus the NAIRU) as functions of exogenous variables relating to "wage pressure" including raw material prices and employment taxes. A production function translates the equilibrium employment rate into equilibrium output. Only if aggregate demand coincides with the level of output can surprises be avoided. Provided that there is some endogenous element in aggregate demand this equilibrium should be attainable.

The major difference between this setup and that considered earlier is the dependence of the NAIRU on a set of variables subject to more frequent and rapid change than its conventional social and demographic determinants. Thus the NAIRU is less of a trend variable and unemployment is less regressive. In this sense it appears to be subject to hysteresis although, in this formulation, it is not the previous level of unemployment as such that determines today's NAIRU. Layard and Nickell have indeed estimated that a very large proportion (75%) of the rise in UK unemployment in recent years is due to relative price, tax and similar changes. This is not the picture that emerges from B/S although L/N also assign a role to aggregate demand.

My own reluctance to accept the L/N estimate of the NAIRU as representing permanent changes stems from a belief that (male) labour supply is highly inelastic and that bargaining structures are unlikely to mask this indefinitely. If there is indeed an underlying NAIRU from which deviations may from time to time occur the evidence as marshalled in both approaches is that the deviations are of considerable persistence. In the B/S case, however, it is more difficult to extract estimates of the NAIRU and its determinants and thus to consider policies other than demand management which might reduce it.

What kind of picture finally emerges from the book read in the light of the reservations expressed above? First that for virtually all countries there is empirical support for the relevance both of classical (real wage) and Keynesian (aggregate demand) factors. Secondly that the application of a uniform framework to the different countries reveals a marked variation in coefficients. This, if it is not a statistical artefact, has two important implications: that national policies should be expected to differ even when policy makers with similar preferences face (apparently) similar problems; and that international transmission can take odd forms.

Thirdly, though less thoroughly, factors such as corporatism, which economists have tended to dismiss as "mere sociology", may indeed be important.

The Bank of England

REFERENCES

BRUNO, M., Aggregate Supply and Demand Factors in OECD Unemployment: an Update, National Bureau of Economic Research Working Paper 1696, September 1985 (forthcoming in *Economica*).

CROUCH, C., The Conditions for Trade Union Wage Restraint, in *The Politics and Sociology of Global Inflation*, L. Lindberg, and C. Maier, eds., Brookings Institute, Washington, 1986.

HENRY, S. G. B., SAWYER, M. C., and SMITH, P. C., Models of Inflation in the U.K: an Evaluation, *National Institute Economic Review*, 77, August 1976, 60–71.

SARGAN, J. D., Wages and Prices in the U.K., in *Econometric Analysis for National Economic Planning*, P. E. Hart, G. Mills, and J. K. Whittaker, eds., Butterworths, London, 1964.

WEITZMAN, M. L., *The Share Economy*, Harvard University Press, Cambridge, Mass., 1984.

CALL FOR PAPERS

The Editors invite submissions for a SPECIAL ISSUE ON PUBLIC ECONOMICS, which should appear in 1989. Submissions on any subject in this area are welcome until Christmas, 1987.

Oxford Economic Papers 38 (1986), 551–565

INPUT PRICE SHOCKS IN THE SMALL OPEN ECONOMY*

By EDWARD F. BUFFIE

1. Introduction

SINCE the first oil crisis in 1973, a substantial literature has arisen analyzing the effects of oil price shocks. The great majority of papers have concentrated on determining the repercussions upon the terms of trade and the balance of payments in models characterized by intertemporal optimization and full-employment (Obstfeld, 1980; Sachs, 1981; Bruno, 1982; van Wijnbergen, 1984; Marion, 1984). By contrast, relatively little progress has been made in understanding the short-run, macroeconomic consequences of oil shocks. According to the conventional wisdom (Rivera-Batiz, 1985, p. 354–356; Blinder, 1979, chapter 5) both supply and demand contract but there is a presumption that the contractionary supply side effect will dominate, giving rise to stagflation. This assertion needs to be subjected to careful, theoretical scrutiny. A priori, it is far from clear whether supply should be expected to contract more or less than demand and consequently whether adverse oil shocks impart inflationary or deflationary pressures to the economy. Furthermore, an oil shock should not be labeled as contractionary merely because it produces a reduction in gross output. It is necessary as well to verify that the contraction in gross output mirrors a contraction in employment.

The main purpose of this paper is to develop a general analysis of the short-run impact of an oil price rise (or, more topically, an oil price decrease) on employment and inflation in the small open economy. Surprisingly, in the small open economy there is no presumption that an oil price rise is stagflationary. A great deal depends on the initial state of the economy and the nature of substitution patterns between domestic factors and oil. If goods markets are initially in equilibrium and, as is frequently asserted, there is little substitutability between domestic factors and oil, then in most cases the outcome is *stag-deflation*: both employment and the rate of inflation decline. When nontradables output is initially demand constrained, it becomes important to distinguish between the impact on gross output and employment. Gross output always declines but the effect on aggregate employment is uncertain. In the nontradables sector, a higher oil price stimulates an increase in employment for technologies exhibiting a modest degree of flexibility.

The paper is organized as follows. Section 2 develops a tradables-nontradables model of the small open economy with a simple specification of demand but a general treatment of production. Oil, capital and labor are factors of production in each sector and duality theory is employed to allow

---

* I am indebted to two anonymous referees and P. J. N. Sinclair for helpful comments.

a general formulation of technology. The money wage and the exchange rate are fixed and demand depends only on current prices and income. Occam's razor justifies this approach. Even neglecting wealth, interest rate and intertemporal substitution effects, in a large number of cases an oil shock will contract demand strongly enough to produce stag-deflation.

In Section 3 the impact effects upon inflation and sectoral employment are analyzed and general conditions are derived under which the outcome will be stag-inflationary or stag-deflationary. The final section summarizes the main results.

2. The model

We assume a small open economy of the Salter–Swan type (Salter, 1959; Swan, 1963) in which a nontraded good and a composite, traded final good are produced domestically. The exchange rate and the world market price of the traded final good are constant, so the domestic inflation rate depends only upon changes in the price of the nontraded good. There are two variable factors of production, labor (L_i) and noncompetitive imported oil (I_i), and fixed, sector-specific capital stocks ($\bar{K}_i$). The traded final good is the numeraire and units are chosen so that its price equals unity. Notational conventions are as follows: a circumflex denotes the percentage change in a variable ($\hat{X} = dX/X$) and T and N subscripts and superscripts stand for the tradables and nontradables sectors, respectively.

Under the assumption that each sector's output is produced by perfectly competitive firms enjoying constant returns to scale, Shephard's lemma may be used to write the sectoral factor demands as

$$L_i = Q^i(L_i, I_i, \bar{K}_i)C^i_1(w, r_i, p) \tag{1}$$

$$\bar{K}_i = Q^i(L_i, I_i, \bar{K}_i)C^i_2(w, r_i, p) \tag{2}$$

$$I_i = Q^i(L_i, I_i, \bar{K}_i)C^i_3(w, r_i, p), \tag{3}$$

where $i = N, T$; Q^i is output in the ith sector; C^i is the ith sector's unit cost function; w is the wage rate; p is the price of oil; r_i is the rental rate on the ith sector capital stock; and a numbered subscript of the cost function denotes a partial derivative with respect to the corresponding argument. The nominal wage is fixed in the short-run by previously negotiated contracts. It is assumed that firms are never rationed in the labor market; labor supply exceeds labor demand both before and after the oil shock.

Equations (1)–(3) together with the zero profit condition

$$P_i = wC^i_1 + r_iC^i_2 + pC^i_3 \tag{4}$$

enable r_i and notional Q^i, L_i and I_i to be solved for as a function of w, p, and P_i. There is no rationing on international markets (i.e., no export quotas or oil embargoes), so in the tradables sector notional and actual output always coincide.

Matters are more complicated in the nontradables sector. Due to temporary price rigidities, the goods market may fail to clear in the short-run. The solutions given by equations (1)–(4) for notional output and factor demands, will be the actual quantities produced and employed only if firms are not thrown off their supply curves by deficient effective demand.[1] (The short side of the market rules.) Notional quantities shall be denoted by an asterisk, their effective, demand constrained counterparts by a lower-case e, and nontradables demand by D^N:

$$Q^N = \text{Min}\,(Q^{N*}, D^N) \tag{5}$$

$$L_N = \begin{bmatrix} L_N^* & \text{if} & Q^N = Q^{N*} \\ L_N^e & \text{if} & Q^N = D^N \end{bmatrix} \tag{6}$$

$$I_N = \begin{bmatrix} I_N^* & \text{if} & Q^N = Q^{N*} \\ I_N^e & \text{if} & Q^N = D^N \end{bmatrix}. \tag{7}$$

For nontradables demand, a very simple specification is adopted:

$$D^N = D^N(P_N, Y) \tag{8}$$

$$Y = P_N Q^N + Q^T - p(I_T + I_N). \tag{9}$$

D^N depends upon the relative price of the nontradable and real income. For simplicity, only real effects are considered; demand effects working through financial channels (i.e., interest rate and wealth effects) are ignored.

Finally, we make the customary assumption that the relative price of the nontradable varies positively with excess demand

$$\dot{P}_N = \psi(D^N - Q^{N*}), \qquad \psi > 0, \tag{10}$$

where an overdot denotes a time derivative.

In light of the large number of recent papers that have derived savings and investment responses consistent with intertemporally optimizing be-havior on the part of consumers and firms, the crude and simple specification of demand in the current model needs some justification. The decision to focus only on the contractionary effect exerted by the immediate worsening in the economy's terms of trade was made in part in an effort to keep the model analytically tractable, but also because the incorporation of other demand effects either gives rise to ambiguous terms or does not alter qualitatively the results obtained here. Van Wijnbergen (1982, 1984) has shown that the impact on investment demand may be positive or negative

[1] Leijonhufvud (1968), Clower (1970), Barro and Grossman (1971, 1976), and Malinvaud (1977) were the most influential in developing the closed economy disequilibrium analysis. For open economy extensions, see Dixit (1978), Neary (1980), Liviatan (1979) and Cuddington (1980).

Observe that with the zero profit condition holding, notional supply for each individual firm is undefined, but aggregate notional supply is nonetheless uniquely determined since the capital market must clear. A more natural interpretation arises if one makes the conventional assumption that all output is produced by a single competitive firm. The Q^{N*} found from (1)–(4) is then the output level that maximizes the return to shareholders subject to $K_N = \bar{K}_N$.

depending on whether capital is putty-clay or putty-putty and that the intertemporal substitution effects which emerge with forward-looking consumers play no role in determining whether in the short-run the shock will create Keynesian or Classical unemployment, though they do affect the results quantitatively. The analysis that follows, therefore, should be viewed as complementary to that developed in the existing literature where demand effects are treated in greater detail.

3. Instantaneous effects

In the disequilibrium model sketched in the previous section, w and P_N are given at any particular point in time. When the shock occurs, the adjusting variables in the short-run are the rate of nontradables price inflation and the sectoral rental rates, output levels, and factor demands. The impact upon the tradables sector will be of a purely classical nature, but in the nontradables sector the shock may bring on either Classical unemployment (CU) or Keynesian unemployment (KU). Besides the nature of technology and sectoral asymmetries, the initial state of the economy is critical in determining the outcome. Section 3.1 develops the analysis under the assumption that the nontradables sector is initially in equilibrium and Section 3.2 deals with the case where firms are initially quantity constrained in the goods market.

3.1. Initial equilibrium in the nontradables sector

The price shock analyzed here is one which appears as a sudden, once-and-for-all worsening in the economy's terms of trade: after the initial discontinuous jump, p remains fixed (or rises at the same pace as the rate of world inflation). To determine which blade of the demand-supply scissors will do the cutting when the nontradables market initially clears at notional quantities, we need to know the sign of $J = \hat{D}^N/\hat{p} - \hat{Q}^{N*}/\hat{p}$, where $\hat{D}^N/\hat{p}$ is the contraction in nontradables demand under the assumption that $Q^N = Q^{N*}$. If J is positive, the shock produces stag-inflationary CU: employment falls and inflation accelerates. When J is negative, stag-deflationary KU results: both employment and inflation decline.

Differentiating (8) and (9) and choosing units so that initially $P_N = 1$, we obtain[2]

$$J = m_N(\theta_L^N \lambda \hat{L}_T^*/\hat{p} - \phi_I/\phi_N) - \theta_L^N(1 - m_N)\hat{L}_N^*/\hat{p} - \theta_I^N \hat{I}_N^*/\hat{p}, \qquad (11)$$

where θ_j^i represents the share of factor j in the total cost of sector i output; $\lambda = L_T/L_N$; m_n is the marginal propensity to consume nontradables; and ϕ_I and ϕ_N are the shares of oil and nontradables output in national income, respectively $[\phi_I = p(I_T + I_N)/Y$ and $\phi_N = P_N Q^N/Y]$.

---

[2] In deriving (11), remember, from the envelope theorem, that if firms are operating on their supply curves small changes in I_T and I_N have no effect on Y. When firms are demand constrained, this is no longer true. See the discussion that follows in Section 3.2.

To solve for the notional labor demands, first logarithmically differentiate equations (1) and (2). Utilizing Uzawa's result (Uzawa, 1962) that the Allen partial elasticity of substitution between factors i and j, σ_{ij}, may be expressed as $\sigma_{ij} = C_{ij}C/C_iC_j$, and substituting for r from (4) gives[3]

$$\hat{L}_i^*/\hat{p} = -\theta_I^i(\sigma_{LK}^i + \sigma_{KI}^i - \sigma_{KK}^i - \sigma_{LI}^i). \tag{12}$$

A higher price for oil lowers the profit maximizing level of output and the market clearing capital rental. With p higher and r lower, the net substitution effect upon labor demand is positve or negative depending on whether $(\sigma_{LI} \gtrless \sigma_{LK})$. At given factor prices, a reduction in output generates a proportionate reduction in labor demand. This contractionary effect is reflected in the term $-\theta_I(\sigma_{KI} - \sigma_{KK})$.

The solution in (12) can be restated in terms of just the cross-partial elasticities of substitution among the three factors. Using the symmetry property and the adding-up conditions on the partial elasticities of substitution

$$-\theta_j\sigma_{jj} = \sum_{i \neq j} \theta_i\sigma_{ji}, \qquad \sigma_{ji} = \sigma_{ij}$$

(12) becomes

$$\hat{L}_i^*/\hat{p} = -[(1 - \theta_I^i)\sigma_{KL}^i + \theta_K^i(\sigma_{KI}^i - \sigma_{LI}^i) + \theta_I^i\sigma_{KI}^i]\theta_I^i/\theta_K^i = -\varepsilon_{wp}^i < 0. \tag{13}$$

For production functions where primary factors are separable from oil $(\sigma_{KI} = \sigma_{LI})$ and all factors are Allen substitutes $(\sigma_{ij} > 0,\ i \neq j)$, labor and oil are gross complements: the contractionary output effect always dominates the ambiguous substitution effect and causes labor demand to decline. This so called normal case (see Radner, 1968)[4] covers all of the standard production functions. An increase in notional labor demand is conceivable, but requires that σ_{KL} and σ_{KI} be *very* small compared to σ_{LI} so that the net substitution effect is favorable and of sufficient magnitude to more than offset the contractionary pull of a lower scale of output. [Note: $\hat{Q}^i/\hat{p} = -\theta_I((1 + \theta_I)\sigma_{KI} + \theta_L\sigma_{KL}).$]

---

[3] $\hat{r}_i/\hat{p} = -\theta_I^i/\theta_K^i$, as the remaining terms drop out thanks to the envelope theorem.

[4] Some estimates for the developed countries (Hudson and Jorgenson, 1974; Berndt and Wood, 1975) suggest that capital-oil complimentary and labor-oil substitutability may be strong enough to make ε_{pw}^N negative, but the reliability of these estimates is open to doubt and, oil aside, there seem to be very few instances in which the σ_{ij} diverge strongly enough to raise labor demand. Humphrey and Moroneys' (1975) estimates for six industries in the U.S. manufacturing sector turned up two cases of capital- natural resource complimentary, but in neither case was the estimated coefficient significantly different from zero. Burgess (1974), in an aggregate time series study for the U.S., found that over the period 1947–68 σ_{KI} was on average more than triple the value of σ_{LI} (3.3 vs. 1.06). The estimates of Laumas and Williams (1981) for nine industry groups in the Indian manufacturing sector show σ_{KI} ranging from 0.663 to 1.077 and σ_{LI} from 0.411 to 1.416. The principal doubt surrounding the Berndt–Wood and Hudson–Jorgenson results is whether time series data are too short-run and too contaminated by cyclical noise to allow reliable estimates of the production function parameters. Ozatalay–Grubaugh–Long II (1979) and Griffin–Gregory (1976) find $\sigma_{KI} > \sigma_{LI}$ using cross-section data.

Following a similar procedure for $\hat{I}_N^*$ gives

$$\hat{I}_N^*/\hat{p} = -\theta_I^N(2\sigma_{KI}^N - \sigma_{II}^N - \sigma_{KK}^N) = -\varepsilon_{pp}^N. \tag{14}$$

ε_{pp}^N must be positive since the output effect cannot dominate the own price substitution effect even for an inferior factor.

Using (13) and (14) to substitute for $\hat{L}_i^*$ and $\hat{I}_N^*$ in (11), we arrive at the critical expression for J:

$$J = \theta_L^N(1 - m_N)\varepsilon_{wp}^N + \theta_I^N\varepsilon_{pp}^N - m_N(\theta_L^N\varepsilon_{wp}^T\lambda + \phi_I/\phi_N). \tag{15}$$

The first two terms represent the increase in excess demand due to the reductions in L_N and I_N while the last two terms measure the contraction in demand stemming from the terms of trade loss and the fall in tradables sector employment. A large number of parameters influence the sign of J. In general, CU is more likely the *more flexible* is nontradables sector technology and the less flexible is tradables sector technology, the smaller is the share of the tradables sector in aggregate employment, the greater is the oil intensity of tradables production (which raises ϕ_I) and the smaller is the marginal propensity to consume nontradables.

With two positive terms weighing in against two negative ones in (15), it is evident that the sign of J will depend in good measure on the structural characteristics of the economy. One result, however, falls out immediately. Consider a *balanced* economy as one in which the trade deficit is initially zero, sectoral production functions are identical and demand is homothetic.[5] With homothetic demand, the marginal propensity to consume good i equals its consumption share α_i, permitting (15) to be expressed as:

$$J = \theta_L\varepsilon_{wp}(\alpha_T - \alpha_N\lambda) + \theta_I\varepsilon_{pp}^N - \phi_I. \tag{16}$$

Moreover, in a balanced economy $\phi_I = \theta_I/(1 - \theta_I)$ and an initially zero trade deficit implies $\alpha_N\lambda = \alpha_T + \phi_I = \alpha_T + \theta_I/(1 - \theta_I)$.[6] Subsituting these expressions into (16) gives

$$J \gtreqless 0 \quad \text{as} \quad -\theta_L\varepsilon_{wp} + (1 - \theta_I)\varepsilon_{pp}^N \gtreqless 1, \tag{17}$$

from which it is easy to see

---

[5] The assumption of an initially zero trade deficit is purely a simplifying assumption. None of the results of Section 3.2 require the trade balance to be zero. In the current section, Proposition 1 holds without modification if the trade deficit (as a percentage of income) is less than ϕ_I and Proposition 2 is amended to read that

$$(\sigma_{KL} - \sigma_{VI})\theta_I\frac{\theta_L}{\theta_K}b(1 - \theta_I) + \sigma_{VI} < 1$$

is a necessary and sufficient condition for a KU outcome, where b is the ratio of the trade deficit to value-added. The term involving b is quantitatively insignificant. Even when σ_{KL} far exceeds $\sigma_{VI}(\sigma_{KL} - \sigma_{VI} = 1)$, nontradables production is highly labor intensive ($\theta_L = 0.60$, $\theta_K = 0.20$), and the initial deficit is extremely large ($b = 0.10$), it does not exceed 0.05.

[6] In a balanced economy, $\phi_I = (\phi_T + \phi_N)\theta_I$. From the definition of value-added, $\phi_I = \phi_T + \phi_N - 1$ or, after substituting for $(\phi_T + \phi_N)$, $\phi_I = \theta_I/(1 - \theta_I)$. λ can be written as $\theta_L^T\phi_T/\theta_L^N\phi_N = \phi_T/\phi_N$ in a balanced economy. When the trade deficit is initially zero, $\phi_T = \alpha_T + \phi_I$ and hence $\alpha_N\lambda = \alpha_T + \phi_I$.

Proposition 1: In a balanced economy, an unconditional own price elasticity of demand for oil less than unity is a sufficient condition for a KU outcome.

Proposition 1 is fairly general in that it imposes no restrictions on the nature of technology. More exact results can be obtained if a particular production function is postulated. The functional form most frequently used in the existing literature has been a CES production function nested at the level of value-added and oil (Findlay and Rodriguez, 1977; Buiter, 1978; Bruno and Sachs, 1979, 1982; Giavazzi, 1980; Katseli-Papaefstratiou, 1980), hereafter referred to as the VAS (value-added separable) production function or VAS technology. In this case, $\sigma_{LI} = \sigma_{KI} = \sigma_{VI}$, where σ_{VI} is the elasticity of substitution between value-added and oil, and straightforward manipulations show that[7]

$$\varepsilon_{pp} = \frac{\sigma_{VI}(1 - \theta_L) + \theta_I\theta_L(\sigma_{KL} - \sigma_{VI})}{\theta_K} \tag{18}$$

$$\varepsilon_{wp} = \frac{\theta_I[\sigma_{KL} + \theta_I(\sigma_{VI} - \sigma_{KL})]}{\theta_K} \tag{19}$$

Substituting the above expressions into (17), there emerges, after simplification
$$J \lessgtr 0 \quad \text{as} \quad \sigma_{VI} \lessgtr 1. \tag{20}$$

Remarkably, the outcome turns exclusively on the magnitude of the elasticity of substitution between value-added and oil, with Cobb–Douglas technology (at the tier of value-added and imported inputs) constituting the dividing line between KU and CU. To summarize, we have demonstrated

Proposition 2: In a balanced economy where production functions are VAS, a necessary and sufficient condition for a KU outcome is $\sigma_{VI} < 1$.

In light of the widely held belief that substitutability between oil and primary factors is limited in the short-run (ε_{pp}^N or $\sigma_{VI} < 1$), the preceding results argue powerfully in favor of the view that KU is to be expected when sectoral asymmetries are of minor importance and consumption patterns are not strongly heterothetic. The conventional wisdom, which holds both that CU is highly probable and that the elasticity of demand for oil is low in the short-run, would appear to be incorrect unless use of oil in the tradables sector is negligible. This case would apply to *certain* LDCs where primary products account for the bulk of export earnings (bauxite in Jamaica; rubber and tin in Malaysia; copper in Zaire; coffee in Uganda etc.)[8] and extreme

---

[7] (19) follows immediately from (12). To derive (18), first substitute for σ_{II} and σ_{KK} in (14) from the adding-up conditions on the partial elasticities of substitution:

$$\varepsilon_{pp}^N = \theta_I\left[\sigma_{KI}\left(2 + \frac{\theta_I}{\theta_K} + \frac{\theta_K}{\theta_I}\right) + \frac{\theta_L}{\theta_I}\sigma_{IL} + \frac{\theta_L}{\theta_K}\sigma_{KL}\right].$$

With VAS technology, $\sigma_{KI} = \sigma_{LI} = \sigma_{VI}$. (18) is obtained after collecting and simplifying terms.

[8] This is not true of many LDCs. In 1979, manufactured goods accounted for more than one-half of all LDC non-fuel exports (Kirkpatrick and Nixson, 1984, p. 19).

protectionist policies (redundant tariffs or widespread use of import quotas) have, in effect, made manufacturing production a part of the nontradables sector. For the sake of brevity, I will call this prototype the PE (Primary Export) economy. In PE economies, the contractionary demand effects of an oil price shock are weaker both because ϕ_I is smaller and because tradables sector employment does not decline. Accordingly, it is easy to establish that the conditions for CU are less exacting than in a balanced economy:

> *Proposition* 3: In a PE economy, a sufficient condition for CU is that the unconditional own price elasticity of demand for oil exceed the marginal propensity to consume the nontraded good.

Proof. With the tradables sector not using oil, J is positive when

$$\theta_L^N \varepsilon_{wp}^N (1 - m_N) + \theta_I^N (\varepsilon_{pp}^N - m_N) > 0. \tag{21}$$

Given that labor and oil are gross complements, $\varepsilon_{wp} > 0$ and hence a sufficient condition for $J > 0$ is $\varepsilon_{pp}^N > m_N$.

> *Proposition* 4: In a PE economy where the nontradables production function is VAS, a sufficient condition for CU is $\sigma_{VI} > m_N$.[9]

Proof. Substituting for ε_{wp}^N and ε_{pp}^N in (21) from (18) and (19) shows $J > 0$ if

$$\sigma_{VI}\theta_I(1 - m_N\theta_L) + \sigma_{KL}\theta_L(m_T + m_N\theta_I) + \theta_K(\sigma_{VI} - m_N) > 0. \tag{22}$$

As the first two terms are positive, a sufficient condition for $J > 0$ is $\sigma_{VI} > m_N$. For notational ease, N superscripts are omitted in (22) and in the remainder of this section.

Propositions 3 and 4 rule out KU under far weaker conditions than Propositions 1 and 2 and, in fact, define a range over which the outcome must differ qualitatively from that in a balanced economy ($m_N < \varepsilon_{pp} < 1$ or $m_N < \sigma_{VI} < 1$). Even under the strong assumption that the tradables sector does not use oil, however, a CU outcome requires that technology exhibit at least a modest degree of flexibility, particularly when the economy is relatively closed at the margin with respect to consumption. This can be seen most clearly by comparing the conditions for CU in the cases of a nonnested CES production function, (Smid, 1979) and a VAS production function in which value-added and oil are used in fixed proportions (Findlay and Rodriguez, 1977; Buiter, 1978; Kateseli-Papaefstratiou, 1980). In the CES case, $\sigma_{VI} = \sigma_{KL} = \sigma$ and (22) simplifies to

$$\sigma > \theta_K/(\theta_I + \theta_K + m_T/m_N), \tag{23}$$

[9] Dixit has shown that with Cobb–Douglas utility and production functions an oil price shock generates a payments deficit in a small economy producing a single traded good. This is a corollary of Proposition 4. (When supply falls by more than demand in a small, totally open economy, the result is a payments deficit). As Proposition 4 makes clear, Dixit's result holds with technology considerably less flexible than Cobb-Douglas and does not require Cobb-Douglas preferences.

whereas, if there is no substitutability between oil and primary factors, $\sigma_{VI} = 0$ and

$$\sigma_{KL} > \theta_K/\theta_L(\theta_I + m_T/m_N) \tag{24}$$

is required for a CU outcome. (24) is a considerably more stringent condition than (23), especially when m_T/m_N is relatively small. For example, with $m_T = m_N$, $\theta_I = 0.20$ and $\theta_K = 0.40$, (23) and (24) state that CU arises when $\sigma > 0.25$ and $\sigma_{KL} > 0.83$. By contrast, in an economy that is more closed (at the margin) with respect to consumption where, say, $m_T/m_N = 0.33$, the borderline value of σ is still only 0.43 but the critical value of σ_{KL} rises to 1.89.

To complete the analysis of the potential impact effects, we need to know how the economy behaves when $J < 0$ and firms are prevented from realizing their notional factor demands by deficient effective demand. If this situation arises because of the shock, the demand constraint forces nontradables employment to fall by an amount exceeding that given in (14).' If, however, KU prevails *initially*, the shock affects the economy through channels very different from those analyzed so far. This is pursued in the next section.

3.2. Demand constrained output

In an economy suffering from KU, the macroeconomic repercussions of an import price shock are much less likely to be adverse. In fact, the price shock could even alleviate the demand constraint faced by firms in the nontradables sector. As before, the terms of trade loss and induced layoffs in the tradables sector lower demand, but substitution away from oil in the nontradables sector pulls in the opposite direction by shifting payments toward domestic factors of production. Though the latter effect is seldom strong enough to generate an increase in nontradables demand, it often prevents a steep decline in the scale of nontradables output which would fully nullify the favorable substitution effect operating on labor demand. Consequently, if technology is fairly flexible, nontradables sector employment increases.

It is assumed that the price shock does not lower notional supply enough to eliminate KU. Firms, therefore, cannot attain their supply curves and factor demands are determined by solving (1)–(3) with D^N substituted for Q^N: [10]

$$\hat{L}_N = \delta_L^N \hat{D}^N + \bar{\varepsilon}_{wp}^N \hat{p} \tag{25}$$

$$\hat{I}_N = \delta_I^N \hat{D}^N + \bar{\varepsilon}_{pp}^N \hat{p}, \tag{26}$$

[10] With $\hat{D}^N/\hat{p} < \hat{Q}^{N*}/\hat{p}$ it can be seen from (2) that r, to ensure equilibrium in the capital market, falls to a level that allows individual firms to earn positive economic profits. Since we have perfectly competitive firms and constant returns to scale, this may seem to contradict the statement that notional output falls. However, if we make the conventional assumption that output is produced by a single representative firm the change in notional supply is still given by $Q^{N*} = Q^N(L_N^*, I_N^*)$, as that is the level of output that maximizes the sum of quasi-rents $(r_N \bar{K}_N)$ and pure profits per unit of capital. (That is, Q^{N*} maximizes $P_N Q^N - wL_N - P_I I_N$.)

where

$$\delta_L^N = 1 - \sigma_{LK}/\sigma_{KK} > 0$$
$$\delta_I^N = 1 - \sigma_{IK}/\sigma_{KK} > 0$$
$$\bar{\varepsilon}_{wp}^N = \theta_I^N(\sigma_{LI} - \sigma_{KI}\sigma_{LK}/\sigma_{KK}) > 0$$
$$\bar{\varepsilon}_{pp}^N = \theta_I^N(\sigma_{II} - \sigma_{IK}^2/\sigma_{KK}) < 0.$$

δ_L^N and δ_I^N will be positive if neither factor is inferior. The σ_{IK}/σ_{KK} terms enter because as output increases the rental rate is driven up to equilibrate the capital market, thus inducing substitution toward L_N and I_N (assuming neither factor is complementary with capital). Concavity of the cost function guarantees that $\bar{\varepsilon}_{pp}^N$ is negative, and with $\bar{\varepsilon}_{pp}^N$ negative, $\bar{\varepsilon}_{wp}^N$ must be positive.[11] Again, the second term in the parentheses in these expressions reflects a cross-substitution effect, this time arising from the increase in the rental rate brought on by an increase in p.

To get the reduction in nontradables demand, differentiate (8) and (9) again—this time with $Q^N = D^N$—and substitute from (26) for $\hat{I}_N$:

$$\hat{D}^N/\hat{p} = -m_N(\theta_L^N \varepsilon_{wp}^T \lambda + \theta_I^N \bar{\varepsilon}_{pp}^N + \phi_I/\phi_N)/\Delta, \tag{27}$$

where

$$\Delta = 1 + \delta_I^N \theta_I^N - m_N.$$

Δ^{-1}, the multiplier, will be positive provided tradables are not strongly inferior. The expression enclosed by parentheses in the numerator gives the overall reduction in real income due to the price shock. The familiar first and third terms represent, as before, the loss in real income arising from the economy's worsened terms of trade and layoffs induced in the tradables sector. The second negative term measures the real income gain accruing on substitution away from imported oil in the nontradables sector. At a *given* level of nontradables output, a reduction in I_N raises national income by lowering the economy's import bill. There is no corresponding term involving I_T because, with output supply determined in the tradables sector, variations in I_T have no impact on national income up to a first-order effect (the envelope theorem). For D^N to increase, the total bill for imported oil in the nontradables sector must decline. This requirement yields the following set of results:

---

[11] Since the cost function is concave, its matrix of second partial derivatives is negative definite and hence

$$C_{33}C_{22} - C_{23}C_{32} > 0$$

Dividing through by $C_3^2 C_2^2$ and multiplying by C^2 gives

$$\sigma_{II}\sigma_{KK} - \sigma_{IK}^2 > 0$$

or

$$\sigma_{II} = \frac{\sigma_{IK}^2}{\sigma_{KK}} < 0$$

Proposition 5: If the nontradables sector is initially characterized by KU, a necessary condition for nontradables demand to increase is $-\bar{\varepsilon}_{pp}^{N} > 1$.

Proof. Even ignoring the term involving ε_{wp}^{T} in (27), $\hat{D}^{N}/\hat{p} > 0$ requires

$$-\bar{\varepsilon}_{pp}^{N} > \phi_{I}/\phi_{N}\theta_{I}^{N} = 1 + \phi_{T}\theta_{I}^{T}/\phi_{N}\theta_{I}^{N}. \tag{28}$$

Corollary 5.1: In a balanced economy, where the nontradables sector is initially characterized by KU, a necessary condition for nontradables demand to increase is $-\bar{\varepsilon}_{pp}^{N} > 1/m_{N}(1 - \theta_{I})$.

Corollary 5.2: If the nontradables sector is initially characterized by KU and technology is VAS, then a necessary condition for nontradables demand to increase is $\sigma_{VI}^{N} \geqslant 1/(1 - \theta_{I})$.[12]

Corollary 5.3: In a balanced economy where the nontradables sector is initially characterized by KU and technology is VAS, a necessary condition for nontradables demand to increase is $\sigma_{VI} > 1/(1 - \theta_{I})^{2}m_{N}$.

A reduction in effective demand seems all but certain. Regardless of the general structural characteristics of the economy, a necessary condition for demand to increase is that the conditional own price elasticity of demand for I_{N} exceed unity. In a balanced economy, the requisite value of $-\varepsilon_{pp}^{N}$ is on the order of 1.5–3.0 ($\theta_{I} = 0.10$–0.30, $m_{N} = 0.40$–0.80), and if technology is VAS, σ_{VI} will usually have to lie between two and four.

These results both complement and contrast with those of the previous section. Consider the results pertaining to VAS technology. When $\sigma_{VI} < 1$, technology is insufficiently flexible to prevent a reduction in effective demand in a KU economy or the emergence of KU in a balanced economy enjoying initial goods market equilibrium. However, for technologies that are more flexible, but not extraordinarily flexible, the results differ sharply: in a balanced economy, if $1 < \sigma_{VI} \leqslant 1/m_{N} (1 - \theta_{I})^{2}$, an oil price shock produces CU when goods markets are initially in equilibrium, but exacerbates the shortfall of effective demand when KU initially prevails.

Provided the degree of substitutability between primary factors and oil is not exceedingly high, the overall effect on nontradables sector employment will consist of an adverse output effect and a favorable cross-substitution effect. Surprisingly, however, it can be demonstrated that in certain plausible cases the substitution effect dominates even for relatively inflexible technologies. Consider a PE economy (or, more generally, any economy where $\theta_{L}^{N}m_{N}\varepsilon_{wp}^{T}\lambda$ is small) in which technology is VAS. In this case (25) yields after using (27) and noting that $\bar{\varepsilon}_{wp}^{N} = \theta_{I}^{N}\sigma_{VI}\delta_{L}^{N}$

$$\hat{L}_{N} \gtrless 0 \quad \text{as} \quad \sigma_{VI} + m_{N}\sigma_{VI}[\theta_{L}^{N} + \theta_{K}^{N} - \theta_{I}^{N}\theta_{K}^{N}\sigma_{VI}/(\theta_{L}\sigma_{KL}^{N} + \theta_{I}^{N}\sigma_{VI})] \gtrless m_{N}. \tag{29}$$

---

[12] This is not inconsistent with assertions found elsewhere in the literature (Katseli, p. 372; Bruno and Sachs, 1979, p. 13–14) that when imported inputs are used only in the nontradables sector (or think of a one good model) the total intermediates import bill at a given level of *notional* output rises or falls depending on whether the elasticity of substitution between value-added and the imported input is below or above one.

Since the minimum possible value of the bracketed term is θ_L (when $\sigma_{KL} = 0$), we have

> *Proposition* 6: In a PE economy where the nontradables sector is initially characterized by KU and technology is VAS, a sufficient condition for employment to increase is $\sigma_{VI} > m_N/(1 + m_N\theta_L^N)$.

Comparing Propositions 4 and 6 makes it evident that, once again, the initial state of the economy is extremely important. When the goods market is initially in equilibrium and technology is VAS, an oil price shock always lowers nontradables sector employment. By contrast, Proposition 6 states that in a KU economy a contraction in employment occurs only if technology is relatively inflexible. If technology is Cobb–Douglas, employment must increase. More generally, the stylized facts ($m_N \approx 0.50$, $\theta_I^N \approx 0.20$, $\theta_K^N \approx 0.40$) suggest that a favorable effect on employment is likely for values of σ_{VI} exceeding 0.42.

Finally, it should be noted that the initial state of the economy could also importantly affect the response of the payments balance. As there is no investment in the current model, the price shock creates a surplus or a deficit depending on whether savings rise or fall. For the simplest possible specification in which savings depend only on current income, a deficit always emerges when goods markets are initially in equilibrium since value-added declines in both the tradables and nontradables sectors.[13] Should KU initially prevail, however, a payments surplus, though improbable, is conceivable; if nontradables sector employment rises enough to offset the worsening in the economy's terms of trade and any reduction in tradables sector employment, the price shock is expansionary and generates an increase in savings and a payments surplus.

4. Concluding Remarks

This paper has investigated the short-run, macroeconomic effects of an OPEC-type price shock in a model with a very general treatment of production. The short-run impact on employment depends sensitively upon the initial state of the economy. If KU initially prevails in the nontradables sector, employment may well increase. In fact, when the tradables sector does not use imported inputs, this is the expected outcome provided that technology is not highly inflexible.

If the nontradables sector is initially in equilibrium, more conventional results emerge. Employment in both the tradables and nontradables sectors falls in all cases save technologies where factoral substitution patterns are strongly biased toward labor. The key variables determining whether the shock shall prove inflationary as well as contractionary are the nature of

---

[13] With forward looking consumers, intertemporal substitution effects come into play and much depends on whether the shock is anticipated and whether the price is expected to rise or fall in future periods. See Marion (1984).

technology, sectoral asymmetries, and the initial state of the economy. Somewhat surprisingly, contrary to many casual assertions found in the existing literature,[14] in numerous cases stag-deflationary, Keynesian unemployment is to be expected.

University of Pennsylvania,
Philadelphia, U.S.A.

REFERENCES

ALLEN, R. G. D., *Mathematical Analysis for Economists.* London: MacMillan Press, 1938.

AIZENMAN, JOSHUA. "Disinflation and Non-Traded Goods," Discussion Paper, University of Pennsylvania, May 1982.

BARROW, ROBERT, J. and GROSSMAN, HERSCHEL L., "A General Disequilibrium Model of Income and Employment," *American Economic Review,* 61, No. 1 (March 1971): 82–93.

——, *Money, Employment and Inflation.* Cambridge, Mass.: Cambridge University Press, 1976.

BERNDT, ERNST R. and WOOD, DAVID O., "Technology, Prices and the Derived Demand for Energy," *Review of Economics and Statistics,* 56, No. 3 (August 1975): 259–68.

BLINDER, ALAN S., *Economic Policy and the Great Stagflation.* New York: Academic Press, 1979.

BRUNO, M., "Adjustment and Structural Change under Supply Shocks," *Scandinavian Journal of Economics* 84, No. 2 (1982): 199–221.

—— and SACHS, JEFFREY., "Macro-Economic Adjustment With Import Price Shocks: Real and Monetary Aspects," *The Maurice Falk Institute for Economic Research in Israel,* Discussion Paper No. 793, January 1979.

——, "Input Price Shocks and the Slowdown in Economic Growth: The Case of U.K. Manufacturing," Review of Economic Studies, 49, No. 159 (Special Issue, 1982): 679–706.

BURGESS, DAVID F., "Production Theory and the Derived Demand for Imports," *Journal of International Economics,* 4, No. 2 (May 1974): 103–18.

BUITER, WILLIAM., "Short-run and Long-run Effects of External Disturbances under a Floating Exchange Rate," *Economica,* 45, No. 179 (August 1978): 251–72.

CLOWER, ROBERT W., "The Keynesian Counter-revolution: A Theoretical Appraisal." In *Monetary Theory,* edited by Robert W. Clower. Baltimore: Penguin Books, 1970.

CUDDINGTON, JOHN, T., "Fiscal and Exchange Rate Policies in a Fix-Price Trade Model With Export Rationing," *Journal of International Economics,* 10, No. 3 (August 1980): 319–40.

DIXIT, AVINASH., "The Balance of Trade in a Model of Temporary Equilibrium With Rationing," *Review of Economic Studies,* 65, No. 3 (October 1978): 393–404.

[14] Bruno and Sachs (1982) assume output to be supply determined and speculate that this is likely to be the case after allowing for contractionary demand effects. Malinvaud argues (1977, p. 90–1) that the oil shock may be treated as a type of technical regress that expands the region of Classical unemployment, but is careful to qualify this conclusion by stating that it is conditional on the assumption that the trade balance remains in equilibrium. Later (p. 109), he notes that the worsening in the terms of trade may give rise to Keynesian unemployment. The simulations performed in Malinvaud (1980, p. 86) show, in fact, that an oil shock produces an initial spell (five years) of Keynesian unemployment. Neary (p. 418–19), like Malinvaud, treats the import price shock as analogous to technical regress, but shows that either Classical unemployment or repressed inflation may result. The latter outcome is possible because when consumers are rationed in the nontradables market labor supply may fall by more than labor demand. This possibility does not arise in the model used here since labor supply is assumed fixed.

DORNBUSCH, RUDIGER., Chapter 5 ("Intermediate Goods and Nontraded Goods") in *Open Economy Macroeconomics*. New York: Basic Books, Inc., 1980.

FINDLAY, RONALD and RODRIGUEZ, CARLOS A., "Intermediate Imports and Macroeconomic Policy under Flexible Exchange Rates," *Canadian Journal of Economics*, 10, No. 2 (May 1977): 208–17.

GIAVAZZI, F., "Exchange Rates and Current Account Dynamics Following Real Disturbances," Paper presented at the Econometric Society meetings, August 1980.

GRIFFIN, JAMES M. and GREGORY, PAUL R., "An Intercountry Translog Model of Energy Substitution Responses," *American Economic Review*, 66, No. 5 (December 1976): 845–57.

HONKAPOHJA, S. and ITO, T., "Stability and Regime Switching," *Journal of Economic Theory*, 29, No. 1 (February 1983): 22–48.

HUDSON, E. A. and JORGENSON, D. W., "U.S. Energy Policy and Economic Growth, 1975–2000," *Bell Journal of Economics*, 5, No. 2 (Autumn 1974): 461–514.

HUMPHREY, DAVID B. and MORONEY, J. R., "Substitution among Capital, Labor, and Natural Resource Products in American Manufacturing," *Journal of Political Economy*, 83, No. 1 (February 1975): 57–82.

KATSELI-PAPAEFSTRATIOU, LOUKA T., "Transmission of External Price Disturbances and the Composition of Trade," *Journal of International Economics*, 10, No. 3 (August 1980): 357–76.

—— and MARION, NANCY P., "Adjustment to Variations in Imported Input Prices: The Role of Economic Structure," Economic Growth Center Discussion Paper No. 360, Yale University, August 1980.

LAUMAS, PREM S. and WILLIAMS, MARTIN., "The Elasticity of Substitution in India's Manufacturing Sector," *Journal of Development Economics*, 8, No. 3 (June 1981): 325–37.

KIRKPATRICK, C. H. and NIXSON, F. I., "Industrial Structure, International Trade and Development," in *Industrial Structure and Policy in Less Developed Countries*. London: George Allen and Unwin, 1984.

LEIJONHUFVUD, AXEL. *On Keynesian Economics and the Economics of Keynes: A Study in Monetary Theory*. London and New York: Oxford University Press, 1968.

LIVIATAN NISSAN., "A Disequilibrium Analysis of the Monetary Trade Model," *Journal of International Economics*, 9, No. 3 (August 1979): 355–78.

MALINVAUD, EDMOND., *The Theory of Unemployment Reconsidered*. New York: Halsted Press, 1977.

——, *Profitability and Unemployment*. Cambridge: Cambridge University Press, 1980.

MARION, N., "Nontraded Goods, Oil Price Increases and the Current Account," *Journal of International Economics*, 16, No. 1/2 (February 1984): 29–44.

MUELLBAUER, J. and PORTES, R., "Macroeconomic Models with Quantity Rationing," *Economic Journal*, 88 (1978): 393–404.

NEARY, J. P., "Nontraded Goods and the Balance of Trade in a Neo-Keynesian Temporary Equilibrium," *Quarterly Journal of Economics*, 95, No. 3 (November 1980): 403–32.

OBSTFELD, MAURICE., "Intermediate Imports, the Terms of Trade, and the Dynamics of the Exchange Rate and Current Account," *Journal of International Economics*, 10, No. 4, (November 1980): 461–80.

——, "Relative Prices, Employment, and the Exchange Rate in an Economy with Foresight," *Econometrica*, 50, No. 5 (September 1982): 1219–1242.

OZATALAY, SAVAS; GRUBAUGH, STEVEN G; and LONG II, THOMAS V., "Energy Substitution and National Energy Policy," *American Economic Review*, 69, No. 2 (May 1979): 369–71.

RIVERA-BATIZ, FRANCISCO, L. and RIVERA-BATIZ, LUIS., *International Finance and Open Economy Macroeconomics*. New York: MacMillan Publishing Co., 1985.

SACHS, J., "The Current Account and Macroeconomic Adjustment in the 1970s," *Brookings Papers on Economic Activity*, 1 (1981): 201–282.

SALTER, W., "Internal and External Balance: The Role of Price and Expenditure Effects," *The Economic Record*, 35, No. 81 (August 1959): 226–38.

SMID, M., "Oil, Employment and the Price Level: A Monetary Approach to the Macroeconomics of Imported Intermediate Goods under Fixed and Flexible Rates," unpublished paper, University of Western Ontario, November 1979.

SWAN, T. W., "Longer-Run Problems of the Balance of Payments." In *The Australian Economy: A Volume of Readings,* edited by H. W. Arndt and W. M. Corden, Melbourne: Cheshire Press, 1963.

UZAWA, H., "Production Functions with Constant Elasticities of Substitution," *Review of Economic Studies,* 29, No. 81 (October 1962): 291–99.

VAN WIJNBERGEN, S., "Oil Price Shocks, Unemployment, Investment and the Current Account: An Intertemporal disequilibrium Analysis," mimeo, 1982.

——, "The Optimal Investment and Current Account Response to Oil Price Shocks under Putty-Clay Technology," *Journal of International Economics,* 17, No. 1/2 (August 1984): 139–149.

VARIAN, HAL R., *Microeconomic Analysis.* New York: W. W. Norton Co., Inc., 1978.

Oxford Economic Papers 37 (1985), 161–195

RATIONAL EXPECTATIONS, INFORMATION AND ASSET MARKETS: AN INTRODUCTION

By MARGARET BRAY[1]

1. Introduction

FINANCIAL markets are a subject of perpetual fascination to economists and others. There are very large sums of money to be gained and lost on them. They are obviously crucially important not only to the people and institutions who invest directly, but also to the many others who invest indirectly through holding unit trusts (mutual funds), pension or life assurance policies. Moreover the financial markets do not operate in isolation; they affect and are affected by the rest of the economy.

One important economic function of such markets is the spreading and sharing of risk. An entrepreneur can reduce the risks which he carries by selling shares in his firm. Investors may be willing to carry some of the risk because they are less risk averse than the entrepreneur. They may also be willing to invest even if they are more risk averse because the market allows them to hold a diversified portfolio which reduces risk. Investing £10,000 in ten different firms whose profits are imperfectly correlated is very much less risky than investing £10,000 in one of the firms. The view that such markets perform a socially important function in spreading risk reasonably well is widely held, (see Arrow (1964) and Diamond (1967) for theoretical models). But there are distinguished dissidents; in Chapter 12 of the General Theory, Keynes argues forcefully that the markets increasingly provide a casino for speculators, rather than a guide for investors, and may be socially useless or even positively dangerous.

Recent theoretical work on asset markets, based on the rational expectations hypothesis, has argued that they may have an additional informational role. Traders have information which affects their evaluation of the value of assets, the demand for the assets, and thus prices. Other traders may attempt to infer the information from prices. The major achievement of recent work has been to develop a coherent description of this phenomenon, and use it to ask how well the markets transmit and aggregate the information.

Much of this literature is highly technical, and inaccessible without a considerable mathematical apparatus. Yet the basic issues can be understood with much less background, as this paper seeks to demonstrate. It is written as an introduction to recent work on information in asset markets, assuming intermediate microeconomics, enough calculus to differentiate a quadratic, a little manipulation of linear equations, and enough probability theory to know about means, variances, and conditional distributions. I use

[1] I am grateful to Craig Alexander, Jeremy Edwards, Anna Lemessany, Peter Sinclair, and Martin Weale for comments on an earlier version of this paper.

expected utility theory, but anyone who does not know the theory, and is willing to take on trust my assertion that it is a sensible way to model choice under uncertainty, should be able to follow the argument.

Much of the paper is concerned with elaborating a simple model. The model introduced in Section 2 is the standard deterministic partial equilibrium model of supply and demand in a spot market, modified by the assumption that production decisions must be made before the market operates on the basis of price expectations. I use this model to introduce a perfect foresight equilibrium; the deterministic version of a rational expectations equilibrium. In Section 3 I introduce a futures market, operating at the date when production decisions are made. A futures contract is a financial asset, whose gross return is the spot price. I argue that arbitrage implies that in this deterministic model, if expectations are held with certainty, the futures price must be equal to the present discounted value of the expected spot price. Section 4 introduces briefly the expected utility theory of choice under uncertainty. Section 5 applies this theory to a stochastic version of the model on the assumption that dealers are risk neutral, using an arbitrage argument to establish that the futures price is equal to the present discounted value of the expected spot price. Section 6 shows how the simple arbitrage argument breaks down when risk neutral dealers have diverse information, introducing the informational role of asset prices. The formal definition of a rational expectations equilibrium in an asset market with asymmetric information is introduced in Section 7. Section 8 introduces risk aversion, simplifying matters mathematically by working with exponential utility functions, and normal random variables. The joint equilibrium of the spot and futures market when dealers are risk averse is calculated, on the assumption that no-one has any private information about the spot price when trading on the futures market. Information is introduced in Section 9, firstly on the assumption that all dealers have the same information, secondly on the assumption that there are informed and uniformed traders, but the informed traders all have the same information, and thirdly on the assumption that dealers have diverse information. In this model the futures market is remarkably informationally efficient; it aggregates information perfectly. Section 10 is concerned with the implications and robustness of the informational efficiency result in this and related models. In the models which I use calculating the rational expectations equilibrium is relatively straightforward, but in Section 11 I introduce a version of the spot and futures market model which has no rational expectations equilibrium. I discuss the nature and significance of the problems associated with the existence of rational expectations equilibrium, and the literature on the subject. Section 12 attempts an evaluation of the models, discussing the assumptions, concentrating largely on the rational expectations assumption, and referring briefly to the empirical and experimental evidence. Section 13 discusses some open questions prompted by these models.

The results which I establish have no claims to originality, the first model which I develop has its origins in the cobweb model (Kaldor 1934), and in Muth's paper on rational expectations (1961). The futures market model is based on Danthine (1978), and related to Grossman (1976 and 1977) and Bray (1981). The non-existence example in Section 11 is new in detail, but is similar to that of Kreps (1977). I give references to other, related literature, where appropriate. A more technical introduction to this and many other topics can be found in Radner's (1982) survey of 'Equilibrium Under Uncertainty' and in the symposium issue (April 1982) of the Journal of Economic Theory on 'Rational Expectations in Microeconomic models', in particular the introduction by Jordan and Radner. Stiglitz (1982) discusses a range of issues concerned with information and capital markets.

2. Supply and demand with a production lag: perfect foresight equilibrium

In the standard model of supply and demand, production and consumption decisions are taken simultaneously, based on the price. If production takes time, production decisions have to be based on the expected price. For example a farmer plants a crop in January which will be harvested and sold in June. To begin with assume that there is no uncertainty, an assumption which will be relaxed in Section 4. Demand $D(p_s)$ is a deterministic function of p_s, the spot price of wheat in June. Supply $S[p_s^e]$ is a deterministic function of p_s^e, the farmers' point expectation belief in January about what the spot price will be in June. For now, assume that all farmers are subjectively certain about what the price will be, and all have the same beliefs. If the market in June clears, supply equals demand. $D[p_s] = S[p_s]$. The expected price determines production which in turn determines the actual price. In fact the price p_s, is a function of the expected price.

In Fig. 1 when the price is p_s^e, $Q = S[p_s^e]$ is produced. When Q is put on

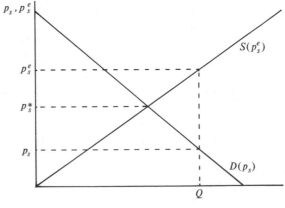

Fig. 1

the spot market in June the price is p_s. If $p_s \neq p_s^e$ the farmers, despite their subjective certainty, are wrong. Beliefs are wrong unless $p_s^e = p_s^*$, the price at which the supply and demand curves intersect so $S[p_s^*] = D[p_s^*]$. This could well be described as a self-fulfilling belief. However the standard terminology is a perfect foresight equilibrium or more recently (following Muth (1961)) a rational expectations equilibrium.

A rational expectations equilibrium can be defined as a situation in which people do not make systematic mistakes in forecasting. In this case where beliefs are point expectations held with certainty, rational expectations equilibrium requires that beliefs be correct, i.e. that people have perfect foresight. The rational expectations assumption is now used very widely, but remains controversial. The assumption avoids many of the difficult dynamic problems apparently associated with expectation formation, making it possible to proceed with other questions. For the time being I will simply assume rational expectations without further discussion, returning to the matter in Section 12.

3. Financing production: futures markets and arbitrage

The revenue from selling the crop arrives some time after most of the production costs are incurred. This leaves a farmer with the problem of finding funds to cover the investment in planting the crop. He may have sufficient wealth to finance this from his own resources. If not he will have to borrow.

Assume that everyone knows that the price in June will be p_s. There are perfect capital markets, that is the farmer can borrow or lend as much as he wishes at the same interest rate. £1 borrowed in January must be repaid with £$(1 + r)$ in June. Suppose that a farmer has wealth W_0 in January, and incurs the costs of producing output y, which have a present discounted value in January of $C(y)$. He invests the remainder of his wealth $W_0 - C(y)$ at interest rate r until June. His wealth in June is the sum of his revenue from output $p_s y$ and the return on his other investment

$$W = p_s y + (W_0 - C(y))(1 + r) = p_s y - C(y)(1 + r) + W_0(1 + r)$$

The value of profits from production in June is $p_s y - C(y)(1 + r)$. Note that $W_0 - C(y)$ may be negative, in which case the farmer is borrowing to cover some of his costs. The farmer maximises his June wealth by maximizing profits. If C is a convex function of y and $p_s > C'(0)(1 + r)$, this is done by setting $p_s = C'(y)(1 + r)$. The value of y is independent of his initial wealth, which simply determines how much, if anything he has to borrow.

The farmer may also finance his production by selling on the futures market. A futures market is an institution on which money is exchanged for promises to deliver goods in the future. For example a farmer may sell wheat in January for delivery in June. As before suppose the farmer has wealth W_0 in January, produces y, incurring costs $C(y)$, and sells z on the futures market at price p_f. This leaves him $W_0 - C(y) + p_f z$ to invest at interest r. In June he sells the remainder of his output $y - z$ on the spot market. His wealth in June is

$$W = p_s(y - z) + (W_0 - C(y) + p_f z)(1 + r)$$
$$= p_s y - C(y)(1 + r) + (p_f(1 + r) - p_s)z + W_0(1 + r). \tag{3.1}$$

The farmer maximises his wealth, as before by choosing output y so $p_s = C'(y)(1 + r)$. If $p_f > p_s/(1 + r)$, so that the futures price exceeds the present discounted value of the spot price, he can make arbitrarily large profits by selling on the futures market. He will increase z indefinitely, and will wish to set $z > y$, selling more on the futures market than he produces, meeting the shortfall $z - y$ by buying on the spot market. However he is unlikely to find a willing buyer at this price. There are two possible classes of buyers, consumers and speculators. Consumers (e.g. food manufacturers and wholesalers) may choose to buy futures in January rather than wanting to buy on the spot market in June, thus hedging against uncertainty about the June spot price. For the sake of simplicity I will assume that consumers do not participate in the futures market; if they did it would complicate the models without substantially affecting the conclusions. Speculators buy futures contracts, which they sell on the spot market, never actually taking delivery of the goods, in the hope of making a profit on the difference between the futures price and the present value of the spot price. Suppose a speculator with wealth W_0 in January buys x futures contracts in January, sells x on the spot market in June, and invests the rest of his wealth in the safe asset paying interest r. His wealth will be

$$W = p_s x + (W_0 - p_f x)(1 + r)$$
$$= (p_s - p_f(1 + r))x + W_0(1 + r). \tag{3.2}$$

If $p_f > p_s/(1 + r)$ both speculators and farmers will wish to sell futures. With no willing buyers the market cannot clear. If $p_f < p_s/(1 + r)$ both speculators and farmers will want to buy futures. Thus the only price at which the futures market can clear is when $p_f = p_s/(1 + r)$. This is an example of an arbitrage argument—these arguments are based on the premise that in equilibrium it cannot be possible for anyone to make arbitrarily large certain profits. If the market is perfectly arbitraged $p_s = p_f(1 + r)$. The wealth in June of farmers and speculators does not depend on the size of their future trades. In this deterministic model with perfect foresight, a futures contract is a safe asset paying interest r. There is no reason for anyone to use the futures market in preference to borrowing or lending at rate r elsewhere. If the futures market ceased to exist no-one would be any better or worse off.

In fact under certainty there seems little reason for the futures market to exist. Any understanding of futures markets, and other asset markets such as the stock market, depends upon introducing uncertainty.

4. Choice under uncertainty

The farmer faces risks in both the quantity and price of output. A futures market allows the farmer to shift the price risks to speculators. If his output y is certain he can completely eliminate the risk by setting $z = y$, selling his entire output on the futures market. But why will the speculator be willing to assume the risk, and at what price? The currently available answers to this, and many other questions about economics under uncertainty, are derived from a widely accepted model of choice under uncertainty: the theory of expected utility. An introduction to the theory can be found in among other places Deaton and Muellbauer (1980), in a survey by Schoemaker (1982) or, in a valuable collection of readings, Diamond and Rothschild (1978).

Assume that an investor has decided to invest a certain amount W_0 for a period. He has a number of different assets to choose between, and a definite set of beliefs about the joint probability distribution of the returns on the different assets. He cares only about the probability distribution of his wealth $\tilde{W}$ at the end of the period, which depends upon the way he allocates his initial wealth W_0 between the different assets. The theory of expected utility shows that if his preferences over the probability distribution of $\tilde{W}$ satisfy some plausible assumptions he will choose a portfolio which maximises the mathematical expectation $EU(\tilde{W})$ of a function $U(\tilde{W})$ given his beliefs about the probabilities. For a discrete probability distribution $EU(\tilde{W}) = \sum_i U(W_i)p_i$ where W_i is wealth in state i and p_i the probability of state i. For a continuous probability distribution

$$EU(\tilde{W}) = \int_{-\infty}^{\infty} U(W)f(W)\,\mathrm{d}W$$

where f is the probability density function. In both cases the probability distribution depends upon the investors beliefs, and his choice of portfolio.

The theory has two essential elements, the utility function, and the probability distribution which determines the mathematical expectation. The functional form of the utility function U describes attitudes to risk. U is increasing provided investors prefer more to less wealth. If $U(\tilde{W}) = \tilde{W}$ the investor is risk neutral, caring only about expected wealth, and not at all about its riskiness. If $U(\tilde{W})$ is strictly concave the investor is risk averse, strictly preferring investments yielding the expectation of $\tilde{W}$ for sure, to random $\tilde{W}$. Risk aversion in investment choices for an individual seems highly plausible, and is often assumed.

The assumption that uncertainty can be described in terms of probability distributions is widely made today, but historically has not commanded universal acceptance. Keynes was a notable dissenter. There is very little controversy about applying the mathematical theory of probability to assess the probabilities associated with a series of similar events, where after a time there is enough data to construct probabilities from frequency distributions, (for example weather or life expectancy data), situations described by Knight (1921) as risk. The argument is rather whether meaningful probabilities can be assigned to unique events, where there is no objective frequency data to rely on, situations described by Knight as uncertainty. The subjectivist or Bayesian viewpoint on probability is that Knight's distinction is invalid. It is always possible to elicit probabilities by forcing people to make bets. (See Raiffa (1968)). There is however no guarantee in subjectivist theory that different people will form the same probability distributions, unless there is frequency data to base them on, which brings us back to Knight's risk. For some purposes it is enough to assume that people act as if they had subjective beliefs expressible as probability distributions. However many models postulate that people have the same correct beliefs about probability distributions, (rational expectations). These models do not seem to be applicable to situations which Knight would describe as uncertain.

I am now in a position to use the theory of expected utility to extend the theory of asset pricing under certainty to uncertainty. Initially I will assume risk neutrality, and then proceed to consider risk aversion.

5. Risk neutrality: arbitrage again

Returning to the futures market example suppose that once farmers have chosen their level of inputs their output y is certain. The June spot price is uncertain because spot demand is uncertain. A risk neutral farmer will choose his output y and futures sales z to maximise the expected value of his wealth, from (3.1) this is

$$E\tilde{W} = E\tilde{p}_s y - C(y)(1+r) + (p_f(1+r) - E\tilde{p}_s)z + W_0(1+r).$$

(Throughout this paper a tilde $\tilde{\ }$ above a variable indicates that it is random.) A speculator will choose his futures purchases x to maximise the expected value of his wealth, from (3.2) this is

$$E\tilde{W} = (E\tilde{p}_s - p_f(1+r))x + W_0(1+r).$$

Decisions depend upon the mathematical expectation $E\tilde{p}_s$ of $\tilde{p}_s$, its average value. The risk neutral dealers do not care about any other characteristics of the probability distribution. $E\tilde{p}_s$ is not a point expectation held with certainty, the dealers are aware that there is uncertainty and would expect to observe that usually $E\tilde{p}_s \neq \tilde{p}_s$.

Precisely the same arbitrage argument as before implies that unless $p_f = E\tilde{p}_s/(1+r)$ there are unlimited positive expected profits to be made and the market cannot clear. The argument is less compelling than under certainty. Although a speculator may wish to exploit opportunities for making positive expected profits he may not be able to do so. Suppose that $E\tilde{p}_s > p_f(1+r)$, so buying futures contracts generates a positive expected return. A risk neutral speculator will choose to spend his entire wealth on futures contracts, he will also wish to borrow without limit to exploit further the opportunity for profit. There is a chance that the spot price will be so low that he cannot repay his debts; lending to the speculator becomes risky. Speculators may face either a higher interest rate than r, or limits on credit, limiting their ability to arbitrage the market.

6. Diverse information

The simple arbitrage argument also breaks down if different dealers (farmers and speculators) have different beliefs about the expected spot price. This is not incompatible with the dealers having rational expectations, if they have access to different information. Suppose for example that $\tilde{p}_s = \tilde{I} + \tilde{e}$ where $\tilde{I}$ and $\tilde{e}$ are independent random variables, $E\tilde{e} = 0$, and so $E\tilde{p}_s = E\tilde{I}$. There are two types of dealers. The informed dealers observe $\tilde{I}$ before the futures market opens; their expectation of $\tilde{p}_s$ is conditional upon $\tilde{I}$, $E[\tilde{p}_s \mid \tilde{I}] = \tilde{I}$. The uninformed dealers observe nothing, their expectation of $\tilde{p}_s$ is $E\tilde{p}_s = E\tilde{I}$. If both types of dealers are risk neutral, face no borrowing constraints, and stick to their beliefs, the informed will want to buy or sell an unlimited amount unless $p_f = E[\tilde{p}_s \mid \tilde{I}]/(1+r) = \tilde{I}/(1+r)$, and the uninformed dealers will want to buy or sell an unlimited amount unless $\tilde{p}_f = E\tilde{p}_s/(1+r)$. Unless by coincidence $E[\tilde{p}_s \mid \tilde{I}] = E\tilde{p}_s$ (i.e. if $\tilde{I} = E\tilde{I}$) the market apparently cannot clear.

It is however most unlikely that the uninformed dealers will stick to their beliefs. Knowing that there are informed dealers in the market whose trading affects the futures price they will try to make inferences from the futures price about the spot price. They are using the price of a financial asset, a futures contract, to make judgements about its quality. Judging quality from price is not confined to financial markets. Consumers may also do so, assuming that cheap goods are also cheap and nasty. One of the major successes of recent economic theory has been the development of models which take this into account.

In these models prices have two roles, their conventional role in determining budget sets for consumers and profit opportunities for firms, and an additional role in transmitting information. Hayek (1945) in a discussion of decentralisation and planning argues that the conventional role of prices must also be understood as an informational one. In standard Walrasian competitive equilibrium models once households and firms know current prices they have no use for any further information about the plans, characteristics and opportunities of others in the economy, they need make no attempt to infer this information from prices. As Grossman (1981) argues recent models of asymmetric information move beyond this, some agents

want some information held by others, in this case information about the
spot price in the future. They try to infer as much information as they can
from current prices. In some cases the price system may be entirely efficient
at transmitting information, prices are so informative that there is no
additional information currently known to anyone in the economy which
would be helpful. In other cases prices may be less informationally efficient,
conveying some information, but still leaving a frustrated desire to see the
current contents of someone else's mind, or computer file. In either case
agents are trying to look beyond prices, to solve an inference problem,
which is unnecessary in standard Walrasian models. The central question
addressed by the models which I am about to discuss is how informationally
efficient are prices? These models make use of the idea of a rational
expectations equilibrium. I will now show how this equilibrium is defined,
and explain how it yields an equilibrium price for this example.

7. Rational expectations equilibrium and risk neutrality

The definition of a rational expectations equilibrium for the spot and
futures markets has four parts. A very similar definition can be formulated
for any asset market model. The first part describes how dealers form their
beliefs.

*Part 1. Each dealer (farmer or speculator) observes some private information
$\tilde{I}_i$ and the futures price $\tilde{p}_f$. Given this information he has beliefs about the spot
price $\tilde{p}_s$ which can be expressed as a conditional probability distribution.*

For example dealer i might believe that given the futures price $\tilde{p}_f$ and
private information, $\tilde{I}_i$, the conditional distribution of $\tilde{p}_s$ was normal with
mean $E[\tilde{p}_s \mid \tilde{p}_f, \tilde{I}_i] = \frac{1}{2}\tilde{p}_f + \frac{1}{4}\tilde{I}_i$ and variance $\frac{1}{8}$. At this stage I have not required
that the beliefs be correct, only that they exist.

The second part of the definition states that given their beliefs dealers
choose their portfolio in accordance with expected utility theory.

*Part 2. Each dealer chooses the holding of futures contracts, and for farmers,
output, which maximises his expected utility given his beliefs about the spot
price, conditional upon his private information and the futures price.*

Parts 1 and 2 of the definition give the supply and demand for futures.
Note that supply and demand are affected by both the numerical value of
the futures price and information, and by beliefs. If a risk neutral dealer
believes that $E[\tilde{p}_s \mid \tilde{p}_f, \tilde{I}_i] = \frac{1}{2}\tilde{p}_f + \frac{1}{4}\tilde{I}_i$, he will buy or sell an unlimited amount
depending on whether $\tilde{p}_f - [\frac{1}{2}\tilde{p}_f + \frac{1}{4}\tilde{I}_i]/(1 + r)$ is positive or negative. To emphasize this point I will write $d_i[\tilde{p}_f, \tilde{I}_i; B_i]$ for dealer i's demand for futures,
where B_i is shorthand for beliefs.

The next part of the definition is

Part 3. The spot and futures prices are at levels where both markets clear.

In different years the information will be different, so if the markets are to clear prices must be a function of the information. Demand and the market clearing prices also depend upon beliefs, so I will write

$$\tilde{p}_f = f[\tilde{I}_1, \tilde{I}_2,..., \tilde{I}_n; B_1, B_2 ... B_n]$$
$$\tilde{p}_s = g[\tilde{I}_1, \tilde{I}_2,..., \tilde{I}_n; B_1, B_2 ... B_n].$$

An omniscient economist could calculate the function f. Knowing the joint distribution of $[\tilde{I}_1, \tilde{I}_2 ... \tilde{I}_n]$ the economist could then calculate the joint distribution of $[\tilde{p}_f, \tilde{p}_s, \tilde{I}_1, \tilde{I}_2 ... \tilde{I}_n]$, and so the conditional distribution of $\tilde{p}_s$ given $\tilde{p}_f$ and $\tilde{I}_i$ for each i. This would tell the economist what the correct beliefs for each dealer would be, call them $\hat{B}_i$. As the joint distributions depend upon the original beliefs, $[B_1, B_2 ... B_n]$, the correct beliefs $[\hat{B}_1, \hat{B}_2 ... \hat{B}_n]$ also depend upon the original beliefs. A more formal way of saying the same thing is that $[\hat{B}_1, \hat{B}_2 ... \hat{B}_n]$ is a function of $[B_1, B_2 ... B_n]$.

The last part of the definition is

Part 4. Each agent has rational expectations. They have correct beliefs about the joint probability distribution of the futures price, spot price and private information, so

$$B_i = \hat{B}_i \qquad i = 1, 2 ... n.$$

Note that this states that beliefs about the entire conditional probability distribution are correct. Much of the macroeconomic literature works with models where only the conditional mean is relevant, but the rational expectations hypothesis is not confined to such models.

This definition may appear unnecessarily long winded. Stating that the beliefs are correct in Part 1 would make for greater brevity, but stating the definition in this way gives more insight. It is helpful in calculating the rational expectations equilibrium in simple models, where making a guess about the functional form of beliefs, calculating supply and demand, and then checking to see if there is indeed a set of beliefs which generates rational expectations often works. This approach is also very helpful in understanding issues associated with the existence and stability of rational expectations equilibrium.

I have stated the definition in terms of a spot and futures market, but very similar definitions can be formulated for any set of financial asset markets. I have not been specific about the information $\tilde{I}_i$. All that is required is that it be a random variable, but it may be continuous or discrete, a scalar or a vector. It may always take the same value, $\tilde{I}_i = 0$, in which case it is effectively no information.

I will now calculate the rational expectations equilibrium for the futures market example with risk neutral dealers. Here the informed agents observe $\tilde{I}$ and the uninformed agents observe nothing. Recall that $\tilde{p}_s = \tilde{I} + \tilde{e}$, $\tilde{I}$ and $\tilde{e}$ are independent and $E\tilde{e} = 0$. In accordance with Part 1 of the definition, suppose that the informed dealers believe that $E[\tilde{p}_s \mid \tilde{I}, \tilde{p}_f] = \tilde{I}$, and the uninformed dealers believe that $E[\tilde{p}_s \mid \tilde{p}_f] = \lambda \tilde{p}_f$ where λ is a constant. Utility maximisation (Part 2 of the definition) for risk neutral dealers implies that the informed dealers will want to buy or sell an unlimited amount unless $E[\tilde{p}_s \mid \tilde{I}, \tilde{p}_f] = \tilde{p}_f(1+r)$, and the uninformed dealers will want to buy or sell an unlimited amount unless $E[\tilde{p}_s \mid \tilde{p}_f] = \tilde{p}_f(1+r)$. Thus market clearing (Part 3 of the definition) implies that

$$E[\tilde{p}_s \mid \tilde{I}, \tilde{p}_f] = \tilde{I} = \tilde{p}_f(1+r)$$

and

$$E[\tilde{p}_s \mid \tilde{p}_f] = \lambda \tilde{p}_f = \tilde{p}_f(1+r).$$

This is impossible unless $\lambda = 1+r$, and $\tilde{p}_f = \tilde{I}/(1+r)$. It remains to check that Part 4 of the definition holds. If $\tilde{p}_f = \tilde{I}/(1+r)$ knowing $\tilde{p}_f$ tells the informed dealers nothing about $\tilde{I}$ and $\tilde{p}_s$ which they did not know already from observing $\tilde{I}$ directly. As $\tilde{p}_s = \tilde{I} + \tilde{e}$, the correct conditional expectation for the informed dealers is $E[\tilde{p}_s \mid \tilde{I}] = E[\tilde{p}_s \mid \tilde{I}, \tilde{p}_f] = \tilde{I}$. The uninformed dealers observe $\tilde{p}_f = \tilde{I}/(1+r)$, so can infer $\tilde{I}$ from $\tilde{p}_f$, knowing that $E[\tilde{p}_s \mid \tilde{I}] = \tilde{I}$, their correct conditional expectation is $E[\tilde{p}_s \mid \tilde{I}] = E[\tilde{p}_s \mid \tilde{p}_f] = \tilde{I} = (1+r)\tilde{p}_f$, which is the form assumed with $\lambda = 1+r$. This is a rational expectations equilibrium.

This is a very striking result, indicating that the market is completely efficient as a transmitter of information from the informed to the uninformed. Much of the recent theoretical work on asset markets has been concerned with investigating the circumstances under which a rational expectations equilibrium exists, and is informationally efficient.

This example has a number of peculiar features. The assumption of risk neutrality is special, and I have argued that even with risk neutrality the market may not be perfectly arbitraged. In equilibrium neither farmers nor speculators have any reason to trade futures. The expected profits from trade are always zero. It seems possible that the futures market will die away. But without a futures market the informational differences will persist, so there will be a motive for trade. These peculiarities stem from the risk neutrality assumption.

8. Rational expectations equilibrium under risk aversion

I will now introduce risk aversion into the model. This can generate considerable mathematical complexities, which I will minimise by assuming that both farmers and speculators have utility functions of the form

$$U_i(\tilde{W}) = -e^{-k_i\tilde{W}} \equiv -\exp(-k_i\tilde{W})$$

where k_i is a positive constant. I will use the second form of notation, which avoids the need for superscripts. Remember that 'exp' is an abbreviation for 'exponential' and not for 'expectation'.

This utility function is widely used and has some attractive properties. Its first derivative is positive $(U' > 0)$ implying that utility is increasing in wealth. The second derivative is negative $(U'' < 0)$ implying risk aversion. The constant $k_i = -U''/U'$ is the coefficient of absolute risk aversion, higher values of k_i imply greater risk aversion. Above all there is the very useful result that if $\tilde{W}$ is normal with mean $E\tilde{W}$ and variance var $\tilde{W}$

$$E\{-\exp(-k\tilde{W})\} = -\exp(-k[E\tilde{W} - \tfrac{1}{2}k \text{ var } \tilde{W}]). \tag{8.1}$$

This result implies that the expected utility maximising portfolio is one that maximises $E\tilde{W} - \tfrac{1}{2}k$ var $\tilde{W}$. As I will demonstrate this makes for a very tractable model of asset demand, which is linear in expected asset return and prices. The major unattractive feature of the utility function, which I will also demonstrate is that asset demand is independent of wealth.[2]

I will now use (8.1) to result to analyse the behaviour of the spot and futures market model under risk aversion. The first step in defining and calculating the rational expectations equilibrium is a description of the information and beliefs. The first case I will look at is where dealers have no private information, each farmer and speculator has the same belief that

$$\tilde{p}_s \sim N(\mu, \sigma^2). \tag{8.2}$$

Later I will look at a version of the model where each agent has the same piece of information, and then at versions with diverse private information. Once the mathematics has been done for the first case the others follow very simply.

Equation (8.2) gives the beliefs described in Part 1 of the definitions of a rational expectations equilibrium. I will use this to derive the utility maximising speculators' demand for futures, and the farmers' demand for futures and spot supply (Part 2 of the definition). I will then make an assumption about spot demand which enables me to write down market clearing conditions for the spot and futures markets (Part 3 of the definition). These conditions will generate a 'correct distribution' for the spot price which will depend upon the parameters of the model, including μ and σ^2. I will show that there are values of μ and σ^2 which generate correct beliefs, (Part 4 of the definition), thus deriving the rational expectations equilibrium.

---

[2] $E(\exp(-k\tilde{W})$ is the moment generating function of the random variable $\tilde{W}$, an object which mathematicians find interesting. The result is proved in most texts on probability, e.g. Meyer (1970).

There are n dealers, m farmers and $n - m$ speculators. Farmers are indexed by $i = 1, 2 \ldots m$, and speculators by $i = m + 1, \ldots n$.

Speculators

Speculator i has a utility function $-\exp[-k_i \tilde{W}_i]$. If he buys x_i futures at price p_f, sells them on the spot market at price $\tilde{p}_s$, gets interest r on a safe asset, and has initial wealth W_{i0}, his final wealth $\tilde{W}_i$ is from (3.2) a random variable

$$\tilde{W}_i = (\tilde{p}_s - p_f(1 + r))x_i + W_{i0}(1 + r).$$

As speculators believe that $\tilde{p}_s \sim N(\mu, \sigma^2)$, they believe that $\tilde{W}_i$ is normal, and

$$E\tilde{W}_i = (\mu - p_f(1 + r))x_i + W_{i0}(1 + r)$$
$$\text{var } \tilde{W}_i = \sigma^2 x_i^2.$$

From (8.1) the speculator will choose x_i to maximise

$$E\tilde{W}_i - \tfrac{1}{2}k_i \text{ var } \tilde{W}_i = (\mu - p_f(1 + r))x_i + W_{i0}(1 + r) - \tfrac{1}{2}k_i \sigma^2 x_i^2.$$

Thus

$$x_i = \frac{1}{k_i \sigma^2}(\mu - p_f(1 + r)) \qquad (i = 1, \ldots n). \tag{8.3}$$

The speculator buys futures if $\mu > p_f(1 + r)$, there is a positive expected profit to be made on holding futures, and sells futures if $\mu < p_f(1 + r)$, there is an expected loss to be made on holding futures. His trades are inversely proportional to σ^2, the variance of the spot price, and to k_i, which measures risk aversion. Note that x_i does not depend on initial wealth W_{i0}, due to the special utility function for which the coefficient of absolute risk aversion $k_i = -U''/U'$ does not depend on wealth.

Farmers

The speculators choose to take on risk by entering the futures market. If the farmers' output is certain they can entirely avoid risk by hedging; selling their entire output on the futures market. If they sell more or less than this they are assuming risk which they could avoid, in pursuit of profits, effectively acting as speculators. If y_i is farmer i's output, and z_i his future sales, $x_i = y_i - z_i$ can be thought of as speculative purchases of futures. The farmer's wealth is from (3.1) a random variable

$$\tilde{W}_i = (p_f y_i - C(y_i))(1 + r) + (\tilde{p}_s - p_f(1 + r))x_i + W_{i0}(1 + r).$$

The first term is profits from production if all output is sold on the futures market. The second term is profits from speculation. The third term is the future value of initial wealth. As he believes that $\tilde{p}_s \sim N(\mu, \sigma)$ he believes that $\tilde{W}_i$ is normal, with mean and variance

$$EW_i = (p_f y_i - C(y_i))(1+r) + (\mu - p_f(1+r))x_i + W_{i0}(1+r)$$
$$\text{var } \tilde{W}_i = \sigma^2 x_i^2.$$

If the farmer has a utility function $-\exp(-k_i \tilde{W}_i)$ from (8.1) he chooses (x_i, y_i) to maximise

$$E\tilde{W}_i - \tfrac{1}{2}k_i \text{ var } \tilde{W}_i = (p_f y_i - C(y_i))(1+r) + (\mu - p_f(1+r))x_i + W_{i0}(1+r)$$
$$- \tfrac{1}{2}\sigma_i^2 x_i^2.$$

I will assume that the farmer's costs are

$$C(y_i) = \tfrac{1}{2}cy_i^2$$

where c is a positive constant. Thus the farmer will maximise

$$(p_f y_i - \tfrac{1}{2}cy_i^2)(1+r) + (\mu - p_f(1+r))x_i + W_{i0}(1+r) - \tfrac{1}{2}\sigma_i^2 x_i^2.$$

The first order condition for y_i implies that $p_f = cy_i$. The futures price determines the level of output, which is set so that the futures price is equal to the marginal cost of production. This result is valid for arbitrary utility functions. In this case it implies that

$$y_i = c^{-1}p_f \qquad (i = 1, \dots m). \tag{8.4}$$

The first order condition for x_i implies that

$$x_i = \frac{1}{k_i \sigma^2}(\mu - p_f(1+r)) \qquad (i = 1, \dots m). \tag{8.5}$$

The farmer's speculative demand for futures is precisely the same as if he were a pure speculator. This result is not valid if output is uncertain, but is convenient. (See Bray (1981).)

The futures market

The futures market clearing condition is

$$\sum_{i=1}^{n} x_i = \sum_{i=1}^{m} y_i. \tag{8.6}$$

The sum of speculative demand for futures from farmers and speculators is equal to farmers' output, sold forward to hedge against uncertainty. Using the expressions for x_i, and y_i, (8.3)–(8.5)

$$\sum_{i=1}^{n} \frac{1}{k_i \sigma^2}(\mu - p_f(1+r)) = \sum_{i=1}^{m} c^{-1}p_f = mc^{-1}p_f. \tag{8.7}$$

Thus the futures price depends upon the distribution of the spot price μ and σ^2. However the spot price depends upon the physical quantity produced, $\sum_{i=1}^{m} y_i$, which in turn depends upon the futures price. The equilibria of the spot and futures markets have to be considered simultaneously.

The spot market

Assumption: Spot demand is

$$D(\tilde{p}_s) = \tilde{a} - b\tilde{p}_s$$

where $\tilde{a}$ is a normal random variable with mean $E\tilde{a}$ and variance var $\tilde{a}$, and b a positive constant.

Thus spot demand is subject to random variation as $\tilde{a}$ varies. Spot supply comes from two sources. Farmers sell any output which they have not already sold on the futures market, so farmer i sells spot $x_i = y_i - z_i$. Speculator i sells spot everything which he bought on the futures market from farmers, x_i. Total spot sales $\sum_{i=1}^{n} x_i$ are thus equal to farmers' total output $\sum_{i=1}^{m} y_i$. (This is implied by the futures market clearing condition (8.6)). As (8.4) implies that $\sum_{i=1}^{m} y_i = mc^{-1}p_f$ the spot market clears when

$$\tilde{a} - b\tilde{p}_s = mc^{-1}p_f. \tag{8.8}$$

Rational expectations equilibrium

Eliminating p_f from the market clearing conditions (8.7) and (8.8) implies that

$$\tilde{p}_s = b^{-1}\tilde{a} - b^{-1}mc^{-1}\phi^{-1}\mu \tag{8.9}$$

where

$$\phi = 1 + r + mc^{-1}\sigma^2 \left[\sum_{i=1}^{n} k_i^{-1}\right]^{-1}. \tag{8.10}$$

As $\tilde{a}$ is normal and all the other terms on the right hand side of (8.9) are constants $\tilde{p}_s$ is normal. The dealers' beliefs about the form of the distribution of $\tilde{p}_s$ is correct. From (8.2) they believe that $\tilde{p}_s \sim N(\mu, \sigma^2)$. Equation (8.9) implies that

$$E\tilde{p}_s = b^{-1}E\tilde{a} - b^{-1}mc^{-1}\phi^{-1}\mu \tag{8.11}$$

and

$$\text{var } \tilde{p}_s = b^{-2} \text{var } \tilde{a}. \tag{8.12}$$

Beliefs about the mean and variance are correct if $E\tilde{p}_s = \mu$ and var $\tilde{p}_s = \sigma^2$. In this case (8.11) and (8.12) imply that the beliefs are correct if and only

$$\sigma^2 = b^{-2} \text{var } \tilde{a} \tag{8.13}$$

$$E\tilde{p}_s = \theta^{-1}\phi E\tilde{a} \tag{8.14}$$

where substituting for σ^2 in (8.10)

$$\phi = 1 + r + mc^{-1}b^{-2} \text{var } \tilde{a} \left[\sum_{i=1}^{n} k_i^{-1}\right]^{-1} \tag{8.15}$$

and

$$\theta = b\phi + mc^{-1}. \tag{8.16}$$

Thus from (8.9), (8.14) and (8.16) as $\mu = E\tilde{p}_s$

$$\tilde{p}_s = \theta^{-1}\phi E\tilde{a} + b^{-1}(\tilde{a} - E\tilde{a}) \tag{8.17}$$

and from (8.8) and (8.17)

$$p_f = \theta^{-1}E\tilde{a}. \tag{8.18}$$

If the futures price is given by (8.18) and dealers' beliefs about the expected spot price by (8.13)–(8.16) the futures market clears. The futures price determines output. Output determines the distribution of the spot price. At this futures price, and this expected spot price, dealers' beliefs about the distribution of the spot price are correct. This is a rational expectations equilibrium.

Introducing risk aversion changes the model in several respects. If all dealers are risk neutral arbitrage implies that $(1+r)p_f = E\tilde{p}_s$: the expected return on risky futures is the same as the return on the safe asset. Dealers are indifferent about how many futures they hold, and have no positive reason to trade on the futures market. In this model with risk aversion (8.14) and (8.18) imply that $\phi p_f = E\tilde{p}_s$, and from (8.15) $\phi > 1 + r$. The risk premium $\phi - (1+r)$ is an increasing function of the variance of the spot price $b^{-2}\,\mathrm{var}\,\tilde{a}$, and each dealer's risk aversion parameter k_i. Speculators are willing to take on some of the farmer's risk in order to earn a positive expected return. This model in fact overemphasizes the riskiness of speculative portfolios, because it considers only a single risky asset. In practice speculators can diminish, but not eliminate risk by holding a portfolio of several risky assets whose returns are imperfectly correlated.

Both speculators and farmers wish to hold definite amounts of futures, and the market will trade actively. As $\mu = E\tilde{p}_s > p_f(1+r)$ (8.3) and (8.5) imply that demand from speculators, and the speculative element of farmer's demand will be strictly positive in equilibrium. Farmers as a whole must be net sellers of futures, to meet the demand from speculators. But an unusually risk tolerant farmer might be a net purchaser.

9. Rational expectations equilibrium and information

In the model which I have just analysed the spot price is stochastic and differs from year to year, but the futures price is a constant, a function of the parameters of the model, including the mean and variance of $\tilde{a}$, the stochastic intercept in the spot demand function, which is by assumption the source of all the uncertainty.

I am now going to modify the model by assuming that dealers have information about $\tilde{a}$ in January when the futures market operates. I will look at three different information structures of increasing complexity, asking in each case how well the futures price reflects the information.

Example 1. *Symmetric Information*
 Assume that

$$\tilde{a} = \tilde{I} + \tilde{e} \tag{9.1}$$

$\tilde{I}$ and $\tilde{e}$ are independent scalar normal random variables, $E\tilde{I} = E\tilde{a}$, and $E\tilde{e} = 0$. As the sum of normal variables is normal $\tilde{a}$ is still normal, var $\tilde{a} =$ var $\tilde{I} +$ var $\tilde{e}$. Assume also that all dealers, farmers and speculators observe $\tilde{I}$ each January. Conditional upon the information $\tilde{I}$ each dealer believes correctly that $\tilde{a}$ is a normal random variable whose mean $E(\tilde{a} \mid \tilde{I}) = \tilde{I}$ is random, whereas var $(\tilde{a} \mid \tilde{I}) =$ var $\tilde{e}$ is not random. The model is unchanged, apart from the fact that beliefs about the mean of $\tilde{a}$ change from year to year. The rational expectations equilibrium can be calculated as before. Paralleling (8.12) and (8.14)–(8.18)

$$\text{var}[\tilde{p}_s \mid \tilde{I}] = b^{-2} \text{var}[\tilde{a} \mid \tilde{I}] = b^{-2} \text{var}\, \tilde{e} \tag{9.2}$$

$$E[\tilde{p}_s \mid \tilde{I}] = \theta^{*-1} \phi^* E(\tilde{a} \mid \tilde{I}) = \theta^{*-1} \phi^* \tilde{I} \tag{9.3}$$

where

$$\phi^* = 1 + r + mc^{-1}b^{-2} \text{var}[\tilde{a} \mid \tilde{I}] \left[\sum_{i=1}^{n} k_i^{-1} \right]^{-1} \tag{9.4}$$

$$\theta^* = b\phi^* + mc^{-1} \tag{9.5}$$

$$\tilde{p}_s = \theta^{*-1} \phi^* E(\tilde{a} \mid \tilde{I}) + b^{-1}[\tilde{a} - E(\tilde{a} \mid \tilde{I})] = \theta^{*-1} \phi^* \tilde{I} + b^{-1} \tilde{e} \tag{9.6}$$

and

$$\tilde{p}_f = \theta^{*-1} E(\tilde{a} \mid \tilde{I}) = \theta^{*-1} \tilde{I}. \tag{9.7}$$

These equations differ from (8.12) and (8.14)–(8.18) in two ways. Firstly the terms relating to the unconditional distribution of $\tilde{a}$, $E\tilde{a}$ and var $\tilde{a}$ in the previous equations, have been replaced by the corresponding terms for the distribution conditional upon the information $E(\tilde{a} \mid \tilde{I})$ and var $(\tilde{a} \mid \tilde{I})$. Secondly the futures price $\tilde{p}_f$ is now a random variable rather than a constant.

The expressions θ^* and ϕ^* are not random because var $(\tilde{a} \mid \tilde{I})$ is not random. Thus provided the numerical values of θ^* and ϕ^* are known it is possible to infer $\tilde{I}$, and $E[\tilde{p}_s \mid \tilde{I}]$ from $\tilde{p}_f$.

$$E[\tilde{p}_s \mid \tilde{I}] = \theta^{*-1} \phi^* \tilde{I} = \phi^* \tilde{p}_f$$

and so the conditional distribution of $\tilde{p}_s$ given $\tilde{p}_f$ is normal

$$E[\tilde{p}_s \mid \tilde{p}_f] = E[\tilde{p}_s \mid \tilde{I}] = \phi^* \tilde{p}_f \tag{9.8}$$

and

$$\text{var}[\tilde{p}_s \mid \tilde{p}_f] = \text{var}[\tilde{p}_s \mid \tilde{I}] = b^{-2} \text{var}(\tilde{a} \mid \tilde{I}) = b^{-2} \text{var}\, \tilde{e}. \tag{9.9}$$

Anyone knowing the numerical value of ϕ^* would form the same conditional expectation of the spot price $\tilde{p}_s$ from the futures price $\tilde{p}_f$, as if he knew the information $\tilde{I}$. This observation is perhaps not very interesting in the context of this example, in which, by assumption all the dealers know $\tilde{I}$, but it is helpful in analysing the next two examples.

Example 2

As in the previous example

$$\tilde{a} = \tilde{I} + \tilde{e}$$

$\tilde{I}$ and $\tilde{e}$ are independent, and normal. $E\tilde{a} = E\tilde{I}$, and $E\tilde{e} = 0$. However now only some of the dealers observe $\tilde{I}$. The others have no private information. In the rational expectations equilibrium the uninformed dealers will infer what information they can about the spot price from the futures price. If the futures price is completely efficient as an information transmitter the uninformed traders will trade as if they had the information.

This observation suggested to Radner (1979) and Grossman (1978) that models with asymmetric information could be analysed by considering the corresponding model in which the information is pooled and made available to all dealers, (called a full communications equilibrium by Radner, an artificial economy by Grossman). If the futures price is a perfect transmitter of information in the rational expectations equilibrium of the original model, dealers' beliefs about the distribution of the spot price given the futures price in the original model will be the same as if they had the information available to them in the full communications equilibrium. Thus supply, demand and prices, will be the same in the full communications equilibrium as in the rational expectations equilibrium of the original model.

Observing this point Radner and Grossman argued that the first step in analyzing this type of model should be to examine the full communications equilibrium. This is much easier than looking at the rational expectations equilibrium with asymmetric information directly, because if dealers know all the information which could possibly be reflected in prices already they have no motive for using prices as information, so prices do not affect beliefs in the full communications equilibrium. Having characterised prices in the full communications equilibrium ask what dealers' correct beliefs would be conditional on the full communications equilibrium prices. In particular ask whether the beliefs are the same as they would be if dealers know all the information. If they are it has been established that a rational expectations equilibrium exists in which beliefs, prices, supply and demand are the same as in the full communications equilibrium.

Consider the four part definition of a rational expectations equilibrium in an asset market with asymmetric information. The first part refers to beliefs, the second to utility maximisation given beliefs, the third to market clearing, and the fourth to correct beliefs. If the full communications equilibrium prices allow dealers to form precisely the same beliefs as if they had all the information, utility maximisation leads to the same trades as in the full communications equilibrium. As the trades are the same the market clears at the same prices. The beliefs generating the trades are correct. This is a rational expectations equilibrium. This argument breaks down if beliefs given the full communications equilibrium prices are not the same as beliefs given all the information. In this case if a rational expectations equilibrium exists prices transmit some, but not all information.

In this example the full communications equilibrium is one in which all dealers observe $\tilde{I}$. This is precisely example 1 where I have already argued that conditioning on the futures price alone leads dealers to the same beliefs as if they knew the information $\tilde{I}$. Thus the full communications equilibrium prices of example 1 are also rational expectations equilibrium prices for example 2. In this rational expectations equilibrium the futures price transmits all the information from the informed to the uninformed dealers.

Example 3. Diverse Information

I now generalise the information structure considerably. Suppose that each dealer observes a random information variable $\tilde{I}_i$. This may be a scalar or a vector, it may be constant, in which case it is effectively no information. The only restriction is that $(\tilde{a}, \tilde{I}_1, \tilde{I}_2 \ldots \tilde{I}_n)$ has a joint normal distribution. It seems an impossible task to ask a single price to aggregate all this diverse information, so that in the rational expectations equilibrium, dealers can trade as if they had all the information. Yet this is in fact so, owing to the following properties of normal random variables.

Lemma: Conditional distributions of normal random variables

If $[\tilde{a}, \tilde{I}_1, \tilde{I}_2 \ldots \tilde{I}_n]$ has a joint normal distribution,

$$\tilde{I} = E[\tilde{a} \mid \tilde{I}_1, \tilde{I}_2 \ldots \tilde{I}_n]$$

and

$$\tilde{e} = \tilde{a} - \tilde{I}$$

then $\tilde{I}$ and $\tilde{e}$ are independent normal random variables, $E\tilde{a} = E\tilde{I}$, $E\tilde{e} = 0$ var $\tilde{a} =$ var $\tilde{I} +$ var $\tilde{e}$. The conditional distribution of $\tilde{a}$ given $\tilde{I}$ is the same as the conditional distribution of $\tilde{a}$ given $\tilde{I}_1, \tilde{I}_2 \ldots \tilde{I}_n$. Both conditional distributions are normal, with mean

$$E(\tilde{a} \mid \tilde{I}) = E[\tilde{a} \mid \tilde{I}_1, \tilde{I}_2 \ldots \tilde{I}_n] = \tilde{I}$$

and variance

$$\text{var}\,(\tilde{a} \mid \tilde{I}) = \text{var}\,[\tilde{a} \mid \tilde{I}_1, \tilde{I}_2 \ldots \tilde{I}_n] = \text{var}\,\tilde{a} - \text{var}\,\tilde{I} = \text{var}\,\tilde{e}.$$

Proof: See appendix.

This result shows that for the purposes of forming beliefs about $\tilde{a}$ knowing $\tilde{I} = E[\tilde{a} \mid \tilde{I}_1, \tilde{I}_2 \ldots \tilde{I}_n]$ gives the same information as knowing $\tilde{I}_1, \tilde{I}_2 \ldots \tilde{I}_n$. The conditional mean $\tilde{I}$, a single number, aggregates perfectly all the diverse information. (It is a sufficient statistic for the information.)

This result can be used to compare two full communications equilibria, for the spot and futures market model. In the first equilibrium dealers observe the vector of random variables $\tilde{I}_1, \tilde{I}_2 \dots \tilde{I}_n$. In the second they observe $\tilde{I} = E[\tilde{a} \mid \tilde{I}_1, \tilde{I}_2 \dots \tilde{I}_n]$. In both equilibria the conditional distribution of $\tilde{a}$ is normal, with the same mean and variance. Thus the equilibrium prices are the same. The equilibrium in which all dealers observe $\tilde{I}$ is the equilibrium of the first model studied in this section. The prices in both equilibria are given by (9.2)–(9.7). In these equilibria, from (9.7)

$$\tilde{p}_f = \theta^{*-1}\tilde{I} = \theta^{*-1}E[\tilde{a} \mid \tilde{I}_1, \tilde{I}_2 \dots \tilde{I}_n] \tag{9.10}$$

and from (9.2) and (9.3)

$$\text{var}\,[\tilde{p}_s \mid \tilde{p}_f] = \text{var}\,[\tilde{p}_s \mid \tilde{I}] = \text{var}\,[\tilde{p}_s \mid \tilde{I}_1, \tilde{I}_2 \dots \tilde{I}_n] = b^{-2}\,\text{var}\,\tilde{e} \tag{9.11}$$

$$E[\tilde{p}_s \mid \tilde{p}_f] = E[\tilde{p}_s \mid \tilde{I}] = E[\tilde{p}_s \mid \tilde{I}_1, \tilde{I}_2 \dots \tilde{I}_n] = \theta^{*-1}\phi^*\tilde{I} = \phi^*\tilde{p}_f \tag{9.12}$$

and

$$\tilde{p}_f = \theta^{*-1}\tilde{I} = \theta^{*-1}E[\tilde{a} \mid \tilde{I}_1, \tilde{I}_2 \dots \tilde{I}_n]. \tag{9.13}$$

Conditioning only on the futures price dealers form the same beliefs about the spot price as they would if they know either $\tilde{I} = E[\tilde{a} \mid \tilde{I}_1, \tilde{I}_2 \dots \tilde{I}_n]$, or the entire information vector $\tilde{I}_1, \tilde{I}_2 \dots \tilde{I}_n$. By the same argument as before these must also be rational expectations equilibrium prices for the model in which dealer i observes information $\tilde{I}_i$.

This is a much stronger result than before. It argues that a market price can not only transmit a single piece of information from one set of dealers to another, but also aggregate a large and diverse set of information perfectly.

10. The robustness of the informational efficiency result

In the previous Section I showed that in a simple futures market model the market price can aggregate diverse information so efficiently that each dealer's beliefs about the return on holding an asset (the spot price) given only its price are the same as if he had access to all the information to the market. He finds his own private information completely redundant.

This surprising result is not limited to futures markets. From a speculator's point of view a futures contract is one of many financial assets, others include shares and bonds issued by firms, and government securities. The original version of this model (Grossman 1976) considered a stock market. The stock lasts for one period, and pays a random gross return $\tilde{R}$. An investor with wealth W_{i0} who buys x_i units of the stock at price p and invests $W_{i0} - px_i$ in a safe asset paying interest r, has final wealth

$$\tilde{W}_i = (\tilde{R} - p(1+r))x_i + W_{i0}(1+r).$$

The gross return $\tilde{R}$ pays a role precisely analogous to the spot price in the futures market. If $\tilde{R}$ is normally distributed and the investor has an exponential utility function $-\exp[-k_i\tilde{W}_i]$ the argument used to derive the speculators demand for futures yields the investors demand for the stock

$$x_i = \frac{1}{k_i \operatorname{var} \tilde{R}}(E\tilde{R} - p(1+r)). \tag{10.1}$$

If there are n investors and a fixed supply of the stock S, market clearing requires that

$$\sum_{i=1}^{n} \frac{1}{k_i \operatorname{var} \tilde{R}}(E\tilde{R} - p(1+r)) = S. \tag{10.2}$$

The stock and futures markets models are mathematically very similar, apart from the fact that the supply of the asset in the stock market is taken as exogenous.

Now suppose the investors have diverse information, $\tilde{I}_1, \tilde{I}_2 \ldots \tilde{I}_n$, and $[\tilde{R}, \tilde{I}_1, \tilde{I}_2 \ldots \tilde{I}_n]$ is joint normal. Experience with the futures market model suggests looking at the full communications equilibria, in which market clearing implies that

$$\sum_{i=1}^{n} \frac{1}{k_i \sigma^2}[E[\tilde{R} \mid \tilde{I}_1, \tilde{I}_2 \ldots \tilde{I}_n] - (1+r)\tilde{p}] = S$$

where $\sigma^2 = \operatorname{var}[\tilde{R} \mid \tilde{I}_1, \tilde{I}_2 \ldots \tilde{I}_n]$ so

$$E[\tilde{R} \mid \tilde{I}_1, \tilde{I}_2 \ldots \tilde{I}_n] = \sigma^2 \left[\sum_{i=1}^{n} k_i^{-1}\right]^{-1} S + (1+r)\tilde{p}. \tag{10.3}$$

Anyone knowing the numerical value of $\sigma^2 \left[\sum_{i=1}^{n} k_i^{-1}\right]^{-1} S$ and $(1+r)$ could infer $E[\tilde{R} \mid \tilde{I}_1, \tilde{I}_2 \ldots \tilde{I}_n]$ from the price $\tilde{p}$, and would form the same beliefs about $\tilde{R}$ as if he knew $\tilde{I}_1, \tilde{I}_2 \ldots \tilde{I}_n$. By a now familiar argument this implies that the full communications equilibrium is also a rational expectations equilibrium; the rational expectations equilibrium price aggregates the information perfectly.

Grossman wrote the paper embodying this result before he had the idea of using an artificial economy, or full communications equilibrium, to analyse the model. He had to use more complex arguments and was not able to prove such a general result. The paper was important firstly because if was the first satisfactory asset market model embracing risk aversion and asymmetric information, and secondly because Grossman pointed out a most important paradox. In Grossman's model, just as in the spot and futures market model, knowing the asset price renders dealers private information redundant. If this information is costly no dealer has any incentive to gather the information, particularly if he knows that another dealer is using the same information. Yet if no-one gathers the information it cannot be reflected in the price, which generates incentives to gather the information.

Grossman and Stiglitz (1980) resolve this paradox by modifying the model slightly. Suppose now that the asset supply is a normal random variable $\tilde{S}$. The relationship between the full communications equilibrium price $\tilde{p}$, $E[\tilde{R} \mid \tilde{I}_1, \tilde{I}_2 \dots \tilde{I}_n]$ and $\tilde{S}$ is given by (10.3), modified only by replacing the constant S by random $\tilde{S}$

$$E[\tilde{R} \mid \tilde{I}_1, \tilde{I}_2 \dots \tilde{I}_n] = \sigma^2 \left[\sum_{i=1}^{n} k_i^{-1} \right]^{-1} \tilde{S} + (1+r)\tilde{p}. \tag{10.4}$$

Even if the numerical values of $\sigma^2 \left[\sum_{i=1}^{n} k_i^{-1} \right]^{-1}$ and $(1+r)$ are known it is impossible to infer $E[\tilde{R} \mid \tilde{I}_1, \tilde{I}_2 \dots \tilde{I}_n]$ from $\tilde{p}$ because $\tilde{S}$ is different each time the market operates. Conditioning on $\tilde{p}$ does not yield the same information as conditioning on $\tilde{I}_1, \tilde{I}_2 \dots \tilde{I}_n$. The full communications equilibrium is not a rational expectations equilibrium. (This is also true in the spot and futures market model, if farmers' output is uncertain, and dealers have information about both spot demand and output (Bray, 1981).)

Grossman and Stiglitz calculate the rational expectations equilibrium for a version of the stock market model in which there are two groups of dealers. The informed dealers all observe the same information, on which they base their expectations. The uninformed dealers form their expectations on the basis of the price. The informativeness of the price increases as the proportion of informed dealers increases. In the absence of information costs the informed dealers have higher expected utility than the uninformed, because they are less uncertain of the asset return (its conditional variance is lower for the informed than the uninformed). If information is costly informed dealers may be better or worse off. If the proportion of informed dealers is large and the price conveys much of the information to the uninformed dealers they are likely to be worse off. If the proportion of informed dealers is small and the price conveys little information to the uninformed they are likely to be better off. Grossman and Stiglitz show that for each level of information costs there is an equilibrium proportion of informed dealers, so that the benefits of the information just balance the costs, and dealers are indifferent between being informed and uninformed. They derive a variety of interesting comparative static results from this model.

11. Existence of rational expectations equilibrium

Expectations play a crucial role in all the models which I have presented, as in many others. Whenever I have needed to close models by specifying expectations I have followed standard practice in postulating rational expectations. In each case I have been able to show that a rational expectations equilibrium exists by solving explicitly for the equilibrium. This is not always possible. Indeed in some examples, such as the one which follows it can be shown that there is no set of prices and beliefs which satisfy Parts 3 and 4 of the definition. There is no rational expectations equilibrium.

The example is similar in form to that of Kreps (1977). It is a somewhat modified version of the spot and futures market model. For mathematical simplicity assume that there is one farmer and one speculator. Each maximises the expectation of a utility function $-\exp(-\tilde{W})$. The speculator believes the spot price $\tilde{p}_s \sim N(\mu, \sigma^2)$. The interest rate $r = 0$. Arguing as before the speculators' excess demand for futures is

$$x_s = \frac{1}{\sigma^2}(\mu - p_f). \tag{11.1}$$

The farmer has a cost function for output $C(y) = sy + \frac{1}{2}y^2$. He also believes that $\tilde{p}_s \sim N(\mu, \sigma^2)$. Utility maximisation for the farmer implies that he sets output so $C'(y) = p_f$ or

$$y = p_f - s. \tag{11.2}$$

He hedges by selling y on the futures market, and in addition speculates by buying futures

$$x_f = \frac{1}{\sigma^2}(\mu - p_f). \tag{11.3}$$

Futures market clearing implies that $x_s + x_f = y$, or from (11.1)–(11.3)

$$\frac{2}{\sigma^2}(\mu - p_f) = p_f - s. \tag{11.4}$$

Spot demand is

$$D(p_s) = \tilde{a} - \tilde{p}_s$$

where $\tilde{a}$ is a normal random variable, and var $\tilde{a} = 1$. Spot market clearing implies that $D(\tilde{p}_s) = y$, that is

$$\tilde{a} - \tilde{p}_s = p_f - s. \tag{11.5}$$

Equation (11.5) implies that

$$E\tilde{p}_s = E\tilde{a} - p_f + s \tag{11.6}$$

and

$$\text{var } \tilde{p}_s = \text{var } \tilde{a} = 1. \tag{11.7}$$

If the farmer and speculator are to form rational expectations $\mu = E\tilde{p}_s = E\tilde{a} - p_f + s$, and $\sigma^2 = \text{var } \tilde{p}_s = 1$. The futures market clearing condition (11.4) becomes

$$2(E\tilde{a} - p_f + s - p_f] = p_f - s$$

so

$$p_f = \frac{1}{5}(2E\tilde{a} + 3s). \tag{11.8}$$

Spot market clearing and rational expectations imply (11.6), which with

(11.8) implies that

$$E\tilde{p}_s = \tfrac{1}{5}(3E\tilde{a} + 2s). \tag{11.9}$$

So far I have had no difficulty in calculating the rational expectations equilibrium, but introducing asymmetric information can cause complications. Suppose that there are only two sorts of weather, good and bad. The farmer observes the weather; the speculator does not. If the weather is good $E\tilde{a} = \tfrac{5}{4}$ and $s = \tfrac{1}{6}$. If it is bad $E\tilde{a} = 1$ and $s = \tfrac{1}{3}$.

There are only two possibilities, either the futures price is different in different weather or it is not. If the futures price is different the speculator can infer the weather from the price. Trades and prices will be the same as if both farmer and speculator knew the weather. In this case in good weather $E\tilde{a} = \tfrac{5}{4}$, $s = \tfrac{1}{6}$, from (11.8) $p_f = \tfrac{2}{3}$ and from (11.9) $E\tilde{p}_s = \tfrac{49}{60}$. In bad weather $E\tilde{a} = 1$, $s = \tfrac{1}{3}$, from (11.8) $p_f = \tfrac{2}{3}$, and from (11.9) $E\tilde{p}_s = \tfrac{44}{60}$. Thus the futures price is the same in both weathers, contradicting the supposition that it was different.

The alternative supposition is that the futures price is the same whatever the weather, in which case the speculator's demand will be the same. If the farmer has rational expectations his excess demand for futures will be using (11.2), (11.3) and (11.6), and recalling that $\sigma^2 = 1$ and $\mu = E\tilde{p}_s$,

$$x_f - y = (E\tilde{p}_s - p_f) - (p_f - s) = E\tilde{p}_s + s - 2p_f$$
$$= E\tilde{a} + 2s - 3p_f.$$

In good weather $E\tilde{a} + 2s = \tfrac{19}{12}$, in bad weather $E\tilde{a} + 2s = \tfrac{5}{3}$. If p_f is independent of the weather the speculator's demand for futures is independent of the weather, but the farmer's is not. The futures market cannot clear at the same price in both weathers. This exhausts the possibilities. In this example the assumptions of market clearing and rational expectations are logically inconsistent. There is no rational expectations equilibrium.

In defining a rational expectations equilibrium for an asset market model in Section 3 I argued that the market clearing condition induces a mapping from the beliefs people hold to the correct beliefs. This is an almost universal feature of models with expectations, it crops up for example in equation (8.11) which gives the correct expected spot price $E\tilde{p}_s$, as a function of the subjectively held expectation μ. A rational expectations equilibrium is a fixed point of this mapping. Fixed point theorems give conditions under which mappings have fixed points; notably continuity. The non-existence problems for rational expectations models with asymmetric information stem from discontinuities in the mapping, where a small change in prices can induce a large change in the information which can be inferred from them. In the example, if prices are identical in both weathers, the speculator cannot infer the weather, but if they are very slightly different he can.

Checking that an equilibrium exists is an essential preliminary to using a model; assuming that an equilibrium exists and arguing from there, can yield no valid conclusions if in fact no equilibrium exists. Knowing the circumstances under which a model has an equilibrium puts logical limits on the range of applicability.

Existence problems are attacked from two directions, existence theorems and non-existence examples. Existence theorems establish that under certain conditions, typically conditions on preferences, technology, and the structure of transactions and information, an equilibrium exists. For some special models equilibrium can be shown to exist by calculating the equilibrium, but in general the problem is attacked indirectly, often using fixed point theorems which establish that a set of equations has a solution, but not what the solution is. Non-existence examples show that in certain cases no equilibrium exists. These examples are helpful because they show certain conjectured general existence results cannot be valid; a claim that *all* models of a certain type have an equilibrium is wrong if a single such model has no equilibrium, just as a single black swan is enough to invalidate the claim that all swans are white.

The non-existence example which I demonstrated earlier is not robust; a small change in the parameters of the model would allow an equilibrium to exist, non-existence is a freak eventuality. Radner (1979) studies a much more general asset market model which shares two features with this example. In both models there are only a finite number of different possible information signals. In the example there are two, good weather or bad weather. In Radner's model there may be a large but finite number of different signals received by a finite number of individuals. The vector of joint signals can only take a finite number of different values. In Radner's model, as in my example, there may be no rational expectations equilibrium. Radner shows rigorously that equilibrium exists generically. Generic existence is defined precisely in the paper; the idea which it captures is that whilst equilibrium may fail to exist in some special cases, almost any perturbation of the model will restore existence. Radner's proof proceeds by considering the full communications equilibrium, in which dealers pool all their information signals before trading. The price vector in the full communications equilibrium $\tilde{p}$ is a function of the joint signal $\tilde{s}$, $\tilde{p} = p(\tilde{s})$. If the price vector is different whenever any element in the signal is different, the price reveals the signal, the full communications equilibrium is a rational expectations equilibrium, in which prices fully reveal the information.

The crucial question is whether the map from the signals into prices is invertible. There are a finite number, m, of signals, whereas prices can be any vector in R^{n+}, so there are an infinity (indeed a continuum) of different possible prices. Radner's result confirms the intuition that if the utility functions generating demand are reasonably well behaved, the map from signals to prices fails to be invertible only in special circumstances, in which case a small perturbation of the model restores invertibility.

The assumption that there are a finite number of different possible signals plays a crucial role in this invertibility argument. If there are a continuum of different possible signals the argument may break down. Jordan and Radner (1982) devise an example with an informed and uninformed dealers and one relative price. The informed dealer observes a signal $\tilde{s}$ in $[0, 1]$. Given the price, the informed dealer's demand changes with the signal, if there are two different signals $s_1 \neq s_2$, with $p(s_1) = p(s_2)$ the informed dealer's demand is different for the two signals, but the uninformed dealer who observes only the price has the same demand. The market cannot clear at the same price for both s_1 and s_2. On the other hand if the function is invertible the uninformed dealer can infer s from p, the prices are the same as in the full communications equilibrium. But Jordan and Radner show that the full communications equilibrium price function has the form shown in Fig. 2, and is not invertible. This is a robust example, changing the parameters of the model changes the price function a little, but does not make it invertible.

The importance of invertibility for the existence of rational expectations equilibria in which prices reveal all the information suggests that the relative dimensions of the signal space and the price space may be important. This is confirmed by Allen (1982) who shows that if the dimension of the signal space is less than the dimension of the price space a fully revealing rational expectations equilibrium exists generically. Jordan (1983) shows that if the dimension of the price space is higher than the dimension of the signal space rational expectations equilibrium exists, generically, but is not fully revealing.

The literature on fully revealing equilibria is concerned with equilibria in which dealers can infer the entire information signal from the prices. This is sufficient to enable them to form the same expectations as if they saw the signal. But it is not necessary; dealers want to know about a vector of asset returns $\tilde{R}$. If $\tilde{R}$ and the information $\tilde{I}$ are joint normal, knowing $E(\tilde{R} \mid \tilde{I})$ tells them as much as knowing $\tilde{I}$. The vector $E(\tilde{R} \mid \tilde{I})$ has the same

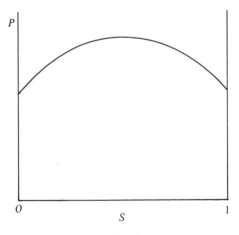

FIG. 2

dimension as $\tilde{R}$, the number of risky assets. This may be much lower than the dimension of $\tilde{I}$. Grossman (1978) uses this result to analyse a stock market model in which returns are normal, and dealers care only about the mean and variance of return. By applying the captial asset pricing model Grossman shows that provided the market portfolio is not a Giffen good dealers can infer $E(\tilde{R} \mid \tilde{I})$ from the information, and so a rational expectations equilibrium exists in which dealers trade as if they had all the information. Grossman also exploits the properties of normal random variables in his paper on futures markets (1977), showing how they can act to transmit information.

The existence of rational expectations equilibrium in asset markets is an attractive and challenging problem for mathematical economists. A more sophisticated discussion, and further references are in Radner (1982), which surveys the literature on 'Equilibrium Under Uncertainty', and by Jordan and Radner (1982) which introduces a symposium issue of the Journal of Economic Theory, on Rational Expectations in Microeconomic Models, which includes a number of related papers. More recent work on the matter includes Jordan (1982a, 1982b), Allen (1983), and Anderson and Sonnenschein (1985).

12. Evaluating the models

A model is a simplified, stylised description of certain aspects of the economy. It omits many details in order to concentrate on certain features and their interrelationships. One of the major objectives of modelling is often to show that the description is logically consistent by demonstrating that an equilibrium exists, an issue which I have discussed at some length. If a model is to be used as a basis for saying something about real economies logical consistency is essential; even grossly unrealistic models may be useful in establishing logical limits to rhetoric. But is is obviously desirable that a model be a correct, as well as a consistent, description.

Unfortunately there is no clear and universally applicable criterion for the correctness of models. Any model omits details, abstracts and simplifies. Reality is too complicated to be thought about in totality. Assumptions in economic models are most unlikely to be completely adequate descriptions of behaviour. The question to ask is whether they are plausible enough to generate implications which say something about the aspects of reality with which the model is concerned. This is inevitably a matter of judgement, and must often depend upon the use to which a model is being put.

The three major assumptions made in the financial market models which I described are that markets clear, that agents are price-takers and that they have rational expectations. These assumptions are very widely made; they are also central to the 'new-classical' macroeconomics (Begg 1982a). Market clearing and price-taking seem in general quite plausible for financial markets, where prices move readily, there is little evidence of sustained excess supply and demand, and a large number of traders.

The rational expectations hypothesis can be stated loosely, that people do not make systematic mistakes in forecasting; more precisely, people's subjective beliefs about probability distributions correspond to the objective probability distributions. Employing the rational expectations hypothesis imposes two logical requirements, that objective probability distributions exist, and that a rational expectations equilibrium exists. In constructing a model an economist creates the objective probability distributions, but these models can only be applied to situations where the distributions could in principle at least be derived from data. This requires that the structure and parameters of the economy are in some way constant through time. Rational expectations models describe long run stationary equilibria.

One important criticism of the rational expectations hypothesis is that it assumes that agents know too much. Consider the spot and futures market model with asymmetric information. In rational equilibrium the uninformed dealers believe correctly that the conditional distribution of the spot price given the futures price is normal, has conditional mean given by (9.8) $E[\tilde{p}_s \mid \tilde{p}_f] = \phi^* \tilde{p}_f$ and a constant conditional variance. All they need to know is the fact of normality, and the numerical value of ϕ^* and var $[\tilde{p}_s \mid \tilde{p}_f]$. The uninformed dealers do not have to know the structure of the model, just two parameters of the reduced form. Further by observing the markets operating in rational expectations equilibrium for a number of years the numbers ϕ^* and var $[\tilde{p}_s \mid \tilde{p}_f]$ could be estimated by standard statistical techniques. Apparently it is quite easy to learn how to form rational expectations.

In financial markets there are very large amounts of money at stake; and there is every incentive to apply the considerable abilities and resources of professional investors to make the best possible forecasts. However the argument that it is easy or even possible to learn how to form rational expectations by applying standard statistical techniques is misleading. Economists are interested in expectations because they believe that expectations affect what happens. This belief is reflected in the models, if agents in these models do not have rational expectations the model behaves differently from the rational expectations equilibrium. In Section 7 I defined a rational expectations equilibrium as a fixed point of the mapping from subjectively held beliefs into 'correct beliefs' induced by the market clearing condition. Outside rational expectations equilibrium subjective beliefs differ from both correct beliefs, and the rational expectations equilibrium beliefs. For example in the spot and futures market model in rational expectations equilibrium dealers believe that $E[\tilde{p}_s \mid \tilde{p}_f] = \phi^* \tilde{p}_f$. If dealers believe that $E[\tilde{p}_s \mid \tilde{p}_f] = \phi \tilde{p}_f$ where $\phi \neq \phi^*$, the correct conditional expectation will be of the form $E[\tilde{p}_s \mid \tilde{p}_f] = \hat{\phi} \tilde{p}_f$ where $\hat{\phi} \neq \phi$, the expectation is incorrect, and $\hat{\phi} \neq \phi^*$, the correct expectation is not the same as in the rational expectations equilibrium. Changing to the 'correct' expectation formation rule $E[\tilde{p}_s \mid \tilde{p}_f] = \hat{\phi} \tilde{p}_f$, changes the behaviour of the model, and this rule becomes incorrect. The obvious question to ask is whether repeated changes of the expectation formation rule ultimately lead to a rational expectations equilibrium. Is it possible to describe a plausible learning process which ultimately yields rational expectations? The answer depends upon how 'plausible' is understood. One possibility is to insist that agents learn using correctly specified Bayesian models. David Kreps and I argue elsewhere (Bray and Kreps, 1986) that is is in fact not plausible, because it in effect assumes a more elaborate and informationally demanding form of rational expectations equilibrium. However if agents do learn in this way and if the model has suitable continuity properties, expectations eventually become rational in the conventional sense.

Another possible way to model learning is to assume that agents estimate the model as if it were in rational expectations equilibrium, for example in the spot and futures market model they regress $\tilde{p}_s$ on $\tilde{p}_f$ using ordinary least squares, and use the estimated regression coefficients in forecasting $\tilde{p}_s$ from $\tilde{p}_f$. In Bray (1982) I studied this procedure for the model of example 2 where there are uninformed dealers, and informed dealers all of whom have the same information. I found that provided the uninformed dealers did not form too large a proportion of the market, the model would eventually converge to its rational expectations equilibrium. Bray (1983)[3] and Bray and Savin (1984) study similar econometric learning processes for a simple macroeconomic model and a version of the cobweb model. In both these models if the parameters of the supply and demand functions have the usual signs agents eventually learn how to form rational expectations. In all these examples agents are estimating misspecified economic models, so convergence to rational expectations equilibrium is not based on standard theorems on the asymptotic properties of estimators, is somewhat surprising, and hard to prove. Convergence to rational expectations equilibrium may be slow, and takes place only if the parameters of the model lies in a certain range. Although many of the examples which have been studied converge in economically plausible circumstances there is no general theory which establishes that convergence will always take place.

Expectations are important for economics; they crop up unavoidably in considering a vast range of issues. The enormous virtue of the rational expectations hypothesis is that it gives a simple, general and plausible way of handling expectations. It makes it possible to formulate and answer questions, for example, on the efficiency of markets as transmitters as information, which would otherwise be utterly intractable. All recent progress on the economics of information is built on the rational expectations hypothesis.

Consider for a moment the alternative hypotheses. One possibility is that

---

[3] Bray (1983) is much the shortest and simplest of these papers on learning, and the best introduction to the issues as I see them. Bray and Savin (1984) contains computer simulations which shed light on the rates of convergence and divergence, and discusses the relationship between this work, and time-varying parameter models in econometrics. Related literature is surveyed briefly in Blume, Bray and Easley (1982). Bray and Savin (1984) contains more recent references.

agents use a simple forecasting rule which generates systematic mistakes. In any application it is necessary to specify the rule, for example adaptive expectations. If there is good evidence that people do forecast in this way this is attractive, but it seems implausible that in the long run in a stable environment they will fail to notice their mistakes and modify the rule. Another alternative is to try to model the dynamics of the learning process. At present this seems to make for models which are too complicated and mathematically difficult to use for addressing most questions. Rational expectations equilibrium is a way of avoiding many difficult dynamic issue; if an issue is intractable in the current state of knowledge circumventing it is probably the most fruitful research stragegy.

Another alternative is to rely on survey data for expectations. Where possible this may be valuable in empirical work, if not very helpful for theorists.

A further alternative is to follow Keynes and argue that expectations cannot be described as probability distributions, they are volatile, and not susceptible to formal description. This makes it impossible to incorporate expectations explicitly into formal models, except by treating them as exogenous. Begg (1982b) argues that this is Keynes' strategy in the General Theory and is followed in traditional text-book treatments of Keynesian theory. In some cases I think this is an entirely defensible, indeed attractive strategy for modelling short-term events. The danger is that if expectations are unobservable, inexplicable, exogenous and volatile it leaves the model with no predictive and very little explanatory power as anything can be attributed to a shift in expectations. The rational expectations hypothesis also postulates unobservable expectations, but otherwise in total opposition to Keynes treats expectations as explicable, exogenous, and stable (unless the underlying model changes in which case expectations change appropriately). In medium to long term models the extreme rational expectations hypothesis is more attractive than the extreme exogenous expectations hypothesis. There is currently no generally acceptable intermediate hypothesis. Note that although Keynes himself would probably shudder if he knew there is no reason why rational expectations should not be incorporated into 'Keynesian' models, which would have quite different properties from the 'new-classical' rational expectations models. (See Begg 1982b.)

The rational expectations hypothesis seems at present much the most satisfactory generally applicable hypothesis on expectations formation. But it must be remembered that rational expectations models describe long run equilibria, on the assumption that the dynamics induced by learning eventually converge to rational expectations equilibrium. We have no good reason to believe that this assumption is always, or even often, valid.

I have discussed the assumptions of the financial market models at some length. The other criteria for the correctness of the models as descriptions is to look at implications of the models, and compare them with data. There are two sources of data, experimental data from laboratory situations, and empirical data from real markets. Ultimately the objective is to understand real markets, but laboratory data generated by setting up a market with groups of students, enables the experimenter to control and design the experiment, eliminating the host of extraneous factors which affect real market data.

Plott and Sunder (1982) set up a series of asset markets with informed and uninformed traders. The return on the asset depended on which of two or three states of the world occurs. The informed traders all had the same piece of information, in most cases telling them which state of the world had occurred. Plott and Sunder calculated two prices for each market, firstly the rational expectations equilibrium price in which the uninformed dealers inferred the as much as possible from the price, secondly the prior information price in which the uninformed dealers traded only on the basis of their prior information. Although the rational expectations model was not a perfect fit, prices did show a tendency to move towards their rational expectations equilibrium level. Plott and Sunder interpret the data as supporting the rational expectations rather than the prior information model.

Real market data has been used to test the efficient markets hypothesis, that using information in addition to the current price of an asset does not make for better predictions, the market price efficiently aggregates all the information. Three different forms of the hypothesis have been considered, the weak form, considering the information in past prices, the semi-strong form, considering more general publically available information, and the strong form, considering private information. The empirical literature is vast; Brealey (1983) provides a very readable introduction, and numerous references. Broadly the literature supports the weak and semi-strong forms of the efficient markets hypothesis, but private information does seem to give some advantage. The efforts of numerous academic investigators have failed to uncover a rule for forecasting market prices in order to manage a portfolio which does significantly better than holding a fixed well diversified portfolio. These results are consistent with the theoretical models which I have been describing and can be taken as support for the application of the rational expectations hypothesis to financial markets.

13. Further questions

These models answer some questions, but provoke others. Many of the models consider asset markets in isolation, taking the return generated by the asset as exogenous. (The spot and futures market model is an exception.) But financial markets are part of a larger system. One of their major functions is to enable enterprises to spread, and share risk, with consequences for output, investment and employment. It now appears that the markets may also have a role as transmitters of information. The ramifications of this role are not understood, but may be investigated using techniques similar to those which I have described.

Another set of open questions concern the mechanism of price formation. In these models price is a function of information, for example in the spot and futures market model where dealers have diverse information the futures price $\tilde{p}_f = \theta^{*-1}E[\tilde{a} \mid \tilde{I}_1, \tilde{I}_2, \ldots \tilde{I}_n]$, (9.10), where θ^* is a parameter, and $\tilde{I}_i$ agent i's information, a normal random variable. As the information varies from year to year the price varies. If the dealers have diverse information no individual dealer can check that the price is at the correct level given all the information. If a dealer thinks that the futures price is high or low given his private information, he can only conclude that other dealers have different information which leads them to expect a high or low spot price. Any numerical value of $\tilde{p}_f$ can clear the market, it is far from clear what pushes $\tilde{p}_f$ to its correct value. (This point is originally due to Beja, (1976)).

Universal price-taking is of course a convenient fiction. People set prices, unilaterally, by auction procedures, or by haggling. If there is a very limited range of prices at which goods can be sold price-taking is a good approximation. It may be necessary to consider the detailed mechanics of price making, the activities of brokers, jobbers, and market makers, to understand some aspects of the determination of prices in asset markets. In discussing their experimental results Plott and Sunder suggest that some of the information is transmitted by the oral auction process which they use, including unaccepted bids and offers. If this is so it provides an additional reason for looking at the institutional details of market structure.

The models which I have a very stark, simple, time structure, things happen at only two dates. In practice many financial markets operate repeatedly, the same asset is traded at a large number of dates, indeed trade may best be modelled as a continuous time process. There is a literature on continuous time models of financial markets (e.g. Black and Scholes (1973), and Merton (1973)), but this literature takes no account of informational asymmetries. Continuous time models with asymmetric information are attractive means of investigating the rate at which markets disseminate information, although they may pose formidable technical difficulties. There is certainly a case for looking at a richer temporal structure than has been considered up to now.

Faculty of Economics and Politics, Cambridge

APPENDIX

Proof of Lemma. Conditional distributions of normal random variables
  Anderson (1958) shows that

$$\tilde{I} = E[\tilde{a} \mid \tilde{I}_1, \tilde{I}_2 \ldots \tilde{I}_n] = E\tilde{a} + \Sigma_{ay} \Sigma_{yy}^{-1} (\bar{y} - E\bar{y}) \tag{A.1}$$

where $\bar{y}$ is notation for the vector $[\tilde{I}_1, \tilde{I}_2 \ldots \tilde{I}_n]$, $\Sigma_{ay} = \mathrm{cov}\,(\tilde{a}, \bar{y})$, $\Sigma_{yy} = \mathrm{var}\,(\bar{y})$. Equation (A.1) implies that $\tilde{I}$ is a linear function of $[\tilde{I}_1, \tilde{I}_2 \ldots \tilde{I}_n]$. As linear functions of normal random variables are normal, $\tilde{I}$ and $\tilde{e} = \tilde{a} - \tilde{I}$ are normal.

$$\text{cov}(\tilde{e}, \tilde{y}) = \text{cov}[\tilde{a} - E\tilde{a} - \Sigma_{ay} \Sigma_{yy}^{-1}(\tilde{y} - E\tilde{y}), \tilde{y}]$$
$$= \Sigma_{ay} - \Sigma_{ay} \Sigma_{yy}^{-1} \Sigma_{yy} = 0.$$

Thus $\tilde{e}$ and $\tilde{y}$ are uncorrelated, and as they are normal independent. Since $\tilde{I}$ is a linear function of $\tilde{y}$, $\tilde{I}$ and $\tilde{e}$ are uncorrelated, that is

$$\text{cov}(\tilde{I}, \tilde{e}) = \text{cov}(\tilde{I}, \tilde{a} - \tilde{I}) = 0 \qquad (\text{A.2})$$

and so $\tilde{I}$ and $\tilde{e}$ are independent.

From (A.1)

$$E\tilde{a} = E\tilde{I} \qquad (\text{A.3})$$

and so $E\tilde{e} = E\tilde{a} - E\tilde{I} = 0$. As $\tilde{I}$ and $\tilde{e}$ are independent

$$\text{var } \tilde{a} = \text{var}(\tilde{I} + \tilde{e}) = \text{var } \tilde{I} + \text{var } \tilde{e}.$$

As $\tilde{I}$ is a function of $\tilde{I}_1, \dots \tilde{I}_n$ and $\tilde{e}$ is independent of $\tilde{I}_1, \tilde{I}_2 \dots \tilde{I}_n$ the conditional distribution of $\tilde{a} = \tilde{I} + \tilde{e}$ given $\tilde{I}_1, \tilde{I}_2 \dots \tilde{I}_n$ is normal (as $\tilde{e}$ is normal), with mean

$$E[\tilde{a} \mid \tilde{I}_1, \tilde{I}_2 \dots \tilde{I}_n] = E[\tilde{I} \mid \tilde{I}_1, \tilde{I}_2 \dots \tilde{I}_n] + E[\tilde{e} \mid \tilde{I}_1, \tilde{I}_2 \dots \tilde{I}_n]$$
$$= \tilde{I} + E\tilde{e} = \tilde{I} = E(\tilde{a} \mid \tilde{I})$$

and

$$\text{var}[\tilde{a} \mid \tilde{I}_1, \tilde{I}_2 \dots \tilde{I}_n] = \text{var}[\tilde{e} \mid \tilde{I}_1, \tilde{I}_2 \dots \tilde{I}_n] = \text{var } \tilde{e} = \text{var}(\tilde{a} \mid \tilde{I}).$$

It can be shown that the conditional expectation of $\tilde{a}$ given $\tilde{I}_1, \tilde{I}_2 \dots \tilde{I}_n$ is the unique linear function of $\tilde{I}$ of $\tilde{I}_1, \tilde{I}_2 \dots \tilde{I}_n$ satisfying (A.2) and (A.3). These equations characterise the conditional expectation of one normal random variable given another. (See Bray (1981) for an application of this fact.)

REFERENCES

ALLEN, B. (1982), "Strict Rational Expectations Equilibria with Diffuseness" *Journal of Economic Theory*, 27, 20–46.

ALLEN, B. (1983), "Expectations Equilibria with Dispersed Information: Existence with Approximate Rationality in a Model with a Continuum of Agents and Finitely Many States of the World" *Review of Economic Studies*, 50 267–85.

ANDERSON, T. W., (1958), *An Introduction to Multivariate Statistical Analysis*, Wiley, New York.

ANDERSON, R. M. and SONNENSCHEIN, H., (1985), "Rational Expectations with Econometric Models", forthcoming, *Review of Economic Studies*.

ARROW, K. (1964), "The Role of Securities in the Optimal Allocation of Risk-Bearing", *Review of Economic Studies*, 31, 91–96.

BEGG, D. K. H. (1982a), *The Rational Expectations Revolution in Macroeconomics*, Philip Allan, Oxford.

BEGG, D. K. H. (1982b), "Rational Expectations, Wage Rigidity and Involuntary Unemployment: A Particular Theory", *Oxford Economic Papers*, 34, 23–47.

BEJA, A. (1976), "The Limited Information Efficiency of Market Processes", Research Program in Finance Working Paper No. 43, University of California, Berkeley.

BLACK, F. and SCHOLES, M. (1973), "The Pricing of Options and Corporate Liabilities", *Journal of Political Economy*, 81, 637–659.

BLUME, L., BRAY, M. M. and EASLEY, D. (1982), "Introduction to the Stability of Rational Expectations Equilibrium", *Journal of Economic Theory*, 26, 313–317.

BRAY, M. M. (1981), "Futures Trading, Rational Expectations, and the Efficient Markets Hypothesis", *Econometrica*, 49, 575–596.

BRAY, M. M. (1982), "Learning, Estimation, and the Stability of Rational Expectations", *Journal of Economic Theory*, 26, 318–339.

BRAY, M. M. (1983), "Convergence to Rational Expectations Equilibrium" in *Individual Forecasting and Aggregate Outcomes*, ed. R. Frydman and E. S. Phelps, Cambridge: Cambridge University Press.

BRAY, M. M. and KREPS, D. M. (1986), "Rational Learning and Rational Expectations", forthcoming in 'Essays in Honor of K. J. Arrow', edited by W. Heller, D. Starrett and R. Starr.

BRAY, M. M. and SAVIN, N. E. (1984), "Rational Expectations Equilibria, Learning and Model Specification", Economic Theory Discussion Paper No. 79, Department of Applied Economics, Cambridge.

BREALEY, R. (1983), *An Introduction to Risk and Return* Second Edition, Blackwell, Oxford.

DANTHINE, J. P. (1978), "Information, Futures Prices and Stabilising Speculation", *Journal of Economic Theory*, 17, 79–98.

DEATON, A. and MUELLBAUER, J. (1980), *Economics and Consumer Behaviour*, Cambridge University Press, Cambridge.

DIAMOND, P. A. (1967), "The Role of a Stock Market in a General Equilibrium Model with Technolgoical Uncertainty", *American Economic Review*, 57, 759–773.

DIAMOND, P. A. and ROTHSCHILD, M. (1978), *Uncertainty in Economics*, Academic Press, New York.

GROSSMAN, S. J. (1976), "On the Efficiency of Competitive Stock Markets Where Traders Have Diverse Information", *Journal of Finance*, 31, 573–585.

GROSSMAN, S. J. (1977), "The Existence of Futures Markets, Noisy Rational Expectations and Informational Externalities", *Review of Economic Studies*, 44, 431–449.

GROSSMAN, S. J. (1978), "Further Results On the Informational Efficiency of Competitive Stock Markets", *Journal of Economic Theory*, 18, 81–101.

GROSSMAN, S. J. (1981), "An Introduction to the Theory of Rational Expectations Under Asymmetric Information", *Review of Economic Studies*, 48, 541–560.

GROSSMAN, S. J., and STIGLITZ, J. E. (1980), "On the Impossibility of Informationally Efficient Markets", *American Economic Review*, 70, 393–408.

HAYEK, F. A. (1945), "The Use of Knowledge in Society", *American Economic Review*, 35, 519–530.

JORDAN, J. S. (1982a), "Admissable Market Data Structures: A Complete Characterisation, *Journal of Economic Theory*, 28(1), 19–31.

JORDAN, J. S. (1982b), "A Dynamic Model of Expectations Equilibrium", *Journal of Economic Theory*, 28(2), 235–54.

JORDAN, J. S. (1983), "On the Efficient Markets Hypothesis", *Econometrica*, 51, 1325–1343.

JORDAN, J. S. and RADNER, R. (1982), "Rational Expectations in Microeconomic Models: an Overview", *Journal of Economic Theory*, 26, 201–223.

KALDOR, N. (1934), "A Classificatory Note on the Determinateness of Equilibrium", *Review of Economic Studies*, 1, 122–136.

KEYNES, J. M. (1936), *The General Theory of Employment, Interest and Money*, Macmillan, London.

KNIGHT, F. H. (1921), *Risk, Uncertainty and Profit*, Houghton Mifflin, New York.

KREPS, D. (1977), "A Note on Fulfilled Expectations Equilibria", *Journal of Economic Theory*, 14, 32–43.

MERTON, M. (1973), "An Intertemporal Capital Asset Pricing Model", *Econometrica*, 41, 867–888.

MEYER, P. L. (1970), *Introductory Probability and Statistical Applications* Second Edition, Addison Wesley, Reading, Massachusetts.

MUTH, J. F. (1961), "Rational Expectations and the Theory of Price Movements", *Econometrica*, 29, 315–335.

PLOTT, C. R. and SUNDER, S. (1982), "Efficiency of Experimental Security Markets With Insider Information: An Application of Rational Expectations Models", *Journal of Political Economy*, 90, 663–98.

RADNER, R. (1979), "Rational Expectations Equilibrium Generic Existence and the Information Revealed by Prices", *Econometrica*, 47, 655–678.

RADNER, R. (1982), "Equilibrium Under Uncertainty" in *Handbook of Mathematical Economics, Vol. II*, Editors K. J. Arrow and M. D. Intriligator, Amsterdam, North-Holland.

RAIFFA, H. (1968), *Decision Analysis: Introductory Lectures on Choice Under Uncertainty*, Addison Wesley, Reading, Massachusetts.

SCHOEMAKER, P. S. H. (1982), "The Expected Utility Model: Its Variants, Purposes, Evidence and Limitations", *Journal of Economic Literature*, 20, 529–563.

STIGLITZ, J. E. (1982), "Information and Capital Markets", in *Financial Economics: Essays in Honor of Paul Cootner*, Editors W. F. Sharpe and C. M. Cootner, Prentice-Hall.

Oxford Economic Papers 38 (1986), 456–480

PRE-SET PRICES, DIFFERENTIAL INFORMATION AND MONETARY POLICY

By T. M. ANDERSEN*

1. Introduction

THE ROLE of monetary policy as a potential stabilizer of economic activity is a controversial issue. The current debate is highly influenced by the New Classical Macroeconomics, according to which any systematic monetary policy is neutral within a setting of i) instantaneous market clearing, ii) rational expectations, and iii) imperfect information.

The question of instantaneous market clearing has often been regarded as the main dividing line between 'Keynesians' and 'Monetarists', and for this reason the assumption of instantaneous market clearing has been widely disputed. Despite this criticism no viable alternative has been developed. Most studies of the implications of fixed, predetermined or 'disequilibrium' prices have taken resort to some *ad-hoc* assumption concerning price formation as for instance the anticipatory price setting rule (Green and Laffont, 1981; Brunner, Cukierman and Meltzer, 1983). According to this price rule prices are predetermined equal to the rationally (homogeneously) expected Walrasian price level. However, this approach does not come to issue with the main criticism of the assumption of instantaneous market clearing, namely, that it does not delegate the price-decisions to well-defined agents pursuing well-defined objectives (Arrow, 1959). Prices remain therefore to be set by a third-party or auctioneer, although not a Walrasian auctioneer. In the present study we shall give up the assumption of instantaneous market clearing and propose a way in which an economy with predetermined prices can be constructed such that the identity and objective of price setters are well-defined.

The present paper starts out from the criticism made by Arrow (1959) of the instantaneous market clearing assumption by delegating the price decisions to well-defined agents (firms) who pursue well-defined objectives. As forcefully argued by Hayek (1945) most economically relevant information is decentralized, and we analyse the coordination problem which arises when numerous price setters quote prices on differential or decentralized information. The differential information structure arises naturally from the fact that each firm observes its own sales (quantity signal) and costs (price signal). Besides this private information agents have access to aggregate information which becomes available to all agents through price figures (price signals) and output figures (quantity signals). These different sources of information are explicitly considered in the present study.

* I am grateful to J. Drèze, P. J. N. Sinclair and two anonymous referees for valuable comments. The usual disclaimer applies. The financial support of the "Danish Social Science Research Council" is gratefully acknowledged.

Giving up the assumption that an economy-wide auctioneer sets prices we have to face the problem of how price decisions become coordinated,[1] since prices will be set by numerous agents each pursuing its own objective under imperfect knowledge about the price decisions made by other agents. Within a setting of monopolistic competition[2] we shall analyse the adjustment to nominal shocks in an economy with many price setting firms, where each firm sets its price under imperfect information about the price set by other firms. Each firm is assumed to be a monopolist in the specific market for the product it produces, but all firms compete for a place in the budget constraint of demanders. To model this we assume that the demand for any commodity depends not only on its own price, but also on the aggregate price level. For this reason each firm is concerned about the price decisions made by other firms, and we shall assume that each firm, conditional on its information set, makes rational expectations of the general price level and the shocks affecting the economy. Within this setting coordination failures are specifically linked to the fact that the price decision is not left to an omnipotent auctioneer, but to the non-cooperative and imperfectly informed decisions of firms.

In the model there are two important sources of aggregate information to the agents, namely information to be inferred from the prices quoted by the firms or the general price level,[3] and (lagged) information on the real outcomes of past contracts (output). The question is whether the monetary authority can and should affect real decisions by relating the money supply to such information.

To prove the case for an active monetary policy requires not only that monetary policy is non-neutral and potentially beneficial, but also that the private sector can not overcome the information and coordination problem without any external intervention. A possible way for the private sector to do so would be by indexing prices on the same aggregate information as constitutes the basis for monetary policy. We shall compare monetary policy and private indexation as potential stabilizers of the economy to nominal shocks.

The main conclusions can briefly be summarized as follows: i) monetary policy is non-neutral and can be arranged so as to eliminate the implications of differential information, and make real output equal to full current information real output, ii) a private indexation scheme can only partially overcome the implications of differential information for the allocation of

---

[1] An alternative way to approach this problem is to assume price decisions to be asynchronized over time, cf. Blanchard (1982).

[2] For recent advances within the theory of imperfect competition and applications in macroeconomics, see Hart (1982, 1985).

[3] Price signals are thus important information signals as in competitive models, but in a qualitatively different way. With pre-set prices the price signal only reveals information on past shocks to the economy, whereas under instantaneous market clearing price signals also reveal information on current shocks to the economy.

economic resources, and hence iii) monetary policy is a potentially better stabilizer than a private indexation scheme.

In a context of non-clearing markets Fischer (1977)[4] has developed a well-known example of how a systematic monetary policy can affect real output.[5] Specifically, the setting is one where the monetary authority has the possibility of reacting to disturbances which occur after nominal wages have been fixed. By so doing the price level and hence the real-wage rate can be affected, and this makes a systematic monetary policy non-neutral. However, indexation can in this setting accomplish the same as monetary policy. The reason why monetary policy is non-neutral in the present paper is related, but qualitatively different to the one outlined above. First, the model is constructed so that the monetary authority has no leverage over the real-wage rate. Secondly, the disturbances which constitute the basis for monetary policy in the present paper do not take place after contracts (nominal prices) have been set. In a decentralized market economy the agents naturally obtain different information on the disturbances to the economy, and this affects their behaviour (price decisions). To the extent that the disturbances are correlated over time this difference in information is important. Moreover, we find that the conditions of the contracts entered into under differential information (prices and quantities) aggregate and disseminate information, and this gives the monetary authority a potential role as a stabilizer of economic activity by basing its behaviour on such information. Obviously, the role for policy hinges on information which becomes available after contractual arrangements have been made, but it is the contracts as such which provide the authority with the information to which it reacts.

Another related paper is that of Green and Honkapohja (1983), where monetary policy is studied within a traditional macro-model with sluggish price adjustment. Specifically, prices are assumed to adjust to the lagged imbalance between demand and supply, and output transacted is determined by the min-rule. The main difference to the present paper is also that here the price decisions are not decentralized.

It is worth while pointing out that the present work is closely related to recent work which has proved systematic monetary policy to be non-neutral within flex-price models with differential information (King (1982, 1983), Weiss (1980, 1982), Canzoneri, Henderson and Rogoff (1983), Andersen (1984a)). In a flexprice model the current equilibrium prices[6] reveal information on the current shocks. In a fix-price model the channels of

---

[4] For an analysis of the conditions for neutrality of monetary policy in the case of 'disequilibrium' prices, see B. McCallum (1980) and Nickerson (1985).

[5] See also Phelps and Taylor (1977). The present work is closely related to that of Phelps and Taylor (1977) in terms of motivation, but differs significantly in respect to both model structure and informational problems.

[6] Quantities transacted may also reveal valuable information, see e.g. Andersen (1985a).

information aggregation and dissemination are different, and it is the object of this paper to study these in relation to the effects on monetary policy.

The paper is organized as follows: Section 2 sets-up the model, which is a modified version of the model developed in Andersen (1985b). The effects of monetary policy and private indexation are analysed in Sections 3 and 4, respectively. Finally, Section 5 summarizes and concludes the paper.

2. The model

2.1. *Single firms*

The basic structure of the model is adopted from Andersen (1985b). Consider a continuum of firms j, $0 \leq j \leq 1$. Time, t, is discrete and $t = 0, 1, 2, \ldots,$. Each firm faces at time t a demand curve given as

$$D_t^j = (Y_t/P_t)^a (P_t/P_t^j)^b E_t^j \qquad b > 1, \quad b > a \qquad (1)$$

where Y_t is aggregate nominal income at time t, P_t is the aggregate price level at time t, P_t^j is the price set by firm j for period t, and E_t^j is a shift-variable to demand at date t. To ensure that aggregate nominal production $(P_t D_t)$ equals aggregate nominal income (Y_t) one has to impose the constraint that a equals one. Imposing this constraint will not change any results in the paper.

Each firm produces output subject to a Cobb–Douglas production technique by use of one variable input, say labour, and the cost function of producing Q_t^j units at time t for firm j is

$$C_t^j(Q_t^j) = W_t^j (Q_t^j)^\alpha, \qquad \alpha > 1 \qquad (2)$$

where W_t^j is the nominal wage rate paid for labour used by firm j at time t.

We shall assume each firm to follow what Leland (1972) has termed "P-behaviour", namely, that the firm determines its price prior to trading and adjusts supply to meet demand at the announced price, i.e.

$$D_t^j = Q_t^j \qquad \text{for all } j, t \qquad (3)$$

An inflexible price within the period can be justified by the existence of adjustment costs (Sheshinski and Weiss, 1977) or information costs (Choudhri and Ferris, 1985).

The firm has to set a price for period t before it knows its input costs, the demand shock, the nominal income and the general price level for the period. The price which firm j sets for period t is chosen so as to maximize expected real profits.
$$E[(P_t^j D_t^j - C_t^j(D_t^j))/P_t \mid I_{t-1}^j] \qquad (4)$$

where I_{t-1}^j is the information set of firm j at the end of period $t - 1$ (to be specified below).

The firm acts as a monopolist in setting its price, but adopts a Nash-behaviour with respect to the general price level, and maximizing (4) given (1), (2), and (3) we find that the nominal price quoted by firm j in logs[7] can be written as[8]

$$p_t^j = \pi_0 + \pi_1 E(w_t^j \mid I_{t-1}^j) + \pi_2 E(p_t \mid I_{t-1}^j)$$
$$+ \pi_3 E(y_t \mid I_{t-1}^j) + \pi_4 E(e_t^j \mid I_{t-1}^j) \tag{5}$$

where

$$\pi_0 = [-\ln(1-b) + \ln b\alpha + \tfrac{1}{2}a^2(\alpha^2 - 1) \, \mathrm{VAR}\,(y_t \mid I_{t-1}^j) + \tfrac{1}{2}\,\mathrm{VAR}\,(w_t^j \mid I_{t-1}^j)$$
$$+ \tfrac{1}{2}((\alpha(b-a)-1)^2 - (b-a-1)^2)\,\mathrm{VAR}\,(p_t \mid I_{t-1}^j)$$
$$+ (\alpha^2 - 1)\,\mathrm{VAR}\,(e_t^j \mid I_{t-1}^j)]\pi_1$$

$$\pi_1 = (1 + b\alpha - b)^1 > 0$$
$$\pi_2 = (1 + b\alpha - b)^{-1}((\alpha - 1)(b - a)) > 0$$
$$\pi_3 = (1 + b\alpha - b)^{-1}a(\alpha - 1) > 0$$
$$\pi_4 = (1 + b\alpha - b)^1(\alpha - 1) = a^{-1}\pi_3 > 0$$

It is easily verified that

$$\pi_1 + \pi_2 + \pi_3 = 1 \tag{6}$$

Aggregate nominal income is assumed to be given as

$$y_t = m_t + n_t \tag{7}$$

where m_t is the money supply under the control of the monetary authority in period t and n_t is an exogenous shock-variable determined as

$$n_t = \rho n_{t-1} + \varepsilon_t \qquad -1 \leqslant \rho \leqslant 1$$

and

$$\varepsilon_t \sim N(0, \sigma_\varepsilon^2)$$

(7) can be interpreted as representing the equilibrium condition of the money market[9] under the special assumption of a zero interest elasticity and a unitary income elasticity of the demand for money.[10] The serial-correlation in the shock n_t is crucial. With serial correlation the information obtained on the current shocks is relevant for the future state of the economy, and hence it is valuable as opposed to the case where there is no serial correlation. As shall be made more clear below, the differential information which the agents obtain on the shock is of importance and

---

[7] For any variable X_t, let x_t be defined as $\ln X_t$. If X_t is log-normally distributed it follows that $\ln E(X_t^a \mid I_t^j) = aE(x_t \mid I_t^j) + \tfrac{1}{2}a^2\,\mathrm{VAR}\,(x_t \mid I_t^j)$, cf. Aitchison and Brown (1957).

[8] For details see Andersen (1985b).

[9] Let the money demand be $m_t^d = r_t + p_t + u_t^d = y_t + u_t^d$, where r_t is the relevant real-income variable for the money demand and u_t^d is a (velocity) shock to money demand, and let total money supply be $m_t^s = m_t + u_t^s$ where u_t^s is a shock to the money supply outside the control of the monetary authority. We find from the equilibrium condition $m_t^s = m_t^d$ that $y_t = m_t + u_t^s - u_t^d$, which reduces to (7) for $n_t = u_t^s - u_t^d$.

[10] This assumption is not crucial.

leaves a role for an active stabilization policy only when there is serial correlation.

The shift variable to demand is determined as

$$e_t^j \sim N(0, \sigma_e^2) \qquad \text{for all } j, t$$

and we shall assume the shocks to demand to vanish upon aggregation, i.e.

$$\int e_t^j f(j) \, dj = 0$$

where $f(j)$ is the density of firms on the unit interval, and

$$\int f(j) \, dj = 1$$

We have assumed that the firms do not know their input costs when they make their price decision. To keep the model tractable we shall not try to endogonise input costs, but assume these to be exogenously determined. To stress the importance of differential information in relation to the coordination of price decisions we do not want to build into the model any nominal wage stickiness or possibility that the monetary authority can affect the real-wage, hence, the nominal cost (wage) rate is assumed to respond proportionally to the nominal variable y_t.[11] In any period firm j does only observe its own input costs assumed to be given as

$$w_t^j = y_t + u_t^j \qquad \text{for all } j, t$$

u_t^j is a local shock (real) to the wage of firm j at time t, determined as

$$u_t^j \sim N(0, \sigma_u^2) \qquad \text{for all } j, t$$

It is assumed that these shocks vanish upon aggregation,[12] i.e.

$$\int u_t^j f(j) \, dj = 0$$

We shall assume that

$$E e_t^j u_t^j = E e_t^j \varepsilon_t = E u_t^j \varepsilon_t = 0 \qquad \text{for all } j, t.$$

To summarize we have two types of shock variables, (i) local or firm specific shocks to costs and demand (u_t^j and e_t^j) which vanish upon aggregation, and (ii) an aggregate nominal shock variable (n_t).

---

[11] It might be argued that it would be more natural to assume the real wage rate to be given as u_t^j, i.e. the nominal wage is indexed proportionally to the price level, $w_t^j = p_t + u_t^j$. It can easily be verified that nothing qualitatively will be changed by this modification, cf. Andersen (1984b).

[12] The model can easily be generalized to allow for aggregate shocks to demand and costs, cf. Andersen (1985c).

2.2. *Information*

The time structure of the model can be outlined as follows. At the end of period $t - 1$ all firms make a price announcement for period t conditional on their information I_{t-1}^j, and these prices become known to all agents initially in period t. The information contained in the vector of announced prices $\{(p_t^j)_{j=0}^1\}$ can usefully be summarized in the mean price level p_t.[13] In period t the j'th firm also observes its costs, w_t^j, and at the end of the period its sales, q_t^j. Furthermore, we shall assume information on mean output to be collected and made publicly known. However, since each firm only knows its own output at the end of the period and the collection and processing of such information takes time, the period $t - 1$ mean output will not be known until period t, i.e. q_{t-1} becomes public knowledge in period t.[14] Let S_t^j denote the set of signals observable to the j'th firm in period t, we have that

$$S_t^j = \{p_t, q_{t-1}, w_t^j, q_t^j\} \tag{8}$$

It is seen that each firm in every period receives public information through a price signal p_t and a quantity signal q_{t-1},[15] and private information through a price signal w_t^j and a quantity signal q_t^j.

The information set of firm j at the end of period t is thus given as

$$I_t^j = \{(S_{t-1}^j)_{i=0}^\infty, n_{-\infty}, m_{-\infty}\} \tag{9}$$

In (9) we have introduced the additional assumption that each agent knows the starting point of the processes determining n_t and m_t.[16]

It should be pointed out that the market structure precludes contingent trading, since a complete set of markets eliminates differences in information and hence coordination problems from the model. The non-existence of a complete set of markets can be justified by either transactions- or information costs.

2.3. *The monetary feedback rule*

The money supply m_t is assumed to be determined by a feedback rule which relates the money supply to information possessed by the monetary authority. We shall assume that the monetary authority is no better informed with respect to any variable than the public, i.e. if S_t^p denotes the set of signals observable to the policy maker in period t we assume that

$$S_t^p \subset S_t^j \qquad \text{for all } j \text{ and } t$$

---

[13] In fact p_t is a sufficient statistic for the information contained in the price vector about n_t.

[14] Notice, that we are not assuming price information to become more quickly available than quantity information, since p_t^j and q_{t-1}^j both are known to the j'th firm at the end of period $t - 1$, but p_t and q_{t-1} are not until the start of period t.

[15] Nothing qualitatively would be changed if w_t becomes public knowledge with a one period lag, since w_t is informationally equivalent to q_t.

[16] This is a technical assumption which is not really needed, but serves the purpose of simplifying and exposition.

Specifically, we shall assume that the monetary authority only observes the public price signal p_t and quantity signal q_{t-1} in period t, i.e.

$$S_t^p = \{p_t, q_{t-1}\} \tag{10}$$

and the information set of the policy-maker in period t is

$$I_t^p = \{(S_{t-1}^p)_{i=0}^\infty, n_{-\infty}, m_{-\infty}\}$$

Again we assume the starting point of the processes n_t and m_t to be known.

Given this information set we shall assume the feedback rule for the money supply to be

$$m_t = g_1 m_{t-1} + g_2 p_t + g_2 q_{t-1} \tag{11}$$

That is, the money supply for period t depends on the two currently observable signals p_t and q_{t-1} and the past history of the economy through the lagged money supply.

It should be pointed out that the role for monetary policy to be found in the present paper does not depend on the monetary authority having access to information which is not publicly known. The role for monetary policy arises here from the possibility of adjusting the money supply to public signals which aggregate decentralized information, viz. the price announcements made for the period (p_t) and information on quantities transacted (q_{t-1}).

Finally, it should be remarked that whether m_t is publicly known/ announced or not any agent j can deduce m_t from (11) and its information set I_{t-1}^j, cf. below. There are no unanticipated changes in the money supply.

2.4. Solution of the model

To solve the model is a bit tricky since the price quoted by each firm depends on its expectations of the aggregate price level (p_t) and the nominal shock variable (y_t), which in turn depends on the price level and the past output level.[17] A fairly easy way to solve the model is to conjecture the price level and the output level to depend on the state variables as follows

$$p_t = \delta_0 + \delta_1 m_{t-1} + \delta_2 n_{t-2} + \delta_3 \varepsilon_{t-1} + \delta_4 p_{t-1} \tag{12}$$

and

$$q_{t-1} = \psi_0 + \psi_1 m_{t-1} + \psi_2 n_{t-2} + \psi_3 \varepsilon_{t-1} + \psi_4 p_{t-1} \tag{13}$$

Given (12) and (13) we can make a more precise statement on the information set of firm j at date t. Since $(p_{t-i}, q_{t-1-i})_{i=0}^\infty$ and $m_{-\infty}$ are known to firm j in period t it follows that m_t is also known in the period t. From knowledge of $(p_{t-i})_{i=0}^\infty$ and $n_{-\infty}$ it follows from (12) that ε_{t-1} is known if $\delta_3 \neq 0$, or from knowledge of $(q_{t-1-i})_{i=0}^\infty$ and $n_{-\infty}$ that ε_{t-1} is known if

---

[17] This interdependence is what constrains us to choose a log-linear model with log-normally distributed variables, since a specific solution is difficult to obtain otherwise.

$\psi_3 \neq 0$. Hence, knowledge of $p_t(\delta_3 \neq 0)$ and/or $q_{t-1}(\psi_3 \neq 0)$ implies that n_{t-2} and ε_{t-1} are known at the end of period t.[18] It follows that the following statement on the information set of firm j at the end of period t can be made:

$$\bar{I}_t \subset I_t^j \qquad \text{for all } j \text{ and } t$$

and

$$\bar{I}_t \subset I_t^p \qquad \text{for all } t$$

where

$$\bar{I}_t = \{m_t, n_{t-2}, \varepsilon_{t-1}\}$$

Consequently, all agents are at the end of period t fully informed on the state of the economy in period $t-1$ and backwards. Informational problems arise because the agents are not fully informed about the state of the economy in period t (ε_t), and this has consequences for future periods due to the serial-correlation in the shock-variable ($n_{t+1} = \rho(\rho n_{t-1} + \varepsilon_t) + \varepsilon_{t+1}$). Before we elaborate on this, let us start by clarifying the information available to agent j at the end of period t on the state of the economy in period t (ε_t). Given the structure of the model ((8), (12) and (13)) it is immediately apparent that only the local wage and the local quantity sold in period t reveals information on ε_t to firm j.

Specifically, we find that q_t^j can be written as

$$\begin{aligned} q_t^j &= a(y_t - p_t) + b(p_t - p_t^j) + e_t^j \\ &= a(g_1 m_{t-1} + g_2 p_t + g_3 q_{t-1} + \rho n_{t-1} + \varepsilon_t - p_t) \\ &\quad + b(p_t - p_t^j) + e_t^j \end{aligned} \tag{14}$$

Given the information set (8) it follows that observation of q_t^j adds information on q_t^j equal to $a\varepsilon_t + e_t^j$ to what is already known from the other signals in the information set I_t^j. Similarly, we find that the observation of w_t^j adds information on $w_t^j = \varepsilon_t + u_t^j$ since

$$\begin{aligned} w_t^j &= y_t + u_t^j \\ &= g_1 m_{t-1} + g_2 p_t + g_3 q_{t-1} + \rho n_{t-2} + \varepsilon_t + u_t^j \end{aligned} \tag{15}$$

Hence, each agent knows at the end of period t the past history of the state of the economy up to and including period $t-1$, and has information on the period t innovation in the nominal shock from knowledge of $a\varepsilon_t + e_t^j$ and $\varepsilon_t + u_t^j$. As shown in the appendix we have that $E(\varepsilon_t \mid q_t^j, w_t^j) = h_1 q_t^j + h_2 w_t^j = H\varepsilon_t + h_1 e_t^j + h_2 u_t^j$, where $H = ah_1 + h_2$.

It is seen that the local or firm specific shocks (e_t^j, u_t^j) to demand and costs imply that the agents are imperfectly and differently informed of the state of the economy ($\sigma_e^2 \neq 0$, $\sigma_u^2 \neq 0$). The importance of this arises because the shocks are correlated ($n_{t+1} = \rho(\rho n_{t-1} + \varepsilon_t) + \varepsilon_{t+1}$) and firms have to make a

---

[18] Hence, n_{t-1} is known since $n_{t-1} = \rho n_{t-2} + \varepsilon_{t-1}$.

price announcement for period $t + 1$ given the information available at the end of period t.

It is worthwhile to stress that the relevant information is available in the market as a whole, but due to the decentralized character of the economy it is not directly pooled. However, the decisions made by the agents embody their information, and in this way it becomes pooled and potentially available for policy makers. In Section 3 we shall explicitly analyse the role of monetary policy within this setting.

We can now proceed to find a solution to the model, and after some tedious manipulations it can be shown (see Appendix) that the coefficients to equation (13) are given as $(g_2 \neq 1)$

$$\delta_0 = \frac{\pi_0}{(\pi_1 + \pi_3)(1 - g_2)}$$

$$\delta_1 = \frac{g_1 + ag_3}{1 - g_2}; \qquad \delta_2 = \frac{\rho^2 + ag_3\rho}{1 - g_2}$$

$$\delta_3 = H(\pi_1 + \pi_2)(\rho + ag_3)K^{-1}; \qquad \delta_4 = \frac{-ag_3}{1 - g_2} \qquad (16)$$

where

$$K = 1 - H\{(\pi_1 + \pi_3)g_2 + \pi_2\}$$

Similarly, we find the coefficients to equation (14) to be

$$\Psi_0 = 0$$

$$\Psi_1 = \Psi_3 = -\Psi_4 = a$$

$$\Psi_2 = a\rho \qquad (17)$$

The question of whether a systematic monetary policy has any role to play as a potential stabilizer which can overcome the coordination problems arising from differential information can now be analysed.

2.5. *Full current information*

As stressed above the coordination problem arises because the agents at the end of period t are not perfectly informed on the current state of the economy. As a point of reference for the analysis of the implications of differential information it is useful to consider the solution of the model under full current information, i.e. all agents know ε_t at the end of period t ($\varepsilon_t \in I_t^{j*} \forall j, t$). In this case there is no information confusion and all agents hold the same information (homogeneous information), and we find the price level to be

$$p_{t+1}^* = \delta_0^* + m_{t+1} + \rho n_t \qquad (18)$$

It is seen that the full current information price level is homogeneous of degree one in the (homogeneously) expected nominal change $(m_{t+1} + \rho n_t)$.

Hence, anticipated nominal shocks do not affect real output (systematic monetary policy is neutral) and we find

$$q_{t+1}^* = a(y_{t+1} - p_{t+1}^*)$$
$$= a(-\delta_0^* + \varepsilon_{t+1}) \tag{19}$$

Notice, that ε_{t+1} affect the period $t+1$ output since it is an unanticipated nominal change.

In comparing the allocation under full current information and differential information, it is immediately clear that they coincide if (i) there is no serial correlation in the nominal shock ($\rho = 0$) or (ii) there is no local shock to either wages or demand ($\sigma_u^2 = 0$ and/or $\sigma_e^2 = 0$). Except in these special cases differential information has real consequences and we shall analyse the role of monetary policy as a stabilizer of economic activity.

3. Monetary policy

We shall in this section consider the optimal monetary policy, i.e. the choice of the parameters in the feedback rule (11). In (11) assumptions concerning the information available to the monetary authorities have already been built in, that is, the monetary authority can react to the mean of the prices quoted by the firms and the past output level which become publicly known after period t prices have been announced.

Encountering non-neutralities raises the difficult problem of the appropriate objective for monetary policy. The criterion is here stated in terms of the gap between the actual and full information mean output, as has become standard in this branch of literature. In doing this we are implicitly assuming more information to be preferable to less information, although the welfare implications of an improvement in information are not in general unambiguous, since an improvement in information can reduce (ex–ante) welfare by eliminating possibilities of risk-sharing (Arrow, 1978). In the present context of risk-neutral firms and absence of contingent markets it can be argued that an improvement in information increases welfare, since it permits an adoption of production to the state of the economy. Specifically, the objective of the monetary authority is to minimize

$$E\{(q_t - q_t^*)^2\} = E(q_t - q_t^*)^2 + \text{VAR}\,(q_t - q_t^*) \qquad \text{for any } t \tag{20}$$

where q_t^* is the full current information output defined in Section 2.5.

The mean output under differential information can from (1) by use of (7), (11) and (12) be written as

$$q_t = a\left[\frac{-\pi_0}{\pi_1 + \pi_3} + \phi\varepsilon_{t-1} + \varepsilon_t\right] \tag{21}$$

where

$$\phi = (g_2 - 1)\delta_3 + g_3\psi_3 + \rho$$

In deriving (21) use has been made of the following relationships

$$(g_2 - 1)\delta_0 = -\pi_0/(\pi_1 + \pi_3)$$

$$(g_2 - 1)\delta_4 + g_3\psi_4 = 0$$

$$g_1 + (g_2 - 1)\delta_1 + g_3\psi_1 = 0$$

$$(g_2 - 1)\delta_3 + g_3\psi_3 + \rho^2 = 0$$

Equation (21) reveals that the choice of g_1 is irrelevant to the probability distribution of mean output, since neither $(\pi_0/\pi_1 + \pi_3)$ nor ϕ depend on g_1. This should come as no surprise since g_1 is the coefficient to the past money supply in the feedback rule for the money supply, cf. (11), and the past money supply is known to all agents, i.e. m_{t-1} belongs to I_{t-1}^j for all j, t. The $g_1 m_{t-1}$ part of the current money supply is therefore homogeneously perceived and affects the price level proportionally without any effects on the mean output, [cf. proposition 2.i. in Andersen (1985b)]. However both g_2 and g_3 are relevant to the probability distribution of output, and this follows from the fact that the monetary reaction to both the price level and the past output level is heterogeneously perceived by the firms when they set prices, [cf. proposition 2.ii in Andersen (1985b)]. We shall consider the choice of g_2 and g_3 which minimize the monetary objective function (20).

Let us consider the two terms in (20) separately, and let us start by analysing the variance of mean-output around the full current information mean output.

$$\text{VAR} (q_t - q_t^*) = a^2\phi^2\sigma_\varepsilon^2 \tag{22}$$

Minimization of (22) seems to be accomplished by either a choice of g_2 or g_3, that is, we have two independent instruments and a choice of either of these should exist such that (22) becomes equal to zero. For g_3 equal to zero we find that[19]

$$\phi = (g_2 - 1)H(\pi_1 + \pi_3)K^{-1} + \rho$$

$$= -\rho(1 + \pi)K^{-1} \tag{23}$$

(23) shows that no choice of g_2 exists for g_3 equal to zero which makes Φ and hence (22) equal to zero, but by making the numerical value of g_2 arbitrary large Φ can be made arbitrary close to zero.

The non-neutrality of money arises here because the monetary authority, when it learns p_t, can change the money supply so as to counteract the effect of the heterogenously perceived nominal shock (ε_{t-1}). This requires that ε_{t-1} can be inferred from p_t given the information available to the monetary authority. We find that for g_2 going to infinity δ_3 goes to zero, but p_t reveals ε_{t-1} only if $\delta_3 \neq 0$. Hence, in the limit the informational basis for the policy disappears because if the monetary policy completely eliminates the effect

---

[19] This is a policy which is only based on the conditions of currently made price decisions (contracts).

of ε_{t-1} on the price, then p_t would obviously no longer depend on ε_{t-1}, contradicting that the monetary authority can infer ε_{t-1} from p_t. In this way an optimal policy based only on the aggregate price signal eliminates the informational assumption on which it relies, and this explains why a choice of g_2 only approximately can make (22) equal to zero.[20]

Let us consider the choice of g_3. We have that

$$\phi = (g_2 - 1)H(\pi_1 + \pi_3)(\rho + ag_3)K^{-1} + ag_3 + \rho \tag{24}$$

It is easily seen from (24) that by setting g_3 equal to $-\rho/a$, ϕ becomes equal to zero no matter the choice of g_2 $(g_2 \neq 1)$.[21]

The policy based on the past output level does not encounter the same problem as the policy based on the price level, because the past output level always depends on ε_{t-1} irrespective of the choice of g_3 $(\psi_3 = a \neq 0)$. Hence, the optimal policy does not in this case eliminate the informational assumption on which it is based.

The optimal choice of g_3 implies that δ_3 and δ_2 becomes equal to zero, and therefore

$$p_t = \delta_0 + \delta_1 m_{t-1} + \delta_4 p_{t-1}$$

The optimal policy eliminates in this way two implications of differential information, namely, i) heterogenous expectations about the period t price level, since $E(p_t \mid I^j_{t-1}) = p_t$ for all j and t, and ii) uncertainty about the period t price level, since $\text{VAR}(p_t \mid I^j_{t-1}) = 0$ for all j and t.

For the nominal variable y_t we find

$$
\begin{aligned}
y_t &= g_1 m_{t-1} + g_2 p_t + g_3 q_{t-1} + \rho^2 n_{t-2} + \rho \varepsilon_{t-1} + \varepsilon_t \\
&= (g_2 \delta_0 + g_3 \psi_0) + (g_1 + g_2 \delta_1 + g_3 \psi_1) m_{t-1} \\
&\quad + (\rho^2 + g_2 \delta_2 + g_3 \psi_2) n_{t-2} + (\rho + g_2 \delta_3 + g_3 \psi_3) \varepsilon_{t-1} \\
&\quad + (g_2 \delta_4 + g_3 \psi_4) p_{t-1} + \varepsilon_t
\end{aligned}
$$

Under the optimal policy $\rho + g_2 \delta_3 + g_3 \psi_3 = 0$, and the heterogenously perceived change ε_{t-1} has no influence on period t conditions. All agents will therefore hold the same expectations on y_t, and the only source of uncertainty about y_t is the unanticipated shock ε_t which is known to nobody at time $t - 1$, i.e.

$$\text{VAR}(y_t \mid I^j_{t-1}) = \sigma^2_\varepsilon \quad \text{for all } j \text{ and } t$$

Turning to the first term of (18) we have for $g_3 = -\rho/a$ that

$$q_t - q_t^* = a\left(-\frac{\pi_0}{\pi_1 + \pi_3} + \frac{\pi_0^*}{\pi_1 + \pi_3}\right)$$

---

[20] A similar result was remarked in the context of a flex-price model under differential information by Weiss (1982, p. 37).

[21] Notice, that this choice of g_3 makes the choice of g_2 $(g_2 \neq 1)$ irrelevant to the probability distribution of output.

Since $\text{VAR}(p_t \mid I^*_{t-1}) = 0$, $\text{VAR}(y_t \mid I^*_{t-1}) = \sigma^2_\varepsilon$ and $\text{VAR}(w^j_t \mid I^*_{t-1}) = \sigma^2_\varepsilon + \sigma^2_u$ we find that $\pi^*_0 = \pi_0$, and hence $q_t = q^*_t$ w.p. 1.

Finally, notice that the optimal monetary policy rule has a very intuitive interpretation. If the nominal shocks are positively correlated over time $(\rho > 0)$ we find that g_3 becomes negative, hence the optimal policy rule simply says that the money supply should be adjusted counter cyclically, i.e. when output increases the money supply should be decreased and vice versa, cf. (11). It can be concluded that there exists an optimal monetary feedback rule $(g_3 = -\rho/a,\ g_2 \neq 1)$ which implies that all implications of differential information are eliminated, and an allocation as under full current information is obtained.

This result can be interpreted as follows. In any period t there is an unanticipated shock (ε_t) which firms receive differential information about due to the local shocks to cost and demand (v^j_t and e^j_t). This lack of information is of importance to real decisions since the nominal shock variable is correlated over time and firms have to determine a price for the next period given their information on the state of the economy. Monetary policy works because the money supply for period $t + 1$ can be adjusted in a way such that ε_t becomes immaterial to all future periods. That is, by changing the money supply such that ε_t only has an effect in period t (this effect cannot be eliminated since it is due to an unanticipated change), but no effect in period $t + 1$, it does not matter whether agents are perfectly or differently informed about ε_t at the end of period t. It is crucial that this argument does not rely on a presumption that the monetary authority is better informed than the private agents, in fact is has been assumed that it is no better informed than the least informed private agent. The rule for an active policy arises because the monetary authority as a central external agent can react to the decentralized information on the state of the economy as it becomes embodied in price and output statistics: that is, coordination in a decentralized market system with decentralized price decisions and information can be improved by an appropriately formulated monetary policy.

4. Indexation

In the preceding section we have seen how monetary policy can be conducted so as to eliminate the implications of differential information about nominal shocks for the allocation of economic resources. This does not, however, necessarily prove the case for an active stabilization policy since the private sector has a possibility of counteracting the effects of differential information by adopting an indexation scheme. The purpose of this section is to analyse the effects of indexation on nominal prices, and to compare this with monetary policy. For the purpose of this section we shall disregard monetary policy, i.e. $g_1 = g_2 = g_3 = 0$, and hence nominal income y_t is equal to the exogenous shock variable n_t.

We shall assume the indexation of nominal prices to operate on the same information set as that which formed the basis for monetary policy, viz. the current price level and the past output level.[22] Denote the indexed price of firm j for period t, $\hat{p}_t^j$, where

$$\hat{p}_t^j = p_t^j + \lambda_1 p_t + \lambda_2 q_{t-1} \tag{25}$$

(25) says that the originally announced price by firm j for period t is changed according to the current mean price level with the coefficient λ_1 and to the past output level with the coefficient λ_2.

The mean price level is ex-post to indexation given as

$$\hat{p}_t = (1 + \lambda_1)p_t + \lambda_2 q_{t-1} \tag{26}$$

The optimal policy for firm j is to set a price for period t so as to maximize

$$E[(\hat{P}_t^j D_t^j - C_t^j(D_t^j))/\hat{P}_t \mid I_{t-1}^j]$$

where demand now depends on the ex-post indexation prices.

The optimal price must be chosen such that[23]

$$E(\hat{p}_t^j \mid I_{t-1}^j) = \hat{\pi}_0 + \pi_1 E(w_t^j \mid I_{t-1}^j) + \pi_2 E(p_t \mid I_{t-1}^j)$$
$$+ \pi_3 E(y_t \mid I_{t-1}^j) + \pi_4 E(e_t^j \mid I_{t-1}^j) \tag{27}$$

where

$$E(\hat{p}_t^j \mid I_{t-1}^j) = p_t^j + \lambda_1 E(p_t \mid I_{t-1}^j) + \lambda_2 E(q_{t-1} \mid I_{t-1}^j)$$

The price set by firm j for period t is found to be

$$p_t^j = \hat{\pi}_0 + \pi_1 E(w_t^j \mid I_{t-1}^j) + \pi_3 E(y_t \mid I_{t-1}^j)$$
$$+ (\pi_2(1 + \lambda_1) - \lambda_1)E(p_t \mid I_{t-1}^j)$$
$$+ \lambda_2(\pi_2 - 1)E(q_{t-1} \mid I_{t-1}^j) + \pi_4 E(e_t^j \mid I_{t-1}^j) \tag{28}$$

To solve the model we proceed as in section 2 by conjecturing a price and output function.[24]

$$p_t = \hat{\delta}_0 + \hat{\delta}_2 n_{t-2} + \hat{\delta}_3 \varepsilon_{t-1} + \hat{\delta}_4 p_{t-1} \tag{29}$$

and

$$q_{t-1} = \hat{\psi}_0 + \hat{\psi}_2 n_{t-2} + \hat{\psi}_3 \varepsilon_{t-1} + \hat{\psi}_4 \hat{p}_{t-1} \tag{30}$$

The solution (see appendix) yields the following coefficients to the price

---

[22] We are analysing the general form of indexation to see how this compares with monetary policy, without any concern whether this is a type of indexing typically experienced. The result of this exercise may provide a partial explanation of why indexation formulas like (25) are rarely encountered in reality. See Fischer (1983) for a theoretical and empirical analysis of the extent to which indexation is inflationary.

[23] The π-coefficients are except for π_0 independent of the information structure.

[24] Obviously m_{t-1} can be left out since we are assuming a passive monetary policy, i.e. m_t is constant and equal to zero for all t.

equation (29)

$$\hat{\delta}_0 = \frac{\hat{\pi}_0}{(\pi_1 + \pi_3)(1 + \lambda_1)}$$

$$\hat{\delta}_2 = \rho(\pi_1 + \pi_3)(\rho - a\lambda_2)L^{-1}$$

$$\hat{\delta}_3 = H(\pi_1 + \pi_3)(\rho - a\lambda_2)L^{-1} \qquad (31)$$

$$\hat{\delta}_4 = \frac{-\lambda_2 a}{\lambda_1 - 1}$$

where

$$L = 1 - H\{\pi_2 - \lambda_1(\pi_1 + \pi_3)\}$$

The coefficients to the output equation (30) turns out to be the same under indexation as under monetary policy, i.e.

$$\hat{\Psi}_i = \Psi_i \qquad i = 0, 2, 3, 4 \qquad (32)$$

The mean output under indexation is found to be

$$\hat{q}_t = a\left[\frac{-\hat{\pi}_0}{\pi_1 + \pi_3} + \hat{\phi}\varepsilon_{t-1} + \varepsilon_t\right]$$

where

$$\hat{\phi} = \rho - (1 + \lambda_1)\hat{\delta}_3 - \lambda_2\hat{\psi}_2$$

Use have been made of the following relationships

$$-(1 + \lambda_1)\hat{\delta}_0 = \hat{\pi}_0/(\pi_1 + \pi_3)$$

$$\rho^2 - (1 + \lambda_1)\hat{\delta}_2 - \lambda_2\hat{\psi}_2 = 0$$

$$(1 + \lambda_1)\hat{\delta}_4 + \lambda_2\hat{\psi}_4 = 0$$

We shall evaluate indexation by the same criterion as in the case of monetary policy, that is, we shall look for a choice of λ_1 and λ_2 which minimizes

$$E\{(\hat{q} - q_t^*)^2\} = E(\hat{q}_t - q_t^*)^2 + \text{VAR}\,(q_t - q_t^*) \qquad (33)$$

where

$$\hat{q}_t - q_t^* = a\left\{\frac{\pi_0^* - \hat{\pi}_0}{\pi_1 + \pi_3} + \hat{\phi}\varepsilon_{t-1}\right\} \qquad (34)$$

From (34) we find

$$E(\hat{q}_t - q_t^*) = a\frac{\pi_0^* - \hat{\pi}_0}{\pi_1 + \pi_3} \qquad (35)$$

and

$$\text{VAR}\,(\hat{q}_t - q_t^*) = a^2\hat{\phi}^2\sigma_\varepsilon^2 \qquad (36)$$

Let us start by considering the minimization of (36). Using (31) we find that

$$\phi = \rho - (1 + \lambda_1)H(\pi_1 + \pi_3)(\rho - \lambda_2 a)L^{-1} - a\lambda_2 \qquad (37)$$

It follows from (37) that the same can be said about the choice of λ_1 and λ_2 as was said about the choice of g_2 and g_3 in the case of monetary policy. Hence, no choice of λ_1 exists for $\lambda_2 = 0$ which makes $\hat{\phi}$ equal to zero. The reason is the same as in the case of g_2, namely that if λ_1 goes to infinity $\mathring{\delta}_3$ goes to zero and the informational basis for indexation disappears. However, a choice of λ_2 exists for any λ_1 that makes $\hat{\phi}$ equal to zero, viz. $\lambda_2 = \rho/a$, and (36) becomes equal to zero.

However, the analogy between a private indexation scheme and monetary policy ends here. To see this, we notice that nominal income is given as

$$y_t = \rho^2 n_{t-2} + \rho\varepsilon_{t-1} + \varepsilon_t \qquad (38)$$

The period t nominal income is thus homogeneous of degree one in the part of the period $t-1$ innovation in the nominal shock variable relevant for period t ($\rho\varepsilon_{t-1}$). So is the ex-post indexation general price level given the indexation parameters which minimize (36).

$$\hat{p}_t = (1 + \lambda_1)p_t + \lambda_2 q_{t-1}$$
$$= (1 + \lambda_1)\mathring{\delta}_0 + \rho^2 n_{t-2} + \rho\varepsilon_{t-1}$$

Hence, the adjustment in period t to the misperceived period $t-1$ shock seems to be accomplished by this indexation scheme[25] since it implies that neither relative prices nor real incomes change since

$$\hat{p}_t^j - \hat{p}_t = p_t^j + \lambda_1 p_t + \lambda_2 q_{t-1} - (1 + \lambda_1)p_t - \lambda_2 q_{t-1}$$
$$= p_t^j - p_t$$

and

$$y_t - \hat{p}_t = -\frac{\hat{\pi}_0}{1 - \pi_2} + \varepsilon_t$$

Given that neither relative prices nor real income comes to depend on the misperceived state variable ε_{t-1} how can it be that indexation can not replicate the full information allocation? This is caused by the fact that although indexation can ensure an optimal ex-post adjustment with respect to the misperceived state variable it leaves ex-ante uncertainty with respect to the actual adjustment, which is reflected in the fact that

$$\text{VAR}\,(\hat{p}_t \mid I_{t-1}^j) = \rho^2\sigma_\varepsilon^2 > 0 = \text{VAR}\,(p_t \mid I_{t-1}^*) \qquad (39)$$

$$\text{VAR}\,(y_t \mid I_{t-1}^j) = \rho^2\sigma_\varepsilon^2 + \sigma_\varepsilon^2 > \sigma_\varepsilon^2 = \text{VAR}\,(y_t \mid I_{t-1}^*) \qquad (40)$$

---

[25] It can easily be verified that the firm-specific prices are homogeneous of degree one in $\rho\varepsilon_{t-1}$ ex-post to indexation.

Compared to the full information case the optimal indexation leaves more uncertainty, and this is of importance because firms have to pre-set prices. We find thus that

$$E(\hat{q}_t - q_t^*) = a\frac{\pi_0^* - \hat{\pi}_0}{\pi_1 + \pi_3} < 0,$$

since the π_0 coefficient (cf. (5)) is increasing in the variances of the nominal variables. Hence, the choice of indexation parameters which minimizes the variability of output causes an output loss.

Looking more closely at the reason for this result we find from (34) that indexation can make the output depend on the state variable ε_{t-1} as under full information, but only at the cost of increased uncertainty as shown by (39) and (40). Still, the result may seem paradoxical since the ex-post indexation prices are homogeneous of degree one in the misperceived nominal state variable $\rho\varepsilon_{t-1}$. The explanation is to be found in (5) which shows that the nominal price quoted by firm j (p_t^j) is homogeneous of degree one in the expected nominal variables, cf. (6), but not homogeneous of degree zero in the variances of the nominal variables (see the expression for π_0). The reason why indexation is unable to eliminate all implications of differential information is thus that indexation can ensure an optimal adjustment of the mean of the nominal variables, so that nominal variables are adjusted proportionally to the nominal change, but this operation is not variance-preserving.

In Section 3 we found that monetary policy can attain the full information allocation, but why this difference between monetary policy and a private indexation scheme? The reason that the latter can never completely eliminate the importance of the heterogeneously perceived change ε_{t-1} for period t market conditions, is that it can only adjust prices to take account of information on ε_{t-1} when it becomes available. It follows from the set-up of the model that this information is uncertain to the agents at the time when they set prices, and hence an allocation different from the full current information allocation results. Monetary policy operating on exactly the same information set as the private indexation scheme can do better, because it completely eliminates the importance of the heterogeneously perceived change ε_{t-1} for period t market conditions. The optimal monetary policy implies that the agents need not worry about ε_{t-1} since under the optimal monetary policy the money supply is adjusted so as to make the ε_{t-1} shock which is heterogeneously perceived irrelevant for period t conditions.

It might be argued that the difference between $\hat{\pi}_0$ and π_0^*, cf. (48) is of second order of magnitude, and not a sufficient reason to regard monetary policy as a generally better hedge against nominal shocks than a private indexation scheme. This argument neglects, however, that there is a significant difference between the two mechanisms because they imply qualitatively different forms of uncertainty. Under an optimal monetary policy all implications of differential information are eliminated and the only uncertainty (exogenous) is with respect to the exogenous nominal shocks about which all agents are equally imperfectly informed. This (exogenous) uncertainty is also found under an optimal indexation scheme, but in addition there is (endogenous) uncertainty because agents possess different information, and agents are uncertain about the information possessed by other agents, and hence the actions taken by other agents. The difference between the two mechanisms is thus more important than the present analysis necessarily makes clear, because we have assumed risk-neutrality, and therefore not allowed the difference in risk between the two systems to play its full force. We can conclude that a private indexation scheme is not able to replicate the effects of a systematic monetary policy. The adjustment to nominal shocks is not a trivial matter which could be overcome by the private sector, but requires the cooperative effort between the private and the public sector.

5. Conclusion

Within a setting of imperfect competition and differential information it has been shown that monetary policy has a role as a stabilizer of economic activity. The assumption of imperfect competition was introduced to allow a rigorous determination of prices, but the coordination problems were solely due to the differential information about the state of the economy.

Harris and Holmstrøm (1983) argue that monetary policy has a nontrivial role in a contractual world to the extent that it conveys information which it would otherwise be more costly for private agents to obtain. Information dissemination by policy actions is thus a substitute for private information acquisition, and this creates room for beneficial monetary policy. This argument is related to results obtained by Weiss (1980, 1982), and King (1982, 1983) in competitive flex-price models with differential information where it is shown that a systematic monetary policy can affect real allocations by improving the information content of prices. The role for an active monetary policy found in this paper is of a qualitatively different nature, since it does not work by improving the information set of the private agents, but by eliminating the implications of differential information for the allocation of economic resources. The result of this paper is thus closely related to the role for an active stabilization policy found in Andersen (1984a) within a competitive flex-price model with differential information.

The assumptions underlying the model of this paper have purposely been chosen so as not 'a priori' to bias the results away from monetarist or classical conclusions and we have only considered purely nominal shocks. This serves the purpose of showing how easily non-classical results can be obtained in models with a classic flavour by simply introducing differential information. The results of this paper have, however, a wider interest since it turns out that the approach generalizes to the more general and interesting case of aggregate real shocks to cost and demand, cf. Andersen (1985c).

Having found a case for an active stabilization policy raises a number of questions concerning the feasibility of implementing such policies. In this respect it is worth pointing out that strong assumptions have been made about the information available to the policy makers (e.g., on the stochastic properties of the model), although the information available to the policy maker is inferior to that possessed by the private agents. Hence, it could be questioned to what extent policy makers in practice have the necessary information to pursue a successful stabilization policy. Moreover it should be pointed out that the cooperative view taken on policy in this paper by-passes the important question of whether policy-makers can credibly commit themselves to policy-rules like those analysed in this paper.[26]

We have compared indexation to monetary policy and found that monetary policy is a potentially better stabilizer than a private indexation scheme. This conclusion holds even though we have considered an ideal indexation scheme which does not take account of the fact that indexation in practice is often incomplete due to the fact that i) indexing is only partial to nominal shocks, ii) indexing is lagged, iii) not all prices are indexed, or iv) indexing is costly.[27]

In comparing private and external intervention it is important to keep in mind that an (implicit) premise of this analysis has been that coordination failures or business cycle fluctuations can only arise under an incomplete market structure. Consequently the private sector has been constrained from the outset not to adopt the first-best response of opening contingent markets, and hence the comparison is biased in favour of external intervention, since policy is compared to indexation which is the second-best response of the private sector.

For analytical convenience use have been made of specific functional forms of the demand and the cost functions. However, the qualitative results of the paper relies more on the differential information structure than the specific functional form of the model. More troublesome is the assumption that demand determines quantities traded given the prices set by firms. This is in a sense a very Keynesian assumption since it implies that effective demand determines output, but the empirical importance of such arrangements remains an open question. This is so because it implies that firms continue to supply at the announced price even if marginal costs exceed the price. It could, of course, be argued that firms have an incentive to act in this way to make their price announcements credible, i.e. to gain reputation that prices announced are reliable signals for consumers' decisions by ensuring that consumers can actually buy at the quoted prices. However, the assumption implies a considerable analytical simplification,

[26] See e.g., Honkapohja (1985) for a survey of some recent game-theoretic approaches to this question.
[27] J. McCallum, (1983).

and it seems difficult to do without it due to the problems of handling the non-linearities which arise under other assumptions, cf. Taylor (1985).

Aarhus University

APPENDIX

A. *Solution of the model under monetary policy*

The information set of agent j at time $t-1$ gives the agent knowledge of m_{t-1}, n_{t-3} and ε_{t-2}, hence we find from (13) and (14) that

$$E(p_t \mid I_{t-1}^j) = \delta_0 + \delta_1 m_{t-1} + \delta_2 n_{t-2}$$
$$+ \delta_3 E(\varepsilon_{t-1} \mid I_{t-1}^j) + \delta_4 p_{t-1} \tag{A-1}$$

and

$$E(q_{t-1} \mid I_{t-1}^j) = \Psi_0 + \Psi_1 m_{t-1} + \Psi_2 n_{t-2}$$
$$+ \Psi_3 E(\varepsilon_{t-1} \mid I_{t-1}^j) + \Psi_4 p_{t-1} \tag{A-2}$$

To find $E(\varepsilon_{t-1} \mid I_{t-1}^j)$ we notice that w_{t-1}^j and q_{t-1}^j are informationally equivalent to $w_t^j = \varepsilon_{t-1} + u_{t-1}^j$ and $q_{t-1}^j = a\varepsilon_{t-1} + e_{t-1}^j$. Using that $(\varepsilon_{t-1}, a\varepsilon_{t-1} + e_{t-1}^j, \varepsilon_{t-1} + u_{t-1}^j)$ is jointly normally distributed we have that (Graybill, 1961, p. 62)

$$E(\varepsilon_{t-1} \mid q_{t-1}^j, w_{t-1}^j) = M_{12} M_{22}^{-1} \begin{bmatrix} q_{t-1}^j \\ w_{t-1}^j \end{bmatrix}$$

where the variance-covariance matrix of $(\varepsilon_{t-1}, q_{t-1}^j, w_{t-1}^j)$ reads

$$V = \begin{bmatrix} \sigma_\varepsilon^2 & a\sigma_\varepsilon^2 & \sigma_\varepsilon^2 \\ a\sigma_\varepsilon^2 & a^2\sigma_\varepsilon + \sigma_e^2 & a\sigma_\varepsilon^2 \\ \sigma_\varepsilon^2 & a\sigma_\varepsilon^2 & \sigma_\varepsilon^2 + \sigma_u^2 \end{bmatrix}$$

The conditional expectation of ε_{t-1} given the information set I_{t-1}^j is now found as

$$E(\varepsilon_{t-1} \mid q_{t-1}^j, w_{t-1}^j) = h_1 q_{t-1}^j + h_2 w_{t-1}^j \tag{A-3}$$

where

$$h_1 = \frac{a\sigma_\varepsilon^2(\sigma_\varepsilon^2 + \sigma_u^2) - a(\sigma_\varepsilon^2)^2}{(\sigma_\varepsilon^2 + \sigma_u^2)(a^2\sigma_\varepsilon^2 + \sigma_e^2) - a^2(\sigma_\varepsilon^2)^2}$$

$$h_2 = \frac{\sigma_\varepsilon^2(a^2\sigma_\varepsilon^2 + \sigma_e^2) - a^2(\sigma_\varepsilon^2)^2}{(\sigma_\varepsilon^2 + \sigma_u^2)(a^2\sigma_\varepsilon^2 + \sigma_e^2) - a^2(\sigma_\varepsilon^2)^2}$$

Given (A-3) we can write (A-1) and (A-2) as

$$E(p_t \mid I_{t-1}^j) = \delta_0 + \delta_1 m_{t-1} + \delta_2 n_{t-2}$$
$$+ \delta_3(h_1 q_{t-1}^j + h_2 w_{t-1}^j) + \delta_4 p_{t-1} \tag{A-4}$$

and

$$E(q_{t-1} \mid I_{t-1}^j) = \psi_0 + \psi_1 m_{t-1} + \psi_2 n_{t-2}$$
$$+ \psi_3(h_1 q_{t-1}^j + h_2 w_{t-1}^j) + \psi_4 p_{t-1} \tag{A-5}$$

The expectation of the nominal variable y_t is found to be

$$E(y_t \mid I_{t-1}^j) = E(m_t \mid I_{t-1}^j) + E(n_t \mid I_{t-1}^j)$$
$$= g_1 m_{t-1} + g_2 E(p_t \mid I_{t-1}^j) + g_3 E(q_{t-1} \mid I_{t-1}^j)$$
$$+ \rho^2 n_{t-2} + \rho E(\varepsilon_{t-1} \mid I_{t-1}^j) \tag{A-6}$$

Using that $E(w_t^j \mid I_{t-1}^j) = E(y_t \mid I_{t-1}^j)$ we find by use of (A-6) and (5) that the price announced by firm j for period t is

$$p_t^j = \pi_0 + (\pi_1 + \pi_3) g_1 m_{t-1} + (\pi_1 + \pi_3) \rho^2 n_{t-2}$$
$$+ (\pi_1 + \pi_3) \rho E(\varepsilon_{t-1} \mid I_{t-1}^j) + \{(\pi_1 + \pi_3) g_2 + \pi_2\} E(p_t \mid I_{t-1}^j)$$
$$+ (\pi_1 + \pi_3) g_3 E(q_{t-1} \mid I_{t-1}^j) \tag{A-7}$$

The aggregate price level is defined as

$$p_t = \int p_t^j f(j) \, dj$$

and we find from (A-7) that it can be written as $(H = ah_1 + h_2)$

$$p_t = \pi_0 + \{(\pi_1 + \pi_3) g_2 + \pi_2\} \delta_0 + (\pi_1 + \pi_3) g_4 \psi_0$$
$$+ \{(\pi_1 + \pi_3) g_1 + \delta_1((\pi_1 + \pi_3) g_2 + \pi_2) + (\pi_1 + \pi_3) g_3 \psi_1\} m_{t-1}$$
$$+ \{(\pi_1 + \pi_3) \rho^2 + \delta_2((\pi_1 + \pi_3) g_2 + \pi_2) + (\pi_1 + \pi_3) g_3 \psi_2\} n_{t-2}$$
$$+ \{(\pi_1 + \pi_3) \rho H + \delta_3 H((\pi_1 + \pi_3) g_2 + \pi_2) + \psi_3 H(\pi_1 + \pi_3) g_3\} \varepsilon_{t-1}$$
$$+ \{\delta_4((\pi_1 + \pi_3) g_2 + \pi_2) + \psi_4(\pi_1 + \pi_3) g_3\} p_{t-1} \tag{A-8}$$

Hence, for the initial conjecture on the price function (12) to be consistent with resulting price function (A-8) we must have that the δ-coefficients fulfill the following restrictions

$$\delta_0 = \pi_0 + \{(\pi_1 + \pi_3) g_2 + \pi_2\} \delta_0 + (\pi_1 + \pi_3) g_3 \psi_0$$
$$\delta_1 = (\pi_1 + \pi_3) g_1 + \delta_1\{(\pi_1 + \pi_3) g_2 + \pi_2\} + (\pi_1 + \pi_3) g_3 \psi_1$$
$$\delta_2 = (\pi_1 + \pi_3) \rho^2 + \delta_2\{(\pi_1 + \pi_3) g_2 + \pi_2\} + (\pi_1 + \pi_3) g_3 \psi_2 \tag{A-9}$$
$$\delta_3 = (\pi_1 + \pi_3) \rho H + \delta_3 H\{(\pi_1 + \pi_3) g_2 + \pi_2\} + \psi_3 H(\pi_1 + \pi_3) g_3$$
$$\delta_4 = \delta_4\{(\pi_1 + \pi_3) g_2 + \pi_2\} + \psi_4(\pi_1 + \pi_3) g_3$$

The output of firm j in period $t-1$ is found from (1) and (3) to be

$$q_{t-1}^j = a(y_{t-1} - p_{t-1}) + b(p_{t-1} - p_{t-1}^j) + e_{t-1}^j$$

and it follows that the mean output in period $t-1$ is

$$q_{t-1} = a(y_{t-1} - p_{t-1})$$
$$= a(m_{t-1} + \rho n_{t-2} + \varepsilon_{t-1} - p_{t-1})$$

It is easily seen that the coefficients in (13) are determined as

$$\psi_0 = 0$$
$$\psi_1 = \psi_3 = a$$
$$\psi_2 = a\rho \tag{A-10}$$
$$\psi_4 = -a$$

Using that $1 - \pi_2 - (\pi_1 + \pi_3) g_2 = (\pi_1 + \pi_3)(1 - g_2)$ we find from (A-9) and (A-10) for $g_2 \neq 1$

that[28]

$$\delta_0 = \frac{\pi_0}{(\pi_1 + \pi_3)(1 - g_2)}$$

$$\delta_1 = \frac{g_1 + ag_3}{1 - g_2}; \qquad \delta_2 = \frac{\rho^2 + ag_3\rho}{1 - g_2}$$

$$\delta_3 = \frac{H(\pi_1 + \pi_3)(\rho + ag_3)}{1 - H\{(\pi_1 + \pi_3)g_2 + \pi_2\}}; \qquad \delta_4 = \frac{-ag_3}{1 - g_2}$$

B. *Solution of the model under indexation*

By use of (29) and (30) we find after some manipulations that (28) can be written as

$$p_t^j = \hat{\pi}_0 + (\pi_1 + \pi_3)(\rho^2 n_{t-2} + \rho E(\varepsilon_{t-1} \mid I_{t-1}^j))$$
$$+ \{\pi_2(1 + \lambda_1) - \lambda_1\}\{\hat{\delta}_0 + \hat{\delta}_2 n_{t-2} + \hat{\delta}_3 E(\varepsilon_{t-1} \mid I_{t-1}^j) + \hat{\delta}_4 \hat{p}_{t-1}\}$$
$$+ \lambda_2(\pi_2 - 1)\{\hat{\psi}_0 + \hat{\psi}_2 n_{t-2} + \hat{\psi}_3 E(\varepsilon_{t-1} \mid I_{t-1}^j) + \hat{\psi}_4 \hat{p}_{t-1}\} \qquad \text{(B-1)}$$

Since the information set is unchanged we have that $E(\varepsilon_{t-1} \mid I_{t-1}^j)$ is unchanged from (A-3), cf Appendix A.

Aggregating $(B - 1)$ to obtain the aggregate price level we find

$$p_t = \{\hat{\pi}_0 + (\pi_2(1 + \lambda_1) - \lambda_1)\hat{\delta}_0 + \lambda_2(\pi_2 - 1)\hat{\psi}_0\}$$
$$+ \{(\pi_1 + \pi_3)\rho^2 + \hat{\delta}_2(\pi_2(1 + \lambda_1) - \lambda_1) + \hat{\psi}_2\lambda_2(\pi_2 - 1)\}n_{t-2}$$
$$+ \{(\pi_1 + \pi_3)\rho + \hat{\delta}_3(\pi_2(1 + \lambda_1) - \lambda_1) + \hat{\psi}_3\lambda_3(\pi_2 - 1)\}H\varepsilon_{t-1}$$
$$+ \{(\pi_2(1 + \lambda_1) - \lambda_1)\hat{\delta}_4 + \lambda_2(\pi_2 - 1)\hat{\psi}_4\}\hat{p}_{t-1} \qquad \text{(B-2)}$$

For the resulting price equation (B-2) to be consistent with the conjecture (29) we must have that

$$\hat{\delta}_0 = \hat{\pi}_0 + \{\pi_2(1 - \lambda_1) - \lambda_1\}\hat{\delta}_0 + \lambda_2(\pi_2 - 1)\hat{\psi}_0$$
$$\hat{\delta}_2 = (\pi_1 + \pi_3)\rho^2 + H\hat{\delta}_2(\pi_2(1 + \lambda_1) - \lambda_1) + \hat{\psi}_2\lambda_2(\pi_2 - 1)$$
$$\hat{\delta}_3 = H(\pi_1 + \pi_3)\rho + H\hat{\delta}_3(\pi_2(1 + \lambda_1) - \lambda_1) + H\hat{\psi}_3\lambda_2(\pi_2 - 1) \qquad \text{(B-3)}$$
$$\hat{\delta}_4 = \hat{\delta}_4(\pi_2(1 + \lambda_1) - \lambda_1) + \lambda_2(\pi_2 - 1)\hat{\psi}_4$$

Mean output is under indexation given as

$$\hat{q}_{t-1} = a(y_{t-1} - \hat{p}_{t-1}) \qquad \text{(B-4)}$$

It is easily checked that the coefficients in (30) are given as

$$\hat{\psi}_0 = \psi_0 = 0$$
$$\hat{\psi}_2 = \psi_2 = a\rho$$
$$\hat{\psi}_3 = \psi_3 = a$$
$$\hat{\psi}_4 = \psi_4 = -a$$

REFERENCES

ANDERSEN, T. M. (1984a), Differential Information and the Role for an Active Stabilization Policy, *Economica* (to appear).

---

[28] Hence, the δ coefficients are uniquely determined and (12) and (13) represent the unique linear rational expectations equilibrium to the model.

ANDERSEN, T. M. (1984b), Pre-set Prices, Differential Information and Monetary Policy, Memo 1984–1, Institute of Economics, Aarhus.

ANDERSEN, T. M. (1985a), The Informational Efficiency of Price and Quantity Signals, *Economics Letters*, 18, 121–124.

ANDERSEN, T. M. (1985b), Price and Output Responsiveness to Nominal Changes Under Differential Information, Memo 85–7, Institute of Economics, Aarhus. *European Economic Review*, 29, 63–87.

ANDERSEN, T. M. (1985c), Uncoordinated Prices and Monetary Policy, *Revue Economique*, Nov, 1247–1270.

ARROW, K. J. (1959), Toward a Theory of Price Adjustment, in *The Allocation of Economic Resources*, M. Abramovitz et al. (eds.), Stanford University Press, 41–51.

ARROW, K. J. (1978), Risk Allocation and Information: Some Recent Theoretical Developments, *Geneva Papers on Risk and Insurance*, 8, 5–19.

BLANCHARD, O. J. (1982), Price Asynchronization and Price Level Inertia, Harvard Discussion Paper.

BRUNNER, K., CUKIERMAN, A. and MELTZER, A. H. (1983), Money and Economic Activity, Inventories and Business Cycles, *Journal of Monetary Economics*, 11, 281–319.

CANZONERI, M. B., HENDERSON, D. W. and ROGOFF, K. S. (1983), The Information Content of the Interest Rate and Optimal Monetary Policy, *Quarterly Journal of Economics*, XCV III 545–566.

CHOUDHRI, E. U. and FERRIS, J. S. (1985), Wage and Price Contracts in a Macro Model with Information Costs, *Canadian Journal of Economics*, XVIII, 766–783.

FISCHER, S. (1977), Long Term Contracts, Rational Expectations, and the Optimal Money Supply Rule, *Journal of Political Economy*, 85, 191–205.

FISCHER, S. (1983), Indexing and Inflation, *Journal of Monetary Economy*, 12, 519–41.

GREEN, J. and HONKAPOHJA, S. (1983), Variance-Minimizing Monetary Policies with Lagged Price Adjustments and Rational Expectations, *European Economic Review*, 20, 123–141.

GREEN, J. and LAFFONT, J.-J. (1981), Disequilibrium with Inventories and Anticipatory Price Setting, *European Economic Review*, 16, 199–223.

HAYEK, F. H. (1945), The Use of Knowledge in Society, *American Economic Review*, XXXV, 519–30.

HARRIS, M. and HOLMSTRØM, B. (1983), Microeconomic Developments and Macroeconomics, *American Economic Review Paper and Proceedings*, 73, 223–227.

HART, O. D. (1982), A Model of Imperfect Competition with Keynesian Features, *Quarterly Journal of Economics*, XCVII, 109–138.

HART, O. D., (1985), Imperfect Competition in General Equilibrium: An Overview of Recent Work, ch. 2 in K. J. Arrow and S. Honkapohja (eds.), *Frontiers of Economics*, Basil Blackwell.

HONKAPOHJA, S. (1985), Expectations and the Theory of Macroeconomic Policy: Some Recent Developments, *European Journal of Political Economy*, 1, 467–483.

KING, R. G. (1982), Monetary Policy and the Information Content of Prices, *Journal of Political Economy*, 90, 247–279.

KING, R. G. (1983), Interest Rates, Aggregate Information, and Monetary Policy, *Journal of Monetary Economics*, 12, 199–234.

LELAND, H. E. (1972), Theory of the Firm Facing Uncertain Demand, *American Economic Review*, 62, 277–291.

McCALLUM, B. T. (1980), Rational Expectations and Macroeconomic Stabilization Policy—An Overview, *Journal of Money, Credit and Banking*, XII, 716–746.

NICKERSON, D. (1985), A Theorem on Policy Neutrality, *European Economic Review*, 28, 331–345.

PHELPS, E. S. and TAYLOR, J. B. (1977), Stabilizing Powers of Monetary Policy and Rational Expectations, *Journal of Political Economy*, 84, 163–190.

SHESHINSKI, E. and WEISS, Y. (1977), Inflation and Cost of Price Adjustment, *Review of Economic Studies*, 44, 287–304.

TAYLOR, J. B. (1985), Rational Expectations in Macroeconomic Models, in Arrow, K. J. and
    S. Honkapohja (eds.), *Frontiers of Economics,* Basil Blackwell.
WEISS, L. (1980), The Role of Active Monetary Policy in a Rational Expectations Model,
    Journal of Political Economy, 88, 221–233.
WEISS, L. (1982), Information Aggregation and Policy, *Review of Economic Studies,* XLIV,
    31–42.

Oxford Economic Papers 38 (1986), 481–500

DEBT POLICY UNDER FIXED AND FLEXIBLE PRICES

By N. RANKIN

1. Introduction

IN THIS paper we contrast the effects of an increase in government debt under the polar assumptions (a) that prices adjust instantaneously to clear markets in the Walrasian manner, and (b) that they are exogenously given and that quantities adjust instead, in the manner of Benassy (1975) or Drèze (1975). To do this we make use of a choice-theoretic macromodel based on overlapping generations and perfect foresight. Such a structure originates in the classic articles of Samuelson (1958) and Diamond (1965), but has only rather recently been employed in the "Keynesian", and—by implication— "short-run", context of fixed prices (see for example Gale (1983 Ch. 1)). The broad aim of this paper, then, is to display the potential of such a framework for analysis of macroeconomic issues, and in particular for providing some formal answers to questions which, because of their eclectic nature, have so far only been treated verbally in the literature.

An excellent example of such a verbal treatment concerning the question at issue is Tobin's (1980) Paish lecture. In this we are reminded that not only are Keynesians opposed to the "Ricardian" doctrine that government debt is neutral, as revived by Barro (1974), but so too are "fiscal conservatives", for whom, in contrast to the Keynesians, government debt is positively harmful. This uneasy anti-Ricardian alliance is, and must be, based on the rejection of the views (a) that capital markets are "perfect", and (b) that the private sector can be treated as a single, infinitely-lived, perfectly-foresighted individual. After Barro's (1974) contribution, the latter has come to mean a denial that a system of inter-generational transfers (bequests or gifts) can make a "dynasty" of overlapping generations equivalent to a single individual. Such a denial is strongly argued informally by Tobin, and in Rankin (1985), the framework of the present paper has been used to examine formally the effect of fixed prices on the implications of infinite lives for debt neutrality. In the present paper, the aim is to dissect the anti-Ricardian alliance by considering formally the exact implications of debt non-neutrality depending on whether prices are flexible or fixed.

The intuitive reasoning on this issue, as provided by Tobin (1980), starts from the proposition that a "helicopter drop" of bonds, which by virtue of finite lives are regarded as net wealth by the recipients, will raise the demand for current consumption. Under flexible prices where there is no involuntary unemployment, the most significant effect of this will be to raise the interest rate and thus crowd out investment and the future capital stock, so reducing long-run output and consumption. Thus more bonds bring lower long-run welfare for the sake of a temporary boost to current consumption: this is the basis for the "fiscal conservatives'" opposition to government debt. Under fixed prices, which are assumed to be at levels generating Keynesian unemployment, the higher consumption demand will call forth higher output via the Keynesian "multiplier". Thus more bonds bring higher welfare in all periods, in stark contrast to the outcome under flexible prices, and are regarded as positively beneficial by Keynesians.

The original motive of the present research was to confirm these intuitive arguments in a unified formal framework. Although this is broadly what the paper achieves, it also reveals a significant counterexample to the general argument. This is more than a mere curiosity, since it derives from an inescapable aspect of the basic situation. It occurs in the second of the two versions of the model considered below, where labour supply is taken to be endogenous. Under fixed prices, if the economy starts off sufficiently close to Walrasian equilibrium, we show that more bonds may *reduce* welfare, despite raising output in the usual Keynesian manner. As explained below, this is a typical instance of the "theory of the second best" at work, since it is caused by the interaction of *two* distortions from Pareto optimality, both of which are quite fundamental to the original arguments.

The paper falls into two sections. In the first, investment and capital accumulation are given full weight, and so the other aspect of the supply side of the economy, labour supply, is treated as exogenous. This is in line with the standard treatment in growth models. In the second section, an endogenous labour supply is allowed, and so to simplify the analysis the capital stock is then made exogenous, as in the simplest models of Barro and Grossman (1971) and Malinvaud (1977).

2. A model with an endogenous capital stock

(i) *Elements of the model*

The structure of this model is very similar to that of Diamond's (1965) growth model, with the simplification that we assume no population growth. It should thus be made clear at the start that, as in Diamond's model, and as also in Samuelson's (1958) model, of which Diamond's can be seen to be an extension, the steady state Walrasian equilibrium is not Pareto-efficient amongst steady states. This does not necessarily mean it is not Pareto-efficient when transition paths are taken into account (indeed, unlike Diamond's model, the interest rate always exceeds the (zero) growth rate). However, it does mean that a government which attaches equal weight to the utility of different generations would have an incentive to intervene to ensure that steady state utility is maximised. This would seem a likely welfare criterion for "fiscal conservatives", who lay emphasis on the long run, and hence we shall use it to distinguish the implications of fixed and flexible prices for a welfare-improving debt policy. Whether it is accepted or not does not of course affect the purely "positive" conclusions of the analysis.

Consumers are assumed to live for two periods, there being a single representative of each generation. They have an endowment of time, L, during the first period of life, which may be used for either leisure or work. Since, in this section, we shall assume no utility of leisure, they always choose to supply this in full to the labour market. Depending on whether prices are flexible or fixed, this supply may or may not be satisfied. During the second period of life consumers have no saleable labour, and so are retired. However, utility is obtained from consumption in both periods of life, and since we assume consumers start life with no assets, they must save in order to provide consumption when retired. This they may do by accumulating any of the three types of asset in the economy: fiat money, government bonds or physical capital (i.e. ownership of firms). Bonds and capital are assumed to be perfect substitutes and hence have an identical real return. Money, however, pays no interest, and hence would not be demanded at all unless it performed some other function than being a mere store of value. Thus we assume it has a transactions role, which can be modelled by supposing real money balances to provide utility, as has commonly been postulated in money-and-growth models (see, e.g., Sidrauski (1967), Brock (1974)). This inclusion of money is the second respect in which the present model differs from Diamond's (1965).

Under the assumption of no utility of leisure, then whether rationed or not in the labour market, the consumer's employment level, l_t, is exogenous to him, being equal to L when not rationed, or $l_t < L$ when rationed. Thus in both cases his lifetime maximisation problem may be stated formally as:

maximise
$$u(c_t^Y, M_t/P_t, c_{t+1}^0) \tag{1}$$

s.t.
$$w_t l_t - \tau_t + v_t = c_t^Y + \{1 - q_t\} \frac{M_t}{P_t} + q_t \frac{P_{t+1}}{P_t} c_{t+1}^0 \tag{2}$$

where c_t^Y, c_{t+1}^0 is consumption when young and old (respectively), M_t is end-of-period money holdings, w_t is the real wage, τ_t is a lump-sum tax, v_t is the net present value of firm ownership (see below), and q_t is the price of government bonds. Bonds are taken to be promises of one unit of currency in one period's time (i.e. "treasury bills"), so the interest rate is $1/q_t - 1$. The end-of-period bond stock will be denoted B_t. Note that B_t does not appear explicitly in (2), since it has been eliminated by combining the consumer's single-period budget constraints to obtain his lifetime constraint.

Since the L.H.S. of (2) consists of the consumer's exogenous (to him) life-time income, and the R.H.S. consists of the choice variables appearing in his utility function, together with their relative prices, his demands when young are clearly given by functions with the forms:

$$c_t^Y = c(w_t l_t - \tau_t + v_t, q_t, P_{t+1}/P_t) \qquad (3)$$
$$(+) \qquad\quad (?) \qquad (?)$$

$$m_t = m(w_t l_t - \tau_t + v_t, q_t, P_{t+1}/P_t) \qquad (4)$$
$$(+) \qquad\quad (+) \qquad (?)$$

Demand for consumption when old, although a function of the same variables, may also be written simply as equal to the old's initial asset stocks plus profit receipts:

$$c_{t+1}^0 = M_t/P_{t+1} + B_t/P_{t+1} + k_t + \pi_{t+1} \qquad (5)$$

where k_t is the end-of-period capital stock and π_{t+1} is the real value of profits. The "expected" signs of the partial derivatives in (3) and (4) are indicated under variables. Taking all commodities to be "normal" goods, we have c_y, $m_y > 0$ (where the "y" subscript indicates the income partial derivative). If, further, all are net substitutes and substitution effects dominate, then m_q, c_p, $m_p > 0$ ("p" indicating the partial with respect to P_{t+1}/P_t), but for c_p and m_p the second assumption would be rather strong. c_q is ambiguous even when income effects are ignored.

The second type of agent is a single representative firm, whose ownership is always in the hands of the old generation. We assume it has a strictly concave production function, $y_t = f(l_t, k_{t-1})$, with, in general, a positive cross derivative, $f_{lk} > 0$. When not rationed, the firm's problem is formally:

maximise $\quad v_t = (f(l_{t+1}, k_t) - w_{t+1}l_{t+1} - \{P_t/P_{t+1}q_t - 1\}k_t)q_t P_{t+1}/P_t$

Note that $P_t/P_{t+1}q_t - 1$ is just the real interest rate. The solution involves the usual first-order conditions, $f_l = w_{t+1}$ and $f_k = P_t/P_{t+1}q_t - 1$. Solving these together gives the capital demand function:

$$k_t = k(q_t P_{t+1}/P_t, w_{t+1}) \qquad (6)$$
$$(+) \qquad\quad (-)$$

and, more simply, from $f_l(l_t, k_{t-1}) = w_t$, labour demand is:

$$l_t = l^d(w_t, k_{t-1}) \qquad (7)$$
$$(-)(+)$$

Concavity ensures that the own-price derivatives have signs as shown, while the assumption that $f_{lk} > 0$ determines the signs of the cross-partials.

When the firm expects to be rationed to sell only y_{t+1} output next period, its problem becomes:

maximise $\quad v_t = (y_{t+1} - w_{t+1}l_{t+1} - \{P_t/P_{t+1}q_t - 1\}k_t)q_t P_{t+1}/P_t$

s.t. $\quad\quad\quad y_{t+1} = f(l_{t+1}, k_t)$

Profit maximisation now simply means cost minimisation, for which the first-order condition is $f_l/f_k = w_{t+1}/\{P_t/P_{t+1}q_t - 1\}$. Using this gives the constrained, or "accelerator", capital demand function:

$$k_t = \bar{k}(y_{t+1}, q_t P_{t+1}/P_t, w_{t+1}) \qquad (8)$$
$$\quad (+) \quad (+) \qquad (+)$$

When the firm faces an output constraint y_t in the current period, its constrained labour demand function is obtainable simply by inverting the production function:

$$l_t = \bar{l}^d(y_t, k_{t-1}) \qquad (9)$$
$$\quad (+) \quad (-)$$

Again, the indicated signs of the partial derivatives follow from concavity and $f_{kl} > 0$.

The third agent in the economy is the government. We ignore government spending, since the concern is only with debt policy, and for the same reason assume that the government keeps the nominal money supply, M, constant. Furthermore, since we shall focus on steady states, we shall assume a continuous balanced-budget policy (apart from the single-period imbalance implied by one-off "helicopter drops" of bonds). Thus, in all periods taxation is set equal to interest on outstanding debt (which, with one-period bonds, means the finance necessary for a repeated re-issue of the same number of bonds):

$$\tau_t = \{1 - q_t\}B/P_t \qquad (10)$$

(For an analysis of the effects of government spending and deficit financing when prices are fixed, see Rankin (1985).)

(ii) The effects of debt under flexible prices

Setting demand equal to supply in the goods, labour and money markets provides equations for determining the equilibrium prices (P_t, w_t, q_t). Making use of (5), note that the goods market identity can be written:

$$y_t = c_t^Y + M/P_t + B/P_t + k_{t-1} + y_t - w_t l_t + \{k_t - k_{t-1}\}$$

Thus

$$w_t l_t = c_t^Y + M/P_t + B/P_t + k_t \qquad (11)$$

Using this simplified form, we can write the market-clearing equations as:

$$w_t L = c(w_t L - \{1 - q_t\}B/P_t + v_t, q_t, P_{t+1}/P_t)$$
$$+ M/P_t + B/P_t + k(q_t P_{t+1}/P_t, w_{t+1}) \qquad (12)$$

$$M/P_t = m(w_t L - \{1 - q_t\}B/P_t + v_t, q_t, P_{t+1}/P_t) \qquad (13)$$

$$L = l^d(w_t, k_{t-1}) \qquad (14)$$

where (10) has been used to substitute out τ_t.

Note that (12) and (13) contain the expectations variables (P_{t+1}, w_{t+1}, v_t), and so an appropriate expectations hypothesis must be introduced before equilibrium can be fully defined. We shall assume throughout the paper that all agents have perfect foresight, since the focus is not on the consequences of incorrect expectations. With an infinitely-lived economy, this then gives rise to the usual feature that the equilibrium sequence $\{P_t, w_t, q_t\}_{t=0}^{\infty}$ is not unique, and to make it so, we must follow the convention (see, for example, Burmeister (1980)) of ruling out divergent sequences. For this to tie down a unique, non-divergent time path, the system must satisfy the appropriate saddlepoint stability condition: namely, that when linearised about its steady state, it should have exactly as many stable eigenvalues as there are predetermined variables (again, see Burmeister (1980)). Although, in this paper, we shall not be directly concerned with behaviour outside the steady state, such behaviour cannot simply by ignored, since if the system is "understable" (i.e. has too few stable eigenvalues), the steady state is unattainable; while if it is "overstable" (i.e. has too many), there are multiple non-divergent equilibrium sequences of which the steady state is only one, meaning that the economy can flip in and out of it quite arbitrarily. Furthermore, by an extension of Samuelson's well-known "correspondence principle" (see, for example, Rankin (1986)), the comparative statics of the steady state are related to its stability properties in such a way that if saddlepoint stability is not satisfied, the sign of the long-run effect of debt on the economy will be reversed. Thus, saddlepoint stability needs to be assumed in what follows.

Unfortunately (from a certain viewpoint), this is not an innocuous assumption for any of the models studied in this paper, i.e. saddlepoint stability is by no means guaranteed simply by taking any set of individually plausible parameter values. Quite a likely property is that of over-stability, implying the existence of multiple convergent time paths. While the existence of multiple equilibria in flexible-price, overlapping-generations economics is quite well-known (see, for example, Hahn (1982)), it does not appear to have been documented—as is done below—for fixed-price economies. Multiple equilibria open up a range of interesting questions of interpretation and of the appropriate policy response, but which go beyond the scope of this paper. Hence we shall here confine attention to cases where saddlepoint stability is satisfied.

It is clear that, since the nominal asset stocks, M and B, are fixed, the steady state of the model (11)–(13) must involve a constant price level. Thus, the steady state (P, w, q, k) may be defined by the equations:

$$wL = c(wL - \{1 - q\}B/P + q\{f(L, k) - wL - \{1/q - 1\}k\}, q, 1)$$
$$+ M/P + B/P + k \tag{15}$$
$$M/P = m(wL - \{1 - q\}B/P + q\{f(L, k) - wL - \{1/q - 1\}k\}, q, 1) \tag{16}$$
$$L = l^d(w, k) \tag{17}$$
$$k = k(q, w) \tag{18}$$

Earlier we stated that the Walrasian steady state was not Pareto efficient amongst steady states. Ignoring utility changes due to changes in real money balances, the resource allocation which maximises the steady state utility of the typical consumer is clearly that which solves the problem:

maximise $$u(c^Y, c^0)$$

s.t. $$c^Y + c^0 = f(L, k)$$

(Note that the temporary sacrifice of consumption which is necessary to raise k is not a constraint here, since we are looking at the optimum steady state, not the optimum transition path.) The problem can be seen to divide into two: first maximise output, by appropriate choice of k; second, maximise utility, by an appropriate division of output between c^Y and c^0. For the first part to have a solution, f_k must eventually fall to zero, so that the optimum capital stock, k^*, is defined by $f_k(L, k^*) = 0$. Note that this is just a special case of the familiar "golden rule" from optimal growth theory: that the capital/labour ratio should be chosen such that $f_k = n$, where n is the rate of population growth. To solve the second part, the necessary condition is that the consumer's marginal rate of substitution between consumption when young and old should be unity. For both these conditions to be satisfied in the Walrasian steady state, we therefore need that the steady state interest rate be zero (i.e. $q = 1$). However, it is readily seen that $q < 1$ in this state, since from the consumer's lifetime budget constraint, (2), $q = 1$ would necessitate that the "price" of real balances, $1 - q$, was zero, and this would only occur if the consumer was satiated with them. Thus the interest rate is in general "too high" for Pareto efficiency. This results in both a "production loss", due to a low capital stock; and a "consumption loss", due to an excessive proportion of output being consumed in old age. By comparison, Diamond (1965) found that the interest rate might be either too high or too low. The latter possibility is clearly ruled out in the present model by the assumption of a zero rate of population growth and the impossibility of a negative interest rate.

From this discussion it can be seen that (ignoring the direct effect on utility of changes in real money balances), a necessary and sufficient condition for a change in the bond stock to increase steady state welfare is that it should reduce the steady state interest rate. Intuitively, we would expect that a rise in the bond stock would raise the interest rate, thus lowering welfare, as feared by the "fiscal conservatives". Differentiating (15)–(18) totally, the following expression for the bond price multiplier is obtained:

$$\frac{dq}{dB} = \frac{\overset{(-)}{-l_w^d}(1 - \overset{(+)}{\{1 - q\}c_y} - \{1 - q\}m_y)MP^{-3}}{D_1} \tag{19}$$

$$(?)$$

The sign of the numerator is readily found to be positive, using the assumptions made earlier, and noting that the "adding-up" constraint for the consumer's income derivatives implies $0 < c_y + \{1 - q\}m_y < 1$. The denominator is a more complicated expression whose sign is ambiguous, as forewarned above. However, using the necessary conditions for saddlepoint stability, it may be determined as negative. This is a tedious algebraic manipulation which we leave to the appendix. Thus the overall sign is negative, i.e. a rise in the bond stock raises the interest rate, tending to lower welfare.

A complete assessment of the welfare effect requires us also to consider the direct effect on utility of the change in real money balances as the price level changes. It would be expected that a rise in the bond stock would raise demand and thus the price level, so lowering real balances (this is proved in the appendix). By itself, this also reduces utility. It is conceivable that the rise in real balances could alter preferences between consumption in the two periods of life in such a way as to reverse the fall in utility due to the rise in the interest rate, but this would clearly be ruled out if preferences were separable in consumption, and more generally could only arise as a pathological case.

(iii) *The effects of debt under fixed prices*

We now assume that the price and money wage are exogenous and constant over time, at such values as to generate excess supply in the goods and labour markets, i.e. "Keynesian unemployment", in Malinvaud's (1977) classification. Output and employment are thus determined only by demand. The bond price continues to adjust instantaneously to clear the money market.

As under flexible prices, we shall focus on the steady state. A more explicit discussion of the dynamics, in order to establish the conditions for saddlepoint stability, is contained in the appendix. Again using the goods market identity (11), the steady state Keynesian unemployment equilibrium (l, q, k) is defined by the equations:

$$wl = c(wl - \{1 - q\}b + q\{f(l, k) - wl - \{1/q - 1\}k\}, q, 1) + m + b + k$$

(20)

$$m = m(wl - \{1 - q\}b + q\{f(l, k) - wl - \{1/q - 1\}k\}, q, 1) \qquad (21)$$

$$k = \bar{k}(f(l, k), q, w) \qquad (22)$$

where $m \equiv M/P$, $b \equiv B/P$.

Before presenting the results of a mathematical examination of the effects of a rise in b on welfare, consider again the intuitive argument. In this model, a helicopter drop of bonds has both a multiplier and an "accelerator" effect on output. The multiplier effect is initiated by the stimulus to the consumption demand of the old generation, through the presence of b on the R.H.S. of (20). The rise in the output constraint makes it worthwhile for firms not only to employ more labour, but also to employ more capital, as indicated by the presence of y (substituted out as $f(l, k)$) in $\bar{k}(.)$. The accumulation of capital then has a reinforcing wealth effect on consumption demand, through the appearance of k on the R.H.S. of (20), and so on. Although this is clearly a very strong expansionary mechanism, two factors must be set against it. First, the interest rate would be expected to rise, which counteracts the positive accelerator effect on the capital stock. Second, for a given level of output, a rise in the interest rate has an adverse effect on steady state utility by increasing the distortion towards consumption in the second period of life, as noted in the previous section. Thus, we need a positive effect on output sufficiently large to outweigh the negative distributional effect if the overall outcome is to be a welfare improvement.

To find the multiplier of the bond stock on output, we differentiate the system (20)–(22) totally. After some simplification, this yields the following expression:

$$\frac{dy}{db} = \frac{-(\{1 - \{1 - q\}c_y\}\overset{(+)}{m_q^c} + \{1 - q\}m_y\overset{(+?)}{c_q^c})k_l^*/\bar{k}_y}{\underset{(?)}{D_2}} \tag{23}$$

where superscript "c" denotes a compensated derivative (i.e. pure substitution effect), and k_l^* is the (positive) derivative of steady state capital with respect to employment (see appendix). The numerator is negative provided that the ambiguous compensated derivative c_q^c is positive (which holds if current consumption is a "closer" substitute for future consumption than for money) or not too negative. The denominator is ambiguous, as pointed out earlier, but for saddlepoint stability must be negative (shown in the appendix). Under these assumptions, an increase in the bond stock thus raises steady state output, confirming the Keynesian intuitive argument. With a positive denominator on the other hand, the response is perverse, but the model then has multiple perfect foresight adjustment paths, which clouds the interpretation of the steady state multipliers, as already observed.

It is also possible to confirm that under the same conditions as necessary for output to rise, steady state utility must rise as well (see appendix). This is despite the rise in the interest rate, which has an otherwise adverse distributional effect on utility, as noted above. Thus the conditions for saddlepoint stability are in broad terms sufficient for government debt to be a beneficial instrument, under Keynesian unemployment.

To summarise this section, we have shown that in a simple general equilibrium model based on maximising behaviour, the non-neutrality of debt can take starkly different forms depending on whether prices are flexible or fixed. Under flexible prices, a higher level of government debt is harmful, in the sense that it reduces the utility of the typical individual; while under fixed prices such as to generate a permanent state of Keynesian unemployment, it is beneficial, in the sense that it raises the utility of the typical individual. This makes it critical to know which of the two cases more closely approximates reality when debt policy is being discussed—an issue which is probably the single most controversial question in contemporary macroeconomics, but which will not be embarked upon here.

3. A model with an endogenous labour supply

(i) *Elements of the model*

The structure of the model we shall consider in this section most closely resembles that of the simple models of Barro and Grossman (1971) and Malinvaud (1977). We assume that leisure, $L - l_t$, enters the utility function. To keep the analysis manageable, the capital stock is taken as fixed, and there is no investment. The firm's profits are assumed to be distributed to the young, rather than to the old: this generates a model as similar as possible to the textbook IS–LM model.

Since labour supply is endogenous, the consumer's demand functions will take different functional forms depending on whether labour supply is rationed or not. In the latter case, the lifetime maximisation problem may be stated formally as:

maximise
$$u(c_t^Y, L - l_t, M_t/P_t, c_{t+1}^0) \tag{24}$$

s.t.
$$w_t l_t - \tau_t + \pi_t = c_t^Y + \{1 - q_t\} \frac{M_t}{P_t} + q_t \frac{P_{t+1}}{P_t} c_{t+1}^0 \tag{25}$$

Solving this generates unconstrained demand and supply functions for the young which clearly have the forms:

$$c_t^Y = c(\pi_t - \tau_t, w_t, q_t, P_{t+1}/P_t) \tag{26}$$
$$\quad (+) \ (+) \ (?) \quad\ (?)$$

$$l_t = l(\pi_t - \tau_t, w_t, q_t, P_{t+1}/P_t) \tag{27}$$
$$\quad (-) \ (+) \ (?) \quad\ (?)$$

$$m = m(\pi_t - \tau_t, w_t, q_t, P_{t+1}/P_t) \tag{28}$$
$$\quad (+) \quad (+)(+) \quad\ (?)$$

Likely signs are again suggested for the partial derivatives. If all commodities are normal and net substitutes, then c_y, m_y, c_w, $m_w > 0$, $l_y < 0$. To get l_w, $m_q > 0$, we assume substitution effects dominate income effects. The same assumption is more contentious for the remaining derivatives, which are left as ambiguous.

When prices are fixed, the inflation term may be dropped, and if the consumer is rationed to $l_t = \bar{l}_t$, his problem becomes:

maximise
$$u(c_t^Y, L - \bar{l}_t, m_t, c_{t+1}^0) \tag{29}$$

s.t.
$$w_t \bar{l}_t - \tau_t + \pi_t = c_t^Y + \{1 - q\}m_t + q_t c_{t+1}^0 \tag{30}$$

$\bar{l}_t$ influences the consumer's choice in two ways. First, it raises his lifetime income, i.e. the L.H. term in (30). Note that, since $\pi_t = y_t - wl_t$, this simply equals aggregate disposable income, $y_t - \tau_t$. Second, since $\bar{l}_t$ enters (29), it may affect preferences between c_t^Y, m_t and c_{t+1}^0. However, if $u(.)$ is weakly separable between leisure and all other goods, this effect will be absent, and since it is unclear a priori in which direction the effect will operate, this provides a useful benchmark case. The constrained demand functions may thus be written as:

$$c_t^Y = \bar{c}(y_t - \tau_t, \; q_t, \; \bar{l}_t) \tag{31}$$
$$\phantom{c_t^Y = \bar{c}(}(+) \quad (?) \;\; (?)$$

$$m_t = \bar{m}(y_t - \tau_t, \; q_t, \; \bar{l}_t) \tag{32}$$
$$\phantom{m_t = \bar{m}(}(+) \quad\;\; (+)(?)$$

When $u(.)$ is separable in leisure, $\bar{c}_l = \bar{m}_l = 0$.

Consumption demand of the old simply equals their initial asset stocks, and is thus:

$$c_t^0 = m_{t-1} + b_{t-1} \tag{33}$$

The firm's decision problem is reduced to that of choosing a single input, employment, and its unconstrained and constrained demand functions (respectively) are given by (7) and (9), with k_{t-1} suppressed. The goods supply function corresponding to (7) we write as:

$$y_t = y^s(w_t) \qquad (=f(l^d(w_t))) \tag{34}$$

(ii) The effects of debt under flexible prices

We focus as before on the steady state, in which $P_{t+1} = P_t = P$. The market-clearing conditions giving the steady state equilibrium prices (P, w, q) are:

$$y^s(w) = c(y^s(w) - wl^d(w) - \{1-q\}B/P, w, q, 1) + M/P + B/P \tag{35}$$

$$l^d(w) = l(y^s(w) - wl^d(w) - \{1-q\}B/P, w, q, 1) \tag{36}$$

$$M/P = m(y^s(w) - wl^d(w) - \{1-q\}B/P, w, q, 1) \tag{37}$$

where π and τ have been substituted out.

In Section 2 we observed that the Walrasian equilibrium was Pareto inefficient amongst steady states, and the same may be seen to be true here. Non-satiation in real money balances ensures a positive "price" of money, $1-q$, and thus a positive interest rate, $1/q - 1$, which is necessarily greater than the rate of zero required by the "golden rule". This results, as before, in a distortion of the allocation of consumption towards the second period of life; and also, now that labour supply is endogenous, in a distortion of the trade-off between leisure and second-period consumption. Since changes in leisure correspond to changes in output, this second distortion means that output could be "too high" or "too low". The direction of the output effect depends on the ambiguous effect which the interest rate has on labour supply: if a higher interest rate raises labour supply (i.e. $l_q < 0$), output will be too high, and vice versa.

For the same reasons as in Section 2, we might therefore expect that a rise in the bond stock would, by raising the interest rate, reduce steady state welfare still further. This would again justify the opposition of the "fiscal conservatives" to increased government debt. However, since we shall see that it is quite likely that at the same time output rises, the argument in this case is more subtle than the simple heuristic one that more debt is bad because it means lower output.

To find, firstly, the effect of a helicopter drop of bonds on output, we differentiate (35)–(37) totally. To reduce the number of conflicting effects at work, it is helpful to consider the value of the multiplier at the point $B = 0$, which is (see appendix for derivation):

$$\frac{dy}{dB} = \frac{\overset{(?)}{(\{m_y l_q^c - l_y m_q^c\}\{1-q\}} - \overset{(-)}{\{l_y c_q^c - c_y l_q^c\}\{1-q\} - l_q^c)MP^{-3}f'/f''}}{\underset{(?)}{D_3}} \quad (38)$$

The most probable sign for the denominator is negative (appendix refers). If all commodities are normal, then it may be shown that when preferences over first-period consumption and leisure are separable, the first two terms in the numerator are positive and zero respectively (see appendix). A sufficient condition for $dy/dB > 0$ is then $l_q^c < 0$, which holds if leisure is a "closer" substitute for future consumption than for money. A positive effect on output is thus quite likely.

Under reasonable conditions, it may also be shown that the interest rate rises (see appendix). However it is less intuitively clear in this than in the exogenous labour supply case that such a change must lower steady state utility, owing to the complications caused by the change in leisure. Thus we proceed directly to calculate du/dB. The following expression for this is readily obtained, using the equilibrium and the consumer's and firm's first-order conditions:

$$\frac{du}{dB} = -u_Y\{1-q\}\frac{d(B/P)}{dB} \quad (39)$$

where $u_Y = \partial u/\partial c^Y > 0$. This is immediately seen to be negative when evaluated at $B = 0$; while more generally it could only be positive in the unlikely event of a rise in the nominal bond stock causing so great a rise in the price level that the real bond stock *falls*.

(iii) *The effects of debt under fixed prices*

Using the consumer's constrained demand functions (31) and (32), the steady state Keynesian unemployment equilibrium (y, l, q) is defined by the equations:

$$y = \bar{c}(y - \{1 - q\}b, q, l) + m + b \tag{40}$$

$$m = \bar{m}(y - \{1 - q\}b, q, l) \tag{41}$$

$$l = \bar{l}^d(y) \tag{42}$$

Note that in the case where $u(.)$ is separable in leisure, l drops out of (40) and (41), as pointed out earlier, so that the system may be solved recursively as in the textbook IS–LM model.

The mechanism whereby an increase in the bond stock may act to raise output is the same as in the model of Section 2, except that we now have just a multiplier and not an accelerator effect. Differentiating (40)–(42) gives the following expressions for the bond stock multiplier:

$$\frac{dy}{db} = \frac{\overset{(+)}{\{1 - \{1 - q\}\bar{c}_y\}\bar{m}_q^c} + \overset{(+?)}{\{1 - q\}\bar{m}_y\bar{c}_q^c}}{\underset{(+)}{\{1 - \bar{c}_y\}\bar{m}_q^c} + \underset{(+?)}{\bar{m}_y\bar{c}_q^c} - \underset{(?)}{\phi}} \tag{43}$$

where

$$\phi = \{\bar{c}_l\bar{m}_q - \bar{m}_l\bar{c}_q\}/f' + \{\bar{c}_l\bar{m}_y - \bar{m}_l\bar{c}_y\}b/f'$$

Since the model contains no inherent dynamics (none of the behavioural equations contain expectations variables), we cannot use saddlepoint stability to sign the denominator. Note that if $u(.)$ is separable in leisure, $\bar{c}_l$, $\bar{m}_l$ and thus ϕ, are all zero. Since it is impossible in general to sign ϕ a priori, we shall take this as the most plausible neutral assumption. In this case $dy/db > 0$ provided that $\bar{c}_q^c$ is positive or not too negative (cf. (23)).

As in Section 2, the effect on welfare cannot be gauged by output alone. This time there are two counter-balancing factors which need to be netted out: the adverse distributional effect of a rise in the interest rate on consumption; and the reduction in leisure caused by the rise in output. From the utility function,

$$\frac{du}{db} = u_Y\frac{dc^Y}{db} + u_0\frac{dc^0}{db} - u_L\frac{dl}{db}$$

where $u_Y = \partial u/\partial c^Y$, $u_0 = \partial u/\partial c^0$, $u_L = \partial u/\partial(L - l)$

$$= u_Y\left(\frac{dc^Y}{db} + q\frac{dc^0}{db} - w^*\frac{dl}{db}\right)$$

using the first-order conditions from the consumer's problem, $u_Y = u_0/q = u_L/w^*$, where w^* is the shadow wage which would induce the consumer to supply freely his ration level (when compensated in real income)

$$= u_Y\left(\left(\frac{dy}{db} - 1\right) + q - \frac{w^*}{f'}\frac{dy}{db}\right)$$

since $y = c^Y + c^0 = c^Y + m + b$, whence $dc^0/db = 1$, $dc^Y/db = dy/db - 1$; and $dl = dy/f'$

$$= u_Y\left(\frac{dy}{db}\left(1 - \frac{w^*}{f'}\right) - \{1 - q\}\right) \tag{44}$$

Note that w^*/f' is a measure of the degree of disequilibrium. If the consumer's supply of labour is rationed, $w^* < w$, and if the firm's supply of output is rationed, $f' > w$. Thus in Walrasian equilibrium, $w^*/f' = 1$; while as output falls, $w^*/f' < 1$. If $f' \to \infty$ as $l \to 0$, then $du/db \to u_Y\{dy/db - 1 + q\} = u_Y q\bar{m}_q\{\{1 - \bar{c}_y\}\bar{m}_q^c + \bar{m}_y\bar{c}_q^c\} > 0$. For sufficiently low levels of output, higher government debt is therefore beneficial, as found in Section 2. However, for high levels of output sufficiently close to the Walrasian equilibrium, $du/db \to -u_Y\{1 - q\} < 0$, so that higher government debt is now harmful. Thus with an endogenous labour supply, there exists a clear exception to the expected Keynesian result. (Note that with an exogenous labour supply, i.e. no utility of leisure, w^* is always zero and hence du/db is always positive.)

This is at first glance puzzling. If both the consumer and firm are rationed, this surely means that each would gain utility or profits by exchanging an extra unit of labour for w units of output. The complication is caused by the interest rate being above its "golden rule" level of zero. The higher output is not allocated entirely to consumption when young, but rather partly to consumption when old. With $q < 1$, however, the consumer is not indifferent to this postponement of the enjoyment of some of the fruits of his labour; only if it is all consumed when young does his utility unambiguously increase. Close to the Walrasian equilibrium where $w^* = f'$ this negative factor becomes decisive, and utility definitely falls. Such a phenomenon may be explained by the fact that in the fixed-price model we have not one, but two, fundamental sources of deviation from Pareto optimality: an excessive interest rate, which is a feature inherited from the flexible-price model; and rigidity of prices. This is a clear "second best" situation, and it is a feature of such situations that the presence of a second distortion may or may not invalidate the standard solution to the first. The general conclusion of the "theory of the second best" is that there are no general conclusions, and this is illustrated by the differing results under fixed prices obtained in Sections 2 and 3.

4. Conclusions

Tobin's (1980) assertion that if government bonds are net wealth, they will have completely different effects on output and welfare if prices are rigid and there is involuntary unemployment, than if prices are flexible and there is no unemployment, is broadly supported by our analysis. However, there is a notable qualification to this which may arise when labour supply is endogenous: we have seen that under fixed prices but close to Walrasian equilibrium, welfare may be reduced by a higher debt. Also, with an endogenous labour supply, a fall in welfare under flexible prices may be accompanied not by a fall in output, but rather by a rise.

Although in this paper we have focused on steady states, which may seem particularly abstract, the importance of the permanent effects of changes in the stock of debt for the more familiar short-run issues of the desirability and effectiveness of tax cuts and spending increases, is much greater than may appear. Fiscal policy is typically perceived as concerned with flow instruments—tax rates and spending levels—while monetary policy is concerned with stock instruments—the levels of various monetary aggregates. Yet if taxation and spending are to have the "pump-priming" effects attributed to them in Keynesian theory, they can do so only because they influence the level of the government deficit and thus, with time, the level of government debt. If government debt is neutral, fiscal policy is reduced to almost complete impotence, as is shown under flexible prices by Barro (1974), and under fixed prices in Rankin (1985). Thus an independent understanding of the effects of debt is crucial for a general understanding of fiscal policy.

Queen Mary College, London University

APPENDIX

(i) *Stability and comparative statics of Section 2(ii) model*

From (14) for $t+1$, $L = l^d(w_{t+1}, k_t)$, or $w_{t+1} = f_l(L, k_t)$. Using this in (6), $k_t = k(q_t P_{t+1}/P_t, f_l(L, k_t))$. Thus, k_t is an implicit function of $q_t P_{t+1}/P_t$ alone: write this as:

$$k_t = k^+(q_t P_{t+1}/P_t) \qquad \text{with derivative } k_q^+ = k_q/\{1 - k_w f_{lk}\} > 0$$

We also have $v_t = (f(L, k_t) - f_l(L, k_t)L - \{P_t/P_{t+1}q_t - 1\}k_t)q_t P_{t+1}/P_t$, which is hence a function only of $q_t P_{t+1}/P_t$. Write this as:

$$v_t = v^+(q_t P_{t+1}/P_t) \qquad \text{with derivative } v_q^+ = \pi + k - qL f_{lk} k_q^+ \gtrless 0$$

—evaluating in the steady state.

Together with (12)–(14), we have:

$$w_t L = c\left(w_t L - \{1 - q_t\}\frac{B}{P_t} + v^+\left(q_t\frac{P_{t+1}}{P_t}\right), q_t, \frac{P_{t+1}}{P_t}\right) + \frac{M+B}{P_t} + k_t$$

$$\frac{M}{P_t} = m\left(w_t L - \{1 - q_t\}\frac{B}{P_t} + v^+\left(q_t\frac{P_{t+1}}{P_t}\right), q_t, \frac{P_{t+1}}{P_t}\right)$$

$$L = l^d(w_t, k_{t-1})$$

$$k_t = k^+(q_t P_{t+1}/P_t)$$

This system we use to define (P_{t+1}, k_t, w_t, q_t) given (P_t, k_{t-1}), i.e. a pair of implicit difference equations in (P_t, k_{t-1}).

Differentiate totally, evaluating in the steady state and, for simplicity, at $B = 0$:

$$
\begin{bmatrix}
-c_y v_q^+ \dfrac{q}{P} - \dfrac{c_p}{P} & -c_y v_q^+ - c_q & \{1 - c_y\}L & -1 \\[2ex]
-m_y v_q^+ \dfrac{q}{P} - \dfrac{m_p}{P} & -m_y v_q^+ - m_q & -m_y L & 0 \\[2ex]
0 & 0 & -l_w^d & 0 \\[2ex]
-k_q^+ \dfrac{q}{P} & -k_q^+ & 0 & 1
\end{bmatrix}
\begin{bmatrix}
d\Delta P_{t+1} \\[2ex]
dq_t \\[2ex]
dw_t \\[2ex]
d\Delta k_t
\end{bmatrix}
$$

$$
=
\begin{bmatrix}
-\dfrac{m}{P} & 1 & -c_y\{1-q\}\dfrac{1}{P} + \dfrac{1}{P} \\[2ex]
\dfrac{m}{P} & 0 & -m_y\{1-q\}\dfrac{1}{P} \\[2ex]
0 & l_k^d & 0 \\[2ex]
0 & -1 & 0
\end{bmatrix}
\begin{bmatrix}
dP_t \\[2ex]
dk_{t-1} \\[2ex]
dB
\end{bmatrix}
\tag{A1}
$$

Denote the L.H. matrix as A. From this solve by Cramer's rule for the coefficient matrix of the system linearised about its steady state:

$$
\begin{bmatrix}
\partial \Delta P_{t+1}/\partial P_t & \partial \Delta P_{t+1}/\partial k_{t-1} \\[2ex]
\partial \Delta k_t/\partial P_t & \partial \Delta k_t/\partial k_{t-1}
\end{bmatrix}
= \frac{1}{|A|}
\begin{bmatrix}
-l_w^d \dfrac{m}{P}\{m_y v_q^+ + m_q + c_y v_q^+ + c_q + k_q^+\} \\[2ex]
-l_w^d \dfrac{m}{P} k_q^+ \left\{ \dfrac{m_p}{P} - m_q \dfrac{q}{P} + \dfrac{c_p}{P} - c_q \dfrac{q}{P} \right\} \\[2ex]
l_k^d L(\{1 - c_y\}\{m_y v_q^+ + m_q\} + m_y\{c_y v_q^+ + c_q + k_q^+\}) \\[2ex]
l_k^d L k_q^+ \left(\{1 - q\}\left\{ \dfrac{m_p}{P} - m_q \dfrac{q}{P} \right\} + m_y \left\{ \dfrac{c_p}{P} - c_q \dfrac{q}{P} \right\} \right) - |A|
\end{bmatrix}
$$

Call this matrix C. Then, after some simplification,

$$
|C| = \frac{\overset{(+)}{(k_q^+ l_k^d L\{1 - c_y - m_y\}} + \overset{(?)}{l_w^d\{m_y v_q^+ + m_q + c_y v_q^+ + c_q + k_q^+\})m/P}}{\underset{(?)}{(k_q^+\{m_p - qm_q\}} + \{m_p - qm_q\}\{c_y v_q^+ + c_q\} - \{c_p - qc_q\}\{m_y v_q^+ + m_q\})l_w^d/P}}
$$
$$
\underset{(-)}{}
$$

In this model, k_{t-1} is predetermined but P_t is free. We treat the system as its differential equation equivalent (which is not strictly rigorous, but amounts to ruling out saddlepoints with oscillatory divergent paths—see Rankin (1986)), and thus require $|C| < 0$ for saddlepoint stability (see, e.g., Burmeister (1980)).

To obtain the steady state multipliers, set $d\Delta P_{t+1} = d\Delta k_t = 0$ in (A1), and solve by Cramer's rule:

$$
\frac{dq}{dB} = \frac{\overset{(-)}{-l_w^d\{1 - \{1-q\}m_y} - \overset{(+)}{\{1-q\}c_y\}m/P^2}}{(l_k^d k_q^+ L\{1 - c_y - m_y\} + l_w^d\{m_y v_q^+ + m_q + c_y v_q^+ + c_q + k_q^+\})m/P}
$$

$$
\frac{dP}{dB} = \frac{\overset{(-)}{(m_y k_q^+\{\{1-q\}l_w^d - qLl_k^d\}} + \overset{(-)}{l_w^d\{m_y v_q^+ + \{1 - \{1-q\}c_y\}m_q + \{1-q\}m_y c_q\})/P}}{\underset{(+)}{(l_k^d k_q^+ L\{1 - c_y - m_y\}} + l_w^d\{m_y v_q^+ + m_q + c_y v_q^+ + c_q + k_q^+\})m/P}
$$
$$
\underset{(?)}{}
$$

The numerator of dq/dB is positive, as noted in the main text. Under the same assumptions, the numerator of dP/dB is negative. The common denominator is the same as the numerator of $|C|$, showing the "correspondence principle" at work. To sign it using the condition $|C| < 0$, we need first to sign the denominator of $|C|$. On direct examination, the latter is highly ambiguous. To help, we appeal to simpler versions of the same model (not presented here): if capital is exogenous, a necessary condition for stability turns out to be $m_p c_q - c_p m_q < 0$. If this component dominates in the more complex model, the denominator of $|C|$ is positive. $|C| < 0$ then requires the denominator of the multipliers to be negative.

(ii) *Stability and comparative statics of Section* 2(iii) *model*

With an exogenous price and wage, substituting out y_{t+1} as $f(l_{t+1}, k_t)$ from (8) gives $k_t = \bar{k}(f(l_{t+1}, k_t), q_t, w)$. Thus k_t is an implicit function of (l_{t+1}, q_t). Write this as $k_t = k^*(l_{t+1}, q_t)$, with derivatives:

$$k_l^* = f_l \bar{k}_y / \{1 - f_k \bar{k}_y\} > 0, \qquad k_q^* = f_k \bar{k}_q / \{1 - f_k \bar{k}_y\} > 0$$

since $1 - f_k \bar{k}_y$ may be shown to be positive under our assumptions. We also have $v_t = (f(l_{t+1}, k_t) - wl_{t+1} - \{1/q_t - 1\}k_t)q_t$, which is hence also a function of (l_{t+1}, q_t). Write this as $v_t = v^*(l_{t+1}, q_t)$, with derivatives:

$$v_l^* = q(\{1 - \{1/q - 1\}\bar{k}_y\}\{1 - f_k \bar{k}_y\}^{-1} f_l - w) > 0$$

$$v_q^* = \pi + k + q\bar{k}_q(\{1 - \{1/q - 1\}\bar{k}_y\}\{1 - f_k \bar{k}_y\}^{-1} f_k - \{1/q - 1\}) > 0$$

since $f_k > 1/q - 1$ when the firm expects future rationing, and $f_l > w$ when the firm is currently rationed.

Keynesian unemployment equilibrium in t can then be written:

$$wl_t = c(wl_t - \{1 - q_t\}b + v^*(l_{t+1}, q_t), q_t, 1) + m + b + k^*(l_{t+1}, q_t)$$

$$m = m(wl_t - \{1 - q_t\}b + v^*(l_{t+1}, q_t), q_t, 1)$$

This system we use to define (l_{t+1}, q_t) given l_t, i.e. an implicit difference equation in l_t.

Differentiate totally, evaluating at the steady state:

$$\begin{bmatrix} -c_y v_l^* - k_l^* & -c_y\{b + v_q^*\} - c_q - k_q^* \\ -m_y v_l^* & -m_y\{b + v_q^*\} - m_q \end{bmatrix} \begin{bmatrix} d\Delta l_{t+1} \\ dq_t \end{bmatrix}$$

$$= \begin{bmatrix} c_y v_l^* + k_l^* - w\{1 - c_y\} & 1 - \{1 - q\}c_y \\ m_y v_l^* + wm_y & -\{1 - q\}m_y \end{bmatrix} \begin{bmatrix} dl_t \\ db \end{bmatrix} \quad (A2)$$

By Cramer's rule,

$$\frac{d\Delta l_{t+1}}{dl_t} =$$

$$\frac{\overset{(+)}{w\{1 - c_y\}m_q} + \overset{(+)}{wm_y\{c_q + b + v_q^* + k_q^*\}} - k_l^*\{m_y\{b + v_q^*\} + m_q\} - v_l^*\{c_y m_q - m_y\{c_q + k_q^*\}\} \overset{(?)}{}}{\underset{(+)}{k_l^*\{m_y\{b + v_q^*\} + m_q\}} + v_l^*\{c_y m_q - m_y\{c_q + k_q^*\}\} \underset{(?)}{}}$$

l_t is non-predetermined, so this must be positive for saddlepoint stability.

To obtain the steady state multipliers dl/db and dq/db, set $d\Delta l_{t+1} = 0$ in (A2) and solve by Cramer's rule:

$$dl/db = (-\{1 - \{1 - q\}c_y\}m_q - m_y\{\{1 - q\}\{c_q + k_q^*\} + b + v_q^*\})/D_2$$

$$dq/db = m_y\{wq + v_l^* + \{1 - q\}k_l^*\}/D_2$$

D_2 is minus the numerator of $d\Delta l_{t+1}/dl_t$, again indicating the "correspondence principle" in operation.

To find dy/db, we have $y = f(l, k^*(l, q))$, so

$$\frac{dy}{db} = \{f_l + f_k k_l^*\}\frac{dl}{db} + f_k k_q^* \frac{dq}{db} = \frac{k_l^*}{\bar{k}_y}\frac{dl}{db} + f_k k_q^* \frac{dq}{db}$$

Substituting from above, the resulting expression simplifies to:

$$\frac{dy}{db} = -(\{1 - \{1 - q\}c_y\}m_q + m_y\{\{1 - q\}c_q + b + \pi + k\})k_l^*/\bar{k}_y D_2$$

Note that from (2), q changes the "price" of both money and future consumption, so that, by the Slutsky equation, $c_q = c_q^c - \{c^0 - m\}c_y$ and $m_q = m_q^c - \{c^0 - m\}m_y$ (superscript "c" denoting a compensated derivative). From (5), $c^0 - m = b + \pi + k$, so that the multiplier may finally be written:

$$\frac{dy}{db} = \frac{-(\{1 - \{1 - q\}c_y\}\overset{(+?)}{m_q^c} + \{1 - q\}m_y\overset{(+)}{c_q^c})k_l^*/\bar{k}_y}{D_2}$$

as in (23). As noted in the main text, the numerator is negative provided c_q^c is positive or not too negative. D_2, which equals minus the numerator of $d\Delta l_{t+1}/dl_t$, is inherently ambiguous in sign. Now the denominator of $d\Delta l_{t+1}/dl_t$ is positive close to the Walrasian equilibrium, since $v_l^* = 0$ here. It will most likely also be positive away from it provided k_q^* is not too large, since $c_y m_q - m_y c_q > 0$ if preferences are intertemporally separable (see appendix sect. (iii)). Thus saddlepoint stability requires that D_2 be negative.

The effect on steady state utility is:

$$\frac{du}{db} = u_Y\frac{dc^Y}{db} + u_0\frac{dc^0}{db} = u_Y\left(\frac{dc^Y}{db} + q\frac{dc^0}{db}\right)$$

—using the consumer's first-order condition $u_0 = qu_Y$;

$$= u_Y\left(\{1 - q\}\frac{dc^Y}{db} + q\frac{dy}{db}\right) \tag{A3}$$

—using $c^0 = y - c^Y$. It has been seen that dy/db is positive. Using (5), $c^Y = wl - k - m - b$, so:

$$\frac{dc^Y}{db} = w\frac{dl}{db} - \frac{dk}{db} - 1 = \{w - k_l^*\}\frac{dl}{db} - k_q^*\frac{dq}{db} - 1$$

using $k = k^*(l, q)$. Substituting from above, the resulting expression simplifies to:

$$\frac{dc^Y}{db} = \frac{-\{c_y m_q - m_y c_q\}\{\{1 - q\}k_l^* + v_l^*\}}{D_2}$$

Intertemporally separable utility gives $c_y m_q - m_y c_q > 0$, as noted, so that with $D_2 < 0$, $dc^Y/db > 0$. Then from (A3), $du/db > 0$.

(iii) *Stability and comparative statics of Section 3(ii) models*

Consider first the signs of the following cross-combinations of consumers' derivatives:

(a) $c_y m_q - m_y c_q$. From (25), note that q_t affects both the "price" of real balances, $1 - q_t$, and the "price" of future consumption, $q_t P_{t+1}/P_t$. Denoting the former as r and the latter as s, and treating them as independent, derivatives with respect to q may be divided up as (evaluating at $P_{t+1} = P_t$) $c_q = c_s - c_r$, etc. Now, from the Slutsky equation, $c_s = c_s^c - c^0 c_y$, $c_r = c_r^c - mc_y$, etc. (superscript "c" denoting a compensated derivative). Hence,

$$c_y m_q - m_y c_q = c_y\{m_s^c - m_r^c - \{c^0 - m\}m_y\} - m_y\{c_s^c - c_r^c - \{c^0 - m\}c_y\}$$
$$= \{c_y m_s^c - m_y c_s^c\} - \{c_y m_r^c - m_y c_r^c\}$$
$$ (+)\quad(-)\qquad\quad(+)\quad(+)$$

If utility is intertemporally separable so that $u = u(v(c^Y, L - l, M/P), c^0)$, then the compensated cross-derivative between c^0 and any other commodity is proportional to the income derivatives (see Deaton and Muellbauer (1980), p. 128), i.e. $c_s^c = \mu c_y c_y^0$, $m_s^c = \mu m_y c_y^0$, $l_s^c = \mu l_y c_y^0$.

The first R.H. expression drops out, leaving an expression which is positive, if all commodities are normal and net substitutes.

(b)
$$m_y l_q^c - l_y m_q^c = \{m_y l_s^c - l_y m_s^c\} - \{m_y l_r^c - l_y m_r^c\}$$
$$= -\{m_y l_r^c - l_y m_r^c\} > 0$$
$$(+)(-)(-)(-)$$

using the same assumptions.

(c)
$$l_y c_q^c - c_y l_q^c = \{l_y c_s^c - c_y l_s^c\} - \{l_y c_r^c - c_y l_r^c\}$$

Here consider $u = u(v(c^Y, L - l), M/P, c^0)$. Separability from c^0 makes the first R.H. term zero, and separability from M/P makes the second R.H. term zero.

In this model, an appeal to saddlepoint stability turns out to be unhelpful in signing D_3, the denominator of the steady state multipliers. This is because although $-D_3$ is the numerator of $d\Delta l_{t+1}/dl_t$, its denominator is highly ambiguous in sign. Thus we consider D_3 directly. Differentiate totally (35)–(37), and simplify by evaluating at $B = 0$:

$$
\begin{bmatrix}
f'/f'' - c_w^c & m/P & -c_q^c \\
1/f'' - l_w^c & 0 & -l_q^c \\
-m_w^c & -m/P & -m_q^c
\end{bmatrix}
\begin{bmatrix}
dw \\
dP \\
dq
\end{bmatrix}
=
\begin{bmatrix}
-c_y\{1-q\}/P + 1/P \\
-l_y\{1-q\}/P \\
-m_y\{1-q\}/P
\end{bmatrix}
dB
$$

Here we have used: $l_w^d = 1/f''$, $y_w^s = f'/f''$, $\partial\{y^s(w) - wl^d(w)\}/\partial w = -l$ since $w = f'$, $c_w + lc_y = c_w^c$ etc., $c_q + bc_y = c_q^c$ etc.

Using Cramer's rule and $dy = dw \, f'/f''$,

$$\frac{dy}{dB} = \frac{(\{m_y l_q^c - l_y m_q^c\}\{1-q\} - \{l_y c_q^c - c_y l_q^c\}\{1-q\} - l_q^c)mP^{-2}f'/f''}{(l_q^c\{c_w^c + m_w^c - f'/f''\} - \{m_q^c + c_q^c\}\{l_w^c - 1/f''\})m/P}$$

$$\frac{dq}{dB} = \frac{(\{1 - \{1-q\}c_y - \{1-q\}m_y\}\{l_w^c - 1/f''\} + l_y\{1-q\}\{c_w^c + m_w^c - f'/f''\})mP^{-2}}{(l_q^c\{c_w^c + m_w^c - f'/f''\} - \{m_q^c + c_q^c\}\{l_w^c - 1/f''\})m/P}$$
$$\quad (?) \qquad (+) \qquad\qquad (+) \quad (?) \qquad (+)$$

The numerator of dy/dB was discussed in the main text. The numerator of dq/dB is positive when the economy is sufficiently close to the optimum so that $q \cong 1$, though farther away from it we additionally need the cross derivatives c_w^c, m_w^c to be sufficiently small to ensure this sign. If the common denominator, D_3, is negative, then $dq/dB < 0$. D_3 is ambiguous given only the basic assumptions of normality and net substitutability. Sufficient but not necessary conditions for it to be negative would be $l_q^c < 0$, $c_q^c > 0$. These hold if, respectively, leisure and first-period consumption are "closer" substitutes for second-period consumption than for money.

REFERENCES

BARRO, R. J. (1974) "Are Government Bonds Net Wealth?" *Journal of Political Economy* 82, pp. 1095–1117.

—— and GROSSMAN, H. I. (1971) "A General Disequilibrium Model of Income and Employment" *American Economic Review* 61, pp. 82–93.

BENASSY, J.-P. (1975) "Neo-Keynesian Disequilibrium Theory in a Monetary Economy" *Review of Economic Studies* 42, pp. 503–523.

BROCK, W. A. (1974) "Money and Growth: The Case of Long-Run Perfect Foresight" *International Economic Review* 15, pp. 750–777.

BURMEISTER, E. (1980) "On Some Conceptual Issues in Rational Expectations Modelling" *Journal of Money, Credit and Banking* 12, pp. 800–816.

DEATON, A. S. and MUELLBAUER, J. (1980) *Economic Theory and Consumer Behaviour* Cambridge: Cambridge University Press.

DIAMOND, P. (1965) "National Debt in a Neoclassical Growth Model" *American Economic Review* 55, pp. 503–511.

DREZE, J. H. (1975) "Existence of Exchange Equilibrium under Price Rigidities" *International Economic Review* 16, pp. 301–320.

GALE, D. (1983) *Money: In Disequilibrium* Cambridge: Cambridge University Press

HAHN, F. (1982) *Money and Inflation* Oxford: Blackwell.

MALINVAUD, E. (1977) *The Theory of Unemployment Reconsidered* Oxford: Blackwell.

RANKIN, N. (1985) "Debt Neutrality in Disequilibrium" in Currie, D. A. (ed.) *Advances in Monetary Economics* London: Croom-Helm.

RANKIN, N. (1986) "On the Extension of the 'Correspondence Principle' to Perfect Foresight Models", Disc. Paper No. 150, Econ. dept., Queen Mary College, London.

SAMUELSON, P. A. (1958) "An Exact Consumption-Loan Model of Interest With or Without the Social Contrivance of Money" *Journal of Political Economy* 66, pp. 467–482.

TOBIN, J. (1980) "Government Deficits and Capital Accumulation" in Tobin, J. *Asset Accumulation and Economic Activity* Oxford: Blackwell.

Oxford Economic Papers 38 (1986), 501–515

MONETARY AND EXCHANGE RATE POLICIES IN AN OPEN MACROECONOMIC MODEL WITH UNEMPLOYMENT AND RATIONAL EXPECTATIONS

By JOHN FENDER

THE MAIN aim of this paper is to analyze the behaviour of an open economy, with unemployment, under the influence of rational expectations about future economic variables. As such, it might be regarded as an attempt to incorporate some of the factors discussed in Neary/Stiglitz (1983) into an open economy temporary equilibrium with rationing framework. The latter approach has been developed by a number of authors recently (see, for example, Dixit (1978), Neary (1980), Cuddington, *et al.* (1984)), and is an extension of the Barro/Grossman analysis (see, for example, Barro/Grossman (1976)) to an open economy. This analysis, by explicitly modeling the constraints faced by agents when markets do not clear, provides a rigorous framework for the analysis of economies with non-market clearing (although the question why markets should be characterized by non-market clearing is not addressed). One defect of the temporary equilibrium with rationing literature is that, in spite of the widely recognized importance of expectations, particularly in open economies, they have received only rudimentary treatment in the literature. An important exception is Neary/Stiglitz (1983), who introduce rational expectations into a temporary equilibrium with rationing framework. In models characterized by market clearing, it is usually sufficient for agents to formulate expectations about future prices; however, in a model where some markets may fail to clear, it will usually be necessary for agents to form expectations over quantities as well. In the Neary/Stiglitz paper, the concept of *rational constraint expectations* is introduced, and it is shown that, in general, the effectiveness of stabilization policy is enhanced, rather than diminished, when expectations are rational (compared with the situation when they are exogenous).

In order to analyze the problem, a two-period framework is developed. Some recent papers have presented open economy models based on such an approach; examples are Aizenman (1983), Greenwood (1983), Persson and Svensson (1983) and Cuddington and Vinals (1984). There seems to be widespread agreement that a number of issues in macroeconomics are most

Acknowledgments: The first draft of this paper was written while the author was on leave from Lancaster University at the Institute for International Economic Studies at the University of Stockholm, and appeared as Seminar Paper No. 305. Versions of the paper were presented in seminars at the Institute and at the University of Uppsala. The author is grateful to participants in the seminars, and to Dean Croushore, Peter Sinclair and Lars Svensson for useful comments and discussion, but accepts full responsibility for all the paper's deficiencies.

appropriately tackled in such a framework. Aizenman and Greenwood develop models with market-clearing in both periods; the Cuddington/ Vinals paper has non-market clearing in the first period, and whilst the Persson/Svensson paper considers non-market clearing in both periods and develop a model which is similar in some respects to that presented here, the authors are interested in rather different questions, such as the implications of optimistic beliefs in a Keynesian economy. It is important to develop a model of this type with disequilibrium in the labour market for a number of reasons. One is that such an assumption would appear to be more satisfactory for a large number of economies than an assumption of labour market clearing would be. Another is that it may be useful to develop models based on non-market-clearing, so that their results can be compared and contrasted with those derived from market clearing models. It then becomes apparent what difference an assumption of market clearing makes.

The analysis of this paper will therefore concern an open economy in which two periods (the present and the future, or periods one and two) are distinguished. We follow Neary (1980), Cuddington/Vinals (1984), Persson/ Svensson (1983) and others in distinguishing between two domestically produced goods, a tradable and a non-tradable. The tradable can be bought and sold on world markets at a given world currency price (it is assumed the country is 'small'). The producers of traded goods are therefore assumed not to face rationing in overseas markets. Output of the tradable is determined on the basis of profit-maximizing behaviour by producers; output of the non-tradable is assumed to be demand determined and its price in both periods is fixed. There is unemployment in both periods; employment is determined through the production technology from the output of both goods. The producers of traded goods offer employment up to the point where the marginal product of labour equals the product real wage. The producers of non-traded goods, on the other hand, are rationed in the product market, and their effective demand for labour is derived by inverting their production function. We are therefore considering a model of two-period Keynesian unemployment. This is but one of many possibilities, yet the one that commands the greatest interest. A constant money wage is assumed; by appropriate choice of units this is equated to unity (as is the foreign currency price of imports). There are two assets in the model, money and (international) bonds, which pay a given world interest rate. At this rate, agents can borrow or lend indefinitely, provided they satisfy their intertemporal budget constraints (this is the assumption of perfect capital mobility; it does not imply, though, that agents can increase their indebtedness without limit).

Consumption and money-holding behaviour are determined through the maximization of an intertemporal utility function subject to the appropriate budget constraint. Both current and future events are likely to influence agents' future income, and hence their current consumption. A two period model with rational expectations enables interdependencies of this type to be analyzed.

The exchange rate may be fixed or flexible in each period; so there are four combinations of exchange rate regimes to be considered. It might be argued that analysis of fixed exchange rate regimes is less relevant today; however, given that governments often intervene in foreign exchange markets, analysis of the fixed rate case still has some relevance. For each case, the effects of monetary policy (actual and anticipated) and, where appropriate, exchange rate policy (actual and anticipated) will be discussed. We shall be primarily concerned with the effects on current period variables.

Of the results which are derived, a number appear surprising. One is the strong possibility that an anticipated increase in the money supply may produce an appreciation of the current exchange rate. Another is the finding that an anticipated devaluation (in a fixed rate world) produces a deterioration in the current balance of trade but an improvement in the overall balance of payments; there is a capital account improvement which outweighs the current account deterioration.

In the next section of the paper, the model is described in more detail and the behaviour of the representative consumer derived; the following section contains an analysis of the effects of monetary and exchange rate policies, and there is a concluding section. More technical material is placed in the Appendix.

I

It is assumed that the representative consumer maximizes a utility function of the form:

$$U = \alpha \log c_1 + \beta \log n_1 + \gamma \log (M_1/P_1)$$
$$+ \Delta[\alpha \log c_2 + \beta \log n_2 + \gamma \log (M_2/P_2)] \tag{1}$$

where c_i is consumption of the tradable in period i.

    n_i is consumption (and output) of the non-tradable in period i.

    M_i is money holdings in period i.

    P_i is the price index for deflating money balances.

    Δ is the discount factor.

A number of features of this approach requires comment. A specific functional form is postulated for the utility function; in this we follow much of the literature, including Aizenman (1983) and Cuddington and Vinals (1984). Although it would be desirable to work with a more general utility function, doing so would make the analysis much less tractable. A second point relates to the incorporation of real money balances in the utility function. This is a widely adopted practice, employed in Sidrauski (1967), Brock (1974), LeRoy (1984), Michener (1984), and elsewhere. It is recognized that the procedure is not fully satisfactory. We adopt it because it does generate a demand for money function with reasonable properties, including interest sensitivity of the demand for money. This is something which is not done by the main alternative, the 'cash in advance' approach (used by Cuddington and Vinals (1984), for example), according to which purchases are constrained by an agent's holding of money balances. (Also, see Brock (1974), pp. 768–9 and LeRoy (1984), pp. 189–195, for defences of the money in the utility function approach). With reference to both the above points, it should be stressed that in deriving our main results, more general functional forms are used and the purpose of the analysis in this section is mainly to suggest appropriate signs for the relevant partial derivatives. So our analysis will be considerably more general than it might appear initially.

A further point relates to the P_i term used to deflate money balances. We would normally expect this to be a function of the prices of consumer goods, however, since it is eliminated in the process of maximization, there is no need to discuss its specification.

The utility function is maximized subject to the following budget constraint:

$$M_1 + e_1 c_1 + q_1 n_1 + \frac{1}{(1+r)} \{M_2 - M_1 + q_2 n_2 + e_2 c_2\} = \Omega \qquad (2)$$

where Ω is wealth (defined below).

e_i is the domestic currency price of the tradable in period i (and also, given the normalization assumption, the exchange rate in the relevant period).

q_i is the price of the non-tradable in period i.

r^* is the world rate of interest.

r is the domestic currency rate of return from investing in foreign assets.

The consumer takes wealth and prices as given. Wealth is defined by:

$$\Omega = \bar{M}_1 + Y_1 + \frac{1}{(1+r)} (\bar{M}_2 + Y_2) \qquad (3)$$

$$Y_i = e_i t^s(e_i) + q_i n_i \qquad (4)$$

where $\bar{M}_i$ is the money transferred to the consumer at the beginning of period i.

Y_i is nominal income received during period i.

$t'_s(\cdot)$ is the domestic supply function of tradables $(\partial t^s(\cdot)/\partial e_i > 0)$

The budget constraint can be explained as follows: in each period the consumer receives a certain transfer of money from the government (this might be described as 'helicopter' money) and receives income generated from the sales of tradables and non-tradables (it is assumed that all income thus generated accrues to the consumer). The present value of these receipts is designated 'Ω' (wealth). Nominal income is defined to be the sum of the values of tradable and non-tradable output. Tradable output depends solely on the domestic currency price of tradables (this is as might be expected on the basis of profit maximizing, price-taking behaviour by producers with one variable factor of production, labour and with diminishing returns). The price of labour is normalized to unity.

There are two assets in the economy, money and foreign bonds, which give a certain rate of return (in foreign currency terms) of r^*. The return to domestic holders is calculated as follows: one unit of domestic currency will purchase $1/e_1$ units of foreign currency, which will produce $(1 + r^*)/e_1$ units of foreign currency in the next period, which can then be exchanged for $e_2(1 + r^*)/e_1$ units of domestic currency. It follows that

$$r = \frac{e_2}{e_1}(1 + r^*) - 1 \tag{5}$$

By maximizing (1) subject to (2), using standard techniques, we can derive the following equations:

$$c_1 e_1 = \alpha X \Omega \tag{6}$$

$$n_1 q_1 = \beta X \Omega \tag{7}$$

$$M_1 = \gamma \frac{(1 + r)}{r} X \Omega \tag{8}$$

$$c_2 e_2 = \Delta \alpha (1 + r) X \Omega \tag{9}$$

$$n_2 q_2 = \Delta \beta (1 + r) X \Omega \tag{10}$$

$$M_2 = \Delta \gamma (1 + r) X \Omega \tag{11}$$

where $X = \{(\alpha + \beta + \gamma)(1 + \Delta)\}^{-1}$.

Current expenditure on both goods is proportional to wealth; this is as expected, given the logarithmic utility function. Equation (8) shows that the current demand for money depends on both wealth and the nominal interest rate. Future demands for goods and the future demand for money are all proportional to wealth, with the factor of proportionality related to the interest rate.

Since wealth depends on non-tradable output, n_1 appears on both sides of equation (7) and n_2 on both sides of equation (10). This represents a type of multiplier process; anything which leads to increased spending on the non-tradable raises income and thus leads to further spending on the non-tradable, and so on. It would be desirable to eliminate n_1 and n_2 from the right hand sides of equations (6) and (11); this is done by substituting equations (7) and (10) into equations (3), using equation (4). Doing this, we obtain

$$\Omega = \frac{(\alpha + \beta + \gamma)}{(\alpha + \gamma)} \phi \tag{11'}$$

where

$$\phi = \{\bar{M}_1 + e_1 t^s(e_1)\} + \frac{1}{(1+r)} \{\bar{M}_2 + e_2 t^s(e_2)\}$$

This, together with equation (5), can be substituted into equations (6) and (11) to give demands for goods and money in both periods as functions of e_1, e_2, $\bar{M}_1$, $\bar{M}_2$ (since changes in q_1, q_2 and r^* are not considered in this paper, we treat these variables as parameters). This gives

$$c_1 = c_1(e_1, e_2, \bar{M}_1, \bar{M}_2) \tag{12}$$

$$c_{11} \gtreqless 0; \quad c_{12}, c_{13}, c_{14} > 0$$

$$n_1 = n_1(e_1, e_2, \bar{M}_1, \bar{M}_2) \tag{13}$$

$$n_{11}, n_{12}, n_{13}, n_{14} > 0$$

$$M_1 = M_1(e_1, e_2, \bar{M}_1, \bar{M}_2) \tag{14}$$

$$M_{11} > 0; \quad M_{12} \gtreqless 0; \quad M_{13}, M_{14} > 0$$

$$c_2 = c_2(e_1, e_2, \bar{M}_1, \bar{M}_2) \tag{15}$$

$$c_{21} \gtreqless 0; \quad c_{22}, c_{23}, c_{24} > 0$$

$$n_2 = n_2(e_1, e_2, \bar{M}_1, \bar{M}_2) \tag{16}$$

$$n_{21} \gtreqless 0; \quad n_{22}, n_{23}, n_{24} > 0$$

$$M_2 = M_2(e_1, e_2, \bar{M}_1, \bar{M}_2) \tag{17}$$

$$M_{21} \gtreqless 0; \quad M_{22}, M_{23}, M_{24} > 0$$

where M_{ij} represents the partial derivative of M_i with respect to its jth argument and similar notation is used for C_{ij} and n_{ij}. In deriving the above condition, it has been assumed that $\partial \phi / \partial e_1$ and $\partial \phi / \partial e_2 > 0$ (or that both a current and a future depreciation tend to increase wealth); these assumptions are discussed further in the Appendix.

The assumptions as to the signs of the partial derivations in equations (12) to (17) can be explained as follows. Increases in e_1, e_2, $\bar{M}_1$ and $\bar{M}_2$ all tend to raise wealth, and hence the *value* of spending on current tradables and non-tradables (see equations (6) and (7)). However, it is clear from equation (6) that a rise in e_1 need not increase the *volume* of purchases of tradables. The demands for money in the two periods and for the two goods in the future also rise with wealth. A future depreciation does, however, also tend to raise the interest rate and this reduces the current demand for money, so that the overall effect in equation (14) is unclear. Similarly, through the interest rate effect, a rise in e_1 will tend to reduce demand for future goods and money, hence imparting an ambiguity to the direction of the total effect of such a change in these variables.

So far, we have described the demands of the representative consumer as functions of the exchange rate and monetary transfer in each period. The next task is to characterize the nature of the equilibrium for the whole economy and to consider the effects of changes in some of the exogenous variables. In doing this, it is necessary only to use the functional forms in equations (12) to (17); it might be suggested that these have very reasonable properties and hence our analysis is considerably more general than inspection of our specific utility function might suggest.

II

It is necessary first of all to specify the exchange rate regime in each period. It is assumed that each period's exchange rate can either be freely floating or fixed, and hence that there are four combinations of exchange rate regimes to analyze. In each of these, the effects of changes in the monetary transfer and (where appropriate) changes in the exchange rate are considered.

1. *Exchange rates flexible in both periods*

This is characterized by the following equations:

$$M_1(e_1, e_2, \bar{M}_1, \bar{M}_2) = \bar{M}_1 \tag{18}$$

$$M_2(e_1, e_2, \bar{M}_1, \bar{M}_2) = \bar{M}_1 + \bar{M}_2 \tag{19}$$

Here, the exchange rates adjust in order to ensure that the demand for money is equated to the exogenously given supply ($\bar{M}_1$ in period 1, $\bar{M}_1 + \bar{M}_2$ in period 2). With e_1 and e_2 determined, the output and consumption of each good can be calculated in a straightforward manner. Tradable output, for example, follows from the relevant exchange rate in each period through the tradable supply function. We are interested here in the effects of changes in $\bar{M}_1$ and $\bar{M}_2$. Accordingly, the above system of equations is differentiated and we solve for changes in the exchange rate in terms of changes in the money supplies; details are given in the Appendix.

The most surprising result here is the strong possibility (a sufficient condition for which is that $M_{12} > 0$) that a future monetary expansion results in an appreciation of the current exchange rate. This is in sharp contrast with virtually all other models which have looked at this link: 'The fact that an increase in the expected future money supply should lead to a depreciation of the current exchange rate ... is a ubiquitous conclusion of simple monetary approach models' (Greenwood (1983) p. 551). The explanation is quite straightforward, though. The increase in the future money supply results in a depreciation of the future exchange rate. This raises the current interest rate, reduces the demand for money and hence the current exchange rate tends to depreciate—this is the channel stressed by conventional models. However, in the current model, there are forces going in the opposite direction. The increase in the future money supply raises wealth (both because of the higher value of the transfer and because of the increased economic activity generated by the monetary expansion) and this raises the current demand for money, hence tending to appreciate the current exchange rate. Hence, the overall effect depends upon the net effect of these two mechanisms: one might be described as an interest rate effect, tending to depreciate the exchange rate, the other being a wealth effect, tending to appreciate it. The latter effect will be stronger, the higher the supply elasticity of tradables.

If the current exchange rate does appreciate in response to a future monetary expanison, current output of tradables falls. However, since wealth rises, consumption of both goods rises; the balance of trade hence deteriorates. Output of non-tradables rises, and so does employment in non-tradable production whereas employment in tradable production falls.

If, on the other hand, the current exchange rate does depreciate in response to an anticipated monetary expansion, then tradable output must rise. Non-tradable output rises as well, provided that wealth rises, as will consumption of tradables.

The other effects in this regime are fairly straightforward. An increase in $\bar{M}_1$, the current money supply, results in a depreciation of both the current and the future exchange rates; accordingly, both tradable and non-tradable output (and consumption) rise, although it seems difficult to sign the overall effect on the balance of trade.

The effects of a temporary monetary expansion can also be compared to those of a permanent one. Analytically, a temporary monetary expansion can be represented by an increase in $\bar{M}_1$ accompanied by an equal and opposite change in $\bar{M}_2$. On the assumption that $\partial e_1 / \partial \bar{M}_2 < 0$, it is apparent that a temporary monetary expansion has a greater effect on the current exchange rate, and hence results in a greater increase in tradable output. However, the increase in both tradable and non-tradable consumption is less with a temporary increase (as the increase in wealth is lower), so the balance of trade is more likely to improve; the (differential) effect on employment is unclear, though.

2. *Fixed exchange rates in each period*

With fixed exchange rates in each period, the levels of output of the tradable can be inferred from the relevant exchange rate, whereas consumption of (and output of) the non-tradable can be deduced from knowledge of both periods' exchange rates and monetary transfers.

It is assumed that foreign exchange reserves are more than sufficient to ensure convertibility of the currency for all the changes considered. Actual money supplies in each period adjust through the balance of payments to ensure money market equilibrium, so that equilibrium is characterized by the following two equations:

$$M_1(\bar{e}_1, \bar{e}_2, \bar{M}_1, \bar{M}_2) = M_1 \qquad (20)$$

$$M_2(\bar{e}_1, \bar{e}_2, \bar{M}_1, \bar{M}_2) = M_2 \qquad (21)$$

Effects on the money supplies in each period (and hence also in the balance of payments) can be derived by differentiating the appropriate equation with respect to the relevant argument.

Increases in current and future monetary transfers (which can be described as monetary policy) have predictable effects. By increasing wealth, they increase demand for tradables and non-tradables without affecting tradable output. Monetary policy is hence expansionary, and leads to a deterioration in the current balance of trade. The effect it has on the current balance of payments depends very much on the period in which the monetary expansion occurs. With a current monetary expansion, a deterioration in the overall balance of payments is to be expected ($\partial M_1 / \partial \bar{M}_1 < 1$); the increase in the monetary transfer is greater than the increase in the demand for money, and economic agents dispose of the excess through the balance of payments, either buying foreign goods or foreign assets. So with current monetary expansion, both the balance of trade and the balance of payments deteriorate. With a future monetary expansion, the current demand for money rises; since the domestic component of the money supply is unchanged, this means that the extra money demanded must be supplied through the balance of payments. So although the current balance of trade deteriorates, the overall balance of payments improves; this implies there must be a capital account improvement which more than outweighs the current account deterioration.

A future devaluation will result in an increase in future tradable output, and so future income and therefore wealth will increase. This raises current consumption of both goods, and is therefore expansionary (as far as current employment is concerned) and worsens the current balance of trade. Whether the balance of payments improves depends upon whether the demand for money increases, and this, in turn, depends upon the sign of M_{12}. The anticipated devaluation raises the interest rate; this reduces the demand for money (and this tends to worsen the balance of payments); however, it increases the demand for money through its effect on wealth. The latter effect is more likely to predominate, the higher the supply elasticity of tradables. In the case where the balance of payments improves, the deterioration in the balance of trade is more than outweighed by a capital inflow.

A current devaluation, on the other hand, has more predictable effects. Since it raises current tradable output, demand for both goods in the first period rises. The interest rate also declines, since the future anticipated exchange rate is unchanged, so the current demand for money must increase. The effect on future variables is less clear (because the interest rate effect and the wealth effect go in opposite directions). So a devaluation is expansionary and improves both the balance of payments and the balance of trade.

It may be noted that the devaluation discussed here might be described as a temporary devaluation, in that the future exchange rate is unaffected. It would be straightforward to analyze the effects of a permanent devaluation (i.e. one in which the future exchange rate is devalued as well).

3. Current exchange rate flexible, future exchange rate fixed

This regime can be characterized by the following equations:

$$M_1(e_1, \bar{e}_2, \bar{M}_1, \bar{M}_2) = \bar{M}_1 \tag{22}$$

$$M_2(e_1, \bar{e}_2, \bar{M}_1, \bar{M}_2) = M_2 \tag{23}$$

In the first period the exchange rate is endogenous and adjusts to ensure money market equilibrium. In the second period, with a fixed exchange rate, the money supply adjusts endogenously through the balance of payments to equate the demand for money. The regime may be of relevance in a situation where the currency has been allowed to float but the government has announced a return to a fixed parity. The above pair of equations is solved in the Appendix for changes in the endogenous variables in terms of changes in the exogenous variables. The effects of a current monetary expansion are, as might be expected, a depreciation in the current exchange rate and an increase in the future money stock. The policy is hence expansionary; current tradable and non-tradable output rise (production of future tradables is unaffected, however). The effects of a future monetary expansion is perhaps of greater interest; the result is an unambiguous appreciation of the current exchange rate. The explanation is that the future monetary expansion increases wealth both directly and through its associated effects on spending on the non-tradable in both periods, and this, in turn, increases the current demand for money. With a flexible exchange rate, this must result in an appreciation of the currency. Tradable output falls, but consumption of both goods rises; the balance of trade hence deteriorates. There is no possible ambiguity here, as there was in the first regime, because the future exchange rate is fixed, and hence the demand for money, at the initial exchange rate, cannot fall because of an increase in the interest rate.

But a future devaluation of the exchange rate will not have such a clear cut effect, though. It does tend to raise future economic activity and hence wealth, so tending to appreciate the current exchange rate. But it also means an increase in the interest rate, which tends to depreciate the exchange rate. The overall effect depends upon which of these factors dominates. If the exchange rate does depreciate, then current tradable output rises, although non-tradable output could change in either direction. If the exchange rate appreciates, then since wealth rises in this case, both tradable and non-tradable consumption rise, so that the balance of trade unambiguously deteriorates.

4. Current exchange rate fixed, future exchange rate flexible

The equations characterizing this regime are

$$M_1(\bar{e}_1, e_2, \bar{M}_1, \bar{M}_2) = M_1 \tag{24}$$

$$M_2(\bar{e}_1, e_2, \bar{M}_1, \bar{M}_2) = M_1 + \bar{M}_2 \tag{25}$$

Most of the results derived in this regime are ambiguous and do not seem particularly interesting. Accordingly, the regime will not be discussed further.

Concluding comments

This paper has developed an intertemporal open macroeconomic model, where agents form rational expectations about future non-market clearing states, and, in the context of the model, has derived a number of results concerning the effects of changes in the money supply and in exchange rates. Some of these results confirm conclusions derived using more conventional models; others do not. Perhaps the following conclusions should be emphasized:

(1) When the current exchange rate is flexible, a future monetary expansion may well result in an appreciation of the exchange rate. The result is unambiguous if the future exchange rate is fixed. When the future exchange rate is flexible, this result is more likely, the higher the supply elasticity of tradables. The assumption that future unemployment occurs is crucial in generating this result; the future monetary expansion raises output, income and employment in the future and this arises the current demand for money, hence appreciating the exchange rate. In the future flexible exchange rate case, then there is an interest rate effect going in the opposite direction, so that the overall effect is unclear.

(2) In a fixed exchange rate world, a future devaluation will be expansionary providing that it raises wealth. A criterion for this can be given; wealth is more likely to rise, the higher the supply elasticity of tradables. Since the current demand for tradables rises, the balance of trade deteriorates whereas the balance of payments improves in order to supply the extra quantity of money demanded.

(3) A current devaluation will be expansionary and improve both the balance of payments and the balance of trade.

(4) A deterioration in the balance of trade may be associated with either an improvement or a deterioration in the balance of payments. The direction of the relationship may well depend upon the nature of the 'shock'. For example, in a fixed rate world, an increase in the current money supply results in a deterioration of both the balance of trade and the balance of payments, whereas a future monetary expansion worsens the balance of trade yet improves the balance of payments.

(5) A number of measures will benefit one sector at the expense of the other. For example, a future monetary expansion in Regime 3 results in an increase in current non-tradable output whereas current tradable output will fall (because of an exchange rate appreciation).

(6) Some conclusions can be drawn about the effects of permanent, as opposed to temporary, changes. For example, a permanent devaluation will be more expansionary than a temporary devaluation if, and only if, the effects of a future devaluation are expansionary.

The model does contain certain features which might be criticized, including the two period nature of the analysis, the way in which money is introduced into the model and the assumption of nominal wage rigidity. However, the two period structure is used so that the influence of the future on the present can be analyzed in a fairly tractable way; it is not meant to be descriptive of reality. The assumption that real money balances enter the utility function may not be particularly palatable, but it does generate demand for money functions with reasonable properties, and there seem to be no fully satisfactory way of incorporating the demand for money into a macroeconomic model. The assumption of money wage rigidity (and the associated rigidity of non-tradable prices) is used as an analytical device to enable unemployment (excess supply of labour) to be analyzed; it is not to be supposed that wages are literally rigid. Inasmuch as prices are not perfectly flexible, it will almost certainly be the case that periods of disequilibrium will occur, and in such circumstances a non-market clearing approach should generate some insight. A more satisfactory theory would explain both price and quantity adjustments; however, we are a considerable way from such a theory at the moment.

Overall, the model should not be taken too literally; rather, it should be regarded as an exploration of the possibilities in an intertemporal open economy with unemployment and rational expectations. There are a number of ways in which it could be extended. One possibility, which is explored in Fender and Nandakumar (1985), is to incorporate government expenditure, taxation and the appropriate government budget constraint into the analysis.

The Pennsylvania State University, USA.

APPENDIX

Differentiation of ϕ using (5) gives:

$$\frac{\partial \phi}{\partial e_1} = t^s(e_1)[1 + \varepsilon_{st}] + \frac{[\bar{M}_2 + e_2 t^s(e_2)]}{e_2(1 + r^*)} > 0$$

$$\varepsilon_{st} = \frac{e_i}{t_s(e_i)} \cdot \frac{\partial t^s(e_i)}{\partial e_i} \qquad 1 = 1, 2$$

ε_{st} is the supply elasticity of tradables, and is assumed constant. Differentiating with respect to e_2, and manipulating, we obtain

$$\frac{\partial \phi}{\partial e_2} = \frac{1}{1 + r}\left[t^s(e_2)\varepsilon_{st} - \frac{\bar{M}_2}{e_2}\right]$$

$$\gtreqless 0 \quad \text{as} \quad \varepsilon_{st} \gtreqless \frac{\bar{M}_2}{e_2 t^s(e_2)}$$

The possible ambiguity is due to the fact that the future devaluation reduces the real value of the future monetary transfer. In the text, it is assumed that $\partial \phi / \partial e_2 > 0$, which will hold if ε_{st} is sufficiently large or if $\bar{M}_2$ is sufficiently small.

Now, the properties of M_1 and M_2.
From (8), (11) and (11'), we have

$$M_1 = \frac{\gamma}{(1+\Delta)(\alpha+\gamma)}\left\{\frac{1+r}{r}\right\}\phi$$

$$M_2 = \frac{\Delta\gamma}{(1+\Delta)(\alpha+\gamma)}(1+r)\phi$$

so

$$M_{11} = \frac{\gamma}{(1+\Delta)(\alpha+\gamma)}\left[\left(\frac{1+r}{r}\right)\frac{\partial\phi}{\partial e_1} - \frac{\phi}{r^2}\frac{\partial r}{\partial e_1}\right] > 0$$

$$M_{12} = \frac{\gamma}{(1+\Delta)(\alpha+\gamma)}\left[\frac{(1+r)}{r}\frac{\partial\phi}{\partial e_2} - \frac{\phi}{r^2}\frac{\partial r}{\partial e_2}\right] \gtreqless 0$$

$$M_{21} = \frac{\Delta\gamma}{(1+\Delta)(\alpha+\gamma)}\left[(1+r)\frac{\partial\phi}{\partial e_1} + \frac{\partial r}{\partial e_1}\phi\right] \gtreqless 0$$

$$M_{22} = \frac{\Delta\gamma}{(1+\Delta)(\alpha+\gamma)}\left[(1+r)\frac{\partial\phi}{\partial e_2} + \frac{\partial r}{\partial e_2}\phi\right] > 0$$

$$\left\{\text{From (5) } \frac{\partial r}{\partial e_1} < 0 \text{ and } \frac{\partial r}{\partial e_2} > 0; \text{ these are used in signing the expressions}\right\}.$$

$$M_{13} = \frac{\gamma}{(1+\Delta)(\alpha+\gamma)}\left\{\frac{1+r}{r}\right\}$$

$$M_{14} = \frac{\gamma}{(1+\Delta)(\alpha+\gamma)}\cdot\frac{1}{r}$$

$$M_{23} = \frac{\Delta\gamma}{(1+\Delta)(\alpha+\gamma)}(1+r)$$

$$M_{24} = \frac{\Delta\gamma}{(1+\Delta)(\alpha+\gamma)}$$

The last four terms are all positive; M_{23} and M_{24} are both clearly less than unity. It will also be assumed that M_{13} and M_{14} are less than unity; this implies that r is 'sufficiently' high. This assumption has the plausible implication that a monetary transfer leads to a less than equivalent increase in money holdings (*ceteris paribus*) in either period.

Regime 1

Totally differentiating the system of equations (18) and (19):

$$\begin{pmatrix} M_{11} & M_{12} \\ M_{21} & M_{22} \end{pmatrix}\begin{pmatrix} de_1 \\ de_2 \end{pmatrix} = \begin{pmatrix} (1-M_{13})\,d\bar{M}_1 - M_{14}\,d\bar{M}_2 \\ (1-M_{23})\,d\bar{M}_1 + (1-M_{24})\,d\bar{M}_2 \end{pmatrix}$$

It follows that:

$$\frac{de_1}{d\bar{M}_1} = \frac{(1-M_{13})M_{22} - (1-M_{23})M_{12}}{D}$$

A sufficient condition for positivity is $M_{12} < 0$.

$$\frac{de_1}{d\bar{M}_2} = \frac{-M_{14}M_{22} + (1-M_{24})M_{12}}{D}$$

A sufficient condition for negativity is $M_{12} > 0$.

$$\frac{de_2}{d\bar{M}_1} = \frac{M_{11}(1-M_{23}) - M_{21}(1-M_{13})}{D}$$

A sufficient condition for positivity is $M_{21} < 0$.

$$\frac{de_2}{d\bar{M}_2} = \frac{(1 - M_{24})M_{11} + M_{21}M_{14}}{D}$$

A sufficient condition for positivity is $M_{21} > 0$.

$$D \equiv M_{11}M_{22} - M_{12}M_{21} > 0.$$

Regime 3

Total differentiation of equations (22) and (23) yields:

$$\begin{pmatrix} M_{11} & 0 \\ M_{21} & -1 \end{pmatrix}\begin{pmatrix} de_1 \\ dM_2 \end{pmatrix} = \begin{pmatrix} (1 - M_{13}\,d\bar{M}_1 - M_{14}\,d\bar{M}_2 - M_{12}\,d\bar{e}_2) \\ -M_{22}\,d\bar{e}_2 - M_{23}\,d\bar{M}_1 - M_{24}\,d\bar{M}_2 \end{pmatrix}$$

So

$$\frac{de_1}{d\bar{M}_1} = \frac{(1 - M_{13})}{M_{11}} > 0$$

$$\frac{de_1}{d\bar{M}} = \frac{-M_{14}}{M_{11}} < 0$$

$$\frac{de_1}{d\bar{e}_2} = \frac{-M_{12}}{M_{11}} \gtrless 0$$

$$\frac{dM_2}{d\bar{M}_1} = \frac{M_{11}M_{23} + (1 - M_{13})M_{21}}{M_{11}}$$

A sufficient condition for positivity is $M_{21} > 0$.

$$\frac{dM_2}{d\bar{M}_2} = \frac{M_{11}M_{24} - M_{14}M_{21}}{M_{11}}$$

A sufficient condition for positivity is $M_{21} < 0$.

$$\frac{dM_2}{d\bar{e}_2} = \frac{M_{11}M_{22} - M_{12}M_{21}}{M_{11}} > 0$$

REFERENCES

AIZENMAN, J., "A Theory of Current Account and Exchange Rate Determination," NBER Working Paper No. 1177, 1983.

BARRO, R. J. and GROSSMAN, H. I., *Money, Employment and Inflation,* Cambridge University Press, 1976.

BROCK, W., "Money and Growth: The Case of Long Run Perfect Foresight," *International Economic Review,* 1974, pp. 750–777.

CUDDINGTON, J. T., JOHANSSON, P. O. and LOFGREN, K. G., *Disequilibrium Macroeconomics in Open Economies,* Oxford: Basil Blackwell, 1984.

CUDDINGTON, J. T. and VINALS, J. M., "Budget Deficits and the Current Account: An Intertemporal Disequilibrium Approach," Stanford University, 1984.

DIXIT, A. K., "The Balance of Trade in a Model of Temporary Equilibrium with Rationing," *Review of Economic Studies,* 1978, pp. 393–404.

FENDER, J., and NANDAKUMAR, P., "An Intertemporal Macroeconomic Model with Oil and Fiscal Policy," Seminar Paper No. 313, Institute for International Economic Studies, Stockholm, 1985.

GREENWOOD, J., "Expectations, the Exchange Rate and the Current Account," *Journal of Monetary Economics,* 1983, pp. 543–570.

LeRoy, S., "Nominal Prices and Interest Rates in General Equilibrium: Money Shocks," *Journal of Business*, 1984, pp. 177–196.

Michener, R., "A Neoclassical Model of the Balance of Payments," *Review of Economic Studies*, 1984, pp. 651–666.

Neary, J. P., "Non-traded Goods and the Balance of Trade in a Neo-Keynesian Temporary Equilibrium," *Quarterly Journal of Economics*, 1980, pp. 403–429.

Neary, J. P. and Stiglitz, J. E., "Towards a Reconstruction of Keynesian Economics: Expectations and Constrained Equilibria," *Quarterly Journal of Economics*, 1983, pp. 199–228.

Persson, T. and Svensson, L. E. O., "Is Optimism Good in a Keynesian Economy?", *Economica*, 1983, pp. 291–300.

Sidrauski, M., "Rational Choice and Patterns of Growth in a Monetary Economy," *American Economic Review Supplement*, 1967, pp. 534–544.

Oxford Economic Papers 38 (1986), 545–550

INTERNATIONAL ECONOMIC POLICY
COORDINATION AND TRANSMISSION:
A REVIEW

By MICHAEL R. DARBY*

OPEN economy macroeconomics rose in fashion as the *General Theory's* jubilee neared. Perhaps no concern in open economy macroeconomics is more fashionable than international economic policy coordination, particularly if fashion is measured by the number of important conferences. An outstanding example of such is the June 1984 London conference jointly sponsored by the Centre for Economic Policy Research and the National Bureau of Economic Research. The proceedings of that conference are reported in Buiter and Marston (1985) which in turn provides the immediate impetus to this essay. This essay is not properly a review of that volume, however, but rather a response to a malaise reflected therein and obvious at other related conferences.

Aside from a brief editors' introduction and concluding panel discussion by Richard N. Cooper, Michael J. Emerson, Louka T. Katseli, and Stephen Marris, the book consists of eight main papers with two comments on each. The main papers can be usefully separated into two groups: those dealing with international transmission and institutions and those utilizing a game-theoretic approach to analyze international coordination or its lack.

W. Max Cordon exposits a graphical model to illustrate why coordinated expansion might be attractive to countries joined by floating exhange rates due to positive externalities in terms of output-inflation tradeoffs. Continuing their ongoing research on the implications of optimizing intertemporal models, Jacob A. Frankel and Assaf Razin demonstrate the theoretical ambiguity of whether the international transmission of fiscal policies is characterized by positive or negative transmission. In their model, whether a government spending increase is permanent or transitory, anticipated or unanticipated, as well as other factors, determines the direction of transmission. Patrick Minford presents and uses an early version of the Liverpool multilateral macroeconomic (simulation) model to analyze the effects of various government policies including most notably U.S. monetary and fiscal policy. In this preliminary version of the model, the builders' priors appear to play an unsurprisingly large role in determining the results obtained. Tomaso Padoa Schioppa demonstrates that the European Monetary System appears to have substantially increased the coordination of policies among its members and discusses the institutions which he believes

* The author acknowledges useful comments on earlier drafts by John Haltiwanger, Ross Levine, and Peter Sinclair, but any opinions expressed are those of the author alone and are not necessarily shared by his employers, past, present, or future. The research reported here is part of the NBER's research program in International Studies.

were central to this process. I believe that this distorts the independent determination of German inflation which permits the other countries to acquiesce or revalue.

I believe that the core of the book is found in the four papers which use the game-theoretic approach. Barry Eichengreen offers an unusual melding of a game-theoretic model and the history of the monetary conflicts among Britain, France, and the United States between the World Wars. Unfortunately, the two-country strategic model was inconsistent with the pursuit of the leadership role by both Britain and the U.S. Marcus Miller and Mark Salmon report computational methods for finding time-consistent solutions in continuous-time models of strategic asymmetry and rational, forward-looking expectations. David Currie and Paul Levine examine simple policy rules in a model which is complex by game-theoretic standards; they find examples of rules which work well for a single nation but are undesirable for all nations to adopt. Finally, Gilles Oudiz and Jeffery Sachs analyze the difference in payoffs between single and multiperiod models when the long-run effects of current policies are considered. On these four papers—and the broader research agenda which they represent—I focus my remarks.

In Section I, I outline what I see as the central issues of concern to macroeconomic policymakers. This appreciation is contrasted in Section II with the literature represented by the game-theoretic core of Buiter and Marston (1985). Conclusions are drawn in Section III.

I. International macroeconomic policy issues

Macroeconomic policymakers in one country are concerned about actions of their foreign counterparts only to the extent that effects of those actions are transmitted internationally.[1] International transmission may have nominal impacts, as on inflation rates, or real impacts, as on the real exchange rate, relative prices, and net foreign investment/current account.

The Bretton Woods system, for example, was established to take advantage of nominal transmission from the United States where the Federal Reserve System was to provide a stable nominal anchor, constrained if need be by the convertibility of gold. In the event, the link to gold proved to be little more than a government price-fixing scheme: In Darby et al. (1983) we found that the Federal Reserve's monetary policy was independent not only of gold reserves but of any other international factors. This exogenous behavior by the central country is appropriate to a linked fiat-currency system. However, the increasingly inflationary American monetary policy after the early 1960s—for domestic political reasons perhaps related to the intellectual ascendancy of ideas of a long-dead academic scribbler—led to foreign imports of unwanted inflation, the

[1] This section draws heavily on work (largely joint) reported in Darby et al. (1983) and Darby (1985, 1986). In what follows I omit actions such as default or expropriation even though they may have macroeconomic impact in order to conform to the issues considered in the subject literature.

breakdown of the Bretton Woods system, and ultimately a painful period of disinflation.[2] Clearly, nominal transmission through a system of pegged exchange rates can create important external effects from policy actions in the reserve country. However, nominal transmission does not appear to be the focus of current policy concerns.

I believe the current concerns focus on these salient facts: the trade-weighted real value of the U.S. dollar and the U.S. after-tax real interest rate were much lower during 1971–1980 than before or after.[3] American policymakers are concerned about the influence of the value of the dollar on producers of traded goods while foreign policymakers find the effects of U.S. interest rates contractionary. Much of the vogue of international macroeconomic policy cooperation seems to be a hope by some that it will provide a club to force a reluctant U.S. President to raise taxes or alternatively (by some in the U.S.) that foreigners can be forced to alter their policies so as to ameliorate the effects of American actions. Presumably cooperation would involve an agreement that the U.S. should raise taxes a bit and other countries cut their taxes.

However, there is no agreement among policymakers or economists that the return of the U.S. real exchange rate and after-tax real interest rate to their Bretton-Woods levels reflects a flaw in American policy. On the one hand, there is specific, empirically based, doubt that the tax cuts have any significant impact on either real interest rates or the real exhange rate.[4] On the other hand, negative after-tax real rates, low investment, and low value of the dollar are not viewed as evidence of a healthy American economy during 1971–1980. If higher real interest rates and capital inflows reflect a renewed confidence in America as a place to invest, this could be counted as a positive change despite real concern over individuals who, through no fault of their own, must shift from traded to nontraded goods production.

Thus, the basic issues on the international macroeconomic policy table appears to be real exchange rates and real interest rates. It is far from clear that 1971–1980 levels were preferable, given their costs, to levels experienced before or since them. Nor is it clear what macroeconomic policy instruments could effect a lasting return to those levels.[5]

II. Game-theoretic policy coordination

The game-theoretic analysis of policy coordination appears to me to be subject to both technical quibbles and a more substantive objection. The

[2] Germany now appears to play the role of a stable nominal anchor for the European Monetary system.

[3] The former point was made by Lothian (1985) who explains about 75 percent of the 1957–1984 variation in real exchange rates by a 1972–1980 dummy variable. Holland (1984) analyzed longer term trends in real interest rates.

[4] I share these doubts for reasons expressed in Darby (1986).

[5] Meese and Rogoff (1983a,b) have demonstrated the inadequacy of standard models as predictors of exchange-rate movements. The Lucas critique would suggest further problems if even reliable predictive relationships were to be exploited by policymakers.

technical quibbles leave one unsure whether the lack of consistency in the literature on such fundamental questions as the magnitude and sign of gains from coordination reflects a fundamental ambiguity or alternative special assumptions made on grounds of computational tractability rather than empirical evidence. For example, is there any firm basis for choosing a loss function quadratic in deviations of output *and* inflation from normal levels? If side payments are to be considered as means to reach cooperative solutions, should we broaden the gains to include noneconomic issues which may be linked in negotiations? Will behaviour vary systematically as governments approach elections and, arguably, become more myopic? Need we be concerned that international coordination typically involves more than two players and may indeed involve negotiations within currency blocs (e.g., the EMS, North America) and across currency blocs (as in the recently formed Group of 7)?[6] Perhaps further theoretical work can resolve such quibbles and provide economic intuition which is currently absent from the literature, but it cannot resolve more fundamental issues of the nature of international transmission.

The game-theoretic literature emphasizes the potential cost of failures to cooperate among nations which have significant and well understood international transmission.[7] This might characterize nominal transmission among countries joined by pegged exchange rates, but surely the large literature on that question suggests that the reserve/nonreserve country pattern exists to reduce the costs implicit in multinational determination of the "world" inflation rate.[8]

I see little relevance of the game-theoretic analysis to a world in which policymakers cannot agree on the causes of the current values or the effects of specific policy actions either domestically or internationally. For example, should foreigners who want lower American real interest rates urge the Federal Reserve (a) to loosen money and so (temporarily) lower the after-tax real rate or (b) tighten to further (permanently) reduce inflation and hence the so-called Darby effect which raises the tax-exempt rate relevant to foreign investors compared to the after-tax real rate determined by U.S. savers and investors?

International policy coordination has become more of a reality since James Baker became Secretary of the Treasury. In part this reflects renewed

[6] Eichengreen (Buiter and Marston, 1985, p. 174) reports that extending his model to three countries does not alter the principal conclusions, but we really do not know what happens in general.

[7] In an insightful panel discussion, Richard Cooper suggests that the arguments for international coordination are principally externalities, public goods, and multilateral monopoly. The former in the form of international transmission is the principal issue in fact. Cooper also suggests that international agreements may speed the process of adjustment which might otherwise slowly reach an acceptable solution iteratively. This is an interesting idea which would seem to invoke at least transitory international transmission.

[8] Or course, the "real business cycle" theorists would assert that the real economy is completely unaffected by money-supply changes so that no determinant solution to the monetary coordination problem would seem possible.

interest in a system of pegged exchange rates. It may also reflect changes in perception of the economic importance of international transmission. I see no evidence that if reflects changes in any of the assumptions underlying the game-theoretic approach or arises from a sudden awareness of the results of such analyses. That is, as a positive matter, I find that these analyses do not help to explain whether international coordination will occur, or what its content will be if it does so.

III. Conclusions

Although acutely aware that an experienced scientist is more reliable on what can be done than what cannot, I have argued in this brief essay that game-theoretic analysis has not been and likely will not be a fruitful way to understand international macroeconomic policy coordination.[9] I believe that the main issues here concern disagreements over the effects of alternative policies and not difficulties in negotiating mutually beneficial cooperative actions. It is at best a second-order question how alternative forms of international coordination effect the transmission process, but even that question cannot be addressed in game-theoretic models which presuppose a known, fixed structure of economic cause and effect.

I see the basic problem being that the assumptions—indeed, the entire literature—appear to be driven by the game-theoretic technique rather than the world so that elegant, enigmatic variations result that seem to offer little guidance for the issue important for understanding international macroeconomic cooperation or its absence. Such a judgment may be wrong, but in a world of scarce time and other resources, such judgments must sometimes be made.

Open-economy macroeconomists know remarkably little about what causes substantial, long-lasting shifts in real interest rates and real exchange rates. Most of our models and empirical analyses deal with the small fluctuations around the level determined by these broader movements. Until we can explain the major movements, coordination of the macroeconomic policies of the major industrial nations is likely to fail from lack of consensus.

U.C.L.A., U.S.A
and National Bureau of Economic Research

[9] Similarly negative views on the contribution of the game-theoretic approach are voiced in the Buiter and Marston (1985) volume, most notably in comments by Ralph Bryant, the paper by Tommaso Padoa Schioppa, and panel discussion by Stephen Marris. The conference reported there was not monolithic and it would be patently unfair to hold responsible individual participants or possibly even its organizers for the theme which I believe has dominated this and other discussions of late.

REFERENCES

BUITER, WILLEM H., and RICHARD C. MARSTON, eds., *International Economic Policy Coordination,* Cambridge: Cambridge University Press, 1985 [ISBN 0-521-30554-3].

DARBY, MICHAEL R., "Monetary Policy in a Large Open Economy," in Albert Ando *et al.,* eds., *Monetary Policy in Our Times,* Cambridge, MA: The MIT Press, 1985.

DARBY, MICHAEL R., "The Internationalization of American Banking and Finance: Structure, Risk, and World Interest Rates," *Journal of International Money and Finance,* 5 (December 1986): in press.

DARBY, MICHAEL R., JAMES R. LOTHIAN, and ARTHUR E. GANDOLFI, ANNA J. SCHWARTZ, ALAN C. STOCKMAN, *The International Transmission of Inflation,* A N.B.E.R. Monograph, Chicago: University of Chicago Press, 1983.

HOLLAND, A. STEVEN, "Real Interest Rates: What Accounts for Their Recent Rise?," *Federal Reserve Bank of St. Louis Review,* 66 (no. 10, December 1984): 18–29.

LOTHIAN, JAMES R., "The Behavior of Real Exchange Rates," paper presented at the U.C.L.A. Workshop in Monetary Economics, May 20, 1985.

MEESE, RICHARD A., and KENNETH S. ROGOFF, "Empirical Exchange Rate Models of the Seventies: Do They Fit Out of Sample?," *Journal of International Economics,* 14 (February 1983): 3–24. (1983a)

MEESE, RICHARD A., and KENNETH S. ROGOFF, "The Out-of-Sample Failure of Empirical Exchange Rate Models: Sampling Error or Misspecification," in J. A. Frenkel, ed., *Exchange Rates and International Macroeconomics,* Chicago: University of Chicago Press, 1983. (1983b)

Oxford Economic Papers 38 (1986), 516–544

AUTONOMY AND THE CHOICE OF POLICY IN ASYMMETRICALLY DEPENDENT ECONOMIES

An investigation of the gains from international policy co-ordination

By A. J. HUGHES HALLETT

1. Introduction

OFFICIAL concern at the multiplying problems faced by policy makers is clearly recognisable in Prime Minister Muldoon's remark: "1983 was the year that interdependence leapt out of the textbooks and landed on ministers' desks everywhere".[1] Persistent recessions since 1974, two oil price shocks and an international debt crisis, have made policy makers all too aware of the links between their economies, and that mutual dependence through trade and capital movements also makes their policy choices interdependent. The problem is serious enough; the average OECD country now exports about 30% of its GNP, so that the "spillover" effects of policy changes from one country to another can be very powerful. Even the US is 20% dependent on foreign activity. How should policy be designed in these circumstances, and could the international coordination of policy lead to better results?

The fact that foreign reactions often interfere with domestic policies has persuaded many politicians to call for coordinated economic policies. Competitive devaluations used to be the standard example, but nowadays few countries can divorce their monetary policies from foreign monetary conditions. Thus not all countries can reduce inflation simultaneously by tight money, high interest rates, or currency appreciation. But if all countries do tighten their policies simultaneously, the losses of output and employment are likely to be larger than any of them planned because of the adverse spillovers between economies. Similarly budget reductions abroad may frustrate domestic reflation plans, while foreign budget deficits can crowd out domestic investment. Given the degree of their interdependence, the European economies have an obvious incentive to export their inflation and unemployment—yet if they all do that, no country will benefit. Similarly, if they all expand together the inflation gains may well be larger, and the employment gains smaller, than expected because of the spillovers.

The problem here is clear enough; uncoordinated policies may actually limit our ability to control individual economies. It therefore seems odd that, after a decade of annual economic summit meetings, there is so little evidence on how interdependence should affect policy design. Similarly, although economic theory has shown that coordinated policies can bring gains, there is no evidence on either whether these gains will be significant over a period of time, nor on how they would be distributed between

[1] Sir Robert Muldoon at an OECD meeting.

countries. This paper therefore analyses the interdependence of the US and EEC economies using an empirical multicountry model, and considers different strategies for the 1974–78 recession which led to the proposal of coordinated policies at the 1978 Bonn Economic Summit Meeting.

Our results confirm Cooper's (1969) theoretical arguments for international cooperation: coordination restores policy effectiveness, and also cuts the cost of intervention by speeding up policy responses. These gains actually arise from coordinated monetary actions—so the "G 5" group of governments are right to try to harmonise their interest rates as a first step. However the central result is that asymmetries between countries play a vital role. Coordination produces better results both because it allows governments greater freedom to *specialise* in those policy instruments which have comparative advantage, and because it allows governments to coordinate the *timing* of their policy impacts. Hence coordination should aim to exploit the differences between economies, and to organise the sequencing of policy actions rather than to promote parallel policies. This implies that the EEC commission is wrong to make the convergence of economic structures a policy goal in itself (EEC [1984]). In fact asymmetric policy responses offer each economy an extra degree of control; and market flexibility, in particular, increases that autonomy because the consequences of external shocks or policy changes are more easily absorbed.[2]

These results are important because they show that previous studies, which have used models of identically symmetric economies and/or static decisions, could not pick up a major part of the gains from policy coordination. For example Cooper (1969), Hamada and Sakuri (1978) and Johansen (1982) have identically symmetric economies and static decisions. Currie and Levine (1985), Miller and Salmon (1985), Oudiz and Sachs (1985), and Taylor (1985) all consider identically symmetric economies but dynamic decisions, while Canzoneri and Gray (1985) allow asymmetric spillovers (in sign but not size) under static decisions. Finally the only empirical study so far, Oudiz and Sachs (1984), considers asymmetric economies but a static decision process, and therefore misses the gains from coordinating the timing of policy interventions.

This paper continues with the empirical approach because it is not always practical to use theoretical models in this context. There are three spillover channels to consider (via income, monetary, and terms of trade linkages) and we need to evaluate *net* spillover effects when all three channels are operating. No theoretical model has yet managed to treat all three channels simultaneously (very few consider more than one) because it is too difficult to sign the sum of all the partial derivatives of different instruments, activated in different periods, on each target in each period. That, as Flood (1979) points out, can be highly misleading. As a result, many theoretical models show an extreme sensitivity to changes in their underlying assump-

---

[2] Similar arguments were put, but not tested, by Koromsay *et al.* (1984) and Katseli (1985).

tions and restrictions. For example, Mundell's (1963) model yields totally opposite results if flexible exchange rates become fixed. Similarly Corden and Turnovsky (1983) can reverse Hamada and Sakuri's (1978) conclusions simply by considering two production sectors per economy instead of one. These examples are a striking illustration of Malinvaud's (1981) warning that the untested restrictions assumed in theoretical models are frequently more extreme in their consequences than those in empirical models.

2. Economic cooperation and world recession: a review

The severity of the recessions which followed the 1973/74 oil price rise has provided good reason to examine the case for internationally coordinated policies. With unemployment rising and output falling worldwide, the US in fact chose to pursue a policy of deficit financing (tax cuts and tight money since 1975; increased public expenditures since 1980), while European governments followed contractionary policies (mainly public expenditure cuts and tight monetary control). Even within these two different strategies, there were many policy changes. Budgetary policy started out by being cautious in 1974; but by 1975 several OECD countries had expanded their public expenditures to compensate for the external deficits caused by the rise in oil prices. In some countries monetary restraint was also eased. Then in 1976–77 most countries restrained their fiscal outlays again, so that output continued to stagnate while unemployment increased and inflationary expectations persisted. In particular the record shows that US and EEC policies, from 1975 up to the second oil price shock, were increasingly divergent. The EEC economies, in particular, resorted to fluctuating (and divergent) fiscal and monetary actions. A large cut of government expenditures in 1976 was followed by a rise in 1977 and a shift from social outlays to government consumption in 1978. During these years there were also alternating changes in the discount rate. Such an erratic and unsynchronised pattern of policy adjustments suggests that the coordination of policy effort between the US and the various EEC governments might bring important benefits; an argument explicitly endorsed by the declarations made during the Bonn Summit meeting of 1978.

Nevertheless many policy makers and economists continue to believe in the virtues of coordinated policies. In 1974 finance ministers of the industrialised economies agreed to avoid competitive deflations which would merely pass current account deficits between partners. In 1978 the US administration called for joint action to expand the major economies as a "locomotive" for world recovery. However, Germany's solo attempt to carry out that programme rapidly ran into trouble—as did later attempts by France and Sweden. Policy makers called again for joint reflation in the 1980–2 recession, although coordinated policies were by then opposed by the US government. More recently it has been argued that European governments should accept greater fiscal expansion in return for reduced US deficits, and that coordinated policies would have helped by reducing exchange rate fluctuations.[3]

However advocating cooperation has led to very little positive action, precisely because there are no estimates of either how large the gains are likely to be, nor of how they might be distributed between countries. Similarly there is little agreement on what exactly determines the size of those gains, so that detailed arguments for cooperation are difficult to establish in practice. In these circumstances, it would have been very hard for any sovereign government to justify surrendering some of its own objectives for the incompletely specified and unquantified benefits of international action; benefits which might, in any case, largely go to the other participants.

The exercises which follow therefore examine the advantages in promoting economic recovery through concerted action by the US and EEC policy makers. The US and EEC are assumed to have the same target variables, but the priorities which governments attach to these targets differ to match their observed policy stances. The choice of the 1974–78 planning period implies that we are looking for improved policy reactions to a common unanticipated shock—the oil price rise of 1973. However the planners are also assumed to be interested in governing supply conditions in 1978 and beyond. Hence the targets combine conventional stabilisation objectives (unemployment, inflation, production growth, the balance of trade) with indicators of potential supply (the real investment/production ratio, and the ratio of profits to national income). The differences in policy stance is represented by giving inflation and production growth a relatively high priority in the US objective function, but weighting production and the balance of trade more heavily for the EEC objectives. Exchange rates float freely throughout.

The following instruments were used by the US and EEC to improve economic performance during this period: government expenditures; social security contributions and expenditures; direct taxes on households and corporations; discount rates; net government borrowing from central and commercial banks. The aim of this exercise is to compare different strategies for generating improved policy responses to a common shock. The ideal values were therefore chosen to reflect the policy makers' preferred policy values. This was done in order to inject something of the policy makers' own preferences into the problem, and so that the variables themselves are all defined as *discretionary adjustments* from some reference path—in this case, that used to linearise the model. Injecting the policy maker's preferences in this way naturally tends to bias the policies towards those actually chosen; but since the purpose was to compare different policy making strategies, each of which contains the same "bias", the comparisons

---

[3] See Helmut Schmidt, V. Giscard d'Estaing, Martin Feldstein, and Laurence Klein in the Economist (between February and June 1983); also Bergsten *et al.* (1982), Begg (1983), and Layard *et al.* (1986).

themselves will not be affected. The instrument variables are defined as adjustments to the average historical choices, so their ideal values are zero. The target variables are adjustments to the values obtained by simulating historical instruments and the OECD's published expectations for the exogenous variables. Their ideal values then represent outcomes better than the policy makers could have hoped for by simulating their own policies. Therefore the ideal values are not a feasible set. The ideal target values may seem controversial, but since virtually none of the outcomes actually reached them (see Table 2 below) their precise values are unimportant. Our results will not be materially affected if the "ideal" annual reduction of unemployment were raised to 2% or 3% of the labour force. Similarly the results will not be affected by increasing the ideal output growth, or the ideal inflation reduction, beyond 3% in each year for 5 years. Hence the focus of the argument will be on the qualitative, rather than quantitative, results.

Finally we found by experimentation that the penalties on instrument changes should be roughly equally distributed, although the targets attract greater penalties as a group. The scope for changing decision values by manipulation of the objective function weights is really quite limited in practice (Brandsma *et al.* [1983]). In this case, even rather modest changes in the specified relative priorities imply movements in the instrument values beyond what governments would normally define as the boundaries of politically or administratively feasible interventions (as distinct from what is technically feasible). Table 1 therefore summarises the policy variables, their ideal values, and an "acceptable" set of priorities.

TABLE 1
The Objectives of Economic Policy 1974–78

	US Ideal	Priority	EEC Ideal	Priority	Symbol	Units
Targets:						
Inflation	−3%	4	−3%	1	P	% annual growth
Output	3%	4	3%	4	X	% annual growth
Balance of trade	1%	1	1%	4	B	% of GNP
Employment	$1\frac{1}{2}$%	1	$1\frac{1}{2}$%	1	E	% of labour force
Investment	3%	1	3%	1	IR	% of GNP
Profit	3%	1	3%	1	PR	% of GNP
Instruments:	*Historical Av.*		*Historical Av.*			
Government expenditure	2%	1	4%	1	G	% annual growth
Social security outlays	15%	1	16%	1	S	% annual growth
Direct tax, households	10%	1	17%	1	TH	% annual growth
Direct tax, companies	9%	1	14%	1	TC	% annual growth
Discount rate	0.4%	1	$-\frac{1}{4}$%	1	R	Level
Central bank loans	5%	1	19%	1	LC	% annual growth
Commercial bank loans	5%	1	19%	1	LB	% annual growth

Note: Social security contributions are restricted to equal outlays in these exercises; there are no deficits on that account.

3. The model and its asymmetric policy responses

The policy dependence between the US and EEC economies has been explored here using a version of the COMET multi-country econometric model (Barten, d'Alcantara, Carrin (1976)). COMET is typical of the empirical models which are currently used for analysing economic inter-dependence. It describes the economies of the EEC countries, the US, the remaining OECD countries, OPEC, the Socialist and the developing countries. The version used here has been re-estimated and contains the following changes: (a) aggregation into three economic blocks, to give a systematic specification across the US and EEC economies; (b) consistent accounts for the Rest of the World; (c) the introduction of financial sectors, international capital movements, and endogenous exchange rates.[4] The importance of having a rest of the world block is that one country's trade deficit is not automatically the other country's surplus. One can then see if policy improvements in the US and EEC are obtained at the expense of other countries. Similarly any spillovers transmitted through third countries are fully accounted for.

The US and EEC blocks, some 200 equations in total, have similar structures based on a conventional Keynesian demand system covering consumption, investment, and foreign trade. Cobb-Douglas production functions determine labour demand and investment. The supply side of both blocks are modelled by similarly specified potential output functions; and the potential and actual outputs are reconciled by a capacity utilisation index. In each block prices are related to import prices and the GDP deflator. The GDP deflator itself is determined by unit labour, capital costs and the utilisation index, while wages depend on consumption prices, productivity, unemployment, taxes and social security contributions.

The monetary sectors describe the financial relations between the central and commercial banks, the government, the private sector, and the foreign sector. Private and government financial surpluses are the main input from the real sector. Interest rates, which affect both real spending and international borrowing, are determined by those surpluses and by the behaviour of the banks. There is an important difference between the US and the EEC here. In either case government expenditures are financed, to a large extent, by loans from the private sector. In the EEC, this involves selling bonds to the banking system which then adjusts its portfolio and offsets any upward pressure on interest rates. Meanwhile the extra government expenditures also pass through the banking system, so that credit creation effects tend to reduce interest rates and increase domestic activity until inflation and wage increases set in to reverse that some periods later. Government expenditures in the US, however, are financed by borrowing savings directly from the private sector and from abroad, or by

---

[4] The model, as used, is described in Van der Windt *et al.* (1984).

tax and other fiscal measures. With a low propensity to save and greater interest elasticity of investment, this leads to the crowding out of private investment followed by higher interest rates and falling activity levels. At the same time prices rise due to higher capital costs. This crowding out process sets in after one year. It is sustained because there is no offsetting expansionary pressure or credit creation.

An analysis of the model's dynamic properties revealed that policy changes in the US generate quicker and stronger responses than those in the EEC (compare tables A2 and A3 in the appendix). This stems principally from reactions of real quantities to price, wage or interest rate changes, which are both larger and faster in the US structural equations. These differences are accentuated on the US side by international capital movements (which depend on relative interest rates, domestic savings, the trade balance, and relative growth rates). For example both economies react in a similar way to a rise in the domestic interest rate, but the US balance of payments alone is affected significantly (and positively). Again the impact of a rise in US interest rates on European targets is roughly equal to that for an equivalent rise in the EEC interest rate; but the EEC rate does not have the equivalent effects on US targets. Hence internal US policies for monetary control, or for financing the budget, tend to attract capital from abroad in a way that EEC policies do not.

Thus, in this model, US policy instruments have more powerful short run multipliers, but less powerful long run multipliers, than their EEC counterparts. These differences of impacts and timing show up clearly in the target responses to changes in interest rates, money supply, and (less clearly) in government and social security expenditures. Only taxation on households generates a larger response in Europe. In the longer run the US multipliers for government and social security expenditures, taxation, and the interest rate weaken to the extent that sign changes appear in all of them, while that for money supply strengthens. The main European multipliers (government expenditures, social security payments and taxation) also weaken slightly, while the monetary instruments (the interest rate and money supply) strengthen. That leaves the US multipliers weaker for all instruments except the interest rate (whose relative strength over its EEC counterpart has fallen) and the money supply (whose relative strength over its EEC counterpart remains about the same).

The spillover effects from one economy to the other show a similar pattern in that the effects of EEC policy changes on the US build up over time, whereas the effects of US policies on the EEC are immediate and do not build up (tables A4 and A5 of the appendix). Moreover the US spillover multipliers are nearly all stronger than the corresponding EEC multipliers. Thus rising public expenditures and high interest rates in the US would only temporarily increase European output, profits and trade balances. This result is broadly consistent with most theoretical models, and with recent history. In contrast, public expenditure cuts and low interest rates in Europe would first add to a US trade deficit (while expanding US output only slightly) but would lead to a reduction of that deficit and extra inflation later on. Recent events, at least, have been consistent with the first part of that finding.

However the monetary instruments are the only variables which actually have strong spillover effects, and here the impact of US monetary policy on the EEC far exceeds that of EEC monetary policy on the US. Moreover that asymmetry becomes more marked the longer the time lag since a policy change. It is important to identify these spillover effects since, as Canzoneri and Gray (1985) point out, the appropriate policy responses for interdependent economies depend on knowing the type of policy regime faced. Canzoneri and Gray consider three regimes defined by the signs of the spillovers: (a) the "beggar-thy-neighbour" case, where money supply expansion in each economy has negative effects on output in the other economy; (b) the "locomotive" case, where money supply expansion has positive effects on output in the other country; and (c) the "asymmetric" case, where the money supply spillovers may be of different sizes but must have different signs. The present model points to the "asymmetric" case for short run effects of US monetary policy on the EEC and vice versa. Expansion of the US money supply has a positive impact on EEC output and employment, whereas expanding the EEC money supply has a negative effect on US output and employment. Thus the tight American monetary policy of recent years, backed up by a relatively tight European money supply, have both worked to the American short term advantage. However the spillovers from that policy will eventually tend to increase output abroad while depressing it domestically; the spillover multipliers are negative, the domestic multipliers positive. This is Mundell's (1963) result: monetary policy turns into a "beggar-thy-neighbour" regime in the long term, but, being dominated by the US money supply, it is certainly not symmetric. That poses an awkward problem of selecting the timing of the interventions so as to get the desired *net* effects in each period, while the policy regime shifts with the passage of time. This implies: (a) a dynamic analysis of policy spillover effects is essential since those effects can, like any policy multipliers, change sign over time and the dynamic consequences of different strategies may be quite different from their impact effects; and (b) the *net* impacts of current and past policy changes (both at home and abroad) will probably have to be evaluated numerically.

Extending this classification to interest rates, we find that the spillovers from lower interest rates on output and employment are all positive while domestic effects are also positive.[5] This variable therefore introduces a

---

[5] The output responses to monetary expansion and falling interest rates are therefore consistent domestically, but conflict in their spillover effects. That is a common empirical result (Helliwell and Padmore [1985]); and, together with the faster US policy responses and the dominance of US monetary spillover effects, it appears in nearly all the models in the Brookings model comparison seminar (Hickman [1986]). In this case it arises from the

"locomotive" policy regime, which will allow an expansion of the international money supply. Once again the US policy spillovers outweigh those from the EEC, particularly those which arise from interest rate changes. Finally public expenditures also offer a "locomotive" regime in the short run which becomes ineffective with respect to output and employment in the longer term. But, as explained above, the US public expenditure domestic multipliers change sign after one year (while their EEC counterparts do not) so that the underlying policy regime now shifts for domestic, rather than international, reasons. Again the timing of policy impacts will be important.

Hence, taking these points together, numerical policy evaluations seem unavoidable because we have to estimate the *net* spillover effects from: (i) a combination of multiple transmission channels between an instrument in one economy and a target in another; (ii) the combined effects of different instruments on a foreign target variable (spillovers may be small individually but substantial in sum); (iii) spillover multipliers which are asymmetric between economies; (iv) dynamic spillover multipliers which may change sign at successive intervals.

4. Noncooperative policies with anticipations

In order to measure the potential gains from cooperative policy making, we must first determine how far each country can expect to satisfy its own objectives when all countries follow noncooperative strategies. To obtain that benchmark each government must condition its decisions on the actions to be expected from rational policy makers abroad. They must also expect that foreign decision makers will, at the same time, be choosing their policies in the same way. This means each decision rule must evaluate the expected foreign responses to domestic policy adjustments, simultaneously with the usual joint determination of the decision values themselves. Otherwise surprises cannot be avoided since it is inconsistent to determine country 2's policies, $x^{(2)}$ say, using a rule which specifies $\partial x^{(2)}/\partial x^{(1)} \neq 0$ but $\partial x^{(1)}/\partial x^{(2)} = 0$, while assuming at the same time that $x^{(1)}$ will depend on a rule in which $\partial x^{(1)}/\partial x^{(2)} \neq 0$ but $\partial x^{(2)}/\partial x^{(1)} = 0$.[6] If the assumed policy responses differ from actual policy reactions (i.e. the conjectured $\partial x^{(2)}/\partial x^{(1)}$ value used to derive the rule for $x^{(1)}$ differs from the value computed when

---

crowding out effects of deficit financing noted above; the real interest rate effects come to dominate the monetary ones. The Federal Reserve's MCM model and the Japanese EPA model also corroborate these multipliers (Oudiz and Sachs [1984]) if Germany is taken to represent the EEC. The same holds for the government expenditure multipliers. The conclusions of this section may therefore be reasonably robust.

[6] Cooper (1985) stresses the same point in his survey of policy interdependence, and argues that the severity of the 1975 and 1979 recessions were exaggerated because countries ignored the predictable policy responses made by others.

evaluating the rule for $x^{(2)}$), then the anticipations generated within the game must be incomplete. Consequently a form of Lucas critique will apply, and policy makers will make systematic "errors" because they fail to base their decisions on rational expectations of future behaviour.

One solution method which does evaluate foreign reactions jointly with domestic decisions in an asymmetric system is discussed in Hughes Hallett (1984) and Brandsma and Hughes Hallett (1984). The multicountry version of this solution runs as follows. Let each country have m_i domestic targets, $y_t^{(i)}$, n_i policy instruments, $x_t^{(i)}$, and be subject to non-controllable (random) events $s_t^{(i)}$ over periods $t = 1 \ldots T$. If there are two countries, the decision variables are $y^{(i)'} = (y_1^{(i)'} \ldots y_T^{(i)'})$ and $x^{(i)'} = (x_1^{(i)'} \ldots x_T^{(i)'})$ for $i = 1, 2$ subject to external shocks $s^{(i)'} = (s_1^{(i)'} \ldots s_T^{(i)'})$. Suppose each country aims for ideal values $y^{(i)d}$ and $x^{(i)d}$, for $i = 1, 2$, so that $\bar{y}^{(i)} = y^{(i)} - y^{(i)d}$ and $\bar{x}^{(i)} = x^{(i)} - x^{(i)d}$ define its decision "failures". The national objectives of each country are represented by the loss functions:

$$w^{(i)} = \tfrac{1}{2}[\bar{y}^{(i)'}B^{(i)}\bar{y}^{(i)} + \bar{x}^{(i)'}A^{(i)}\bar{x}^{(i)}] \qquad i = 1, 2 \tag{1}$$

where $B^{(i)}$ and $A^{(i)}$ are positive definite and symmetric matrices. Let the two economies be linked via the world economic system

$$y_t = f(y_t, y_{t-1}, x_t^{(1)}, x_t^{(2)}, e_t) \tag{2}$$

where e_t represents any noncontrollable variables. The constraints on each country's targets can now be condensed to

$$y^{(i)} = R^{(i,1)}x^{(1)} + R^{(i,2)}x^{(2)} + s^{(i)} \qquad i = 1, 2 \tag{3}$$

where $R^{(i,j)}$, $j = 1, 2$, are $(m_i T \times n_j T)$ matrices containing submatrices of dynamic multipliers $R_{tk}^{(i,j)} = \partial y_t^{(i)}/\partial x_k^{(j)}$ if $t \geq k$, and zeros elsewhere. Hence $R^{(i,i)}$ measures the responses of country i's targets to its own instruments, and $R^{(i,j)}$ the spillover effects from country j's decisions.

Each policy maker will find his own decision variables constrained by $\bar{y}^{(i)} = R^{(i,i)}\bar{x}^{(i)} + [R^{(i,j)}\bar{x}^{(j)} + c^{(i)}]$ where $c^{(i)} = s^{(i)} - y^{(i)d} + \Sigma_j R^{(i,j)}x^{(j)d}$. Each country's optimal strategy therefore depends on, and must be determined simultaneously with, the decisions to be expected abroad. In the absence of cooperation, the optimal decisions $(x^{(1)*}, x^{(2)*})$ will satisfy $w^{(i)}(x^{(i)*}, x^{(j)*}) \leq w^{(i)}(x^{(i)}, x^{(j)*})$ for $i = 1$ and 2, and all feasible $x^{(i)} \neq x^{(i)*}$. This equilibrium holds only when both countries perceive that no further gains can be made by varying their reactions to the decisions currently expected from their opponent, because to do so would trigger optimal counter-reactions (in the opponent's interest) which more than offset any gains made by the first country.[7] But whenever net gains could be made, despite foreign responses, a further round of policy adjustments must be expected. The necessary

---

[7] See Bresnahan (1981), Ulph (1983), Holt (1985) for the conjectural variations method, and Basar (1986) for a technical summary. Brandsma and Hughes Hallett (1984) extend it for any number of targets and time periods, and for asymmetric decision makers.

conditions for jointly optimal decisions by both countries are therefore satisfied by solving

$$\partial w^{(i)}/\partial x^{(i)} + [(\partial y^{(i)}/\partial x^{(j)})\partial x^{(j)}/\partial x^{(i)} + \partial y^{(i)}/\partial x^{(i)}]'\partial w^{(i)}/\partial y^{(i)} = 0 \qquad (4)$$

for $i = 1$ and 2 simultaneously. Let $D^{(j)} = \partial x^{(j)}/\partial x^{(i)}$. Inserting trial values, $D_s^{(1)}$ and $D_s^{(2)}$, into (4) automatically generates the policy adjustments:[8]

$$\begin{bmatrix} I & -D_{s+1}^{(1)} \\ -D_{s+1}^{(2)} & I \end{bmatrix}\begin{bmatrix} \bar{x}_{s+1}^{(1)} \\ \bar{x}_{s+1}^{(2)} \end{bmatrix} = \begin{bmatrix} F_{s+1}^{(1)}c^{(1)} \\ F_{s+1}^{(2)}c^{(2)} \end{bmatrix} \qquad (5)$$

where $F_{s+1}^{(i)} = -(G_s^{(i)'}B^{(i)}R^{(i,i)} + A^{(i)})^{-1}G_s^{(i)'}B^{(i)}$ with $G_s^{(i)} = R^{(i,i)} + R^{(i,j)}D_s^{(j)}$, and where

$$D_{s+1}^{(i)} = F_{s+1}^{(i)}R^{(i,j)} \neq D_s^{(i)}. \qquad i = 1, 2 \quad \text{and} \quad j \neq i \qquad (6)$$

Unfortunately this iteration may fail to converge and, in any case, it typically yields multiple solutions. However we need to check that these adjustments do provide gains for one or both countries at each stage, since equilbrium requires a solution in which both countries enjoy the best objective function values available simultaneously. To that end, $D_{s+1}^{(i)}$ is replaced by $\gamma_i D_{s+1}^{(i)} + (1 - \gamma_i)D_s^{(i)}$ where $0 \leq \gamma_i \leq 1$ is chosen (at each step) so as to force $x_{s+1}^{(1)}$ and $x_{s+1}^{(2)}$ "downhill"—i.e. so that $w^{(i)}(x_{s+1}^{(1)}, x_{s+1}^{(2)}) \leq w^{(i)}(x_s^{(1)}, x_s^{(2)})$ for $i = 1, 2$. This modification introduces a directed search such that at least one country is better off (and neither worse off) at each step. An exhaustive search will then identify the optimal decisions $(x^{(1)*}, x^{(2)*})$ as defined by the joint minima specified above.[9]

This solution procedure explicitly recognises that a player should only alter his conjectures about an opponent's reactions in a way which is Pareto improving for both players, since otherwise the opponent simply will not react in the way conjectured. In this context, one cannot expect any sovereign government to adjust its responses *unilaterally* against its own interests because that would amount to imposing inter-country comparisons without any compensating policy bargain. In any case, to establish an equilibrium position requires a solution yielding the best available objective function values for both countries simultaneously. Finally, the purpose of (7) is to eliminate inconsistencies between conjectured responses, $D_s^{(i)}$, and optimised reactions, $D_{s+1}^{(i)}$. But, as Basar (1986) shows, consistency with real valued policy reactions is not always possible. Nevertheless, the Pareto improving property eliminates surprises, and any incentive to deviate unilaterally from the final decisions, by picking the *best* of the real valued solutions subject to no country being worse off than it would be with alternative conjectures.

[8] To save introducing new notation, s is an iteration index for the entire $x^{(i)}$ vector, while $x_t^{(i)}$ defines the subvector of $x^{(i)}$ active in period t.
[9] The starting point is arbitrary, but could be the zero conjectures (open loop Nash) solution. Since the latter exists (Aubin, 1979), this search will terminate.

This "downhill" search ultimately yields the optimal decisions

$$\bar{x}^{(i)*} = -[G_*^{(i)'}B^{(i)}G_*^{(i)} + A^{(i)}]^{-1}G_*^{(i)'}B^{(i)}E_{1i}(d_*^{(i)}) \qquad i = 1, 2 \qquad (7)$$

where $G_*^{(i)} = R^{(i,i)} + R^{(i,j)}D_*^{(j)}$ and $d_*^{(i)} = c^{(i)} + R^{(i,j)}F_*^{(j)}c^{(j)}$ depend on $F_*^{(j)}$ which is defined by (6) but evaluated at the terminal values $D_*^{(1)}$, $D_*^{(2)}$.[10] Certainty equivalence has been applied to each objective, $E_{ti}(w^{(i)})$, where $E_{ti}(.) = E(. \mid \Omega_{ti})$ denotes an expectation conditional on country i's information at t. The computed policies are therefore conditioned on a single information set representing either one or the other government's view of the past and future at a given moment. They would be revised by explicit reoptimisations conditional on subsequent information sets (Ω_{ti}, for $t = 2 \ldots T$ and $i = 1, 2$). Notice that these decisions are identical to the optimal decisions for a closed economy whose targets behave as

$$y^{(i)} = (R^{(i,i)} + R^{(i,j)}D_*^{(j)})\bar{x}^{(i)} + d_*^{(i)} \qquad (8)$$

Thus the *net* effect of domestic action and foreign reactions is to change the policy responses from those in (3) to those in (8).

One objection to standard game theory solutions is that the conjectures which agents are presumed to hold in the standard case are usually wrong (Ulph, 1983). The open loop Nash solution, for instance, requires each policy maker to base his actions on the assumption that the other will not react to any policy adjustments, although both economies will be affected. That assumption nevertheless generates nonzero reactions, i.e. $D_1^{(1)}$, $D_1^{(2)}$ given $D_0^{(1)} = 0$, $D_0^{(2)} = 0$, which falsify the original conjectures. This is true for all solutions except those at the point where the conjectures turn out to equal the optimal reactions. The inconsistencies at earlier steps of (6) are therefore just a demonstration of the *Lucas critique*. The policies of one country, based on certain conjectured responses abroad, automatically generate different reactions from those conjectured; and that discrepancy invalidates the original policy selection because the spillovers from the new reactions alter the responses of the first country's targets to its own instruments. For instance, the open loop Nash solution generates policies for country 1 assuming that $R^{(1,1)}$ describes the target responses to domestic policy changes, whereas $R^{(1,1)} + R^{(1,2)}D_1^{(2)}$ will actually determine those responses. Country 1 then has to modify its proposed action to account for the changed dynamics induced by foreign reactions. More generally the responses change from $R^{(i,i)} + R^{(i,j)}D_s^{(j)}$ to $R^{(i,j)} + R^{(i,j)}D_{s+1}^{(j)}$. Only at termination is the Lucas critique satisfied because, if one country then tries to gain by altering its reactions, the other will be made worse off and would retreat to a position which makes them both worse off. Notice also that neither $D_*^{(j)}$ nor $D_*^{(j)}$ are block lower triangular, even when $D_0^{(j)} = 0$. Hence the conjectures are intertemporal; current decisions will allow for any foreign policy threats which may lie in the future.

[10] The reader is referred to Hughes Hallett (1984) for the derivation of (8), and its reoptimisation on subsequent information sets.

5. Cooperative decision making

Noncooperative decisions are known to be socially inefficient in the absence of side payments. Da Cuhna and Polak (1967), for example, showed that the entire set of nondominated (Pareto efficient) decisions can be generated by minimising

$$w = \alpha w^{(1)} + (1 - \alpha)w^{(2)} \qquad 0 < \alpha < 1 \qquad (9)$$

subject to (3). Hence, once a collective objective (or α value) is agreed, both countries could gain by solving one global policy problem. But whether those gains would be worthwhile compared to the loss of individual sovereignty is an empirical issue for which evidence has yet to be produced. Moreover, cooperation may entail redistributing the policy gains in a way which agrees poorly with national priorities or bargaining power.[11] It is therefore important to estimate both the size and distribution of the gains from cooperation, compared to those of a noncooperative strategy, in order to say anything about the value or sustainability of cooperation in practice.

A second set of questions concerns the qualitative differences between cooperative and noncooperative policies. Do the gains from cooperation derive from smaller interventions, or from better target realisations, or from the fact that policy goals can be reached earlier under coordinated policies? Cooperation also permits countries to exploit any asymmetries between their policy responses more efficiently. Three types of asymmetry are relevant here: (i) asymmetric domestic impacts of different instruments (leading to policy specialisation); (ii) asymmetric spillovers between countries (leading to unequal bargaining strengths); and (iii) asymmetric distributions of responses over time (leading to differing speeds of adjustment).

6. Empirical results: cooperative and noncooperative strategies

Table 2 presents optimised decisions (averaged over the period 1974–78) for the US and EEC under three different strategies:

(i) Isolationist policies which ignore interdependence; i.e. decisions by (4), with the restriction $\partial y^{(i)}/\partial x^{(j)} = R^{(i,j)} = 0$, but target outcomes by (3).

(ii) Noncooperative policies, including anticipated reaction terms, by (7).

(iii) Cooperative (Pareto efficient) policies, on an equal shares basis, by minimising (9) with $\alpha = \frac{1}{2}$ subject to (3).[12]

[11] A "real world" illustration is provided by the rise in inflation and current account deficit suffered by Germany after the cooperative policies, agreed at the Bonn Summit meeting in 1978, were enacted. Those policies were rapidly abandoned.

[12] This cooperative solution is a convenient point of reference since it corresponds to weighting national interests by relative GNP size (1978 figures). Alternative α values can be considered provided that the outcomes *strictly* dominate the best noncooperative solution, but the results do not change much (Hughes Hallett, 1985).

TABLE 2
Mean Interventions under Isolationist, Optimal Noncooperative, and Cooperative Strategies (1974 Information Set). Adjustments to the Historical values

Instruments	Isolationist US	Isolationist EEC	Noncooperative US	Noncooperative EEC	Cooperative US	Cooperative EEC
G	−0.96	+0.52	+0.18	+0.68	+0.23	+1.01
S	−2.38	+0.26	−1.11	+0.13	−0.61	+0.32
TH	−0.73	+0.41	−0.67	−0.62	−0.40	−0.59
TC	−0.44	−0.03	−0.23	−0.10	−0.14	−0.06
R	−0.21	−0.81	−0.49	−0.51	−0.43	−0.15
LC	+0.10	+0.01	−0.05	+0.03	+0.03	0.00
LB	−0.24	−0.18	−0.72	−0.04	−0.27	−0.19
Targets						
P	−1.6	−2.2	−2.2	−2.3	−2.3	−2.1
X	+1.9	+2.4	+2.3	+2.3	+2.7	+2.4
B	−2.1	−0.1	−0.5	+0.3	−0.2	+0.4
E	+0.9	+0.8	+1.2	+0.8	+1.2	+0.9
IR	+1.5	+3.8	+1.8	+3.3	+2.0	+3.7
PR	+1.2	+3.4	+1.5	+3.6	+1.3	+3.6

These three strategies represent the three fundamental choices facing policy makers at the start of the planning exercise. They can decide to ignore interdependence, or to set their policies competitively, or to accept an equitable compromise by cooperating. Detailed questions about the exact intervention paths can then be settled once the fundamental strategy has been selected. The noncooperative strategy provides the benchmark against which the gains from cooperation, and the characteristics of a cooperative policy, may be measured. The isolationist policies are used here to establish the *scale* of the changes resulting from cooperative rather than competitive policy making; although they also show some of the costs of ignoring interdependence. All the values reported in Table 2 are computed using the initial (1974) information set. They therefore represent the options as they would have appeared when the policy makers had to choose their fundamental strategy.

A popular objection to policy analysis based on noncooperative decisions is that those decisions are often time-inconsistent; with the passage of time policy makers may find that they can improve their economy's performance, for the planning periods which remain, by reneging on their previously announced policies. If that can be predicted in advance, the noncooperative policies will cease to be credible. However, as far as the noncooperative decisions of this paper are concerned, explicit reoptimisation of $E_{ti}(w^{(i)})$ shows that the revised decisions for $x_t^{(i)} \ldots x_T^{(i)}$, for each t in turn, remain identical to those expected earlier if there are no changes in the information set (Hughes Hallett (1984)). There is nothing here to stop agents attempting to make extra gains by reoptimising the purely future elements in $E_{ti}(w^{(i)})$, but if they manage to do so the performance index for the planning interval *as a whole* will be made worse.[13] Therefore the noncooperative decisions defined by (8) will be credible since any decisions on fundamental strategy will be taken with respect to their currently expected value for the entire planning period, and not on the basis of potential improvements to the later periods, which would yield a worse performance taking all periods together. This property may seem rather specialized, but it is consistent with the aim of establishing a reputation over a period of time and with the fact that policy makers will be judged on the sum of their achievements over a given period.

(i) Optimal policies ignoring interdependence

The isolationist policies for the US involve a cut of 1% p.a. in government expenditures, and of $2\frac{1}{2}$% p.a. in social security expenditures, while both quantities rise in the EEC. This US fiscal disengagement is due to the fact that domestic deficit financing in the US induces crowding out effects which lead to contractions in output, followed by upward pressure on both prices and interest rates. This was pointed out in Section 3. Consequently, if one ignores spillovers from abroad, the US budget deficit should be cut as the economy moves into recession. This is accomplished here by expenditure cuts, combined with tax cuts of $1\frac{1}{4}$% p.a. favouring first the corporate sector and then households. The US government did in fact introduce such a strategy (defence expenditures excepted) for the 1979–81 recession.

In contrast, deficit financing in the EEC has expansionary effects on output and inflation in the first few years, and adverse effects only later. So expenditures are increased to start with, while taxes are sharply reduced. This pattern is, however, reversed in the final two years.[14] Thus the EEC budget deficit would increase, while that in the US would decrease, over this five year period.

These fiscal changes mainly affect the household sector in both the US

---

[13] This happens because the constrained objective has an intertemporal rather than the usual time-recursive structure, so that the decisions cannot be separated into a time nested sequence of actions; Hughes Hallett (1984). There are several other ways of specifying time-consistent behaviour which depend on memoryless rules for re-establishing equilibrium at each t (Oudiz and Sachs, 1985). Such rules ignore the intertemporal elements of the constrained objective. In contrast, time consistency holds here because each government recognises that if it were to renege, then so will the others. Each country can only gain from time inconsistent decisions if the other country, despite being made worse off, sticks to its original policies. If both countries are simultaneously time-inconsistent (whether in an attempt to realise those gains, or in order to minimise the damage caused by time-inconsistency abroad), they will *both* end up worse off. Once this is understood, the incentive for time-inconsistent behaviour vanishes. Hence the need to predict future foreign decisions restricts each government's freedom of action and ensures revised decisions which are consistent with previous announcements/expectations. That is a formalisation of the Oudiz–Sachs (1985) "reputation" equilibrium.

[14] The year-by-year policy changes are reported in the appendix; table A1.

and the EEC; and the fact that social security cuts are more intensively used in the US is the product of real wage rigidity found in the US economy compared to the real disposable wage rigidity of the European economies (Branson and Rotemberg, 1980). Hence real wage flexibility is crucial for analysing not only an economy's responses to shocks from abroad, but also for determining what kind of policies are appropriate.

The monetary variables show that the change in European budgets is not financed by loans from the central banks (LC) and that the loans from commercial banks (LB) cause no extra money creation. The main European instrument, the discount rate, is lowered throughout the period. After a few years, however, balance of payments and deficit financing difficulties lead to the fiscal switch noted above. In the US, the dependence of budget financing on savings requires a more sophisticated strategy. First a lowering of the discount rate has to induce a fall in interest changes to stimulate economic activity. A rise of the discount rate (R) is then used to acquire savings until the loans from the banks to the government start to decline, after which the discount rate is lowered again.

The basic position is therefore one of standard Keynesian deficit financing in Europe, to stimulate aggregate demand and output, with monetary control and falling interest rates to reduce inflation. Meanwhile policies which have come to be associated with "supply side" economics operate in the US; a reduction in government intervention, especially in social security outlays and taxation, is coupled with a tight monetary policy.

(ii) Noncooperative (competitive) strategies

Turning to the noncooperative policies, recognition of their interdependence should lead both economies to introduce rising government expenditures, although the change is only marked in the US. The US social security cuts are halved, and in Europe they turn positive in 1975–1977. Once again tax cuts appear in both economies, although they are more variable than in the previous case. To the extent that these corporate tax and social security cuts benefit firms by cutting unit labour costs, this strategy appears to be aimed at boosting price flexibility in the US economy. That flexibility will give it the ability to adjust faster and more fully to changes in conditions abroad.

The US fiscal position is now broadly neutral with reduced, but more flexible, interest rates to offset any crowding out of the expansionary impulse. The EEC, on the other hand, switches to fiscal expansion with an accommodating monetary policy. The changes in monetary policy are more complicated because policy makers must allow for the possibility that their budget deficits will be financed from abroad. An initial rise in European discount rates attracts American capital, as witnessed by lower loans to the US government. The US has to resort to increasing interest rates; but rational expectations of the US monetary policy, together with the destabilising interest rate fluctuations in the US, then lead to larger adjustments in both monetary and fiscal policy in Europe. Indeed Table 2 shows that the main changes are in the monetary variables; the US follows a more restrictive policy but reduces interest rates, while the EEC now intervenes more actively both with loans and the discount rate.

Finally recognising interdependence has had a greater effect on US policies than on EEC policies. The US fiscal disengagement is halved, while its monetary policy more than doubles in overall impact. Meanwhile monetary expansion is reduced in the EEC and fiscal neutrality becomes fiscal expansion. Thus policy interactions have led to some convergence in the national policies. The US has dropped its "supply side" stance in favour of some demand creating measures; and the EEC intervenes with a more active monetary policy, using alternately the discount rate and money supply.

(iii) *Cooperative policies*

Cooperation between the US and the EEC takes the optimal policies a step further towards convergence; but the changes are now larger for the EEC than the US, and appear in government and social expenditures and in the monetary instruments. Government expenditures rise faster in both economies, and the US social security cuts are halved once again while those in the EEC lose their vigour. Tax cuts are still in evidence, although less prominent in the US.

Overall the cooperative policies call for reduced interventions in the US, and for more stable policies in both economies compared to the non-cooperative strategies. Indeed Fig. 1 shows that the US interventions are smoother than their EEC counterparts, and that (for both countries) the degree of smoothness increases with coordination. But for the EEC it is the optimal noncooperative interventions which are least smooth. Thus the EEC has to work harder, and has greater difficulty in controlling the spillovers, in a noncooperative environment. Moreover, the activism of monetary policy has now vanished—most noticeably the sharp restrictions of money supply and interest rate policy which appeared in the US noncooperative solution. Both loans to the government and the discount rates follow either constant or steadily changing paths. This suggests that it is important to coordinate the *timing* of monetary changes, and that the gains to cooperation may be significant only when that is done. Indeed the dominance of US monetary instruments among the spillover multipliers, and the asymmetry of the strategies which anticipate policy actions abroad (the US specialising in monetary control, the EEC in fiscal expansion), indicate that the important spillovers were caused by monetary rather than fiscal action. Therefore international policy should perhaps concentrate on the coordination of monetary policy, leaving fiscal instruments free for domestic purposes.

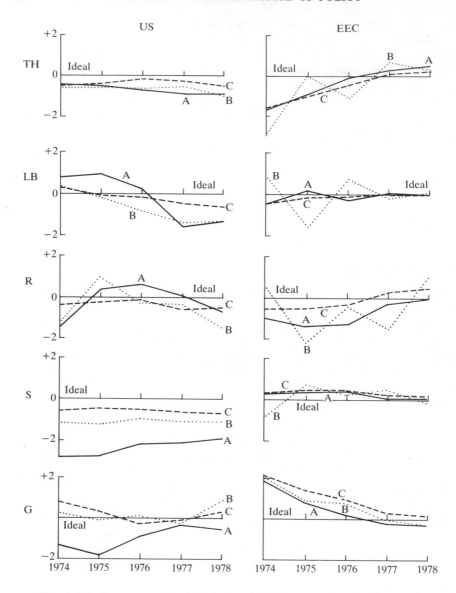

FIG. 1. The Instruments; A = Isolationism, B = Noncooperative, C = Cooperative

7. The gains from cooperation

(i) *Comparative advantage and policy specialisation*

One striking feature of the results in Table 2 is the increasing specialisation in the noncooperative and cooperative solutions. Both the US and the EEC concentrate on the instruments with more powerful domestic multipliers; the monetary instruments (R and LB) for the US, and the fiscal instruments (G and TH) for the EEC. This specialisation can be explained by the comparative advantage of the policy instruments under each strategy.

In the cooperative solution each country uses its instruments to "produce" several target values in the global objective (9), where $w^{(i)} \geq 0$. It therefore pays each country to put most effort into those instruments with the lowest opportunity costs; i.e. those with the largest (absolute) multipliers. Specialisation according to comparative advantage always makes it possible to reallocate the intervention effort between countries so as to get improved outcomes for both components in a global objective, since both countries are directly or indirectly "producing" some of the changes in both $w^{(1)}$ and $w^{(2)}$.

In noncooperative problems there is no global objective, so comparative advantage is restricted to the different instruments in the home country. That explains the different specialisation patterns in the noncooperative and the cooperative solutions of Table 2. Tables A2 and A3 of the appendix show that government and social expenditures, interest rates, and loans to the government (G, S, R and LB) have comparative advantage among the US instruments, while government expenditures, taxes, and interest rates (G, TH and R) have it among the EEC instruments. But the comparative advantage of G and S in the US, and of R in the EEC, disappears when compared to the same instrument in the other economy. Hence the noncooperative solutions show specialisation in all those instruments; but those without any *international* comparative advantage (i.e. G and S for the US, and R for the EEC) are phased out in the cooperative solution. That leads to a shift in the policy mix in both countries; the US tends to specialise in monetary policy, and the EEC in fiscal actions.

Hence the opportunity to reallocate instruments according to international (in addition to national) comparative advantage is one important reason why a cooperative solution can always produce a *better* outcome than the optimal noncooperative solution. Policy makers can then exploit the comparative advantage of the same instrument in different countries, as well as that of different instruments within one country. This is a general comparative advantage argument, closely related to Mundell's "principle of effective market classification". But in this context we must distinguish the cooperative from the noncooperative case, and also provide for policy specialisation rather than for a strict allocation of instruments.

(ii) *The expected target values*

Table 2 shows the average expected changes in the target variables compared to the values which could have been expected by simulating the historical instrument choices. These expected outcomes are better for all variables in both economies, excepting the US balance of trade. This is consistent with theory, which predicts that expansion will generate an improved balance of trade in a Keynesian economy with sticky wages but no such improvement for a classical economy with flexible wages and prices. Section 6 highlighted the wage/price flexibility of the US economy. However, expansion does little to meet the EEC employment target, indicating that European unemployment will be hard to eliminate.

Overall the US targets improve as we move from the isolationist to the cooperative solution (especially for production, balance of trade, and investment), but the EEC targets are not much affected by the type of strategy chosen. Once again we have evidence of asymmetry in US–EEC economic relations. Figure 2 sketches those target values in more detail, and

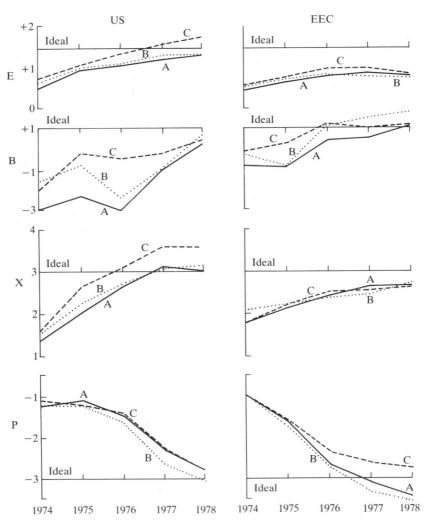

FIG. 2. The Targets; A = Isolationism, B = Noncooperative, C = Cooperative

makes clear where cooperation is advantageous. Under cooperation the US in fact does uniformly better only in employment, output, and the trade balance. The EEC does uniformly better only in employment and the trade balance; and both countries do worse with inflation. Nevertheless gains arise in all cases because cooperation *both* advances the timing *and* increases the speed with which the target variables approach their ideal values. That is to say, both countries tend to reach their minimum target "failures" earlier, and the rate of approach is faster, under cooperative policies. The upshot is better expected outcomes for most targets in terms of smaller average deviations from their ideal paths. These results therefore confirm one of Cooper's (1969) arguments: policy coordination damps out the transitory effects of shocks more rapidly and hence lowers the costs of reaching a given performance level in terms of the targets.

(iii) *Externalities*

The results in Table 2 showed that the gains from cooperation would take the form of both smaller instrument interventions and better expected target values in the US; but in the EEC those gains arise from a reduction in intervention effort rather than from improved target values. Thus the EEC would exploit the US economy as a locomotive; improvements in the US would enable the EEC to reach the same target values with less effort, both because the favourable spillovers are enhanced and because the un-favourable spillovers are blocked. Similarly an improved EEC economic performance means that the US instruments need to intervene less strongly in order to start a recovery following the oil price shock, and to a certain extent they can switch to achieving better outcomes for their own targets. These points are illustrated in greater detail by Table 3, which distinguishes target "failures" ($\frac{1}{2}\bar{y}^{(i)*'}B^{(i)}\bar{y}^{(i)*}$) from instrument "failures" ($\frac{1}{2}\bar{x}^{(i)*'}A^{(i)}\bar{x}^{(i)*}$) in each objective function. Adopting a competitive rather than isolationist strategy yields a large gain in US target performance, but only a slight improvement in its instrument values; the target failures fall by 79%, compared to only 11% for the instruments. That pattern is not repeated on the EEC side, where the target failures fall by 46% but the instrument failures actually rise by 3%. Those figures confirm that the US should act as

TABLE 3

The Total Target and Instrument Failures Within Each National Objective Function

Strategy	Isolationist		Noncooperative		Cooperative ($\alpha = \frac{1}{2}$)	
	Tgts	Instruments	Tgts	Instruments	Tgts	Instruments
US	170.6	18.3	35.9	16.3	40.5	7.0
EEC	56.7	10.2	30.2	10.5	27.1	7.1

the locomotive for recovery, and that the EEC is vulnerable to adverse spillovers from US actions. Meanwhile cooperative rather than competitive strategies produce a substantial fall in the US instrument failures (down 58%) at the cost of a slightly worse target performance (up 13%), while the EEC enjoys a significant reduction in both target and instrument failures (they both fall by 33%). Thus cooperation significantly reduces the conflicts between instruments: the US can scale down its role as locomotive, and the EEC is freed from the need to block spillovers from the US. Moreover, since most of the EEC targets fail to improve on average, while the target failures are reduced in aggregate, the gains to cooperation must have come from better timing of the policy impacts. Similarly the US targets behave worse overall, so cooperation prevents the US dictating the sequence of events to its own advantage. That is the price of being released from the burden of being the locomotive.

Cooperation therefore reduces policy "externalities". In this case it reduces the cost (to the EEC) of blocking spillovers from US policy, and the cost (to the US) of generating a recovery. Consequently the US and EEC target responses to domestic instrument changes appear to be stronger under cooperative policies than under competitive policies. That result illustrates Cooper's second argument for cooperation: coordination restores the policy impacts weakened by interdependence.

(iv) *The gains from coordination*

The objective function evaluations in Table show that accommodating economic interdependence brings larger gains to the US than the EEC, but the gains to explicit cooperation are significantly smaller and mainly benefit the EEC. Thus the US can expect to gain nearly twice as much as the EEC from competitive policy making (72% vs. 39%), whereas the subsequent gains from cooperation are smaller (9% vs. 33% respectively) and favour the EEC by 3 to 1. This cooperative solution therefore dominates the best competitive outcome.

To place these results in context, the gains to cooperation can be expressed in units of equivalent GNP growth; that is the average rate of GNP growth, all other decision variables remaining fixed, which would yield the same objective function gains for each economy. Here the gains to cooperation for the US is equivalent to an extra 0.47% annual GNP growth for 5 years, while for the EEC it is worth an extra 1.35% annual GNP

TABLE 4
The Performance Indices Under Different Strategies

Strategy	Isolationist	Noncooperative	Cooperative ($\alpha = \frac{1}{2}$)
US objectives: w_{US}^*	188.9	52.2	47.5
EEC objectives: w_{EEC}^*	66.9	40.7	27.2

growth for 5 years. This is a comparison advocated by Oudiz and Sachs (1984) who obtained the equivalent of 0.2% and 0.3% GNP growth for the US and West Germany in a static decision framework. This suggests again that coordinating the *timing* of policy effects can be at least as important as coordinating the impacts of contemporaneous instruments. It also suggests that the lion's share of the EEC's gains will go to the weaker European economies. That makes it important to extend this study to analysing the distribution of gains within the EEC, since if the gains go to the weaker countries while the burden of adjustment falls mainly on the stronger economies it will become extremely difficult to maintain economic cooperation within the European community.

8. Conclusions

A. In the light of the large gains which the US can secure simply by exploiting noncooperative policies, compared to smaller gains from cooperation, it is easy to understand why the Americans regard competitive decision making as the important issue in international economic policy. Indeed, the American position has been clearly stated in such terms by Feldstein (1983).[15] Nevertheless the European need for cooperation in order to overcome the spillovers from the US, while the US operates as the engine of recovery, is also clear enough.

B. Three important arguments for the coordination of economic policy have emerged:

(i) Coordination restores policy effectiveness weakened by interdependence and by foreign reactions. Cooperation involves trading reductions in foreign externalities caused by domestic action against reduced externalities from foreign reactions. As a result, smaller interventions can achieve better expected outcomes on average.

(ii) Coordination speeds up an economy's responses to policy action, and damps out the transitory effects of external shocks more rapidly.

(iii) Coordination enables governments to extend the range of comparative policy advantage, and hence the policy *specialisations*, which they can exploit. Thus, paradoxically, coordination helps restore a degree of autonomy in policy choice to the policy makers and the loss of sovereignty may be more apparent than real.

C. The first two arguments above confirm the theoretical results due to Cooper (1969): coordination cuts the cost of intervention since one needs to intervene less and for shorter periods. But the third argument shows that coordination brings additional benefits to countries which have asymmetric

---

[15] Feldstein's argument is that one only needs a full exchange of information (about aims, policies etc.) between countries. Each country is then free to set its own policies as it sees fit, offsetting any unwelcome spillovers as necessary. Ultimately that is the same as arguing for competitive decision making in a full information framework.

policy responses. These additional gains cannot be detected in Cooper's analysis since that was based on a model of two identically symmetric economies. Similarly, while the gains from cooperation are relatively small here, they are significantly larger than previous estimates which have been based on static decision procedures (Oudiz and Sachs [1984]). That suggests a major part of the gain comes from coordinating the *timing* of policy impacts—particularly with respect to monetary policy.

D. Asymmetries in policy responses allow greater autonomy in responding to external shocks. In this case the US should concentrate on monetary policy, while the EEC concentrates on fiscal interventions. The opportunity for specialisation arises here from different methods of financing fiscal expansion and because market responses to price, wage and interest changes are larger and faster in the US.

E. The poor performance of the isolationist strategy underlines the importance of allowing for international repercussions when selecting national economic policies. At a minimum, each country needs to learn something of the priorities, assumptions, and expectations which go into the decision making of its partners. If this takes the form of an information exchange under competitive policy making, then we have "coordination" of a different type. That yields the greater part of the benefits of explicit cooperation.

F. Some important issues which require further research are:

(i) This paper assumes unified EEC policies. Are the gains from coordination *within* the EEC larger than those from coordination with the US? How are those intra-EEC gains distributed?

(ii) Can international cooperation in fact be sustained? Are the results sensitive to the (perceived) bargaining strengths of the participants? Are the incentives to cheat sufficiently small, or must punishment schemes be introduced?

(iii) To what extent are these results dependent on one particular model? The model used here is a conventional one, with rational expectations being generated by game theoretic behaviour. Both the domestic and international policy responses are very similar to those in other empirical and theoretical models. But even if the numerical results reported here are sensitive to the model, the conclusions drawn are all qualitative and are therefore necessarily less sensitive.

University of Newcastle Upon Tyne, U.K.

TABLE A1

Optimal Isolationist, Competitive, and Cooperative Policy Adjust-ments for the US and EEC economies (1974 Information Set)

	Isolationist		Optimal non-cooperative		Cooperative $\alpha = \frac{1}{2}$	
Variables	US	EEC	US	EEC	US	EEC
1974: G	−1.33	1.88	0.31	1.99	0.78	2.04
S	−2.83	0.29	−1.20	−0.86	−0.62	0.28
TH	−0.44	−1.74	−0.62	−2.91	−0.53	−1.60
TC	−0.87	−0.21	−0.70	−0.50	−0.37	−0.19
R	−1.44	−1.01	−1.33	0.60	−0.39	−0.57
LC	0.39	−0.02	0.22	0.18	0.10	−0.01
LB	0.76	−0.53	0.35	0.88	0.28	−0.53
1975: G	−1.78	0.84	−0.07	0.87	0.37	1.44
S	−2.80	0.39	−1.22	0.75	−0.55	0.42
TH	−0.56	−0.94	−0.59	0.00	−0.42	−1.05
TC	−0.62	−0.03	−0.35	0.01	−0.26	−0.06
R	0.37	−1.41	0.99	−2.22	−0.29	−0.55
LC	0.19	0.03	0.11	−0.12	0.04	0.01
LB	0.89	0.09	−0.20	−1.61	−0.18	−0.20
1976: G	−0.88	0.31	0.06	0.81	−0.24	1.00
S	−2.20	0.39	−0.95	0.28	−0.56	0.39
TH	−0.78	−0.08	−0.63	−1.14	−0.24	−0.47
TC	−0.36	0.03	−0.15	−0.02	−0.08	−0.03
R	0.67	−1.32	−0.27	−0.44	−0.13	−0.38
LC	0.09	−0.01	0.07	0.09	0.07	−0.01
LB	0.19	−0.33	−0.92	0.71	−0.20	−0.20
1977: G	−0.32	−0.19	−0.25	−0.03	−0.14	0.38
S	−2.13	0.11	−0.09	0.54	−0.61	0.31
TH	−0.97	0.24	−0.58	0.63	−0.29	0.07
TC	−0.26	0.03	0.02	0.07	−0.01	0.00
R	0.04	−0.28	−0.35	−1.47	−0.78	0.29
LC	−0.11	0.02	−0.07	−0.02	−0.01	0.01
LB	−1.64	0.02	−1.43	−0.23	−0.53	−0.00
1978: G	−0.49	−0.26	0.86	−0.22	0.38	0.20
S	−1.96	0.10	−1.08	−0.06	−0.72	0.22
TH	−0.91	0.46	−0.93	0.32	−0.53	0.10
TC	−0.11	0.02	0.03	−0.04	0.01	−0.01
R	−0.69	−0.01	−1.49	0.97	−0.58	0.44
LC	−0.09	0.00	−0.10	0.00	−0.05	−0.00
LB	−1.39	−0.02	−1.40	0.03	−0.71	−0.02

Legends and units: see Table 1.

TABLE A2
Selected US Instruments, Domestic Multipliers

Impact multipliers:

target / instr.	G	S	TH	TC	R	LB
P	−0.07	0.04	0.04	0.04	0.48	−0.21
X	0.42	0.14	−0.07	−0.03	1.14	0.25
B	−0.89	−0.38	0.06	0.02	2.10	−1.00
E	0.21	0.05	−0.05	−0.02	−0.50	0.09
IR	0.58	0.10	−0.16	−0.05	−0.78	−0.06
PR	0.52	−0.24	−0.29	−0.01	−1.63	0.21

Dynamic (5 year lag) multipliers:

target / instr.	G	S	TH	TC	R	LB
P	0.23	0.11	−0.07	−0.01	0.17	0.59
X	−0.13	−0.02	0.05	0.01	−0.94	2.22
B	0.66	0.13	−0.17	−0.10	−0.39	−3.72
E	−0.06	−0.02	0.02	0.00	−0.46	0.98
IR	−0.37	−0.09	0.12	0.02	1.29	1.52
PR	−0.14	−0.04	0.05	0.02	1.49	−1.27

TABLE A3
Selected EEC Instruments, Domestic Multipliers

Impact multipliers

target / instr.	G	S	TH	TC	R	LB
P	−0.07	0.11	0.35	0.03	0.04	0.00
X	0.49	0.21	−0.19	−0.01	−0.38	−0.01
B	−0.20	−0.03	0.13	0.02	−0.09	−0.01
E	0.14	0.06	−0.06	−0.00	−0.07	−0.00
IR	0.61	0.16	−0.50	−0.02	−0.46	−0.01
PR	1.00	0.27	−0.66	0.03	−1.36	−0.02

Dynamic (5 year lag) multipliers:

target / instr.	G	S	TH	TC	R	LB
P	−0.16	0.14	0.19	0.02	0.59	0.18
X	0.30	0.06	0.03	−0.01	−0.31	0.15
B	−0.11	0.13	0.41	0.04	−0.21	−0.33
E	0.12	−0.01	−0.03	−0.01	−0.14	−0.01
IR	0.39	0.02	0.09	−0.03	−0.82	−0.06
PR	0.60	0.23	0.18	0.01	−0.28	−0.27

Selected US Instruments, Spillover Multipliers

Impact multipliers:

target \ instr.	G	S	TH	TC	R	LB
P	−0.04	−0.01	0.01	0.01	0.13	−0.02
X	0.23	0.06	−0.05	−0.02	−0.68	0.04
B	0.30	0.06	−0.08	−0.03	−0.87	0.08
E	0.07	0.02	−0.02	−0.01	−0.18	0.01
IR	0.28	0.08	−0.06	−0.03	−0.83	0.05
PR	0.46	0.12	−0.11	−0.04	−1.52	0.10

Dynamic (5 year lag) multipliers:

target \ instr.	G	S	TH	TC	R	LB
P	0.10	−0.01	−0.00	0.00	0.60	−0.94
X	0.06	0.02	0.00	−0.01	−0.47	−0.04
B	0.28	0.09	−0.05	−0.04	−1.77	1.10
E	−0.02	−0.01	0.01	0.00	−0.00	−0.08
IR	−0.01	−0.01	0.03	−0.00	−0.33	−0.12
PR	0.39	0.10	−0.07	−0.06	−1.89	−0.04

TABLE A5
Selected EEC Instruments, Spillover Multipliers

Impact multipliers:

target \ instr.	G	S	TH	TC	R	LB
P	−0.06	−0.01	0.04	0.00	0.31	0.00
X	0.11	0.06	−0.03	−0.00	−0.50	−0.01
B	0.55	0.26	−0.30	−0.00	0.95	−0.02
E	0.05	0.03	−0.01	0.00	−0.20	−0.00
IR	0.09	0.06	−0.00	0.00	−0.17	−0.00
PR	0.14	0.06	−0.07	−0.00	−0.65	−0.01

Dynamic (5 year lag) multipliers:

target \ instr.	G	S	TH	TC	R	LB
P	−0.49	−0.04	0.23	0.03	0.63	−0.03
X	0.25	0.08	0.04	−0.01	−0.43	−0.00
B	−0.45	−0.02	0.55	0.05	−0.12	−0.45
E	0.09	0.04	0.04	−0.00	−0.18	−0.01
IR	0.06	0.04	0.12	0.00	0.37	−0.07
PR	−0.00	−0.03	0.05	0.00	0.78	−0.11

REFERENCES

AUBIN, J. P. (1979) "*Mathematical Methods of Game and Economic Theory*", North Holland, Amsterdam.

BARTEN, A. P., d'ALCANTARA, G. and CARRIN, C. J. (1976) "COMET: A medium-term macroeconomic model for the European Economic Community", *European Economic Review*, 7, 63–115.

BASAR, R. (1986) "A Tutorial on Dynamic and Differential Games" in T. Basar (ed) "*Dynamic Games and Applications in Economics*" Springer Verlag, Berlin and New York.

BEGG, D. (1983) "The Economics of Floating Exchange Rates: the lessons of the 70s and the research programme for the 80s" Memorandum in *International Monetary Arrangements: vol. III* (p. 4–56), HMSO, London.

BERGSTEN, C. FRED et al. (1982) "*Promoting World Recovery*" (a statement on global economic strategy by 26 economists from 14 countries), Institute for International Economics, Washington, D.C.

BRANDSMA, A. S., HUGHES HALLETT, A. J. and VAN DERWINDT, N. (1983) "Optimal Control of Large Linear Models: An Efficient Method of Policy Search Applied to the Dutch Economy" *Journal of Policy Modelling*, 5, 253–270.

BRANDSMA, A. S. and HUGHES HALLETT, A. J. (1984) "Economic Conflict and the Solution of Dynamic Games" *European Economic Review*, 26, 13–32.

BRANSON, W. H. and ROTEMBERG, J. (1980) "International Adjustments with Wage Rigidity" *European Economic Review*, 13, 309–32.

BRESNAHAN, T. F. (1981) "Duopoly Models with Consistent Conjectures" *American Economic Review*, 71, 934–45.

CANZONERI, M. and GRAY, J. A. (1985) "Monetary Policy Games and the Consequences of Noncooperative Behaviour", *International Economic Review*, 26, 547–64.

COOPER, R. N. (1969) "Macroeconomic Policy Adjustment in Interdependent Economies" *Quarterly Journal of Economics*, 83, 1–24.

COOPER, R. N. (1985) "Economic Interdependence and Coordination of Economic Policies" in R. W. Jones and P. B. Kenen (eds) "Handbook of International Economics: Vol. II" North Holland, Amsterdam.

CORDEN, W. M. and TURNOVSKY, S. J. (1983) "Negative Transmission of Economic Expansion" *European Economic Review*, 20, 289–310.

CURRIE, D. and LEVINE, P. L. (1985) "Macroeconomic Policy Design in an Interdependent World" in W. H. Buiter and R. C. Marston (eds) "International Economic Policy Coordination" Cambridge University Press, Cambridge and New York.

DA CUHNA, N. and POLAK, E. (1967) "Constrained Minimisation of Vector-Valued Criteria in Finite Dimensional Spaces", *Journal of Mathematical Analysis and Applications*, 19, 103–24.

EEC (1984) "The Annual Economic Report 1984–5" *The European Economy*, No. 23, The European Economic Commission, Brussels.

FELDSTEIN, M. (1983) "The World Economy Today", *Economist*, June 11, 1983.

FLOOD, R. P. (1979) "Capital Mobility and the Choice of Exchange Rate System" *International Economic Review*, 20, 405–16.

HAMADA, K. and SAKURI, M. (1978) "International Transmission of Stagflation under Fixed and Flexible Exchange Rates" *Journal of Political Economy*, 86, 877–95.

HELLIWELL, J. F. and PADMORE, T. (1985) "Empirical Studies of Macroeconomic Interdependence" in R. W. Jones and P. B. Kenen (eds) "Handbook of International Economics: Vol. II" North Holland, Amsterdam.

HICKMAN, B. G. (1986) "The US Economy and the International Transmission Mechanism: A Structural Comparison of 12 Models" Paper presented to the Conference on Empirical Macroeconomics for Interdependent Economies, Brookings Institution Washington, DC.

HOLT, C. A. (1985) "An Experimental Test of the Consistent Conjectures Hypothesis" *American Economic Review*, 75, 314–25.

HUGHES HALLETT, A. J. (1984) "Noncooperative Strategies for Dynamic Policy Games and the Problems of Time Inconsistency" *Oxford Economic Papers,* 36, 381–99.

HUGHES HALLETT, A. J. (1985) "How Much Could the International Coordination of Economic Policies Achieve? An Example from US–EEC Policy Making" Discussion Paper No. 77, Centre for Economic Policy Research, London.

JOHANSEN, L. (1982) "The Possibility of International Equilibrium at Low Levels of Activity" *Journal of International Economics,* 13, 257–65.

KATSELI, L. (1985) Contribution to the Panel Discussion, p. 376–9 in W. H. Buiter and R. C. Marston (eds) "International Economic Policy Coordination" Cambridge University Press, Cambridge and New York.

KOROMSAY, V., LLEWELLYN, J. and POTTER, S. (1984) "Exchange Rates and Policy Choices: Some Lessons from Interdependence in a Multilateral Perspective" *American Economic Review* (papers and proceedings) 311–315.

LAYARD, R., BASEVI, G., BLANCHARD, O., BUITER, W. and DORNBUSCH, R. (1986) "Europe: the Case for Unsustainable Growth" in O. Blanchard, R. Dornbusch and R. Layard (eds) "Restoring Europe's Prosperity" MIT Press, Cambridge, Mass.

MALINVAUD, E. (1981) "Econometrics Faced with the Needs of Macroeconomic Policy" *Econometrica,* 49, 1363–75.

MILLER, M. and SALMON, M. (1985) "Policy Coordination and the Time Inconsistency of Optimal Policy in Open Economies" *Economic Journal* (supplement 124–35).

MUNDELL, R. A. (1963) "Capital Mobility and Stabilisation Policy Under Fixed and Flexible Exchange Rates" *Canadian Journal of Economics,* 29, 475–85.

OUDIZ, G. and SACHS, J. (1984) "Policy Coordination in Industrialised Countries", *Brookings Economic Papers* (1), 1–64.

OUDIZ, G. and SACHS, J. (1985) "International Policy Coordination in Dynamic Macroeconomic Models" in W. H. Buiter and R. C. Marston (eds) "International Economic Policy Coordination" Cambridge University Press, Cambridge and New York.

TAYLOR, J. B. (1985) "International Coordination in the Design of Macroeconomic Policy Rules" *European Economic Review,* 28, 53–82.

ULPH, D. (1983) "Rational Conjectures in the Theory of Oligopoly" *International Journal of Industrial Organisation,* 1, 131–54.

VAN DER WINDT, N., SIEBRAND, J. C., SWANK, J. and PIJPERS, J. R. (1984a, b) "Rasmus: an annual model of the US and EEC economies" Discussion Papers 8405/G and 8411/G, Erasmus University, Rotterdam.

Oxford Economic Papers 38 (1986), 354–361

"OF MARX AND KEYNES AND MANY THINGS"*

By F. H. HAHN

NEAR the end of this long book Marglin writes: "By contrast (to the neo-classical model), if one follows the neo-Marxian lead, one will look to the relations of production and focus on the balance of class power. It will come as no surprise that I find the second a more useful starting point." (p. 469). Well, as a matter of fact, it does come as a bit of a surprise. For up to this point class power or struggle hardly made an appearance and apart from Marglin's well known views on the division of labour, neither did the relations of production. There are obiter dicta on these matters and here and there a speculative paragraph. But in the formal analysis—and most of the book is formal analysis—these Marxian preoccupations are absent. There is no attempt to bring game theory to the aid of an analysis of class war and of social equilibrium and even Schumpeter's stimulating reformulation of some Marxian insights is absent; indeed Schumpeter appears neither in the index nor in the bibliography. To this one must now add that Keynes too appears in emasculated form. The result, paradoxically, is that neo-classical methodology comes off best since models using it are not put on the short rations meted out to Keynes and Marx. So it comes about that while this is a remarkably honest book with careful attention to the details of arguments and a number of quite excellent insights it must also be judged a failure relatively to the author's main intention. This I take to have been a clear presentation of what he regards as canonical examples of Neo-classical, Neo-Keynesian and Neo-Marxian theorising. A secondary intention was to present his own theory of savings and a synthesis of Keynes and Marx. This secondary intention is carried out well but does not convince.

The vehicle chosen by Marglin for his enterprise is post war growth theory without too many complications (e.g. no putty-clay etc.). This means that he concentrates attention on steady states and on small neighbourhoods of such states. The teacher in him is relentless. We start with fixed coefficient one commodity models, move on to a spectrum of techniques and thence to continuous substitutability. After that it is the turn of multiple commodities, von Neumann, double-switching etc. In each of these simplifications the three "schools" are distinguished as follows. The Neo-Classical model is based on the maximisation of the intertemporal utility function subject to a budget constraint and the requirement of labour market clearing (the natural rate of growth = warranted rate). The Neo-Marxian and Neo-Keynesian models define the warranted growth rate using a Pasinetti description of saving which in turn depends on whether capitalists

---

* A review article of: *Growth Distribution and Prices* by Stephen A. Marglin, Harvard University Press, Cambridge, Massachusetts, 1984.

own a negligible fraction of wealth or not. The Neo-Marxians "close" the model by setting the real wage at a (socially determined) subsistence level while the Keynesians "close" it by an investment function—animal spirits depending on the rate of profit. In none of the models is there durable capital nor are financial assets of any kind formally included. (Thus Keynes is studied without Liquidity Preference.)

It is proper to start with praise. First of all, the models are lucidly and clearly presented, with lots of diagrams to help the algebra. They are also studied and manipulated with care. Secondly Marglin, unlike many others in revolt against Neo-Classical theory, understands what he is doing. Here he is on marginal productivity: "There is first of all the *general* theory that assumes nothing more controversial than continuous substitution, constant returns to scale, and competitive profit maximisation. This theory, far from being unique to one school of thought, is—or at least ought to be—the common property of all three approaches" (p. 223). He has other things to say on marginal productivity to which I return below but here I note that he would have been a welcome ally in the Cambridge (England) of the sixties. Or again on using class analysis: "the harmonisation of class interests is a real problem for Marxian theory. . . " (p. 472, see also the excellent page 473). Or on $g = s_c r$ "It is misleading to characterise the role of technology in a model by its role in one of *two* equilibrium conditions, namely by its absence in the saving equation" (p. 128). When one recalls the nonsense that has been written on all these matters one can only give thanks for Marglin. There are many other instances of his perspicacity, intelligence and above all understanding even of uncongenial theories which one could quote. Thirdly and lastly Marglin combines intellectual honesty with serious thought. This last is best seen when he stands back and comments on the formalities: "the labour theory of value is a theory of class relationships, a theory of the *source* of value rather than a theory of growth, distribution and relative prices" (p. 45). But it is also seen in his careful and interesting empirical chapters on savings.

Had this book been published in the sixties it would surely have made its mark. As it is there must be some doubt. The theory of growth is now definitely somewhat in eclipse and I am not sure that this fate is not deserved. The major part of this theory was concerned with steady states and it was never clear why, even given the commitment to equilibrium analysis, this particular equilibrium should be of central interest. Moreover the models invariably failed to show concern for the real engines of growth: innovations and perhaps population growth. Indeed most of them are simply mechanical toys sans history and sans human ingenuity. Certainly they taught us something but in retrospect, what they taught was elementary and quite palpably only the beginning of a story. Perhaps it is not possible to do more—a theory of history is not self-evidently a plausible aim. But it is surprising in an author of Marxian sympathies to have opted for so uncompromising a concentration on the most visible nuts and bolts.

Consider Marglin's characterisation of the three schools. He argues that the postulate of intertemporal utility maximisation leaves one sufficient flexibility as to adapt it to most purposes (e.g. it is easy to specify utility functions which make savings proportional to current income). So, of itself, this postulate cannot be a necessary distinguishing mark. The critical feature which for Marglin distinguishes the Neo-Classical from other theories, is the postulate of continuous market clearing. In this characterisation he must have been much influenced by the current American scene, in particular in the Mid-West. Indeed he quotes one of Lucas's more remarkable methodological claims in support. But I very much doubt that this goes to the heart of the matter. Were those writing on general equilibrium and stability (e.g. Arrow and Hurwicz) not in the Neo-Classical tradition? Indeed why bother with "existence" proofs if it is an axiom that markets always clear?

Marglin's view of Neo-Classical economics does not, so it seems to me, dig deeply enough. Neo-Classical economics has, I think, two fundamental characterising features. It seeks understanding which is rooted in that of the rational agent—that is an agent who knows what he wants and knows how to get it. Secondly it therefore requires explanation, at the level of the individual agent, if it is claimed that in such and such an economy what seem to be Pareto-improving transactions fail to be undertaken. For instance such explanations may be found in the informational structure of the situation. A good example is the Stiglitz–Weiss (1981) account of credit rationing. Here at the going interest rate the demand for loans may exceed supply but it is shown that this is not a sign of unexploited Pareto-improvements. In the same way if workers were to incur social stigma from undercutting others, an excess supply of labour would not signal Pareto-inefficiency.

I labour these points because I confess to some resentment at having the whole Neo-Classical methodology defined by an elementary (American) textbook or by economists who have not thought beyond it. In particular the axiom of continuous market clearing is not only not self-evident (as axioms are often defined) but vastly disabling for the theorist since it removes such a large array of intellectually taxing questions from consideration. I know of no instance of such a step being advocated by any of the great post-war codifiers of Neo-Classical economics.

There is a third aspect of much of Neo-Classical economics which I have not taken as characterising it, namely the assumption of perfect competition. Much of Neo-Classical economics proceeds on this assumption although it is due to Neo-Classical economists that we now understand not only its precise logical entailment but also its range of applicability. I have not taken perfect competition as "characterising" because it seems to me senseless to adopt a classification which leads to a proliferation of "schools". Surely one is justified in thinking of the splendid work now being done in Industrial Organisation Theory, for instance, as fully in the Neo-Classical tradition?

So much for this, perhaps not fundamentally important, general matter. In his manipulation of the traditional Neo-Classical growth models Marglin is on the whole sure-footed and thorough. But that is not always so. Thus he considers "life-cycle" savings to be the leading example of Neo-Classical models. (He does not discuss the much researched infinitely lived agent case.) But he does not construct an explicit model of overlapping generations and this leads to certain obscurities. For instance on p. 152 Marglin argues that in a life-cycle model a higher level of per capita wages leads to a higher level of profits. This in turn entails a lower profit rate and a higher capital intensity and so more saving (by the young). This may be correct reasoning but it is hardly transparent. For instance if there is a unique steady state and if all of this is to apply to steady states, then we are only at liberty to consider a "higher wage" when we are thinking of another steady state with a different technology. But then the argument does not follow. If it is not meant to be steady state analysis then all sorts of other elements would be up for consideration.

But this is a small matter. More important is Marglin's preoccupation with one version or another of the "Cambridge Savings Equation". He is to be praised for his discussion of the "anti-Pasinetti" regime (in which capitalists own a negligible fraction of the total capital stock) and for his careful analysis of the destination of household savings (housing, pension funds, etc.). But he attaches too much significance to that story and his treatment is not always convincing.

In a thesis which I wrote in 1951 the central message of which was published in 1952 and the whole of which was published in 1972, I developed a distribution theory based on different savings propensities out of profits and out of wages. The model was closed by an investment function rather than by a "full employment" postulate. My conclusion was (and is) that these kind of theories (a) are very crude (the "profits" "wages" division is far too rough) and (b) that such merit as they do have relates largely to the "short run". By this I mean that one can think of strong reasons why marginal product equations need not hold in the short run which leaves the way open for other mechanisms operating via the distribution of income and its effect on savings. In the short run with commodity market clearing and production lags one can indeed rehabilitate a sort of "Wages-Fund" doctrine. But in the long run with a choice of technique and no precommitments nothing fundamentally new seems to be added to the Neo-Classical story by recognising the dependence of the savings ratio on the distribution between wages and profit.

At least that is true as far as steady state equilibrium goes. Marglin however argues that the stability properties of such an equilibrium are very much affected. He supports this view by means of a model of "out-of-equilibrium behaviour" in the vicinity of steady state. The point is well worth making but as usual one reserves judgment since there is so little either theoretically or empirically justified which underlies our adjustment hypotheses. Nonetheless the distribution-dependent savings function may indeed turn out to be an important stabiliser.

One of the difficulties with this approach to savings is that there seems no immediate reason, (unless profits go entirely to the young in an overlapping generations model), why there should be a higher saving propensity out of profits. Very early on in the literature an appeal was made to the role of undistributed profits—the saving propensity of corporations does indeed seems clearly higher than is that of persons. To this there is an obvious objection. Corporations are owned by persons through the holding of shares and in a properly functioning share market, existing share-holders will receive (neglecting taxes) in the form of an appreciation what is withheld through retained profits. If that is so then corporations as such cannot influence the savings ratio. If the share market functions only imperfectly then it may yet be insufficient to appeal to retained profits to justify the basic feature of this approach to savings.

It is clear that Marglin understands all of this but what he has to say on the matter is quite inadequate. (See e.g. 6.26 on p. 130 and the discussion on pp. 378–9.) He seems muddled and appears to believe that because shareholders do not directly control the actions of corporations one can neglect the effect of retentions on shareholders' disposable income via share price changes. In an age of take-overs it is odd not to see them mentioned. In a situation where profit distribution normally carries tax penalties a theorist far from taking retention as disadvantageous to persons would, in the first instance, be inclined to assume the reverse. But if he does not then he has a lot of explaining to do and Marglin's efforts here are far from sufficient.

Indeed he has espoused a somewhat extreme view of savings by persons insofar as they are directed to productive investment (rather than housing and pensions etc.). This is the proposition that persons will plan to spend the whole of their income (including on housing etc.). and that such saving as they do is entirely due to income being higher than "normal". "In short household saving is hypothesized to be a disequilibrium phenomenon. . . that occurs only when income is increasing at a faster rate than households can learn to spend it" (p. 144). In a lengthy empirical chapter this hypothesis is compared with others with the conclusion that "the disequilibrium hypothesis may explain the behaviour of the bottom 80 to 90 percent of the income distribution". The chapter is interesting and well argued but I am too inexpert in these data to allow me to comment. On the whole it is certainly not implausible.

But when incorporated in the theoretical model and treated formally there are certain difficulties. When income is increasing less fast than households have learned to spend it then they decumulate (according to the equation). It is unclear to me what it is that they have to decumulate (I believe they do not, and cannot, borrow according to Marglin), and we are not told. Next, Marglin applies the "disequilibrium hypothesis" to workers and capitalists separately and goes through the arithmetic of steady state. One notices that the hypothesis is not very convincing for capitalists and that is the reason Marglin espouses the treatment of retentions which I have already discussed. But what has puzzled me most is the importation of the "disequilibrium" parameter θ into the steady state equation. In steady state there is nothing to learn and as far as I can see Marglin's hypothesis would lead to zero household savings. I may have misunderstood him but I must report that I could not fathom the economics of pp. 145–152.

Given the large space devoted to savings it is a disappointment that Marglin was unwilling to analyse the fruits of savings as represented by the asset structure. This is particularly disabling when it comes to Keynes and it is surprising in view of some of his own insightful remarks, e.g. when speaking of the "Widow's Cruse" he writes "capitalists' priority is built into the model *in the assumption that capitalists have a monopoly of bank credit*" (p. 94, italics in original). But he has not formally modelled either banks, nor credit nor any other financial instruments. The section entitled "Money" (pp. 89–93) is pretty unsatisfactory since no-one seems to be holding the stuff and the stability story is unconvincing.

In the context of steady state analysis (an enterprise unlikely to have recommended itself to Keynes) the most interesting "Keynesian" feature is the investment function. As long as one sticks to exogenously given "animal spirits" certain difficulties of analysis can be avoided. But in this book the desired rate of capital accumulation (which is not the same thing as investment) is simply written as a function of "the" rate of profit. If there are alternatives to productive investment, say land, existing buildings, government debt, leave alone foreign assets, then this will not do. Such alternatives surely help one, at least partly, to understand the differences in capital accumulation in the seventeenth and eighteenth century in Britain and, say, Spain. But in any case one would have thought in view of the quotation already given that the terms on which capitalists can borrow will have some effect on their accumulation of productive capital. If it is maintained that in equilibrium the borrowing rate of interest must equal the profit rate then this needs arguing and it requires a theory of borrowing and lending (Keynes, Kalecki etc. etc.). Moreover there are a number of instances where Marglin has an essentially Wicksellian story (of inflation) to give but only tells half of it. If memory serves, Harrod did not base his arguments on fixed coefficients of production but rather on the Keynesian ground that the convenience of holding money sets a lower bound on the rate of profit and he envisaged the possibility of a "liquidity stop" which would prevent deepening being an available resolution of the conflict of a warranted growth rate which exceeded the natural rate. Marglin says nothing in either criticism or support of this view because he is generally silent on these characteristically Keynesian features. Had we had less on Pasinetti and Cambridge arithmetic and more on the financial nitty gritty of investment this would, in my view, have been a great improvement.

(Incidentally it should be remarked that the whole investment story is deeply mysterious under perfect competition and steady state at constant prices. Perfect competitors do not have to predict demand—only prices. Why do they invest at a constant rate? Is it "finance" which limits the amount of investment which they can do? Or perhaps "adjustment costs"? None of this is discussed).

There are of course many more things to discuss in a book of this length. But I content myself with only one more specific topic.

I have always been puzzled by what Marglin discerns as a characterising feature of Neo-Marxian economics—the subsistence wage. We all understand that subsistence is to be given a "social" interpretation. Puzzle number one is this. If the "social" is a reflection of the mode of production then so presumably is the subsistence wage. In economy A where labour is highly productive (has a high marginal product) are we allowed to hypothesise that the subsistence wage will be higher than in economy B where labour is of low productivity? If yes then what *exactly* is the connection between labour's productivity and the subsistence wage? If no then how do we account for some rather obvious stylised facts on these matters?

Puzzle number two concerns the related "aspiration" theory of wages (popular with some of my Cambridge colleagues and treated kindly by Marglin). According to that theory workers insist on, or set, the aspiration (subsistence?) real wage. How exactly do they manage to do that? Are they always winners in the class struggle as exemplified by wage bargaining? I am aware that this bargain may be in terms of money wages. But while I can see that workers may demand the money wage which given their price expectations yields the desired real wage, I do not see why they always get what they demand. Bargaining theory does not suggest that to be the case.

Puzzle number three concerns the reserve army in its role of preventing the wage rising above its subsistence level. Marglin here appeals to the importation of foreign labour and that does have some plausibility. But one could also maintain that this importation was occasioned by native workers raising their wage by undertaking more skilled jobs and leaving an excess demand for unskilled jobs to be filled by foreigners. This did not stop native workers in raising their wage above subsistence in their jobs but did prevent unskilled jobs paying above subsistence. Apart from this one would like to have an explanation for the increasing international disparity in real wages.

All these seem to me genuine puzzles and some more help in resolving them would have been appreciated.

So to the summing up. Marglin is clearly an economist of very high intelligence and he has thought deeply and honestly. For reasons unknown to me he chose to set the stage in the context of the growth debates of the sixties. While this has not prevented him giving us many valuable insights into alternative models it has prevented consideration of deep and fundamental matters such as a proper account of class conflict, or of innovations and incentives, of financial assets etc. etc. It is something of a mystery that he felt it necessary to devote so much space for instance to a model which presupposes a hereditary class of workers and capitalists (Pasinetti). Clearly Marglin believes that there are genuinely alternative theories on offer (and he complains about the dominance of one of them in America and elsewhere). But from what he gives us here it is hard to agree with him. He himself attempts a hybridisation between Keynes and Marx. But he could have gone further. As I have already argued the axiom of continuous competitive market clearing does not constitute a theory—for one thing we cannot understand it. Granted that we are all, as Marglin argues, moved by ideology as indeed we are by our mothers and fathers, it is still the case that when we speak with precision we can often understand each other and suspend judgment. For instance one feels sure that there is something to class conflict but as far as I know it has never been described with sufficient clarity and precision to allow one to use it for analysis or to understand it. Marglin is one of those who could remedy that. Perhaps he will do so in his next book.

Churchill College,
Cambridge, U.K.

REFERENCES

STIGLITZ, JOSEPH E. and WEISS, A. (1981). "Credit rationing in markets with imperfect information". *American Economic Review,* Vol. 71, No. 3 (June), pp. 393–410.
HAHN, F. H. (1952), "The Share of Wages in the National Income". *Oxford Economic Papers.*
HAHN, F. H. (1972), *The Share of Wages in the National Income,* Weidenfeld and Nicolson.

Oxford Economic Papers 37 (1985), 353–361

A DUAL DECISION APPROACH TO DISEQUILIBRIUM GROWTH

By V. GINSBURGH,* P. Y. HENIN** and PH. MICHEL**

1. Introduction

ITO'S (1978, 1980) basic model of disequilibrium growth retains Solow's (1956) neoclassical assumption of a constant exogenous saving rate. Recently, in a critical survey, Ito himself (1982) questions the assumption and recognizes that endogenizing the saving rate would be more consistent with optimizing behavior.

To achieve this, one has to consider the optimal consumption and saving program of households which may happen to be constrained on the labor or the goods market. The generalization of Ito's model requires thus a dynamic counterpart to the static Dual Decision Hypothesis (DDH for short) introduced by Clower (1965) and Barro and Grossman (1976).

Henin and Michel (1982a and b) have considered the disequilibrium growth path of an economy with price and wage rigidities, given .by the optimal accumulation program of firms. A dual decision extension of this work is provided here, in which it is assumed that households also are intertemporal utility maximisers. Both households and firms have a fully rational (perfect foresight) behavior: their expectations are always equal to the actual solution of the intertemporal model.

Section 2 discusses a simple model, in which consumers decide on the growth of capital, and firms simply adapt employment to the given capital stock. Section 3 is concerned with an extension which takes into account dual decisions of consumers and producers, in a growth framework; it is shown that four temporary equilibrium regimes will emerge, while in the long run, full employment growth is achieved. Conclusions are offered in Section 4.

2. A simple model

In the usual formulation of the Dual Decision Hypothesis, agents perceive constraints limiting their transactions in the current period. Neary and Stiglitz (1983) generalized the idea to two period models. We consider that agents optimize over an infinite horizon, and perceive not only to-day's but also all future constraints.

We shall cope at first with the case where the dynamics results only from

* University of Brussels.
** University of Paris I.
The authors are grateful to C. Chamley and P. Pestieau for highly clarifying discussions of a first version of this paper. As well as to an anonymous referee of the Journal for his helpful comments.

households behavior: this is the symetric of the Ito's or, more specifically, of Hénin and Michel (1982a and b) optimizing model. Next section will be devoted to the general case where both agents are optimizing over time.

The economy produces a single commodity at a rate $Y(t)$, using two factors, labor $L(t)$ and capital $K(t)$. The production function F is concave, differentiable and homogenous of degree one:

$$Y(t) = F(K(t), L(t)).$$

Assuming that firms are carrying no inventories, output is either consumed ($C(t)$) or invested ($I(t)$)

$$Y(t) = C(t) + I(t).$$

The evolution of the capital stock is given by

$$\dot{K}(t) = I(t) - \delta K(t)$$

where $\dot{K}(t)$ is the rate of change of the capital stock, which decays at a rate δ. Labor supply $L^s(t)$ is exogenous and increases at a given natural rate n

$$L^s(t) = L_0 e^{nt}.$$

Households choose the path of the saving rate $s(t)$ (and hence of investment, and the capital stock) so as to maximize[1] discounted utility streams:

$$\int_0^\infty e^{-(r-n)t} U(c(t)) \, dt \tag{2.1}$$

subject to

$$\dot{k}(t) = s(t) F(k(t), l(t)) - (\delta + n) k(t) \tag{2.2}$$

$$0 \leq s(t) \leq 1; \quad l(t) \text{ is exogenous} \tag{2.3}$$

where $c(t) = (1 - s(t)) Y(t) / L^s(t)$, $k(t) = K(t)/L^s(t)$ and $l(t) = L(t)/L^s(t)$; $U(\cdot)$ is concave, differentiable and satisfies $U'(\cdot) > 0$, $U'(0) = +\infty$. This is the usual optimal growth model, in which labor demand $l(t)$ is exogenous to the decisions of households, and full employment does not necessarily prevail.

To solve the model, consider the following Hamiltonian function:

$$H^H = U[(1-s)F(k, l)] + q^H[sF(k, l) - (\delta + n)k] \tag{2.4}$$

where q^H is the costate variable associated with the evolution of the capital stock, with:

$$\dot{q}^H = (r + \delta)q^H - F_k'(k, l)[(1-s)U'(\cdot) + q^H s]. \tag{2.5}$$

Households decide on their saving rate $s(t)$ by maximizing H^H over $s(t), 0 \leq s(t) \leq 1$, leading to:

$$s(t) = 0 \quad \text{and} \quad U'(\cdot) \geq q^H(t) \tag{2.6a}$$

or

$$0 < s(t) < 1 \quad \text{and} \quad U'(\cdot) = q^H(t). \tag{2.6b}$$

[1] See Arrow and Kurz (1970) for a justification of discounting the utility of per capita consumption at the rate $(r-n)$.

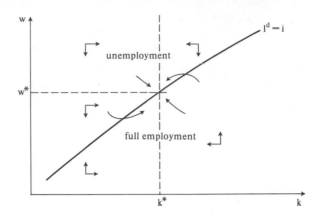

FIG. 1. Dynamics of the simple growth model.

For interior solutions, (2.5) can be written:

$$\dot{q}^H = [r + \delta - F'_k(k, l)]q^H. \tag{2.7}$$

While the saving rate is decided by households, firms simply choose at every time t the level of employment $l(t)$ so as to maximize current profits

$$F(k(t), l(t)) - w(t)l(t) \tag{2.8}$$

subject to

$$0 \leq l(t) \leq 1; \quad \text{for given } k(t) \text{ and } w(t). \tag{2.9}$$

This leads to the usual static optimality condition

$$F'_l(k, l) = w(t) \tag{2.10}$$

which defines the optimal labor demand $l^d(t)$. Effective employment is $l(t) = \min \{l^d(t), 1\}$.

The locus of equilibrium points on the labor market can be defined by the $F'_l(k, 1) = w$ curve represented in Fig. 1. In this simple model, there are only two possible disequilibrium regimes: there is unemployment above the curve, for $l^d(t) < 1$, and excess demand for labor under the curve where $l^d(t) > 1$.

If one assumes a competitive adjustment for the wage rate[2]

$$\dot{w}(t) = \lambda[l^d(t) - 1], \qquad \lambda > 0, \qquad w(0) = w_0 \tag{2.11}$$

dynamics can be studied as follows.

First, on the steady state path, $q^H(t) = \dot{w}(t) = 0$ and from (2.7), (2.10) and

[2] While the assumption of a competitive adjustment of wage is theoretically important for the long run convergence towards the market clearing value, the particular linear formulation (2.11) is inessential, and may be seen as a linear approximation of a more general adjustment process.

(2.11) one has

$$F'_k(k, l) = r + \delta; \qquad F'_l(k, l) = w; \qquad l = 1$$

which defines a point (k^*, w^*) on the curve $l = 1$ in the (k, w)-plane. The wage rate increases or decreases according to whether $l^d(t) > 1$ or $l^d(t) < 1$. The capital stock increases or decreases according to whether $k(t) < k^*$ or $k(t) > k^*$. The dynamic behavior, represented in Fig. 1, is similar to that of an economy with constant saving rate,[3] like in Ito (1978). This is not surprising, since in our model, the endogenous saving rate converges to $s^* = (\delta + n)k^*/F(k^*, 1)$.

3. A dynamic dual decision extension

The model studied in Section 2 is not symmetric, since households behave dynamically, whereas the behavior of firms is myopic. One could of course study the situation in which the behavior of firms is intertemporal, while households make short term decisions.

An approach in which both agents behave dynamically is necessary to deal with the dynamics of the dual decision hypothesis. The growth path of the economy is then the result of two optimizing agents, in which each agent has perfect foresight and takes the decisions of the other agent as given.

Therefore, the model involves basically an intertemporal Nash equilibrium because each agent does not take into account the effect of his own decisions on other's behavior.

We consider a model in which

(a) households decide on their saving rate (but not on total savings or consumption), and take as given future employment and future rates of output;

(b) firms have perfect foresight of future saving rates, and decide on the level of employment and the rate of output. As a consequence, they influence the level of investment, and capital is not given anymore, like in the simple model of Section 2.

The optimizing behavior of consumers is thus given by (2.1)–(2.3), while the problem of firms is[4]

$$\max \int_0^\infty e^{(r-n)t}\{[1 - s(t)]F(k(t), l(t)) - w(t)l(t)\}\, dt \qquad (3.1)$$

---

[3] The only difference between the two models is that in figure one, capital per head k converge directly towards k^* in every regime while in Ito's model, k decrease in the North-West quadrant of the (w, k) plane, which precludes any direct convergence to equilibrium and requires a much larger decrease in the real wage as to restore full employment. This difference provides an interesting illustration of the cost in terms of adjustment of an exogeneous saving rate in the place of an optimally flexible one.

[4] The fact that the criterion for firms is different from the utility function of households may be justified on the grounds that firms' ownership is unequally distributed across households. Owing to the homogeneity of degree one of the profit function, the expression (3.1) where profit per head is discounted at the rate $(r - n)$ is identical to discounting the level of profits at rate r.

subject to

$$\dot{k}(t) = s(t)F(k(t), l(t)) - (\delta + n)k(t) \tag{3.2}$$

$$0 \leqslant l(t) \leqslant 1; \quad s(t) \text{ and } w(t) \text{ are exogenous.} \tag{3.3}$$

The economy follows a path defined by the simultaneous solution of problems (2.1)–(2.3) and (3.1)–(3.3). Since we assume that agents are rational, the constraints they anticipate are identical with the actual constraints obtained by solving (2.1)–(2.3) and (3.1)–(3.3).

Define the Hamiltonian functions of problems (2.1)–(2.3) and (3.1)–(3.3) as functions of the decisions of each agent, the decisions of the other being given:

$$\begin{aligned} H^H &= U[(1-s)F(k, l)] + q^H[sF(k, l) - (\delta + n)k] \\ H^F &= (1-s)F(k, l) - wl + q^F[sF(k, l) - (\delta + n)k] \end{aligned} \tag{3.4}$$

where q^H and q^F are the costate variables associated with the evolution of the capital stock in the households' and firms' problems respectively, with

$$\begin{aligned} \dot{q}^H &= (r+\delta)q^H - F'_k(k, l)[(1-s)U'(\cdot) + q^H s] \\ \dot{q}^F &= (r+\delta)q^F - F'_k(k, l)[(1-s) + q^F s]. \end{aligned} \tag{3.5}$$

Households decide on their saving rate $s(t)$, given by max H^H over $s(t)$, $0 \leqslant s(t) \leqslant 1$, leading to

$$s(t) = 0 \quad \text{and} \quad U'(\cdot) \geqslant q^H(t) \tag{3.6a}$$

or

$$0 < s(t) < 1 \quad \text{and} \quad U'(\cdot) = q^H(t). \tag{3.6b}$$

Likewise, firms decide on their demand for labor $l(t)$ given by max H^F over $l(t)$, $0 \leqslant l(t) \leqslant 1$, leading to

$$l(t) = 1 \quad \text{and} \quad v(t)F'_l(\cdot) \geqslant w(t) \tag{3.7a}$$

or

$$0 < l(t) < 1 \quad \text{and} \quad v(t)F'_l(\cdot) = w(t) \tag{3.7b}$$

where

$$v(t) = 1 - s(t) + q^F(t)s(t) \tag{3.8}$$

is the value for firms of one unit of output, obtained as a weighted average of 1, the value of one unit sold to households, and q^F the value of one unit of investment (the weights are evidently $1-s$ and s).

The notional employment rate of firms $l^d(t)$ is obtained by solving (3.7b) for $l(t)$; (3.7b) equalizes the marginal productivity of labor $F'_l(\cdot)$ valued at $v(t)$, with the real wage rate $w(t)$. The usual marginal productivity condition $F'_l(\cdot) = w(t)$, corresponding to a myopic behavior, is optimal only if $v(t) = 1$, implying $q^F(t) = 1$ or $s(t) = 0$. The effective employment rate is given by $l(t) = \min \{l^d(t), 1\}$.

It is straightforward to analyze temporary equilibria on the labor market: there is unemployment if $l^d(t) = l(t) < 1$, excess demand if $l^d(t) > 1$ and equilibrium if $l^d(t) = 1$.

On the market for goods, there can be no discrepancy between effective demand and supply.[5] If, by assumption, households are never rationed, firms may however perceive constraints: they may be willing to sell more (which corresponds to excess supply) or to invest more (excess demand) since saving (and consumption) is decided jointly by households and firms. The possibility of adjustment by varying the level of inventories is ruled out by assumption. The two regimes can be characterized as follows:

(i) excess supply: when $v(t) < 1$, it is easy to see from (3.8) that we must have $s(t) > 0$ and $q^F(t) < 1$. Since $\partial H^F / \partial s(t) = (q^F(t) - 1) F(k, l)$ is then negative, firms are willing to invest less, or, in other words, they would find profitable an increase in households' consumption. To reduce further undesired capital accumulation, firms have to reduce their demand for labor, obtained by (3.7b) as $l^d(w(t)/v(t)) < l^d(w(t))$ for given $w(t)$ and $v(t) < 1$. There is thus a negative spillover of the effective demand constraint (excessive saving rate) on labor demand;

(ii) excess demand: when $q^F(t) > 1$, $\partial H^F / \partial s(t) > 0$ and an increase in the saving rate would allow firms to increase their discounted profits by investing more. If $s(t) > 0$, $v(t) > 1$ and the labor demand $l^d(w(t)/v(t))$ is larger than in the myopic case $l^d(w(t))$; there is thus a positive spillover of the goods market (which is rationed) on the labor market.

The various temporary equilibrium regimes obtained are similar to the ones obtained in the standard case; these similarities should however not overcast the specific implications of the dynamic dual decision hypothesis.

On the goods market, we have singled out the cases of an insufficient or an excessive saving ratio. These two cases point to traditional business cycle theories, with their distinction between situations of "lack of saving" and "underconsumption with excessive saving".[6] Before the Keynesian revolution, the tradition, starting with Tugan–Baranovsky, and continued by Cassel (1932) and Hayek (1931), was to explain cyclical peaks by a lack of saving with respect to the needs of the process of capital deepening; these theories are very different from those based on the accelerator, which discuss overcapitalization with respect to demand. These references suggest the following interpretations of the regimes generated by our model, and represented in Fig. 2.

(i) unemployment associated with a "too high" saving rate is the analogue of Keynesian unemployment, and will be called "underconsumption unemployment";

(ii) unemployment associated with a lack of saving appears as "Hayekian unemployment", a variety of classical unemployment;

---

[5] This results from the absence of money; this is also the case in Solow's (1956) and Ito's (1980) models of which ours is a straightforward generalization.

[6] See e.g. Haberler (1943).

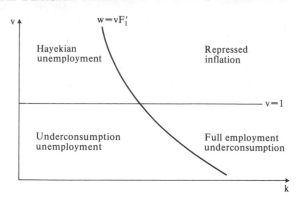

FIG. 2. Representation of temporary equilibria.

(iii) excess labor demand together with excessive saving is termed "full employment underconsumption", close to the "underconsumption" situation of the standard model;

(iv) excess demand on the labor market while firms experience rationing on investment possibilities, corresponds to the "repressed inflation" regime.

In Fig. 2, the horizontal line $v(t) = 1$ separates the "excess demand" $(v(t) > 1)$ region from the "excess supply" region $(v(t) < 1)$ on the goods market; since $F''_{kl}(\cdot) > 0$, $v(t) = w(t)F'_l(\cdot)$ is a decreasing function of $k(t)$, which separates unemployment from excess demand on the labor market.

The dynamics of the model, for a given initial capital stock $k(0)$ are fully defined by the differential equations associated with the two optimization problems of households and firms

$$\dot{k}(t) = s(t)F(k(t), l(t)) - (\delta + n)k(t) \tag{3.9}$$

$$\dot{q}^H(t) = (r + \delta)q^H(t) - F'_k(k(t), l(t))[(1 - s(t))U' + s(t)q^H(t)] \tag{3.10}$$

$$\dot{q}^F(t) = (r + \delta)q^F(t) - F'_k(k(t), l(t))[1 - s(t) + s(t)q^F(t)] \tag{3.11}$$

to which we add an equation explaining wage adjustments as a function of the excess demand for labor

$$\dot{w}(t) = \lambda[l^d(t) - 1], \qquad \lambda > 0, \qquad w(0) = w_0 \tag{3.12}$$

while $s(t)$ and $l(t)$ satisfy the optimality conditions (3.6)–(3.7).

We first examine the steady state solution $(\bar{k}, \bar{s}, \bar{q}^F, \bar{q}^H, \bar{l}, \bar{w}, \bar{v})$ and show that, if it exists, it is uniquely determined and satisfies all the optimality conditions. Indeed, for $\dot{w} = 0$, $l^d = \bar{l} = 1$; for $\bar{k} > 0$ and $\dot{k} = 0$, it follows from (3.9) that $\bar{s}F(\cdot) = (\delta + n)\bar{k}$ and $\bar{s} > 0$; then, from (3.6b), we have $\bar{q}^H = U'(\cdot)$; replacing this in (3.10) with $\dot{q}^H = 0$ leads to $F'_k(\cdot) = r + \delta$ (which is the usual condition on a stationary path); this in turn defines a unique value of $\bar{k}$ and $\bar{s}$ (using $\bar{s}F = (\delta + n)\bar{k}$), and of $\bar{q}^H$. Replacing $F'_k = r + \delta$ in (3.11) gives $\bar{q}^F = 1$, and hence, using (3.8), $\bar{v} = 1$; finally, from (3.7b) it follows that $\bar{w} = F'_l(\bar{k}, \bar{l})$.

Under the usual concavity assumptions on the utility and production functions, $U(\cdot)$ and $F(\cdot)$, the stationary solution is unique and is an optimal solution for the consumers and the firms.

Any trajectory of the system (k, q^F, q^H, w) which converges to the unique stationary state is an intertemporal equilibrium of the economy. Indeed, when the economy is following such a trajectory, for each agent the path of the variables under his control is optimal for a given path of uncontrolled variables: it satisfies the sufficient conditions of Arrow and Kurz.

It is not possible to give a picture of the full dynamics of such trajectories lying in a four-dimensional space. Moreover, the dynamics of the model will in general involve changes in regimes. At these points, a change in differential equations occurs. Thus, the four state variables, either predeterminated like k and w, or forward looking as q^F and q^H are continuous but their time derivatives are not continuously differentiable functions. There are no stability conditions available for such systems (Honkapojha et Ito 1983). Only for paths belonging for ever to a same regime do standard stability conditions apply.[7]

In the present case, one may hazard the following appreciation: On the one hand, the transversality conditions are stability conditions for forward looking variables. On the other hand, the dynamics of pre-determined k and w is similar to this one represented in Fig. 1. This gives some intuitive support to the idea that stability prevails.

4. Concluding comments

The model discussed provides a dynamic extension of the basic static dual decision hypothesis, and a more satisfactory formulation of a disequilibrium version of the neoclassical growth model.

Like in the Solow–Ito tradition, money is not explicitly introduced, and there is no possibility for effective (or ex post) disequilibria to appear on the goods market; however, the value of implicit prices provides information on notional (or ex ante) disequilibria, and restores the existence of four regimes of temporary equilibria, instead of two as is the case in Ito's model.

When the assumption is made that the wage rate adjusts to excess demand for labor, disequilibria will only be temporary, and it appears that full employment growth is the only sustainable steady state.

Finally, by assuming non-competitive wage adjustments, like Pitchford and Turnovsky (1978) or Picard (1982) it is possible to obtain non-Walrasian steady states, with lasting unemployment; this is clearly a decisive step away from neoclassical conclusions, using a neoclassical framework.

Universite de Paris I-Pantheon-Sorbonne, France.

[7] According to the now classical stability conditions, as two state variables are predeterminated, k and w, and two are forward looking, q^H and q^F, the convergence towards the steady state requires that, among the roots of the linearized system, two have a positive real part and two have a negative one.

REFERENCES

ARROW, K. and KURZ, M. (1970, *Public Investment, the Rate of Return and Optimal Fiscal Policy*, Baltimore: The Johns Hopkins Press.

BARRO, R. and GROSSMAN, H. (1976), *Money, Employment and Inflation*, Cambridge University Press.

CASSEL, G. (1932), *The Theory of Social Economy*, Harcourt.

CLOWER, R. (1965), The Keynesian Counterrevolution: A Theoretical Appraisal, in F. Hahn and F. Brechling, eds., *The Theory of Interest Rates*, London: McMillan.

HABERLER, G. (1943), *Prospérité et Dépression*, Genève: Société des Nations.

HAYEK, F. (1931), *Prices and Production*, London: Routledge and Kegan Paul.

HENIN P. Y. (1981), Equilibres avec Rationnement dans un Modèle Macroéconomique avec Investissement Endogène, *Economie Appliquée* 4, 697–728.

HENIN, P. Y. and MICHEL, PH. (1982a), Théorie de la Croissance avec Rigidité Salariale et Contrainte de Demande Effective: une Reformulation, in P. Y. Henin et Ph. Michel, eds., *Croissance et Accumulation en Déséquilibre*, Paris: Economica.

HENIN, P. Y. and MICHEL, PH. (1982b) Harrodian and Neoclassical Paths in a Constrained Growth Model, Economic Letters, 10, pp. 237–242.

HONKAPOHJA, S. and ITO, T, Stability with Regime Switching, Journal of Economic Theory, 1983, Vol. 29, n° 1, pp. 22–48.

ITO, T. (1978), A Note on Disequilibrium Growth Theory, *Economics Letters* 1, 45–49.

ITO, T. (1980), Disequilibrium Growth Theory, *Journal of Economics Theory*, 23, 380–409.

ITO, T. (1982), Disequilibrium Growth Theory, a Critical Survey, in P. Y. Henin and Ph. Michel, eds., *Croissance et Accumulation en Déséquilibre*, Paris: Economica.

MALINVAUD, E. (1981), *Profitability and Unemployment*, Cambridge University Press.

NEARY, P. and STIGLITZ, J. (1983), Towards a Reconstruction of Keynesian Economics, *Quarterly Journal of Economics*, Vol. 98, pp. 199–228.

PICARD, P. (1982), Inflation and Growth in a Disequilibrium Macroeconomic Model, *Journal of Economic Theory*.

PITCHFORD, J. and TURNOVSKY, S. (1978), Expectations and Income Claims in Wage Price Determination: an Aspect of the Inflationary Process, in A. Bergstron, A. J. Catt, M. H. Preston and B. D. Silverston, eds., *Stability and Inflation: Essays in Honor of A. W. Phillips*, London: Wiley.

SOLOW, R. (1956), A Contribution to the Theory of Economic Growth, *Quarterly Journal of Economics*, 70, 65–94.

Oxford Economic Papers 38 (1986), 367–385

REFLECTING ON THE THEORY OF CAPITAL AND GROWTH

By E. MALINVAUD[1]

IMPROVING the understanding and theoretical analysis of economic growth has been one of the main motivations of Sir John Hicks through many of his writings. Since this is also for me a strong motivation, I find it proper on this occasion to discuss the full range of theories in which the essential role of time is recognized.

One may say that these theories aim at providing a conceptual system that should permit rigorous study of the reasons why some economies grow faster and perform better than others, or than the same economies in different historical phases. Experience has taught us the difficulty of such an ambitious aim. This is why we often view the theory of capital and growth as dealing more modestly with the representation of medium and long term economic evolution under steady conditions.

Even when its scope is so limited, the ideal theory is not available today. We have some notions on what it should be; but we do not hope to be able to specify it properly right away. We are rather striving to make some sure steps toward its construction. Hence, two questions: are the steps sure? Do they go in the right direction?

The whole of Hicks' research applies this strategy. He made some important steps, probed their reliability, argued for their significance. Since I walked behind him, but sometimes stepping a few feet out of his way in the hope of finding a better path, I may sit down today, look around and wonder where he and his colleagues or students have led us on the way toward this ideal theory that appears in the far distance, still quite fuzzy for our eyes.

While I do so, you will notice a difference in style, since you are all faithful readers of Hicks. I am indeed unable to convey, as well as he does in his writings, the feeling that the choice of the best specification for the theoretical analysis of complex phenomena is a very delicate problem, the solution of which can always be questioned. As for me, I like to stress the parts that I think to have been firmly established, often fooling myself in behaving as if these parts at least were unquestionable.

The first phase in our search for the theory of growth has been to reach a clear understanding on what would be a stationary equilibrium. I shall have relatively little to say on the microeconomic field of this well explored area. But it also contains macroeconomic bushes and swamps, through which the best way to choose is less apparent. Later, our discussion will concern

---

[1] Text of the Hicks Lecture, given on May 1st, 1986.

whether and how, starting from a given initial situation, but still operating under stationary conditions, economic growth will reach an equilibrium: what Hicks called "the traverse". From there on, we shall have to explore a few tentative ways to go over the many difficulties of the study of growth under disequilibrium prices.

1. Microeconomic equilibrium theories

The ultimate aims of theories of capital and growth are the understanding and analysis of macroeconomic phenomena. But solid foundations are mainly microeconomic. I am one of those who think that macroeconomic specifications do not arise only from abstract reflection but also from econometric induction (even though this induction is often at present not formalized and quite loose; even though it will seldom be quite conclusive and never be easy). Nevertheless even simply embedding econometric results within the main theories requires a careful study of their relations to the microeconomic environment from which they come and of the various aspects of aggregation.

Microeconomic theories providing the required foundations must then be general. Of course, this does not mean that general models only are admissible in the research process on microeconomic theory. Quite the contrary, the building of present theories of capital and growth most often proceeded from the careful study of special models: the point-input point-output case of the exploitation of growing forests, the "Akerman problem", Samuelson's chocolate economy, and so on. But those must in the end be viewed as intermediate steps toward the derivation of general microeconomic theories, from which macroeconomic theories ought to be derived by a process of aggregation and econometric selection.

In other words, research typically moves to and fro. It does not need to, and in fact cannot, specify from the beginning the appropriate general fundamental models that will later be accepted. But we must from time to time try to be precise on our general theories. This is why I want to stress here the two features of these theories that I consider as being essential: economic activity proceeds recursively, growth results from a sequence of temporary equilibria.

But before I do so, I should like to draw your attention to two somewhat puzzling sections at the beginning of *Capital and Time* (I.3 and I.4), where Hicks discusses what he calls "the *disintegration* of the productive process". Considering how we can represent production in our theories of capital and growth, he there distinguishes three methods, which he respectively calls the "method of sectoral disintegr\tion" (some firms produce capital goods, others use these goods), the " .nethod of von Neumann" (production lasts just one period, inputs occurring at the beginning, outputs at the end), the "method of separable elementary processes" (a process uses only primary inputs and produces only outputs directly used in consumption). We there have the vision of production taking place before us in the economy, like in a living organism. Hicks asks us to wonder how we should disintegrate this organism so as to understand how its functions.

If I am drawing your attention to these sections, it is because they seem to suggest that, in contradiction to what I shall assume here, microeconomic concepts may not be the most fundamental ones. They may already be the result of simplifications, abstracting from important features of a reality that might better be described with less disintegration. Let us keep this query in mind for future research.

Without now choosing between Hicks' three methods, I want to stress here that they have in common two features. First, the notions of goods and commodities are the same in the three cases. They accept the idea, clearly expressed for instance by Debreu, that two equal quantities of the same physical good are not fully substitutable for one another if they are available at different times; these two quantities then correspond to different commodities. But, when listing the commodities, the specifications keep the notion of goods that remain physically the same through time. The index of a commodity specifies the good as well as the time concerned. Indeed, the very concept of growth requires that some things are directly comparable from one period to the next, and it seems to be admissible for general theories that all goods (and services) keep a constant meaning through time.

The second common feature is that, in all three methods, each elementary productive operation only concerns a finite number of periods, although production can proceed for ever into the future, although the periods of elementary operations can overlap. This is what I mean when I say that production proceeds recursively. But our general theories must recognize that this feature does not apply only to production but to any economic activity; generations of consumers also live finite times. This is why the recent study of overlapping generation models has been a major achievement of the last three decades for the development of the general microeconomic theories of capital and growth. I am sure that this specification with overlapping generations will more and more be recognized as the proper one.[2]

These theories have used two equilibrium concepts. One, the "full general equilibrium" concept, simply generalizes the corresponding concept of static timeless theories. The identity of individual goods then matters very little; but a high degree of consistency is required from the full set of individual plans, no matter how remote in the future they may be. The alternative concept, the "temporary general equilibrium" was lucidly discussed in *Value and Capital* (in particular chap. 9), transposing to general equilibrium the analysis of Alfred Marshall; its exact definition, involving in

---

[2] The first introduction of overlapping generation models is usually attributed to P. Samuelson (*Journal of Political Economy*, December 1958). I recently discovered that it may be found in M. Allais (*Economie et Intérêt*, Imprimerie Nationale, Paris 1947).

particular expectations of agents as to future prices and other conditions, is familiar and will not be repeated here. Clearly this second concept is much better suited than the first one for positive theories of capital and growth. But the distinction is sometimes forgotten.

This may result from the fact that the two concepts happen to coincide for stationary economies, in which expectations not only keep constant values, as all other variables do, but are quite naturally assumed to be also exact. The coincidence even extends to proportionally growing economies, which are hardly different from stationary ones, but were often considered during these past decades as providing a better reference. The coincidence may seem trivial; it requires however the proof of a stationarity property for the structure of the full general equilibrium price system of a stationary economy. This proof actually gave me a hard time when I worked at it thirty-five years ago.[3]

But the coincidence is not always a blessing, because it may lead the theorist to overlook the distinction between the two concepts of equilibrium and therefore to pay too little attention to some special features of the temporary equilibrium definition.

I must now turn attention to the distinction between Hicks' three methods of disintegration for the representation of the productive system. I shall not quarrel with him by arguing that the first method, at least in the way it was used so far, is a particular case of the second. The important point is to discuss the role of the third method, by comparison with the second. Clearly, Hicks likes it and I do as well. But what are his reasons, before I give mine?

In chapter I of *Capital and Time,* he gives two reasons. In section I.3, speaking of the second method, he says: "the categories with which it works are not very recognizable as economic categories"; then at the beginning of the following section: "Thus there should be room for a third method, expressible more naturally in economic terms". The argument is surprising: since the second method is quite flexible in its definition of goods, it can be applied to all conceivable cases, even though it may be cumbersome when it has to identify many kinds of more or less used equipment goods; on the contrary by limiting itself to primary factors and consumption goods, the third method forces the analyst to simplifications that are not so natural.

But Hicks goes on to argue, in section I.6, that the special usefulness of the third method is for the analysis of "the traverse", i.e. for growth outside of the steady state.[4] The main feature that ought to appear is "extensive *complementarities over time*" (italics in the text); the second method would

---

[3] *Econometrica,* April 1953. The proof was not even quite complete, as was later pointed out in D. Gale and R. Rockwell, "On the interest rate theorems of Malinvaud and Starrett", *Econometrica,* March 1975.

[4] This second argument, but not the first one, is repeated in "Time in Economics", published in 1976, and appearing as essay 21 in John Hicks, *Collected Essays on Economic Theory,* Vol. II, Basil Blackwell, Oxford 1982.

make "the economy too flexible", whereas the third would recognize its inflexibility. This is an interesting point, but so far only based on intuition. I do not think it has ever been proved; it would certainly be a worthwhile question to clear up for a mathematical economist. My own guess is that no general formal proof of the difference will be found; it is indeed known that, within the second method, the putty–clay specification (not to speak of the clay–clay) introduces a good deal of complementarity over time.

Actually, if Hicks asserts the third method to be particularly appropriate for the study of the traverse, it is because he is becoming more and more motivated by a particular issue in this study, namely what I shall call the "Impulse problem": how does a technical innovation change the structure of production and consumption, as well as the price structure, this change being traced from the initial introduction of the innovation to its exclusive use. A number of Hicks' writings reveal the importance he gave to this problem after 1970. I shall come back to it. Whenever the innovation amounts to the discovery of a new elementary process for transforming primary factors into consumption goods, then clearly the third method has a definite advantage.

Beyond these two reasons there may also be a sentimental attachment of Hicks for the third method which, after Böhm-Bawerk and Wicksell, he extended in *Value and Capital* ("in one of the less read chapters" as he revealingly writes in "Time in Economics", op. cit.). It may moreover be that Hicks will agree with me when I give my own argument as follows: as an alternative analyzing to the second method, the third one provides a different way of analyzing the same basic issues; its occasional use should be recommended because it may lead us to see better some important points. In theoretical analysis it is indeed often rewarding to look at the same questions through different glasses. The main reason for arguing in favour of the third method may then simply be that it is too neglected nowadays.[5]

2. Macroeconomic analysis

After this initial discussion on methods, let me come closer to the substance of the theories of capital and growth. We cannot do so without often speaking in macroeconomic terms. Indeed, the largest part in the content of these theories is macro. A good deal of the irritation that participants in, and observers of, debates on these theories suffered, could have been avoided if the conditions applying to the edification of macroeconomic theory had been better recognized from the beginning. Here, I shall express agreement with Hicks on his main statements but I may appear to be more dogmatic in my assessment of fundamental difficulties.

Let me first quote an important excerpt from "Methods of dynamic analysis", an article presented by Hicks in his collected essays as being

---

[5] A careful reader of my writings may note that I was less favourable to the method in the last sentences of my 1960 *Review of Economic Studies* article. Age may make me less dogmatic.

particularly important but hardly even read (essay number 18 in volume II). Evaluating the relative merits and conditions of static and dynamic analyses, he there makes a comparison with economic history, which has both to survey the state of a given economy at a given epoch, stressing differences with other economies or epochs, and to present a narrative of some process of economic change. He then writes: "it is in fact exceedingly difficult to cast economic history into a narrative form without becoming *more* abstract than one has to be on the survey method; greater realism in the matter of time-sequence has to be purchased by a higher level of abstraction in most other respects. We are, I believe, in substantially the same case in economic theory. . . . It is no accident that dynamic theory tends so largely to run in terms of simple aggregative models".

Before we discuss some of these models, it is worth considering briefly the mere definition of the main concepts of macroeconomic analysis. By doing so we are faithful to Hicks, who very substantially contributed to the subject.

I shall submit here that the main point is to decide whether a capital aggregate is a different kind of animal from a production aggregate. As soon as the question is phrased in this way, the answer is obvious: it is not a different kind of animal, but simply a more difficult animal.

The production flow and the capital stock are both made up of many different goods. Speaking in macroeconomic terms we aggregate these many goods; the only way we do it in practice is by valuing them with prices. They may be prices varying through time; we then speak of value aggregates. They may be fixed prices resulting in volume aggregates. (In order to avoid complications, I shall limit attention here to two periods, and hence neglect volume aggregates defined from chain indices). The problems begin when we try to be precise on what are these prices. Statisticians would like them to be actual prices, current prices for value aggregates, average prices of a given period for volume aggregates. Theoreticians would moreover like these prices to correspond to those of their theories, most often to be purely competitive prices. Both must recognize that some prices have to be imputed because some goods in the production flow and still more in the capital stock are not actually traded.

It is, of course, an important question to decide about the principles that may lie behind the determination of these imputed prices, in particular behind the choice of prices to be applied to old equipment. Similarly it is important, for capital still more than for production, to deal clearly with the treatment of new goods and to know which base period prices will be given to them in the computation of volume aggregates. Economic statisticians have discussed these issues many times, using in particular Hicks' lucid writings on the subject.[6] A simple reason explains why the discussion is

---

[6] After his important writings on the definition and measurement of social income, those on capital appear as essays 8 and 9, published respectively in 1958 and 1969, in *Collected Essays on Economic Theory*, Volume I. See also chapter 13, in *Capital and Time*, 1973.

neither very convincing, not even always conclusive: indeed the problems, as they are posed, have no good solution; capital aggregates, but also production aggregates, will never be rigorously defined in such a way that, in all conceivable applications, they can perfectly replace the microeconomic entities that they represent.

It is my view that, in order to be useful, the study of these questions must be fully reoriented. We need as many theories of aggregation as we have types of macroeconomic analysis and each one of these theories must consider several cases of microeconomic environment, in each case clarifying the meaning of macroeconomic results and the errors to which they may be exposed. Some general principles may help in the building of these theories. I considered them long ago[7] and stressed in particular the role of aggregate quantities, seen as imperfect representations of corresponding microeconomic quantities. But a general study of aggregation can only be a first step, without much interest if other steps are not made.

This being my position, let me consider for instance one type of macroeconomic analysis that plays an important role in the study of economic growth: the analysis of productivity trends. Whenever we assess the past, present or future role of capital accumulation on productivity trends, we are using some sort of capital volume aggregate and some sort of macroeconomic production function, whether explicitly or implicitly. Those who objected to the use of such tools had no impact on actual macroeconomic analyses because they neither proved that we need not study the role of capital accumulation on productivity trends, or found out another way of doing it. On the contrary a careful and positive study of the aggregation problems in this context will improve the methodology actually used and throw light on the significance and pitfalls of the results.

There is a literature on this problem. Indeed, the irritating debates between the two Cambridges can coolly be read again with benefit as a contribution to the problem (if one has the time necessary to read it again). Cases have been found in which the use of proper aggregates does not run the risk of erroneous assessments, such as the case discussed by Samuelson in his 1962 article on "the surrogate production function".[8] But other cases have also been found in which no technical change occurs and the set of competitive stationary states has a different structure from the one that could be derived from a sensible aggregate production function.

Actually, these latter cases are better understood if one refers to the technical literature on the aggregation of production functions.[9] It dealt

[7] E. Malinvaud, "L'agrégation dans les modèles économiques", *Cahiers du Séminaire d'Econométrie,* No 4, 1956, Paris, C.N.R.S.

[8] P. A. Samuelson, "Parable and realism in capital theory, the surrogate production function", *Review of Economic Studies,* June 1962.

[9] See F. Fisher, "The existence of aggregate production functions", *Econometrica,* October 1969; L. Johansen, *Production Functions: an Integration of Micro and Macro, Short Run and Long Run Aspects,* North Holland Pub. Co., Amsterdam 1972; F. Fisher, R. Solow and J. Kearl, "Aggregate production functions: some CES experiments", *Review of Economic Studies,* June 1977.

rather fully with the situation of a competitive environment, labour inputs being perfectly mobile and capital inputs immobile. But in macroeconomic analysis, other situations have also to be considered, whether perfect competition does not apply or labor is not perfectly mobile. Hence, other significant aggregation problems have to be discussed.[10]

3. Comparative dynamics

Some important conjectures concerning macroeconomic properties must also be studied by what Hicks called "comparative dynamics".[11] Two such properties have a long history in economic theory, technology being assumed fixed in the two cases and perfect competition assumed to prevail: a higher capital per unit of labour input requires a lower real interest rate; a lower real interest rate implies a longer production process. Both properties associate capital deepening with a falling interest rate (or a falling rate of profit, if the two rates are identified). The first property often was in the background of the debates between the two Cambridges and the second property was discussed by Hicks several times, notably in *Value and Capital* and *Capital and Time*. The properties hold in the most aggregated models: the case of a single produced good serving both as capital in a one period production function and for consumption, or the case of a single final good obtained from labour by a point-input point-output process. The problem is to know whether they are generally valid.

The first source of confusion concerns the way in which the properties ought to be specified in general, when the relative prices of the various goods are not the same in the two hypothetical situations to be compared (stationary states or proportional growth paths). Speaking in broad terms, one may say that, when comparing the capital aggregates or the average periods of production in the two situations, these aggregate quantities should be computed with the same prices. If not, the properties would have an ambiguous meaning with respect to the notion of capital deepening. The confusion arose time and again about the capital aggregate, changes in the value of capital being mistakenly considered when changes in the volume really mattered. The same confusion would undoubtedly arise, if the average period of production became more familiar, for instance as a result of wide adoption of Hicks' third method. In other words, the capital aggregate and the average period of production are considered as reflecting quantitative features of production, but their measures also imply prices used as weights; when comparisons are aimed at revealing quantitative

---

[10] I have tried to discuss a wide range of situations in section 5, chapter 4 of *Théorie Macroéconomique,* vol. I, Dunod, Paris 1981.

[11] J. Hicks, "'A Value and Capital' growth model", *Review of Economic Studies*, June 1959.

changes associated with a change in interest rate, the prices used for the aggregate measure of quantities must be kept fixed.[12]

But even when they are adequately specified, the two properties cannot be proved to hold in full generality. The theoretical work of the last thirty years has shown that the interest rate is related in a very complex way to the many exogenous determinants of equilibrium and that changes of relative prices, which are associated with changes of interest, may be responsible for paradoxical effects in the simultaneous variations of the interest rate and of quantitative characteristics of the equilibrium.

For the relation between the volume of capital and the interest rate, I may first refer here to the article I wrote on the occasion of my 1959 visit to Professor Hicks at Oxford, where I showed that a general comparative dynamics approach did not lead to the conjectured property, even simply in a three commodity world.[13] Later, some counterexamples to the property were explicitly worked out. Finally, the conditions under which the conjectured "capital deepening response" to changes in interest rate held were greatly clarified by E. Burmeister and J. Turnovsky.[14]

All this work concerned what Hicks calls "the second method of disintegration". What about the changes in the length of the production process? The question has been seriously concerning Hicks. He dealt with it in *Value and Capital* (chapter 17) and discussed it again in *Capital and Time* (chapter 12), essentially restating more neatly the results established more than thirty years earlier. I read his contribution as having been to make rigorous a property that previously was loosely stated, or proved only in very special cases. He showed that, for the conjectured property to apply, one needed to define the average period of production properly, each lag being weighted not exactly by the net input that it concerned, but by this input capitalized at the current rate of interest; moreover when the impact of a change in interest on the timing and quantity of net inputs was being considered, one needed to maintain fixed, in the measurement of the average period of production, the coefficients by which inputs were capitalized.

However, his proof concerned only the case in which there would exist just one primary factor and one final good. It is legitimate to ask whether the property generalizes to several primary factors and final goods. Since the question has not been extensively studied, I cannot be absolutely sure, but I feel quite confident that no generalization of the property will be

---

[12] I may mention in passing that the same kind of confusion nowadays threatens comparative statements involving Tobin's q indicator in theoretical disequilibrium economics, since computation of this indicator involves quantities as well as prices. When its change are considered as reflecting changes of relative prices, quantities must be kept fixed.

[13] E. Malinvaud, "The analogy between atemporal and intertemporal theories of resource allocation", *Review of Economic Studies*, vol. XXVII, no 3, 1961.

[14] E. Burmeister and J. Turnovsky, "Capital deepening response in an economy with heterogeneous capital goods", *American Economic Review*, December 1972.

found: the "capital deepening response" to change of the interest rate ought to be subject, in this formulation, to the same kind of limitations that appeared with the second method. If I am rather confident in this statement, it is because I looked carefully at a completely neglected article by John Sargan, who seriously tried to apply the third method in the general case of several primary factors and final goods and to derive comparative dynamics properties.[15]

What are the implications of these theoretical developments for applied macroeconomic analysis? At this point, it is natural to wonder whether any use should be made in applications of the average period of production. Hicks never suggested it; his earlier writings may already have led readers to conclude that he considered his third method as being appropriate only for theoretical exploration. This conclusion was later made explicit in *Capital and Time* or still better in an article published at about the same time, where it is explained that the joint production resulting from the durable use of fixed capital makes roundaboutness a confusing concept: "There is no period of production", he writes.[16] Indeed, attempts at direct determination of the average period of production by statisticians would meet insuperable difficulties, since it would require detailed data on the use of old equipment, data that are not available, even simply within the firms. Indirectly, one could use the approximation derived by Maurice Allais, according to whom, under perfect competition, the average period of production may be approximated by the ratio between the value of productive capital and the income earned by primary factors of production.[17] But this would mean only another way of looking at essentially the same macroeconomic variables, and with little benefit since it would require an increased degree of abstraction.

More usefully, we must wonder whether the lapses from the conjectured capital deepening response, whatever the approach from which it is specified, have real significance. For lack of accurate econometric evidence the question must be left open. In my work as an applied macroeconomist, whenever this capital deepening response is assumed, I am, however, not really disturbed. My subjective evaluation gives very low probability to the risk of mistakes resulting from the assumption. I know of too many other cases of theoretical possibilities, such as upward sloping demand curves, that have little bearing on actual phenomena. But of course this intuition of mine ought to be substantiated, for instance by an approach similar to the

---

[15] J. Sargan, "The period of production", *Econometrica,* April 1955.

[16] "The Austrian theory of capital and its re-birth in modern economics", essay No 8 in volume III of *Collected Essays on Economic Theory.*

[17] M. Allais, *Economie et Intérêt,* Paris, Imprimerie Nationale, 1947. The approximation is given on page 132 for a stationary economy. It holds for proportional growth as well, if the interest rate is not very different from the growth rate.

one used by W. Hildenbrand to demonstrate that aggregate demand curves are downward sloping.[18]

4. Proportional growth and the traverse

When attention turns from stationary equilibria or proportional growth paths to less special evolutions, we must on this occasion speak of "the traverse", the denomination used by Hicks. My first reflection will then be to wonder whether this is such a good word that we should always use it in preference to any other.

So far as I understand, it evokes a path that permits us to reach, rather directly, a main road. If so, its exclusive usage may convey a misleading image because, even in a stationary environment, evolution outside the feasible stationary equilibrium may fail to converge with it and may indeed not be geared to join it.

Actually, Hicks was clear on the limitations of the concept. For instance, in *Capital and Time,* when introducing the study of cases in which the economy is not in a steady state, he writes: "In most of the cases which we shall examine there will prove to be a tendency to equilibrium; so that our sequence can properly be considered as a *Traverse* from one steady state to another. But, as we shall see, it is far from clear that this is generally true. There are other possibilities" (p. 82).

But another aspect of the concept is also disturbing me. Taking a traverse implies the intention to join a main road. Is economic growth far sighted enough to make the image appropriate in this respect? The question actually raises an issue which is at the core of a conflict of opinions concerning the operation of our economic system. Some economists claim that, when proper account of expectations and market forces is taken, the economy is stable and naturally finds the efficient growth path; a good model should then be one of competitive growth with perfect foresight; the image of a traverse should well suit these economists. But other economists do not share this optimistic thesis. I find it a bit troublesome that our vocabulary may seem to prejudge the solution of this big unsolved issue.

In fact, it is curious to note that, for the study of the traverse, Hicks only considers models in which economic growth is absolutely myopic, even blind: the conditions of the current period fully determine investment, without conditions in subsequent periods playing any role, expectations being assumed static when they have to occur. Hicks even says that a theory with correct expectations is not "the kind we are here endeavouring to construct" (CT, p. 56). Convergence to the steady state may then perhaps

---

[18] W. Hildenbrand, "On the law of demand", *Econometrica,* 1983, 997–1019; K. and W. Hildenbrand, "On the mean income effect: a data analysis of the U.K. family expenditure survey", Bonn discussion paper, November 1985.

better be described as a situation in which the forest, through which the blind walker moves, gently slopes down to an unexpected main road.

Let us, however, speak of the traverse, since it is a handy short expression for economic growth outside the steady state. I see the study of the traverse as having three possible objectives: (i) description of qualitative features of economic growth, after the steady state has been disturbed, (ii) convergence to a steady state, (iii) possibility of overcapitalization or of overexhaustion of resources. The available literature mainly concentrates on problem (ii), whereas Hicks is also quite interested in problem (i) and I think problem (iii) ought not to be neglected.

For the organization of what I should like to say, I find it convenient to sharply distinguish between the flexprice case, which is going to be the subject of this part, and the fixprice case, which I shall consider only in the following and last part of my talk. Let us then now discuss the properties of a full employment growth path made of a sequence of competitive temporary equilibria.

What is the ultimate aim of this discussion? Can it be to sharpen our intuition about the evolution of quantities and prices in a real economy? Such was certainly the aim of Ricardo and other great economists of the nineteenth century. Such is also one important motivation of Hicks. Indeed, he often presented his study of the traverse as being intended to provide the missing last chapter of his book *A Theory of Economic History*.[19] Since he sees the "mainspring of economic growth" as being technical progress, he wants to study how, after each invention, resource allocation and relative prices change and evolve. This is a main theme in the second part of *Capital and Time*.

So far as I know, no other mathematical economist today entertains the same hope of being able to trace through time the impact of each new change in economic environment on equilibrium prices and quantities. We have become more modest. When we want to know the effects of technical progress, increased scarcity of some resources and other changes, we most often neglect to consider transitory phases.

Indeed, the theoretical answers that we are deriving at present come most often from the comparative dynamics of steady states, either stationary states or rather proportional growth paths in which some form of technical progress is recognized. The answers precisely follow from the kind of properties that I examined in the preceding section. Considering what can be, and cannot be, achieved by a purely theoretical analysis, I indeed think the comparative dynamics of steady states essentially provides the proper background for our intuition on such issues. I do not expect many extra insights resulting from attempts at precisely studying flexprice growth out of the steady states, which would then have to be in an evolving environment.

---

[19] See for instance page xvii in the Preface of J. Hicks, *Economic Perspectives, Further Essays on Money and Growth*, Clarendon Press, Oxford 1977.

The ultimate aim of the discussion of the traverse in a flexprice setting is rather, I believe, a better understanding of the role of the price system in our economies, a better understanding of whether and why it has, or ought, to be supplemented by other guides for long term decisions. My own conclusion of what I learned from this theory can be stated as follows: orderly convergence of economic growth to a steady, sustainable and efficient path could not be taken for granted, and would even appear unlikely, if the price system alone was operating. I think I then see a little better the meaning of the following questions: why is the price system not alone to operate? Which ones of the many mechanisms, that operate besides it and interfer with it, play a useful role? Which ones ought to be removed and which ones maintained, reactivated or even added?

With this concern in mind, we cannot but be impressed by the complexity of the model to be tackled by a fully convincing theory. "The task thus outlined is formidable" writes Hicks (CT, p. 82); and I can paraphrase one of its following sentences by saying: "most of what we theorists can offer is not more that solutions for quite special cases".

But when clearcut results in favor of one thesis fail to be obtained on most of the special cases studied, we at least know that truth of the thesis in the complex conditions of the real world is unlikely. This is precisely the situation we are facing about the convergence hypothesis. Without attempting to survey the relevant literature on this hypothesis, I may briefly recall some of its main findings.

The mathematical exploration of the problem is fairly advanced for one case, which makes the recursive structure of economic growth quite simple, the case in which the value of consumption is assumed to be equal to wages and in which labor is the unique primary factor of production (I suppose the hypothesis made in *Capital and Time,* according to which wages are consumed and consumption out of profits is constant, makes little difference). In the classical two sector model, with one consumption good and one capital good, one knows, in particular from Hicks' discussion in *Capital and Growth,* that converge may fail to hold if production of the capital good is more capital intensive than production of the consumption good. Taking the multiplicity of capital goods into account requires an hypothesis about expectations, the easiest one being perfect myopic forecast: the instantaneous changes in the prices of the various capital goods are correctly expected. Since the initial work of F. Hahn on this model,[20] it is known that dynamics in the neighbourhood of the steady state usually has the saddle-point property, which means that convergence requires very particular and unlikely initial conditions. The joint production case, which would properly deal with complementarity over time, has, however, been little studied in the framework of this model, which applies the second "method of disintegration".

---

[20] F. Hahn, "On warranted growth paths", *Review of Economic Studies,* 1968.

More generally, convergence depends on what are the characteristics of technological constraints, of saving behavior and of expectations formation. But introduction of alternative hypotheses, concerning in particular savings, does not make convergence more likely than in the case I just discussed. This conclusion applies for instance when one studies the implications of the two main theories of saving: the permanent income hypothesis[21] and the life cycle hypothesis embedded in the overlapping generation model.[22]

Considering the aim I attribute to the study of convergence, one understands why I insist also on the study of questions that more explicitly belong to the welfare economics of growth, even though one might dispute their classification under the heading of the traverse problem. Over-capitalization could occur in a proportional growth path. Even though consideration of exhaustible resources rules out proportional growth, it can still be conceived in the framework of a regular and typical pattern playing the same role in the theoretical elaboration as does the steady state. But the possibility of overcapitalization or overexhaustion fundamentally concerns efficiency of the price system, in the same way as possible lack of convergence.

Actually, the two possibilities of overcapitalization and overexhaustion raise different problems. Overcapitalization is well defined now, after the success of the golden rule literature. The question of knowing whether it occurs is mainly econometric. Theory can, however, clear the ground and help in the specification of the hypothesis to be tested. It can study under which conditions overcapitalization might result from too high saving propensities, from the high pure profit rates that risk taking in business may require, or from non competitive market structures and behavior. I believe this study does not attract the attention it deserves.[23]

Overexhaustion may on the contrary appear to be an elusive concept. Its study requires a rigorous definition of the efficient speed of exhaustion of natural resources. If a formal definition can be derived from macroeconomic specifications that are similar to those used in the optimal growth literature, one may feel that these specifications assume as given some parameters whose determination precisely is at the root of the problem, such as the rate at which utilities of future generations should be discounted. However, an elusive concept is not necessarily a void concept. In this instance public interest, as well as reflection, proves that it is not void. I believe that theory should aim at making it less elusive and at studying the conditions of its actual occurrence.

---

[21] T. Bewley, "The permanent income hypothesis and long-run economic stability", *Journal of Economic Theory,* June 1980.
[22] I discussed this case in *Théorie Macroéconomique,* chap. 6, Dunod, Paris 1981.
[23] I devoted a few pages to it in *Théorie Macroéconomique,* op. cit.

5. Growth under sticky prices

We owe the distinction flexprice–fixprice to Hicks. Was it pure co-incidence if the distinction was first clearly introduced and discussed in *Capital and Growth*? Few economists share the extreme view according to which a fixprice theory cannot teach anything that would be relevant to the real world. On the other hand, few economists believe that the fixprice hypothesis can be appropriate anywhere in a theory of economic growth. Hicks is, however, among those few since in *Capital and Time,* published eight years later, he again treats on a par the two fixprice and flexprice cases.

I am also among those few. More precisely, in what would, I believe, be an appropriate theory, the temporary equilibrium would assume most prices to be fixed, i.e. exogenous; prices would then move from one temporary equilibrium to the next, but not by the full extent that would have been required to clear all excess demands and supplies; moreover, they would be subject to autonomous trends and shocks. Such an appropriate growth theory is, however, quite complex to deal with and has many degrees of freedom; hypotheses intended to make it simpler or more precise can seldom avoid the criticism of being "*ad hoc*". Under these circumstances, I see the two growth theories, built respectively under the flexprice and the fixprice assumptions, as playing complementary roles and as enlightening two sides of the same reality. This is probably also the view held by Hicks who wrote in *Capital and Growth,* p. 77: "Though our ultimate preference may be for something which lies between [flexprice and fixprice], anything which does so must partake to some extent of the difficulties of both. It is the extremes which are (relatively) simple, so that it is with them that it is best to begin".

One must recognize, however, that they apply to different time perspectives: the real long run for the flexprice growth theory, the transition from the short to the medium run for the fixprice. One might even entertain a synthesis, according to which the flexprice theory would provide the relevant reference for long run growth, whereas evolution around this long term trend would be properly understood by reference to the fixprice theory. Although at some places, for instance when he considers the traverse as "the passage to equilibrium", Hicks might be understood as accepting this synthesis, a careful reader will probably conclude that he does not. For instance on page 131 of *Capital and Growth,* he writes: "It is essentially this method [of endogenous determination of prices] which is the basis for what has been presented by a number of economists . . . as *Growth Theory*: a general theory . . . of long-term Economic Growth. I would not myself claim for it that it is a theory of Economic Growth, if by that one means a theory that can hope to give at all an adequate explanation of actual Growth phenomena".

Now, I think we have to be more clear. Either we completely discard the flexprice growth theory as empirically irrelevant, as some radical economists undoubtedly do, and then we should no longer pay any attention to it in our reflections. Or we believe that it provides a useful first approximation for some phenomena, and then we ought to say which phenomena. As for me, I am confident that the flexprice theory gives us the adequate framework for the explanation of most long term trends of relative prices, as I already hinted earlier. Therefore it is also reliable when we want to understand such things as long term changes in consumption patterns, or to discuss at least some of the likely impacts of such institutional changes as fiscal reforms or trade liberalization.

On the other hand, I do not find in this flexprice theory some of the ingredients that seem to be required for the understanding of relative growth performances of various industrial countries, for instance of England and France through the eigthteenth, nineteenth and twentieth centuries. Why is it so? Because I agree with economic historians in thinking that an essential element in the explanation is the course of business profitability, while this latter is precisely a deviation from the flexprice equilibrium.

Business profitability may be characterized by the anticipated marginal pure profit rate (excess over the real interest rate or, if I may use this word in order to avoid being misunderstood, excess over the marginal productivity of capital). Over decades and excepting cases of major shocks, this can be properly measured by the mean realized pure profit rate. So far as we now know, such a measure shows substantial differences from one economy to another, from one decade to another. The existence of a non-zero pure profit rate is inconsistent with existing flexprice growth theories. Taking explicit account of uncertainties and of risk aversion into account, one could certainly build a flexprice theory that would explain a positive pure profit rate. But this would still not suffice for the explanation of some growth phenomena, since the observed differences, with at some times and places negative, at others high pure profit rates, cannot be mainly explained by differences in risk exposure or business attitudes toward risk. They truly reveal what is best interpreted as disequilibria of the price system.

It is common sense to believe that these disequilibria play an important role in explaining relative growth performances. They may themselves result from inadequate economic policies or from the working of the socio-economic system, for instance along lines stressed by M. Olson.[24] But they certainly also have to do with the institutional changes that Hicks emphasized in his book, *A Theory of Economic History*. More precisely, a good understanding of the interplay between the institutional environment

---

[24] M. Olson, *The Rise and Decline of Nations,* Yale University Press, 1982.

and economic performances requires consideration of business profitability, which is a very important link between the two.[25]

The existence of disequilibria, leading to durable differences in profitability conditions, shows that something else than our present flexprice growth theories is required. Fixprice growth theories offer an alternative view. I agree with Hicks in thinking that, at the present phase of development of our economic theories, a research programme on economic growth under the fixprice hypothesis is quite warranted. Indeed, I like to think that I am taking part in this programme. But I certainly would not claim that it will be the end of our efforts. Even if purely real and wholly aggregated, consisting only of one real wage rate and one real interest rate, the price system has, according to the fixprice hypothesis, full exogeneity, which is difficult to swallow within a theory of economic growth and can be maintained only for some limited purpose. Intermediate specifications will have to be found and worked out.

I also agree with Hicks in thinking that "the traverse" may be the domain of questions for which we shall most often refer to the fixprice kind of growth theory. Keynesian long term stationary equilibria are also relevant. But if a change is being brought to their determinants, for instance a change in the real wage rate, it is interesting to study not only the long term effect and its stability, but also the path through which it is achieved, and in particular the short term effect, which may go in the reverse direction. This is precisely the study I tried to present in "Wages and Unemployment".[26] The same framework may be used in order to understand why a deliberate policy of low real interest rates should be favourable to economic growth, but not always in the long run to employment.

Rather than considering shifts of the fixed prices, Hicks focused his attention on changes in the physical determinants of growth, and in particular on technical progress. In *Capital and Time* he took again the old but still significant problem studied by Ricardo, namely whether technical progress may result in unemployment. Another similar problem is to know whether an acceleration of participation to the labour force may induce some increase in unemployment. The popular belief, and even the intuition of some economists, is indeed that such an effect should occur. Hence, a careful study makes sense. Using the flexprice, and therefore full employment, hypothesis cannot be appropriate. Therefore one should, at least for the time being, use the alternative fixprice hypothesis.

The answer given by Hicks is that, if the real wage rate remains fixed, the

[25] So far as I can see, Hicks never explicitly stressed in his writings the importance of profitability as a driving force of economic growth. Considering both his role in promoting the fixprice approach and his vision about the driving force of modern economic growth, I find this lack of interest curious.

[26] *Economic Journal*, March 1982.

introduction of new machines could induce a temporary surge of unemployment, but that eventually employment will on the contrary increase faster. One should, however, remember that this is proved within a model of capital shortage, whose relevance has to be assessed in actual economies to which the conclusion would be applied: employment is a function of existing productive capacities, which depend on capital accumulation, hence on profit margin. The introduction of a new more efficient process of production both decreases the labour requirement per unit of capacity and increases the profit margin. The first effect may dominate in the short run, but will eventually be superseded by the second.

Clearly the examples that I have just considered, namely the effect of an exogenous change in real wages and the unemployment that can result from inventions, are only two among the many questions to be clarified by the theory of growth under imperfectly flexible prices. In order to emphasize the point at the end of this talk, let me consider briefly Hick's vision about the driving force of the actual modern growth process. This is presented at the end of his Nobel lecture[27] and developed more fully in an essay published a little later.[28] The intention there is to supplement the book *A Theory of Economic History* which, stressing the role of the merchants in the emergence of a market system, was mainly addressed to growth before the Industrial Revolution.

The mainspring of industrialism is "science-based technical progress embodied in physical equipment". Each new invention gives an Impulse that works through a temporary rise in the rate of profit, the latter generating the necessary saving for implementation of the invention. The Impulse eventually peters out because of scarcity of primary resources, most often in modern times scarcity of labour. But new inventions, some of them induced, come in and maintain economic growth.

This process does not work as well in all times and places. "The individual Impulse has two dimensions, since it is spread out over time. Its size and its time-shape depend partly upon the nature of the improvement which has initiated it, partly on the characteristics of the economy in which it is carried through" (p. 31 of the 1977 reprint of "Industrialism"). Where the "English sickness" prevails, technical progress is threatened or twisted, by a "sectional struggle" of each industry trying to gain against the others, by improving its terms of trade (p. 38). In such distortions of the price system with respect to what "economic criteria" would require, the formation of wages plays a special role. Not only are wages to a large extent protected against the ups and downs that the law of supply and demand would imply, but they are also subject to a "social spreading" (p. 41).

[27] "The mainspring of economic growth", *Swedish Journal of Economic*, 1973, reprinted in *American Economie Review*, December 1981.
[28] "Industrialism", *International Affairs*, April 1974, reprinted in J. Hicks, *Economic Perspectives: Further Essays on Money and Growth*, Clarendon Press, Oxford, 1977.

I do not want to comment here on this vision of modern economic growth and to compare it with the ones proposed by others (actually many economists do accept it). I should just like to stress that it raises a large number of theoretical questions if we begin to look at it closely. It recognizes the existence of some disequilibria between demands and supplies, or within the price structure, but it does not make them fully explicit, neither does it study under which conditions the conjectured effects of these disequilibria will occur. Hence, it suggests an important research programme for the theory of capital and growth.

In the Preface of *Economic Perspectives* Hicks explains that *Capital and Time* was the ladder by which he climbed to his present point of view; it provided the formal argument; but before the point of view could be stated clearly, he had to diminish his dependence on the formal argument. "In the essay on "Industrialism" the ladder has finally been kicked down" he wrote (p. xvi). I would like to conclude this talk in announcing that many of us are now putting our own ladders up around the tree on top of which Sir John is sitting.

I.N.S.E.E., Paris

Oxford Economic Papers 38 (1986), 386–402

A DISAGGREGATED DISEQUILIBRIUM MODEL OF THE LABOUR MARKET

By MARTYN ANDREWS* and STEPHEN NICKELL†

Introduction

WE NOW possess a considerable body of evidence which suggests that the wage does not adjust in such a way as to equate the demand and supply of labour in every period.[1] If this is true, then we are confronted with the double problem of what determines both employment and the wage. Theories of non-market clearing wage determination are numerous and varied and many such theories imply a theory of employment determination as well.[2] Most of these theories are, however, difficult to operationalise and it is traditional in the empirical modelling of markets in disequilibrium simply to assume that the wage adjusts towards some long run level which may or may not be the market clearing value.[3] We intend to follow this tradition. Given the wage, the standard disequilibrium market model then asserts that employment is determined on the short side of the market.[4] A typical example would have the following form

$$n^d = n^d(w/p, z^d) \tag{1a}$$

$$n^s = n^s(w/p, z^s) \tag{1b}$$

$$n = \min(n^s, n^d) \tag{1c}$$

$$w/p = f((w/p)_{-1}, (w/p)^*, z^w) \tag{1d}$$

where $(w/p)^*$ satisfies

$$n^d(w/p, z^d) = n^s(w/p, z^s) \tag{2}$$

w is the nominal wage, p is the price level, n is employment and z^d, z^s and

* Macroeconomic Modelling Bureau, Warwick University.
† Institute of Economics and Statistics, Oxford University.

We are grateful to the Economic and Social Research Council, the Department of Employment and the Esmee Fairbairn Trust for financial assistance. We should also like to thank Mark Stewart, Peter Sinclair, three referees and participants of seminars at Warwick, Dublin and Oxford for helpful comments on earlier drafts of this paper.

[1] See, for example, Ashenfelter and Ham (1979), Ham (1985), Altonji (1982), Hall (1980), Rosen and Quandt (1978), Romer (1981), Andrews (1983), Nickell and Andrews (1982), Muellbauer and Winter (1980).

[2] A large number of theories of this type are discussed in Stiglitz (1984) and Johnson and Layard (1984).

[3] The classic model of this kind as applied in the labour market context is set out in Rosen and Quandt (1978).

[4] Of course, in the standard income expenditure models built in the 1960's wages do not adjust to clear the market but employment is determined on the demand side of the market. This was, for many years, the standard method of dealing with the "disequilibrium" problem. In the model set out here, however, it is simplest to imagine that the goods market is competitive with price taking firms.

z^w are other variables which influence labour demand, labour supply and wages respectively. $(w/p)^*$ is the market clearing real wage.

There are a number of problems with this formulation, particularly with regard to the specification of labour demand which is normally used. The standard specification includes the current level of output as one of the z^d variables.[5] This is not, of course, a contentious issue in the sense that it is always possible to write down factor demands conditional on output with the price terms simply capturing substitution possibilities. However, if the output variable is treated as exogenous then there is a serious problem. If firms take their own output as given then the model set out above in (1), (2) makes little sense. The labour demand equation is then a disequilibrium equation for it implies that the firms are constrained in the amount of output they can produce and sell. This is somewhat at variance with the rationale underlying this kind of model where the basic equations are supposed to capture the "notional" supplies and demands. Thus, for example, suppose "exogenous" output rises. Thus n^d rises and at some point it moves beyond n^s and so employment is then fixed. Suppose output continues to increase. With employment fixed, it is not clear how the extra output gets produced. Under these circumstances, output is surely constrained by the labour supply restriction. Consequently output cannot conceivably be exogenous in this framework and to treat it as such tends to undermine the whole exercise.

A second problem with model (1) and (2) which is mentioned in Rosen and Quandt (1978) and emphasised in Muellbauer (1978) and Muellbauer and Winter (1980) arises when it is used in aggregate. Casual observation reveals that it is possible for some labour markets to be in excess demand while others, which are spatially or occupationally distinct, are in excess supply. This has the powerful implication that total observed employment will be less than both n^s and n^d and the aggregate "min" model will not accurately describe the data.

It is our purpose in this paper to take account of both the above problems. In the next section we set out a model where aggregate employment is generated by adding up over a large number of sub-markets each of which is potentially out of equilibrium. In Section 2 we discuss the specification of both the supply and demand equations and the estimation of the model and this is followed by a discussion of our results.

1. Aggregation over markets in disequilibrium[6]

Suppose we have N separated labour markets with a uniform wage. Suppose further that labour demand and supply functions in the ith market are given by

$$n_{it}^d = \bar{X}_t \bar{\alpha} + \bar{u}_t + u_{it}; \qquad n_{it}^s = \bar{Z}_t \bar{\beta} + \bar{v}_t + v_{it} \qquad (3)$$

[5] For example, Rosen and Quandt (1978), Lewis and Makepiece (1981).

[6] The notion of smoothing by aggregation utilised in this model has a long history stretching back to Roy (1930) (other references may be found in Muellbauer 1978) and an example of its

where $\bar{u}_t$, $\bar{v}_t$ are white noise error terms, $\tilde{X}_t$, $\tilde{Z}_t$ are sets of variables including wages, and u_{it}, v_{it} are independently distributed across i although they may be serially correlated.[7] If we define U as the set of markets where firms are unconstrained (excess supply) and C as the set of markets where firms are constrained (excess demand), then we have

$$i \in U \text{ iff } v_{it} - u_{it} > \tilde{Y}_t\tilde{\gamma} + \tilde{\eta}_t; \qquad i \in C \text{ iff } v_{it} - u_{it} \leqslant \tilde{Y}_t\tilde{\gamma} + \tilde{\eta}_t$$

where

$$\tilde{Y}_t\tilde{\gamma} + \tilde{\eta}_t = \tilde{X}_t\tilde{\alpha} - \tilde{Z}_t\tilde{\beta} + \bar{u}_t - \bar{v}_t. \tag{4}$$

So if λ_t is the proportion of labour markets in XS supply and N is "large" we may write

$$\lambda_t = \Pr\,(v_{it} - u_{it} > \tilde{Y}_t\tilde{\gamma} + \tilde{\eta}_t) = f_1(\tilde{Y}_t\tilde{\gamma} + \eta_t), \text{ say} \tag{5}$$

$$\sum_{i \in U} u_{it} = \lambda_t N E_i(u_{it} \mid v_{it} - u_{it} > \tilde{Y}_t\tilde{\gamma} + \tilde{\eta}_t) = \lambda_t N f_2(\tilde{Y}_t\tilde{\gamma} + \tilde{\eta}_t), \text{ say} \tag{6}$$

$$\sum_{i \in C} v_{it} = (1 - \lambda_t) N E_i(v_{it} \mid v_{it} - u_{it} \leqslant \tilde{Y}_t\tilde{\gamma} + \tilde{\eta})$$
$$= (1 - \lambda_t) N f_3(\tilde{Y}_t\tilde{\gamma} + \tilde{\eta}_t), \text{ say} \tag{7}$$

Note that $\sum_{i \in U} u_{it}$ is the sum of the market specific errors in the demand equation in those markets in excess supply. The conditional expectation f_2 is the average error in these markets which is likely to be negative because those markets which have negative demand errors are more likely to fall in the excess supply category. An exactly similar argument applies with regard to the supply side errors in the excess demand markets.

Assuming that employment is determined on the "short" side in each sub-market we have aggregate employment, n, given by

$$n_t = \sum_{i \in U} (\tilde{X}_t\tilde{\alpha} + \bar{u}_t + u_{it}) + \sum_{i \in C} (\tilde{Z}_t\tilde{\beta} + \bar{v}_t + v_{it})$$

$$= f_1 N(\tilde{X}_t\tilde{\alpha} + \bar{u}_t) + \sum_{i \in U} u_{it} + (1 - f_1) N(\tilde{Z}_t\tilde{\beta} + \bar{v}_t) + \sum_{i \in C} v_{it}$$

---

use in empirical work is presented in Batchelor (1977). The model discussed in this section is set out in Nickell (1980) and has been published in Nickell (1984). Subsequently, we discovered that the employment equation has been written up in an unpublished manuscript by Kooiman and Kloek (1979) although it is not related to a wage model. Martin (1985) also contains an extensive discussion of this model. An alternative although related framework is provided by Lambert (1984) and is used by Sneessens and Drèze (1985) in a macro-model of the Belgian economy.

[7] Note that in this model, all the regressor variables are identical across markets with u_{it}, v_{it} being the only terms which vary over i. This is, to some extent, simply a matter of expositional convenience. The markets can be of varying sizes so long as the supply and demand functions have the same structure and thus can be aggregated in a natural fashion.

or, using (6), (7),

$$n_t = f_1 N(\tilde{X}_t \tilde{\alpha} + \bar{u}_t + f_2) + (1 - f_1) N(\tilde{Z}_t \tilde{\beta} + \bar{v}_t + f_3) \tag{8}$$

Next we may generate an aggregate equation by defining

$$N(\tilde{X}_t \tilde{\alpha} + \bar{u}_t) = X_t \alpha + u_t, \quad N(\tilde{Z}_t \tilde{\beta} + \bar{u}_t) = Z_t \beta + v_t,$$
$$N(\tilde{Y}_t \tilde{\gamma} + \tilde{\eta}_t) = Y_t \gamma + \eta_t. \tag{9}$$

This adding up procedure clearly involves either adjustment of the coefficient if the variable is a (common) price or adjusting the variable if it is a quantity. Writing (8) out in full thus yields

$$n_t = f_1 \left[\frac{Y_t \gamma + \eta_t}{N} \right] (Y_t \gamma + \eta_t) + Z_t \beta + N f_1 \left[\frac{Y_t \gamma + \eta_t}{N} \right] f_2 \left[\frac{Y_t \gamma + \eta_t}{N} \right]$$
$$+ N \left[1 - f_1 \left[\frac{Y_t \gamma + \eta_t}{N} \right] \right] f_3 \left[\frac{Y_t \gamma + \eta_t}{N} \right] + v_t$$

If we now suppose v_{it}, u_{it} are bivariate normal with zero mean and parameters $(\sigma_1, \sigma_2, \rho)$ and define $\sigma_3 = N(\sigma_1^2 + \sigma_2^2 - 2\sigma_1 \sigma_2 \rho)^{\frac{1}{2}}$ then, by using standard results on conditional normal expectations, it may be shown that the employment equation reduces to

$$n_t = -\Phi \left[\frac{Y_t \gamma + \eta_t}{\sigma_3} \right] (Y_t \gamma + \eta_t) + X_t \alpha - \sigma_3 \phi \left[\frac{Y_t \gamma + \eta_t}{\sigma_3} \right] + u_t \tag{10}$$

where ϕ, Φ are the standard normal density and CDF respectively. Both σ_3 and $(Y_t \gamma + \eta_t)$ clearly play an important role in this equation which can be clarified if we rewrite (10) as

$$n_t = (X_t \alpha + u_t) - \left[\Phi \left[\frac{Y_t \gamma + \eta_t}{\sigma_3} \right] (Y_t \gamma + \eta_t) + \sigma_3 \phi \left[\frac{Y_t \gamma + \eta_t}{\sigma_3} \right] \right]$$
$$= \text{aggregate demand for labour} - g(Y_t \gamma + \eta_t, \sigma_3)$$

where g is a non-negative function with derivatives $g_1 > 0$, $g_2 > 0$. σ_3^2 / N^2 is the variance of $(u_{it} - v_{it})$ and σ_3 thus measures the variability of disequilibrium across markets whereas $(Y_t \gamma + \eta_t)$ is a measure of the aggregate excess demand for labour. Thus for a given level of aggregate demand for labour, any increase either in the extent of aggregate excess demand or in the variability of excess demand across markets will lead to lower employment. These results are both in accord with intuition. Notice further that if both σ_3 and $(Y_t \gamma + \eta_t)$ are zero, g is zero and we have the equilibrium model. On the other hand if σ_3 only is zero, we have the standard (min condition) disequilibrium model, for the right hand side of (10) is $X_t \alpha + u_t$ (demand) if $Y_t \gamma + \eta_t < 0$ (excess supply) and is $Z_t \beta + u_t$ (supply) if $Y_t \gamma + \eta_t > 0$ (excess demand).

It is clear that estimation of an equation such as (10) on its own will present serious problems, not least because identification will be so weak. The introduction of a wage equation of the type (1d) may, however, lead to large gains in efficiency. Suppose we introduce a simple partial adjustment equation of the form

$$(w/p)_t = \delta_0 + \delta_1(w/p)_t^* + (1 - \delta_1)(w/p)_{t-1} + \sum_{i=2} \delta_i z_{it}^w, \quad 0 \le \delta_1 \le 1 \quad (11)$$

where $(w/p)^*$ is the equilibrium real wage. This seems a natural, although somewhat *ad hoc*, formulation for a real wage adjustment equation. If $\delta_0 = 0$ and if either $z_i^w = 0$ in the long run or $\delta_i = 0$, $i \ge 2$ then the real wage converges in the long run to its equilibrium level. Otherwise it will converge to a value away from the competitive market clearing level as it may do in the presence of unions, for example. Note that in the equilibrium model $\delta_0 = \delta_i = 0$, $i \ge 2$ and $\delta_1 = 1$ and then $(w/p)_t = (w/p)_t^*$ for all t. The equation contains no apparent error term although both supply and demand equation errors enter via $(w/p)^*$.[8]

It order to see how this equation combines with the employment model (10), it is convenient to rewrite the aggregate demand and supply functions with the wage term separated out. Thus we have

$$n_t^d = X_t\alpha + u_t = \alpha_1(w/p)_t + \bar{X}_t\bar{\alpha} + u_t,$$
$$n_t^s = Z_t\beta + v_t = \beta_1(w/p)_t + \bar{Z}_t\bar{\beta} + v_t \quad (12)$$

where

$$X_t = ((w/p)_t, \bar{X}_t), \quad \alpha' = (\alpha_1, \bar{\alpha}'), \quad Z_t = ((w/p)_t, \bar{Z}_t),$$
$$\beta' = (\beta_1, \bar{\beta}')$$

We now define the equilibrium real wage $(w/p)^*$ as the solution to

$$X_t\alpha + u_t = Z_t\beta + v_t$$

which, with the notation in (12), yields

$$(w/p)_t^* = (\beta_1 - \alpha_1)^{-1}(\bar{X}_t\bar{\alpha} - \bar{Z}_t\bar{\beta} + \eta_t) \quad (13)$$

where remember that $\eta_t = u_t - v_t$. This may also be written

$$(w/p)_t^* - (w/p)_t = (\beta_1 - \alpha_1)^{-1}(Y_t\gamma + \eta_t) = (\beta_1 - \alpha_1)^{-1}(n_t^d - n_t^s)$$

using (12). If we substitute this expression into the adjustment equation

---

[8] Note that the adjustment equation (11) can be rewritten $\Delta(w/p)_t = \delta_0' + \delta_1'(n_t^d - n_t^s) + \sum_{i=2} \delta_i' z_{it}^w$ which is identical to that used by Rosen and Quandt (1978) with the exception of the missing error term ($\delta_0' = \delta_0/(1 - \delta_1)$, $\delta_1' = \delta_1/(\beta_1 - \alpha_1)(1 - \delta_1)$, $\delta_i' = \delta_i/(1 - \delta_1)$). This restriction is forced upon us in order to make estimation feasible. It is also worth noting that the assumed adjustment process is rather restrictive. Generalisation to the less restrictive error correction format (i.e. adding a term $\delta_2((w/p)_{t-1}^* - (w/p)_{t-1})$) leads to problems which appear very difficult to resolve.

(11), we obtain after some manipulation

$$n_t^d - n_t^s = Y_t\gamma + \eta_t = \frac{\beta_1 - \alpha_1}{\delta_1}\left[(1 - \delta_1)\Delta(w/p)_t - \delta_0 - \sum_{i=2}\delta_i z_{it}^w\right] \quad (14)$$

If we now substitute (14) into (10) and (13) into (11) we then obtain the two equation model

$$n_t = X_t\alpha - \Phi(A_t/\sigma_3)A_t - \sigma_3\phi(A_t/\sigma_3) + u_t \quad (15a)$$

$$(w/p)_t = \delta_0 + \frac{\delta_1}{\beta_1 - \alpha_1}(\bar{X}_t\bar{\alpha} - \bar{Z}_t\bar{\beta})$$

$$+ (1 - \delta_1)(w/p)_{t-1} + \sum_{i=2}\delta_i z_{it}^w + \frac{\delta_1}{\beta_1 - \alpha_1}\eta_t \quad (15b)$$

where

$$A_t = \frac{\beta_1 - \alpha_1}{\delta_1}\left[(1 - \delta_1)\Delta(w/p)_t - \delta_0 - \sum_{i=2}\delta_i z_{it}^w\right] \quad (15c)$$

$$= n_t^d - n_t^s,$$

the excess demand for labour (see 14). The parameters of the model are α, β, σ_3, δ_0, δ_1, δ_i, $i \geq 2$. As we have already noted, $\sigma_3 = \delta_0 = \delta_i = 0$, $i \geq 2$, $\delta_1 = 1$ generates an equilibrium model but if only $\sigma_3 = 0$ then the model reduces to one of the standard disequilibrium models described in Quandt (1978), namely that in which the price (i.e. wage) equation error is identically zero. Although the model has a recursive form in the sense that the wage equation (15b) does not have employment on the right hand side, it is in fact genuinely simultaneous because of the natural correlation between u_t and $\eta_t = u_t - v_t$. The next stage is to consider the empirical specification of the demand and supply functions and the estimation of the model in the light of this specification. This is the topic discussed in the next section.

2. Specification and estimation

Starting with the demand side, the actual equation which we estimate has the following structure

$$n_t^d = \alpha_0 + \alpha_1(w(1 + t_1)/p)_t + \alpha_2 n_{t-1} + \alpha_3 n_{t-2}$$
$$+ \alpha_4(p_m/p)_{t-1} + \alpha_5 k_t. \quad (16)$$

$$\alpha_1 < 0, \qquad \alpha_5 > 0.$$

n = employment, w = nominal wage, t_1 = employers' tax rate on labour, p = output price, p_m = price of materials/energy, k = capital stock. The basic form of this equation is that for a profit maximising firm with a predetermined capital stock and one other factor of production aside from labour (namely materials/energy). A number of points are worth noting. First, the actual lag structure is the one we finally employ. This is the consequence of a limited amount of experimentation. Second, the lags on the dependent variable may arise as a consequence of adjustment costs. However, such costs will also imply that the demand for labour is a function of future wage/price expectations. Here we simply suppose these to have been substituted out.[9] Third, it is worth re-emphasising that we are not conditioning labour demand on the level of output. Aside from the reasons discussed already this does have the further advantage that it enables us to read off directly the (capital stock constant) elasticity of employment with respect to the real wage, a not uninteresting parameter.

Looking now at the supply equation, we simply set down the function which is consistent with intertemporal optimisation on the part of individual agents.[10] Thus we have

$$n_t^s = \beta_0 + \beta_2 \left[\frac{w(1-t_2)}{p(1+t_3)} \right]_{t-1} + \beta_3 W_t^{**} + \beta_4 n_{t-1} + \beta_5 n_{t-2}$$
$$+ \beta_6 (r_t + r_{t-1}) + \beta_7 \text{POP}_{t-1} + \beta_8 \rho_t. \qquad (17)$$
$$\beta_2 > 0, \qquad \beta_3 < 0, \qquad \beta_7 > 0, \qquad \beta_8 < 0.$$

t_2 = income tax rate, t_3 = tax rate on goods, W^{**} = normal or long run real wage, r = real interest rate, POP = population of working age, ρ = replacement rate (the ratio of unemployment benefit to post tax hourly earnings). As before, the lags on this equation are those finally estimated. The general structure implies that individuals may respond differently to temporary and permanent shifts in real wages. The normal real wage W^{**} measures the long run level of real wages and so the impact of a permanent shift in real wages is $\beta_2 + \beta_3$ in contrast to that of a temporary shift which is simply β_2. Standard theory (see Lucas and Rapping 1969) implies $\beta_2 > 0$, $\beta_3 < 0$ and thus $\beta_2 + \beta_3 < \beta_2$. Intertemporal substitution possibilities also imply a positive real interest rate effect on labour supply ($\beta_6 > 0$). The working population is included as an obvious normalisation factor and the replacement rate (unemployment benefits/post tax earnings) captures the impact of the unemployment compensation system.[11] The lags on employment may arise as a consequence either of costs of adjustment or habit persistence. Finally it is worth noting that we found no role for the current

---

[9] This implies, of course, that the equation should contain all variables which are used to forecast the real wage. In fact, however, given the lagged real wage, other variables seem to add no useful information.

[10] See Lucas and Rapping (1969) for the two period model and Sargent (1979) p. 367–373 for the general version.

[11] Note that although the latter contains earnings, it may safely be taken as exogenous because the authorities will typically set benefits in relation to the general standard of living. That is they decide on the replacement rate and then work out the benefit level which will generate it.

real wage in this equation implying some delay in the response of suppliers of labour. This is not particularly surprising given the fact that it probably takes some little time for most suppliers of labour, who are employees, to learn about and respond to real wage shifts. This has important consequences for it implies that $\beta_1 = 0$ in the model (15) with the lagged real wage term entering the variables $\bar{Z}$.

In order to estimate the parameters of the demand and supply functions we must first discuss the relationship between the actual form of the demand and supply functions set out in (16), (17) and the basic micro model in (3). At the sectoral level, (16) becomes (with errors added)

$$n_{it}^d = \tilde{\alpha}_0 + \tilde{\alpha}_1(w(1 + t_1)/p)_t + \tilde{\alpha}_2 n_{it-1} + \tilde{\alpha}_3 n_{it-2}$$
$$+ \tilde{\alpha}_4(p_m/p)_{t-1} + \tilde{\alpha}_5 k_{it} + \tilde{u}_t + \tilde{u}_{it}. \tag{18}$$

The form of this equation is different from the micro equation set out in (3) where none of the regressors is sector dependent. The capital stock term may be dealt with simply by noting that we have labour markets of identical size and hence k_{it} can be rewritten as k_t/N, N being the number of markets. However, although the markets are "identical", it is clear that n_{it-1}, n_{it-2} differ across i. To deal with this point we define the following additional (mean zero) error components

$$\varepsilon_{it-1} = n_{it-1} - n_{t-1}/N, \qquad \varepsilon_{it-2} = n_{it-2} - n_{t-2}/N$$

(18) can then be rewritten

$$n_{it}^d = \tilde{\alpha}_0 + \tilde{\alpha}_1(w(1 + t_1)/p)_t + \tilde{\alpha}_2 n_{t-1}/N + \tilde{\alpha}_3 n_{t-2}/N$$
$$+ \tilde{\alpha}_4(p_m/p)_{t-1} + \tilde{\alpha}_5 k_t/N + \tilde{u}_t + u_{it} \tag{19}$$
$$u_{it} = \tilde{u}_{it} + \tilde{\alpha}_2 \varepsilon_{it-1} + \tilde{\alpha}_3 \varepsilon_{it-2}$$

u_{it} thus contains the underlying error plus lagged deviations of sector employment from average sector employment. These latter terms imply that u_{it} is serially correlated but we may still assume independence across i. The serial correlation in the u_{it} is of no consequence since they do not influence the aggregate error term.

Equation (19) thus corresponds to the demand side of (3) and a similar argument applies on the supply side. So we have

$$\tilde{X}_t \tilde{\alpha} = \tilde{\alpha}_0 + \tilde{\alpha}_1(w(1 + t_1)/p)_t + \tilde{\alpha}_2 n_{t-1}/N + \tilde{\alpha}_3 n_{t-2}/N$$
$$+ \tilde{\alpha}_4(p_m/p)_{t-1} + \tilde{\alpha}_5 k_t/N$$

and when we aggregate this over markets (see 9), we simply multiply through by N. Thus comparing (16) with (18) we see that $\alpha_0 = N\tilde{\alpha}_0$, $\alpha_1 = N\tilde{\alpha}_1$, $\alpha_2 = \tilde{\alpha}_2$, $\alpha_3 = \tilde{\alpha}_3$, $\alpha_4 = N\tilde{\alpha}_4$ and $\alpha_5 = \tilde{\alpha}_5$.

Having dealt with this point, we now consider the model which is actually estimated based on (16), (17). (15a, b, c) become

$$n_t = \alpha_0 + \alpha_1(w(1+t_1)/p)_t + \alpha_2 n_{t-1} + \alpha_3 n_{t-2}$$
$$+ \alpha_4(p_m/p)_{t-1} + \alpha_5 k_t - \Phi(A_t/\sigma_3)A_t - \sigma_3\phi(A_t/\sigma_3)$$
$$+ u_t \tag{20a}$$

$$(w/p)_t = \delta_0 + \frac{\delta_1}{|\alpha_1|(1+t_{1t})}\left[(\alpha_0 - \beta_0) + (\alpha_2 - \beta_4)n_{t-1}\right.$$
$$+ (\alpha_3 - \beta_5)n_{t-2} + \alpha_4(p_m/p)_{t-1} + \alpha_5 k_t$$
$$- \beta_2\left[\frac{w(1-t_2)}{p(1+t_3)}\right]_{t-1} - \beta_3 W_t^{**} - \beta_6(r_t + r_{t-1})$$
$$\left. - \beta_7 POP_{t-1} - \beta_8\rho_t\right] + (1-\delta_1)(w/p)_{t-1}$$
$$+ \sum_{i=2} \delta_i z_{it}^w + \frac{\delta_1}{|\alpha_1|(1+t_{1t})}\eta_t \tag{20b}$$

where

$$A_t = \frac{|\alpha_1|(1+t_{1t})}{\delta_1}\left[(1-\delta_1)\Delta(w/p)_t - \delta_0 - \sum_{i=2}\delta_i z_{it}^w\right] \tag{20c}$$

Estimation of this model is straightforward. We multiply (20b) through by $(1+t_{1t})$ and then assume that u_t, $\frac{\delta_1}{|\alpha_1|}\eta_t$ are bivariate normal and serially uncorrelated. Since n_t does not appear in (20b), maximum likelihood estimates may be obtained simply by minimising the log determinant of the error variance matrix. Non-linearity ensures that this is not a trivial computational exercise but it may be performed without great difficulty.

Three final points before looking at some results. First it is clear that the real interest rate cannot be treated as exogenous so we replace it by its fitted value from a regression on a set of exogenous variables. Second, we define the normal real wage, as in Andrews and Nickell (1982), by

$$W_t^{**} = \sum_{1=-2}^{2}\left[\frac{w(1-t_2)}{p(1+t_3)}\right]_{t+i}$$

where the current and future values are fitted values from a regression on a set of exogenous regressors. A somewhat longer moving average would have been preferable but too many degrees of freedom would be lost.[12] Third, the variables included in z_{it}^w must be considered. There are two types

---

[12] Two points are worth noting about this. First, we include lagged as well as future real wages to capture the initial wealth variable which we have omitted from the labour supply function (for want of a decent appropriate measure). Second, the fitted values represent agents' forecasts of the unobserved future components.

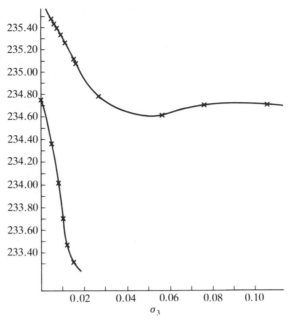

FIG. 1. Log-likelihood values corresponding to variations in σ_3

of variables which may enter here. Those which represent exogenous shocks which may induce short run deviations of the real wage from its equilibrium level and those which represent factors inducing a permanent discrepancy between the real wage and its equilibrium (as defined by the supply/demand system). The most important factor in this latter category is the existence of unions and we capture their importance by including union density (the proportion of the employed who are unionised). The variable we use to capture exogenous shocks is the change in real government expenditure.[13] The data used are those in Nickell and Andrews (1983) and Andrews and Nickell (1982) and description and sources are set out in the Appendix. Finally, it is worth noting that the equations are run in levels, not in logs, and that all variables aside from the real interest rate are normalised to have a unit mean. The corresponding coefficients thus have an elasticity interpretation.

Results

Before considering parameter estimates it is worth discussing our experience in estimating this model. First it is extraordinarily difficult to pin down an estimate of the σ_3 parameter. In order to give a flavour of the problem we present in Fig. 1 a graph of the maximised log likelihood for various imposed values of σ_3. The line BB represents a sequence of local

---

[13] Other variables have been tried in this context without success.

maxima whereas AA represents the global maxima (as far as we can tell). We have included BB for reasons which will become apparent although AA estimates are obviously superior in a statistical sense. We obtained estimates for the standard min condition model ($\sigma_3 = 0$) on the BB line but we were unable to find corresponding estimates on the AA line which therefore stops short of the axis. We were not able to obtain convergence in this region.[14] Although the variations in the log likelihood appear quite dramatic, a glance at the left-hand scale reveals that the difference between the two-lines is not large in likelihood terms. However, this does not apply to some of the parameter estimates as we shall see.

In Table 1, we report results for the equilibrium model (column E), the two disequilibrium models corresponding to $\sigma_3 = 0.01$ where D1 is on the BB line and D2 is on the AA line and the Rosen/Quandt type min condition model D3 at the left-hand end of the BB line. We only report these four sets of estimates because the parameter values are extremely close for all points on either AA or BB (for example, compare D1 and D3). There is a significant gain in likelihood in moving from the equilibrium model (E) to the disequilibrium model (D1), twice the difference in the log-likelihood being $13.94(X^2(5)_{0.05} = 10.95)$. So the disequilibrium models provide a significantly better description of the data than the equilibrium version which certainly accords with the generally accepted view of the UK labour market.

Looking more closely at the parameter estimates, we see that with the exception of D2, the long-run wage elasticities are very similar across all the models but the short run supply elasticity is higher in the disequilibrium versions.

The long-run wage elasticities of supply tend to be negligible whereas in the short run they are around one-half. Furthermore, we were able to obtain a reasonably well-determined real interest rate effect on labour supply, something which is quite rare in this context.[15] The (capital fixed) real wage elasticity of demand appears to be around one-half except in model D2 where it is more than three times as big. This is one of the larger discrepancies between the D1 and D2 results, another being the size of the union effect on wages which is considerably bigger, although badly determined, in the latter case. However, the wage adjustment parameter appears to be around 0.5 in all cases.

The biggest difference between the D1 and D2 equations becomes apparent when we look at the measures of the excess demand for labour

---

[14] It is clear from all this that identification of σ_3 is problematic, presumably because aggregate data is being used to try and capture a disaggregated phenomenon. Attempts to tie it down by allowing it to vary on a trend or with measures of mismatch were unsuccessful and free estimation also proved impossible. The evidence does, of course, suggest that its maximum likelihood estimate is negative in turn suggesting an inappropriate distributional form for the unobserved market heterogeneity.

[15] See Lucas and Rapping (1969) and Altonji (1982), for example.

TABLE 1

Labour supply, demand and wage adjustment equations United Kingdom 1954–79

Model number		Equilibrium				Disequilibrium			
		E		D1		D2		D3 (Rosen–Quandt)	
Labour demand (n_t^d)									
Constant	(α_0)	0.51	(0.15)	0.60	(0.24)	0.68	(0.94)	0.61	(0.30)
$(w(1+t_1)/p)_t$	(α_1)	−0.30	(0.070)	−0.28	(0.14)	−0.55	(0.56)	−0.30	(0.15)
n_{t-1}	(α_2)	1.22	(0.41)	1.13	(0.50)	1.00	(0.64)	1.14	(0.40)
n_{t-2}	(α_3)	−0.70	(0.49)	−0.68	(0.55)	−0.34	(1.50)	−0.71	(0.48)
$(p_m/p)_{t-1}$	(α_4)	−0.078	(0.025)	−0.082	(0.043)	−0.14	(0.07)	−0.086	(0.053)
k_t	(α_5)	0.35	(0.08)	0.32	(0.17)	0.43	(0.85)	0.34	(0.17)
Labour supply (n_t^s)									
Constant	(β_0)	−0.77	(0.34)	−1.07	(0.42)	−1.11	(0.37)	−1.02	(0.37)
$w(1-t_2/p(1+t_3)_{t-1}$	(β_2)	0.20	(0.11)	0.53	(0.44)	0.37	(0.13)	0.48	(0.48)
W_t^{**}	(β_3)	−0.34	(0.22)	−0.41	(0.39)	−0.65	(0.24)	−0.74	(0.82)
n_{t-1}	(β_4)	0.81	(0.41)	0.40	(0.54)	0.53	(0.27)	0.44	(0.62)
n_{t-2}	(β_5)	−0.76	(0.27)	−0.77	(0.53)	−0.75	(0.31)	−0.79	(0.46)
$r_t + r_{t-1}$	(β_6)	0.21	(0.12)	0.26	(0.15)	0.26	(0.12)	0.25	(0.17)
POP_{t-1}	(β_7)	1.69	(0.62)	2.35	(0.70)	2.31	(0.63)	2.29	(0.72)
Wage adjustment									
Constant	(δ_0)	0.0		−0.26	(0.10)	−0.51	(0.53)	−0.25	(0.10)
Adjustment coefficient	(δ_1)	1.0		0.50	(0.43)	0.59	(0.56)	0.58	(0.44)
Union density	(δ_2)	0.0		0.58	(0.21)	0.91	(1.01)	0.54	(0.21)
Δ government expenditure	(δ_3)	0.0		0.50	(0.22)	0.51	(0.31)	0.43	(0.25)
σ_3		0.0		0.01		0.01		0.00	
log likelihood		226.68		233.66		235.2		234.75	
short run wage elasticity (demand)		−0.30		−0.28		−0.55		−0.30	
short run wage elasticity (supply)		0.20		0.53		0.37		0.48	
long run wage elasticity (demand)		−0.63		−0.51		−1.82		−0.53	
long run wage elasticity (supply)		−0.15		0.086		−0.23		−0.19	

(i) We have no formal serial correlation statistics. The correlograms for all the equations are, however, very flat. Standard errors appear in parentheses.

(ii) n = employment, w = wage, p = output price, p_m = material/energy input price, t_1 = employers' labour tax rate, t_2 = income tax rate, t_3 = indirect tax rate, $W_t^{**} = \frac{1}{5}\sum_{i=-2}^{2}\left[\frac{w(1-t_2)}{p(1+t_3)}\right]_{t+i}$, k = capital stock, r = real interest rate, POP = population of working age. The real interest rate is defined as $r_t = R_t - (\hat{P}_{t+1} - P_t)/P_t$ where r is the Treasury Bill Rate, P is the retail price index and $\hat{P}_{t+1}$ is the expected price. The future components of W^{**} and r are dealt with by using fitted values from regressions on a set of exogenous and predetermined variables, namely n_{t-1}, n_{t-2}, $(w(1-t_2)/P)_{t-1}$, $(w(1-t_2)/P)_{t-2}$, $(w(1+t_1)/P)_{t-1}$, p_m/P_{t-1}, POP_{t-1}, k_t, Union density, T, DUM, QPW, QPW_{t-1}. The last four instruments are described in the Data Appendix (11, 14 and 20).

(iii) Note that the equations are not in logs but variables have been normalised to have a sample mean of unity allowing the coefficients to have an elasticity interpretation except in the case of the real interest rate.

implicit in these models. A good measure in this context is $\hat{A}_t$ since, as (15c) indicates, A_t is the excess demand for labour.

In Table 2, we report $\hat{A}_t$ for models D1, D2, D3 as well as the vacancy rate and minus the unemployment rate for comparison purposes. As we can see, the overall impression is that the estimated excess demand series move in the same broad direction as the vacancy rate and the negative of the unemployment rate. However, there are big differences between D2 and D1, D3. The latter two both exhibit a percentage change between the 1950's and the late 1970's which is in close accord with the change in the unemployment rate. D2, on the other hand, has a percentage change which

TABLE 2

Measures of the excess demand for labour
(percentages)

	$\hat{A}_t$	$\hat{A}_t$	$\hat{A}_t$	$-U_t$	V_t
	(D1)	(D2)	(D3)		
1954	2.2	13.9	2.1	−1.4	5.1
1955	0.9	11.7	1.1	−1.1	6.2
1956	−0.2	10.0	0.2	−1.2	5.3
1957	0.3	10.9	0.6	−1.6	4.1
1958	1.4	13.1	1.5	−2.2	3.0
1959	−0.4	10.2	0.1	−2.4	3.5
1960	0.6	11.4	0.9	−1.8	4.6
1961	−0.2	10.3	0.2	−1.7	4.5
1962	−0.6	9.9	−0.1	−2.3	3.1
1963	0.0	10.9	0.4	−2.8	3.0
1964	−0.6	9.6	−0.1	−2.0	4.6
1965	0.1	10.7	0.4	−1.7	5.4
1966	0.1	11.2	0.5	−1.8	5.2
1967	−1.8	8.3	−1.0	−3.0	3.6
1968	0.1	11.3	0.5	−3.3	4.0
1969	−0.2	9.3	0.1	−3.3	4.2
1970	−0.4	7.3	−0.1	−3.6	4.0
1971	−2.3	4.7	−1.6	−4.7	2.6
1972	−1.5	5.8	−0.9	−5.1	2.9
1973	−4.5	1.5	−3.3	−3.6	5.6
1974	−3.6	2.5	−2.6	−3.6	5.1
1975	−4.1	1.1	−3.1	−5.5	2.6
1976	−6.0	−1.4	−4.5	−7.1	2.1
1977	−5.0	−1.8	−3.8	−7.4	2.5
1978	−2.9	1.7	−2.2	−7.2	3.1
1979	−4.7	−1.6	−3.6	−6.8	3.2

U_t is the male unemployment rate. V_t is the vacancy rate (vacancies/employment) where registered vacancies are adjusted for the greater market penetration of the Government Employment Services in recent years (see Jackman, Layard and Pissarides, 1983 for details).

is more than twice as great. Furthermore, D2 indicates that there was excess demand for labour almost throughout, with the level of excess demand being around 10 percent until 1970. This seems a very large value and the D1, D3 series are much more closely in accord with our prior expectations. However, none of the fitted series capture the 1973 boom although they all capture the sharp rise in unemployment in 1967, 1971–72 and 1976. This is quite encouraging in the sense that there is nothing in the data we have used which is directly related to the unemployment series (in particular, the broad structure of the employment series is completely different from the unemployment series).

To summarise, therefore, we find that the results generated by models on the BB line in Fig. 1 which correspond to local maxima seem to be somewhat more persuasive than those produced by statistically superior models on the AA line in Fig. 1. Overall the parameter estimates seem quite sensible but the models are not well identified with respect to the σ_3 parameter. There seems to be a certain lack of robustness about these models which is by no means unusual in the world of disequilibrium modelling and is, perhaps, a consequence of the assumed price taking behaviour of firms when computing their notional demand for labour. It would, perhaps, be more appropriate to suppose that firms set prices and then simply supply whatever is subsequently demanded along the lines set out in Layard and Nickell (1986), for example. In any event, the results reported here, although quite encouraging, indicate that a great deal more needs to be done before anything really convincing is likely to emerge.

DATA APPENDIX

All data used in estimation can be obtained on request from the authors, together with copies of a computer run replicating equations E and D1, using TSP. The "computer names" are given in parentheses.

1. n. Employees in employment, males and females, mid-year GB. ETAS (N).
2. $\{w(1 + t_1)/p\}$. Real product wage. See 4, 6, and 8 below (WPP).
3. $\{w(1 - t_2)/P\}$. Real consumption wage. See 4, 5, and 10 below (WCP).
4. w. Pre-tax wage rate. This is calculated as follows. We first take the following data: E, average weekly earnings of full-time male manual workers (21 years and over), at the October in each year, for all industries covered; H, average weekly hours of . . . (as E above); N^h, average normal weekly hours of male manual workers, for all industries and services.

    The overtime premium, π, can be given a value of 0.3, whence $E = wN^h + 1.3w$ $(H - N^h)$ and w is easily calculated. We also adjust w by a factor that captures the decline of normal hours in total hours, namely $(1 - N^h/45)*1.3 + N^h/45$, which makes workers relatively better off at lower normal hours for a given hourly wage.

    All data for E, H, N^h are published in BLSHA YB and DEG.
5. P. Retail price index. General index of retail prices, all items, 1975 = 100. ETAS.
6. p. Firm's output price index. This we define as the retail price index, P, divided by $1 + t_3$. (see 10 below).
7. p_m/p. p_m is the price of materials and fuels. The series used was the 'wholesale price index of materials and fuel purchased by manufacturing industry', 1975 = 100. From 1954–1979 the series is published in ETAS. However observations for 1950–53 were generated by

splicing the above with the following series, which is published in various issues of MDS between December 1954 and August 1958, namely the 'price index of basic material used in broad sectors of industry, excluding fuel used in non-food manufacturing industry', 1949 = 100. (QP).

8. $(1 + t_1)$. t_1 is tax on employment borne by the firm. Series is calculated by taking the ratio of two indices; 'total labour costs per unit of output for the whole economy', 1975 = 100 and 'wages and salaries per unit of output for the whole economy', 1975 = 100. BLSHA, YB, DEG and ETAS. (T1).

9. $(1 + t_3)$. t_3 is the tax rate on goods. This is the ratio of the GDP deflator at market prices, 1975 = 100 to the GDP deflator at factor cost, 1975 = 100. The measures of GDP are all expenditure based. Note that the series is an index. All series taken from ETAS. (T3).

10. t_2. Average rate of income tax. The series taken reflects the direct tax rate on income, namely 'total personal disposable income', £ million, current prices, divided by 'total income before tax', £ million, current prices. In contrast to $(1 + t_1)$ and $(1 + t_3)$ this series is an actual tax rate, not an index. Both constituent series are published in ETAS. (T2).

11. T. $\log(1 + t_1) + t_2 + \log(1 + t_3)$. Variables described above.

12. k. k is the capital stock. The series used is 'gross capital stock at 1975 replacement cost', in £ thousand million. Data is available yearly from 1958 onward in successive issues of the BB, at various base years (which were easily 'spliced' together). Before 1958 only the 1954, 1951 and 1948 observations were published. Data was interpolated using real investment data, namely 'total gross domestic fixed capital formation' £ million at 1975 prices, using the usual technique involving the estimation of a decay parameter $\hat{\delta}$ from the postulated relationship,

$$K_n = \sum_{i=1}^{n} (1 - \delta)^{n-i} I_i + (1 - \delta)^n K_0 \qquad (A.1)$$

where K_n, K_0 are end of period and beginning of period capital stocks, I_i is investment. The missing K's are calculated recursively from (A.1) by setting $n = 1$ each time, and using $\hat{\delta}$. The investment series is published in ETAS. (K).

13. r. Real rate of interest, calculated as $R_t - (\hat{P}_{t+1} - P_t)/P_t$. R is the rate of discount for 91-day Treasury bills after the weekly tender, and is expressed as a yield (per cent per annum of 365 days). Averaged over last working day of each month. BESA, BEQB. (I).

14. DUM. Labour supply dummy whose value is zero up to 1966; unity thereafter. (DUM2).

15. POP. Population of working age. Total population, mid-year estimates, males and females between ages 15 and 64. Taken from AAS. (POP).

16. UD. Union density. The proportion of employees unionised. DEG.

17. U. Male unemployment rate. The series used is 'males wholly unemployed as a percentage of the number of employees (employed and unemployed) at the appropriate mid-year, for the UK. The numbers unemployed exclude 'temporarily stopped' but include school-leavers. The data is published in BLSHA, YB and DEG.

18. XMW. XMW is world trade in manufactures. The series used is the 'quantum index for world manufacturing exports', 1975 = 100. UNB.

19. G. G is real government expenditure. Series is calculated from 'general government expenditure on goods and services', in £ million, which is divided by the GDP at factor cost deflator. The GDP factor cost deflator was used because the equivalent series at constant prices do not exist. ETAS. (a).

20. QPW. Is the pound price of materials/fuel (P_m) divided by the world export unit value index converted from dollars to pounds using the current exchange rate. UNB, ETAS.

ABBREVIATIONS

| BB | 'Blue Book', National Income and Expenditure (yearly) |
| BEQB | Bank of England Quarterly Bulletin |

BESA 70   Bank of England Statistical Abstract, 1970
BESA 75   As above, 1975 (only published twice)
BLSHA   British Labour Statistics, Historical Abstract, 1886–1968
DEG   Department of Employment Gazette (monthly)
ETAS 81   Economic Trends Annual Supplement, 1981
ET   Economic Trends (monthly)
FS   Financial Statistics (monthly)
LBB 81   'Light Brown Book', 'Abstract of Statistics for Index of Retail Prices, Average
           Earnings, Social Security Benefits and Contributions', published by DHSS, May
           1981
MDS   Monthly Digest of Statistics
UNB   United Nations Quarterly Bulletin
YB   British Labour Statistics, Year Book, 1969–1976, (published 8 times, between
           1969 and 1976).

REFERENCES

ALTONJI, J. (1982), "The Intertemporal Substitution Model of Labour Market Fluctuations: An Empirical Analysis", *Review of Economic Studies*, 5, 159.

ANDREWS, M. (1986), "The Aggregate Labour Market: An Empirical Investigation into Market Clearing", forthcoming, *Economic Journal*.

ANDREWS, M. and NICKELL, S. J. (1982), "Unemployment in the United Kingdom Since the War", *Review of Economic Studies*, October.

ASHENFELTER, O. and HAM, J. (1979), "Education, Unemployment and Earnings", *Journal of Political Economy*, Vol. 87, No. 5, Pt. 2.

HALL, R. E. (1980), "Labour Supply and Aggregate Fluctuations", Carnegie–Rochester Public Policy Conference, Vol. 12, (*Journal of Monetary Economics*, Supplement).

HAM, J. (1985), "Testing Whether Unemployment Represents Intertemporal Labour Supply Behaviour", forthcoming, *Review of Economic Studies*.

JACKMAN, R., LAYARD, R., and PISSARIDES, C. (1984), "On Vacancies", London School of Economics, Centre for Labour Economics, revised mimeo, 9th April 1984.

JOHNSON, G. and LAYARD, R. (1983), "Long Run Unemployment and Labour Market Policy", forthcoming in O. Ashenfelter and R. Layard (eds.), *Handbook of Labor Economics*, North-Holland.

KOOIMAN, P. and KLOEK, T. (1979), "Aggregation of Micro-Markets in Disequilibrium", Working Paper, Econometric Institute, Erasmus University, Rotterdam.

LAMBERT, J. P. (1984), *Disequilibrium Macro Models Based on Business Survey Data: Theory and Estimation for the Belgian Manufacturing Sector*. Doctoral Dissertation, Université Catholique de Louvain: forthcoming, Cambridge University Press.

LAYARD, R. and NICKELL, S. (1986), "Unemployment in Britain", London School of Economics, Centre for Labour Economics, DP No. 240, forthcoming in *Economica*.

LEWIS, P. E. T. and MAKEPIECE, G. H. (1981), "The Estimation of Aggregate Demand and Supply curves for Labour in the UK", *Applied Economics*, pp. 289–298.

LUCAS, R. E. and RAPPING, L. A. (1969), "Real Wages, Employment and Inflation", *Journal of Political Economy*, September/October.

MARTIN, C. (1985), "A General Framework for Disequilibrium Modelling", Birkbeck College, mimeo.

MUELLBAUER, J. (1978), "Macrotheory vs. Macroeconometrics: the Treatment of 'Disequilibrium' in Macromodels", Birkbeck College, mimeo.

MUELLBAUER, J. and WINTER, D. (1980), "Unemployment, Employment and Exports in British Manufacturing: A Non-Clearing Markets Approach", *European Economic Review*, May.

NICKELL, S. J. (1980), "Some Disequilibrium Labour Market Models: Further Formalisation of a Muellbauer Type Analysis", London School of Economics, Centre for Labour Economics, Working Paper No. 205.

NICKELL, S. J. (1984), "The Modelling of Wages and Employment", in D. F. Hendry and K. Wallis, eds., *Econometrics and Applied Economics,* Basil Blackwell, London.

NICKELL, S. and ANDREWS, M. (1983), "Unions, Real Wages and Employment in Britain 1951–79", *Oxford Economic Papers,* November.

ROMER, D. (1981), "Rosen and Quandt's Disequilibrium Model of the Labour Market: A Revision", *Review of Economics and Statistics,* 62, pp. 145–146.

ROSEN, H. S. and QUANDT, R. E. (1978), "Estimation of a Disequilibrium Aggregate Labour Market", *Review of Economics and Statistics,* 60, August, pp. 371–379.

ROY, R. (1930), "La Demande dans ses Rapports avec la Repartition des Revenues", *Metron* 8, no. 3, 101–153.

SARGENT, T. J. (1979), *Macroeconomic Theory,* Academic Press, London.

SNEESSENS, H. R. and DRÈZE, J. H. (1985), "A Discussion of Belgian Unemployment, Combining Traditional Concepts and Disequilibrium Econometrics", forthcoming, *Economica,* Special Issue on Unemployment.

STIGLITZ, J. E. (1984), "Theories of Wage Rigidity", paper presented at the conference on Keynes' Economic Legacy, Delaware, January 12–13.

Oxford Economic Papers 38 (1986), 403–423

WAGES, TAXES AND THE UTILITY-MAXIMIZING TRADE UNION: A CONFRONTATION WITH NORWEGIAN DATA

By TOR HERSOUG, KNUT N. KJAER *and* ASBJORN RØDSETH*

1. Introduction

THE IDEA that trade unions maximize utility functions can be traced back to Dunlop (1944), but the amount of model-building which explicitly includes unions as rational economic agents has not been overwhelming. In recent years, however, the interest in this idea has had an upsurge, cf. Oswald (1979, 1982, 1985) for an example and further reference.

The major part of this literature has been purely theoretical. The labour economics literature is abundant with attempts at measuring effects of trade unionism, but this work is usually based on rather ad hoc assumptions regarding union behaviour.[1]

In this article we estimate a simple macroeconomic model for the determination of nominal wages by a utility maximizing trade union. The model can briefly be described as follows: There exists one dominating trade union with the ability to determine the expected nominal wage rate of the economy. The employers adjust employment to this wage rate.[2] The arguments in the union's utility function are real disposable wage and employment. When determining its optimal wage rate, the union will consider the price and employment effects of its wage decision and take into account income tax rates, expected competitive prices, and factors influencing the demand function for labour. Actual wage rates are equal to the rates planned by the union, times a random disturbance.

To our knowledge, ours is the first econometric study at the macro level based on the concept of a utility-maximizing trade union. (Later we have become aware that Pencavel (1985) is working on Swedish data with a similar approach.) Andrews and Nickell (1982) studied union impact at the macro level for postwar UK. They did not model union behaviour explicitly, but instead applied *ad hoc* measures of union power such as the rate of unionization and the union "mark-up". The approach we are taking has already been adopted in a number of theoretical studies which deal with

---

* We are grateful for comments on earlier versions of this paper from Lars Calmfors, Aanund Hylland, Nils Gottfries, Andrew Oswald, and two anonymous referees.

[1] Cf. Lewis (1963) and Parsley (1980) for surveys of this literature. Freeman and Medoff (1982) presents a schematic grouping of results. Exceptions, who based their work on utility maximization, are Rosen (1970) and Dertouzos and Pencavel (1981).

[2] This approach differs from that of de Menil (1971) and McDonald and Solow (1981), who assume that the union and the employer bargain over both the wage rate and employment. That assumption seems inappropriate for our purpose since employment commitments are not part of the central wage bargaining in Norway.

policy problems, e.g. Calmfors (1982), Calmfors and Horn (1985), Gylfason and Lindbeck (1982) and Hersoug (1984). We thus think it is high time for these ideas to be made operational and to be subjected to empirical tests.

The article is organized as follows. Section 2 describes the institutional background of wage setting in Norway. Section 3 presents the theory in detail and shows how the wage equation is derived in a form which can be estimated. Section 4 briefly describes the data and the estimation procedure. Section 5 displays and discusses the results, and section 6 contains some concluding comments.

2. Institutional background

In 1982 about 65 per cent of Norwegian wage earners were organized. The largest union is the Norwegian Federation of Trade Unions (LO), which organizes 43 per cent of all employees. Its member unions operate both within the private and the public sector.

The organized employers are together employing 59 per cent of the wage earners. Most important is the Norwegian Employers' Confederation (NAF), with members mainly in the manufacturing sector and a coverage of 22 per cent of all employees.

The bargain between LO and NAF settles wages and working conditions for practically all workers in manufacturing. The contract period is sometimes one year, but more often two years. In the latter case, however, there are always negotiations about wage increases in the mid-year, but strikes and lock-outs cannot be used during these mid-year negotiations.

The organizations in the other parts of the labour market await the results from the LO–NAF bargaining, and their contract is regarded as a norm in the following negotiations. In these the discussion seem to be largely about how the LO–NAF contract is to be adapted to the particular area.

In certain sectors, particularly in manufacturing, the central bargaining sets minimum wages only, while local unions and firms are free to bargain for local additions to these (strikes and lock-outs are prohibited in this local bargaining). The difference between the wage increase which comes as a direct consequence of the central contract and the ex-post measured increase in average wages, is termed wage drift. A major part of wage drift is a result of local bargaining. In recent years about half the wage increases in manufacturing stems from wage drift.

In the LO–NAF negotiations the parties use forecasts of wage drift, and the attention of the public is focused on the expected increases in average wages. The union leaders talk as if they first decide on a goal for the overall change in wages and then subtract the wage drift to find what should be obtained at the central bargaining.

Local bargaining differs from central bargaining in that manning rules and other regulations directly affecting employment can often be included in the former, while they are never a subject in the latter (at least not in the private sector).

Our model presupposes one central trade union which alone decides the wage level of the economy. This union is concerned with the employment rate in the whole economy. Given the wage rate, employment is determined unilaterally by the individual employers.

Applying this model to the Norwegian economy seem to require that

(i)   LO has the power to dictate its wages to NAF.

(ii) LO is able to make fairly accurate and unbiased forecasts of the total wage given the outcome of the central bargaining.

(iii) LO influences the wage levels in the whole economy, and perceives itself this way.

(iv) LO cares equally for the employment of both members and non–members (LO has no statistics on unemployed members, and because members are spread throughout the economy, unemployment rates for LO cannot be derived from official statistics).

These assumptions may seem overly strong. Still there is nothing in the institutional setting which denies that they could hold to a sufficient degree of approximation for the model to be of interest. As mentioned in the introduction, models with the same general structure has been used in policy analysis. It is hard to find many countries where such models could have more relevance than in Norway. Thus, Norway should be a good test case for whether these models have any empirical relevance at all.

3. From theory to application

Union utility is a function of the real disposable wage, R, and of the employment rate, E:

$$V = v(R, E) \qquad v_R > 0, \quad v_E > 0 \tag{1}$$

E is defined as total employment relative to the labour force, or, equivalently as one minus the rate of unemployment. Real disposable wage is defined as:

$$R = \frac{W - \tau(W)}{P} \tag{2}$$

W is the nominal wage rate for someone working a standard number of hours per year, $\tau(W)$ a tax function and P the consumer price index.

The trade unions' conjectures about how their wage setting influences prices and employment are given by the two functions:

$$P = P(W, z_1) \qquad P'_W > 0 \tag{3}$$

$$E = (W, z_2) \qquad E'_W < 0 \tag{4}$$

z_1 and z_2 are exogenous variables influencing the consumer price index and labour demand. Conjectured government accommodation of wage increases by increased public expenditure is included in the functional form.

From (2), (3), and (4) we eliminate W and P and get a relationship between R and E (conditional on the exogenous variables and the tax function):

$$R = R(E) \qquad (5)$$

(5) represents the union's opportunity locus. We assume that the union is facing a trade-off between real disposable wage and employment, i.e. $R' < 0$. Behind this is an assumption that a rise in nominal wages will increase the real disposable wage. This is less likely to be true the more progressive is the tax system and the stronger is the effect of wages on the price level, cf. Calmfors (1977) and Rødseth (1984).

The union will maximize (1) with respect to R and E and subject to (5). The corresponding optimal nominal wage can be found from (4). The outcome of the maximization is the central trade union's *planned* level of nominal wages, employment etc.

The question now is how to specify the four functions (1)–(4) in order to make the model amenable to estimation. We start with the tax function. The income tax function is progressive, and has become increasingly so over the years. The degree of progressivity is clearly important for the steepness of the trade-off which the union faces. To summarize the actual tax schedule in a convenient way, we choose to approximate it by

$$\tau(W) = W - bW^{1-g}$$

where b and g are estimated from the actual tax functions of each of the years in question. We use b and g as exogenous variables instead of the actual tax rates and tax brackets. A property of the tax function is that g equals the difference between the marginal and average tax rates divided by one minus the average tax rate. The variable g can thus be interpreted as a measure of the degree of progressivity of the tax system. For a proportional tax system $g = 0$. The more progressive is the tax system, the higher is g. The tax function is described more closely in Hersoug (1984), which also demonstrates how the optimal union wage changes with different types of tax changes. When the wage contracts are negotiated, the tax schedule of the year in question has already been decided by the Norwegian Parliament, and is thus known to the parties.[3] Given our tax function, the after tax real

---

[3] Exceptions to this were the years 1974–77 and 1980. During the LO–NAF negotiations these years the government promised to reduce the tax rates which had already been enacted by Parliament. The intention was to reduce wage demands, and in some cases it was said that the tax rebates were conditional on wage increases being kept within reasonable limits. It is a debatable question whether LO took these conditionality clauses seriously, or just took the new tax rates for granted. If the clauses were taken seriously, we should expect our equation to overpredict wages in the years in question. This is not the case, c.f. Fig. 5. A direct test is impossible, since the government never published the exact conditions. However, complaints from the government about too high wage increases were common, but in no case resulted in revocation of the tax rebates.

wage is

$$R = \frac{W - \tau(W)}{P} = \frac{bW^{1-g}}{P} \qquad (2')$$

We now turn to conjectures about prices. Before every major wage negotiation in Norway a committee of economic experts, popularly known as the Aukrust-committee, makes a report on the prospects for inflation, the extent of wage drift etc. The committee's model for price formation described in Aukrust (1977) is based on the well-known distinction between traded and non-traded goods. The prices of the former are assumed given from world markets, while the prices of the latter are determined by constant mark-up over wage and materials cost. In addition there are some exogenous prices (of public services, domestically produced agricultural goods etc.).

For these publicly regulated prices we assume the same pricing rule as for non-traded goods, i.e. constant factor shares. (This seems to be particularly well justified for agricultural prices, since Parliament has indexed agricultural income to the wages of male workers in manufacturing.) Predictions for each year take as their starting point the observed price level of the preceding year. On these assumptions the ratio between the expected price level this year and the actual price level last year, is equal to a weighted average of the two corresponding ratios for traded goods prices and for unit wage costs in the non-traded sector. Thus, our counterpart to (3) can be summarily expressed as

$$P = P^0(W/W_{-1})^\alpha \qquad (3')$$

where P^0 is an index for the price level which is expected to prevail if wages are unchanged from last year, and α is the weight of unit wage costs in the above mentioned weighted average. P^0 depends on the development in labour productivity, indirect taxes, and prices of traded goods, as well as on the actual price level last year.[4] Since we know the model used for price level predictions, we can calculate α directly from it. On this basis we did set $\alpha = 0.6$. When α is known, P^0 can be computed from the data provided we assume a known mechanism for the generation of expectations of traded goods prices.

In order to simplify later formulae it is convenient to define a new variable which summarizes all the exogenous influences on the real disposable wage.

---

[4] The formula for P^0 is

$$P^0 = P_{-1}\left(\frac{1+t}{1+t_{-1}} \cdot \frac{a_{s,-1}}{a_2}\right)^\alpha \left(\frac{P^e_*}{P_{*,-1}}\right)^{1-\alpha}$$

t is the rate of pay-roll tax, a_s is the average labour productivity in the non-traded sector and P_* the price of traded goods. Superscript e stands for expectation. Additional corrections were made for the changes in sales tax in 1967 and for the introduction of VAT in 1970. For further details on this as well as on the fixing of α, see the authors, (1984).

From equations (2') and (3') we can calculate the nominal wage which is expected to make this year's real disposable wage equal to last year's. It turns out to be

$$W_R = (R_{-1}P^0/bW^{\alpha}_{-1})^{1/\varepsilon}$$

where $\varepsilon = 1 - g - \alpha$. Provided $\varepsilon > 0$, the required wage, W_R, increases with the price level and the level of taxes. Fortunately $\varepsilon > 0$ everywhere in our sample. With W_R defined, the real disposable wage this period can be expressed as

$$R = R_{-1}(W/W_R)^{\varepsilon} \tag{6}$$

ε is thus the elasticity of the real disposable wage with respect to the nominal wage.

Unfortunately the LO did not, during our period of observation, use a formal model to predict employment. Therefore, we may be on weak foundations when we assume that their employment conjectures are described by

$$E = E_{-1}(W/W_K)^{-\mu} \tag{4'}$$

E_{-1} is the employment rate of the preceding year, W_K the wage rate which is expected to give unchanged cost competitiveness from last year, and $-\mu$ the (constant) elasticity of labour demand with respect to the wage rate.[5] The conjecture is thus that if cost competitiveness is unchanged, the employment rate will also stay constant. W_K is equal to last year's wage corrected for changes in pay-roll tax, productivity growth in the traded-goods sector and expected changes in unit costs abroad.[6]

It should be emphasized that the lagged employment rate is included in (4') only as a proxy for the union's conjecture about the level of the demand curve for labour. In accordance with the general set up of the model in (1)–(4) the union assumes that there are no lagged effects of wages on employment. The level of this year's demand curve is independent of last year's wage rate, but the realized level of demand last year in conjunction with last year's realized wage rate is used to judge what level of demand for labour should be expected this year.

Obviously (4') may be oversimplifying the union's view of the world. It

---

[5] In Rodseth (1984) a major point is that the elasticity of the aggregate demand for labour with respect to the wage rate depends on the degree of progressivity. This is neglected in (4').

[6] The formula for W_K is

$$W_K = W_{-1} \frac{1 + t_{-1}}{1 + t} \cdot \frac{a_K}{a_{K,-1}} \cdot \frac{W^e_*}{W_{*,-1}}$$

where a_K is average labour productivity in the traded-goods sectors and W_* is a weighted average of the unit labour costs of our competitors measured in domestic currency. Equation (4') could be generalized by the inclusion of a trend. This would yield a final equation operationally equivalent to the one we estimate, cf. the authors (1984).

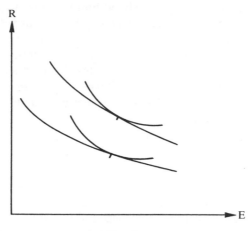

FIG. 1

may take account of lagged responses to wage changes, and it may use various additional sources of information on the level of the demand curve for labour. The response parameter μ might change with different governments. However, the only way to get started in this field is with highly simplified models, and as an estimate of the union's expected level of employment (4') need not be too far off the mark.

By combining (6) and (4') we find that the union's opportunity locus is

$$R = R_{-1}(E/E_{-1})^{-\varepsilon/\mu}(W_K/W_R)^\varepsilon \qquad (5')$$

Provided $\mu > 0$ and $\varepsilon > 0$, R is a decreasing, convex function of E, as the opportunity locus depicted in Fig. 1. The locus shifts inwards with increased W_R and outwards with increased W_K. When progressivity is reduced (g is reduced, ε is increased) it becomes steeper everywhere.

It only remains to specify the utility function. Dunlop (1944) proposed the wage bill. Rosen (1970) and deMenil (1971) use the union rent, i.e. union utility equals employment times the difference between union and non-union wages. More popular in recent years has been the utilitarian utility function, or equivalently, union utility equals the expected utility of a representative member, on the assumption that each member has the same probability of becoming unemployed, see Oswald (1982, 1985) and Calmfors (1982). This approach suffers from the assumption that workers are either employed or unemployed for the whole period, which is far from realistic when the contract period is one year or more. Gylfason and Lindbeck (1982) apply an additively separable quadratic form, and Dertouzos and Pencavel (1981) postulates a Stone–Geary utility function. MaCurdy and Pencavel (1983) allow for a wider class of functions, having the above mentioned as special cases. On the basis of their data for local newspaper typographer unions MaCurdy and Pencavel reject the simpler functional forms.

We take a pragmatic approach without going too deeply into the micro-economic foundations. We want the functional form to be flexible in the sense that there should be independent parameters determining income and substitution effects. We want the parameters to be easily interpretable, and we need to find an explicit solution for the planned wage. Finally, we want to allow for non-linear Engel-curves, since one expects the union's "expansion path" to be more biased towards real disposable income the closer it is to full employment.

The utility function we have used is

$$V = \frac{\kappa_1 \nu_1}{\nu_1 - 1} R^{(\nu_1 - 1)/\nu_1} + \frac{\kappa_2 \nu_1}{\nu_1 - \nu_2} E^{(\nu_1 - \nu_2)/\nu_1} \tag{1'}$$

where κ_1, κ_2, ν_1 and ν_2 are positive constants.

Note the similarity between (1') and a CES utility function.[7] Indeed, if $\nu_2 = 1$, (1') *is* a CES utility function with elasticity of substitution equal to ν_1. A high level of ν_1 will in general indicate large possibilities for substitution between employment and disposable income. ν_2 can easily be shown to equal the ratio between the Engel-elasticities for real disposable wage and relative employment. A value of ν_2 greater than 1 means that the Engel-curve with E on the abscissa is a convex function. At least when we are close to full employment to begin with, this seems reasonable, and thus we expect to find $\nu_2 > 1$.

Maximizing (1') with respect to R and E under the constraint (5'), solving the first order conditions for E, inserting the result into (4'), and solving this expression for W, we get that the union's optimal wage is

$$W = [\kappa(\varepsilon/\mu)^{\nu_1} R_{-1}^{-(1-\nu_1)} E_{-1}^{\nu_2 - \nu_1} W_R^{\varepsilon(1-\nu_1)} W_K^{\mu(\nu_2-\nu_1)}]^{1/h} \tag{7}$$

---

[7] A referee has pointed out to us that our utility function is nearly equivalent to the one in Pencavel (1984). The differences (except for differences in notation) are that Pencavel has *total* employment where we have *relative* employment, and he has gross real wages minus a reference real wage where we have the real after tax wage. Pencavel studied local union contracts and could thus use the observed average wage in the region as reference. The natural candidate for a reference wage in our context would be unemployment benefits. However, in Norway unemployment benefits are linked to the wage level when becoming unemployed. The only major change in the system was in January 1980 when benefits became taxable. At the same time, rates were adjusted with the intention that the average recipient should be unaffected. There has also been a gradual lengthening of the maximum period for which benefits can be paid.

It is hard to see how unemployment benefits in this system could be included in the union utility function as a reference wage in a meaningful way. In particular it would be difficult for the period when benefits were not taxed, because when marginal tax rates rose to higher levels in the seventies, wage earners could gain from being laid-off part of the year. In any case the after tax income differential between employed and unemployed depended strongly on how long the spells of unemployment were, and this poses a difficult aggregation problem.

Another alternative also suggested in Pencavel (1984) would be to use a constant parameter as the reference real wage (or a parameter growing with the rate of productivity growth?). Since our results indicate that the model is already overparametrized, we have not gone further with this.

where, to simplify the expression, we have set $\kappa = (\kappa_1/\kappa_2)^{v_1}$ and

$$h = \varepsilon(1 - v_1) + \mu(v_2 - v_1)$$

It can be shown that the second order condition is equivalent to $h > 0$. This is always satisfied when $v_1 < 1$ and $v_2 > v_1$. Since we are maximizing along a convex opportunity locus, the indifference curves have to be sufficiently curved (v_1 small enough) for the second-order condition to be satisfied.

The interpretation of (7) becomes easier when one exploits that the first order condition is equivalent to

$$\kappa(\varepsilon/\mu)^{v_1}R^{-(1-v_1)}E^{v_2-v_1} = 1 \tag{8}$$

Thus, if last year's real disposable wage and employment ratio were at the optimal levels, and if the degree of progressivity was the same then as now, this year's nominal wage will simply be

$$W = W_R^{\varepsilon(1-v_1)/h}W_K^{\mu(v_2-v_1)/h}$$

Since the exponents add to one (cf. the definition of h), the new rate is simply a weighted geometric average of the wage rates required to keep competitiveness and real disposable wage unchanged from last year. If the union never makes any mistakes in its predictions of wages, prices, and employment, and if the degree of progressivity is never changed, wages W simply continue to develop as a weighted average of W_R and W_K. There will be no Phillips-curve effects or the like, since any unemployment level there is, will be planned by the union, and the union will have no reason to change it unless one of the exogenous variables changes.

In reality the union's conjectures will not be perfect forecasts. In (7) the weighted average of W_R and W_K is augmented by terms which together represents the deviation from optimality last year. Unexpectedly high employment last year would be a sign that wages should be changed this year. If $v_2 - v_1 > 0$, they will be increased. This introduces a kind of short-run Phillips-curve effect. Correspondingly, if the real disposable wage were higher than planned last year, wages this year will be lowered, provided $v_1 < 1$.

The ambiguities in the signs of the effects on wages is caused by the curvature of the opportunity locus. As an example, look at what happens when W_R increases (e.g. because taxes are increased), as it is illustrated in figure 1. The opportunity locus will obviously shift inwards. From (5') it is seen that for any given employment level, the locus also becomes flatter. The inward shift leads to income effects, which, when both goods are normal ($v_2 > 0$), should mean less of both E and R. That the opportunity locus has become flatter, will induce substitution towards more E. If $v_1 > 1$, the substitution effect will dominate the income effect, and the optimal level of employment increases; if $v_1 < 1$ it decreases. In this example nominal wages and employment have to move in opposite directions, and ambiguity in one is ambiguity in the other.

More progressivity makes the opportunity locus less steep, see Hersoug (1984). This leads to substitution towards lower real disposable income and higher employment, i.e. to a lower W. Furthermore, more progressivity (lower ε) means a lower weight on W_R and a higher weight on W_K. When employment becomes cheaper in terms of disposable income, the employment determining variables in W_K get increased weight relative to the income determining variables in W_R. Correspondingly a higher value of μ will also increase the weight on W_K.

(7) is the equation for the union's planned wage. The actual wage W_A is

$$W_A = W e^u \tag{9}$$

where u is assumed to be a normally distributed and serially uncorrelated random error with mean zero and constant variance. The interpretation is that the final outcome is influenced by local bargaining and decisions by individual employers, and thus the actual wage will deviate from the planned wage, but in a random way. The stochastic term could also capture other errors such as e.g. omitted variables.

4. Data and estimation

The important data are displayed in Figs. 2, 3, and 4, and some summary statistics are contained in Table 1. For further information we refer to the

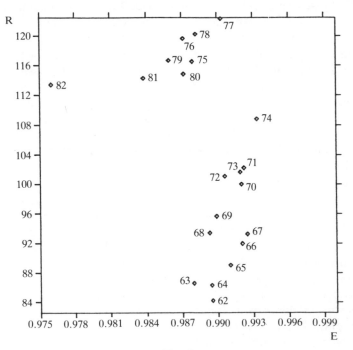

FIG. 2

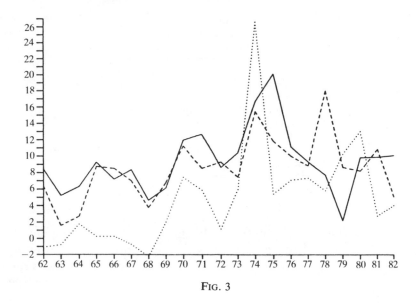

FIG. 3

authors (1984). Figure 2 pictures the development of unemployment and
real disposable wage. There has been a strong upward trend in the real
disposable wage and no marked trend in unemployment. The variation in
unemployment is relatively small. Figure 3 shows the percentage increase in
wages from last year together with the percentage increase that would keep
competitiveness unchanged. These curves move quite closely together with

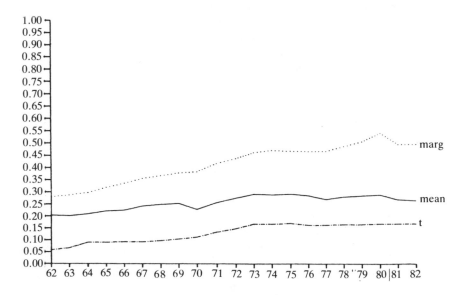

FIG. 4

TABLE 1

Growth rates for wages and some explanatory variables 1962–82

Variable[1]	Mean	Standard deviation
$(W - W_{-1})/W_{-1}$	9.34	3.96
$(W_K - W_{-1})/W_{-1}$	8.52	3.83
$(W_R - W_{-1})/W_{-1}$	-4.46	16.30
$(W_* - W_{*,-1})/W_{*,-1}$	5.58	3.59
$(P_* - P_{*,-1})/P_{*,-1}$	4.86	6.39

[1] Ex-post realized values are used, not expectations.

wages overshooting in 1963/64, in 1971 and in 1975, and falling behind in 1978 and 1979. A strictly monitored wage and price freeze lasted from September 1978 and throughout 1979. Because of this, 1979 was excluded from our sample. The wage freeze may even have biased wage increases in 1978 slightly downwards, although extra wage drift in the fourth quarter would only have a modest impact on the yearly average. Figure 3 also displays the rate of change in import prices (the index for all imports except ships and oil platforms). Clearly import prices are positively correlated with the other variables, but swings with greater amplitude. The swings in import prices translate into even larger swings in the rate of increase in wages which is required to keep real disposable income constant, c.f. the standard deviation in Table 1. The various tax rates in Fig. 4 shows, on the other hand, more trend-like movements, except for 1980 which has markedly more progressivity. When $W_R - W_{-1}$ is negative on average, the main reasons are that productivity growth in the non-traded sector lowers prices, and that there has almost every year been nominal reductions in tax rates.

The yearly wage rate is defined as the hourly wage rate of male workers in manufacturing multiplied by 52 times the standard weekly number of working hours. The hourly wage rate is without overtime compensation and vacation allowances. The method is the same as the one which is used by the main organizations during the negotiations. Male manufacturing workers were used in spite of the group's small share of total employment (19 per cent) because no data of comparable quality are available for the whole labour force. Besides, the group constitutes the core of LO and is used by other groups as the benchmark for comparison. From the available statistics it appears that the wages for other large groups follow those for male manufacturing workers rather closely.

For the expectations of import prices and unit wage costs abroad we used three alternatives:

A. The expected level is equal to the level one year before times one plus a three-year moving average of the growth rate of the variable in question.
B. Same as A for unit wage costs for the whole period and for import prices

until 1965. After that year the predictions from the Aukrust-committee for import prices are used, or, when they were not available, predictions from the National Budgets of the government.
C. "Perfect foresight": both expectations are set equal to their realized values.

The labour productivities are normal productivities measured as three-year moving averages of current productivity. Similar calculations are behind the series for unit wage costs abroad.

The tax function has been estimated for each year from the actual Norwegian tax schedules of that year. This has been done for two types of households: 1. Singles. 2. Families with one income and two children. Details of the estimations are given in Hersoug (1983), which also shows that the estimated tax functions fit quite well to the actual tax functions over a wide range. When nothing else is said, we have used a tax function which represents a geometric average of the two types of households.

Employment is the number of man-years according to the national accounts. To get the total labour force we added to this the average number of unemployed registered. This figure is subject to a number of biases, the most important probably being that not all those registered want full-time work, and that many who want part-time work do not register. Because the labour force includes a large and growing share of part-time workers, measuring the labour force in numbers only may give a seriously biased picture of the labour market as regards demand and supply of man-hours.

(7) includes four unknown parameters: κ, v_1, v_2, and μ. (Remember ε is treated as an observed variable.) These are estimated by the method of maximum likelihood, which in our case is equivalent to minimizing the sum of squares of the logarithmic residuals in (9). The data set is complete only for the period 1962–1982. As mentioned above, the year 1979 was excluded from the sample because of the wage- and price-freeze. Most estimations were done for the sub-period 1962–1978, 1980, because we wanted to have a couple of sample points left for comparing predictions and actual developments.

The estimated equation is highly nonlinear, mainly because of the way the variable g appears in it. Only asymptotic properties of the estimators are known. Since lagged endogenous variables appear on the right hand side, small sample bias is suspected. The reported standard deviations are calculated from the inverse of an approximation to the information matrix, and may be rather unreliable. With lagged endogenous variables, the Durbin–Watson statistic is suspected to be biased towards the value 2.

5. Empirical results

Table 2 presents results for the alternative mechanisms of expectation formation. Coefficients are very close in alternatives A and B. In all alternatives μ and v_2 are in the expected range, while v_1 is negative, but not

TABLE 2
Parameter estimates for alternative expectations

			Parameters				Summary statistics		
No.	Type	Period	v_1	v_2	μ	κ	$\bar{R}^2$	SER	DW
1	A	1962–78, 80	−0.12	52.83	0.26	1.49	0.997	0.0285	1.45
			(0.32)	(79.47)	(0.26)	(1.08)			
2	B	1962–78, 80	−0.10	59.55	0.26	1.67	0.997	0.0286	1.47
			(0.36)	(93.83)	(0.26)	(1.27)			
3	C	1962–78, 80	−0.15	14.72	0.68	0.79	0.996	0.0335	1.56
			(0.26)	(46.16)	(2.05)	(0.86)			
4	A	1962–78, 80	—	63.31	0.29	1.92	0.997	0.0276	1.47
				(104.88)	(0.28)	(1.29)			
5	B	1962–78, 80	—	68.35	0.28	2.03	0.997	0.0277	1.47
				(114.06)	(0.28)	(1.40)			
6	C	1962–78, 80	—	10.69	1.28	0.99	0.996	0.0326	1.48
				(58.36)	(6.67)	(0.64)			

Standard deviations in parantheses.
SER: Standard error of regression.
DW: Durbin Watson statistic.
$\bar{R}^2$: Multiple correlation coefficient adjusted for degrees of freedom.

significantly different from zero. Alternative C gives quite different estimates of μ and v_2 than the others. The same pattern in the estimates of μ and v_2 also appears when v_1 is set equal to zero a-priori (no substitution). In terms of explanatory power little seems to be lost by imposing this restriction.

With $\bar{R}^2$ (R^2 adjusted for degrees of freedom) at 0.997 or 0.996 the fit might seem good were it not that the equation is in logarithms of levels. The standard error of the regression is 0.0285 in equation 1 in table 2 (alt. A). One alternative hypothesis is a short-run-version of the Scandinavian model of inflation saying that wages are adjusted every year in order to keep competitiveness unchanged from last year, or in other words $W_A = W_K e^u$. The standard error of $\log W_A - \log W_K$ is 0.0343 (alt. A) or 20 per cent higher than the standard error of regression in our model. If we use actual instead of expected wage levels abroad, the corresponding figures are 0.0335 for our model and 0.0847 for the alternative.[8] It is easy to produce *ad hoc* models which have an even better fit than ours; e.g. a simple linear regression of $\log W_A$ on $\log W_K$ has a standard error of 0.0285 (alternative A). The usefulness of such *ad hoc* models is doubtful, though. Still, we cannot claim that the finer details of our model are contributing much to the explanation of wage developments in Norway.

[8] The high correlation between W_A and W_K gives rise to a worrying question about exogeneity and reverse causation. Throughout the estimation period the exchange rate for NOK was fixed in terms of either USD or some basket of currencies. During 1971–82 Norway devalued seven times and revalued once. Most of the parity changes were officially justified by external events such as devaluations by other countries, but we cannot exclude that even these devaluations were undertaken with an eye on W_A and its relation to W_K.

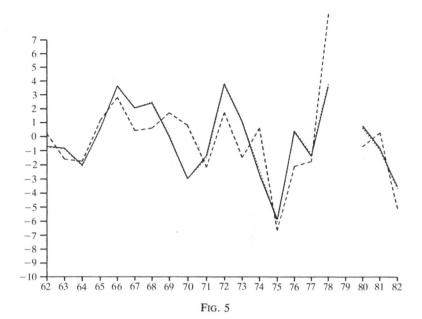

FIG. 5

Percentage differences between actual and predicted wage levels for the top three equations in Table 2 are on average in the sample period 2.0 for alternatives A and B and 2.1 for alternative C. The two largest deviations are

Alt. A	− 5.9 in 1975	+ 3.8 in 1972
B	− 6.0 in 1975	+ 3.8 in 1978
C	− 6.6 in 1975	+ 8.9 in 1978

A plus means that the prediction overrates the actual wage level. Average errors are not frightening, but the largest errors are so large as to make the equations of little use in actual forecasting. Post-sample predictions are not too bad with average deviations for 1981–82 of 2.2 per cent in alternative A, 2.3 in B and 2.7 in C. In Fig. 5 one can compare the actual wage increases with those predicted by equation (1).

Table 3 shows that including just one more year has dramatic quantitative effects on the estimates, but no qualitative effects. Table 4 shows the results of three alternative specifications. Changing α from 0.60 to a low value of 0.45 has a rather strong effect on the estimate of v_1 (equation (10)). Varying the weight on each type of household has no marked effect on the estimates. In no cases are there qualitative changes in the results.

The results show a tendency to positive autocorrelation in the residuals. In all the estimations the Durbin–Watson statistic is around 1.5. If this stochastic had its usual distribution, then 1.5 had been in the inconclusive range for rejecting independence at the 5 per cent level.

The general impression can be summarized as follows: The model fits

TABLE 3
Estimates for alternative sample periods.

No.	Type	Period	Parameters				Summary statistics		
			v_1	v_2	μ	κ	$\bar{R}^2$	SER	DW
7	A	1962–78	−0.45	5.97	0.83	0.42	0.997	0.0286	1.52
			(0.21)	(29.38)	(3.38)	(2.27)			
1	A	1962–78, 80	−0.12	52.83	0.26	1.49	0.997	0.0285	1.45
			(0.32)	(79.47)	(0.26)	(1.08)			
8	A	1962–78, 80–81	−0.14	51.33	0.28	1.48	0.998	0.0276	1.47
			(0.30)	(77.55)	(0.27)	(1.07)			
9	A	1962–78, 80–82	−0.15	26.70	0.52	1.68	0.998	0.0276	1.46
			(0.29)	(52.11)	(0.82)	(0.82)			

reasonably well. The estimates of individual parameters are highly unreliable, v_1 consistently gets a negative (but hardly significantly so) value in contradiction to prior assumptions.

Some ideas of what the estimation results mean, can be obtained from Table 5, where we have given the elasticities of the wage rate with respect to some of the variables in equation (7) for a typical value of g. One should bear in mind that the elasticities are partial and short run. We see that for the three alternative estimates for which we report elasticities, W_K has an overwhelming weight compared to W_R (0.99 against 0.01). Still a progressivity-neutral tax increase (a fall in b) has some effect on W, because the small value of ε (0.15) means that a large increase in W is required in order to give only a modest compensation for a reduction in b. The same effect is behind the result that the elasticities with respect to t and with respect to proportional change in import prices P_* and foreign unit wage costs W_* are slightly greater than unity in absolute value.

The small weight on W_R relative to W_K is easily explained when we look at their standard deviations in table 1. Anything which has such strong

TABLE 4
Estimates for alternative import price share and tax functions.

No.	Type	Period	Parameters				Summary statistics		
			v_1	v_2	μ	κ	$\bar{R}^2$	SER	DW
10	A1	1962–78, 80	−0.49	42.06	0.26	1.43	0.997	0.0280	1.44
			(0.63)	(56.84)	(1.07)	(1.04)			
11	A2	1962–78, 80	−0.16	52.54	0.24	1.35	0.997	0.0285	1.44
			(0.25)	(70.87)	(0.21)	(0.94)			
12	A3	1962–78, 80	−0.03	54.26	0.30	1.79	0.997	0.0285	1.47
			(0.42)	(93.25)	(0.33)	(1.30)			

A1: $\alpha = 0.45$, expectations on import prices and foreign unit wage costs as in type A.
A2: Tax function for household of type 1 (singles).
A3: Tax function for household of type 2 (family with two children and one income).

TABLE 5
Estimated elasticities of the wage level. g = 0.25.

Eq.	W_R	W_K	E_{-1} [1]	b	t	P_*	P_* and W_* [2]
		With respect to					
1	0.01	0.99	3.80	−0.08	−1.04	0.03	1.02
4	0.01	0.99	3.42	−0.05	−1.02	0.02	1.01
9	0.01	0.99	1.90	−0.08	−1.04	0.03	1.02

[1] Partial, i.e. unexpected change.
[2] Proportional rise in P_* and W_* (corresponding to a devaluation of the domestic currency).

variation as W_R must have a small coefficient in an equation where both the explained and the other explanatory variables are relatively stable. The reason for the large fluctuations in W_R is, of course, that with a strong influence of wages on prices and a high degree of progressivity, huge changes in nominal wage rates are required to compensate for changes in the exogenous variable affecting real disposable income.

When we are close to full employment, a one per cent decrease in employment E_{-1}, means an increase of slightly less than one percentage point in the unemployment rate. When this comes as a surprise to the union, next year's wage rate is reduced by 3.8 per cent according to the estimate from 1962–1980. This estimate is cut in half when the sample is extended to 1982. 1981 was the year with the highest unemployment rate registered so far. Apparently that did not have much impact on 1982-wages, and thus the large change in the estimates. The new estimates do not give competiveness lower weight, however. Instead they say that changed wage rates have a larger impact on employment (μ is greater). Since 1982 gave still higher rates of unemployment, we suspect that including 1983 will again give large changes in the estimates.

A change in g will change both the marginal and the average tax rate. We have looked at the effects of simultaneous changes in g and b which are designed to keep constant the average tax rate at the initial nominal wage level. Such a change means that the opportunity locus is twisted around the old equilibrium. Thus it will always enable the union to reach a higher indifference curve, while there will also be substitution effects. The result depends on what the initial values of the other variables are, since the weights on the different terms in (7) depends on g through ε. A simulation shows that according to the estimates in equation 1, a compensated 5 per cent increase in the marginal tax rate at the wage level of 1971 (g up from 0.216 to 0.284) would have given 0.4 per cent higher wages that year. Similarly a 5 per cent compensated reduction in the marginal tax rate in 1981 (g down from 0.310 to 0.242) would have given 1.3 per cent lower wages that year. More progressivity makes the opportunity locus flatter. This should induce substitution towards more employment and lower real disposable income, i.e., a lower nominal wage. Since we have estimated a negative value of v_1, the substitution effect comes out with the wrong sign.

Some further insights into the results can be obtained by looking more closely at the data as they are depicted in figure 2. What we are trying to do is to describe each point in this diagram as a tangency point of the kind depicted in figure 1. The indifference map is the same from year to year. The explanation will have to come from shifts in the opportunity locus. There are two marked features of the data:

(i) They fall in three distinct groups: 1962–74, 1975–81, and 1982. The observations in the second group are up and to the left of the observations in the first. Unemployment in 1982 has not influenced our estimates and thus will not be commented on in the present connection.
(ii) Within each subperiod the observations are rather closely grouped around a relatively steep line going in the north-east direction. In the first sub-period the time trend is an upward movement along the line, in the second period one moves up and then down again.

Trendlike movements in the north-east direction are easily explained by productivity increases which shifts the opportunity locus in figure 1 outwards. When both goods are normal the optimum should move towards north-east. That the movement along the trend is not regular from year to year, can in part be explained by changes in the level of taxation, which sometimes moves the opportunity locus outwards (1970, 1974), sometimes inwards (1978, 1979, 1980). Some movement across the trend in the left-right direction can be explained by the event of unexpectedly high or low demand for labour. Corrective action in the subsequent year(s) then should bring the observations in line.

The big problem is to explain the shift from 1974 to 1975. The main candidate for explaining a movement in the north-west direction is substitution. If the opportunity locus became steeper between 1974 and 1975, this could have induced the union to choose higher real disposable income and less employment. The main determinant of the steepness of the opportunity locus is the degree of progressivity. As can be seen from figure 4 the trend was towards a higher degree of progressivity until 1981. More progressivity means a flatter opportunity locus. Since there was on average more progressivity after 1975 than before 1975, substitution should have given us observations in the second period to the right of those in the first period. History gave the opposite result, and therefore our estimated direct substitution effects are positive instead of negative. They are not strong and significant (v_1 is not significantly different from zero), because if they were, we should have seen more movement to the left in figure 2 also before 1975, since the degree of progressivity increased considerably even in the sixties. Furthermore, 1975 itself cannot be explained by increased progressivity, and thus the large residuals for this year.

The high estimated values of v_2 means that the expansion paths of the utility function are almost vertical in a diagram with E on the abscissa. This is the main reason for the high weight on W_K relative to W_R. When the opportunity locus moves inwards or outwards, most of the response is in *R*. This means that when factors which influence *R* directly, but not *E,* change, very little change in *W* is called for. When on the other hand, factors influencing *E* directly, but not *R,* change, a relatively large change in *W* is required in order to shift the burden of adjustment from *E* to *R*.

6. Concluding remarks

It may seem foolhardy to estimate a model of wage formation based on utility maximization by a single trade union which on its own determines the one and only expected wage level. What we want to capture with our model, however, is not all factors influencing wages, just the major ones. The hypothesis that in a highly unionized economy with highly centralized unions, union decisions are the major influence on wages, seems to us worthwhile of serious examination. Earlier approaches based on expectations-augmented Phillips curves or on the Scandinavian model of inflation, may depend on even more restrictive, although less explicit, assumptions.

The results so far are mixed. As we have seen, the finer ideas of the model are only of moderate help in explaining the wage developments. Our model performs slightly better than a simple alternative which assumes that wages always adjust to keep competitiveness unchanged from last year. It still outperforms with a wide margin the strongest version of the Scandinavian model of inflation where wages are determined by a requirement that competitiveness stays constant throughout the period. A simple estimate of this alternative model gives an average percentage deviation of 5.5, which should be compared to the 2.0 of eq. 1.

After all, we find the results sufficiently encouraging that the main ideas may be worth pursuing further. We may not have given the idea of a utility maximizing trade union a fair trial yet. In particular our relation for employment conjectures could probably be improved upon. Some of the observations might be regarded as corner solutions at full employment. Perhaps a dynamic model where the union takes account of lagged effects of wages on employment or prices, is called for. Additional variables, e.g. government expenditure[9] or normal working hours, may be included in the utility function. These refinements must not require too many new parameters, lest the model shall lose its empirical usefulness.

Calmfors and Horn (1985) and Hersoug (1985), among others, have emphasized the importance of government reactions to unemployment and

[9] Even though the level of public services may affect the utility level of union members, it is not obvious that it has affected wage demands, at least not in the short run. In spite of the fact that public consumption—in part—is financed by personal income taxes, the level of public services during the observation period was never mentioned by Norwegian unions (at least not in public) as a factor influencing their wage demands. Public pension schemes and other cash benefits from the government have been mentioned, though, and these might be included on the line with taxes.

wages for the union's choice of wage level and employment. Possibly we could explain the Norwegian development better by taking account of shifts in the government reaction pattern. In Norway we have some particular reasons to believe that a change in the reaction pattern developed during the years 1973–75. Before 1973 concern about the country's balance of payments had always represented a check to expansionary policies. Then, especially through a government report in early 1974, the huge size of Norway's future oil revenues was realized, as was the freedom of action that they would give us. The government boosted domestic demand and introduced selective employment policies on a large scale. It may be that these events brought μ down, and thus made increases in the real disposable wage cheaper in terms of employment foregone. This can explain why the observations from 1975 on so markedly forms a separate group above and to the left of the earlier observations (cf. figure 2).

To capture this effect we allowed μ to take separate values before 1974 and from 1974 on. The result was that the different estimation algorithms at our disposal refused to converge, or, when the required accuracy was reduced, converged to wildly different parameter values depending on starting points etc. The likelihood became very flat in certain directions; a clear sign that the data do not contain enough information to determine all the parameters. In some directions the likelihood was not so flat, however. Thus the result of the different runs had some robust features: μ after 1974 were only 10–20% of μ before 1974, the weight on W_R was very low compared to that on W_K, and v_1 was very close to zero. We have already explained why the data should make us expect these results.

If we have to resort to changes in policy reactions to explain the actual development, the theory of the utility maximizing trade union is somewhat incomplete until one has specified criteria for determining when there has been a change in policy. Otherwise everything can be explained by referring to policy shifts. Thus, more work in this direction may be one way to go.

This way of gradually changing the model as a result of our experience with the data will of course deprive all test statistics and significance levels of their usual meaning. Consequently, we will not be able to perform any rigorous test of the theory. Still, the way we proceed is probably the only way one can proceed when trying out a theoretical idea on data for the first time. One rarely has enough insight to form satisfactory auxiliary hypotheses before the first look at the data. The real test will come when we use the model to predict the future, or, possibly, if we apply the model to data from other countries with a similar structure. Before such a test has been passed, we will not rely much on our estimates when we are evaluating economic policy.

REFERENCES

ANDREWS, M. and NICKELL, S. (1982), "Unemployment in the United Kingdom since the war," Review of Economic Studies 49, Special Issue, 731–759.

AUKRUST, O. (1977), "Inflation in the Open Economy. A Norwegian Model", in Krause, L. B. and W. S. Salant (eds.), *Worldwide Inflation. Theory and recent experience* (Brookings, Washington, D.C.).

CALMFORS, L. (1977), "Inflation in Sweden", in Krause, L. and W. Salant (eds.), *Worldwide Inflation* (Brookings, Washington, D.C.).

CALMFORS, L. (1982), "Employment Policies, Wage Formation and Trade Union Behaviour in a Small Open Economy", *Scandinavian Journal of Economics 84*, 345–373.

CALMFORS, L. and HORN, H. (1985), "Classical Unemployment, Accomodation Policies and the Adjustment of Real Wages", *Scandinavian Journal of Economics, 87*, 234–261.

DERTOUZOS, J. N. and PENCAVEL, J. H. (1981), "Wage and Employment Determination under Trade Unionism. The International Typographical Union", *Journal of Political Economy 89*, 1162–1181.

DUNLOP, J. T. (1944), *Wage determination under trade unionism* (Macmillan, New York).

GYLFASON, T. and LINDBECK, A. (1982), "The Macroeconomic Consequences of Endogenous Governments and Labor Unions", Seminar Paper No. 232, Institute for International Economic Studies, University of Stockholm.

FREEMAN, R. B. and MEDOFF, J. L. (1982), "The Impact of Collective Bargaining: Can the New Facts be Explained by Monopoly Unionism?" Working Paper No. 837, National Bureau of Economic Research.

HERSOUG, T. (1983), "Utvikling i Personlig Inntektsbeskatning i Norge 1957–83", Memorandum No. 9, from Department of Economics, University of Oslo.

HERSOUG, T. (1984), "Union Wage Responses to Tax Changes", *Oxford Economic Papers 36*, 37–51.

HERSOUG, T. (1985), "Workers vs. Government—Who Adjusts to Whom?", *Scandinavian Journal of Economics 87*, 270–292.

HERSOUG, T., KJAER, K. and RØDSETH, A. (1984), "Wages, Taxes and the Utility Maximizing Trade Union: A Confrontation with Norwegian Data", Memorandum No. 12, Department of Economics, University of Oslo.

LEWIS, H. G. (1963), *Unionism and relative wages in the United States* (University of Chicago Press, Chicago).

MACURDY, T. E. and PENCAVEL, J. H. (1983), "Testing between Competing Models of Wage and Employment Determination in Unionized Markets", Research Paper No. 37, Stanford Workshop on Factor Markets, Department of Economics, Stanford University.

MCDONALD, I. M. and SOLOW, R. M. (1981), "Wage Bargaining and Employment", *American Economic Review 71*, 896–908.

DEMENIL, G. (1971), *Bargaining. Monopoly power versus union power* (MIT Press, Cambridge, Mass.).

OSWALD, A. J. (1979), "Wage Determination in an Economy with Many Trade Unions", *Oxford Economic Papers 31*, 369–385.

OSWALD, A. J. (1982), "The Microeconomic Theory of the Trade Union", *Economic Journal 92*, 576–595.

OSWALD, A. J. (1985), "The Economic Theory of Trade Unions: An Introductory Survey", *Scandinavian Journal of Economics 87*, 160–193.

PARSLEY, C. J. (1980), "Labor Union Effects on Wage Gains. A Survey of Recent Literature". *Journal of Economic Literature 18*, 1–31.

PENCAVEL, J. H. (1984), "The Trade-off between Wages and Employment in Trade Union Objectives", *Quarterly Journal of Economics 99*, 215–231.

PENCAVEL, J. H. (1985), "Wages and Employment under Trade Unions: Microeconomic Models and Macroeconomic Applications", *Scandinavian Journal of Economics 87*, 197–225.

RØDSETH, A. (1984), "Progressive Taxes and Automatic Stabilization in an Open Economy", *Journal of Macroeconomics 6*, 265–282.

ROSEN, S. (1970), "Unionism and the Occupational Wage Structure in the United States", *International Economic Review 11*, 269–286.

Oxford Economic Papers 38 (1986), 424–442

CASH CROP PRODUCTION AND THE BALANCE OF TRADE IN A LESS DEVELOPED ECONOMY: A MODEL OF TEMPORARY EQUILIBRIUM WITH RATIONING

By TESSA A. VAN DER WILLIGEN*

1. Introduction

THE search for microeconomic foundations to the macroeconomics of industralized economies has recently brought sharply into focus the impor- tance of adjustment dynamics. Clower's (1965) insight into the General Theory—the fact that markets do not generally clear instantaneously—has led to a series of models investigating "temporary equilibrium with rationing" (Grandmont, 1977), where agents' decisions are no longer based merely on price signals, but also on quantity signals. While there seems to be general agreement that these models have yielded useful insights, there is also widespread disillusionment with their fundamental assumption that prices are rigid in the short period, an assumption for which no convincing rationale in terms of optimising behaviour has yet been put forward (see e.g. Fitoussi (1983)).

It is therefore surprising that few attempts have so far been made to apply these models explicitly to economies with centrally planned prices—that is not just communist countries but also the many developing countries with largely controlled price systems. It is all the more surprising if one considers that fixprice models can readily be made to yield policy conclusions concerning the level of planned prices, and indeed that market—clearing models will be misleading in this respect.

In order to avoid the pitfalls of generalizations about "the Third World", this paper develops such a model of temporary equilibrium with rationing with one particular less developed economy in mind, Tanzania. It is well-known that since 1978 Tanzania has been plunged into a severe economic crisis, with very large falls in per capita GDP and real output, great capacity under-utilization, high inflation and pervasive shortages of essential consumer goods. The trade deficit has regularly exceeded 10% of GDP.

This external imbalance is widely recognized as the major proximate cause of the crisis, and can in turn be traced partly to a serious decline in cash crop production, on which the balance of trade is heavily dependent. Most observers, led by Ellis (1982), put the blame for this decline squarely

* Present address: Ministry of Finance, P.O. Box 443, Mbabane Swaziland. This paper is part of a M. Phil. thesis submitted to the University of Oxford in April 1984. I am grateful to David Bevan, Chris Gilbert, Sudhir Anand, Ravi Kanbur, Manic Sen, Simon Burgess and Jon Walters for helpful comments and discussions.

on the downward trend in cash crop prices; the emphasis is put variously on the evolution of cash crop prices relative to the general level of prices (the net barter terms of trade confronting producers), or on the evolution of cash crop prices relative to food crop prices. This diagnosis leads to the obvious conclusion that the reduction in the output of export crops could be stemmed by increasing their producer prices, relative either to the general price level or to the prices of food crops.

While it does not need stating that in a partial equilibrium or market-clearing general equilibrium model a price increase will normally call forth an increase in supply, it is not obvious that this proposition will carry over to a model of temporary equilibrium with rationing. Broadly speaking this is because, when agents are faced with quantity signals as well as price signals, no price ratio will adequately capture incentives. So the general line of questions addressed in the present paper is as follows: what are the possible reasons and remedies for a decline in cash crop production? Is an increase in the producer prices of cash crops sufficient to generate an improvement? Is it necessary? Will there be an improvement if an increase in cash crop prices is accompanied by an increase in food crop prices?

The following section provides a description of the model along with some comments on its major shortcomings. Sections 3 and 4 investigate the model's notional and effective equilibria respectively, and conclusions are presented in Section 5.

2. Structure of the model

The centrepiece of the model is the agricultural sector and its decisions to produce cash crops or subsistence crops; this is embedded in a very simple macroeconomic model using rudimentary representations of the industrial sector and of foreign trade. There are four goods:-

  (i) a cash crop (e.g. coffee, tea, cashewnuts)
 (ii) a subsistence crop (e.g. maize, rice, cassava)
(iii) an industrial consumer good (e.g. soap, kerosene, sugar)
 (iv) an imported raw material used in the production of the industrial good (e.g. oil).

The goods are traded on three markets, the subsistence crop market, the industrial good market, and "foreign trade" in which cash crops are exchanged for raw materials. Money is present implicitly as a medium of exchange, but the model is strictly atemporal and there is no store of value.

In addition to government and marketing authorities whose role is strictly to serve as an intermediary, there are two types of actors, peasants and firms. In each case I consider a representative agent, thus ignoring distributional factors.

The peasant grows the subsistence crop and the cash crop on a small holding,[1] where the acreage devoted to each crop is assumed fixed—a consequence of the short run nature of the model—and the only variable input is the peasant's labour.

The peasant sells both crops to the marketing authorities, which will buy any quantities at prices set by them, so that the peasant is never rationed as a supplier. He consumes the subsistence crop and the industrial good, and maximizes utility, a function of his consumption of these two goods and of leisure. Buying and selling prices of the subsistence crop are assumed to be equal, and there are no transaction costs, so that under unrationed circumstances it is immaterial whether we assume that the peasant consumes his own produce, or that he sells his produce to the marketing authority and then buys back the amount he wishes to consume. I assume that the marketing authorities are unwilling or unable to run down stocks, so that the peasant may be rationed as a consumer of the subsistence crop. He may also of course be rationed as a consumer of the industrial good.

Alongside the representative peasant I consider a representative firm, which produces the industrial good while using the imported raw material as its only variable input. The firm has a fixed stock of capital and operates under constant returns to the variable input up to the point of full capacity utilisation; it is government-controlled and the government dictates that whenever possible—that is unless it is rationed on one or other of its markets—it should operate at the point of full capacity utilisation (there is no special significance in its being in the public sector, other than that it avoids the problem of indeterminate output levels under constant returns). The firm may be rationed as a supplier of the industrial good, and also as a buyer of the raw material: there are no stocks of the cash crop or reserves of foreign exchange, hence the firm's demand for the raw material will be satisfied only if current cash crop production is sufficient to provide the foreign currency required. Neither the industrial good nor the raw material are storable.[2]

---

[1] The modelling of a smallholding should not unduly restrict the applicability of the model to economies where estate production is the dominant form of production of cash crops. Though labour supply and demand decisions are made simultaneously by the smallholder and separately by the estate and the labourer, the wage providing a link between the two, all the same variables will nevertheless enter into the labour demand and supply decisions in each case, provided the rural labourer, like the smallholder, has access to a subsistence plot.

[2] It may be objected that under constant terms of trade between the cash crop and the raw material and under constant returns to the use of the raw material in industrial good production, little is gained by modelling the country's own industrial sector: foreign trade could instead be modelled as a direct exchange of cash crops for industrial goods, so that for instance a trade surplus would be synonymous with excess supply of the industrial good. However this ignores the capacity constraint: in the present model not only is it *notionally* possible to have, say, a trade surplus with excess demand for the industrial good (if the foreign exchange from cash crop production exceeds the firm's 'full capacity' requirement while the demand for the industrial good exceeds the 'full capacity' supply), but it is also not immediately obvious that this combination is impossible in *effective* terms. In practice we shall see that the peasant's effective behaviour does indeed make this combination impossible; but this is something that requires proof.

Finally there is a fixed demand for foreign exchange on the part of the government. The government controls the sources of foreign exchange and accords highest priority to its own demand for foreign exchange.

Note that while the government's budget constraint in terms of foreign exchange must be satisfied (foreign exchange from the sale of the cash crop = government's autonomous demand for foreign exchange and foreign exchange allocated to the industrial sector), there is no consideration of what should be its budget constraint in terms of domestic currency (excess of revenue over outlays of the marketing authorities and firm = 0). The implicit assumption, common to most models of this type, is that the government may be saving or dissaving, that is running a budget surplus or deficit, in terms of domestic currency.

Prices on each market are fixed. World prices of the cash crop and raw material are given on the world market (the country is small in world trade), and these are translated into domestic currency by means of a fixed exchange rate. The price of the industrial good is set by the government such that, given the price of the raw material and the (linear) production technology, the firm makes zero profits. I choose the price of the industrial good as numeraire, and consider the conditions for equilibrium in the subsistence crop market, the industrial good market and in foreign trade; first the conditions for notional equilibrium, that is when the agents take only prices into account, and secondly the conditions for effective equilibrium, when agents also take into account the quantity constraints which they face on all other markets (this corresponds to the notion of effective behaviour in Benassy (1975), not the alternative notion of Drèze (1975), where constraints on *all* markets are taken into account).

Two important defects of the general framework of the model need to be stressed. The first is the complete neglect of the urban sector: labour does not enter into the firm's production function, and there are no mouths to feed other than the peasant's. By contrast, in economies like Tanzania the urban sector often does play a part in the links between agriculture and the balance of trade, by creating a need for food imports when the marketed surplus of subsistence crops is insufficient—a need which never arises in the present model since it is assumed that each peasant can grow all the food he needs himself. The present model ignores this possibility and thereby focusses rather narrowly on the cash crop problem.

The second defect in the general framework is the complete neglect of parallel markets and other illegal trading activities, which undermine the credibility of the assumption that prices are fixed at their controlled levels. Yet there can be no doubt that a model of temporary equilibrium with rationing constitutes a better first approximation than a market-clearing model, if only because even where parallel markets in industrial goods are widespread, they too are often subject to rationing: especially in the rural areas it is by no means always, or even usually, certain that a good can be obtained at the "going" black market price. As for illegal trading of crops, the emerging consensus concerning the role of government-controlled prices in production trends (see Section 1) leaves no room for such illegal trading happening on a large scale: no-one, for instance, has yet suggested that apparent declines in production in Tanzania are merely the result of increased illegal activity; and it is the relevance of this consensus that the present model seeks to investigate.

I use the following notation and assumptions:

p_s, p_c = domestic prices of the subsistence crop and cash crop resp.

p_I = domestic price of the industrial good

        $\equiv 1$ as a normalization

P_R = world price of the raw material, in domestic currency

p_c^w = world price of the cash crop, in domestic currency

β = barter terms of trade

        $\equiv p_c^w/p_R$

X_s, X_I = peasant's consumption of the subsistence crop and industrial good resp.

X_R = firm's input of raw material

X_G = government's demand for foreign exchange, in units of domestic currency

Q_s, Q_c = peasant's production of the subsistence crop and cash crop resp.

Q_I = firm's production of the industrial good

L_s, L_c = peasant's labour supply to the production of the subsistence crop and cash crop resp.

T = peasant's total time

l = peasant's leisure

        $\equiv T - L_s - L_c$

$f_s(\cdot), f_c(\cdot)$ = production functions for the subsistence crop and cash crop respectively; defined on labour, L_s and L_c resp.; twice differentiable, increasing and concave

$f_I(\cdot)$ = production function for the industrial good, defined on X_R, the input of raw material; increasing and linear up to X_R^* the "full capacity" input

$U(\cdot)$ = peasant's utility function; defined on consumption of the two goods and leisure, i.e. X_s, X_I and l; twice differentiable, increasing and concave in all three arguments; additively separable.

First derivatives are denoted by dashes (') or subscripts indicating the argument w.r.t. which the derivative is taken, second derivatives by double dashes or double subscripts.

3. Notional equilibrium

Notional behaviour of the agricultural sector

The peasant maximizes utility subject to a budget constraint:

$$\underset{X_s, X_I, L_s, L_c}{\text{Max}} \quad U(X_s, X_I, T - L_s - L_c) \quad \text{s.t.} \quad p_s X_s + X_I = p_s f_s(L_s) + p_c f_c(L_c)$$

Under certain simple assumptions[3] the partial derivatives of the peasant's demands and supplies w.r.t. the two prices p_s and p_c can be unambiguously signed; these signs are given in the following demand and supply functions:

$$X_s = X_s(p_s, p_c) \qquad Q_s = Q_s(p_s, p_c)$$
$${-} \quad {+} \qquad\qquad {+} \quad {-}$$

$$X_I = X_I(p_s, p_c) \qquad Q_c = Q_c(p_s, p_c)$$
$${+} \quad {+} \qquad\qquad {-} \quad {+}$$

Notional behaviour of the industrial sector

Under government instructions the firm produces at full capacity, using an amount of raw material X_R^* and producing Q_I^*. It makes zero profits, since the price of the industrial good has been set at the level required to ensure this.

Notional equilibrium loci

The notional equilibrium loci are defined as follows:

Subsistence crop market equilibrium locus (SCMEL):

$$X_s(p_s, p_c) = Q_s(p_s, p_c) \tag{1}$$
$${-} \quad {+} {+} \quad {-}$$

Industrial good market equilibrium locus (IGMEL):

$$X_I(p_s, p_c) = Q_I^* \tag{2}$$
$${+} \quad {+}$$

Balance of trade locus (BTL):

$$X_R^* + X_G/p_R = \beta Q_c(p_s, p_c) \tag{3}$$
$${-} \quad {+}$$

(there is balance of trade when the foreign exchange required by the industrial sector and by the government equals the foreign exchange earned by exports of the cash crop).

That the three loci intersect is easily shown by simple manipulation of the equilibrium conditions, the peasant's budget constraint, and the

---

[3] These assumptions are: (i) forward-sloping labour supply ($\partial l/\partial p_s < 0$ and $\partial l/\partial p_c < 0$) and (ii) monotonicity throughout price space of the peasant's notional responses to changes in p_s, i.e. the peasant's responses to changes in p_s are not reversed in sign as he changes from being a notional net supplier to being a notional net buyer of the subsistence crop.

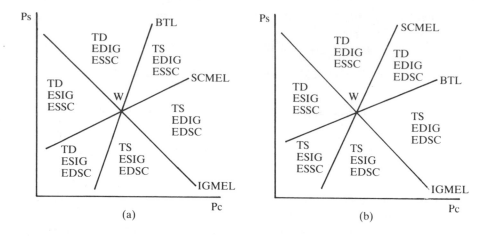

FIG. 1. Notional equilibrium loci

government's budget constraint in terms of foreign exchange. At the point of intersection of the SCMEL and IGMEL, the government's budget constraint requires that

$$X_G = (P_c^w - P_c^*)Q_c^* \tag{4}$$

(asterisks denote variables associated with this equilibrium point).[4] (4) at the same time ensures that this point is also a point of balance of trade.

From (1)–(3) it is clear that the SCMEL and BTL are both upward-sloping in (p_s, p_c) space, while the IGMEL is downward-sloping, so that the relative slopes of the SCMEL and BTL are ambiguous; the two possible configurations are shown in Fig. 1 below. In what follows I set out the argument in detail for the case of Fig. 1(a), and I shall then briefly show that Fig. 1(b) yields identical results.

The abbreviations used in Fig. 1 and in what follows are:

> TD = trade deficit
> TS = trade surplus
> EDIG = excess demand for the industrial good
> ESIG = excess supply of the industrial good
> EDSC = excess demand for the subsistence crop
> ESSC = excess supply of the subsistence crop

Asterisks (*) are used to denote prices and quantities associated with the Walrasian equilibrium point W.

---

[4] If at this point of intersection, $P_c^w = P_c^*$, X_G would have to be negative for there to be balance of trade. This could be taken to represent a foreign financial inflow.

5. Effective equilibrium

I consider the different sectors' responses to rationing on different markets in turn. Rations are denoted by a bar over the variable $(-)$, and effective demands and supplies by a tilde $(\sim)$.

The agricultural sector under excess demand for the industrial good

The peasant's consumption of the industrial good is limited to $\bar{X}_I <$ $X_I(p_s, p_c)$; his demand and supply functions become rationed or effective demands and supplies, $\tilde{X}_s(\cdot)$, $\tilde{Q}_s(\cdot)$ and $\tilde{Q}_c(\cdot)$, into which $\bar{X}_I$ enters as an argument in addition to p_s and p_c. Using simple comparative static techniques, which are more appropriate here than the elegant techniques of Neary and Roberts (1980), owing to the peculiar form of the budget constraint, it is easy to show that, compared to his notional supplies and demands, the peasant increases his demand for the subsistence crop and reduces his supply of both crops:

$$\tilde{X}_s > X_s \tag{5}$$

$$\tilde{Q}_s < Q_s \tag{6}$$

$$\tilde{Q}_c < Q_c \tag{7}$$

The agricultural sector under excess demand for the subsistence crop

The peasant's consumption of the subsistence crop is limited to $\bar{X}_s =$ $Q_s(p_s, p_c) < X_s(p_s, p_c)$: while he was hoping to buy more from the marketing authority than he sold to it, he finds this is impossible since he himself is the sole source of supply of the subsistence crop. This is a peculiar case, rather different from the ones normally considered in rationing theory, since here the peasant is not bound to to the consumption ration $\bar{X}_s$, since he is in control of his own produce and may choose to produce more of the subsistence crop and consume this additional produce himself, without going through the market; his consumption level can therefore rise above the ration $\bar{X}_s$. Therefore in this case it is all four of the notional functions $X_I(\cdot)$, $Q_s(\cdot)$, $Q_c(\cdot)$ and $X_s(\cdot)$ that become rationed functions, $\tilde{X}_I(\cdot)$, $\tilde{Q}_s(\cdot)$, $\tilde{Q}_c(\cdot)$ and $\tilde{X}_s(\cdot)$.

It is easy to show that for any degree of rationing of the subsistence crop, the peasant reduces his supply of the cash crop and his consumption of the subsistence crop, and increases his production of the subsistence crop relative to their notional levels:

$$\tilde{X}_s < X_s \tag{8}$$

$$\tilde{Q}_s > Q_s \tag{9}$$

$$\tilde{Q}_c < Q_c \tag{10}$$

It can also be shown that for infinitesimal rationing (from points where $X_s = Q_s$) the peasant increases his demand for the industrial good relative to its notional level:

$$\tilde{X}_I > X_I \tag{11}$$

No general result is available in this case since for very severe rationing (the peasant was producing very little of the subsistence crop and hoping to consume a large amount of it, e.g. because p_s was very low) the peasant may have to devote so much more labour to the subsistence crop, in order to bring his effective demand and supply of it into equality, that his effective cash crop production can no longer cover even his notional expenditure on the industrial good, let alone an increase in it. However I abstract from this case and assume that (11) holds for more severe rationing as well.

The agricultural sector under double rationing

The peasant's consumption of the industrial good is limited to $\bar{X}_I < X_I(p_s, p_c)$, and his consumption of the subsistence crop to $\bar{X}_s = Q_s(p_s, p_c) < X_s(p_s, p_c)$. The notional functions $Q_s(\cdot)$, $Q_c(\cdot)$ and $X_s(\cdot)$ become the rationed functions $\tilde{Q}_s(\cdot)$, $\tilde{Q}_c(\cdot)$ and $\tilde{X}_s(\cdot)$, which must satisfy $\bar{X}_s = \tilde{Q}_s$. It can be shown that under these circumstances, as might be expected, the peasant reduces his supply of the cash crop and increases production of the subsistence crop:

$$\tilde{Q}_c < Q_c \tag{12}$$

$$\tilde{Q}_s > Q_s \tag{13}$$

(the change in his demand for the subsistence crop is ambiguous: if rationing of the industrial good is severe enough it is conceivable that supply of labour to the production of the cash crop should fall so much that the peasant would find it worthwhile to increase production of the subsistence crop beyond his original demand for it).

In addition under double rationing the peasant's responses to changes in p_s and p_c are modified; in particular:

$$\tilde{Q}_s = \tilde{Q}_s(p_s, p_c) \quad \text{(compare: } Q_s = Q_s(p_s, p_c)) \tag{14}$$
$$\phantom{\tilde{Q}_s = \tilde{Q}_s(}0 \quad + \phantom{\text{(compare: } Q_s = Q_s(p_s, p_c))}+ \quad -$$

$$\tilde{Q}_c = \tilde{Q}_c(p_s, p_c) \quad \text{(compare: } Q_c = Q_c(p_s, p_0)) \tag{15}$$
$$\phantom{\tilde{Q}_c = \tilde{Q}_c(}0 \quad - \phantom{\text{(compare: } Q_c = Q_c(p_s, p_0))}- \quad 0$$

The price of the subsistence crop has become irrelevant since the peasant no longer has anything to do with the subsistence crop market. (15) is a simple consequence of the modified budget constraint, $\bar{X}_I = p_c \tilde{Q}_c$: cash crop production is now determined by the need to pay for one's ration of the industrial good; if the price of the cash crop goes up a smaller supply will be sufficient to raise the required cash. Since a smaller supply of the cash crop, other things being equal, means a lower marginal utility of leisure, this will incite the peasant to substitute away from leisure and into labour supply to the production of the subsistence crop, hence (14).

The industrial sector under trade deficit

The firm is rationed to an amount of the raw material $\bar{X}_R = \beta Q_c(p_s, p_c) - X_G/p_R < X_R^*$; it will produce a correspondingly smaller amount of the industrial good:

$$\bar{Q}_I = f_I(\beta Q_c - X_G/p_R) < Q_I \tag{16}$$

It still makes zero profits since there are constant returns to the use of the raw material over the entire range from 0 to X_R^*.

The industrial sector under excess supply of the industrial good

The firm can only sell an amount $\bar{Q}_I < Q_I$; since it is assumed not to hold inventories it will produce only that amount and its raw material requirement will be correspondingly smaller:

$$\bar{X}_R = f_I^{-1}(Q_I) < X_R^* \tag{17}$$

Again the firm continues to make zero profits.

Effective equilibrium loci

Figure 2 below shows the direction of the shifts of the equilibrium loci when quantity constraints are taken into account, the numbers in brackets referring to the inequalities in the above discussion of rationed behaviour.

It is not immediately obvious how far the loci shift in each case; the following two sections present a detailed analysis of the extent of the shifts in the left-hand and right-hand half of Fig. 2 resp.

Coincidence of the left-hand branches of the BTL and IGMEL

Between the left-hand branches of the BTL and IGMEL there are two regions of double rationing of the industrial sector (TD/ESIG/ESSC and TD/ESIG/EDSC), and it is easy to show that these regions can no longer exist after the firm has recalculated its decisions in accordance with these constraints.

If the firm is rationed on both markets, one or other of these constraints must be "more binding": either the raw material constraint is more binding

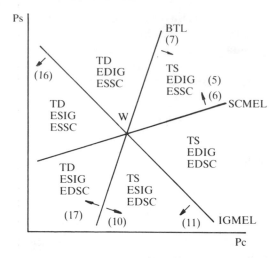

FIG. 2. Directions of the notional-to-effective shifts

and if the firm recalculates in accordance with this there will be excess *demand* for the industrial good; or the supply constraint is more binding and if the firm recalculates in accordance with this there will be a trade *surplus*. Since the firm recalculates in accordance with whichever constraint is more binding, its constrained behaviour cannot give rise to TD/ESIG: it will either give rise to TD/EDIG (recalculation on the basis of the TD constraint) or TS/ESIG (recalculation on the basis of the ESIG constraint).

Thus the arrows labelled (16) and (17) in Fig. 2 must cause the left-hand branches of the BTL and IGMEL to collapse onto each other; but their position relative to the left-hand branch of the SCMEL remains to be established. The following argument demonstrates that they coincide *above* the SCMEL, thus creating a region of TS/ESIG/ESSC.

From the above argument we know that if, on the left-hand branch of the SCMEL, the TD constraint is "more binding", the SCMEL will be in a TD/EDIG region (BTL and IGMEL coincide below SCMEL); whereas if the ESIG constraint is "more binding", the SCMEL will be in a TS/ESIG region (BTL and IGMEL coincide above SCMEL). What determines which constraint is "more binding"? The rationed supply of the industrial good, $\tilde{Q}_I$, as set by the TD constraint is $\tilde{Q}_I = f_I(\beta Q_c - X_G/p_R)$, or, since the firm makes zero profits, $\tilde{Q}_I = p_c^w Q_c - X_G$; while as set by the ESIG constraint it is $\tilde{Q}_I = X_I$ and hence, by the modified form of the peasant's budget constraint when $Q_s = X_s$, as is the case on the SCMEL, $\tilde{Q}_I = p_c Q_c$. If $p_c^w Q_c - X_G < p_c Q_c$ the TD constraint is more binding, if $p_c^w Q_c - X_G > p_c Q_c$ the ESIG constraint is more binding.

At W we had $p_c^w Q_c^* - X_G = p_c^* Q_c^*$. As we move left along the SCMEL p_c falls from p_c^*, and, since we enter a region of notional trade deficit, Q_c falls from Q_c^*. Therefore $p_c Q_c$ falls by more than does $p_c^w Q_c$ as we move left along the SCMEL, so that $p_c Q_c < p_c^w Q_c - X_G$; the ESIG constraint is more binding and so we are in a TS/ESIG region.

Creation of a large TD/EDIG/EDSC region

This section will show that recalculation of decisions in the face of quantity constraints leads to the creation of a large region of TD/EDIG/EDSC ("generalized excess demand") on the right-hand side of Fig. 2. This region takes up most of the space previously occupied by two other regions, TS/EDIG/EDSC and TS/EDIG/ESSC, and the first step is to show that these regions can no longer exist when decisions have been recalculated.

In the TS/EDIG/EDSC region the firm is completely unrationed so, since its decisions are independent of p_s and p_c, it must be producing and demanding the same quantities as at the full equilibrium point W: $Q_I = Q_I^*$ and $X_R = X_R^*$. The peasant, on the other hand, is rationed on both the subsistence crop and the industrial good market. Since he is rationed in the subsistence crop he becomes self-sufficient in it ($\bar{Q}_s = \bar{X}_s$); with his ration of the industrial good set at $\bar{X}_I = Q_I = Q_I^*$, this makes his budget constraint $p_c \bar{Q}_c = \bar{X}_I = Q_I^*$, so that $\bar{Q}_c = Q_I^*/p_c$. At W we had $Q_c^* = Q_I^*/p_c^*$ (since there the budget constraint dictated $X_I^* = p_c^* Q_c^*$ and industrial good market equilibrium ensured $X_I^* = Q_I^*$); in Fig. 2 this TS/EDIG/EDSC region lies entirely to the right of W, so that, if we are investigating its continued existence in this area of the diagram, we hae $p_c > p_c^*$. Using $\bar{Q}_c = Q_I^*/p_c$ and $Q_c^* = Q_I^*/p_c^*$, we immediately get $\bar{Q}_c < Q_c^*$. Since X_R is the same as at W and Q_c is lower, there must be a trade deficit rather than a trade surplus; hence the TS/EDIG/EDSC region cannot exist, at least anywhere to the right of W (I return to this qualification below).

The other region that disappears in this area of the diagram is the TS/EDIG/ESSC region. Once again the firm is completely unrationed so that $Q_I = Q_I^*$ and $X_R = X_R^*$. The peasant is rationed on the industrial good market, to an amount $\bar{X}_I = Q_I = Q_I^*$, so that his effective supplies must satisfy

$$p_s(\bar{Q}_s - \bar{X}_s) + p_c \bar{Q}_c = \bar{X}_I = Q_I^* \tag{18}$$

For there to be excess supply of the subsistence crop it must be the case that $\bar{Q}_s - \bar{X}_s > 0$; for there to be a trade surplus, given that $X_R = X_R^*$, it must be the case that $\bar{Q}_c > Q_c^*$. At W we had

$$p_c^* Q_c^* = X_I^* = Q_I^* \tag{19}$$

But comparing (18) and (19), using $\bar{Q}_s - \bar{X}_s > 0$ and $\bar{Q}_c > Q_c^*$, and noting from Fig. 2 that if it exists this region must be to the North-East of W so that $p_c > p_c^*$ and $p_s > p_s^*$, we have a contradiction; therefore the TS/EDIG/ESSC region cannot exist.

The result that these two regions disappear seems to indicate that the right-hand branch of the BTL follows the direction of arrow (7) (Fig. 2) *past* the right-hand branch of the SCMEL, so that it coincides with the right-hand branch of the IGMEL. The following argument confirms that the BTL must at least shift past the SCMEL.

Consider a point on the SCMEL in the region of excess demand for the industrial good. Since $Q_s = X_s$ the peasant's budget constraint is $\bar{X}_I = p_c \bar{Q}_c$. If this were a point of balance of trade, or of trade surplus, then the firm would be unrationed, with $Q_I = Q_I^*$ and $X_R = X_R^*$, and the budget constraint could be rewritten $Q_I^* = p_c Q_c$. Comparing the budget constraint at W, $Q_I^* = p_c^* Q_c^*$, and remembering $p_c > p_c^*$, we would have $\bar{Q}_c < Q_c^*$, which given $X_R = X_R^*$ is inconsistent with balance of trade or trade surplus. Therefore the SCMEL under excess demand for the industrial good must lie in a region of trade deficit: the BTL must at least shift past the SCMEL.

Once the BTL shifts past the SCMEL it finds itself in a region of excess demand for the industrial good and the subsistence crop, and it was shown that in this region the signs of the partial derivatives of $\bar{Q}_c$ w.r.t. p_s and p_c change, so that the slope of the BTL, defined by the equation $X_R + X_G / p_R = \beta \bar{Q}_c(p_s, p_c)$, is radically altered. Since

$$\bar{Q}_c = \bar{Q}_c(p_s, p_c) \qquad (15)$$
$$\phantom{\bar{Q}_c = \bar{Q}_c(}0 \quad - $$

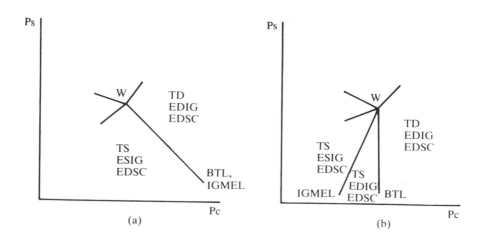

FIG. 3. Two possible configurations of the right-hand branches of BTL and IGMEL

the BTL turns vertical, with a trade deficit on its right and a trade surplus on its left.

All this seems to confirm that the right-hand branch of the BTL comes to coincide with the right-hand branch of the IGMEL; but this would be the case only if the right-hand branch of the IGMEL, which itself shifts left as indicated by (11) in Fig. 2, does not shift past the vertical. If it did the right-hand branch of the BTL, which is vertical in EDIG/EDSC regions, would no longer coincide with it, and a TS/EDIG/EDSC region would appear between the vertical BTL and the IGMEL (remember that the above proof of non-existence of the TS/EDIG/EDSC region is valid only to the right of W). The two possibilities are illustrated in Fig. 3, and below I show that Fig. 3(a) is the correct one.

It is clear from Fig. 3 that an answer to the question "Is the right hand branch of the BTL in a region of excess demand for the industrial good?" would allow us to discriminate between the two possibilities. Consider a point on the BTL; since it is in a region of excess demand for the subsistence crop $\tilde{Q}_s = \tilde{X}_s$, and the peasant's budget constraint becomes $\tilde{X}_I = p_c \tilde{Q}_c$. Since we are on the BTL and either on the IGMEL or in a region of EDIG, the firm is unrationed, hence $Q_I = Q_I^*$ and $X_R = X_R^*$. Since there is balance of trade equilibrium $X_R^* = \beta \tilde{Q}_c - X_G/p_R$, from which we know that $\tilde{Q}_c = Q_c^*$. Since $\tilde{X}_I = p_c \tilde{Q}_c = p_c Q_c^*$ and since, if we are to have EDIG, p_c is equal to p_c^* (see Fig. 3(b)), we have $\tilde{X}_I = p_c^* Q_c^* = Q_I^* = Q_I$, and this rules out excess demand for the industrial good. Therefore the BTL and IGMEL must coincide as in Fig. 3(a).

Configuration of the effective equilibrium loci

Pulling together the elements of the previous two sections we get the following notional-to-effective shifts and effective equilibrium loci:

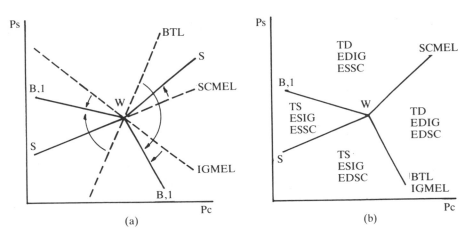

FIG. 4. Notional-to-effective shifts when BTL is steeper than SCMEL

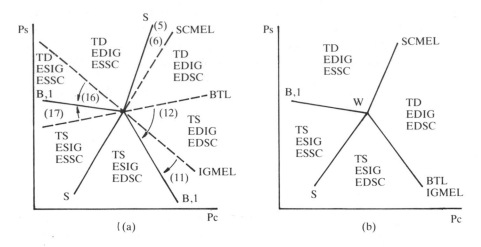

FIG. 5. Notional-to-effective shifts when SCMEL is steeper than BTL

This is also qualitatively exactly the configuration one would obtain if one started with the other possible notional partitioning (Fig. 1(b)), where the relative slopes of the BTL and SCMEL are reversed. The analysis of this case is much simpler and Fig. 5 below should be self-explanatory if it is remembered that (i) TD/ESIG regions cannot exist, and (ii) the BTL is vertical in EDIG/EDSC regions. The names of the regions in Fig. 5(a) are those of notional regions, and the numbers in brackets refer to the inequalities in the discussion of rationed behaviour (these numbers correspond to those in Fig. 2, except that (7) and (10), shifts of the BTL in regions where peasants are rationed on a single market, are replaced by (12), the shift in a region of double rationing of peasants).

5. Conclusions

Figures 4(b) and 5(b) can be used to examine the potential of the two possible remedies to balance of trade problems in a country like Tanzania as outlined in Section 1: increases in the producer prices of cash crops relative to those of subsistence crops, and manipulation of the "rural-urban" terms of trade.

The relative price of the cash crop in Figs. 4(b) and 5(b) is given by the slope of a ray from the origin passing through the point representing the economy's price vector; an increase in the relative price of the cash crop can be represented as a clockwise rotation of this ray. It can be seen from the diagrams that starting from certain areas of trade deficit (that is mainly those which also exhibit excess supply of the subsistence crop), such a clockwise rotation would be an improvement, in the sense that it might take the economy directly to the Walrasian equilibrium W, or at least would bring the relative prices more into line with their levels at W (a change in the absolute levels of p_s and p_c would then be required to take the economy to W). These are regions characterized by too low a relative price for the cash crop. But other areas (mainly those which exhibit excess demand for the subsistence crop) are instead characterized by too *high* a relative price for the cash crop, and increasing it further would merely move the economy away from W.

Thus the direction in which the relative price of the cash crop should change is ambiguous, and this very ambiguity is of interest since it would not have arisen in a market-clearing model. Much depends on the state of the subsistence crop market, though the correct direction of change cannot be deduced merely from this since the slope of the subsistence crop market equilibrium locus is not necessarily the same as the slope of the ray through W from the origin. All that can be said is that if there is excess supply of the subsistence crop it is likely that the relative price of the cash crop should be increased, whereas if there is excess demand for the subsistence crop the relative price of the cash crop should probably be reduced.

In attempting to draw some very tentative policy conclusions from this simple model it should be emphasized that "excess demand for the subsistence crop" as defined here is characterized not merely by inadequate food production, but by there being no marketed food production at all: each peasant must be consuming the whole of his own production of the subsistence crop. However, even if it is not the case in aggregate that there is no marketed production at all, this may mask regional or individual differences: if producers of the cash crop are not able to obtain all the food they want from the market, then an increase in the relative price of the cash crop will have adverse effects. Therefore much more information is needed before policy conclusions can be drawn—but this *caveat* is itself an important conclusion.

The second remedy suggested in Section 1 is manipulation of the "rural-urban" terms of trade. In this model an improvement in the terms of trade facing the peasant can be represented as a movement outward along a ray from the origin. It can be seen from Figs. 4(b) and 5(b) that this move by itself cannot correct a trade deficit; indeed it is only in very small parts of the trade deficit regions that it will take the economy towards rather than away from W: most often it is a *worsening* of the rural-urban terms of trade that is required, e.g. through an increase in the price of the industrial good. The reason is of course that when there is rationing the terms of trade do not adequately capture incentives to produce. Here the effect of the price terms of trade is perverse: the incentives to earn cash are determined entirely by the consumer good rations, and given this target cash income the only effect of the price terms of trade is to set the incentives to produce, so that the higher the crop prices, the less the peasants will produce.

This clear-cut perverse result is due to the extreme simplicity of the model, which allows for only one use of cash, expenditure on the industrial good, so that rationing on this one market immediately gives rise to the notion of a target cash income. Three possible extensions of the model, all of them conducive to realism, would undermine this notion, essentially by allowing markets in which the peasant would be an unrationed buyer: higher crop prices mean improved terms on which leisure can be transformed into consumption on these markets, so that the incentives to produce more are partly restored. These extensions are:

(i) introducing several industrial consumer goods; all of these would have to be rationed for the notion of target cash income to remain relevant.

(ii) relaxing the assumption that peasants are identical; if some peasants produced only the cash crop, or, in a more realistic multi-crop model, if they did not produce the entire range of subsistence crops, they would rely on the market for their consumption of the subsistence crop, or of those subsistence crops which they did not produce themselves. They would then be unrationed in those markets unless there were excess demand in aggregate.

(iii) introducing saving; this could be in the form of assets (e.g. housing, livestock...), the markets for which could be unrationed; or it could be simply in the form of money.

Any of these extensions would go some way towards restoring the incentive effect of better rural-urban terms of trade; but the perverse effect highlighted in the present model cannot for that reason be ignored: if rationing on some markets leads the peasant to practice what Kornai (1979) calls "forced substitution" into less preferred goods, this will increase the probability that additional consumption will not compensate for the loss of additional leisure, and hence increase the probability that effective labour supply will be backward-bending.

Thus the possibility that increases in cash crop prices will have perverse effects must at least be taken seriously, along with its converse, that the trade balance may improve if the rural-urban terms of trade are turned against the peasant. This is most easily done by increasing the prices of industrial goods, which the government may have kept low in an attempt to keep down the cost of living. With severely restricted availability of these goods the effect of this policy may have been, as suggested by the model, to keep down the cost of living in terms of leisure, with severe consequences for the balance of trade.

All this suggests what must rank at least as an alternative explanation and remedy for declines in cash crop production, alongside the orthodox ones of Section 1: cash crop production may decline as a direct consequence of industrial good rationing, and it may be that improvements in the supply and distribution of consumer goods would then bring about an improvement in the balance of trade.

The policy of increasing the overall supply of consumer goods can be represented in the present model as an increase in the availability of foreign exchange to the industrial sector through a reduction in X_G, the government's foreign exchange requirement. This can only be discussed heuristically, since the present model does not allow for variations in X_G. It is clear, however, that in the regions of trade deficit the peasant's target cash income is determined by the ration of the industrial good; if X_G were reduced, this ration would increase and so would cash crop production (and subsistence crop production if the economy was not in a region of excess demand for the subsistence crop). Thus diverting foreign exchange from public investment (which, under conditions of capacity underutilisation, must be relatively unproductive at least in the short run) or, more painfully, from services such as health and education, into production of consumer goods should allow the mobilization of unutilized resources for export production, such that ultimately the required reduction in investment or services will be less than the initial reduction; indeed it is conceivable that resources will be mobilized in such quantities that this more than makes up for the initial "sacrifice" of foreign exchange.

This effect is readily identified as a "supply multiplier" of the type of Barro and Grossman (1974): there is an increase in total foreign exchange availability as a result of an increase in the amount allocated to the consumer goods sector—and being a multiplier it owes its existence directly to the move to a framework of temporary equilibrium with rationing. Whether this multiplier is greater than one, that is whether a reallocation of foreign exchange would allow both private consumption *and* investment (or services) to go up, remains to be investigated; but the role of incentive goods and the slightly unconventional view of the consumer goods sector as a spur to resource mobilisation and development rather than a drain on potential investment resources cannot simply be ignored.

Wolfson College, Oxford

BIBLIOGRAPHY

BARRO, R. J. and GROSSMAN, H. I. (1974), 'Suppressed Inflation and the Supply Multiplier'. *Review of Economic Studies* 41: 87–104.

BENASSY, J. P. (1975), 'Neo-Keynesian Disequilibrium in a Monetary Economy'. *Review of Economic Studies* 42: 502–523.

CLOWER, R. W. (1965), 'The Keynesian Counterrevolution: A Theoretical Appraisal'. In F. H. Hahn and F. Brechling (eds) *The Theory of Interest Rates*. London, Macmillan.

DREZE, J. (1975), 'Existence of an Equilibrium under Price Rigidity and Quantity Rationing'. *International Economic Review* 16: 301–320.

ELLIS, F. (1982), 'Agricultural Price Policy in Tanzania'. *World Development,* 10: 1–20.

FITOUSSI, J. P. (1983), 'Modern Macroeconomic Theory: An Overview'. In J. P. Fitoussi (ed) *Modern Macroeconomic Theory.* Oxford, Basil Blackwell.

GRANDMONT, J. M. (1977), 'Temporary General Equilibrium Theory'. *Econometrica* 45, 535–573.

KEYNES, J. M. (1936), *The General Theory of Employment, Interest and Money.* Cambridge, Macmillan and Cambridge University Press.

KORNAI, J. (1979), 'Resource-Constrained versus Demand-Constrained Systems'. *Econometrica* 47: 801–819.

NEARY, J. P. and ROBERTS, K. W. S. (1980), 'The Theory of Household Behaviour under Rationing'. *European Economic Review* 13: 25–42.

Oxford Economic Papers 38 (1986), 443–455

SIGNALLING IN A MODEL OF MONETARY POLICY WITH INCOMPLETE INFORMATION*

By JOHN VICKERS

1. Introduction

WHEN a new policymaker comes into office, the public might not know his preferences for certain. For example, they might be unsure whether he is a *wet,* more worried about unemployment than inflation, or a *dry,* more worried about inflation than unemployment. The expectations formed by the public have an important influence on the economy, and these expectations are influenced by the policymaker's behaviour. It is therefore possible that the policymaker would try to *signal* his preferences by his behaviour after he comes into office. If, for example, it were advantageous to be perceived as a dry rather than a wet, then a dry policymaker would try to signal his dryness, but a wet would try to masquerade as a dry. This signalling activity can have interesting implications for the time paths of inflation and unemployment, and for welfare.

To investigate this problem, we employ a version of the natural rate model proposed by Barro and Gordon (1983a, b). In this model, inflation is bad but surprise inflation is good—because it causes unemployment to fall below its natural rate, which is assumed to be too high. With complete information (i.e. no uncertainty about the policymaker's preferences) there is positive inflation but no surprise inflation at equilibrium, unless the policymaker can somehow precommit himself to a policy rule (say zero inflation), in which case he can achieve better results than he obtains with discretion. An important question is that of how the policymaker can commit himself to such a rule. Backus and Driffill (1985a, b) and Barro (1985) have drawn on related work in oligopoly theory by Kreps and Wilson (1982a) and Milgrom and Roberts (1982a) to show how *reputation* may enable a policymaker effectively to commit himself to a rule, provided that there is at least some uncertainty about his preferences or opportunities. Incomplete information is also the main feature of the model below, but our approach, and some of our results, differ from those of Backus–Driffill and Barro, as will be explained below. Reputation and signalling in a model of monetary policy has also been investigated by Yoon Ha Yoo (1985), whose work is closely related to that reported here.

* I am grateful to David Backus, John Driffill, Christopher Harris, Paul Klemperer, Jim Mirrlees, Torsten Persson and Peter Sinclair for their helpful comments and suggestions. Particular thanks are due to John Hawksworth for correcting an error in an earlier version, and to Ulrich Zachau for numerous illuminating discussions of signalling models. Remaining errors are mine.

The analysis below is based on the discussion of limit pricing under uncertainty by Milgrom and Roberts (1982b).[1] It is therefore another application of ideas from oligopoly theory to questions of macroeconomic policy. We choose to explore those ideas using the model proposed by Barro and Gordon because of its convenient properties and for the sake of comparison with the other work. Whether or not it is an appropriate representation of an economy for the purposes of monetary policy is of course another matter.

The analysis proceeds in two steps. Initially we employ a notion of equilibrium that is essentially the same as Kreps and Wilson's (1982b) sequential equilibrium (as do Milgrom and Roberts (1982b)). There is usually a great multiplicity of equilibria, which are of two kinds. First, there are *separating* equilibria, in which a dry policymaker does signal his dryness successfully, and thereby reveals his preferences early in his term of office. With a dry policymaker, inflation is initially lower than expected, and unemployment is correspondingly higher. The opposite is true for a wet policymaker, whose true preferences are also revealed by the policies that he initially adopts. Secondly there may exist *pooling* equilibria, in which wets and drys initially behave alike, so that the public cannot initially make inferences as to the policymaker's true preferences. At the end of the period of office, however, wets and drys each behave according to their true preferences. At that point, inflation is unexpectedly low and inflation is unexpectedly high when the policymaker is really dry, and the opposite holds when he is truly wet.

Next, we ask whether the multiplicity of equilibria can be reduced. First, we exploit the idea that it is common knowledge that dominated strategies would not be employed. This eliminates all but one of the separating equilibria and eliminates some remaining pooling equilibria (and maybe all of them, depending on parameter values). Secondly, we employ the ideas described in Kreps (1985), which usually remove any remaining pooling equilibria leaving only the separating equilibrium in which a dry policymaker does the minimum necessary to persuade the public that he is dry, and a wet policymaker behaves as he would with complete information.

An interesting result to emerge is that the outcome under incomplete information may be markedly superior to that under complete information. That is because the policymaker may be encouraged to keep initial inflation down for reasons of signalling, whereas no such motive exists under

---

[1] Paul Klemperer has suggested to me that the literature on limit pricing under uncertainty may have further applications to the question of signalling in monetary policy. In Barro and Gordon's (1983a, b) macroeconomic models it is assumed that the government can choose the rate of inflation. However, it is perhaps more realistic to suppose that the rate of inflation depends on government policy *and* other influences, all of which are unobservable. When the public then observes (say) a low inflation rate, they cannot infer with certainty what was government policy—the low inflation might be due to the other factors. This is formally similar to the limit pricing problem investigated by Matthews and Mirman (1983) in which a potential entrant attempts to infer an incumbent firm's output level—and hence its cost—from market price in the presence of demand uncertainty. Essentially the same signal extraction problem is involved in both cases.

complete information. This effect being anticipated, inflation expectations are lowered.

The model is presented and the analysis of equilibrium is begun in Section 2. The diagrams used to illustrate equilibrium are like those in Kreps (1985). Ways of reducing the multiplicity of equilibria are analysed in Section 3, and Section 4 concludes.

2. The model

The following analysis employs a version of the model of monetary policy proposed by Barro and Gordon (1983a, b). In their model, the costs to the policymaker in period t depend on actual and unanticipated inflation:

$$z_t = z(\pi_t, \pi_t - \pi_t^e), \tag{1}$$

where π_t is actual inflation and π_t^e is expected inflation. It is assumed that costs rise with the magnitude of inflation $|\pi_t|$, but fall with surprise inflation, $\pi_t - \pi_t^e$. Surprise inflation may be beneficial because the equilibrium level of unemployment is too high without it. Alternatively, surprise inflation may be beneficial because it acts as a lump-sum tax on money balances and unindexed bonds, hence allowing lower distortionary taxes elsewhere. We shall use the former interpretation. It is assumed that the policymaker can choose π_t via his choice of monetary policy.

To simply the analysis, we suppose that z takes the form

$$z_t = \tfrac{1}{2}\pi_t^2 + c(\pi_t^e - \pi_t); \qquad c > 0. \tag{2}$$

Thus c represents the weights in the policymaker's objective function attached to inflation and unemployment: a higher value for c reflects greater concern for unemployment relative to inflation.

The public do not know the preferences of the policymaker *ex ante*. Suppose that there are two 'types' of policymaker—type D and type W. The preferences of a policymaker of type $i(=D, W)$ are given by the cost function

$$z_t^i = \tfrac{1}{2}\pi_t^2 + c_i(\pi_t^e - \pi_t), \tag{3}$$

where $0 < c_D < c_W < \infty$. Thus policymakers of type D are 'drys' and those of type W are 'wets'. The prior probability that the policymaker is dry is p, where $0 < p < 1$. He is wet with probability $1 - p$. The game has two periods: $t = 1, 2$. The duration of the game may be thought of as the period of office of the policymaker.

We analyse this game of incomplete information by following Harsanyi's (1967–8) suggestion of replacing it by a game of complete but imperfect information, and regarding the equilibria of the latter game as the equilibria of the former. Thus we suppose that, at the outset of the game, 'Nature' chooses the type of policymaker, according to the probabilities stated above. The policymaker knows what Nature has chosen, but the public do not (although they do know the value of p). Two equivalent interpretations may be given to this construct. The first is that there is initially just one policymaker, who is informed of his type by Nature. This policymaker's strategy specifies his actions contingent upon the type chosen for him. The second interpretation is that there is a population of potential policymakers, one of whom is selected by Nature to play in the game itself. Each of the potential policymakers knows his type, and chooses a strategy before he knows whether Nature has selected him to play in the game itself.

A *strategy* for the policy maker consists of a quadruple $s = (\pi_1^D, \pi_1^W, \pi_2^D, \pi_2^W) \in R^4$ that specifies the inflation rate chosen in each period by the policymaker, contingent upon each of his possible types. We do not model the behaviour of the public explicitly—each member of the public is regarded as being 'small'. Instead, we suppose that the behaviour of the public in period t depends upon π_t^e (and perhaps π_t). The *expectations* of the public consist of a pair $e = (\pi_1^e, \pi_2^e(\cdot))$, where $\pi_1^e \in R$ is the inflation expected in period 1, and $\pi_2^e \colon R \to R$ specifies the inflation expected in period 2, contingent upon that observed in period 1.

The *payoff* of the policymaker is

$$
\begin{aligned}
Z &= pZ_D + (1-p)Z_W \\
&= p[\tfrac{1}{2}(\pi_1^D)^2 + c_D(\pi_1^e - \pi_1^D) + \tfrac{1}{2}(\pi_2^D)^2 + c_D(\pi_2^e(\pi_1^D) - \pi_2^D)] \\
&\quad + (1-p)[\tfrac{1}{2}(\pi_1^W)^2 + c_W(\pi_1^e - \pi_1^W) + \tfrac{1}{2}(\pi_2^W)^2 + c_W(\pi_2^e(\pi_1^W) - \pi_2^W)] \quad (4)
\end{aligned}
$$

An *equilibrium* is a pair (s, e) such that

  (i) s minimises Z given e, and
  (ii) e is correct given s.

Strategy s minimises Z if and only if (π_1^D, π_2^D) minimises Z_D and (π_1^W, π_2^W) minimises Z_W. Condition (ii) means that $\pi_1^e = p\pi_1^D + (1-p)\pi_1^W$, and that π_2^e is equal to the expectation of π_2 conditional upon s and the observation of π_1.

The main factor to note is that the public make inferences about the policymaker's type on the basis of his action in period 1. There are two types of equilibrium. If $\pi_1^D \neq \pi_1^W$ we have a *separating* equilibrium, and the public can infer the type of the policymaker from π_1. From then on, it is as if the game were one of complete information, since π_1, together with s, has revealed the policymaker's type. If, however, $\pi_1^D = \pi_1^W$, we have a *pooling* equilibrium, and the public gain no information from observing π_1. In that event they do not update their prior probabilities, so $\pi_2^e = p\pi_2^D + (1-p)\pi_2^W$. Propositions 1 and 2 below respectively characterise and state conditions for the existence of separating equilibria. Propositions 3 and 4 do likewise for pooling equilibria.

As a first step it is useful to note that s is optimal only if

$$
\pi_2^D = c_D \quad \text{and} \quad \pi_2^W = c_W, \tag{5}
$$

irrespective of π_2^e. The functional form has the useful property that the policymaker has a dominant strategy in period 2. It follows that π_2^e cannot be less than c_D or greater than c_W. A second convenient feature of the functional form is that the π_1^e term enters as an additive constant. The two variables of particular interest are therefore π_1 and π_2^e, and we can use diagrams (like those in Kreps (1985)) to illustrate the analysis.

Before proceeding further, let us define K_i as the lowest level of π_1 such that a policymaker of type i is indifferent between

(a) choosing $\pi_1 = K_i$ and being believed to be dry – in which case $\pi_2^e = c_D$—and
(b) Choosing $\pi_1 = c_i$ and being believed to be wet—in which case $\pi_2^e = c_W$.

Define $r = c_W/c_D > 1$ as the ratio of c_W to c_D. Then it turns out that

$$K_D = c_D[1 - \sqrt{2(r-1)}] \tag{6}$$
$$K_W = c_W[1 - \sqrt{2(r-1)/r}] \tag{7}$$

It is easy to show that $K_W > K_D$ iff $r < 9$. We now characterise separating equilibria.

Proposition 1: Assume that (s, e) is a separating equilibrium. Then $\pi_1^D \in [K_D, K_W]$ and $\pi_1^W = c_W$.

Proof:
To show that $\pi_1^W = c_W$, suppose for a contradiction that there exists a separating equilibrium in which $\pi_1^W \neq c_W$. In that equilibrium $\pi_2^e(\pi_1^W) = c_W$, because expectations are correct at equilibrium. This is the most unfavourable π_2^e for the policymaker, because Z is increasing in $\pi_2^e \in [c_D, c_W]$ by previous argument. So $\pi_1^W = c_W$ could not worsen π_2^e for a wet policymaker, and it would improve his period 1 payoff. Since a wet policymaker could therefore improve his overall payoff, we do not have an equilibrium after all.

Next, π_1^D cannot be less than K_D. For otherwise a dry policymaker would do better to choose $\pi_1^D = c_D$ even if the public then believed him to be wet. This follows from the definition of K_D. Finally, π_1^D cannot exceed K_W. For otherwise a wet policymaker would choose the same π_1 as a dry, and would be believed to be dry (because $\pi_2^e(\pi_1^D) = c_D$ at a separating equilibrium). This would improve his payoff, by the definition of K_W. ■

We now demonstrate the existence of a class of separating equilibria. Fig. 1 illustrates.

Proposition 2: Assume that $r < 9$, in which case $K_W > K_D$. Let k be some number such that $K_D \leq k \leq K_W$. Then there exists a separating equilibrium in which

$$\pi_1^D = k; \qquad \pi_2^D = c_D; \qquad \pi_1^W = \pi_2^W = c_W$$

$$\pi_1^e = pk + (1-p)c_W; \qquad \pi_2^e = \begin{cases} c_D & \text{if } \pi_1 \leq k \\ c_W & \text{otherwise} \end{cases}$$

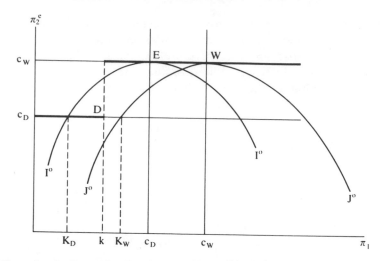

FIG. 1. Example of a Separating Equilibrium. Curves I^0 and J^0 are indifference curves for dry and wet policymakers respectively. Each type of policymaker optimises by choosing his best point on the heavy line that represents π_2^e as a function of π_1. Thus a dry chooses point D (which is better than E, his best point such that $\pi_2^e = c_W$). A wet chooses W (which is better than D, his best point such that $\pi_2^e = c_D$)

Proof:

It is easy to see that the expectations of the public are correct, given the policymaker's strategy. We have already established that $\pi_2^i = c_i$ is optimal $(i = D, W)$. It remains to check (a) that Z_D is minimised by $\pi_1^D = k$, and (b) that Z_W is minimised by $\pi_1^W = c_W$.

(a) Since Z_D as a function of π_1^D is strictly decreasing on $(-\infty, k]$, it follows that $\pi_1^D = k$ is optimal in the domain $(-\infty, k]$. The optimal value of π_1^D in the domain (k, ∞) is c_D. Therefore we need to compare (using natural notation):

$$Z_D(k) = \tfrac{1}{2}k^2 + c_D(\pi_1^e - k) + \tfrac{1}{2}c_D^2, \tag{8}$$

and

$$Z_D(c_D) = \tfrac{1}{2}c_D^2 + c_D(\pi_1^e - c_D) + \tfrac{1}{2}c_D^2 + c_D(c_W - c_D). \tag{9}$$

Define

$$\alpha = Z_D(k) - Z_D(c_D) \tag{10}$$

as the incentive to reduce unemployment in period 1 even at the expense of higher inflation in period 1 and higher unemployment in period 2. We have

$$\alpha = \tfrac{1}{2}k^2 - c_D k + (\tfrac{3}{2} - r)c_D^2$$

$$\alpha = \tfrac{1}{2}(k - c_D[1 + \sqrt{2(r-1)}])(k - c_D[1 - \sqrt{2(r-1)}]). \tag{11}$$

The first term on the RHS of (11) is negative. Therefore $\alpha \leqslant 0$, because $k \geqslant K_D$. Thus there is no incentive to depart from $\pi_1^D = k$.

(b) By the same reasoning as above, we need to compare

$$Z_W(k) = \tfrac{1}{2}k^2 + c_W(\pi_1^e - k) + \tfrac{1}{2}c_W^2 + c_W(c_D - c_W), \tag{12}$$

and

$$Z_W(c_W) = \tfrac{1}{2}c_W^2 + c_W(\pi_1^e - c_W) + \tfrac{1}{2}c_W^2. \tag{13}$$

Define

$$\beta = Z_W(c_W) - Z_W(k) \tag{14}$$

as the incentive to mimic dry behaviour in period 1 in order to reduce unemployment by surprise inflation in period 2. We have

$$\beta = -\tfrac{1}{2}k^2 + c_W k - \left(\frac{1}{r} - \frac{1}{2}\right)c_W^2$$
$$= -\tfrac{1}{2}(k - c_W[1 + \sqrt{2(r-1)/r}])(k - c_W[1 - \sqrt{2(r-1)/r}]) \tag{15}$$

This expression is negative, because $k \leqslant K_W$ from (7). Then there is no incentive to depart from $\pi_1^D = c_W$. We have shown that if $K_D \leqslant k \leqslant K_W$ then the policymaker is behaving optimally given the expectations of the public. ■

The system of expectations in Proposition 2 is not the only one that can support a separating equilibrium in which $\pi_1^D = k$ and $\pi_1^W = c_W$, but it is perhaps rather natural.

In order to characterise pooling equilibria, it is useful to define the following. Let L_i^- (resp. L_i^+) be the lowest (resp. highest) level of π_1 such that a policymaker of type i is indifferent between

(a) choosing $\pi_1 = L_i^-$ (resp. L_i^+) and the public remaining in ignorance of his type—in which case $\pi_2^e = \bar{c}$, where $\bar{c} = pc_D + (1-p)c_W$ is the weighted average of the c_i; and
(b) choosing $\pi_1 = c_i$ and being believed to be wet—in which case $\pi_2^e = c_W$.

It is straightforward to show that

$$L_D^- = c_D(1 - \sqrt{2p(r-1)}), \tag{16}$$

and

$$L_W^- = c_W(1 - \sqrt{2p(r-1)/r}). \tag{17}$$

The expressions for L_D^+ and L_W^+ are obtained by changing the sign in front of the square root from minus to plus in (16) and (17) respectively. Finally, define L as follows:

$$L = [L_D^-, L_D^+] \cap [L_W^-, L_W^+] \tag{18}$$

The set L is nonempty if

$$p \geqslant \frac{(\sqrt{r} - 1)}{2(\sqrt{r} + 1)} \tag{19}$$

We can now characterise pooling equilibria.

Proposition 3: Assume that (s, e) is a pooling equilibrium. Then $\pi_1^D = \pi_1^W \in L$.

Proof:

In a pooling equilibrium, the public cannot infer the policymaker's type from π_1, and therefore $\pi_2^e = \bar{c}$. There could not be a pooling equilibrium with $\pi_1 \notin L$, because in that event at least one type of policymaker would prefer to choose $\pi_1 = c_i$ even if he were then believed to be wet. This follows from the definition of L. ∎

In fact there are pooling equilibria associated with all $\pi_1 \in L$.

Proposition 4: Assume that (19) holds, in which case L is nonempty. Let $l \in L$. Then there exists a pooling equilibrium in which

$$\pi_1^D = \pi_1^W = l; \qquad \pi_2^D = c_D; \qquad \pi_2^W = c_W;$$

$$\pi_1^e = l; \qquad \pi_2^e = \begin{cases} \bar{c} & \text{if } \pi_1 = l \\ c_W & \text{otherwise} \end{cases}.$$

Proof:

Omitted.

The proof is omitted because the expectations π_2^e in Proposition 4 are intuitively odd, especially because $\pi_1 < l$ causes wetness to be inferred although $\pi_1 = l$ does not. Nevertheless Proposition 4 does describe an equilibrium inasmuch as the policymaker is optimising given expectations, and expectations are correct. This suggests that the equilibrium concept needs strengthening, which is the task of the next section. It is worth noting, however, that if $l < c_D$ and $l \in L$, then $\pi_1 = l$ can be supported as a pooling equilibrium by beliefs about π_2 of the form

$$\pi_2^e = \begin{cases} \bar{c} & \text{if } \pi_1 \leq l \\ c_W & \text{otherwise} \end{cases}$$

which are intuitively more appealing than those in Proposition 4 – at least π_2^e is increasing in π_1. Figure 2 is an example of this.

The time paths of inflation and unemployment (which is a function of surprise inflation) are as follows. In separating equilibria, if the policymaker is dry then period 1 inflation is lower than expected, and unemployment is higher than expected; the opposite is true if he is wet. In period 2 there is no surprise inflation, and so unemployment stays at its natural rate, but a dry policymaker has succeeded in getting inflationary expectations down. In pooling equilibria, there is no surprise inflation in period 1. In period 2, if there is a dry policymaker, inflation is lower then expected and unemployment is higher than expected. The reverse holds for a wet policymaker.

It is interesting to compare the payoffs of the two types of policymaker in the game with incomplete information to their payoffs when there is complete information. With complete information, a policymaker of type i

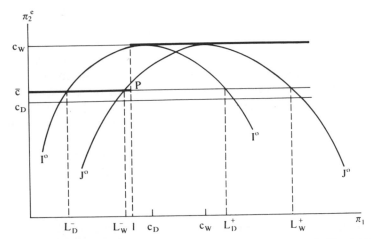

FIG. 2. Example of a Pooling Equilibrium. The indifference curves are as in Fig. 1. The heavy line represents π_2^e as a function of π_1. Point P is the best point such that $\pi_2^e = \bar{c}$ both for wets and dries; and they both prefer it to any point such that $\pi_2^e = c_W$

chooses, and is expected to choose $\pi_1^i = \pi_2^i = c_i$. The payoffs of each type of policymaker are therefore

$$Z_D = c_D^2, \tag{20}$$

and

$$Z_W = c_W^2. \tag{21}$$

In separating equilibria, the payoffs are

$$Z_D^s = \tfrac{1}{2}k^2 + (1-p)c_D(c_W - k) + \tfrac{1}{2}c_D^2, \tag{22}$$

and

$$Z_W^s = c_W^2 - pc_W(c_W - k), \tag{23}$$

where $k \in [K_D, K_W]$. It is straightforward to show that $K_W < c_D$. A dry policymaker gains from the presence of incomplete information insofar as his incentive to signal lowers expected inflation in period 1; but he loses insofar as the possible presence of a wet policymaker raises π_1^e. The overall effect is ambiguous, but if p is close enough to 1, a dry policymaker does better when there is incomplete information. A wet policymaker unambiguously does better when there is incomplete information—he benefits from the lowering of inflationary expectations that results from the possible presence of a dry. The weighted average of Z_D^s and Z_W^s is superior to that of Z_D and Z_W. Thus the presence of incomplete information is "on average" beneficial to the policymaker.

In pooling equilibria, the payoffs are

$$Z_D^P = \tfrac{1}{2}l^2 + \tfrac{1}{2}c_D^2 + (1-p)c_D(c_W - c_D), \tag{24}$$

and

$$Z_D^P = \tfrac{1}{2}l^2 + \tfrac{1}{2}c_W^2 - pc_W(c_W - c_D),\tag{25}$$

where $l \in L$. If $l < c_D$ then it is ambiguous whether a dry policymaker prefers his pooling equilibrium with incomplete information to his payoff with complete information, for the same reason as with separating equilibria. (If $l \geq c_D$, which we argued above to be intuitively odd, the dry policymaker does unambiguously worse at the pooling equilibrium). A wet policymaker certainly prefers his pooling equilibrium payoff to his payoff when there is complete information, again for the reason given before. "On average" the pooling equilibrium is better for the policymaker than the equilibrium with complete information.

3. Refining the set of equilibria

In the previous section it was shown that there may exist continua of both pooling and separating equilibria. It was seen how the form of the public's expectations about period 2 inflation could be such as to support a wide range of equilibria (Recall the discussion after Proposition 4). It is natural to ask whether reasonable restrictions can be placed on these expectations so as to reduce the set of equilibria, ideally to a unique form of equilibrium.

In this section we reduce the set of equilibria in two ways. First, we suppose that it is known that dominated strategies would never be played. (This is in the spirit of the Kohlberg example on p. 884 Kreps and Wilson (1982b)). This is a very natural step to take. It eliminates all separating equilibria except those in which $\pi_1^D = K_W$, and it eliminates some (and maybe all) of any remaining pooling equilibria. The second step is to apply the ideas of Kreps (1985) concerning "stable equilibria". These eliminate all pooling equilibria (if indeed any remain to be eliminated).

The first step involves the removal of dominated strategies. Consider a separating equilibrium (see Proposition 1) in which $\pi_1^D < K_W$. By the construction of K_W, a wet would never choose $\pi_1 < K_W$ even if he thereby convinced the public that he was dry. Therefore any observed $\pi_1 < K_W$ should convince the public that the policymaker is dry. Suppose that x is such that $\pi_1^D < x < K_W$. By choosing $\pi_1 = x$, a dry should therefore convince the public that he was dry, and would improve his payoff relative to his hypothesised "equilibrium" payoff (because $x < K_W < c_D$). Fig. 3 illustrates. We should therefore reject all separating equilibria in which $\pi_1^D < K_W$. This leaves only the separating equilibria in which $\pi_1^D = K_W$. In these equilibria a dry does the maximum necessary to convince the public that he is dry.

This method also succeeds in eliminating some (and maybe all) of any remaining pooling equilibria, because a dry policymaker may improve on his pooling equilibria payoff by choosing $\pi_1 < K_W$ and convincing the public that he is dry.

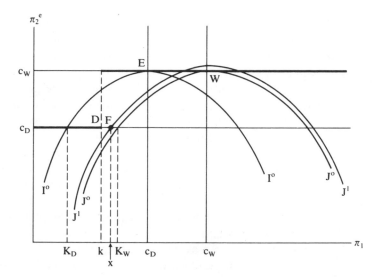

FIG. 3. The case for rejecting the separating equilibrium with $\pi_1 = k$. The diagram is basically the same as Fig. 1. The equilibrium such that $\pi_1 = k$ should be rejected, because if (say) $\pi_1 = x$ were observed, it would be apparent that the policymaker was dry. For a wet can guarantee utility J^0 by choosing $\pi_1 = c_W$, whereas he gets only J^1 at point F. Therefore only a dry would choose $\pi_1 = x$

If any pooling equilibria remain, they can usually be eliminated if a second restriction on beliefs is adopted (see Kreps (1985) for a full discussion). Consider a pooling equilibrium and suppose that there exists x such that

  (a) A wet prefers his pooling equilibrium payoff to the payoff that he would obtain if he chose $\pi_1 = x$ and were believed to be dry; and
  (b) A dry's pooling equilibrium payoff is worse for him than the payoff he would get if he chose $\pi_1 = x$ and were believed to be dry.

Then it can be argued as follows that the pooling equilibrium should be rejected. The public realise that a wet has no incentive to depart from the postulated equilibrium by choosing $\pi_1 = x$ no matter what is then inferred about his type. Therefore $\pi_1 = x$ reveals that the policymaker is dry. A dry does have an incentive (relative to his pooling equilibrium payoff) to choose $\pi_1 = x$ if he thereby reveals himself as dry. He would therefore choose $\pi_1 = x$ rather than behave in accordance with the postulated equilibrium. That equilibrium should therefore be rejected.

It can be demonstrated for a large set of parameter values—roughly speaking, when the relevant inflation rates are positive—that for all pooling equilibria there exists an x satisfying (a) and (b) above. It follows that no pooling equilibria then survive, and we are left only with separating equilibria in which a dry policymaker chooses $\pi_1 = K_W$.

4. Conclusion

It is a commonplace to say that expectations about government policy have an important influence on private sector behaviour, and that these expectations depand partly upon the public's beliefs about government objectives. The resulting incentive and opportunity for the government to signal its objectives have been explored in the context of the natural rate model proposed by Barro and Gordon. The justification for using their model is that its relatively simple structure facilitated the analysis, which nevertheless became quite messy in places. While there exists no definitive solution concept for games of incomplete information it is appropriate to use simple models despite the fact that they have shortcomings in other respects.

It was shown in the model that signalling affects the time path of inflation and unemployment. For example, the election of a dry (though not transparently dry) policymaker may result in a period of high unemployment, accompanied by unexpectedly low inflation, followed by a reduction in inflationary expectations. The presence of incomplete information was shown to have broadly desirable welfare consequences. The reason is that it enables signalling behaviour that would otherwise not occur. This behaviour is anticipated, and inflationary expectations are reduced, which is desirable in the model.

Various techniques were used to reduce the multiplicity of equilibria. One type of equilibrium survived all these techniques, namely that in which a dry signalled his dryness by doing the minimum necessary to persuade the public that he was dry. Whereas others (e.g. Backus–Driffill and Barro) have studied models in which wets successfully masquerade as dries (at any rate for much of the time), in our model it was shown that dries successfully distinguish themselves from wets. These contrasting findings are a subject for further research.

Nuffield College, Oxford.

REFERENCES

BACKUS, D. and DRIFFILL, J. (1985a) 'Inflation and Reputation', *American Economic Review*, 75, 530–538.
—— and ——, (1985b) 'Rational Expectations and Policy Credibility Following a Change in Regime', *Review of Economics Studies*, 52, 211–221.
BARRO, R. (1985) 'Reputation in a Model of Monetary Policy with Incomplete Information', unpublished manuscript, University of Rochester.
—— and GORDON, D. (1983a) 'Rules, Discretion and Reputation in a Model of Monetary Policy', *Journal of Monetary Economics*, 12, 101–121.
—— and ——, (1983b) 'A Positive Theory of Monetary Policy in a Natural Rate Model', *Journal of Political Economy*, 91, 589–610.

HARSANYI, J. (1967–8) 'Games with Incomplete Information Played by 'Bayesian' Players', Parts I, II and III, *Management Science,* 14, 159–182, 320–334, 486–502.

KREPS, D., 'Signalling Games and Stable Equilibria', Stanford mimeo 1985.

—— and WILSON, R. (1982a) 'Reputation and Imperfect Information', *Journal of Economic Theory,* 27, 253–279.

—— and ——, (1982b) 'Sequential Equilibria', *Econometrica,* 52, 863–894.

MILGROM, P. and ROBERTS, J. (1982a) 'Predation, Reputation and Entry Deterrence', *Journal of Economic Theory,* 27, 280–312.

—— and ——, (1982b) 'Limit Pricing and Entry under Incomplete Information: An Equilibrium Analysis', *Econometrica,* 50, 443–459.

MATTHEWS, S., and MIRMAN, L. (1983) 'Equilibrium Limit Pricing: The Effects of Private Information and Stochastic Demand', *Econometrica,* 51, 981–996.

YOON HA YOO, (1985) 'Reputation and Signalling in a Model of Monetary Policy', unpublished manuscript, UCLA.

INDEX